*The Political Culture
of the New West*

Published in cooperation with the William P. Clements Center for Southwest Studies, Southern Methodist University

The Political Culture of the New West

Edited by Jeff Roche

Foreword by David Farber

University Press of Kansas

© 2008 by the University Press of Kansas
All rights reserved

Published by the University Press of Kansas
(Lawrence, Kansas 66045),
which was organized by the Kansas Board of Regents
and is operated and funded by Emporia State University,
Fort Hays State University, Kansas State University,
Pittsburg State University, the University of Kansas,
and Wichita State University

Library of Congress Cataloging-in-Publication Data

The political culture of the New West / edited by Jeff Roche ;
foreword by David Farber.
p. cm.
Includes bibliographical references and index.
ISBN 978-0-7006-1613-8 (cloth : alk. paper)
ISBN 978-0-7006-1614-5 (paper : alk. paper)
1. West (U.S.)—Politics and government—20th century.
2. West (U.S.)—Politics and government—21st century.
3. Political culture—West (U.S.) 4. West (U.S.)—Ethnic
relations—Political aspects. 5. Cultural pluralism—Political
aspects—West (U.S.) 6. West (U.S.)—Social conditions.
I. Roche, Jeff.
F595.2.P64 2008
306.20978—dc22
2008027429

British Library Cataloguing in Publication Data is available.

Printed in the United States of America

10 9 8 7 6 5 4 3 2 1

The paper used in this publication is acid free and meets the minimum
requirements of the American National Standard for Permanence of
Paper for Printed Library Materials Z39.48-1992.

To the bravest kid in the world, Christopher

Contents

Foreword ix
  —David Farber

Acknowledgments xi

Introduction 1
  —Jeff Roche

PART ONE
1. The Western Hero in Politics: Barry Goldwater, Ronald Reagan, and the Rise of the American Conservative Movement   13
  —Robert A. Goldberg
2. Agricultural Politics in the Twentieth-Century American West   51
  —R. Douglas Hurt
3. The Illusions of Independence: Texas Oilmen and the Politics of Postwar Petroleum   74
  —Karen R. Merrill
4. "They Locked God outside the Iron Curtain": The Politics of Anticommunism and the Ascendancy of Plain-Folk Evangelicalism in the Postwar West   97
  —Darren Dochuk

PART TWO
5. The Politics of Place: Carey McWilliams and Radical Regionalism   135
  —Michael Steiner
6. Latinos in the Politics of the West   166
  —Ignacio M. García

7. *The Evolution of Modern American Indian Politics* 195
   —Bradley Glenn Shreve
8. *Becoming the New Objects of Racial Scorn: Racial Politics and Racial Hierarchy in Postwar San Francisco, 1945–1960* 219
   —Scott H. Tang

PART THREE

9. *Remaking Urban in the American West: Urban Environmentalism, Lifestyle Politics, and Hip Capitalism in Boulder, Colorado* 251
   —Amy L. Scott
10. *Free Minds and Free Markets: Counterculture Libertarians, Natural Capitalists, and an Alternative Vision of Western Political Authenticity* 281
    —Andrew G. Kirk
11. *The Call in the Wild: Nature, Technology, and Environmental Politics* 310
    —John P. Herron
12. *The Politics of Western Memory* 332
    —David M. Wrobel

List of Contributors 365
Index 369

Foreword

David Farber

In the American West, where self-invention has been unusually prized, politics have been unusually creative. In recent decades, westerners have led the way in changing the game of politics by expanding the boundaries of the political—sometimes in the name of condemning the whole enterprise. The "art of the possible" in the American West has, arguably, been about "dreaming the impossible" more often than in any other region in the American political landscape. From Orange County archconservatives to the druidic environmentalists of the desert Southwest, politics have been much more than partisan contestation played along fixed lines; they have been a form of collective reckoning in which, often enough, the stakes are perceived to be planetary—whether in the historic Cold War struggle against global communism or the contemporary wrangling over global warming.

Why the American West has been the site of such intense political expression and paradigm-breaking political activism has no easy answer. The essays in this collection, however, take us a long way down the road to figuring out what has made the arid American West such a fertile ground for political experimentation and postpartisan politics. Several of the writers herein make a convincing case that at the heart of Western politics is a paradox. On the one hand, people in great swaths of the West have given claims of regional cultural authenticity—in this case, based broadly on an individualistic frontier ethos—a power such claims no longer possess in any other part of the United States. On the other hand, the West, at least along its big border states, California and Texas, and in its many spectacularly fast-growing cities such as Phoenix, Houston, and Las Vegas, is suffused with a multiethnic diversity that ensures that cultural markers and political blocs are constantly shifting and under pressure to reflect new social and economic realities. Stated simply, the American West is a place where a fixed regional character is celebrated even as the populace of that place (and the way its changing populations make their livings) is ever fluid. In the twinned but sometimes contradictory pull of that frontier ideal and the demands of a new demographic lies a political friction that can be polarizing, leading to politics of reaction, but also libratory, leading to unexpected coalitions and demand for new solutions to collective challenges.

At a practical level the West's swirling cultural and social mix makes for a region open to political bargaining and swing vote behavior (though not, of course, in every state or congressional district). The American West, as several of the essayists instruct, will be for the foreseeable future a region in which no sure outcome can be predicted in electoral politics. And the West seems certain to be, as it has long been, a place at the leading edge of American politics. Broadly, the region's voters will continue to demand that elected officials challenge conventional wisdom, break out of partisan bickering, and offer leadership that honors a hard-to-pin-down frontier tradition but reckons with the realities of cultural pluralism and technology-driven economic globalization. This political dance may well set the style for the nation as a whole.

The cultural pulls and demographic storms of the American West are also likely to continue offering people the wide-open intellectual free spaces that make the region's politics more than a story of red, blue, or even purple states. Reading herein about utopian technologists, activists for Native American sovereignty, populist moralizers, hipster capitalists, borderlands sojourners, and others who defy easy labels shows off the West as an uncanny place in which the American political tradition is being reinvented at breakneck speed. The most exciting aspect of this daring collection of essays is the authors' willingness to see politics as more than cyclic electioneering and cynical fencing for partisan advantage. Grounded in historical study, the essays portray an American West in which people are imaginatively rethinking democratic practice and constantly forging new political publics.

Scholars today tend to dismiss Frederick Jackson Turner's late nineteenth-century claim that it was Americans' frontier experience, above all else, that gave shape to the American character and vitality to the democratic institutions of the United States. Turner, undoubtedly, overargued his case. But readers of this collection will happily discover how a new generation of scholars makes a provocative case for the massive importance of the West in Americans' political imagination and public policy debates.

Acknowledgments

This book started with a set of conversations about western politics and western history. These discussions evolved into more practical ideas about what a book of essays on western politics should look like, who should be involved, and what the best process for creating a more symbiotic and holistic edited volume might be. Quickly, a wish list emerged: the involvement of the University Press of Kansas and the William P. Clements Center for Southwest Studies at Southern Methodist University (SMU) topped that list. Like a lucky kid at Christmas, I got both my wishes within a few hours of one another.

The incredibly generous support of the William P. Clements Center for Southwest Studies at Southern Methodist University was crucial to the completion of this volume. Its director, David J. Weber, has been an enthusiastic partner from the first moment I mentioned the possibility of a book on western politics. I remember fondly our first discussion of the project during an early morning walk through Chinatown. His first question was how SMU's Clements Center might be involved. Also from SMU, Sherry L. Smith has provided more encouragement and mentoring than she'll ever know. Thanks to David and Sherry, the Clements Center not only sponsored a symposium in Dallas that featured early versions of the essays within but also brought contributors together at SMU's Fort Burgwin campus in Taos, New Mexico, to discuss each others' work and the volume as a whole. These intellectually stimulating and enjoyable meetings created a sense of community that guided our vision and led to a truly collaborative effort, which I believe sets this work apart from most books of collected essays. Neither of these events could have conceivably come off without the incredible hard work of Andrea Boardman. It would be impossible to overestimate the debt that everyone associated with this book owes to Andrea for her hard work.

I would also like to thank the College of Wooster for its continued support of this and other projects. It provided a very generous leave, travel money, and three different research assistants. More important, perhaps, has been the intellectual support and stimulation that I enjoy every day. The students in my American West class have forced me over the years to articulate many of the ideas that inform this volume. My colleagues are an excellent group of scholars and, more important, friends. I am in particular indebted to Marc Goulding, Jeff Lantis, and Greg Shaya for all they have done for this volume. Several students helped with various aspects of this project as my research assistants and in other capacities. I would like to thank Sarah Coffin, Anna Courtney, Grace Hansen, Andy Kissinger, Ted Pogue, Heather Williams, and Joe Witkowski. Megan Pritchard and Lindsay Kerr were especially helpful in its early stages. Caitlin Tyler-Richards helped keep me organized. Melanie Walsh was as good a research assistant as anyone could ever hope to find.

Thanks also to Michelle Nickerson and Ben Johnson for all their help with this project and for their continued engagement in and challenges to western history.

I am proud to call the people in this volume my friends. So big, big thanks to Bob, Doug, Karen, Darren, Mike, Ignacio, Brad, Scott, Amy, Andy, John, and David. Special thanks to David Farber for everything he's done for me over the years up to and including his foreword to this volume. The field of western history suffered quite a blow when Nancy Jackson left the University Press of Kansas for a new career. It was at her urging that I took on this project, and she was instrumental in crafting its design and conceptual framework. I, and everyone involved in this project, owe her a hefty and hearty thank you. Fortunately, Nancy left us in the very capable hands of Fred Woodward, the director of the press, who has been remarkable at shepherding it through the publication process. He too deserves mighty thanks for his wisdom and patience.

Just as this book was reaching its final stages, my family confronted a very serious medical crisis that left me unable to attend to any of those hundreds of small details that one must address in order to get a book on the shelves. I turned to one of my oldest and most trusted friends, John Herron, who stepped in and did an outstanding job. In many ways this is as much his book as mine. Thank you, John.

Lastly, I want to thank my family. They put everything into perspective. Thank you, Cathy and Christopher.

The Political Culture
of the New West

Introduction
Jeff Roche

On the night of the 2000 presidential election, all four major television networks along with the major cable news outlets used the same color scheme to demonstrate which candidate had captured each state's electoral votes. The graphic, if by now clichéd, red state–blue state scheme made an indelible impression on viewers and provided television's talking heads with a cool, seemingly undeniable way to explain American voting patterns. The color-coded U.S. maps that appeared countless times over the next month demonstrated a crystal-clear regional divide. The voters of the interior American West along with those of the South voted for Republican George W. Bush, and the voters on the East and West coasts and those on the Great Lakes voted for Democratic Al Gore. America, it seemed, had once again split along regional lines.[1]

Over the next few years, journalists, pundits, and other political observers spent enormous time and energy describing the ramifications of this new regionalism. To listen to this discussion was to come away with the impression that the differences between the red staters of the great American heartland and the blue staters hugging America's shores boiled down to divergent views on God, guns, and gay marriage. Blue came to mean liberal, secular, and urban. Red meant conservative, Christian, and small-town. But where the terms "liberal" and "conservative" had previously applied to individuals or identifiable groups, the new red state–blue state rubric characterized the politics of millions using a grossly simplified analysis of electoral maps.

What those maps appeared to show was a majority of westerners identifying with a conservative Republican Party. Despite the obvious shortcomings of sweeping political generalizations, pundits still seemed genuinely shocked when, over the next few years, western voters elected Democrats to statewide office. In 2007, for instance, Democrats sat in the governor's offices of Montana, Wyoming, Arizona, Oklahoma, Colorado, and Kansas—states that had gone solidly for Bush in 2000 and 2004. In one representative and hotly contested 2006 midterm election, Montana Democrat Jon Tester, an organic farmer from Big Sandy, defeated the powerful Republican incumbent Conrad Burns for his seat in the U.S. Senate. Tester's campaign was, in crucial ways, a demonstration of the *purpleness* of the West. While he took progressive stances on campaign finance reform, the environment, health care, and the minimum wage, he also made support of gun ownership central to his campaign and explained his conservation ethic within the context of "protecting clean places for hunting, fishing, and recreation."[2]

Most easily identified by their independence, Tester and his class of western Democrats tend toward a populist and unpretentious style buttressed by an optimistic pragmatism.[3] Moderate in their approach and drawing upon more than a century of western political thinking, they promise to look out for the little guy and bring common sense to governing. While hardly monolithic in their beliefs, their positions on controversial issues like gay marriage and abortion reflected the traditional western attitude of "Live and let live." Fiscally conservative and probusiness, the new western Democrats also recognized the need to control growth in sprawling western cities. A major reason for their successes was that they approached specific *western* issues with regional solutions not dictated by the national party. Their environmentalism, for example, focused on keeping public spaces open for the benefit of all who enjoy the outdoors. Echoing Tester, Colorado congressman Mark Udall explained, "Our economy depends on healthy public lands and clean water in which to hunt, fish, mountain bike, and ski."[4] Or consider immigration. Recognizing the reality of a large population of undocumented workers central to the economic well-being of their states, most western Democrats have again taken a pragmatic approach, calling for increased border security as well as a guest worker program.

Central to the popularity of these new politicians is their ability to adopt an authentic western mantle. They wear boots, jeans, and Stetsons. They own guns and know how to use them.[5] On the campaign trail, Tester would often rub his flattop haircut or his fairly large belly and tell the crowd that he didn't look much like the U.S. Senate, but then, to the delight of the crowd, he would thunder that it was time the U.S. Senate looked more like Montana. As Ken Salazar, Democratic senator from Colorado, described his like-minded brethren, "the one thing we have in common is our style."[6] Even if skeptics view Democrats' wearing of boots and bolo ties as part of a deliberate public relations strategy to compete with the cowboy conservatives in the GOP, we must also understand such behavior as an effort to reclaim westernness.

In many ways, this reclamation project reflects a long-term struggle to control the symbols of western politics that define (and defend) a regional political ideology. For much of the past half century, however, it was conservatives within the Republican Party who were more effective in linking the West to an ideology. Beginning with Barry Goldwater and continuing through George W. Bush, western conservative leaders on the national stage have rarely missed an opportunity to, as historian Anne Butler once put it, "put on the [cowboy] hat." With the recent electoral success of these Republicans, it would be easy to conclude that western political culture has always been conservative. But that perception makes the post-Bush victories by Tester and others all the more interesting; they were able to articulate a progressive/Democratic message that was, more importantly, an authentic *western* progressive/Democratic message.[7]

What the Democratic resurgence reveals is a set of competing western political traditions that now have an enormous influence on national politics. And a recognition of that influence brings us to *The Political Culture of the New West*. This book began with a simple premise: Regionalism is important to the American political dynamic, and more fundamentally, within that context, western politics matter. The regional influence on national politics includes everything from the anticommunist rhetoric emanating from the military-industrial strongholds of Texas and California to issues of environment and environmental justice to questions of immigration and the resulting construction of interracial political coalitions. Such uniquely western interest groups as wildcatting oilmen, Great Plains wheat farmers, and Colorado rock climbers have all framed their approach to national political interests around personal versions of western individuality and authenticity. Interestingly, once thrust into modern political discourse, these ideas have been appropriated by both the Left and the Right. As a result, we see a recasting of regional politics into something less about historical continuity or cultural exceptionalism and more about political ideas that reflect a broader American political culture.[8]

For more than a century, few disputed what it meant to be a real westerner; the bold and proud pioneers established a legacy that left little room for interpretation. Among the many attributes of regional identity, being a westerner often meant getting there first, whether to Oregon Country, the Kansas prairie, or the mining camps of Montana. Getting there first continues to drive much of western politics. Whether the setting is the Boulder city council dealing with a "hippie problem" or Mexican American leaders in San Diego discussing immigration restrictions, the coincidences of chronology continue to get serious play because with authenticity comes moral authority. Claims to that authority are fraught with political import, as the ability to define the West and interpret its past is also the power to define the region's economy, culture, and politics. Consequently, generations of westerners—most often male, white, and middle or upper class—used the structures of established authority to form and then protect a social, geographic, and economic status quo.

Since the end of World War II, however, calls for expanding the definitions of western authenticity have come from many sources, especially among racial and ethnic minorities. Competing for power and space within the limits of western places, groups committed to social justice have aspired to create a moral geography that reflects the reality of regional diversity and to put an end to the spatial segregation that has accompanied urban sprawl. Rather than acknowledging a top-down authority based on the pioneering claims of Anglo settlers, these regional residents made holistic arguments based on bottom-up desires for a revamped western political order. In many cases, this desire hinges on reconfiguring the unique relationships these groups have with the state. For example, Native Americans' association with the federal government has been both direct and in constant redefinition, while legal classifications, cultural mores, and immigration statutes have stymied other minorities' efforts to achieve increased representation. No group has felt this impact more than Mexican Americans and other Latinos, who have struggled for generations to articulate a political ideology flexible enough to serve the incredible diversity of agendas within the West.[9]

As African Americans, Native Americans, Asian Americans, Latinos, and other racial and ethnic groups fought for political power, they found a powerful ally among a new group of westerners who proved remarkably adept at redefining the cultural and political landscape of the region. These new progressives were concerned not only with the moral geography of the West as it is expressed in how humans should live with each other, but also with how humans should live on the land.[10] They value the natural West, celebrate its multiculturalism, and revere individual freedom, but on hearing these constituencies articulate their view of the West, it becomes obvious that their inspiration comes more from Henry David Thoreau and John Muir than from Frederick Jackson Turner or John Ford. Found in disproportionate numbers in tourist and college towns, these new western progressives have begun to articulate an alternative western political culture defined by moral geographies and a moral economy. Clearly influenced by the intentional communities and communes that flourished across the West in the late 1960s and throughout the 1970s, these voices have found new authority as an alternative voice of authentic western political ideas.[11]

The battles over who is the more "authentic" westerner—the rancher, claiming independence yet reliant upon federally subsidized cheap grazing land, or the backpacking, environmentally conscious Boulder attorney determined to keep snowmobiles out of national parks—was once again brought into brilliant focus in the 2004 presidential election, when the national media seemingly never tired of contrasting the images of the Patagonia-clad John Kerry snowboarding in Aspen and the Stetson-topped George W. Bush clearing brush in Crawford. While Kerry could hardly claim authentic western status (and some of those who slap "Native Texan" bumper stickers on their pickup trucks might question Bush's), the fact remains that they represented these competing visions of the authentic West.

But like the red-blue scheme that opened this essay, these symbols represent a political culture with multiple layers. As just one example, consider the links between western liberalism and western conservatism. It should not surprise anyone that each philosophy differs from its eastern counterpart, but internally, the two sides are marked by a shared history, mythology, language, and identity. Speaking broadly, western politics tend toward the individualistic, and westerners are often leery, if not distrustful, of centralized authority. By putting greater faith in individuals and communities than in institutions, especially national institutions, western voters consistently demonstrate their affinity for local authority. This too has a deep history. During the last decade of the nineteenth century, populists promised to protect the region's farmers and laborers from unscrupulous bankers, railroad owners, and other money-grubbing middlemen.[12] During the Progressive Era, the railroads and other powerful institutions came under even more serious attack, and western voters, led by those in Oregon, worked to put more political power in the hands of the voter.[13] And western supporters of the New Deal, from Marvin Jones, head of the House Agricultural Committee, to John Collier of the Bureau of Indian Affairs, sought to protect local communities from the ravages of economic and ecological disaster.

But certain aspects of populism, progressivism, and the New Deal also made many westerners uncomfortable with the heightened role of federal agencies in governing agricultural production, wages, access to reclamation water, and other aspects of everyday life. This discomfort was often expressed by both sides as an antagonism toward the federal government.[14] During the Cold War, anticommunism provided a handy and powerful language to voice discontent with omnipresent federal power. Led by Barry Goldwater and Ronald Reagan, western conservatives expressed their individual initiative and intention to protect the average citizen by painting the federal government, the "Eastern Establishment," and the cultural elite as the powerful forces aligned against everyday Americans.[15] As the GOP became entrenched in the post-Reagan years, however, more westerners began to see the Republicans as the party of special interests and, as we have seen, Tester and other western Democrats can now proudly wear the maverick label.[16]

This kind of political restlessness has its roots in the nineteenth century. Many western states endured long territorial apprenticeships that dampened partisan rivalries. One result was that, then as now, westerners at least claimed to vote for their preferred candidate regardless of party.[17] Further, they based their votes on particular sets of issues rather than demonstrating the sort of party loyalty that marks voters in other parts of the country. Weak party structures also permitted issue-based movements and parties to influence and occasionally dominate state politics. Further complicating the region's politics is the simple fact that massive population growth makes change a constant.[18] While the instability of political institutions and loyalties might frustrate the pundit, the casual observer, and certainly the campaign manager, for the historian interested in the recent politics of the American West, the last sixty years of regional growth provides a revealing glimpse into the creation, expression, implementation, and eventual evolution of a national political culture. What we see unfolding before our eyes is a grand narrative where competing ideologies, issues, characters, symbols, and languages all vie for attention on our national stage.

In this drama, the stakes couldn't be higher. The demographic growth and economic prosperity of the West since World War II now helps determine our national political agenda. Overall, the seventeen states of the American West have tripled in population since 1940. California, Washington, Idaho, and Texas have all quintupled; New Mexico and Colorado have quadrupled. Arizona has grown by a factor of twelve, and, most spectacularly, Nevada by more than a factor of twenty. Three of the top ten largest cities in the United States are in Texas; three more are in California. Economic and political powerhouses, these two states wield incredible influence in Washington, D.C., and on Wall Street. Any presidential candidate who wins both Texas and California is shy only a third of the votes he or she needs to win the White House. Most political observers believe that New Mexico, Oregon, Colorado, and Nevada, although smaller in size and influence, will be the crucial swing states in the next few election cycles. What does all this mean? From 1952 to 2008, all but one presidential election has featured a westerner at the top of either the Republican or Democratic ticket, a trend that shows no signs of abating.

The region that future national leaders with western roots will represent is only getting more complex. Beyond its racial and ethnic diversity, the West is marked by significant class divides, great differences in lifestyles, ecological distinctions throughout the region (which are often reflected in local economies), an urban-rural rift, and other cultural differences. With immigration and emigration into the West a near constant, the region will continue to find itself in flux. Consequently, what we see in the West is an ever-evolving political culture. The issues that drive and define western politics are forever in motion as well. Some of the complicating factors center on the aforementioned issues of demographic growth and race and ethnicity, but economics, religion, state power, resource management, and memory are sure to remain significant as well.

As contests over these issues played out in the past, westerners crafted unique definitions of liberal and conservative, forged their own connections between culture and politics, and redefined the relationships between economic and political power. If we can agree with historian Gerald Nash, who argued many years ago that the postwar West had become the "pacesetter" for the nation, then the consequences of this regional political refashioning will only grow in significance. We could, for instance, reasonably expect the new ethnic models coming out of the West to continue to inform our national conversation about race, just as issues with a deep western flavor, like immigration and the environment, dominate our current political discourse.[19] Operating from a position of power, western political actors will seek national influence in the western mode, complete with western symbols and, no doubt, with western solutions.

With *The Political Culture of the New West*, then, we seek to explore the consequences of the divergent views of western authenticity in public life. Borrowing the concept of political culture from political scientists (an expansion of the traditional definition of politics to include the belief systems, iconography, and language used to express political situations),[20] we are also interested in the activities that citizens use to "articulate, negotiate, implement, and enforce the competing claims they make upon one another and upon the whole."[21] We recognize, however, that in the West, myth, history, and geography have restricted the ideological marketplace and have made claims to authenticity a powerful part of the region's political culture. It is with this in mind that the essayists in this volume examine competing claims for legitimacy in the western public sphere.[22] In the twelve essays that follow, the authors explore how westerners have expressed themselves within a complex, often contradictory, and constantly changing political culture.

Since only a few of the contributors would identify themselves as "political" historians, the essays herein come to politics from a variety of perspectives. From religion, popular culture, business history, consumerism, environmental history, ethnic history, organizational history, and agricultural history, the contributors ask new questions about the American West. Our goal was to move western political history beyond the standard discussions that dominate political history, elections, parties, and policy, and beyond the standard discussions that dominate western political history, water, progressivism, and the relationship between states and the federal government, to understand how politics are negotiated and articulated among different groups in the postwar West. In no way is this volume meant to be comprehensive, let alone exhaustive; instead, consider it an introduction to some of the ways that western political culture has been articulated by divergent constituencies.

NOTES

1. I say split "again" as the divide broke along nearly exactly the same lines as the 1896 presidential election, in which "the Great Commoner," William Jennings Bryan (the Democratic and Peoples Party candidate), won the South and West, and the candidate of industrial America, William McKinley (Republican of Ohio), won the East and Midwest.

2. Conrad Burns was, of course, not without negatives. He was linked to the infamous lobbyist Jack Abramoff and the scandals of that connection played a role in the campaign. See Matthew Continetti, "How the West Was Won," *Weekly Standard*, 30 October 2006. For more on Burns and Abramoff, see Peter H. Stone, *Heist: Superlobbyist Jack Abramoff, His Republican Allies, and the Buying of Washington* (New York: Farrar, Straus & Giroux, 2006), 109. For quote see Jon Tester for U.S. Senate, "Jon Tester on the Issues," http://www.testerforsenate.com/issues.

3. These new western Democrats began to gain national attention shortly after the 2004 elections. See Matt Welch, "Democrats Need a Breath of Mountain-Fresh Air," *Los Angeles Times*, 2 November 2005; Timothy Egan, "Montana Democrats Reflect on Success," *New York Times*, 14 November 2004, "Drilling in West Pits Republican Policy against Republican Base," *New York Times*, 22 June 2005.

4. Mark Udall, "Why Democrats Are Winning in the West," *Hill*, 2 January 2005.

5. Montana Governor Brian Schweitzer makes much of his and his fellow western Democrats' support of gun ownership. See Mark Sundeen, "The Big-Sky Dem," *New York Times*, 8 October 2006.

6. Ken Salazar, quoted in Joe Klein, "What Democrats in the West Can Teach Their Party," *Time*, 29 January 2007, 23–28.

7 Anne M. Butler, "Selling the Popular Myth," in *The Oxford History of the American West*, ed. Clyde A. Milner II, Carol A. O'Connor, and Martha Sandweiss (New York and Oxford: Oxford University Press, 1994), 771–801, quote on page 784. Thomas B. Edsall, "Democratic Saviors: West Wing," *New Republic*, 20 November 2006, 9–12; Fred Brown, "Hold Your Breath until You Turn Blue," *Denver Post*, 12 November 2006; Mark Sandalow, "Red West Shifting to Blue," *San Francisco Chronicle*, 1 October 2006.

8. The regionalism expressed in this volume closely resembles that described by

Edward L. Ayers and Peter S. Onuf, who argue that regions are "places where discrete, though related structures intersect and interact in particular patterns. The region *is* climate and land; it *is* a particular set of relations between various ethnic groups; it *is* a relation to the federal government and economy; it *is* a set of shared cultural styles." Edward L. Ayers and Peter S. Onuf, "Introduction," in *All Over the Map: Rethinking American Regions*, ed. Edward L. Ayers et al. (Baltimore and London: The Johns Hopkins University Press, 1996), 1–10, quote from page 5. See also David M. Wrobel and Michael C. Steiner, "Many Wests: Discovering a Dynamic Western Regionalism," in *Many Wests: Place, Culture, and Regional Identity* (Lawrence: University Press of Kansas, 1997), ed. David M. Wrobel and Michael C. Steiner, 1–30.

9. Roger W. Lotchin argues that the successes of Hispanic women in western urban politics makes the West unique. Lotchin, "Hispanics, Women, and Western Cities: 'Setting the Pace'—Political Emergence and the Renaissance of Western Exceptionalism," *Western Historical Quarterly*, 29 Autumn 1998, 293–315.

10. For more on how these concepts have been more widely articulated, see E. P. Thompson, *Customs in Common: Studies in Traditional Popular Culture* (New York: New Press, 1993), 185–189.

11. One can find critiques of these New Westers in Michael L. Johnson, *The New Westers: The West in Contemporary American Culture* (Lawrence: University Press of Kansas, 1996), and of like-minded individuals in David Brooks, *Bobos in Paradise: The New Upper Class and How They Got There* (New York: Touchstone, 2000).

12. The populist movement enjoys a long and distinguished historiographic tradition. For some representative samples, see John D. Hicks, *The Populist Revolt: A History of the Farmers' Alliance and the People's Party* (Lincoln: University of Nebraska Press, 1961); Lawrence Goodwyn, *Democratic Promise: The Populist Movement in America* (Oxford: Oxford University Press, 1976); Robert C. McMath Jr., *American Populism: A Social History, 1877–1898* (New York: Hill & Wang, 1993); Peter H. Argersinger, *The Limits of Agrarian Radicalism: Western Populism and American Politics* (Lawrence: University Press of Kansas, 1995).

13. The literature on western progressivism is far too rich to detail here, but for an interesting analysis of its legacy on western political culture, see William Deverell, "Politics and the Twentieth-Century American West," in his fine edited collection *A Companion to the American West*, ed. William Deverell (Boston: Blackwell, 2007), 442–459.

14. The best book about the New Deal in the western states remains Richard Lowitt, *The New Deal and the West* (Bloomington: University of Indiana Press, 1984). See also Karen Merrill's astute analysis of the New Deal's legacy and its historiography, "The New Deal's West," in Deverell, *A Companion to the American West*, 346–360. See also Leonard J. Arrington, "The Sagebrush Resurrection: New Deal Expenditures in the Western States, 1933–1939," *Pacific Historical Review* 52 (February 1983): 1–16.

15. See Barry Goldwater, *The Conscience of a Conservative* (Shepherdsville, Ky.: Victor, 1960), and Phyllis Schlafly, *A Choice Not an Echo* (Alton, Ill.: Pere Marquette Press, 1964). See also Robert Alan Goldberg, *Barry Goldwater* (New Haven, Conn.: Yale

University Press, 1995), and Thomas W. Evans, *The Education of Ronald Reagan* (New York: Columbia University Press, 2006).

16. Political scientists call this switch "realignment." For more on the Republican ascendance in the mountain West, see Peter F. Galderisis et al., eds., *The Politics of Realignment: Party Change in the Mountain West* (Boulder, Colo., and London: Westview Press, 1987).

17. For more on this period, see Earl S. Pomeroy, *The Territories and the United States: 1861–1890* (Philadelphia: University of Pennsylvania Press, 1947), and Howard Roberts Lamar, *The Far Southwest, 1846–1912* (New York: Norton, 1970). For two very nice historiographic and interpretive essays, see Kenneth N. Owens, "Government and Politics in the Nineteenth-Century West," in *Historians and the American West*, ed. Michael P. Malone (Lincoln: University of Nebraska Press, 1983), 148–176, and Jeffrey Ostler, "Empire and Liberty: Contradictions and Conflicts in Nineteenth-Century Western Political History," in Deverell, *A Companion to the American West*, 200–218.

18. See Paul Kleppner, "Politics without Parties: The Western States, 1900–1984," in *The Twentieth-Century West: Historical Interpretations*, ed. Gerald D. Nash and Richard W. Etulain (Albuquerque: University of New Mexico Press, 1989), 295–338; Michael P. Malone and F. Ross Peterson, "Politics and Protest," in *The Oxford History of the American West*, ed. Clyde A. Milner II, Carol A. O'Connor, and Martha Sandweiss (New York and Oxford: Oxford University Press, 1994), 502–503, 523–532; Michael P. Malone and Richard W. Etulain, *The American West: A Twentieth-Century History* (Lincoln and London: University of Nebraska Press, 1989), 54–119; and Gerald D. Nash, *The American West in the Twentieth Century: A Short History of an Urban Oasis* (Englewood Cliffs, N.J.: Prentice Hall, 1973), esp. 254–255.

19. See Nash, *American West in the Twentieth Century*, 6.

20. For a good introduction to these ideas, see Lucian W. Pye, "Introduction: Political Culture and Political Development," in *Political Culture and Political Development*, ed. Lucian W. Pye and Sidney Verba (Princeton, N.J.: Princeton University Press, 1965), 7–8. See also Daniel Elazar and Joseph Zikmund, eds., *The Ecology of American Political Culture* (New York: Crowell, 1975), and Walter Rosenbaum, *Political Culture* (New York: Praeger, 1975).

21. Keith Michael Baker, *Inventing the French Revolution: Essays on French Political Culture in the Eighteenth Century* (Cambridge, Mass., and New York: Cambridge University Press, 1990), 4. See also Roger Chartier, "Text, Symbols, and Frenchness," *Journal of Modern History* 57 (1985): 682–695. For a concise discussion on the evolution of cultural history, see Lynn Hunt, "Introduction: History, Culture, and Text," in *The New Cultural History*, ed. Lynn Hunt (Berkeley and Los Angeles: University of California Press, 1989), 1–22.

22. We are also indebted to the pioneering efforts of historians who work at the nexus of politics and culture. For some excellent examples, see François Furet's groundbreaking work *Interpreting the French Revolution*, trans. Elborg Forster (Cambridge: Cambridge University Press, 1981); Mary Ryan, "The American Parade: Representations of the Nineteenth-Century Social Order," in Hunt, *New Cultural History*, 131–153; and Baker, *Inventing the French Revolution*.

PART ONE

In the crucial month after the 2000 presidential election, as the heavily partisan election cases wrangled through the legal system, Americans witnessed a powerful reminder of the significance of western imagery. Anyone who even occasionally tuned in to CNN or Fox News saw Al Gore, the consummate Washington technocrat, retreat inside the Beltway and, fortified by an arsenal of personal electronics, micromanage his postelection legal campaigns by e-mail, fax, and cellular phone. Bush, on the other hand, headed for his "little slice of heaven"—the Crawford, Texas, ranch he had purchased the previous summer. The visual contrast could not have been more striking: Gore, holed up in the vice president's residence, frantically punching commands into his PalmPilot, and Bush roaming the Central Texas plains on his John Deere Trail Gator. Every few days, in carefully choreographed media events, Bush, dressed in boots, jeans, and a Carhartt jacket, ambled up to the edge of his property and spoke with reporters. Ignoring the television cameras, one might think a Bush barbed-wire press conference was a group of neighbors just shootin' the breeze about the weather, the Dallas Cowboys, or feed prices.

Although frontier images have been an important part of American political culture since the nineteenth century, in the postwar years these symbols were often closely identified with conservatives. Our first group of essays explores the various claims and contests over western authenticity among groups most commonly associated with western conservatism. Some, like prominent national politicians, made this association consciously. Others, like oil producers or farmers, used western mythology and symbolism to express inchoate ideas about much-desired political and economic independence. For still others, like the growing evangelical movement in Southern California, western symbolism and language provided the means to lessen the burdens of southern provincialism and to finally participate in a national political dialogue. Regardless of perspective or intent, all claimed westernness as the fount of their particular brand of moral authority.

Robert Alan Goldberg leads off this section in a carefully nuanced study in which he explains the synergy between the symbols of western myth and the rise of conservative politics. His examination of the ways Barry Goldwater and Ronald Reagan used carefully honed western images to preach their Cold War anticommunist sermons bursts through the false barriers that have divided cultural and political history. Moreover, he clearly demonstrates the *western* nature of contemporary conservative politics and moves the most vibrant political movement of the postwar era into its natural historic and historiographic home—the West.

That agricultural interests dominate western politics shouldn't surprise anyone. But, as R. Douglas Hurt argues in his essay, the political philosophy that guides those interests has undergone an elemental shift over the last century. This shift, from being concerned about the larger commonweal to naked (and very often corporate) self-interest, has had a titanic impact on how western politicians operate within the Beltway. Like so many western constituencies, however, modern agribusiness has clearly recognized the value of authenticity and the powerful hold the farmer still has on the American imagination.

In her essay on the oil business, Karen R. Merrill shows us two competing visions for how best to marshal the potential for that significant resource in the light of a growing world market. Beyond simply explaining the relationship between the West and global politics and the way the region's development has been intimately tied into the exploitation of natural resources, Merrill takes us deeper into the debates over the proper role of the federal government in extractive industry. Moreover, she shows how the "illusion of independence" both constrained the oil industry and glamorized its wheeler-dealers.

Darren Dochuk explains the rise of conservative religion and conservative politics in Southern California in his essay "'They Locked God Outside the Iron Curtain.'" As he traces the interconnectedness of regions, politics, and religion, he demonstrates the importance of the West in nationalizing what had been a traditional southern form of religion. More important, however, he demonstrates how a generation of southern transplants transformed the political, social, and cultural life of California and the West. The politicization of this generation has had, as he clearly shows, a tremendous impact on the development of a *western* conservatism.

CHAPTER 1

The Western Hero in Politics: Barry Goldwater, Ronald Reagan, and the Rise of the American Conservative Movement
Robert A. Goldberg

Americans like the cowboy who leads the wagon train by riding ahead alone on his horse, the cowboy who rides alone into the town, the village, with his horse and nothing else. Maybe even without a pistol, since he doesn't shoot. He acts, that's all, by being in the right place at the right time. In short, a Western.[1]
Henry Kissinger, 1972

The long march to power of American conservatives ended in 1980 with the election of Ronald Reagan to the presidency. Since then, conservative ideas have framed debate and dominated political discourse. In light of the new political reality, the academic community, somewhat reluctantly, shifted its research agenda. Radicals, progressives, and liberals now had to compete for center stage as fieldwork on conservative activists and their movements began in earnest. Biographers published numerous works on the standard bearers of the cause. Historians and political scientists explored the creation of the conservative coalition and the mobilization of groups like the John Birch Society, the Young Americans for Freedom, the Moral Majority, and Right to Life. Similarly, communication scholars studied the means of conservative persuasion, scrutinizing political ads frame by frame to gauge voter reaction. The result has been a more nuanced conceptualization of recent American political and social history. No longer perceived as reactionaries and spoilers, conservatives have begun to take their rightful place as agents of change dedicated to their visions of the good society.[2]

Nevertheless, the scholarly advance has been uneven. The focus of research has been narrowly preoccupied with concrete details and the mechanics of mobilization. There is now an extensive literature about the political strategy and tactics of conservative generals and foot soldiers. Ideological debates within the ranks have been keenly judged for their rhetorical effectiveness. Meanwhile, conservative success has been placed in broader social, economic, political, and demographic contexts. Domestic and international events figure into interpretations and vie for influence alongside shifts in campaign spending, changing means of soliciting voter support, evolving coalitions, growth in regional populations, and variations in ethnic and racial voting.

While vital to an understanding of American politics, such approaches lack depth, for they ignore the symbolic nature of American politics. Beyond individuals, numbers, and events, politics express a people's core myths, beliefs, dreams, and fears. In the political arena, men and women contest values and confirm identities. There, versions of Americanism are celebrated and defended. During campaigns, voters and their candidates are in dialogue about the meaning of America and the relationship of its past and present to the future. The vote is thus more than a means to power. It is also an affirmation of self and group.

Early in their challenge, conservatives saw persuasive advantage in symbols, wrapping themselves in the flag, espousing the American dream, and championing the family. Less obvious was another means of symbolic power. Key to the movement's success was its identification with the American West, past and present, imagined and real. Not only did conservatives develop a base of power in the region; they cloaked themselves in its mythical power. Much of this was the work of Barry Goldwater and Ronald Reagan. During the 1950s and 1960s, their style, words, and deeds conjured up the classic western hero of popular culture. They rode with him in defense of rugged individualism. In the process, they began a conservative politics of inclusion that nationalized western fears of federal authority. When drawing charismatic advantage from identification with the mythical West, neither man offered explanation nor justification. None was needed. Conservatives understood and had already saddled up. Many others would follow them on the trail.

The cult of "true westernness," as the essays in this book reveal, was never, despite claims to the contrary, solely the property of conservative politicians. The western image has always been both constructed and vigorously contested. Karen Merrill's Texas oilmen costumed themselves in Stetsons and cowboy boots as they pursued power at home and abroad in the twentieth century. Doug Hurt reminds us that agricultural organizations vied for authority by making the yeoman farmer a western hero who fought to defend family values and moral America. Andy Kirk's "countercultural entrepreneurs" arrayed themselves in all sorts of Patagonia gear to shape a westernness in their own image—an alternative to federal control and grasping economic development. Nor were conservatives monolithic in their understanding of true westernness. As Darren Dochuk's essay reveals, western conservatism absorbed "the plain-folk evangelicalism" of Oklahoman and Texan Protestantism to find moral traction and bolster a fierce individualism. If Barry Goldwater and Ronald Reagan stood tall in the western sun, there were others who saw high noon as their opportunity to stake a claim to western authority.

"The mid-1950s," recalled Arizona Senator Goldwater, "were very tough days for a conservative."[3] Despite the stirring of movement with the appearance of William F. Buckley's *National Review* and a growing net of right-wing talk-radio programs, conservatives could offer only feeble resistance to "vital center" liberalism. A leadership vacuum stifled mobilization. Ohio Senator Robert Taft was dead, General Douglas MacArthur was retired, and Wisconsin Senator Joseph McCarthy was disgraced. A new generation of leaders had yet to find the will or following to lay claim to the conservative mantle. In this vacuum of authority, conservatives remained fixed in warring ideological camps unable to come to common ground. Even supposed friends raised suspicion. President Dwight Eisenhower proposed a "Modern Republicanism" that accepted the reforms of Franklin Roosevelt's New Deal and continued the expansion of federal bureaucracy and power. Conservatives found little to cheer about on the international front. The president had appeased the communists by "surrendering" in Korea, giving up the rhetoric of rollback, and pursuing summits with the Soviets. In a betrayal of their dreams, conservatives had power to resent but not resist.

Conservatives also had image problems. In the eyes of many Americans, they were out of touch, a rearguard tilting recklessly against the modern world. Leaders like William Knowland, John Bricker, Bourke Hickenlooper, and William Jenner represented an older America in manner and thought. Though competent, they were also colorless, stodgy, cranky, and devoid of charisma. Opposition to social and economic reforms tarred them as elitist and privileged. They were the "standpatters," opposed to change on principle. Others remembered them as isolationists before World War II and as tainted with anti-Semitism. During the Red Scare of the early 1950s, Joseph McCarthy had helped fashion a conservatism of vitriol and character assassination that held the nation's attention only briefly and rapidly became a source of embarrassment. White southern resistance to racial change only added to the indictment against conservatism. In persuading fellow Americans of their case, conservatives were hard-pressed to claim a politics of inclusion that offered a vision of tomorrow. The search for a charismatic paladin was only part of the answer. The meaning of the cause had to change.

Some conservatives sensed that part of the solution was ready-made and close at hand. In film and television westerns, they found the catechism of conservatism and the "new" conservative riding a white horse and dressed in buckskin or chaps. Writing in the *American Mercury* in 1959, Donald Teeple observed, "No western hero ever had any question in his mind about what was *right* and what was *wrong*. No western movie implied that the hero should compromise with evil. . . . There was a constant respect for God, women and the home." For Teeple, westerns were short courses in American diplomacy: "Wouldn't it be a good idea for our diplomats and political leaders to watch these shows? Would a Wyatt Earp stop at the 38th Parallel, Korea, when the rustlers were escaping with his herd? Ridiculous!"[4] Conservative William Rickenbacker echoed Teeple in his *National Review* column. Westerns, he wrote, "speak a language very close to the heart of the American dream: the dream of righteousness, the flowering of personal virtue and the power that flows there from the selfless battle against Evil, the simple moral code, the sense of community, the respect for the poor, for the downtrodden, for the tempest-tossed."[5]

There were plenty of western heroes available on which to model a new conservatism. During the 1950s, Hollywood made more than 800 westerns, including such classics as *High Noon* (1952), *Shane* (1953), *Vera Cruz* (1954), *The Searchers* (1956), *Gunfight at the O.K. Corral* (1957), and *Rio Bravo* (1959). A western series first reached the top-ten television list in 1957. The following year five made the cut, and in 1959, eight. That year there were twenty-eight western programs in prime time, including *Death Valley Days* (1952–1975), *Gunsmoke* (1955–1975), *Have Gun—Will Travel* (1957–1963), *Bonanza* (1959–1973), *Life and Legend of Wyatt Earp* (1955–1961), and *Rawhide* (1959–1966). By the hour and half hour, Americans followed the exploits of Matt Dillon, Paladin, Maverick, Cheyenne, Rowdy Yates, and Johnny Yuma, among others. They learned the ways of men of action, virtue, and grit. In total, westerns accounted for nearly a quarter of all evening programming. Viewers did not always find relief from the western landscape or hero during commercial breaks. Manufacturers exploited the craze with western wear for every member of the family. The Marlboro Man, who exuded "masculine confidence," appeared in 1954 and appeared exclusively as a cowboy in 1964.[6] On the freeways, Americans felt the "freedom" of the West by driving Mustang, Pinto, Bronco, or Maverick automobiles. Meanwhile, sales of paperback westerns shot up and made up more than 10 percent of all works of published fiction by the end of the 1950s.[7]

Film and television present openings to the past, for they reflect the attitudes and values of a people and their time. Their messages reveal a society's hopes and anxieties while nurturing identities. But motion pictures and television programs are more than mirrors. Disguised as entertainment, they play an opinion-shaping role. They engage events and debate ideas. They praise and condemn, teach what is right and wrong, and distinguish friend from foe. More specifically, the western is often a paean to patriotism reminding audiences of their common heritage, shared values, and identity as a people. In the process, legend overcomes history and myth becomes the new reality. The power of filmmakers and television producers to mold perceptions cannot be underestimated. In the twentieth century, they were our most influential teachers.

Generations of Americans have absorbed the formula of the western through dime novels, pulp magazines, radio, motion pictures, or television. Audiences know what to expect; there are few surprises. The drama unfolds in the period between the end of the Civil War and the coming of the automobile in the early twentieth century. The scene opens to a beginning of time when men and women were nothing before land and sky. The West is a raw and unfinished place, where the bareness of life is apparent. It is desert and rock, or wind and rolling prairie, nearly empty of human things. Here tension more than beauty impresses, for it is a space in time where the future is still contested. Savagery grapples with civilization for authority. Danger threatens, help is far distant, and, as film critic Jane Tompkins observes, "there is no place to hide." For the protagonist, this is the testing ground where "what matters is that he be a man."[8] For men, it is a holy place.[9]

This is the site of our creation myth. America was not forged at Plymouth Rock, Bunker Hill, or Gettysburg. Rather, this new man, the American, was birthed in the womb of the frontier. Historian Frederick Jackson Turner was especially articulate in its celebration. In 1893, he observed: "To the frontier the American intellect owes its striking characteristics. That coarseness and strength combined with acuteness and inquisitiveness, that practical, inventive turn of mind, quick to find expedients, that masterful grasp of material things . . . that dominant individualism, working for good and for evil, and withal that buoyancy and exuberance which come with freedom, these are the traits of the frontier."[10]

Out West, Theodore Roosevelt claimed to have encountered firsthand the frontier's offspring. Admiringly, he wrote, "A cowboy will not submit tamely to an insult, and is ever ready to avenge his own wrongs; nor has he an overwrought fear of shedding blood. He possesses in fact, few of the emasculated, milk-and-water moralities admired by the pseudo-philanthropists; but he does possess, to a very high degree, the stern manly qualities that are invaluable to a nation."[11] Surely such men were well prepared for any test.[12]

Film and television fine-tuned the image. With the frontier in wide-angle, long shot, the camera pans to a close-up of the western hero. Its gaze reveals a handsome and virile man, taut, broad shouldered, and lean. He sits tall in the saddle, alert, his face creased, jaws tight, and stare fixed. We need no reminding that "a hero is one who looks like a hero."[13] Recall the casting for the role: Gary Cooper, John Wayne, Gregory Peck, Henry Fonda, Kirk Douglas, James Arness, Richard Boone, and Clint Eastwood. These are men who stand their ground, calmly, when evil comes their way. While they never seek it out, evil in the human guise invariably does approach. The western hero's moral and physical courage builds from a personal code of honor and a sense of integrity. He knows instinctively that truth is simple and justice is clear. The showdown allows no compromise, no retreat. He responds to an inner voice, realizing that neither words nor God will bring salvation. As a character in the film *The Cowboys* (1972) reminds us, "There ain't no Sundays west of Omaha." These plain-speaking warriors are hardly savage men. Those domesticated by television, especially, have a social conscience and act in the defense of women, family, and community. There is no mistaking the western marshal for a southern sheriff. Once evil is gunned down and the test passed, progress resumes in the region of infinite possibilities. Law and order are established, property secured, freedom protected, and a model of proper manhood passed to the next generation. Only then does the western hero mount his horse and ride in search of still-dangerous places.[14]

Box-office revenues and television rating shares demonstrated that the western resonated with audiences in the 1950s and 1960s. Historians and sociologists have suggested that postwar America was particularly susceptible to hero worship. Other-directed men confined to the bureaucratic mazes of white-collar organizations or the drudgery of factory assembly lines perhaps found escape in the Wild West. The vicarious thrill of facing down a desperado may have offered some relief from the suburban constrictions of mortgage payments, dental bills, and Cub Scout meetings. If there was a sense of lost autonomy, television daily brought proof that one man could still make a difference. In a world enmeshed in complications and contradictions, the simple solutions of the nonconformist man of action would surely have appeal. American men certainly learned something from these heroes. So, too, would boys who needed such role models to counteract threats to their masculinity from a feared overmothering.[15]

The western's appeal also lies in its expression of unifying myths and retelling of cherished legends. In a nation lacking the unity of race, ethnicity, or religion, the western story provides common ground. Americanism is shared experience and heritage. Belief is the touchstone of patriotism. As such, westerns are value laden and embedded with political, cultural, and social messages. They teach about progress and the equality of opportunity that is the openness of America. In the land of the second chance, there are no extremes of wealth and only hard-working, rugged individualists seeking their place in the sun. Western heroes aid them by fighting to keep options open and the dream of abundance alive. By defending law and order, they protect society from its most wicked foes, whether criminal, corporate, or tribal. Evil, according to American tradition, does not infect institutions. It is the work of corrupt men and can be expunged by driving them from the temple. Reflecting its time, western heroes are white, yet they display no markers of class or religious denomination. When fighting indigenous peoples, they are duty bound and act without vindictiveness or desire for personal gain. Audiences expect that their heroes will follow the Golden Rule, or what television and film star Gene Autry called the "Ten Commandments of the Cowboy."[16] The cowboy promised to tell the truth, to help people in distress, and never to tolerate racial or religious prejudice. If in the breach, our heroes must cover baser instincts with noble words.[17]

Significantly, the western hero is self-made and self-reliant. He looks to no one for help in fulfilling his mission. Despite the federal government's historic and indispensable role in building the West, Washington is noticeable on-screen by its absence. When it does make the script, it is usually in the shape of the U.S. Cavalry as a deus ex machina when Indians threaten. A growing sensitivity to the plight of Native Americans eventually heaped controversy and derision even on that role. In other instances, the federal government appears in the form of overweight, meddling eastern bureaucrats insensitive to community needs. The western offered one other cue to Cold War audiences: When it was time to protect their families and communities, western heroes drew a line in the sand and dared the wicked to cross. Appeasement was seldom a word heard in the western lands.

It is no wonder that conservatives saw their future in the western past. Americans, wrote Donald Teeple, are looking for a hero and "want a return to the fundamental *virtues* which made this nation great—death rather than dishonor, justice, liberty, honesty, and human dignity . . . [a return] to the days when things were either black or white—right or wrong."[18] *National Review*'s William Rickenbacker agreed: "These glorious shows, year in and year out, draw the greatest audiences in the country, and that's because people [would] much rather live on the Old Frontier than the New Frontier." He conjured up television's Wyatt Earp as a hero for conservatives and predicted in 1962 that if "somebody from Arizona or Texas with the glint of the Western mountains in his eye gets up some day in front of a really mammoth-size Town Meeting and offers himself as a candidate on a platform of Running the Rascals Out of Town, sixty million of us Westerners will put him in office. Belly up to the bar, boys; good days are coming."[19] Merely a man from the western region would not do. Thus, Californian Richard Nixon did not get the role. Acceptable candidates would have to find authenticity within the myth.

In this quest for authenticity, Senator Barry Goldwater of Arizona had clear advantages. No one could contest his pedigree. Goldwater was born in territorial Arizona, the son of a pioneering family. His grandfather, Michel Goldwater, was a Polish Jew who migrated to California in the wake of the Gold Rush. Bankrupted in the Golden State, he packed his wagon with dry goods in the 1860s and followed his mules to the goldfields of Gila City, Arizona. In the desert, hard work brought rewards. "Big Mike," as he was known to the miners, expanded and diversified his business and soon opened shop in other Arizona towns. Abetting his rise were federal dollars. Arizona was an important theater of operations for the U.S. Army after the Civil War. Not only did the army provide security, but it also awarded Big Mike government contracts to ferry troops, grain, and freight to a growing network of forts. Barry Goldwater denied this history, as do many westerners. He remembered instead: "We didn't know the federal government. Everything that was done, we did it ourselves."[20] This version of family lore became hallowed, a patrimony passed from one Goldwater generation to the next.[21]

Goldwater's mother, JoJo, was another self-made Arizonan. Suffering from "lung fever," she came alone to the territory in 1903 hoping that the dry climate would improve her health. For months, she lived with other "lungers" in an army tent several miles north of Phoenix. Her health gradually returned, and she began work as a nurse in a local hospital. Three years later, she met Michel Goldwater's son Baron, who managed the family's Phoenix store. They married in 1907. Barry was born in a fashionable section of Phoenix on 1 January 1909.[22]

Six decades later, in a speech entitled "The West That Was," Barry Goldwater declared, "People—not stereotypes, but individuals—inhabited the West that proved to be a land of opportunity for my immigrant grandfather, my uncles, and father. . . . There was a future for the bold."[23] Their struggle in the desert was an important lesson for Goldwater. Throughout his life he returned to it in body and mind to draw inspiration. From a barren desert, men and women had reaped the promise of America. Success had not come easily, and it was all the more dear because they had begun with so little and

GRANDFATHER MICHAEL, (Big Mike) Goldwater emigrated from Poland in 1852 and started the American (and Arizonan) branch of the Goldwater family.

UNCLE MORRIS GOLDWATER (son of Mike), who first interested Barry Goldwater in politics. He served as Mayor of Prescott for 21 years, and was one of the founders of the Democratic Party in Arizona.

BARON GOLDWATER, father of Barry. Known as a superb merchandiser. He started in the family business in 1896 and built Goldwaters into one of the most outstanding retail operations in the country.

BARRY'S MOTHER, "MUN," who came to Arizona from Nebraska in 1906 for her health. She met Baron while she was shopping in the store. Today, at 88 or 90 (she won't tell), spry and active, she maintains her own home in Phoenix.

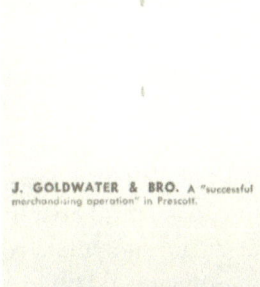 

J. GOLDWATER & BRO. A "successful merchandising operation" in Prescott.

A Goldwater family portrait. Used in campaigning, such images identified Barry Goldwater with a rugged frontier heritage. Note that Michel's name has been anglicized. Arizona Historical Foundation.

the desert foe had been so unyielding. The federal government may have been a prime mover in their history, yet it was the deeds of individuals that filled his memory. The immigrant peddler Michel Goldwater was the core of the family legend. Baron and JoJo were the living embodiments of the self-made. "We don't find people like that today," said Barry Goldwater. "People want it handed out to them. Even people on relief don't want to work. There was no such a thing in those days. You either worked or you starved. People who lived then were a different breed."[24] This legacy was Barry Goldwater's lodestone and it privileged him by ties of blood and opportunity as a legitimate son of the Old West. The Arizona senator's staff would ensure that the story went public. It appeared as background in a multitude of magazine and newspaper articles that helped propel his rise to national political power in the 1950s and 1960s.

To many Americans, coming of age in Arizona suggested the rigors of homesteading and a hardscrabble life. Yet the Goldwater family was part of the Phoenix social and economic elite and experienced little hardship. "I guess I was a spoiled well-off kid," Goldwater would later joke. "I've often told people that I was born in a log cabin equipped with a golf course, a pool table, and a swimming pool."[25] If unable to boast of a personal pioneering experience, Goldwater had the opportunity to pursue a diversity of interests and lead the strenuous life. These activities did much to develop his western persona. His mother encouraged his mechanical abilities and skills in working with his hands. Throughout his life he tinkered on a wide assortment of gadgets and played with inventions. JoJo, afraid only of lightning and tornados (her midwestern legacy), packed provisions and her shotgun and went alone with Barry and his siblings into the backcountry. They took these trips at a time when there were few marked or paved roads in Arizona. The excursions doubled as learning sessions, with JoJo schooling her children in camping, hunting, and fishing. In 1916, when Goldwater was seven years old, they visited Old Orabi on the Hopi Tribe's Third Mesa, kindling in him an appreciation for Native American customs and arts. In his teens, he traded for the first of what would become a collection of more than 400 Hopi kachina dolls. Eventually a Phoenix museum would build a wing to house his collection. Other outings brought the family to Navajo country. As an adult he opened a trading post on the Navajo Reservation and began collecting rugs and artifacts. Other trips took him to ghost towns, mining areas, and mountain regions, and he remained addicted to the Arizona outback all his life. In times of stress as an adult, he disappeared for days in the desert, camping and exploring.[26]

Barry Goldwater took his first pictures with his mother's box camera. By the late 1930s, his interest in photography had evolved from a hobby to a serious pursuit. In 1939 he sold his first photographs to *Arizona Highways*. Eventually, almost 200 of his pictures appeared in the magazine. He published *Arizona Portraits*, the first volume appearing in 1940 and the second in 1946. For the books, he chose from 5,000 negatives to create a montage of photographs that vividly contrasted Arizona's wide vistas with intimate portraits of native peoples. Goldwater's remarkable photographic ability is evident in a self-portrait done at this time. His self-image has him silhouetted and in shadow, wearing a cowboy hat and holding a cigarette. The impression is less of a working cowboy than of an urban one.[27]

Of all of his hobbies, flying was Goldwater's greatest passion. He learned to fly in 1930, soloing after only ten hours of instruction. Flights around Phoenix and Arizona quickly lengthened, and Goldwater made his first cross-country trip, to Los Angeles, in 1931. He would, over his lifetime, clock 12,000 hours of flight time in 165 different types of aircraft, including hel-

In profile, the cowboy Goldwater. This self-portrait offers an image in transition. Here Goldwater resembles the singing cowboy movie-matinee star of the 1930s. Courtesy Bill Saufley.

icopters and gliders. For Goldwater, flying was an experience that confirmed the majesty of God and realized the "ultimate extension of individual freedom."[28] Combining hobbies, he discovered a natural bridge while flying over the Grand Canyon. Flying proved more than a leisure-time pursuit. During the severe winter of 1936 Goldwater helped organize relief flights that dumped hay and feed to save stranded Navajo livestock. On other occasions he delivered medicines to Native American reservations and flew the sick to hospitals.[29]

Goldwater enhanced his reputation as an adventurer and outdoorsman when he joined the Norman Nevills party on a trip down the Colorado River in 1940. Nevills had warned him that "the Colorado is just as tough[,] rough[,] and dangerous as it was when our forerunners Powell, Stone, Stanton, and others took it."[30] Despite the pleading of his wife, who was pregnant with their third child, Goldwater would not be denied. He met the expedition at Green River, Utah, and for forty-two days ran the rapids in a plywood boat. The river and the Grand Canyon awed him: "At this sunset hour the canyon walls are indescribably beautiful, and I fear the magic of photography can never record what I see now. The tall spires near the canyon's top and the walls of the canyon up there look as if God had reached out and swiped a brush of golden paint across them, gilding these rocks in the bright glow of the setting sun."[31]

His naturalist instincts were aroused: "We are on the Colorado . . . that means something more to me than thoughts of electrical power or a harnessed river."[32] Typically western, Goldwater's appreciation for the river only temporarily quieted his enthusiasm for boosterism and economic development. On reaching Lake Mead, he became just the seventy-first known person to travel the Colorado's length. Important to his future, Goldwater recorded the trip on film. He would later, in preparation for a political career, crisscross the state showing this film. "I got to showing that thing as often as five times a day."[33] By April 1941, audiences had surpassed 19,000 people. Those who attended the showings took in more than rapids-running and Grand Canyon scenery. Before them on film and in person was Barry Goldwater, the rugged individualist and courageous adventurer living the life of their dreams. To a ten-year-old who attended a showing in Jerome, Arizona, Goldwater appeared as a "bronze god who had just beaten the river."[34] He only enhanced the mystique by flying his plane to movie exhibitions.[35]

After service as a pilot in World War II, Barry Goldwater returned to Phoenix and entered politics in a run for the city council. He appeared as the citizen-politician, called by the people to service and away from family and career. Leading a good-government ticket composed of business and civic leaders, he joined his fellow candidates in charging opponents with corruption and with having ties to the criminal underworld. He won that election in 1949 and was reelected in 1951, but his sights were already set on a bigger prize. Goldwater announced that he would run against Arizona's U.S. senator Ernest McFarland. Few were surprised by the challenge. Goldwater had made his first public political statement in 1938. Despite the flood of New Deal funds that had stabilized the Arizona economy during the Great Depression, he criticized President Franklin Roosevelt for raising taxes and increasing government spending. "I would like to know," he wrote, "just where you are leading us. Are you going further into the morass that you have led us into or are you going to go back to the good old American way of doing things where business is trusted, where labor earns more, where we take care of our un-employed[?]"[36] Now running for the Senate, Goldwater's main issue was the collectivist threat, both at home and abroad. The New Deal–Fair Deal, he claimed, was a "devilish plan to socialize this country."[37] The stakes were clear: slavery or freedom, right against wrong. This was a war for America's future. Overcoming Arizona's traditional Democratic allegiance and benefiting from General Dwight Eisenhower's coattails, he won narrowly.[38]

In Washington, D.C., he became his own man by attacking the Eisenhower administration. He accused the president of operating a "dime-store New Deal" and "bow[ing] to the siren song of socialism" by failing to cut taxes, balance the budget, and reduce federal power.[39] Goldwater was not jockeying for advantage with the president or in the coming Senate session. Less a legislator than a salesman for a cause. The Arizona senator saw himself as the defender of the people, whose freedom and property were in jeopardy. Goldwater also gained a national reputation by attacking the power of organized labor. He argued that not only did unions rob Americans of their right to work, but as special interests they posed a threat to the democratic process itself.[40]

Given Goldwater's stature, it was not surprising that his 1958 reelection campaign, again against McFarland, attracted national media attention. Most interesting was the way reporters sized him up as a candidate. Paul Healy's *Saturday Evening Post* article titled "The Glittering Mr. Goldwater" was highly laudatory of the Arizona senator: "In his flying clothes he could pass for a character in the Steve Canyon comic strip; . . . As a man's man, he also appeals to women."[41] *Time* magazine's correspondent drew a similar sketch, characterizing Goldwater as a "tall, bronzed, lean-jawed, silver-haired man of 49." He completed Goldwater's portrait: "An experienced pilot, he flew over all 114,000 square miles of his state, landed long enough to fall in love with the landscape and the Indian tribes, snap thousands of color pictures, race down the perilous Colorado River in a flatboat—making friends everywhere."[42] Goldwater would not always find the national media so complimentary, but his campaign against special interests played well in Arizona and voters found convincing his casting of McFarland as a pawn of labor bosses. Goldwater defeated his opponent handily.[43]

This victory had more than local significance. His triumph came in the context of a Republican rout. Of the ten Republican senatorial candidates running for election west of the Mississippi River, Goldwater was the lone victor. Defeat claimed conservatives William Knowland, John Bricker, William Jenner, and George Malone. The election had a critical, defining

In the cockpit of an air force fighter. Photographs like this one frequently decorated newspaper and magazine articles about Goldwater. Arizona Historical Foundation.

effect for Goldwater and the Republican Party. In surviving the Democratic wave, the Arizona senator had enhanced his standing with the Republican rank and file and found open the leadership of the party's conservative wing.

Goldwater's success as a politician was only part of his growing appeal. Victory, after all, had come in remote Arizona, not the best lever with which to raise a national presence. More compelling, the Goldwater persona tripped the folk memory of the western hero. Goldwater was a westerner—a man of action, a rugged individualist, direct, virile, and tough. "For us," wrote conservative James Roberts, "the senator was the knight on the white horse, the Lochinvar riding out of the West to do battle with evil."[44] The image was in part real, in part promoted. On the stump or before television cameras, Goldwater evoked the western hero standing alone against all odds, imbued with frontier virtues, refusing to compromise his beliefs or country. The Arizonan's speaking style enhanced the impression. "His slightly twangy, dehydrated voice," wrote speech professor Ernest Wrage, "suggests that of cowboys of TV westerns."[45] With his no-nonsense tone, ramrod-straight body, and grim face behind black horn-rim glasses, the Arizonan always appeared as if he were facing down wrongdoers at high noon. Even Goldwater's tinkering with gadgets brought to mind the frontiersman, inventive, practical, and utilitarian. The senator's staff nourished the mystique, distributing publicity photographs of Goldwater clad in jeans and cowboy hat astride a horse. At other times he was pictured mounting the modern equivalent—an air force jet fighter. The national press picked up the theme and described Goldwater as the archetypical "cowboy" who, with "jaw squared," was "dynamic, lean, and bronzed."[46] If critics derided Barry as the Marlboro Man who shot from the hip, their words betrayed them. They, too, were captives of the myth.

The flow of tough talk accelerated in the 1960s as Goldwater stumped the nation in search of conservatives. Knowing that the road to victory lay through the Republican Party, he challenged his supporters to "grow up. . . . if we want to take this party back—and I think we can some day—let's get to work."[47] Sounding the traditional western cry against colonialism, he rallied conservatives to fight the "East Coast elite" of Wall Street, Madison Avenue, and Harvard University that dominated the party and dictated its standard bearers.[48] This meant a campaign, without compromise and down to the grass roots, to purge moderates and liberals from the ranks.

In 1960, Goldwater's book *The Conscience of a Conservative* appeared and quickly became a best seller, going through twenty printings in four years and eventually selling 3.5 million copies. The 123-page primer was bold and blunt. Goldwater demanded that Americans awaken to the dangers of liberalism and to the truth of conservative principles. The foe was the federal government, which had become "a Leviathan, a vast national authority out of touch with the people, and out of their control." Forcing government to relinquish its grip on power would mean "freedom" for farmers, labor, and ordinary citizens. He demanded a retreat from the welfare state, "the currently favored instrument of collectivization"; he rejected the income tax as "confiscatory" and demanded cuts in the federal bureaucracy and spending. The book was a call to battle: "I have little interest in streamlining government or in making it more efficient, for I mean to reduce it in size. I do not intend to promote welfare, for I propose to extend freedom. My aim is not to pass laws, but to repeal them." On the foreign front, Goldwater insisted that the United States repudiate all self-imposed restraints on the exercise of power and pursue total victory. He rebuffed negotiations and summit conferences that would not offer the United States substantive gains, and he called for a "reexamination" of America's commitment to the United Nations and for the resumption of nuclear testing.[49] It was now time to make credible the policies of brinkmanship and communist rollback that the Eisenhower administration had decreed and then deserted. "In addition

Claiming a western heritage. In this photo taken during his political rise, a determined Goldwater posed for the camera in cowboy hat, buckskin jacket, and jeans and with shotgun at the ready. Note the contrast between myth and reality: The photographer posed Goldwater standing guard over plastic patio furniture arranged around a swimming pool. Copyright Yousuf Karsh, courtesy Retna Ltd.

to guarding our frontiers," he wrote, "we must try to puncture his. In addition to keeping the free world free, we must try to make the Communist world free." Under a Goldwater presidency, the United States would actively support liberation movements in China and Eastern Europe to compel communist withdrawal. Here was the domino theory in reverse. He reiterated this message two years later in *Why Not Victory?* Goldwater reassured Americans: "Every time we have stood up to the Communists they have backed down. Our trouble is we have not stood up to them enough."[50] The book became an instant best seller.

To anticommunism, fiscal responsibility, and limited government, the Arizonan added a theme that befitted his western aura. Goldwater echoed the sheriff of the Old West when he introduced the issue of law and order, previously a local concern, into presidential politics. He derided U.S. Supreme Court decisions for coddling criminals and attributed rising crime rates to declining moral standards. He condemned the "bullies and marauders" who acted without fear of retribution and made Americans anxious even in their own homes. "I don't have to quote statistics to you," he said grimly. "You know. Every wife and mother—yes every woman and girl knows what I mean."[51] With outlaws on the loose, it was time to put a western lawman in the White House.

Looking to the future, Barry Goldwater reached beyond the conservative rank and file. He preached the politics of inclusion and attempted to enlist what he called the "forgotten" and "silent" Americans "who quietly go about the business of paying and praying, working and saving. They mind their own business and meet their responsibilities on a day-to-day basis. They are the group who, for too long, have had their voices drowned out by the clamor of pressure groups which increases in volume as their numbers decline." To turn the nation, conservatives had to win their support, retrieve their liberty, and "stem the seemingly inexorable march toward the automation of human beings."[52] The media gave Goldwater's "Platform for the Forgotten American" extensive coverage and trumpeted its positive approach and appeal across class, racial, ethnic, and religious lines. Yet the politics of inclusion rang hollow in many Americans' ears. In crafting a campaign strategy that relied on a coalition of white voters in the South and West and then voting against the 1964 Civil Rights Act, Barry Goldwater appeared to betray his own principles.

By 1964, conservatives had completed the capture of the Republican Party and nominated Barry Goldwater for president. He set the tone for the campaign during his acceptance speech at the Republican National Convention in July. Standing before the delegates, he was tight, unsmiling, and uncompromising. He responded to the cheering delegates with neither joy nor excitement. Goldwater drew his line in the sand: "Any who join us in all sincerity, we welcome. Those who do not care for our cause we do not expect to enter our ranks in any case." He railed against "false prophets" and the "swampland of collectivism." It was time for Americans to reclaim their role as "freedom's missionaries in a doubting world." Toward the end of the speech, in a phrase underlined for emphasis, he declared, "Extremism in the defense of liberty is no vice. Moderation in the pursuit of justice is no virtue."[53] Said a reporter, "My God, he's going to run as Barry Goldwater."[54] The Arizonan was not the only westerner in the race. Lyndon Baines Johnson was Texas born, proudly wore a Stetson, was often photographed on horseback, and laid claim to a ranch. Nevertheless, Goldwater trumped LBJ, for the president's liberal rhetoric and position as a Washington insider compromised his western persona.

Long protected by a sympathetic local and national press, the Arizona senator had never learned the politician's art. In presidential politics, his shoot-from-the-hip style became rash and reckless, and his every gaffe was exploited. He grew brittle under the intense scrutiny and criticism. On the campaign trail, his speeches lost their western bearings and resembled Old Testament jeremiads. His out-thrust jaw and defiant stance no longer evoked the western hero's spirit of confidence and optimism. With a prosperous economy, Vietnam still distant, the nation numbed by tragedy, cities yet to explode in racial violence, Barry Goldwater, by his own hand, was slaughtered at the polls. The conservative deliverer had not yet come. What was needed was a different kind of western hero. Soon, out of the West, came a man who smiled rather than scowled, who waved rather than shook his fist.

Western wear was not a natural or obvious fit for Ronald Reagan. Barry Goldwater was typecast, but Reagan's image was more complex and subtle. Reagan was neither born a westerner nor came to it instinctively. He liked to ride horses, yet he always preferred an English saddle. In Hollywood, he played a diversity of roles and was the western hero in only a handful of his more than fifty films. He hosted a western series on television for just a year. In making Reagan western, film and television producers drew from his previous roles. His western hero would be within his range: righteous but charming, resolute but relaxed. Nor did Reagan desire to cast a dark shadow. He remained in character, only now in a western setting. This media-made identification was sufficient to begin authorizing Reagan's credentials as a western hero.

Reagan's look and manner facilitated the transformation. He was more than six feet tall, handsome, and athletic. He impressed audiences as a man of integrity who would not compromise his principles. He talked tough and stood for law and order. Off the set, he played to the image by wearing cowboy hats and jeans and occasionally making public appearances on horseback. On the heels of Barry Goldwater, a conservative activist as western hero did not give Americans pause, and they had no trouble drawing the connection. At the same time, Reagan softened the hard edge of his beliefs by leavening speeches with humor and an optimistic glimpse of a promising future. Whereas Goldwater was the rough-hewn son of the frontier, Reagan was the likable son of the Golden West, a role that would become Ronald Reagan's most recognizable persona. Reagan did not intentionally deceive his fans. Although the role was constructed, he had internalized it and believed passionately in its reality. The effort was not forced and came naturally.

Ronald Reagan was born on 6 February 1911 in Tampico, Illinois, in the front bedroom of a five-room flat above the general store where his father worked. "Our family," Reagan recalled, "didn't exactly come from the wrong side of the tracks, but we were certainly always within sound of the train whistle."[55] Tampico was only briefly home, for father Jack Reagan, an itinerant shoe salesman, chased success through the small towns and cities of Illinois. By age nine, Dutch, as his father nicknamed him, had lived in Chicago, Galesburg, Monmouth, again in Tampico, and Dixon. His mother worked in dress shops, devoting her spare time to her children, alcoholic husband, church and charity work, and theater productions. At age fifteen, Dutch Reagan began the first of seven summers working seven days a week as a lifeguard at a particularly treacherous stretch of the Rock River. He recorded seventy-seven saves, notching his triumphs on a log. In 1929 he won a scholarship to the Christian Church's Eureka College, where he joined a fraternity, played football, and majored in economics and sociology. He graduated at the depth of the Great Depression but secured a job as a sports announcer on radio in Davenport, Iowa. He later moved to Des Moines when a better opportunity appeared. He was popular, and listeners enjoyed his mellifluous voice and easy manner on the air. In Des Moines he pursued his love for horseback riding by joining the Fourteenth Cavalry Regiment of the Iowa National Guard and became an accomplished horseman.[56]

Dutch Reagan's dream, however, outgrew the Midwest. As it did to so many others, the West beckoned him to a brighter future. He set his sights on Hollywood and the movies and parlayed a contact in the film industry into a screen test. He signed with Warner Brothers in 1937 at the age of twenty-six. Apart from short trips to California relating to his job as a sports broadcaster, he was a stranger to the West. Although given ten days to report to work at the studio, he raced from Des Moines to the shining city in the West in three, stopping briefly in Cheyenne, Wyoming, and Nephi, Utah. He remembered only the last segment of the trip: "I crossed the burning desert, and sundown saw me driving that long stretch between the banked orange trees down from San Bernardino to Los Angeles."[57] Reagan was always proud of his rise. As a Horatio Alger, he had proven that the traditional means of hard work and self reliance brought success in a land of opportunity.[58]

The casting department at Warner Brothers began Dutch's apprenticeship in the industry as a lead in quickly and cheaply made B movies, or the second feature on a double bill. He debuted in June 1937 in *Love Is on the Air* as a fast-talking, crusading radio announcer fighting organized crime. In *Submarine D-1* (1937), he had a bit part as a Navy flyer. He appeared several times as Brass Bancroft, U.S. Secret Service agent, who broke up counterfeit money rings and arrested spies conspiring to steal American military secrets. "I became," wrote Reagan, "the Errol Flynn of the B's. I was as brave as Errol, but in a low-budget fashion."⁵⁹ He also played a classic pianist, a Broadway hustler, a military school cadet, and an American pilot in the Royal Air Force. Dutch eventually graduated to supporting roles in A movies. In *Santa Fe Trail* (1940), he was the likable George Custer who loses the girl to best friend Jeb Stuart, played by Errol Flynn. His most memorable parts were as George Gipp, the fallen football hero in *Knute Rockne, All American* (1940) and the tragic Drake McHugh in *Kings Row* (1942). In his first western, *The Bad Man* (1941), Reagan was neither bad nor the man. He was billed behind Wallace Beery, who starred as the lovable bandito Pancho Lopez, and Lionel Barrymore, who played the wheelchair-bound ranch owner. Reagan at least got the girl. In his first five years in Hollywood, Ronald Reagan made thirty-three films, averaging one every eight weeks. With the coming of World War II, he entered the Army Air Corps and was assigned to the motion picture unit in Culver City, California, where he made training films and starred in *This Is the Army* (1943), which brought together stars serving in the armed forces. Following the war, he was the lead in several light romantic comedies, including *That Hagen Girl* (1947), *John Loves Mary* (1949), and *The Girl from Jones Beach* (1949). Looking at the rushes to his movies, Dutch gained new perspective and learned lessons that proved valuable beyond Hollywood: "What a shock this was! It has taken me many years to get used to seeing myself as others see me, and also seeing myself instead of my mental picture of the character I'm playing."⁶⁰

Ronald Reagan had long chafed under studio resistance that kept him from starring in what he called "a cavalry and Indian epic."⁶¹ Movie producers, he complained, "didn't think I was the ranch type."⁶² But Reagan was insistent about getting "a crack at that outdoor stuff."⁶³ He cherished boyhood memories of western heroes at Saturday matinees: "I'd had an affection for those scenes when a troop of Cavalrymen in blue tunics and gold braid, flags raised and bugles blowing, raced across the prairie to rescue beleaguered pioneers."⁶⁴ His friends John Wayne and Gregory Peck had been cast "saber in hand. . . . Everybody rode into the sunset behind the fluttering cavalry guidons." In the waning years of his film career, Reagan got the chance to play the western hero. Of his last thirteen movies, four were westerns.

In 1951 *The Last Outpost* (later released as *Cavalry Charge*) put him in the saddle in old Arizona. Instead of a blue tunic, he wore Confederate gray. He played Vance Britten, a southern cavalry captain sent west to intercept gold being shipped to the Union. In a tired plot device, his brother commands the local Union garrison and has orders to catch him and secure the gold trail. Meanwhile, Britten's ex-fiancée appears in the thick of the action and rekindles their prewar romance. This does not bode well for a movie that deals in grave matters. People are murdered, negotiations grow tense, and Indian attacks are beaten back, but the music and dialogue are, at times, whimsical and serve to lighten the plot. A clownish Washington politician provides comic relief. Nor does Reagan give bite to his role. He proves a crafty foe, repeatedly outsmarting the larger and better equipped U.S. Army. Yet it all seems like a game. He is boyish, charming, and playful. He never sweats, and his uniform remains clean and fresh. He deals in death but only indirectly, for deceased adversaries never appear in the same frame. Here was a sunny western hero without a gritty side, who did not need the contrast of evil to reveal his inherent goodness.

The movie did not receive strong reviews, but it did begin the process of layering Reagan's persona. Against the big southwestern sky and the barren desert, Dutch cut a dashing figure. Ignoring the petty regional quarrels between North and South, he charged with saber drawn, handsome in the saddle, to make America safe. In the process, he never lost his winning smile or disarming manner. Reagan was disappointed with the final cut because "it wasn't an epic." But he saw the bright side: "It was in color, [and] it was loaded with action."[65]

Nor was Reagan pleased by his next western, *Law and Order* (1953), though it served to enhance the mystique. Reagan played Frame Johnson, the lawman said to have cleaned up Tombstone. The trailer announced that "For half a century the West[,] wild[,] magnificent[,] untamed was ripped by outlaw bullets . . . lashed by outlaw fear." To save "an aroused and fearful population" came the "fighting marshals" Wyatt Earp, Wild Bill Hickok, and "the legendary Frame Johnson of Arizona. . . . Law was his pledge, order . . . his creed." The movie immediately testifies to Johnson's credentials. Asked if he had killed all the men buried in Boot Hill, Johnson replies, "Only those that didn't get hung." When an angry mob tries to lynch an outlaw without a trial, he faces it down. "You wanted law and order in this town," he shouts, "you've got it. And you're going to keep having it as long as I'm marshal." That tenure proves brief, for Johnson is disgusted with the town folk and resigns. In true western fashion he says his few words: "We're pulling out . . . I'm all through." He leaves town to get married and run cattle on his new ranch. But no western will let a lawman ride away so easily. A tyrannical rancher, cattle rustlers, a corrupt sheriff, and the death of his brother force Johnson to pin the badge back on and wage war against the "sinkhole of violence and evil." He goes to fight even as his fiancée pleads, "Must you always think like a marshal? Can't you think like a human being just this once?" We knowingly nod at the response of his sidekick: "It's the way he is. You can't ask a man to change." The movie's conclusion offers no surprises. Peace, justice, and civilization return to the West.

In *Law and Order*, Reagan's broad shoulders, tough talk, and gunplay distinguished him as one of the breed of western heroes. Yet despite the intensity of the dialogue and the high body count, Reagan underplayed his role. His was a soft presence, moving with little energy or grit. He appeared domesticated, sprucing up the ranch house for his fiancée and washing dishes; a tender and patient beau in his scenes with her. Dutch was relaxed, not cool, courageous yet unable to evoke the tension inherent in confrontation. He grappled with evil but was untainted by its embrace. The end is optimistic and comforting. Without hesitation or decompression, Johnson settled down to raise a family, his past having no bearing on his future.

Reagan made *Cattle Queen of Montana* (1954) and *Tennessee's Partner* (1955) in succession. In both, he received second billing. Shot against the Technicolor backdrop of Glacier National Park, *Cattle Queen* tells the story of Nevada Smith, played by Barbara Stanwyck, who drives a herd of Texas cattle to Montana only to have it rustled on arrival. The cattle king of Montana does not want competition and has supplied Indians with guns to chase away interlopers. Reagan appears as a U.S. Army officer named Farrell who has secretly infiltrated the cattle king's empire to investigate his illegal activities. The script is mediocre and the ending predictable. A romance develops between Stanwyck and Reagan, the Indians are restrained, and the cattle baron's plot is foiled. Just before the credits roll, the two lovers ride off to build their own cattle empire. Primarily a vehicle for Stanwyck, Reagan is undercover and often off screen. He takes the foreground, on occasion, to show off some fancy gunplay. At other times, he stands off to the side, observing the action or preparing to rescue his romantic interest. Even if not the lead, Reagan still grew western from association. He stood tall and handsome as the big blue sky and snow-covered mountains of Montana country filled the frame.

Reagan also supported John Payne in *Tennessee's Partner*. The film opens with Reagan, looking authentic as Cowpoke, riding through the desert scrub on his way to the mining camp of Sandy Bar. Despite this promising beginning, the western man disappears from the screen for a dozen minutes while the scene shifts to more important happenings in town. Reagan's character finally arrives in Sandy Bar and saves the life and becomes the partner of the slick gambler Tennessee, Payne's character. "I saw a fella in trouble," Cowpoke explains, "I tried to help him out." The action then centers on Tennessee, who is not only good at cards but experienced with the ladies. Meanwhile, Cowpoke's focus is on marriage. The subplot thickens when Tennessee recognizes his sidekick's intended bride as one of his "discards" and a "rattlesnake" and notorious "gold digger." Playing the innocent, Cowpoke fusses over his fiancée, buys her a wedding dress, and denies himself

Ronald Reagan as lawman Frame Johnson in *Law and Order*. From such films, audiences learned the difference between a western marshal and a southern sheriff. Courtesy Wisconsin Center for Film and Theater Research.

all vices. The male bond, although tested, remains firm, and Tennessee saves his friend from an unfaithful partner. Unfortunately, the loyal Cowpoke must take a bullet for his friend and dies. Living and dying by the cowboy code, he passes from the scene without muttering a last word.

Critics judged Reagan a competent actor, but panned him as an action-adventure hero. Garry Wills found Reagan "too light and likable to have the menace needed for such roles. . . . [He was] a light romantic leading man, with a good voice, good timing in the reading of his lines, [and] skill in handling dialogue."[66] Stephen Hunter agreed: "He appeared not to harbor dark longings, or nurse grudges, or fester with bitterness. He had no tragic dimension. He seemed moodless, unsomber, never a dark or looming presence, always a reassuring presence."[67] Yet in the age of television, Reagan offered Americans the kind of hero they wanted. As Richard Corliss observed, "A movie star typically projects danger and a TV star comfort and familiarity. Reagan had this domesticated appeal."[68] Dutch Reagan was confident in the face of adversity, certain that good would triumph. His characters were not violent men even when they killed. They did not brood, harbor prejudice, or reveal a tragic flaw. In just one movie, his last, did he play a villain. Viewers felt that they could trust him. They were attracted by his appearance, not his depth. In Reagan's nonthreatening presence, Hunter notes, we discerned that, "He was what we liked best about ourselves." Critics would never list his films among the best westerns, but these roles reinforced his heroic persona and extended its range. When he walked away from the western set, he carried a new authority. The memory would become the reality and stronger in the telling. According to the *Washington Post*'s Thomas Szasz, writing in 1971: "Mr. Reagan seemed to possess all the virtues of the Western hero he portrayed so often and so well on the screen."[69] In the first rank of believers in the myth was Ronald Reagan himself.

Off the set, Dutch Reagan pursued the outdoors, even if only a brief drive from Hollywood. He bought a 300-acre ranch in the Malibu Hills and bred and raised thoroughbred horses. He loved to ride clad in jodhpurs, posting in the English style: "There is no place on earth I'd rather be than in a saddle, on the back of a horse."[70] In addition to the horses, he ran fifty head of cattle on the ranch. Meanwhile, he felt the yearnings of the homesteader and considered retirement: "To tell the truth, I'd run out of things to do and wanted to really farm." He grew hay and enjoyed "the thrill of looking back at a furrow you've plowed in your own ground." Working the land reinforced self-perceptions. "My every instinct is to turn down an acting job if it interferes with getting the plowing done."[71] Like others before him, he would leave the plow for a higher calling.

Reagan's career took another track when the General Electric Corporation (GE) asked him to host its weekly television program, the *General Electric Theater*. Part of his job description was personal appearance tours of GE plants to boost worker morale. Reagan went on the road giving workers a glimpse of the movie star, telling stories about his fellow actors and the Hollywood scene. His pitch gradually changed and became more political, reflecting a growing disenchantment with liberalism and his battle against

Ronald Reagan, self-portrait, 1981. Courtesy Ronald Reagan Library.

"fellow travelers" and communists in Hollywood. When his assignment expanded to community relations, the speech gradually lost its show business themes and began to strike out at the "rising tide of collectivism." Like Barry Goldwater, he hit the "mashed potato circuit" to target the federal bureaucracy for instigating the assault on liberty. "Freedom," he warned, "has never been so fragile, so close to slipping from our grasp." He ticked off the stories of ordinary men and women enslaved by red tape and federal regulations. Not only had government robbed Americans of their wealth, but it also weakened their self reliance, initiative, and moral fiber. Like the western hero, he cut to the chase: "We are told that the problem is too complex for a simple answer. They are wrong. There is no easy answer, but there is a simple answer." He declared an end to "appeasement" at home and abroad and called on all Americans to confront "the most evil enemy mankind has known in his long climb from the swamp to the stars."[72] The words were tough and frightening, but the speaker was handsome, friendly, relaxed, and charming. He spoke without animosity and served God beyond denomination. Clear and direct, sincere and resolute, he was intensely persuasive.[73]

In 1962 *General Electric Theater* was canceled after losing a ratings war with the Cartwrights of *Bonanza*. GE had also found that its star had become too controversial for the corporate image and did not renew his contract. Although deeply involved in conservative politics and particularly the Goldwater for President campaign, Ronald Reagan signed on in 1964 as host, commercial pitchman, and occasional star of the television western series *Death Valley Days*—"Where western history comes alive." To the sight and sound of the U.S. Borax twenty-mule team tramping through Death Valley, Reagan was again before the viewing public. The series would reconfirm and fine-tune Reagan's identity as a western hero.[74]

Dutch Reagan's western persona played well on television and was particularly suited to the style of *Death Valley Days*. The program avoided "gunplay-and-gore plots" for dramatic, human-interest tales that showcased individuals who were challenged by crisis and emerged as heroes.[75] Repeatedly, Reagan was cast in episodes about selfless men of integrity who calmly take the initiative and make a difference for community and nation.

In "Tribute to a Dog," he played attorney George Vest. Vest risks a promising political career to bring a lawsuit against the local power broker, who had recklessly shot a young boy's dog. "I'm warning you," he threatens Reagan, "drop this case or face the consequences!" But simple truths and the weak must be defended, regardless of the danger. In his appeal to the jury Reagan observes, "Justice is a funny thing. If you put too many wrongs on the scale, it gets awfully hard to make it balance out right again."[76] No jury could deny that truth.

Reagan is the young naval captain David Farragut in "The Battle of San Francisco." News reaches Reagan that the city has "gone mad" when 8,000 vigilantes riot, loot, and take to lynching innocent citizens. Unable to contact superiors for instructions and fearing that California might be split from the Union, the naval captain goes into action. Although determined, he knows the risks: "I might get myself a court martial, but I've got no choice." Reagan single-handedly faces down the Barbary Coast mob, and with the threat of a naval bombardment, restores order to the community. An admiring subordinate observes, "He expects as much of others as he can do himself, but he's the only one of his kind."[77]

Reagan also comes to the defense of the City by the Bay in "Raid on the San Francisco Mint." The crisis now is financial, and as banker William

Chapman Ralston, he is willing to gamble fortune and future for his community. Vowing "I won't let San Francisco die," Reagan outwits a vain federal bureaucrat and secures tons of gold bullion, restoring the confidence of depositors and ending the run on the banks.[78]

In "No Gun behind His Badge," the scene is lawless Abilene, Texas, where three marshals have been murdered in just two months. Reagan plays ex–New York City policeman Thomas Smith, a man of principle, fierce in his convictions, who has contracted with the law-and-order committee to clean up the town. To the disbelief of his employer, Reagan announces that while he once "threw a lot of lead," he no longer carries a gun. Refusing to be mocked for his ideals, the new marshal brings civilization to Abilene without gunplay. His work is cut short when the town bully shoots him with a concealed pistol. Wild Bill Hickok, who just happens to be on the scene, offers a hopeful epitaph: "You know, maybe he was right, just a little bit too soon."[79]

Reagan appeared in his last *Death Valley Days* episode in October 1965. Anticipating a run for the governorship of California the following year, he canceled his contract with the show's producers, ending a twenty-eight-year career in show business. Close friends John Wayne and Chuck Connors, both men with strong western film and television credentials, offered to replace him if necessary to facilitate his withdrawal. *Death Valley Days* had served Reagan well and proved an excellent platform from which to launch a political campaign. The series had reinvigorated his western persona, enabling him to portray and identify with men who had the courage of their convictions, were rugged individualists, and fought for the right. It broadcast images of conservative moderation and civic responsibility that put Reagan in sharp contrast to the politics of extremism that had played so poorly in 1964. Such messages became more convincing as domestic events threatened American stability and defied liberal solution. As the western legend and the man continued to merge for viewers, the boundary between the real and the fanciful blurred for the messenger. As Dutch remembered it: "I didn't even have to get out of my ranch clothes for the filming."[80]

Echoing Barry Goldwater's entry into politics, Ronald Reagan made his first bid for office in 1966 as the reluctant citizen-politician called from private life by public duty. He pledged to start a "prairie fire of reform," to rekindle traditional values of hard work, self reliance, and personal morality.[81] Declaring government the people's enemy, he promised to rein in its power by cutting waste, taxes, and bureaucracy. In the fashion of the Old West, Reagan made law and order his priority, and voters had no doubt about his targets. Students of the University of California, Berkeley, had drawn his ire since the Free Speech Movement had mobilized in the fall of 1964. He decried their growing resistance and continuing demand for authority as well as the "moral collapse" on campus. It was time, he announced, "to clean up the mess at Berkeley." Racial problems in the Golden State were also a police matter for the conservative. In a veiled reference that no one needed to decode, he warned, "Our city streets are jungle paths after dark with more crimes of violence than New York, Pennsylvania, and Massachusetts combined."[82] Reagan, who believed that federal social programs promoted crime and incited racial violence, repeatedly assured anxious white Californians that a Watts riot could never occur on his watch. Although Reagan noted that he would never have voted for the Civil Rights Act of 1964, he declared his willingness to enforce it "at gunpoint if necessary."[83] Few blacks were comforted. Governor Edmund G. "Pat" Brown believed that the election would hinge on the issues. Yet Ronald Reagan counted on more than his conservative agenda. Tall and tanned, he was at once celebrity, patriot, and westerner. According to a newspaper journalist who had observed him on the campaign trail: "He glows with good health. His appearance is statuesque. He will overwhelm the ladies and charm the gentlemen. As Reagan faced the flag . . . he was heroic."[84] Not every candidate could have pulled off that effect.[85]

As a newcomer to politics and uninformed about state issues, Reagan hired the consulting firm of Spencer Roberts to manage his race. It, in turn, contracted with Stanley Plog's and Kenneth Holder's Behavioral Science Corporation to prepare the candidate for the campaign. Reagan's handlers found their candidate weak on the issues and tailored position papers to fit his conservative philosophy. They also taught him to stop "overanswering" questions and make his responses "short and snappy." Encouraging his "sense of righteousness," they trained him to keep "his cool in all kinds of situations."[86] These were minor adjustments, for they were convinced that Reagan was his own greatest asset. "No producer," Stuart Spencer insisted, "should ever mess with this guy."[87] Voters already knew him. Through film and countless public appearances, he had impressed them as warm, sincere, humble, and confident. Film and television had also embedded the image of the western hero in their minds. Thus, crowds were not surprised when the candidate rode in parades on horseback dressed as a cowboy. Chuck Connors and John Wayne made frequent appearances with their friend and added naturally to the campaign ambience. Nor was this a difficult role for Reagan. Said Spencer, "That was him. He adopted the West. He didn't put on a western thing. It was natural for him. He loved the West, the horses, the cavalry, and his ranch. He was comfortable with that. That was him."[88]

Reagan's efforts, alone, did not prompt the appearance of the western hero in the campaign. The *San Francisco Chronicle* found Reagan's western aura so recognizable that it used that guise to picture him in political cartoons. In June 1966 the newspaper portrayed Reagan as a two-gun sheriff walking through Sather Gate on the Berkeley campus to bring order to the university. Later in the month, the *Chronicle* guessed at Reagan's higher political ambitions and showed him in western attire riding a Republican elephant and galloping past Richard Nixon to Washington, D.C. In another cartoon, Governor Brown was enveloped in Reagan's western persona and outfitted as a cowboy in a "high noon" face-off. The *Los Angeles Times* also found the gunfighter analogy appropriate and had Reagan and Brown in a similar pose. Meanwhile, Brown misjudged his opponent's appeal. He played into the myth by running ads titled "Man versus Actor," with Reagan appearing in western costume. This did not help Brown's cause. Nor could Brown overcome the heavy liabilities of events at Berkeley and in Watts. Comforted by Ronald Reagan's rhetoric and persona, California voters in November elected him by a margin of almost a million votes out of 6.5 million cast.[89]

Even as the western film and television series faded from view in the early 1970s, Ronald Reagan's aura remained vibrant and meaningful. His return to the spotlight occurred when traditional values came under attack, America retreated before its enemies, and financial futures eroded under inflation. In 1980, in Marlboro Man fashion, Reagan posed wearing cowboy hat and shirt on billboards, buttons, and posters that announced "America is Reagan Country." His message of morality, strength, renewal, and optimism had not changed. The answers were still simple, and he quoted the John Wayne character in the movie *The Alamo* to remind Americans that "there's right and there's wrong. You gotta do one or the other."[90] In his acceptance speech at the Republican National Convention, he scorned the nation's leaders for betraying the people: "Adversaries large and small test our will and seek to confound our resolve, but we are given weakness when we need strength; vacillation when the time demands firmness."[91] He took office pledging to defeat "special interests" and return the nation and the future to the people. Soon he would set his sights on the "evil empire," keeping his words tough as befitting the western hero. He claimed progress at the end of his first term, announcing that "America is back and standing tall."[92] In his farewell address in 1989, he was straightforward and plainspoken, reminding Americans never to let down their guard: "It's still trust but verify. It's still play, but cut the cards. It's still watch closely. And don't be afraid to see what you see."[93] By the time former Soviet leader Mikhail Gorbachev visited the Reagan ranch, he had earned a white cowboy hat. Tellingly, he put it on backward.[94]

During his White House years, President Reagan maintained a high western profile. He made frequent visits to his 688-acre Rancho del Cielo in the

The cowboy on parade during the 1966 election. On the ranch, Reagan preferred jodhpurs and an English saddle. AP/Wide World Photos.

"Bring on them beatnik varmints!"

The western hero at Berkeley. *San Francisco Chronicle*, reprinted with permission.

Santa Ynez Mountains near Santa Barbara. The official photographer and press releases caught him in Stetson and blue jeans living the strenuous life, riding horses, mending fences, clearing brush, and chopping wood. Echoing the line from a *Death Valley Days* episode and reaffirming his egalitarian nature, a friend who had helped him restore the adobe ranch house recalled, "He never asked me to do anything he wouldn't do."[95] Secret Service agents caught the spirit and gave the president the code name "Rawhide."[96] Even the attempt on Reagan's life enhanced the image. The *Boston Globe*'s liberal columnist David Nyhan wrote, "Reagan won our hearts the day he was shot. He almost became JFK and settled for John Wayne, becoming legend with a wince and a wisecrack: 'I hope all you doctors are Republicans.'"[97] For conservatives, the magic of the western hero remained potent long after Reagan had left the White House. Some even hoped that it was transferable and could still be bartered for votes into the next century.

At Ronald Reagan's death in June 2004, his most poignant and recognizable persona was western. Both *Time* and *Newsweek* magazines put the Rea-

At home on the range. Courtesy Ronald Reagan Library.

gan-as-cowboy photograph on their covers. *USA Today* offered its readers a commemorative portrait of Ronald Reagan in a ten-gallon cowboy hat. At the National Cathedral, President George W. Bush eulogized Reagan and measured him by the cowboy code: "He believed that the gentleman always does the kindest thing. He believed that the people were basically good and had the right to be free. He believed that bigotry and prejudice were the

The Bush campaign, 2000. Author's collection.

worst things a person could be guilty of." When Reagan "saw evil camped across the horizon, he called that evil by name." If he "showed what a president should be, he also showed what a man should be." He was, concluded Bush, the people's president and "wore his title lightly and it fit like a white Stetson."[98] The funeral that Reagan had begun planning in 1981 took up the myth. The ceremonies moved out West to his presidential library, whose entrance is graced by a larger-than-life statue of Dutch in full cowboy regalia. Appropriately, the sun set in the western sky. The western hero departed according to legend. No one was surprised. American audiences had seen the ending so many times before.

During the 1950s and 1960s, conservatives sought standard bearers to lead them from the political wilderness. They first fell in line behind Senator Barry Goldwater of Arizona. When he stumbled, they turned to the actor, then activist Ronald Reagan. Although very different in background, Goldwater and Reagan invoked the creation myth of the American West and appeared as Turnerian frontiersmen. Goldwater from the Arizona territory had the hard edge of the classic western hero in demeanor, rhetoric, and style. Reagan, with his roots in the Midwest and with years of training as an actor, offered a more carefully constructed image that encompassed Horatio Alger, the Hollywood star, and the western man. In the part, they could persuasively decry the decline of American society and champion the return of the rugged, self-reliant westerner of yesteryear who moved by a personal code of morality and honor. With that return, they were certain, there would come an American rebirth. People believed, for both men had internalized the role and were convinced of their own authenticity. Their projection worked well, and few ever contested the claim. Context, meanwhile, offered them opportunity, and they began the transformation of the conservative movement by tapping into the popular western wave that swept film and television. In the guise of western heroes, they proclaimed a conservatism of inclusion that rallied "forgotten" Americans across class, ethnic, gender, religious, and regional lines and against government and the "special interests." The celebration often disguised their partisanship. Even if not personally prejudiced, the conservatives' message had limits. In coded calls for states' rights and law and order, they marked the boundaries for exclusion. The western hero of film and television has since disappeared except in reruns. Yet he retains his relevance, a political symbol that reveals what we dream and also what we fear.

NOTES

1. Oriana Fallaci, *Interview with History* (Boston: Houghton Mifflin, 1976), 41.

2. For examples, see Jonathan Schoenwald, *A Time for Choosing: The Rise of Modern American Conservatism* (New York: Oxford University Press, 2001); John Andrews, *The Other Side of the Sixties* (New Brunswick, N.J.: Rutgers University Press, 1997); Gregory Schneider, *Cadres for Conservatism* (New York: New York University Press, 1999); Jerome Himmelstein, *To the Right: The Transformation of American Conservatism* (Berkeley and Los Angeles: University of California Press, 1990); Mary Brennan, *Turning Right in the Sixties: The Conservative Capture of the GOP* (Chapel Hill: University of North Carolina Press, 1995); Dan T. Carter, *The Politics of Rage: George Wallace, the Origins of the New Conservatism, and the Transformation of American Politics* (New York: Simon & Schuster, 1995); Lee Edwards, *Goldwater: The Man Who Made a Revolution* (Washington, D.C.: Regnery, 1995); Robert Alan Goldberg, *Barry Goldwater* (New Haven, Conn.: Yale University Press, 1995); Peter Iverson, *Barry Goldwater, Native Arizonan* (Norman: University of Oklahoma Press, 1997); Rick Perlstein, *Before the Storm: Barry Goldwater and the Unmaking of the American Consensus* (New York: Hill & Wang, 2001); Matthew Dallek, *The Right Moment* (New York: Free Press, 2000); Kurt Schuparra, *Triumph of the Right* (New York: M. E. Sharpe, 1998); Lisa McGirr, *Suburban Warriors* (Princeton, N.J.: Princeton University Press, 2001); Sara Diamond, *Not by Politics Alone* (New York: Guilford Press, 1998); Joanne Morreale, *A New Beginning: A Textual Frame Analysis of the Political Campaign Film* (Albany: State University of New York Press, 1991).

3. Barry Goldwater, *Goldwater*, with Jack Casserly (New York: Doubleday, 1988), 116.

4. Donald Teeple, "TV Westerns Tell a Story," *American Mercury*, April 1958, 115–116.

5. William Rickenbacker, "60,000,000 Western Viewers Can't Be Wrong," *National Review*, October 1962, 322.

6. Elliott West, "Selling the Myth: Western Images in Advertising," in *Wanted Dead or Alive: The American Western in Popular Culture*, ed. Richard Aquilla (Urbana: University of Illinois Press, 1996), 283.

7. J. Fred MacDonald, *Who Shot the Sheriff? The Rise and Fall of the Television Western* (New York: Praeger, 1987), 11, 55–57; John G. Cawelti, *The Six-Gun Mystique* (Bowling Green, Ohio: Bowling Green University Press, 1984), 2–3; William Boddy, "Sixty Million Viewers Can't Be Wrong: The Rise and Fall of the Television Western," in *Back in the Saddle Again: New Essays on the Western*, ed. Edward Buscombe and Roberta E. Brown (London: BFI, 1998), 119–120, 125; West, "Selling," 277, 283; George Eells, "TV Western Craze: How Long Will It Last?" *Look*, 24 June 1958, 68.

8. Jane Tompkins, *West of Everything: The Inner Life of Westerns* (New York: Oxford University Press, 1992), 18, 71.

9. Ibid., 70, 73; West, "Selling," 271–272; Lee Clark Mitchell, *Westerns: Making the Man in Fiction and Film* (Chicago: University of Chicago Press, 1996), 3–4, 6–8, 153, 159.

10. Frederick Jackson Turner, "The Significance of the Frontier in American History," in *The Early Writings of Frederick Jackson Turner* (Madison: University of Wisconsin Press, 1938), 227–228.

11. Quoted in William W. Savage Jr., *The Cowboy Hero: His Image in American History and Culture* (Norman: University of Oklahoma Press, 1979), 96.

12. Robert G. Athearn, *The Mythic West in Twentieth Century America* (Lawrence: University Press of Kansas, 1986), 273–274.

13. Robert Warshow, *The Immediate Experience: Movies, Comics, Theatre, and Other Aspects of Popular Culture* (Garden City, N.Y.: Doubleday, 2001), 152.

14. Tompkins, *West*, 12, 34, 49, 51, 71, 75; Mitchell, *Westerns*, 156–158, 161, 167; Cawelti, *Six-Gun Mystique*, 55, 59, 60, 78; Will Wright, *Six Guns and Society: A Structural Study of the Western* (Berkeley and Los Angeles: University of California Press, 1975), 58; Stephen Tatum, "The Classic Westerner: Gary Cooper," in *Shooting Stars: Heroes and Heroines of Western Film*, ed. Archie P. McDonald (Bloomington: Indiana University Press, 1987), 61–62, 65; Philip French, *Westerns: Aspects of a Movie Genre* (New York: Oxford University Press, 1977), 48; Janice Hocker Rushing, "The Rhetoric of the American Western Myth," *Communication Monographs* 50 (March 1983): 25; Robert Warshow, "Movie Chronicle: The Western," in *Focus on the Western*, ed. Jack Nachbar (Englewood Cliffs, N.J.: Prentice Hall, 1974), 48, 56; James Lenihan, *Showdown: Confronting Modern America in the Western Film* (Urbana: University of Illinois Press, 1980), 14.

15. West, "Selling," 277, 279; Mitchell, *Westerns*, 153; Elaine Tyler May, *Homeward Bound: American Families in the Cold War Era* (New York: Basic Books, 1988), 20–21.

16. Gary A. Yoggy, "Prime-Time Bonanza! The Western on Television," in Aquilla, *Wanted Dead or Alive*, 164.

17. Liza Jane Nicholas, "Culture and the Cowboy State: The Making of Westerners" (Ph.D. diss., University of Utah, 2001), 184, 205; Mitchell, *Westerns*, 3–5; Richard Slotkin, *Gunfighter Nation: The Myth of the Frontier in Twentieth-Century America* (New

York: Atheneum, 1992), 255, 257, 505–506; Walter Fisher, "Romantic Democracy, Ronald Reagan, and Presidential Heroes," *Western Journal of Speech Communication* 46 (Summer 1982): 301; Cawelti, *Six-Gun Mystique*, 74–75; Lenihan, *Showdown*, 14; Wright, *Six Guns and Society*, 152; Tatum, "Classic Westerner," 73, 83.

18. Teeple, "TV Westerns," 117.
19. Rickenbacker, "60,000,000 Western Viewers," 324.
20. Goldwater with Casserly, *Goldwater*, 28.
21. See Goldberg, *Barry Goldwater*, 3–22.
22. Ibid.
23. Barry Goldwater, "The West That Was," Arizona Historical Foundation (Tucson: Western History Association, 1968), 13, 16.
24. Barry Goldwater, interview by author, 24 September 1992, Phoenix, Ariz.
25. Quoted in Burton Bernstein, "AuH2O," *New Yorker*, 25 April 1988, 49.
26. Goldberg, *Barry Goldwater*, 28, 55.
27. Ibid., 53.
28. Barry Goldwater, *With No Apologies: The Personal and Political Memoirs of Barry M. Goldwater* (New York: William Morrow, 1979), 28.
29. Goldberg, *Barry Goldwater*, 41.
30. Norman Nevills to Barry Goldwater, 22 January 1940, box 10, Norman D. Nevills Papers, Salt Lake City: University of Utah.
31. Barry Goldwater, *An Odyssey of the Colorado and Green Rivers* (Phoenix, Ariz.: Privately printed, 1940), 62.
32. Ibid., 14.
33. Barry Goldwater, interview by author, 30 August 1990, Phoenix, Ariz.
34. Jim Byrkit, interview by author, 15 November 1990, Phoenix, Ariz.
35. William Saufley, interview by author, 31 August 1990, Phoenix, Ariz.; Robert Goldwater, interview by author, 17 November 1989, Phoenix, Ariz.; Goldwater with Casserly, *Goldwater*, 78.
36. *Phoenix Gazette*, 23 June 1938.
37. *Arizona Republic*, 25 April 1952.
38. Goldberg, *Barry Goldwater*, 87, 93–99.
39. Goldwater's comments are in the context of the debate on the Eisenhower Administration's proposed budget for 1957–58. U.S. Senate, 86th Cong., 1st sess., *Congressional Record* 105 (8 April 1957): 5259–5261.
40. Goldberg, *Barry Goldwater*, 121–124.
41. Paul Healy, "The Glittering Mr. Goldwater," *Saturday Evening Post*, 7 June 1958, 39.
42. "Personality Contest," *Time*, 29 September 1958, 15.
43. Goldberg, *Barry Goldwater*, 125–131.
44. James C. Roberts, *The Conservative Decade: Emerging Leaders of the 1980s* (Westport, Conn.: Arlington House, 1980), 26.
45. Ernest J. Wrage, "The Little World of Barry Goldwater," in *Methods of Rhetorical Criticism*, ed. Robert Scott and Bernard Brock (New York: Harper & Row, 1972), 115.
46. "This Lively Man—Goldwater," *Newsweek*, 4 July 1960, 26; "The Conservative

King," *Time*, 8 August 1960, 16; "A New Force for '64: Goldwater Builds a Following," *U.S. News and World Report*, 10 April 1961, 65.

47. *New York Times*, 28 July 1960.

48. Goldwater with Casserly, *Goldwater*, 115.

49. Barry Goldwater, *The Conscience of a Conservative* (Shepherdsville, Ky.: Victor, 1960), 20, 23, 38, 62, 69, 89, 100, 107, 111, 118, 120–122.

50. Barry Goldwater, *Why Not Victory? A Fresh Look at American Foreign Policy* (New York: McGraw-Hill, 1962), 154.

51. "The 'Something's Wrong' Theme," *Time*, 28 August 1964, 24.

52. Goldwater's comments are in context of a speech that he was making at the time and then delivered in Congress. U.S. Senate, 87th Cong., 1st sess., *Congressional Record* 107 (11 January 1961): 576–585.

53. Barry Goldwater, acceptance speech, 16 July 1964, reprinted in *Where I Stand* (New York: McGraw-Hill, 1964), 9–17.

54. Quoted in Theodore White, *The Making of the President 1964* (New York: Atheneum, 1965), 228.

55. Ronald Reagan, *Where's the Rest of Me?* with Richard G. Hubler (New York: Dell, 1965), 49.

56. On Ronald Reagan, see Reagan with Hubler, *Where's the Rest of Me?*; Bill Boyarsky, *The Rise of Ronald Reagan* (New York: Random House, 1968) and *Ronald Reagan: His Life and Rise to the Presidency* (New York: Random House, 1981); Lou Cannon, *President Reagan: The Role of a Lifetime* (New York: Simon & Schuster, 1991); Edmund Morris, *Dutch: A Memoir of Ronald Reagan* (New York: Random House, 1999); Garry Wills, *Reagan's America* (New York: Penguin Books, 1988).

57. Reagan with Hubler, *Where's the Rest of Me?* 90.

58. Morris, *Dutch*, 133.

59. Reagan with Hubler, *Where's the Rest of Me?* 96.

60. Ibid., 93 (quote), 100–117, 121, 124, 132, 140, 218; Wills, *Reagan's America*, 91–92; Tony Thomas, *The Films of Ronald Reagan* (Secaucus, N.J.: Citadel Press, 1980), 115–116.

61. Reagan with Hubler, *Where's the Rest of Me?* 233–234.

62. Quoted in Morris, *Dutch*, 294.

63. Ibid., 245.

64. Ronald Reagan, *Ronald Reagan: An American Life* (New York: Simon & Schuster, 1990), 75.

65. Reagan with Hubler, *Where's the Rest of Me?* 245.

66. Wills, *Reagan's America*, 210–211.

67. Stephen Hunter, "Reagan in Hollywood, Warming Up for Bigger Roles," *Washington Post*, 6 June 2004.

68. Richard Corliss, "His Days in Hollywood," *Time*, 14 June 2004, 61.

69. Thomas Szasz, *Washington Post*, 6 May 1971.

70. Reagan, *Ronald Reagan*, 75.

71. Reagan with Hubler, *Where's the Rest of Me?* 215–216.

72. Ronald Reagan, "A Time for Choosing," 27 October 1964. This address was

also known as "The Speech." www.reaganlibrary.com/reagan/speeches/rendezvous.asp.

73. Reagan with Hubler, *Where's the Rest of Me?* 286, 293, 300, 303.
74. Boyarsky, *Ronald Reagan*, 79, 81.
75. Gary A. Yoggy, *Riding the Video Range: The Rise and Fall of the Western on Television* (Jefferson, N.C.: McFarland, 1995), 80.
76. "Tribute to a Dog," *Death Valley Days*, 27 December 1964.
77. "The Battle of San Francisco," *Death Valley Days*, 18 March 1965.
78. "Raid on the San Francisco Mint," *Death Valley Days*, 10 March 1965.
79. "No Gun behind His Badge," *Death Valley Days*, 25 March 1965.
80. Reagan, *Ronald Reagan*, 138.
81. Stanley Plog, interview by Stephen Stern, 5 June 1981, Oral History Program, Special Collections, University of California, Los Angeles.
82. *Los Angeles Times*, 5 January 1966.
83. Quoted in Matthew Dallek, *Right Moment*, 199.
84. Leo E. Litwack, "The Ronald Reagan Story, or Tom Sawyer Enters Politics," *New York Times Magazine*, 11 November 1965, 174.
85. Dallek, *Right Moment*, xi, 191, 195–198, 226–227.
86. Plog interview.
87. Quoted in Edwin Diamond and Stephen Bates, *The Spot: The Rise of Political Advertising on Television* (Cambridge, Mass.: MIT Press, 1992), 287.
88. Stuart Spencer, telephone interview by author, 28 January 2004.
89. *San Francisco Chronicle*, 6 and 17 June, 12 August 1966; *Los Angeles Times*, 21 September, 3 November 1966.
90. Ronald Reagan, "Unforgettable John Wayne," *Reader's Digest*, October 1979, 118.
91. Ronald Reagan, acceptance speech, Republican National Convention, 17 July 1980, Detroit, Mich. www.nationalcenter.org/ReaganConvention1980.html.
92. Quoted in Paul D. Erickson, *Reagan Speaks: The Making of an American Myth* (New York: New York University Press, 1985), 98.
93. Speeches: Ronald Reagan, farewell address, 11 January 1989. www.ronaldreagan.com/sp_21.html.
94. Cannon, *President Reagan*, 763.
95. Peter Hannaford, *Ronald Reagan and His Ranch: The Western White House: 1981–1989* (Bennington, Vt.: Tordis Ilg Isselhardt, 2002), 45.
96. Cannon, *President Reagan*, 2.
97. David Nyhan, quoted in *Washington Post*, 6 June 2004.
98. "Remarks by President George W. Bush," *New York Times*, 11 June 2004, www.nytimes.com/2004/06/11/politics/TEXT-GWBUSH.html.

CHAPTER 2

Agricultural Politics in the Twentieth-Century American West
R. Douglas Hurt

On 18 January 1978, some 3,000 farmers descended on Washington, D.C. Driving tractors and pickup trucks, they demanded that Congress take immediate action to benefit farmers. Word of their impending arrival had reached the halls of Congress days earlier, but the sight of these rough-handed farmers driving monstrous tractors on streets normally the domain of taxi cabs, limousines, and buses excited nearly everyone. Politicians of every bent joined their staffers as they flocked to watch the demonstration. One member of the American Agriculture Movement (AAM), the organizing force behind the event, spoke for all when he reflected, "They poured out of every corner to meet with us—when I saw all of that, I knew we were damned important." A fellow AAM protester remembered, "We thought we owned the damned town, we knew it, by God."[1]

Until that cold January morning, the men and women who, by political ideology, associated with the American Agriculture Movement had not felt important for a long time. Indeed, they saw themselves as America's forgotten citizens. Unlike other protesters at the nation's capital in recent years, these farmers were demanding not more freedom, but rather the more mundane cost-of-production prices plus a profit for their produce. Despite the democratic symbolism of western farmers parading on tractors around the Mall and Capitol Hill, all of which reinforced, or even reawakened, public association of farmers with the Jeffersonian tradition that held agriculturists as the best champions of democracy, the AAM sought to continue the politics of dependency that had kept farmers tied to the federal government for most of the twentieth century. By the late twentieth century, western farmers could not reach a political consensus on federal agricultural policy. Western agricultural interests were too diverse and specialized for regulation or support by any single agricultural policy. Unity among farmers as a class became impossible to achieve, even in the major political parties. As a result, special-interest farm organizations increasingly became the political home of western farmers. Indeed, by the mid-twentieth century, many western farmers understood that they had no choice but to organize as special-interest groups in order to wield political power. These organizations offered a strong voice calling for the federal government to guarantee the Jeffersonian tradition and keep family farmers on the land to ensure American freedom, democracy, and values. By the 1970s, however, few people cared about farmers. Although the Democratic and Republican parties gave lip service to the needs of farmers, these political entities as a whole did not need the farm vote because it had declined to near insignificance outside of a few rural areas clearly devoted to agriculture, particularly to family farming. In the absence of major party concern for agriculture, western farmers increasingly relied on their commodity organizations to address their concerns and meet their needs.[2]

The failure of farmers to organize a viable national political party at the end of the nineteenth century created a political vacuum that several agricultural groups rushed to fill. These farm organizations, however, were not political parties but agricultural associations designed to achieve economic gains that the People's Party had failed to achieve. Organizations such as the Farmers Union, the Nonpartisan League, and the American Farm Bureau Federation attempted to meet economic and social needs while pursuing agendas that required political action by the major parties. These early twentieth-century agricultural organizations became a bridge between the major political parties and the agricultural commodity groups that emerged about midcentury and grew in political influence, if not power.

In another age, public perception of the political importance of farmers in the Republic had been far different. Thomas Jefferson persuasively argued for the moral superiority of farmers. On the farm, men and women could live independent, egalitarian, and democratic lives and provide the economic and political foundation of the Republic. In 1785, Jefferson wrote, "Cultivators of the earth are the most valuable citizens. They are the most vigorous, the most independent, the most virtuous, and they are tied to the country, and wedded to its liberty and interests, by the most lasting bonds." Two years later, Jefferson reaffirmed this belief: "Those who labor on the earth are the chosen people of God, if ever he has a chosen people, whose breasts he has made his peculiar deposit for substantial and genuine virtue." Jefferson, then, like most Americans, believed that small farmers would support government that protected property while they lived honest, independent lives, and that their integrity would ensure the strongest link between self-interest and the public good, that is, the commonweal. During the nineteenth century, most Americans agreed with Jefferson, believing that farming was the most desirable, perhaps even ideal, way of life. Like Jefferson, they assumed that a nation of small-scale farmers would be ensured freedom, independence, and democracy. They also considered farmers morally superior to city dwellers. In 1896, William Jennings Bryan, then a candidate for the presidency, captured this sentiment when he said, "Burn down your cities and leave our farms, and your cities will spring up again as if by magic; but destroy our farms and the grass will grow in the streets of every city in the country."[3]

By the early twentieth century, however, any hope of achieving the Jeffersonian ideal of an agrarian society lay in the distant past. Yet that ideal remained as an important symbol that farm organizations and others used throughout the century to justify favorable government policies. As late as 1913, one North Dakotan who supported the Farmers Union wrote, "There is no more useful, more fascinating occupation than that of the farmer. Our high standards and ideals are more nearly preserved in their simple dignity and purity by the dwellers upon the farm than by any other class of citizens." While Jeffersonian rhetoric still echoes across the political landscape, farmers have come to rely on the much more down-to-business tactics of interest-group lobbying. They have, however, over the last century sometimes resorted to radicalism and even violence when the government failed to meet their needs.[4]

In the twentieth-century American West, then, farmers used a careful combination of lofty rhetoric, occasional violence, and practical politics to emerge as a central force in American politics. The political orientation of western farmers is the product of long-held agrarian values based on cumulative historical experience. It is important to note that these agrarian values have not been uniform across the West in time and space. During the early twentieth century, for example, western farmers held substantially different views about the role of government than they would come to appreciate in the post–New Deal years.

The political agendas of westerners are broad, and they vary across time, space, and circumstance as well as in relation to ethnicity, gender, and locale. During the early twentieth century, western farm men and women generally believed that politics and the federal government should champion the public welfare, that is, the commonweal. In this sense, western farmers often considered that the government had a responsibility to intervene in private affairs when necessary to protect the public interest, such as the ownership of public utilities. This belief was essentially progressive because many western farmers advocated the use of government to regulate society, particularly corporate society, for the common good.

After the New Deal years, western farmers became more concerned with government agricultural policies that benefited themselves as producers of particular commodity groups. Put differently, after the 1930s, the individualistic political goals of western farmers emphasized the need for government support and regulation of the agricultural economy, usually with price-support programs. Their political work had little ideological base. Instead, western farmers had their eyes focused on the proverbial bottom line. Party politics made little difference. Only the result mattered. Increasingly, western farmers relied on group loyalty rather than political parties to achieve desired economic goals through government. In this sense, after the watershed years of the New Deal, western farmers became more conservative because they sought individual economic protection rather than policies designed to benefit the commonweal.

To fully put this transformation in perspective, we need to examine the political culture of farmers during the years after the Populist era and before the New Deal years. First, in this respect, as the century opened, western farmers conceived the political order as a commonwealth—a state in which the people cooperated to create and maintain the best government possible for the benefit of the public as a whole, based on generally accepted moral principles. Second, they considered government as a marketplace where action resulted from political bargaining and group self-interest. During the early twentieth century, then, western farmers had a shared vision of agrarian values that posited the best government as supportive of a commonwealth made up of self-governing freeholders, that is, property owners, each with a stake in the community. They believed that a good society was created and perpetuated by self-reliant individuals and families who cooperated to achieve common goals. Put differently, they usually viewed politics as a means to achieve economic ends for a common good. After the New Deal, however, they came to equate the common good with their own self-interest. They considered government legitimate if it supported their concept of agrarian values as the foundation of the commonweal.[5]

The farm politics of the early twentieth century reflected farmers' Populist heritage, manifested in the utilitarian premise that government existed to provide the greatest good to the greatest number rather than to serve elitist or privileged groups. This political lineage dated to the agrarian revolt of the late nineteenth century. In 1894, Frank Doster of Kansas expressed the Populist sentiment best when he said, "It is the business of government to do that for the individual which he cannot successfully do for himself and which other individuals will not do for him upon just or equitable terms." The politics of western farmers, however, were not ideological even when their goals seemed radical. The occasional "radicalism" of Great Plains farmers during the early twentieth century, for example, stemmed from their demand that the federal government aid and protect society from railroads, banks, and monopolistic corporations so the public could compete fairly and equitably in the marketplace. Western farmers believed, then, that government should serve the commonweal by providing regulatory legislation for the benefit of society.[6]

The application and results of this belief can be seen on both the state and national levels. The Norwegians, for example, who settled in North Dakota and who had a strong cultural tradition of using government to support the commonweal, organized the Nonpartisan League (NPL) in 1915. Although the NPL had little influence beyond North Dakota, its member farmers advocated economic reform through moderate socialist action in the state legislature. Led by organizer Arthur C. Townley, the NPL sought the establishment of a state-owned terminal grain elevator to ensure accurate grading and fair pricing of grain; it also advocated the creation of state-owned banks, flour mills, and meatpacking plants to guarantee fair credit and purchasing practices. Townley gained considerable allegiance from Norwegians, whose political culture customarily supported government-operated programs in the market place.

In 1916, when the Republican Party failed to meet NPL demands, the league, under Townley's guidance, brilliantly and effectively used the direct primary system to elect Democratic and Republican candidates who supported NPL goals. The NPL elected a governor, gained control of the state's lower house, and became a strong minority in the state senate. A year later, the legislature enacted the NPL program, including a grain-grading system, guaranteed bank deposits, and a nine-hour workday for women. The legislature also provided regulations for the railroads operating in North Dakota to prevent rate discrimination, and it authorized the vote for women in state elections. Although the Nonpartisan League never became a third party in North Dakota, Townley effectively used the direct primary to force the Republican Party, which had dominated state politics, to support the will of the majority, that is, farmers. Until the NPL merged with North Dakota's Democratic Party in 1956, it united farmers in the Flickertail State as no other agricultural organization or party did, and it transformed Populist principles into a workable program.[7]

Beyond North Dakota, few western farmers enjoyed a cultural heritage of using government to ensure social and economic equity. In Nebraska, for example, the NPL met failure, although farmers in the Cornhusker State agreed with many of its goals. Many problems prevented political unity. In

1917, when the NPL began organizational efforts in Nebraska, another organization, the Farmers Union (FU) had a significant presence in the state, and its members enjoyed rapidly increasing prosperity from high wartime prices. Moreover, the NPL began organizational activities in June, one month after the formation of the Nebraska Council of Defense, which suspected the league of disloyalty, given its opposition to the war. In addition, the efforts of the NPL to recruit German farmers for membership antagonized many Nebraskans. Although the NPL had an estimated membership of 5,000 by the end of the war, it could not overcome the opposition of the Farmers Union to the league goal of state ownership of certain agricultural industries. Farmers Union leaders admitted that they had not been able to obtain the legislative goals they sought, particularly cost-of-production prices plus a profit, but in the words of one, they saw "no good reason why our members should divide their efforts between two organizations when the one they have has proved itself so valuable and effective." The inability of Nebraska's farmers to organize and unite for political purposes both indicated their past problems and foretold the future. Western farmers would organize politically, but they would do so increasingly as interest groups, particularly commodity groups, rather than as farmers as a class. In other words, the NPL and Farmers Union provided models for political organization outside the major parties. They focused on limited economic goals, which presaged the even more tightly focused lobbying efforts of the agricultural commodity organizations after World War II, which, in turn, often forced the major political parties to act.[8]

In Idaho, farmers chose a different route for political action. During the first decade of the twentieth century, many farmers had moved onto federal lands administered by the Bureau of Reclamation. This agency contracted with private entrepreneurs to develop irrigation projects and sell the water to farmers. Mismanagement prevailed, and while farmers received little water, they did get high bills for undelivered services. By 1910, angry farmers were refusing to pay for the water they never received. Resentment festered, litigation mushroomed, and farmers sought political relief. They criticized the state legislature and the Bureau of Reclamation with increasing animosity for permitting irrigation companies to "farm the farmers." By 1914, a neo-Populist protest emerged among reclamation-project farmers and dry-land grain farmers. Two years later, these farmers, who believed state government, federal officials, and irrigation "trusts" had conspired against them, formed the Idaho Federation of Agriculture. They intended to wield enough political clout to vote their opponents out of the state legislature. They failed to mobilize sufficient support, however, and the Democratic majority continued to ignore their needs.[9]

Although the state legislature turned its back on the farm problem, Arthur Townley saw an opportunity, and in 1917, he began efforts to organize the NPL in Idaho. He preached the advantages of state-operated banks to improve agricultural credit. While arguing against a third party, he spoke the gospel of nonpartisan political action, including advocating state-owned agricultural processing plants and electric companies. By August 1917, some 4,000 Idahoans had joined the NPL. Although the competing Farmers Union "fairly howled" its opposition because FU leaders felt threatened, the NPL continued its political activities, but not as a lackey of the national league. Idahoans insisted on controlling the leadership and political agenda. In 1918, NPL voters primarily came from the Democratic Party, although they endorsed Republican senator William Borah. The stalwart Democrats and Republicans, however, recovered quickly and passed legislation banning the direct primary in Idaho, thereby ensuring the NPL would never gain control of either the Democratic or Republican Party or the state legislature. The NPL did not disappear, but in 1922, it joined the newly created Progressive Party, through which Idaho's farmers continued to seek economic reform through political action. During the same time, the Patrons of Husbandry, also known as the Grange, in Washington State continued to function as a nonpartisan political pressure group.[10]

At the national level beyond North Dakota, western farmers pursued federal regulation of the economy to benefit the commonweal, although much of their desired legislation benefited them greatly. Farmers in the Great Plains, for example, advocated government regulation to prevent abusive business practices. They urged their congressional delegations to address agricultural grievances in relation to transportation, credit, and marketing, and the congressional response substantially increased the regulatory power of the federal government. Great Plains farm men and women worked through the Democratic and Republican parties to achieve their goals, but they increasingly relied on specific agricultural organizations and commodity groups to lobby for their desired economic reforms. As a result, these groups increasingly became the instruments of political power for commercial farmers during the early twentieth century.[11]

The different agendas of the early twentieth-century farm organizations clearly indicates that the political interests of western farmers had become so diffuse that no group could speak for all farmers. Wheat farmers on the Great Plains had different economic and, therefore, political needs than did vegetable farmers in California. In North Dakota, for example, the political influence of the FU collapsed when it joined with the NPL. In Oklahoma, the Farmers Union wielded more political influence because it did not have competition from another agricultural organization, such as the

NPL. In 1916, John A. Simpson became president of the FU in the Sooner State, and he proclaimed his intent to organize to present the "farmers' side," saying, "The unorganized man has no more to say in affairs of government than his horse or his mule." Simpson's attacks on the federal government soon brought accusations of "un-American" behavior during World War I. He weathered the critics, however, and used the FU to pressure the state legislature to regulate the sampling, grading, and classification of cotton and to create cooperative banks.[12]

In general, during the first two decades of the twentieth century, then, western farmers and their political organizations, such as the Farmers Union and the Nonpartisan League, worked locally and nationally to attack monopolistic corporate practices that they believed discriminated against farmers, lowered their income, and harmed the commonweal. Strong political support from western farmers enabled Congress to set equitable railroad rates and prohibit rebates and rate discrimination. Republicans and Democrats formed various urban and rural coalitions among those who also had grievances against the railroads. With the support of western farmers, Congress passed the Hepburn Act (1906), which authorized the Interstate Commerce Commission (ICC) to set maximum reasonable railroad rates as well as to inspect the financial records of the railroads to ensure good bookkeeping practices. Southern agricultural interests played a role in the passage of the Hepburn Act, but western farmers particularly considered it a major achievement for the regulation of private industry.[13]

In 1910, many western farmers supported further railroad regulation as achieved by the Mann-Elkins Act, which gave the ICC additional power to set railroad rates and required shippers to prove their rates were reasonable, rather than leaving the burden on farmers to prove the rates were unreasonable. By World War I, western farmers could look to the federal government to ensure competition among carriers, set reasonable rates, break up monopolies, and end favoritism for large-scale shippers. In 1913, Congress also approved the Federal Reserve Act, which was intended to bring about greater order and stability in a banking system that had been volatile and chaotic. Farmers particularly benefited because the Federal Reserve banks increased the money supply to member banks, which, in turn, lent to farmers. But the Federal Reserve Act also benefited the commonweal by improving the money supply and credit system, especially in the West.[14]

During the Progressive Era, then, western farmers amply demonstrated that they welcomed the expansion of federal power to support and protect the general welfare. They also became increasingly agreeable to the creation of a distant bureaucracy of experts who influenced their lives through legislation and regulation for the public good. Great Plains farmers and their congressional representatives did not agree among themselves on all issues, but they had sufficient unity to wield political power. Usually Great Plains reformers joined urban reformers, because both groups advocated the benefits of a regulatory state, administered by a bureaucracy of experts in an agency, such as the U.S. Department of Agriculture (USDA), that served urbanites as well as country people. Even though the composition of farm leadership in the region had changed since the late nineteenth century, and while coalitions formed and dissolved over various issues, and although the urban middle-class base of the Progressive movement cannot be denied, western farmers helped achieve considerable regulation of corporate enterprise and industrialist capitalism. By so doing, they played an important role in the creation of the regulatory state for the benefit of the commonweal.[15]

By 1920, then, western farmers increasingly looked to the federal government for help to solve their economic problems. In doing so, they departed from the Jeffersonian ideal that advocated minimal government activity and maximum personal independence. Instead, during the early twentieth century, western farmers sought a fundamental and major expansion of federal regulatory power to aid agriculture, an expansion that they also believed would benefit society. During the 1920s, western farmers and their congressional representatives worked with their counterparts in the Midwest and the South to improve agricultural conditions, particularly after the collapse of commodity prices following World War I. This coalition became known as the farm bloc. The congressional composition of the farm bloc changed periodically, but it initially included Senators George Norris of Nebraska, John Kendrick of Wyoming, Arthur Capper of Kansas, Morris Sheppard of Texas, Edwin Ladd of North Dakota, and Charles McNary of Oregon, as well as Representatives Charles A. Christopherson of South Dakota and James H. Sinclair of North Dakota. The American Farm Bureau Federation (AFBF), which represented many farmers in the Great Plains, urged the farm bloc to improve credit opportunities, protect cooperatives, regulate meatpacking companies and trading in grain futures, and improve farm-to-market roads. The farm bloc operated on the premise that national prosperity depended primarily upon agricultural prosperity. At the same time, the legislative achievements of the farm bloc increased the administrative and regulatory power of the federal government. Through the farm bloc, western farmers welcomed the regulation of meatpackers and stockyards, improved agricultural credit banking systems, and the Highway Act of 1921, which provided funding for the construction of secondary highways, or farm-to-market roads. The farm bloc also achieved regulation of the grain-futures market and higher tariff rates on agricultural commodities. The success of the farm bloc proved that the western farm lobby could form bipartisan policy agendas for the improvement of farm life and the public good.[16]

At the organizational level, the Farmers Union continued to champion federal intervention in the agricultural economy to guarantee farmers cost-of-production prices and a 5 percent profit. As the agricultural economy declined, some FU members even advocated a "farm holiday," during which farmers would neither buy nor sell until the government promised cost-of-production prices plus a profit. Herbert Hoover, however, refused to support federal programs that would provide substantive economic relief to farmers during his administration (1929–1933). Although the call for a farm holiday essentially ended with the election of Franklin Delano Roosevelt to the presidency in 1932, farmers increasingly looked to the federal government for a solution to the agricultural problems that became inextricably linked to the Great Depression.[17]

With the election of Roosevelt, western farmers anticipated some form of economic relief while they battled drought, dust, and depression. Roosevelt had promised farmers economic relief during the presidential campaign, although neither he nor his advisers knew precisely the nature of that aid. Farm experts and government officials, however, had discussed a plan to pay farmers for reducing production for nearly a decade. During the first hundred days of the Roosevelt administration, Congress, with the support of the American Farm Bureau Federation and Secretary of Agriculture Henry A. Wallace, passed the Agricultural Adjustment Act (AAA). This legislation provided for an acreage-reduction program that theoretically would end the problem of crop surpluses and boost commodity prices. The philosophy guiding those western farmers who supported the AAA posited that a strong national economy depended on a prosperous agricultural economy. By paying farmers to produce less of some crops, such as wheat and cotton in the West, the federal government assumed responsibility for the general welfare of at least a portion of the agricultural community.

The Agricultural Adjustment Administration, which administered the AAA, did not require farmers to participate in the crop-reduction program. It did not need to; for many farmers it was their main source of income. Politically, western farmers were divided over New Deal agricultural programs. They needed economic support, but many viewed the New Deal as an imposition by the Roosevelt administration rather than as a reform.[18]

The Agricultural Adjustment Administration's wheat-reduction program provides an example of the decentralized, locally controlled organizational structure that made participating farmers part of the regulatory process. Federal and state officials of the Agricultural Adjustment Administration appointed farmers to local committees, which supervised the program. The county agent also worked with the representatives of agricultural organizations, such as the Farm Bureau and the Farmers Union, to convince members to support the AAA program. Participating farmers elected officers to the county committees. These officers usually had been active in various agricultural organizations, farm cooperatives, and community activities, some of them political. As western farmers, then, participated in the wheat-reduction program, they became part of the program administration and fostered a more democratic bureaucracy. At this point, they supported the AAA primarily for their own personal economic gain rather than for the benefit of the commonweal. In Kansas, for example, farmers cared little about the philosophy behind the AAA program regarding economics, national "necessity," and world prices. Instead, they wanted only to learn how they could participate, the extent of their acreage reduction, and, most important, the amount of money they would receive from the federal government for joining the program. Put simply, they supported the AAA wheat program because they needed the money.[19]

Kansas also provides an example of the shift away from considering government a progressive agent to support society and toward depending on the government for personal economic gain. Consider the acceptance of the AAA by farmers in the Sunflower State. In late May 1935, the Agricultural Adjustment Administration held a nationwide referendum on the question, "Are you in favor of a wheat production–adjustment program to follow the present one which expires with the 1935 crop year?" The agency asked farmers who had signed wheat acreage reduction contracts as well as those who did not participate in the crop-reduction program to vote by secret ballot issued through their local offices of the Agricultural Adjustment Administration. In Kansas, more than 82,000 farmers voted. Nearly 72,000 farmers supported the continuation of the wheat acreage allotment program. Of the 73,000 Kansas farmers who had signed wheat acreage reduction contracts, more than 65,500 favored continuation of the program in some form. Federal officials used these and similar returns from other western wheat-producing states to draft a new four-year program, which became known as the Soil Conservation and Domestic Allotment Act. By the time the Agricultural Adjustment Act of 1938 institutionalized the acreage-reduction and crop-payment programs, western farmers had begun to consider such federal support an entitlement; they had become dependent on it. During the first four years of the AAA program in Kansas, for example, the agency paid wheat farmers $23.2 million in 1933, $25.6 million in 1934, $28.3 million in 1935, and $15.7 million in 1936 for decreasing their wheat acreage. For many Kansas farmers, the checks received from the Agricultural Adjustment

Administration for participation in the wheat acreage reduction program became their only cash income, particularly during 1933 and 1934.[20]

Similarly, cattle raisers began looking to the federal government for economic aid. Although western cattlemen refused to accept production controls for money under the Agricultural Adjustment Act of 1933, they too needed money, and they soon envied the wheat farmers who received government checks for crop reduction. Soon ranchers began urging their congressional delegations to provide a similar cattle-reduction and price-support program, and Congress responded. Between June 1934 and January 1935, more than 110,000 Texas cattle raisers participated in the program. By all accounts, they cooperated eagerly and indicated no fear of federal control, particularly when their checks arrived. In fact, when the federal government announced the termination of the program, Texas cattle producers protested loudly to their congressional representatives, and they insisted that ending the program would ruin the Texas cattle industry. Cattlemen, livestock organizations, newspaper editors, and congressmen demanded the continuation of the cattle-purchase program, that is, economic aid. When the surplus problem ended and feed supplies returned to normal along with the annual precipitation, western cattle raisers abandoned their support for a regulated-production program, even with federal payment for participation. Thereafter, western cattle raisers would pursue economic gains through interest-group politics directed at the U.S. Forest Service and Bureau of Land Management in the executive branch rather than through political activities in Congress.[21]

Overall, however, the economic problems of the 1930s changed government aid. For the remainder of the twentieth century (with an aberration of a short-lived policy change in 1996), western farmers worked through their commodity and organizational groups to influence Congress. They particularly wanted Congress to provide agricultural programs that enhanced individual farm income, usually through various price-supporting and crop-reduction programs. These groups became skilled, professional, and effective lobbyists in Congress. But their lobbying came at a price; they sought out policies that would satisfy individual needs and wants rather than those that would apply to all farmers across the nation. As a result, the politics of western agriculture departed from the Progressive approach, which sought regulation of the economy for the general good. Instead, western farmers became increasingly individualistic and conservative in their thinking about agricultural politics. Put differently, western farmers became less interested in agricultural reforms that would aid society by using government as a tool, in the Progressive tradition, to achieve economic and social change and more interested in policy provisions that would aid themselves.

Regardless of which party held the presidency or provided the majority in Congress, the problems of overproduction and low commodity prices persisted. As a result, western politicians continued to support federal aid to agriculture because the farm vote remained important. Western farmers also continued to lobby Congress through their agricultural organizations to keep the needs of farmers known. Moreover, the farm organizations also helped shape the desires of their members and, thereby, played a doubly important role in the formation of farm policy.[22]

After World War II, officials in the U.S. Department of Agriculture (USDA) continued to consult with agricultural organizations in the West to develop farm policy. When the USDA acted alone, it often confronted angry farmers who objected not only to the proposed policy but also to being left out of the political process. In 1949, for example, Secretary of Agriculture Charles F. Brannan attempted to institute a new policy designed to increase farm income. Known as the Brannan Plan, this policy offered to replace the parity price index with direct monetary payments to farmers. These payments would support their income at a calculated and acceptable level. The plan obligated farmers to observe production controls that would benefit most agriculturists. Brannan's plan, however, generated considerable controversy. While some critics complained about the cost, western wheat, rice, and cotton farmers objected because, compared to then-current policy, it could restrict the amount of money they received from the federal government. Farmer-stockmen objected because the plan would increase feed-grain prices. The Farmers Union, the organization of smaller, less prosperous farmers, supported the plan, but the American Farm Bureau Federation, made up of larger, more affluent farmers, opposed it because the plan would enlarge federal regulation of the agricultural economy. More important, the Farm Bureau Federation argued against it because Brannan had not solicited the advice of the major farm organizations (particularly the Farm Bureau Federation) before devising and announcing this new policy proposal. Clearly, the "old liberalism" or "progressivism" of the New Deal had become the "new conservatism" of western agriculture. Indeed, western farmers preferred New Deal–based farm programs that provided government loans and purchases as well as production allotments and marketing agreements rather than direct cash payments, which they equated with welfare. As a result, the Farm Bureau Federation marshaled enough congressional votes to kill the Brannan Plan. Agricultural policy remained based on the Agricultural Adjustment Act of 1938 as amended by the Agriculture Act of 1949.[23]

The differences over the Brannan Plan between the Farmers Union and the American Farm Bureau Federation show that agricultural organizations often pursued their own agendas. In 1902, for example, the Farmers Union organized in Texas. Originally, it sought "to secure equity, establish justice and apply the Golden Rule," but it later advocated direct regulation of the agricultural economy. Ultimately, the Farmers Union primarily represented small, low-income wheat and cotton farmers on the Great Plains. The Farmers Union considered the American Farm Bureau Federation an auxiliary of chambers of commerce and big business. In contrast, the American Farm Bureau Federation, which organized in 1919, represented large, more financially secure farmers. The Farm Bureau Federation did not favor government regulation of agriculture to control production and to guarantee prices and profits; rather, it considered surplus production a marketing and distribution problem that could be solved by a national farm policy. One Oklahoman who grew up on a farm reflected, "We always believed that the AFB was made up of country club farmers and the FU looked out for the little man. Simplistic yes, but accurate in an Oklahoma way."[24]

Although American Farm Bureau Federation and Farmers Union members did not support each other on all issues, and while some commodity groups, such as the wheat growers' associations, took narrow and particularly self-interested views of agricultural policy, collectively, the voice of western farmers reached Congress. As a result, the secretary of agriculture invariably sought the advice of major farm leaders and their organizations before submitting legislation to Congress. At the same time, the farm lobby enjoyed nearly unrestricted access to Congress. Democratic and Republican politicians knew that termination of New Deal support programs would cause economic havoc for farm families—with resulting political disaster for themselves and their party. Western farmers enjoyed the political power they exercised at the ballot box on election day as well as through the lobbying activities of their organizations.[25]

Despite considerable political success in achieving economic support, some western farmers believed that Congress consistently failed from one farm program to another to meet their economic needs. They occasionally responded with a flash-in-the-pan radicalism. For example, when the National Farmers Organization (NFO) and the American Agriculture Movement spread across a portion of the Great Plains during the middle 1950s and late 1970s, respectively, participating farmers used radical rhetoric and physical intimidation in the hope of influencing Congress to provide an agricultural policy that guaranteed cost-of-production prices plus a profit.

The NFO, for example, sought cost-of-production prices plus a profit by negotiating contracts with food processors through collective-bargaining agreements similar to those won by organized labor. The NFO also supported withholding actions, that is, farm strikes, to gain its objective. This principle quickly gained the NFO a reputation for radicalism, particularly in the wheat-producing states of the Great Plains. During the 1960s, near Ellis, Kansas, a roadside sign read: "The NFO says higher prices or else." Violence, however, marred several NFO strikes, proving that the organization misjudged public opinion. Indeed, the public recoiled from NFO violence and shunned the organization rather than supporting it. Violence exerted by some NFO members against farmers who attempted to reach markets and televised hog and cattle kills that were intended to demonstrate that farmers could not afford to feed their livestock given market prices drove potential supporters away. These activities also proved that the NFO lacked the unity, organization, and discipline to compel economic change through political action. Thereafter, the NFO struggled for the remainder of the twentieth century to regain respectability.[26]

In 1977, the American Agriculture Movement (AAM) emerged as a new political force in the West. Similar to the NFO, the AAM had a flare for radicalism and used intimidation to achieve economic ends through political means. Primarily made up of wheat farmers, the AAM exhibited all the fiery political rhetoric of the Populist movement of the 1890s and more than a few of the intimidating tactics used by the Farm Holiday Association and the National Farmers Organization. Farmers who associated with the AAM (the movement did not have membership roles) believed the federal government should aid farmers by guaranteeing cost-of-production prices plus a profit. Its leaders advocated a farm strike if their goals went unmet. The AAM intended to organize local chapters similar to those of the American Farm Bureau Federation and to establish an office in Washington, D.C., to lobby Congress. From the beginning of the AAM's organization in Campo, Colorado, during summer 1977, however, it espoused an ideology of anticorporate neo-Populism. The message rang sharp and clear: Cheated farmers could exercise considerable political power, if they joined the organization.[27]

The AAM, however, showed a remarkable ignorance of history when it planned a strike during which farmers would neither plant nor purchase until the federal government guaranteed cost-of-production agricultural prices. Naively, AAM members believed that the family farm remained the foundation of the national economy in the Jeffersonian tradition. If the family farm failed only to be replaced by large-scale corporate farms, they believed, the American standard of living as people knew it would crumble. Local AAM demonstrations, such as the one in Lubbock, Texas, during the Christmas shopping season of 1977, when farmers parked large equipment across parking slots at the local mall, annoyed shoppers and denied merchants needed holiday business. This demonstration proved counterproductive and only earned the movement ill will. AAM "tractorcades," that is, demonstrations, in the nation's capital during the next two years also failed to achieve a new farm policy that would guarantee cost-of-production prices plus a profit because the AAM drove political supporters away with its intimidating tactics. Moreover, the AAM never had the numerical strength or political understanding to achieve its goals through the political process.[28]

The AAM glorified family farmers and criticized the federal government and other farm organizations for not working to solve the farm problem, which it defined as low prices and inadequate agricultural income, both of which created an unacceptably low standard of living. Most western farmers and the major commodity organizations, however, did not support a farm strike for economic and political reasons. Without the support of western farmers and having alienated the public, the AAM remained on the fringe of western agricultural politics. Most western farmers had become tied to commodity groups and rejected the pan-farmer argument of the AAM. The AAM proved, once again, that direct action did not achieve political gains. Professional lobbying through the commodity groups, such as the wheat, rice, and cotton associations, gained access to Congress and influenced agricultural policy for western farmers.

By the 1980s, the political strength of western farmers had clearly solidified in the commodity groups, particularly those serving wheat, cotton, and rice growers. These growers' associations maintained offices in the nation's capital, where they had quick and easy access to Congress. By the late twentieth century, western farmers had essentially accepted the farm programs that had emanated from Congress since the New Deal. Although not all farm groups favored acreage- or production-control legislation, they all invariably sought farm policies that benefited them economically. Simply put, western farmers were too different in their needs to support a general farm policy that affected them equally. Instead, they competed with each other to gain as much federal economic support as possible, often at the expense of other farmers or agricultural groups.

Indeed, by the late twentieth century, western farm politics had become interest-group politics par excellence. Much like ranchers, whose political agenda also emphasized personal or interest-group economic benefit and who organized effectively to influence, even capture, the U.S. Bureau of Land Management and the U.S. Forest Service, western farmers relied on their own particular commodity groups to influence public policy. Their primary goal was not to rewrite agricultural policy for all farmers but to ensure that they used their political influence to gain as much benefit for themselves as possible. Indeed, by the end of the twentieth century, western farmers who organized by commodity groups or growers' associations cared little for agricultural legislation that benefited the commonwealth unless it benefited them first and foremost.

Yet while interest-group action dominated agricultural politics, western urban growth created new agricultural issues, the response to which farmers could not control politically. During the late twentieth century, consumers became more concerned about the foods they ate. Chemical additives in the form of growth hormones for beef and dairy cattle made many consumers question the safety of eating beef and drinking milk. Consumers also worried about the consumption of genetically modified crops (GMOs) because no one knew their long-term effects on health. Increasingly, consumer-interest groups pressured food-processing firms to stop buying certain agricultural commodities that they deemed unsafe, even though scientific evidence had not proven those commodities dangerous to human health. In 2000, for example, Frito-Lay, the Gerber Products Company, and the Archer Daniels Midland Company stopped buying or severely restricted the purchase of genetically engineered agricultural products, such as corn and soybeans. Consumer pressure that can only be called political forced the Burger King Corporation to forego buying genetically altered potatoes for its French fries, even though western potato farmers contended that such potatoes not only were safe but also were more productive and profitable than traditional varieties. A spokesman for the USDA affirmed the altered power of western farmers when he said, "The customer is king or queen. Eventually customers around the world are going to be the ones who decide the extent to which they are going to embrace or ignore biotech crops." Consumers also wanted safe drinking water, that is, water, uncontaminated by agricultural pesticides, herbicides, and fertilizers or by runoff from large-scale cattle and hog lots.[29]

By the late twentieth century, urban residents began to control the western environmental agenda. Nonfarming, voting westerners became politically concerned about environmental policy that affected their lives, and they did not particularly care about the ramifications of that policy for western farmers. No matter whether the nonfarming public lived in cities or towns, they did not want to drink water that had to be treated to remove agricultural chemicals, nor did they want to breath the smells of livestock feedlots or confinement facilities. This public demanded government regulation to ensure consumer safety and prohibit agricultural nuisances. By the late twentieth century, western farmers knew that consumer and environmental groups wielded sufficient collective political power to influence federal agricultural policy.[30]

While the political power of western farmers increasingly concentrated in the commodity groups following World War II, and while new environmental groups began to assert political influence, agribusiness corporations dramatically expanded their political power in Congress. Beginning with World War II, western agribusiness—that is, those businesses that financed, marketed, transported, processed, manufactured, and sold agricultural products and equipment—gradually integrated into the national and international economy. Western agribusinesses could not be distinguished from other large-scale corporations at home or abroad. They too had become large-scale and multinational. Western agribusiness corporations became so diversified that few Americans knew who owned such traditionally western brand names as Carnation, Del Monte, and Sun-Maid. By 1970, Transamerica, the one-time parent company of Bank of America and Occidental Life Insurance Company, both major agricultural lenders, provides an example of the far-flung nature of western agribusiness. If western farmers flew via the charter service Trans International Airlines, they traveled on an airplane operated by TransAmerica. If they rented a car from Budget Rent A Car, they rented from TransAmerica. If they saw a movie in town produced by United Artists, they watched a TransAmerica film. Clearly, western agribusinesses no longer primarily engaged in the financing of farming, food processing, or agricultural marketing and transporting operations. Many western agribusinesses held large-scale farms from which they produced gas and petroleum rather than crops, and some preferred to sell acreage to suburban developers rather than produce agricultural commodities. Western agribusinesses continued to sell goods and services to farmers, but agriculturists had virtually no political influence with these corporations.[31]

Beyond the complicated business of knowing who owns what lies the more important matter of the expansive political power that western agribusinesses wielded in Congress. From banking regulations to interest rates to agricultural subsidies, agribusinesses wielded immediate political power largely because of their nearly limitless ability to hire lobbyists to present their needs to western politicians. The deep pockets of western agribusinesses gave those corporations a loud voice in the shaping of policy in a host of contexts, while the internal politics of western agribusinesses, with the mergers, friendly and hostile takeovers, and leveraged buyouts, seemingly resurrected the stereotypical shootout of the Old West. In relation to agriculture, that influence meant that large-scale agribusinesses or corporate farmers received the most economic support via farm legislation and programs.[32]

At the same time, although many western farmers supported the Federal Agriculture Improvement and Reform Act of 1996, which attempted to wean farmers from agricultural subsidies and free them from mandated acreage reductions and price supports, the perennial problem of surplus production and low agricultural prices persisted. Western farmers responded through their commodity groups to force both Democratic and Republican members of Congress to provide an economic safety net. Congress complied with the Farm Security and Rural Investment Act of 2002, which provided additional economic support over the next decade and increased payments to farmers for certain commodities provided they agreed to specific production controls. Western farmers had played a fundamental role in achieving that legislation, but nearly everyone familiar with agricultural policy considered it either a return to the past or a stopgap measure to solve an immediate political problem. Still, no one really knows what to do about overproduction and low prices except to throw more money at producers.[33]

At the dawn of the twenty-first century, the future of farmers looked bleak: The economic situation remains precarious, and their declining numbers did not bode well for the exercise of political power. In 2000, for example, only 4.4 million people lived on 2.1 million farms nationwide, a considerable decrease from 1900, when 29.8 million people lived on 5.7 million farms. Put differently, only 1.6 percent of the population nationwide lived on farms, and fewer than 25 percent of the counties in the United States depended on farming for their primary income. The small percentage of farmers in the total population decreased their political influence; their only power resided in their ability to produce interest-group politics.[34]

In retrospect, then, during the twentieth century, first Progressivism and then conservatives influenced the pursuit of agricultural politics in the American West. It is not too much to say that western farmers used the federal government to achieve agricultural policies that are essentially economic. The result has been a paradoxical combination of populism, progressivism, and conservatism and a narrowing of the political agenda to more self-centered economic goals. Indeed, during the twentieth century the individualistic "I" became more important than the commonweal "we" in the formulation of agricultural policy for western farmers.

By the end of the twentieth century, western farmers spoke for themselves through their commodity groups rather than as farmers as a class through political parties. Western farmers were wheat, cotton, or rice farmers, not just farmers, and their political activities reflected their specializations. In many respects, their politics also indicated the increasing isolation of western farmers from mainstream society, which often had considerably different needs and concerns. Western farmers, then, confronted political forces not in the shape of political parties but, rather, in the form of strong interest groups whose members came and went as their causes were won or lost. The political opposition changed rapidly, and the response of western farmers through their own interest groups was at some times loud and unsophisticated and at other times deft and professional. Western farmers, however, understood that they wielded considerably less political power than Jefferson had wished for them as a class in the early days of the Republic.

Indeed, in 1964 the political power of the western farm states decreased rapidly after the U.S. Supreme Court required reapportionment based on population and as the farm population declined. The Supreme Court based its reapportionment mandate on the principle of one person, one vote. Prior to the Supreme Court's decision, congressional districts gave farmers greater representation than urbanites. Representation favored geography and farmers, but during the 1950s urban citizens began demanding congressional districting based on population, not land area. The Supreme Court agreed. Thereafter, as the number of farmers continued to drop, agricultural organizations represented fewer constituents. Congressional representation also became more urban. As a result, farmers and their organizations lost some political power. Agricultural organizations did not lose all influence, of course, because congressional representatives relied on them for expertise rather than party leadership. Indeed, the commodity organizations continued to exert political power because they did not have an ideological commitment. The commodity groups, for example, rejected the desires of the Farm Bureau Federation for a laissez-faire government relationship with agriculture as well as the call of the Farmers Union for extensive federal intrusion in the agricultural economy. Instead, the commodity groups essentially only wanted more economic aid for member farmers, and these agricultural organizations did not frighten politicians. Rather, the commodity groups helped members of Congress understand specific farm-related issues, because congressional representatives could not afford the technical expertise or the time to master the complexities of agricultural policy making. Consequently, the farm lobby, in the absence of party leadership, provided reliable information to Congress about agricultural problems. The farm lobby in the form of the commodity groups also offered solutions that agricultural constituents favored, and it marshaled the farm vote to support or reject representatives and senators based on their support of agriculture. Once the commodity groups gained access to Congress, they remained a powerful influence on the formulation of farm policy. As a result, western members of Congress usually supported the farm lobby, which included large umbrella organizations such as the Farm Bureau Federation and the Farmers Union, even at the expense of party discipline, if its proposals helped their constituents. If the proposals of the farm lobby did not affect their constituents, members of Congress usually voted according to party line. Equally important, the farm lobby kept the Jeffersonian image alive in the public mind even though its validity lay in the distant past.[35]

Despite the fragmentation and decline of agrarian political power and the inability of western farmers to achieve the Jeffersonian ideal, the public continued to perceive farmers according to old national myths. Indeed, the public kept alive the image of family farmers as an independent people who lead a preferred way of life far from the madding crowd. Late in the twentieth century, most Americans considered farm life preferable to urban living. A poll indicated that 58 percent of the people questioned believed that farm life was more honest and moral than city life, while 64 percent of the interviewees contended that farm men and women worked harder than urbanites, and 67 percent thought that farmers had closer ties to their families than did other people. Those who had incomes below the poverty line were most inclined to believe that farm men and women were especially moral and honest. Interviewees over sixty-five years of age and who depended on agriculture for a living or who lived in communities with fewer than 50,000 residents primarily assumed that farmers had closer family ties than other Americans. Moreover, the poll showed that the poor and less educated preferred life on a farm if they could earn a decent living, while 53 percent of the men and 44 percent of the women interviewed thought they would like to live on a farm. By the turn of the end of the twentieth century, then, the Jeffersonian ideal died hard, if it died at all. Western farmers intended to use their political power to fulfill their own conservative economic ends as well as ensure that they remained in the public mind in myth, if not in reality.[36]

NOTES

1. Quoted in William P. Browne and John Dinse, "The Emergence of the American Agriculture Movement, 1977–1979," *Great Plains Quarterly* 5 (Fall 1985): 225.

2. Catherine McNicol Stock, *Rural Radicals: Righteous Rage in the American Grain* (Ithaca, N.Y.: Cornell University Press, 1996), 153.

3. Adrienne Koch and William Peden, eds., *The Life and Writings of Thomas Jefferson* (New York: Random House, 1944), 377; Thomas Jefferson, *Notes on the State of Virginia*, ed. William Peden (New York: W. W. Norton, 1954), 164–165; William Jennings Bryan, *Speeches of William Jennings Bryan* (New York: Funk & Wagnalls, 1913), 248.

4. Larry Remele, "North Dakota's Forgotten Farmers Union, 1913–1920," *North Dakota History* 45 (Spring 1978): 5.

5. Although I use different terminology, I have drawn on Daniel J. Elazar's *American Federalism: A View from the States*, 2nd ed. (New York: Thomas Y. Crowell, 1972) and "Political Culture on the Plains," *Western Historical Quarterly* 11 (July 1980): 260–283.

6. Doster quoted in Michael J. Brodhead, *Persevering Populist: The Life of Frank Doster* (Reno: University of Nevada Press, 1969), 91.

7. David Danbom, "North Dakota," in *Heartland: Comparative Histories of the Midwestern States*, ed. James H. Madison (Bloomington: Indiana University Press, 1988), 114; Robert L. Morlan, *Political Prairie Fire: The Nonpartisan League, 1915–1922* (St. Paul: Minnesota Historical Society Press, 1985); Larry Remele, "Power to the People:

The Nonpartisan League," in *The North Dakota Political Tradition*, ed. Thomas W. Howard (Ames: Iowa State University Press, 1981), 66–92; Robert H. Bahmer, "The Economic and Political Background of the Nonpartisan League" (Ph.D. diss., University of Minnesota, 1941); Scott Allen Ellsworth, "Origins of the Nonpartisan League" (Ph.D. diss., Duke University, 1982).

8. Douglas Bakken, "NPL in Nebraska, 1917–1920," *North Dakota History* 39 (Spring 1972): 26–31, quote on 29.

9. Hugh T. Lovin, "The Farmer Revolt in Idaho, 1914–1922," *Idaho Yesterdays* 20, no. 3 (1976): 2–6.

10. Ibid., 6–15; Carlos A. Schwantes, "Farmer-Labor Insurgency in Washington State," *Pacific Northwest Quarterly* 76 (January 1985): 1.

11. Theodore Saloutos and John D. Hicks, *Twentieth-Century Populism: Agricultural Discontent in the Middle West, 1900–1939* (Lincoln: University of Nebraska Press, [1951]), 219–254; Remele, "North Dakota's Forgotten Farmers Union," 4–21; R. Douglas Hurt, *Problems of Plenty: The American Farmer in the Twentieth Century* (Chicago: Ivan Dee, 2002), 17–21.

12. Remele, "North Dakota's Forgotten Farmers Union," 16–17, 19; James C. Milligan and L. David Norris, "Organizing Wide-Awake Farmers: John A. Simpson and the Oklahoma Farmers' Union," *Chronicles of Oklahoma* 74 (Winter 1996–1997): 358–359, 363, 370, 374.

13. Elizabeth Sanders, *Roots of Reform: Farmers, Workers, and the American State, 1877–1917* (Chicago: University of Chicago Press, 1999), 199–202.

14. Ibid., 256–261, 301–303; Hurt, *Problems of Plenty*, 24, 26.

15. Hurt, *Problems of Plenty*, 35.

16. Ibid., 39–40, 54; Saloutos and Hicks, *Twentieth-Century Populism*, 336; James H. Shideler, *Farm Crisis, 1919–1923* (Berkeley and Los Angeles: University of California Press, 1957), 151–188, 217–242.

17. David Hamilton, *From New Day to New Deal: American Farm Policy from Hoover to Roosevelt, 1928–1933* (Chapel Hill: University of North Carolina Press, 1991); Van L. Perkins, *Crisis in Agriculture: The Agricultural Adjustment Administration and the New Deal* (Berkeley and Los Angeles: University of California Press, 1969), 10–35; John L. Shover, *Cornbelt Rebellion: The Farmers' Holiday Association* (Urbana: University of Illinois Press, 1965), 200–216.

18. Hurt, *Problems of Plenty*, 67–83.

19. R. Douglas Hurt, "Prices, Payments, and Production: Kansas Wheat Farmers and the Agricultural Adjustment Administration, 1933–1939," *Kansas History* 23 (Spring–Summer 2000): 72–87.

20. Ibid.

21. C. Roger Lambert, "The Drought Cattle Purchase, 1934–1935: Problems and Complaints," *Agricultural History* 45 (April 1971): 85–93, and "Texas Cattlemen and the AAA, 1933–1935," *Arizona and the West* 14 (Summer 1972): 137–154. For the relationship of western cattle raisers to the federal government, see Paul J. Culhane, *Public Lands Politics: Interest Group Influence on the Forest Service and the Bureau of Land Management* (Baltimore: Published for Resources for the Future, Inc., by the Johns

Hopkins University Press, 1981); Paul F. Starrs, *Let the Cowboy Ride: Cattle Ranching in the American West* (Baltimore: The Johns Hopkins University Press, 1998); William D. Rowley, *U.S. Forest Service and the Rangelands: A History* (College Station: Texas A&M University Press, 1985); Karen R. Merrill, *Public Lands and Political Meaning: Ranchers, the Government, and the Property between Them* (Berkeley and Los Angeles: University of California Press, 2002); Debra L. Donahue, *The Western Range Revisited: Removing Livestock from Public Lands to Conserve Biodiversity* (Norman: University of Oklahoma Press, 1999); William D. Rowley, "From Open Range to Closed Range on Public Lands," in *Land in the American West: Private Claims and the Common Good*, ed. William G. Robbins and James C. Foster (Seattle: University of Washington Press, 2000), 96–118.

22. John Mark Hansen, *Gaining Access: Congress and the Farm Lobby, 1919–1981* (Chicago: University of Chicago Press, 1991); William P. Browne, *Cultivating Congress: Constituents, Issues, and Interests in Agricultural Policy Making* (Lawrence: University Press of Kansas, 1995).

23. Hurt, *Problems of Plenty*, 108–109.

24. Gilbert C. Fite, *American Farmers: The New Minority* (Bloomington: Indiana University Press, 1981), 39; Saloutos and Hicks, *Twentieth-Century Populism*, 219–229, quote on 220; private letter to the author, August 2005.

25. Hansen, *Gaining Access*, 97.

26. Personal observation of the author; Fite, *American Farmers*, 158–164; John T. Schlebecker, "The Great Holding Action: The NFO in September 1962," *Agricultural History* 43 (October 1969): 204–213; Willis Rowell, *Mad as Hell* (Corning, Iowa: Gauthier, 1984), 54; Fite, *American Farmers*, 162.

27. William P. Browne, "Mobilizing and Activating Group Demands: The American Agriculture Movement," *Social Science Quarterly* 64 (March 1983): 19–34.

28. Personal observation of the author; Fite, *American Farmers*, 209–217; Browne and Dinse, "Emergence of the American Agriculture Movement," 221–235.

29. Hurt, *Problems of Plenty*, 159–63, quote on 162.

30. Ibid., 164–166.

31. Harry C. McDean, "Agribusiness in the American West," in *The Rural West since World War II*, ed. R. Douglas Hurt (Lawrence: University Press of Kansas, 1998), 213–244.

32. Ibid.

33. Hurt, Problems of Plenty, 166–170.

34. *Historical Statistics of the United States: Colonial Times to 1970*, pt. 1 (Washington, D.C.: U.S. Department of Commerce, Bureau of the Census, 1975), 457; *Agricultural Statistics, 2001* (Washington, D.C.: Government Printing Office, 2001), ix–2; *Perceptions of Rural America* (Battle Creek, Mich.: W. K. Kellogg Foundation, 2001), 4.

35. Hansen, *Gaining Access*, 7, 76, 111, 177, 227; Fite, *American Farmers*, 150–152.

36. R. Douglas Hurt, *American Agriculture: A Brief History*, rev. ed. (West Lafayette, Ind.: Purdue University Press, 2002), 401. For slightly different statistics that address similar questions concerning rural, rather than farm, life, see *Perceptions of Rural America*, 4–10.

CHAPTER 3

The Illusions of Independence: Texas Oilmen and the Politics of Postwar Petroleum

Karen R. Merrill

Oil fuels almost every feature of our twenty-first-century life, but while it comes out of the ground with distinct physical traits—it can be sticky or fluid, dense or light, and is even described as "sweet" or "sour"—by the time it is refined and transformed into a multitude of products (from gasoline to polyester fleece), most people have little material sense for its ubiquitous place in the modern world. Oil remains an abstract part of our ordinary existence, in other words, despite our absolute dependency on it. And outside of the anxiety we feel when its price rises, oil still does not absorb a great deal of public attention nationally, even though recent presidential elections have featured some debate about the future prospects of our oil policy and our energy policy more generally. In large measure, Americans haven't had to ask too many questions about our dependency on oil: Despite a handful of supply disruptions over the last sixty years, oil has been cheap and plentiful.[1]

But underlying this story of petroleum plenty is the fact that the United States has had to rely increasingly on oil from other countries. In 1950, oil from beneath American ground not only provided nearly all the nation's needs, but it also served over 50 percent of the world's needs. In contrast, the United States now needs to import about 60 percent of its oil from overseas, with Canada, Mexico, and Saudi Arabia leading the list of countries that export oil to the United States.[2] That tectonic shift in *where* oil comes from has involved tremendous political questions for both the producers of oil and the American government, and as we face a world in which we will have to depend yet more on other countries, especially in the Middle East, where the largest oil reserves now lie, American consumers will probably have to weigh our country's oil policy with greater frequency and intensity.

With the Persian Gulf War of 1991 and the Iraq War of 2003, the American government has already gone so far as to deploy the military to secure access to the vast stores of oil in the Middle East, and these events have their roots in World War II, when men in Washington and in the petroleum business began directing the future of Americans' role in the exploration and production of oil worldwide.[3] The American oilmen present in such conversations ranged from high-placed executives of the "majors" to small-time independent operators, but a great many of them had come of age in the great oil booms in Texas and Oklahoma (or what was then considered the "Southwest") in the early twentieth century, where a political culture revolving around oil developed.[4] Not only were the states financially dependent on the revenues oil brought in, but the oil industry had also helped incubate certain political ideals about keeping the federal government's involvement in the business to a minimum. Those ideals were hitched to an almost iconic figure in the region: the "independent" oilman who put together his own investment deals, who operated outside corporate hierarchies, and who wasn't afraid to take risks to strike it big in "black gold." But when the U.S. government confirmed in 1944 that enormous volumes of oil existed in the Middle East, particularly in the Persian Gulf region, and that the United States had a profound interest in staking a claim to that oil, southwestern oilmen were clearly facing a new world.

This essay explores the emerging political and economic ideologies of southwestern oilmen as they imagined and then entered that postwar world. First, it examines how independent operators began to carve out a response to the discoveries in the Middle East. Having supplied most of the Allies' oil needs throughout the war, and having staked that enormous job on the lofty goals of the Allied effort, what would become of the domestic oil industry's standing if the American petroleum industry shifted its gaze to the Persian Gulf? What would it mean to the United States if it began relying on oil that came out of the ground in the Saudi Arabian desert, as opposed to, say, West Texas or Oklahoma? With the petroleum industry encompassing widely different kinds of operations and people with extraordinarily different interests, one cannot easily sum up the reactions by American oilmen to the discoveries in the Middle East. Certainly, oilmen the world over recognized that Persian Gulf oil was The Next Big Thing, and those with the capital resources were chomping at the bit to drill and get the oil to market, despite the minimal presence that American oil companies had there at that point. However, the oil discoveries in the Middle East seemed to threaten everything the independents of the Southwest had worked for.

While relatively few of them participated in the highest-level conversations, plenty of them had opinions about the course of American oil policy as they looked toward the postwar period. At root, southwestern oilmen were deeply concerned about the economics of the Middle East reserves and whether these would put online a surplus of oil that would drive down the prices domestic producers received—both at the wellhead and at the refinery—for their oil. They had just survived a difficult period of overproduction in the 1930s, in which the price of oil hit rock-bottom, so this was a reasonable and still-fresh fear. But their concerns went far beyond the economics of the new petroleum order, for in fact independent producers had a significant place in the political debate that occurred about that new order. Indeed, the World War II years, particularly after 1943, provoked intense discussion over a variety of issues related to what "independence" meant to these men: whether they themselves would be able to operate as "independent" producers in the postwar period; whether the southwestern states would be able to regulate oil production independent of the federal government; whether the United States would maintain its independence from foreign oil imports.

These concerns led Texas independents into what might be termed the politics of "oil isolation," as I will explain in more detail below. In contrast, another vantage point will illuminate a more internationalist perspective on postwar oil production, and to explore that, this essay will then focus on one Texas oilman in particular, Everette DeGolyer, who rather reluctantly entered the global politics of oil in the 1940s. As both a world-renowned petroleum geologist and an investor in many domestic operations, and one of the most astute observers of the oil industry during the war and immediate postwar years, DeGolyer was uniquely positioned to study the complexities of America's *and* the Southwest's interests at a moment of great transformation in the global petroleum order. He, too, was interested in the meanings of "independence" at a time when the major oil companies were joining to do business in Saudi Arabia. Like his fellow Texans, DeGolyer had concerns about the maintenance of the "free-enterprise system" in the American oil industry—specifically, the ability of the petroleum business to operate outside government control. But those concerns led him in different directions from Texas independents: As he schooled himself in the history and the politics of the Middle East, DeGolyer became most interested in how American oil operations in the Persian Gulf could avoid the entanglements of British-style colonialism. That DeGolyer became drawn to the image of the pioneering Texas oilman as a model for independence tells us a lot, as I will suggest, about the power of western American icons to shape ideas about U.S. oil operations in the Middle East.

By bringing these two vantage points together, I want to do a couple of things. First, it is important simply to recover the history of the American oil industry, particularly as it made the transition into the postwar years. For some time—probably since J. R. Ewing, from the television show *Dallas*, became a popular figure in the 1980s, but certainly in the last few years with George W. Bush as president—Americans have imagined an almost cartoonish character when they think of the Texas oilman. In part, that figure is a creation of southwestern oilmen themselves, as they have crafted a uniquely western look for the Texas oilman, with cowboy boots and a Stetson hat as indispensable sartorial accessories. These are choices, as Robert Goldberg's essay in this volume underscores, with significant political meanings. But beyond noting the image of the Texas independent, we need to bring greater historical understanding to the widely different interests that oilmen in the region had and to their role in American politics and the positions they staked out. Why, then, turn to *this* moment, the mid-1940s, when it became clear that the center of worldwide oil production was moving to the eastern hemisphere? Because these two different political views—oil isolationism and oil internationalism—nonetheless shared a deeply anachronistic, even nostalgic, understanding of the oil industry's capacity to generate different kinds of independence, whether that meant the autonomy of individual oil operators, of oil-producing regions, or of the nation. This understanding—or more specifically, this postwar business ideology—exerted a real influence on American politics, and at the same time, it stood at great odds both with the actual structuring of the American oil industry in the Persian Gulf after the war and with the political economy of oil in the United States.

One last introductory note: in addition to my employing the term "the Southwest" to indicate Texas and Oklahoma, as was commonly done in the 1940s, I will make use of a couple of other shorthand terms. First, I will refer to the players in the petroleum industry as "oil*men*." While there were some women involved in southwestern oil production—largely in selling leasing rights to property they owned—the industry was so completely dominated by men that the term is appropriate. Second, I will sometimes refer to these players, as I do in the title, as "*Texas* oilmen," although obviously there were many independent oil producers who were not from Texas. But I do so because the oil discoveries in Texas in the early twentieth century put it on the global oil map, and by the 1940s, the American independent oil industry certainly located its own "center of gravity"[5] in that state. Moreover, given the dominance of Texas oilmen in current international politics, such a term appropriately highlights the continuities between mid-twentieth-century concerns about the world oil supply and our own time.

A NEW ROLE FOR GOVERNMENT AND
AMERICAN OIL PRODUCERS

The position that independent producers carved out for themselves in the mid-1940s emerged directly out of their experience of the 1930s and the war years. During the Great Depression, the domestic oil industry was faced with its worst economic crisis to date because of the tremendous flood of oil on the market from the newly opened, colossal fields in East Texas. This oil glut created serious problems, not the least of which was that the pace of oil production in East Texas caused the pressure to drop beneath the oil fields, which made it difficult to recover as much oil as operators should have. But the most pressing concern for large and small oilmen alike was the plummeting price: At its lowest, East Texas crude garnered ten cents a barrel in the summer of 1931, about the price of a loaf of bread.[6] Moreover, accusations flew—some founded, some unfounded—that East Texas operators were engaging in the sale of "hot oil," that is, stolen oil.[7] Ultimately, the crisis came under control with the emergence of different regulatory structures: The state of Texas empowered the Texas Railroad Commission to begin restoring the balance between output and market demand, and in the mid-1930s the Interstate Oil Compact Commission was formed, a commission of oilmen who made recommendations about supply levels among the oil-producing states.[8]

Thus, independent operators found themselves in the 1930s increasingly either tied into regulations or exposed to ideas about economic planning in ways they had not experienced at all before the Depression. But this contact with the government was nothing compared to the relationship that was suddenly forged during World War II between American oil producers and the federal government. It is at this point that Everette DeGolyer became important. The son of a father who never found luck in the oil and minerals business, DeGolyer was by all measures a kind of prodigy in the field of geology. Having first traveled to Mexico under the apprenticeship of U.S. Geological Survey director C. Willard Hayes in 1909, in 1910 he located North America's greatest-producing oil well—Portrero del Llano no. 4—at the age of twenty-one, before he had even received a college degree (and making him the richest college student at the University of Oklahoma when he returned from Mexico). By this point, DeGolyer had caught the attention of Sir Weetman Pearson, Lord Cowdray, who had been sinking money in dry wells in Mexico for years before DeGolyer's discovery. With the vast amounts of oil that would flow from this field, however, Pearson built up his Aguila Oil Company (or Mexican Eagle) into "one of the most promising financial ventures in the world," with DeGolyer occupying the post of chief geologist of the firm.[9]

DeGolyer stayed in Mexico with Aguila until 1914, and within five years, he helped found the Amerada Corporation with Lord Cowdray and other associates from Mexican Eagle. Amerada had operations both in Mexico and in the United States, and the corporation provided him with the resources and support to become the leading proponent of using scientific means to determine oil reserves in any given field. As DeGolyer biographer Lon Tinkle wrote, "For at least a decade" after the founding of Amerada, DeGolyer "was to know more about [geophysical exploration] than any other living soul."[10] But DeGolyer also had aspirations to work independently, both as a scientific consultant and as an operator, and thus he left Amerada in 1932. Because most of his own properties were in Texas, he, his wife, Nell, and their four children relocated to Dallas, and it was there that in 1936 he established the firm with which he was most associated: the DeGolyer and McNaughton Corporation. Although DeGolyer cofounded the firm with fellow geologist Lewis McNaughton, DeGolyer was the man that oil companies and potential exporting companies sought, as he was highly regarded for giving perhaps the most accurate estimates of oil reserves—a not-inconsequential skill in the world of oil investment, which involves a great deal of financial risk.[11]

By the time America stood on the verge of entering World War II, DeGolyer was widely recognized as one of two authorities on the question of how large the remaining oil reserves of the United States were. This question was of consuming interest to government and business leaders, given that over 50 percent of the world's oil came from American oil fields, and particularly to leaders in such states as Texas, Oklahoma, and Louisiana, whose economies relied on the money that flowed from this production. DeGolyer had become a pessimist on this issue, convinced that America would never again be home to enormous oil strikes; Wallace Pratt, a geologist and old friend of DeGolyer's from their days in Mexico and at the time vice president of Standard Oil of New Jersey, was the leading optimist, believing that new and productive oil fields remained to be found in the United States. Because new exploration in the 1930s had, in fact, hit pay dirt in Texas and Oklahoma, many public commentators—including southwestern oil independents—shared Pratt's view. But in Washington, D.C., as Roosevelt and his administration prepared for war, the mood was much more in keeping with DeGolyer's assessment, and at the urging of Secretary of Interior Harold L. Ickes, Franklin Roosevelt established what would become known as the Petroleum Administration for War (PAW) to manage American oil needs. Headed by Ickes, it consisted largely of men with recognized technical expertise in the oil industry; Ickes thus appointed DeGolyer the director of conservation.

DeGolyer was a reluctant participant in politics; like many other men in the business, his appetite was large when it came to exploring for oil—and he was, in addition, a voracious book collector—but he clearly found the political machinations surrounding the petroleum industry a roadblock to the job that he enjoyed doing most: finding oil. Nonetheless, he took on political work as a way to bring greater order and efficiency to the industry, two goals that were close to his heart as a petroleum geologist who had long supported the greater use of scientific equipment in the search for oil. And the task before him and the other officials within the PAW was indeed enormous. Although World War I was said to have been won, in a famous phrase of Lord Curzon's, on a "wave of oil," the petroleum needs for the military in World War II were staggering. As DeGolyer's biographer noted, "In less than two months the United States Fifth Fleet consumed 630 million gallons of fuel oil; to move an armored battalion one hundred miles required 17,000 gallons of gasoline; the Far Eastern Forces used nearly 150 million gallons of aviation gasoline in a single month of attacks on Japanese shipping."[12] In fact, throughout the war, American oil provided on average between 60 and 70 percent of the Allies' needs.[13] With vast demand for oil in the domestic sphere, and despite strict gas rationing during the war, the PAW had to find answers to two questions: How would it keep the fuel supply running at home and to the military in the short term, and did the country have adequate reserves for the long term?

It was in the context of the latter question that DeGolyer became a central player in the political questions about the global search for oil. In the summer of 1943, and under a veil of secrecy, Roosevelt approved the establishment of a new agency, to be headed by Ickes: the Petroleum Reserves Corporation (PRC), whose goal was to investigate whether the U.S. government should become directly involved in oil production overseas through owning some or all of the concession in Saudi Arabia. (That concession was currently held jointly by two American companies, Standard Oil of California and the Texas Company, which would soon join with Standard Oil of New Jersey and Socony-Vacuum to become Aramco.) Under the auspices of the PRC, Ickes sent DeGolyer and several other officials on what was originally supposed to be a secret mission to the Middle East to provide a technical assessment of oil reserves there, to give the government a more realistic basis on which to judge how it might get involved.

That mission occurred during the late fall of 1943 and early winter of 1944 and took DeGolyer to Saudi Arabia, Iraq, Iran, Bahrain, and Kuwait, as well as to Egypt and Palestine and then eventually to London, where he met with British oilmen.[14] It was the British industry, of course, that had the most solid foothold in the Middle East: Parliament had decided in 1914 that the government would hold a 51 percent share in the Anglo-Persian Oil Company (later, the Anglo-Iranian Oil Company, or AIOC), and thus Iran had seen three decades of British oil production by the time DeGolyer arrived for his tour. In contrast, American oil interests had only begun to build up their facilities, with small operations in Kuwait (carried out in combination with the British), Bahrain, and Saudi Arabia. While the mission was purportedly only a technical one—the State Department, in fact, forbade the mission's participants from "discuss[ing] petroleum matters with members of the local governments," presumably meaning the local leaders of the exporting countries—politics clearly occupied a great deal of discussion.[15]

And politics were front and center when the mission returned, as news of its conclusions became public. "The center of gravity of world oil production," DeGolyer wrote in the mission report,

> is shifting from the Gulf-Caribbean area to the Middle East area—to the Persian Gulf area—and is likely to shift until it is firmly established in that area. . . .
>
> When one considers the great oil discoveries which have resulted from the meager exploration thus far accomplished in the Middle East, the substantial number of known prospects not yet drilled, and the great areas still practically unexplored, the conclusion is inescapable that reserves of great magnitude remain to be discovered.[16]

THE EMERGING WORLDVIEWS OF SOUTHWESTERN INDEPENDENTS

The government's response to DeGolyer's report went through several stages as the Roosevelt and Truman administrations considered how best to secure America's future oil supply, starting with the secret negotiations of the PRC to own part of the Saudi Arabian concession, then moving on to the government's plan in 1944 to build a pipeline across Saudi Arabia, which would transport the oil to the eastern Mediterranean, and finally culminating in the government's push to enter into a treaty with Great Britain, with the hope that the treaty would establish an international commission to estimate world oil demand and allocate production output. Behind these three wartime initiatives stood, in particular, military men who embraced the idea of U.S. involvement in foreign oil development through the PRC's owning—wholly or in part—the Saudi Arabian concession. They were drawn to the example of the AIOC, and they hoped to secure their supplies for years to come. In contrast, the domestic oil industry was by and large skeptical and even hostile to the government's entering the foreign oil business in any way. One cannot overestimate how critical the timing of the mission to the Middle East was, for it came at the very moment that the domestic oil industry was chafing under wartime controls, and the debate over how the government should involve itself in oil production in the Middle East helped develop independents' emerging role in national politics. That all three government proposals went down in defeat also indicates that independents entered the postwar period in a position of political strength.[17]

But what did it mean to be an independent oilman? It could mean many things, as it turns out. At one end were the wildcatters, men like Columbus Marion "Dad" Joiner. Joiner had made and lost a lot of money on oil in Oklahoma before he began drilling in the Woodbine sands of East Texas in 1930. Driven further and further into debt after his first attempts were dry holes, he finally struck oil with his Daisy Bradford no. 3 well, and the East Texas oilfields ended up being the largest oilfield in the world at the time, with a recovery of over 5 billion barrels of oil over the years.[18] Like many wildcatters, Joiner would later face financial problems, and by the time of his death, his estate had little value. Dad Joiner represented the classic image of the wildcatter—someone willing to risk everything for the next big "play"—but other independents played their cards with a greater eye to building a business. H. L. Hunt, for instance, began his career as a small-time operator in Arkansas in the 1920s, buying and selling oil leases and eventually breaking into drilling. Hearing rumors of a big discovery in East Texas, Hunt traveled there and bought Dad Joiner's discovery well, along with other, adjacent leases. Joiner would contest these sales in court, but the result was a financial bonanza for Hunt, which ended up providing the foundation for the Hunt Oil Company, established in the mid-1930s, and making Hunt one of the richest people in the United States by the 1940s. Engaged for years in many aspects of the domestic oil industry, Hunt Oil expanded its operations abroad in the 1960s and is currently one of the largest independent energy firms in the world.[19]

But whether one was a wildcatter like Joiner or an assertive businessman like Hunt—or, most likely, someone in between—being an independent oilman in the 1940s meant engaging in the oil business purely on the domestic front and shying away from the large corporate structures of such "majors" as the Standard Oil companies. By 1945, there were thousands of oilmen who called themselves "independents" (there were probably about 3,000 in Texas alone),[20] and their main concern was getting rid of wartime regulations that set limits on what price they could earn for their oil on the market. They believed that by removing such constraints, the government would free up the industry to find more oil. The prospect of the American government's actually getting involved in the postwar petroleum industry abroad thus raised critical concerns in the minds of independents about what the future shape of their industry would be.

At the most basic level, southwestern independents did not want to compete with cheap oil from the Middle East, and they believed that any of the three wartime measures would quickly open up the world oil market to Persian Gulf oil. More specifically, they worried a great deal that Middle Eastern oil might be produced so cheaply that it would undercut their domestic market, particularly on the East Coast.[21] Texas oilmen were anxious about the standing of the independent producers as a whole, they believed that the government was intent on continuing wartime regulation even after the war, which, they believed, would squelch individual initiative and "free enterprise." And the figure at the center of independents' concern and anger was Secretary of the Interior Ickes. As Lawrence Goodwyn has written, Ickes was in fact one of the New Dealers more sympathetic to small oil producers, but "at the policy level . . . he had less faith in small producers and consumers than he did in his own personal capacity to serve as their protector. Ickes was a definite believer in big government, particularly in that sector of the government headed by himself."[22] Indeed, Ickes was one of the New Deal's most outspoken proponents, and previous policy battles with westerners showed how deeply he believed that the federal government should be in charge of resource management. Although Ickes spoke of his support for "the little man," in fact the independents, much like small ranching operators in the region, believed he was simply bent on seizing as much power as he could.[23]

In contrast to that specter, independents raised the figure of "the wildcatter" as the man who formed the bedrock of the industry. This intense attachment to the wildcatter stood as an integral part of what William R. Childs has termed the "civil religion of Texas oil," by which he means that the region had produced, by the 1930s, a set of symbols and values that gave nearly mythological meaning to the place of oil in the region's economy and social and political life.[24] As one producer noted in testimony before the Senate Committee on Foreign Relations,

> It has been the little fellow in the oil industry, the wildcatter, the pioneer, the American, who is resolute, thrifty, ambitious, hard working and willing to take a chance, who has discovered practically every important new oil field ever found in our land. He is the indispensable man in the oil industry. His problem is harder today, but it is upon him we must largely depend if our nation is to escape subservience to those who own foreign oil.[25]

If the "wildcatter" was the hero of the independents' political rhetoric, increased "wildcatting" was their answer to the administration's fear that the United States would run out of oil. As an editorial in the *Oil and Gas Journal* pronounced in January 1944, "What is needed now is the ending of unwarranted restrictions in operations extending from the initial exploratory efforts to the completed well. . . . Past history leaves no doubt as to the success of an all-out wildcat campaign once such a campaign is under way."[26]

But, perhaps surprisingly, despite their fears about competing with imports and about the status of the "little fellow," Texas independents, on the whole, made few criticisms of the majors' desire to gain concessions in Saudi Arabia and their investment in developing them. In their commentary in the *Oil and Gas Journal* and in testimony before congressional committees, they repeatedly expressed support for the majors' efforts to set up operations in the Persian Gulf. As one witness from Denver noted to the Senate Committee on Foreign Relations in 1947, after objecting to the Anglo-American Treaty, "I am not criticizing the importing oil companies. Rather, I commend their enterprise and zeal. . . . I am not opposed to our foreign oil companies engaging in foreign trade, nor to reasonable help our Government may give them in doing so."[27] What he and the vast majority of independents objected to was the federal government's getting directly involved in the oil industry in any foreign country, beyond offering diplomatic protection to American nationals. More generally, while the prospect of government involvement in Persian Gulf operations offered up the specter of, in the words of the president of Sun Oil Company, a "super-state cartel," southwestern independents aimed all their fire at the potential concentration of government power that such a path might involve rather than at the concentration of economic power that was already evident in Aramco's exclusive concession on Saudi oil.[28]

Closer to home, the independents were also well aware of the dependence that Texas and Oklahoma had on the income from taxation on oil profits, particularly for schools, and they were convinced that opening up the Middle East would sharply cut that source of funding.[29] Beyond discussing the economics of the problem, Texas independents partook in an emerging and widespread political discourse that embraced the power of the states as against that of the federal government. As one Texas witness noted in 1947,

> We do not want to see the control over this great industry . . . [taken from] the oil-producing States. During the war we gladly surrendered that control unto the Federal Government. We want it returned to the States under State control—under State control it has grown into a

giant industry. . . . We do not want the bureaucrats in Washington to be our bosses. Under State control, free enterprise has enjoyed its fairest days. Under it men have gone from rags to riches. Everybody has a chance.[30]

Southwestern independents continually connected the American government's imperial design on Saudi Arabian oil to what they saw as the Roosevelt administration's imperial design at home. Again, this had an economic and a political component. Analysts among independents argued that the administration's wartime petroleum measures would give the government "the power" not only to control the world price of oil but also "to control domestic-crude prices within the United States without openly appearing to do so."[31] At the political level, they were particularly concerned about the establishment of an international commission, as outlined by the proposed Anglo-American petroleum agreement, to oversee the flows of supply and demand on the world oil market. As Daniel Yergin has written, "It was one thing to have oil production rates set by the Texas Railroad Commission, whose members were elected in Texas, but quite another to have it done by a commission that was half 'limeys' and half appointees of Franklin Roosevelt."[32] They also expressed concern about the dangers of foreign entanglements, especially following such a devastating war. In the weeks of discussion about the PRC's plan to build a pipeline across Saudi Arabia, independents argued that, rather than providing a secure source of oil for America, the pipeline would open up the United States to further military engagement. As the *Oil and Gas Journal* reported in 1944, in an article about Oklahoma senator E. H. Moore's opposition to the pipeline plan, "Instead of preventing wars . . . the pipe line would be a provocative [*sic*] to war. It would be impossible, [Moore] declared, for the Government to develop foreign oil reserves or maintain a transportation system without maintaining also a military force to protect proprietary rights."[33]

In outlining the independents' objections to the U.S. government's wartime petroleum measures, and in noting that those views represent a politics of oil isolation, at the beginning of this essay, I have wanted to draw out the fundamentally inward-looking nature of their politics. Skeptical or hostile to the powers amassed by the New Deal and wartime administrations of Roosevelt, they rejected outright the role that any international commission might play in planning for world oil production. And although their work had contributed directly to the Allied victory in World War II, they did not see themselves as part of a world oil market or network. In their most expansive moments, they understood that the oilfields of Texas and Oklahoma were part of the dominance of the western hemisphere in world oil production—Mexico and Venezuela were giant producers of oil, too—but as they looked to the future, their concern focused almost exclusively on how to expand their production rates and how to protect their domestic market.[34] Keeping that market to themselves was their first order of business in the postwar world. "Do not let it be subject to the temptation of anybody," one independent from Denver said in a Senate hearing. "Let us keep it free to support the American oil-producing industry, which is necessary for our independence and possibly for our salvation."[35]

The independents thus sustained their political position with the core belief that it would best protect the independence of their industry, the political autonomy of their region, and the independence and national security of the nation. From the perspective of our own time, in which we have to reckon with the future dwindling of oil supplies worldwide, it is clear they could not see that all these realms of independence had, at their center, the oilmen's *dependence* on a dwindling domestic resource. Everette De-Golyer might have reminded them of this fact, but he, too, could not escape the powerful hold that ideals of independence had over the oil industry.

EVERETTE DEGOLYER'S MIDDLE EAST EDUCATION

While DeGolyer went to the Middle East in 1943–1944 ostensibly under government auspices, the record he left behind suggests he viewed himself very much as an independent agent. On the one hand, he was a more iconoclastic thinker about the role of the federal government than were most of his Texas colleagues in the oil industry. For one thing, he had gone to work for Washington in the hope of shaping a better oil-conservation policy.[36] And as he noted to a congressional committee in 1948: "I have not any desire to see government in business, but . . . I don't share the apprehension of a great many of my fellow-Texans that every move the Government makes puts the Government in business."[37] In fact, DeGolyer at this time believed that the government could potentially have a legitimate role, albeit a limited one, in the Middle East by subsidizing the building of a pipeline to transport Saudi Arabian oil to the Mediterranean.[38]

Still, he would never have considered himself a New Dealer in any form, and he valued his independence from the government. Unlike Ickes and America's top military men, he saw the government's role in the Middle East oil operations as simply a temporary expedient. In addition, he had over the years carved out a role for himself as an oil insider who nonetheless made his professional name as an outside consultant, a technical expert, and he relished and felt most comfortable in that position. To represent any institution or organization beyond himself was clearly a stretch for him. Ickes clearly would have been glad to have DeGolyer continue working in an official capacity for the PRC and even offered him the position of vice president. DeGolyer turned it down, adding, however, that he would be happy to advise Ickes in the negotiations to work out a partnership deal with the British in the Middle East. (Ickes did not take him up on that offer, and the deal eventually fell apart.) He returned home to Dallas in March 1944 and noted in his diary on the nineteenth: "I worked on Arabian history most of the day."[39]

That DeGolyer would spend the day working on "Arabian history" signifies a tremendous shift in the mental map on which he charted his life's work, and the trip to the Middle East fully convinced him that the world's biggest oil play would change the compass of Texas oilmen.[40] Up until the mission, DeGolyer's primary attachment was to the Southwest, but his regionalism crossed national boundaries. Thoroughly infatuated with all things Mexican, devoted to a constellation of Mexican geologists and scholars with whom he corresponded regularly and whom he visited whenever he could, he nonetheless had also been part of an exploitative industry that became a target of the Mexican Revolution and was ultimately kicked out of the country in 1938. In the years following the Mexican government's decision to nationalize the oil industry, he noted that he had devoted a great deal of time to trying to understand why that had happened—and even admitted to his associates that he eventually came to sympathize with many of the claims made by Mexicans who wanted to see American and British interests leave the country. He went to Mexico, in other words, as a budding geologist who was compelled by its resources, grew to genuinely love the country and its culture and history, but in the end, and much against his own temperament and inclination, was forced to reckon with its politics.

This experience helps explain why he devoted himself early on to trying to understand the history and politics of the Middle East, and particularly the quest by companies in Great Britain, Europe, and the United States to gain secure access to its petroleum. In anticipation of the mission, he not only read the available scientific information about the geology of the Middle East but also began reading widely among historical accounts and travel writings. After he returned from his trip, when he decided to write a book about the oil industry in the Middle East (a book he never completed), he settled down to his task by taking quite extensive notes on his reading and trying to get his hands on more books.

From these notes and from his correspondence, one can see DeGolyer's undertakings in pursuit of his topic. Foremost among them was his attempt to understand the role of the British. This was a subject that had its own peculiar burdens on DeGolyer, because of his long-standing employment under Lord Cowdray with Aguila and then Amerada. The latter operation drew particular fire after World War I from American oilmen, who loathed the fact that British interests were reaping wealth out of ground within the United States when Great Britain did not allow American companies to explore for oil in India and Trinidad, the two countries that produced oil within the Commonwealth. In 1921, DeGolyer wrote to Wallace Pratt: "So far as my own connections with English capital and foreign enterprise are concerned, I have no apology to make in respect of the benefits which have come to my country," that is, in supplying oil to America.[41] DeGolyer's history, in other words, did not set him against the British; by contrast, many American oilmen deeply resented the head start England's oil industry had taken in foreign oil exploration and production. And in the matter of doing oil business, DeGolyer clearly had plenty of respect for the British industry and its ability to work in foreign lands. "The British have done a good job," he noted. "They pioneered Middle Eastern oil and have built up the world's greatest refinery and one of the world's truly great refining and marketing systems."[42] In contrast, he worried that U.S. naiveté in international oil production had left it "ill prepared" to enter the Middle East.[43]

But DeGolyer's Middle Eastern education, starting as it did at the end of World War II, with the decline of British and French empires around the world, seemed to open up a new window for him on British oil operations, and that was on the question of how oil companies doing business in foreign countries treated their foreign employees. For instance, in a *New York Times* article from 1946 that DeGolyer clipped, he was clearly drawn to information about British labor relations with its Iranian workers, as indicated by his underlining: "British officials do not deny that there *is great room for improvement of the Anglo-Iranian Company's labor standards* but they contend that standards are still above average in Iran."[44] Indeed, over the next several years, DeGolyer would dedicate himself to learning about working conditions in the AIOC operations in Iran and in the Aramco operations in Saudi Arabia, which resulted in several presentations he gave at conferences. One paper in particular shows that DeGolyer was both unusually attuned to labor problems in the oil fields and refineries of the Middle East and captured by the prevailing logic of petroleum development. He thus, on the one hand, strongly recommended better training and housing programs for Saudi workers, noting that "nationals should be trained to perform the work of the skilled and more highly paid jobs" and that "permanent workers and their families must be properly housed, their health protected and they must be provided with adequate educational and recreational facilities. . . . the worker should have these advantages whether provided by the state, the companies or a combination of state and companies."[45] On the other hand, DeGolyer was also fully a creature of his time who believed not only that petroleum development was an unalloyed good but also that the American industry had the potential to offer the Middle East development without the vestiges of colonial practices. "To the poverty stricken lands of the Middle East," he wrote, "the development of the Petroleum Industry promises emancipation. . . . As the Arab awakens and feels the urge to improve his environment, American enterprise will furnish the means."[46] He had faith, in other words, in the claim of American "exceptionalism"—the belief that because the United States had broken away from the British government in 1776, its economic and political development did not replicate that of European nations and therefore followed its own, unique path. Such uniqueness, DeGolyer and others argued, would define the projection of American economic power abroad.

DeGolyer's internationalist sentiments clearly set him apart from many of the independent producers around him: He schooled himself in the history of the battle among the Great Powers over Middle Eastern oil, and he believed that there was no turning the clock back when it came to America's entry into Middle Eastern oil production. But his interests also led him to take up pressing questions about the meanings of "independence" in the changing world petroleum order. With the experience of Mexican nationalization of oil behind him, and with his fears about the legacies of British colonialism, he understood that American and British operations in the Middle East had to contribute to the exporting countries' independent political development by raising the standard of living of its people.

But this vision, which was actually in keeping with the internationalist ideals of the Roosevelt administration, was fraught with tensions about the capacity of the oil business to produce "independence"—tensions that also mark the political vision of Texas independents.

"FREE ENTERPRISE" AND THE "OCTOPUS" OF SAUDI ARABIA

To understand more fully the tensions produced in the worldviews of both DeGolyer and the southwestern independents, it is important to remember that they had in fact established themselves in the oil business during an unusually fluid time in the industry and in an unusually fluid *place* in the industry. Most of them came of age at the time of the breakup of John D. Rockefeller's Standard Oil empire, which occurred in 1911, a time when America was in the midst of a lively antimonopoly discourse. In addition to this national sentiment were the particular patterns emerging out of the Texas attorney general's office, which vigorously pursued antitrust violations in the oil industry as it operated in the state.[47] The powerful antimonopolistic values that circulated in the largely rural state (Texas had been a center of southern Populism in the 1880s and 1890s) found expression in the actual development of the state's oil wealth; indeed, the problems of overproduction in the East Texas fields were the consequences of so many individuals engaged in small, uncoordinated attempts to strike it rich. And although DeGolyer was still involved with British oil interests until 1932, he clearly enjoyed the wide swath of autonomy he had at Amerada for engaging in independent scientific investigation and investment opportunities.

Thus, when they faced the postwar world, DeGolyer and the Texas independents did so with the experience of four decades in the peculiar political economy of Texas oil. While it would be a stretch to say that that experience was "a model of democratic equity," it nonetheless had emphasized, in the minds of those who participated in it, that the industry could produce a large number of enterprising men who generated wealth for themselves and the state by being their own bosses.[48] Clearly, Texas independents worried that the glut of Persian Gulf oil would jeopardize this state of affairs, but they rarely openly criticized the creation in Saudi Arabia of Aramco, a consortium of companies built largely out of the fragmented Standard Oil.[49] That is, they were extremely hesitant to deride the apparent concentration of American economic power in Saudi Arabia, despite the fact that it could undermine their economic interests, because of their commitment to freeing their industry from what they saw as excessive government regulation.

DeGolyer, too, worried about the place of the independent oil producer in the postwar world but never saw the contradiction between his attachment to "free enterprise" and Aramco's presence in Saudi Arabia. By way of conclusion, we can see why that contradiction remained hidden to him by looking at a speech he gave January 10, 1951, at the fiftieth anniversary celebration of Spindletop, the oil gusher that launched Texas as one of the world's premier centers of petroleum production. In the first part of the speech, DeGolyer celebrated the two men responsible for succeeding in drilling Spindletop, Patillo Higgins and Anthony Lucas, and in doing so he lauded America's "free economy" in which "every man is a potential manager which makes it work so well." Implicitly noting the contrast between the United States and the Soviet Union, DeGolyer asked rhetorically—and in keeping with the politics of the independent producers—"Who can believe that if our country in 1901 had been ruled by the hampering hand of bureaucracy and crushed under a pyramid of strict regimentation we would be celebrating one of the greatest oil discoveries of all time?"[50] This paean to the individual takes a fascinating turn at the end of the speech, however, through an anecdote he tells the audience:

> I once traveled over the countryside of Cape Breton for some weeks. It was a hard land. "What does this country produce?" I asked. The reply was from a dour Scot. He looked me squarely in the eye and replied, "Men." And so it was with Spindletop.
>
> This was the hotbed in which were nurtured the seeds of great enterprises notable among which are the Gulf Oil Corporation, The Texas Company and Houston Oil Company.[51]

What is striking about this quotation is the quick shift he makes from men to corporations (and we should note that two out of the three corporations he mentioned were at that moment building their operations in the Persian Gulf—the Texas Company in Saudi Arabia and the Gulf Corporation in Kuwait). That is, his understanding of the "free economy" or the "free-enterprise system" revolved around seeing in it the work and energy of individual men, and he shared with the southwestern independents the belief that, on the whole, the oil industry both ran on and produced risk-taking men of pluck and character. At least, this was his experience with his Anglo-American colleagues. When it came to thinking about Arabs or Iranians in the oil industry, his views were much more limited. He certainly spent more time thinking about their labor conditions and possibilities for job advancement than did his fellow Texans—and he roundly condemned the quasi-colonial practices of the British in Iran—but ultimately, he accepted the companies' line that they were providing for their workers' well-being and long-term prospects in the oil industry.[52] As someone invested in the examples of Patillo Higgins and Anthony Lucas of Spindletop, DeGolyer did not ask or seem to care whether the oil "plays" in Saudi Arabia produced *men;* he also did not comment on the starkly different political economies of the oil industry in Texas and in Saudi Arabia—the former filled with independent producers, the latter run by only one company. Indeed, Aramco showed little interest in producing "independence" among the Saudis actually doing the labor in the oilfields and refineries. Saudi workers were segregated in separate camps and kept out of entertainment facilities, and in fact, they engaged in labor protests and strikes, replicating the experience of nationals working in foreign-owned operations around the world.[53]

DeGolyer and the Texas independents had different kinds of attachments to that most cherished American word, "independence"; as he himself acted independently, so, too, did DeGolyer see the oil industry as one in which other Anglo-American men should be free to manage their economic activities as they saw fit; as they wanted to regain their pre–World War II "independence," so, too, did southwestern oilmen see that sloughing off government involvement in oil matters would produce more profitable oil operations, a more politically autonomous region, and a self-sufficient nation. But independent oilmen and DeGolyer alike rarely questioned where the gigantic corporate structures of businesses like Aramco or the AIOC fit within these peculiarly southwestern views. How would they have reacted, for instance, to the observation by the U.S. ambassador to Saudi Arabia in 1947, J. Rives Childs, who noted that Aramco was an "'octopus' whose tentacles 'extend into almost every domain and phase of the economic life of Saudi Arabia'"?[54] The metaphor, as political scientist Robert Vitalis notes, may have emerged from the wrong industry, coming from Frank Norris's muckraking novel about the railroads instead of Ida Tarbell's exposé of Rockefeller's anticompetitive tactics. But given Texans' love of the wildcatter and the state's own antimonopoly tradition in the petroleum industry, such a metaphor might have given pause to the oilmen of Texas. For in focusing on the ideals of independence, they rarely reckoned with the profound structural changes that would redirect the way oil flowed on the worldwide market and alter the very fabric of life in the newly emergent center of oil production, the Middle East. Such transformations, as we know today, would have extraordinarily long-lasting consequences.

NOTES

1. It is also true that American historians have paid relatively little attention to the role that oil has played in the history of the twentieth century, especially in the domestic political economy. As Carl Coke Rister noted in 1949, "The significance of petroleum, its constant, pervasive influence, is so thoroughly neglected as to constitute a major flaw in historical writing." Rister, *Oil! Titan of the Southwest* (Norman: University of Oklahoma Press, 1949), xi. Outside of pockets of interest by historians—in the history of Texas oil and in the role oil has had in American foreign policy—the historiography is relatively thin.

2. See David S. Painter, "Oil," in *Encyclopedia of American Foreign Policy*, ed. Alexander DeConde et al., 2nd ed. (New York: Charles Scribner's Sons, 2002), 1, 15; and Gibson Consulting, "Some Interesting Oil Industry Statistics," http://64.233.161.104/search?q=cache:hc8hXz55e2EJ:www.gravmag.com/oil.html+history+oil+imports+&hl=en, which provides accurate information up to spring 2004.

3. Michael Klare rightly notes that, in fact, the United States has been involved in four military engagements in the area under the responsibility of the U.S. Central Command. In addition to the two wars mentioned, the United States invaded Afghanistan in 2004, and during the Iran-Iraq War of the 1980s, the Reagan administration "tilted" toward Iraq in providing such things as "loans, intelligence support, and covert arms transfers." Klare, *Blood and Oil: The Dangers and Consequences of America's Growing Dependency on Imported Petroleum* (New York: Metropolitan Books, 2004), 48, 3.

4. Although a historiography exists about these southwestern oilmen, very little work investigates the development of their political ideology in response to the growth in American oil operations in the Persian Gulf. The best account is Lawrence Goodwyn's study of the Texas Independent Producers and Royalty Owners Association in *Texas Oil, American Dreams* (Austin: Texas State Historical Association, 1996), esp. chaps. 2 and 3. The work of Roger M. Olien and Diana Davids Olien has given us a rich account of the domestic oil industry, particularly in Texas, although their interest has revolved largely around the pre–World War II industry. See Olien and Olien, *Oil in Texas: The Gusher Age, 1895–1945* (Austin: University of Texas Press, 2002) and *Oil and Ideology: The Cultural Creation of the American Petroleum Industry* (Chapel Hill: University of North Carolina Press, 2000).

5. As we will see, "center of gravity" is the very powerful term that DeGolyer used to describe the prospective shift in world oil production to the Middle East. See "Preliminary Report of the Technical Oil Mission to the Middle East," box 52, folder 3459, Everette Lee DeGolyer Sr. Collection, DeGolyer Library, Southern Methodist University (hereafter DeG), Dallas. There was never a final version of the report from the government, but it was published in the *Bulletin of the American Association of Petroleum Geologists* 28, no. 7 (July 1944): 919–923.

6. Excellent descriptions of the East Texas oil boom can be found in Olien and Olien, *Oil in Texas*, 167–192; Goodwyn, *Texas Oil*, 30–48; and Rister, *Oil!* 306–326.

7. See, for instance, Harold L. Ickes, *Fightin' Oil* (New York: Alfred A. Knopf, 1943).

8. See Goodwyn, *Texas Oil*, 48, and Olien and Olien, *Oil and Ideology*, 188–208.

9. Lon Tinkle, *Mr. De: A Biography of Everette Lee DeGolyer* (Boston: Little, Brown, 1970), 52.

10. Ibid., 158.

11. Ibid., 224–226.

12. Ibid., 267. Tinkle noted that "the peak daily production in 1944 of 100-octane gasoline alone was 450,000 barrels" (258).

13. The figures are sometimes quoted as higher, but this seems to be the most consistently quoted percentage. See "Workable World Pattern," editorial, *Oil and Gas Journal*, 19 August 1944, 71.

14. For an account of DeGolyer's trip, see Daniel Yergin, *The Prize: The Epic Quest for Oil, Money, and Power* (New York: Simon & Schuster, 1991), 391–393.

15. Acting Secretary of State Edward Stettinius to Abe Fortas (who accompanied the mission), 23 October 1943, DeG, box 52, folder 3459.

16. DeGolyer, "Preliminary Report," *Bulletin*, 919, 921.

17. For two accounts of these initiatives, see Yergin, *Prize*, 391–408, and, especially, David S. Painter, *Oil and the American Century: The Political Economy of U.S. Foreign Oil Policy, 1941–54* (Baltimore: Johns Hopkins University Press, 1986), chaps. 2 and 3.

18. The figure can range as high as 6 billion barrels of oil recovered from the East Texas field; the number cited here can be found in "The Handbook of Texas Online" under the listing of "East Texas Oilfield" by Julia Cauble Smith at http://www.tshaonline.org/handbook/online/articles/EE/doe1.html. For Joiner's brief biography, see http://www.tshaonline.org/handbook/online/articles/JJ/fjo40.html.

19. See Olien and Olien, *Oil in Texas*, 167–175; Goodwyn, *Texas Oil*, 30–39; and Yergin, *Prize*, 244–248.

20. H. J. Porter, testimony in U.S. Congress, Senate, Committee on Foreign Relations, *Petroleum Agreement with Great Britain and Northern Ireland: Hearings on Executive H* (hereafter *Hearings on Executive H*), 80th Cong., 1st sess., 2–9 and 23–25 June 1947, 287. Porter was the president of the Texas Independent Producers and Royalty Owners Association (TIPRO).

21. See Warrick Downing's testimony in ibid.: "I am not an expert... but it is my understanding, and it has been often stated, that the cost of laying down Arabian oil at a profit on the eastern seaboard is less than the cost of transporting oil from the Rocky Mountain region to the same market, without giving any consideration to the finding cost, to the producing cost, or the profits and the high American wages and all those sorts of things" (202). Downing was a Denver attorney who specialized in oil matters.

22. Goodwyn, *Texas Oil*, 49.

23. See my discussion of ranchers' political ideology during the 1940s in Merrill, *Public Lands and Political Meaning: Ranchers, the Government, and the Property between Them* (Berkeley and Los Angeles: University of California Press, 2002), chap. 6.

24. William R. Childs, "The Transformation of the Railroad Commission of Texas, 1917–1940: Business–Government Relations and the Importance of Personality, Agency Culture, and Regional Differences," *Business History Review* 65 (Summer 1991): 285–344.

25. Downing testimony in *Hearings on Executive H*, 199. This rhetoric about the significance of the "little fellow" was also very much a feature of western ranchers' political discourse before the passing of the Taylor Grazing Act in 1934. See Merrill, *Public Lands and Political Meaning*, 135–168, and, for a discussion of that discourse during the Progressive Era, 37–66. Clearly, what such a rhetorical move accomplished for both ranchers and independent oilmen was to fashion an iconic, pioneering figure on which to hang their postwar political goals. In western ranchers' case, the centrality of the "little fellow" in the early twentieth century also indicated a shift in how many ranchers imagined the future of the land they would need to use to raise livestock. While this appears not to be the same for independent oilmen, I would nonetheless hypothesize that the turn to the pioneering wildcatter probably did more work than simply presenting a popular Texas character to advance their political agenda.

26. Editorial, *Oil and Gas Journal*, January 27, 1944, 109.

27. Downing testimony in *Hearings on Executive H*, 203–204.

28. J. Howard Pew, president of Sun Oil Company, made his remarks in response to the proposed Anglo-American Treaty. Quoted in Painter, *Oil and the American Century*, 64.

29. Testimony of Ghent Sanderford, *Hearings on Executive H*, 211. Sanderford was a lawyer in Austin who was the cochair of the committee that had been organized in Texas to oppose the treaty.

30. Ibid., 212.

31. Charles J. Deegan, "Middle East Pipe Line Proposal May Upset Entire U.S. Petroleum Industry," *Oil and Gas Journal*, 24 February 1944, 59.

32. Yergin, *Prize*, 403.

33. "Moore Wins Audience Victory in Debate on Arabian Pipe Line," *Oil and Gas Journal*, 23 March 1944, 63.

34. An editorial in the *Oil and Gas Journal* envisioned that in the future, "the Eastern Hemisphere probably will become independent of the Western Hemisphere, releasing large supplies wherever they are needed." "A Realistic Oil Policy," editorial, *Oil and Gas Journal*, 2 March 1944, 33. I should note that in using the term "isolationist" to describe the Texas independents, I do not mean to suggest they turned their backs utterly on the rest of the world. As should be clear from this discussion, their opposition to the wartime oil initiatives reflected their real engagement with international oil policy. And yet their positions sought to keep U.S. policy decisively focused on the domestic industry rather than on the emergence of U.S. petroleum operations in the Middle East.

35. Downing testimony in *Hearings on Executive H*, 203.

36. DeGolyer wasn't the only oilman to contribute his efforts to the PAW. In fact, loads of southwestern oilmen did so, and their anti–New Deal values had the chance to cook even longer. See the correspondence, for instance, between DeGolyer and Oklahoman Holley Poe, who was the head of the Natural Gas and Natural Gasoline Division, DeG, box 5, folder 647. See also Painter's brief discussion of the founding of the Office of Petroleum Coordinator, the predecessor to the PAW, in *Oil and the American Century*, 11–14.

37. Tinkle, *Mr. De*, 286–287.

38. See ibid., 271–274; also see "Immediate Development of Oil Supplies in Middle East Recommended by DeGolyer," *Journal of Commerce*, 14 March 1944, n.p., in DeG, box 52, folder 3459, where DeGolyer comes out publicly in support of the PRC's proposal to build a pipeline from the Persian Gulf to the Middle East.

39. Diary, 19 March 1944, DeG, box 206, folder 9. See the diary entries on 13, 15, and 17 March 1944 about his conversations with Ickes.

40. See, for instance, the *Dallas Morning News* article "Dallas Expert Surveys Oil in Persian Gulf" about DeGolyer on 6 February 1944: "His trip was somewhat a preview of the world travel which businessmen will make in the future, DeGolyer asserted, as fairly heavy commercial airline traffic to that section of the world will no doubt be established after the war."

41. Quoted in Tinkle, *Mr. De*, 151–152.

42. Handwritten notes, no date, but probably 1951, DeG, box 52, folder 3460. The refinery he refers to was located in Abadan, Iran.

43. From uncited notes he took on articles about "the Middle Eastern problem." From his notes, he wrote the following (it's unclear whether it's an excerpt from an article or DeGolyer's paraphrasing): "The United States, traditionally wedded to isolation and still strongly inclined toward laisser faire, is ill prepared in intimate knowledge of the territories involved and in experiences in international affairs readily to adapt its foreign policy to issues of such scope and consequence." DeG, box 52,

folder 3452. These notes were probably taken around 1946. It seems that despite America's naiveté about foreign petroleum operations, Texas had some important if weird effects on the British. Apparently, in the final set of conferences in London that DeGolyer's mission had with Sir William Fraser, head of the AIOC, the mission members found it difficult to obtain any of the geological information they sought, information they believed the British had. DeGolyer noted in his diary that "after none too friendly a preliminary," Sir William finally agreed to share such information, but "barked" in response—and in an assumed Texas accent—"not to push me too far ma frien'." See 1944 diary, DeG, box 206, folder 9.

44. DeG, box 53, folder 3464.

45. DeG, box 22, folder 2387.

46. Ibid.

47. See Jonathan W. Singer, *Broken Trusts: The Texas Attorney General versus the Oil Industry, 1889–1909* (College Station: Texas A&M University Press, 2002). Singer argues that while litigation against vertically integrated companies expressed sincere antitrust motives within the Attorney General's office, in the end the efforts were largely ineffective.

48. See Goodwyn, *Texas Oil*, 54, who observed that "it could not be said that the development of the East Texas field was a model of democratic equity."

49. The Texas Company was the only member of that consortium that had not previously been part of Standard Oil. The rest of the consortium, by 1948, consisted of Standard Oil of California (later Chevron); Standard Oil of New Jersey (later Exxon); and Socony-Vacuum (Socony had been Standard Oil of New York, and Socony-Vacuum later became Mobil). Today, out of these four companies, we have the two merged majors ExxonMobil and Chevron Texaco.

50. See his Spindletop speech in DeG, box 22, folder 2384.

51. Ibid. What follows in this passage is then a list of individual men whom DeGolyer thinks particularly worthy of mention.

52. One reason that he accepted the companies' view more fully is that the Cold War seemed to constrict his typically iconoclastic mind. His correspondence—especially with the editor of the *Saturday Review of Literature*, Norman Cousins—shows that he was quite concerned about the spread of Soviet communism, and he generally supported the government investigations into alleged communists through the late 1940s and early 1950s. It seems he made the kinds of conclusions about the Middle East that many Americans (especially in the government) did during the early Cold War: namely, that the West needed to keep the Middle East within its sphere of influence, especially given the Soviet Union's claims to Iran in 1946. That belief may have trumped his concern over how Aramco and the AIOC were developing, respectively, Saudi Arabia and Iran.

53. See Robert Vitalis, "ARAMCO World: Business and Culture on the Arabian Oil Frontier," in *The Modern Worlds of Business and Industry: Cultures, Technology, Labor*, ed. Karen R. Merrill (Turnhout, Belgium: Brepols, 1998), and *America's Kingdom: Mythmaking on the Saudi Oil Frontier* (Palo Alto, CA: Stanford University Press, 2006).

54. Quoted in Vitalis, "ARAMCO World," 24.

CHAPTER 4

"They Locked God outside the Iron Curtain": The Politics of Anticommunism and the Ascendancy of Plain-Folk Evangelicalism in the Postwar West

Darren Dochuk

Western culture and its fruits had its foundation in the Bible, the Word of God.... Communism, on the other hand, has decided against God, against Christ, against the Bible, and against all religion. Communism is not only an economic interpretation of life—Communism is a religion that is inspired, directed, and motivated by the Devil himself who has declared war against Almighty God.... The Fifth Columnists, called Communists, are more rampant in Los Angeles than any other city in America.... In this moment I can see the judgment hand of God over Los Angeles.

I can see judgment about to fall.[1]
Billy Graham, 1949

When God gets ready to shake America, he might not take the Ph.D. and the D.D. and the Th.D. God may choose a country boy! God may choose a man no one knows, a little nobody to shake America for Jesus Christ in this day. A hillbilly, a country boy! who will sound forth in a mighty voice to America,"Thus saith the Lord!"[2]
Billy Graham, 1949

With index fingers pointed like pistols and forearms slashing like sabers, southern evangelist Billy Graham assailed the thousands huddled before him with an ultimatum from God: Repent or face judgment; reform or see the City of Angeles crumble. Delivered nightly during the fall of 1949 in the "Canvas Cathedral" in downtown Los Angeles, Graham's sermons were anything but refined in their delivery but could hardly be questioned for their earnestness. A gangly, thirty-year-old rookie itinerant, Graham arrived in Southern California with a surplus of brashness that flowed from a simple but genuine conviction that he had a date with destiny.[3] World events convinced him of this. Just two days before the opening of Graham's Los Angeles crusade, President Harry Truman had announced that the Soviet Union had successfully detonated an atomic bomb. No longer the lone beneficiaries of nuclear weaponry, Americans now faced a more uncertain future as reluctant players in the Manichaean melodrama of the Cold War. Adding to their anxiety were other immediate signs of ultimate consequence: Israeli statehood, the fall of China, and the rise of the United Nations. Certain, therefore, that Los Angeles was not only targeted for the first Soviet warhead but ultimately destined to be the front line in the impending millennial struggle, Graham thundered not simply for theatrical effect but out of honest fear that anything less than complete repentance and utter dedication to the cause of Christianity would result in apocalyptic ruin.

Graham garnered little attention at first, but by the third week of his crusade, word of his timely message spread. Their curiosities tweaked by the conversion of some of the city's brightest stars, citizens, luminaries, and reporters soon packed Graham's tent eager to hear what all the fuss was about. With audiences spilling out into the street, campaign organizers hurriedly expanded the makeshift auditorium to seat 9,000 (up from 6,000), extended the crusade another five weeks, and pressed harder for advertising time.[4] Additional publicity might have been redundant by that point. While locals found themselves chatting about the revival in "barber shops, at newsstands, in stores and factories, on street cars, in buses, everywhere," a hungry press corps dutifully spread the word of Graham's monumental success. Soon *Time* and *Newsweek* had joined the rush to "puff Graham" by profiling "the new evangelist." When news leaked of other celebrity converts, such as mobsters Jim Vaus and Mickey Cohen, and American Olympian Louis Zamperini, the "headlines screamed again."[5] Buoyed by his new fame, Graham, meanwhile, continued delivering his fire-and-brimstone message while speaking simply but robustly about the perils of communism and the benefits of Christ.

So it was that a self-proclaimed "hillbilly" preacher changed the complexion of America's postwar religious culture. As contemporary media accounts documented in rich detail, the tremors set off by the 1949 Los Angeles crusade reverberated throughout the entire country, and the aftershocks continued to be felt for a long while. By the mid-1950s Graham was consulting with presidents and touring the world as the ambassador of a reinvigorated New Evangelical movement. Head of a media conglomerate by the 1960s,

America's so-called Protestant Pope was truly an institution in his own right.[6] Seeking to account for Graham's meteoric rise, scholars and pundits have, of course, offered assessments that range in scale from the sweeping to the anecdotal and in tone from serious misgiving to unabashed praise.[7] Lost in this scholarly conversation, however, has been the question of local origins. What factors indigenous to Southern California and the Cold War West helped Graham and plain-folk evangelicalism enter the cultural mainstream? How did this historic event reflect larger alterations to the religious landscape of this region and to what end in its political development?[8]

Graham's crusade was indeed symbolic of a turning point in post–World War II national culture, but for reasons that must be attributed to the unique environment of the modern West. First, it marked the beginning of a transformation in this region's religious culture brought on by sweeping social changes associated with defense migration from the South. As Graham himself intimated, those evangelical plain folk and preachers who moved west during the Cold War years did so ready, able, and eager to remake Southern California Protestantism. Their roots in the "burned-over" cultural soil of Oklahoma, Texas, and Arkansas had much to do with this confidence.[9] Collectively, their assertiveness stemmed from abiding loyalties to denominations that made up the distended evangelical middle of these states, religious bodies (Cumberland Presbyterian, Campbellite, Pentecostal, Methodist, and especially Baptist) whose doctrinal offerings were distinct but were essentially variants of a central theme of evangelical egalitarianism.[10] Even more important than these corporate ties, however, were their personal convictions. Working from an epistemology of common-sense realism that structured religious belief according to appeals of reason, conscience, and experience, that made the transcendent realm intuitively comprehensible, and that made truth—spiritual, moral, physical, and social—genuinely accessible, plain-folk evangelicals were sustained by an assurance of individual agency in religious processes.[11]

"Texas theology" was what some liked to call the social ethic that complemented this emphasis.[12] Certain of the absolute rightness of their doctrine, impassioned with the cause of evangelical democracy, and dedicated to those leaders most willing to flex their muscles on behalf of such sacred causes, evangelicals nurtured in this belief system exuded a gritty, distinct determination. Compared to northern evangelicals, who turned "serious, quiet, intense, humourless, sacrificial, and patient" in the peak religious experience, southern evangelical church folk were always "busy, vocal, and promotional" and "task-oriented."[13] Much more than an abstraction of theological principles, in other words, plain-folk evangelicalism embodied the cultural values of the region in which it had long enjoyed custodial rights:

social conservatism blended with an entrepreneurial spirit, moral steadfastness combined with physical toughness, fierce individualism supported by strong local communities. In the postwar West, where a frontier spirit of pragmatism still prevailed, these tendencies molded plain-folk evangelicalism into an aggressive, enterprising force.

Second, more than a spark for religious awakening, Graham's crusade was a trigger for political transformation. As it had long been evinced throughout the South, plain-folk evangelicalism served a critical function as a medium through which a set of principles rooted in early nineteenth-century American thought continued to rouse the political imagination: free-market capitalism, unbridled optimism about the freedom and power of the individual conscience, a belief in the rightness of government by popular consensus, and most important, a commitment to the sanctity of the local community. From out of this populist outlook came a clear agenda for political action that was less concerned with maintaining partisan lines than with protecting the interests of "ordinary people" against concentrated power, privilege, and moral pollution, near and far.[14] Organized religion in this political culture assumed the role of political watchdog. Fully committed to an ongoing process of democratization, evangelical leaders and institutions assumed responsibility for protecting society from those who would undermine this "godly" endeavor.[15] Distinctions between religion and politics ultimately held little meaning in this crusade; a threat to independence in one sphere was considered a threat in both. Apolitical in its emphasis on altering social and political systems through acts of individual initiative rather than institutional restructuring, plain-folk evangelicalism was, in other words, never unpolitical or antipolitical; quite the contrary.[16] The myth of the spiritual church notwithstanding, proud southerners always knew "how to play political hardball when the prayer meeting let out."[17]

Once settled on the West Coast, plain-folk evangelicals hesitated little to incorporate politics in their prayer meetings. Here, it seemed, egregious threats to their custodial rights in American culture were cause for a more urgent and aggressive display of politicization. Spurred by fears of a rapidly expanding liberal cosmopolitanism that advocated a centralized state and progressive legislation in church, home, and neighborhood—initiatives that seemed to be overtaking Southern California with arresting force—plain-folk evangelicals entered the public sphere louder than ever, ready to do battle for Christian America. Once their adverse reaction to liberal cosmopolitanism nudged plain-folk evangelicals into the political realm, their confrontation with communism entrenched them there. Convinced that the West Coast was the front line in America's battle against global and domestic communism, evangelicals armed themselves for a war they believed would determine the future of Christian democracy and Christianity itself. In this contestation of ultimate meaning—of God versus anti-Christ, right versus wrong—all remaining distinctions between politics and religion, church and state became fictitious ones. Indeed, spiritual warfare on this scale, it was believed, could not be waged in the human heart alone; evangelical believers needed to be ready to fight with Bibles, bullets, and ballots.[18]

The prevailing political culture of anticommunism on the West Coast thus galvanized plain-folk evangelicalism. Internally, it set in motion among one of Southern California's fastest growing constituencies—southern defense migrants—a move away from the New Deal and toward the New Right. While the politics of organized labor, race, home ownership, and taxation certainly contributed to this shift, many crossed this threshold as they worshipped in one of the thousands of evangelical churches in Southern California.[19] It was here they first articulated their collective longings for a simpler America, voiced their displeasure with an overbearing conglomerate of centralized state and religious organizations, and begged for the social and hence political reclamation of a morally centered, tradition-bound Christian America. It was in the pulpits and pews that small-town Democrats became the New Right's suburban warriors.

Plain-folk evangelicalism's determination to meet communism head on, meanwhile, raised its profile within the wider nexus of postwar, Sunbelt conservatism. Anticommunism was surely a creed that helped unite many people from a variety of ideological and religious backgrounds and consolidate them in a broad-based political right, but its importance was never as great as it was for plain-folk evangelicals, who used it as their entry into the mainstream.[20] Enabled by trends within their changing religious subculture, self-designated "country preachers" like Graham were nevertheless vaulted to fame because of their ability to meet the political demands of a burgeoning conservative movement that relied heavily on the support of traditional Protestants and Catholics. Like other clerics "burdened" with the same cause, plain-folk preachers viewed communism as the ultimate spiritual and political threat, but theirs was an especially loud and effective endorsement of the anticommunist Right.[21] Able to deliver a hard-hitting, black-and-white message of traditional Christian values and populist antistatism in a folksy manner that appealed to the domestic yearnings of the new middle class, these crusaders gained a particularly wide audience in the sprawling suburbs of California's Southland. Here churches joined kitchens as staging areas for grassroots anticommunist crusades. At the same time, these preachers brought incredible institutional resources with them into the conservative alliance—media and educational empires that spanned the entire Southwest—which rendered them especially valuable to Sunbelt conservative leaders like Barry Goldwater and Ronald Reagan. By the early 1960s, efforts at religious institutional expansion and network building would have a profound effect, not only on realignments within the Republican Party facilitating the rise of a western conservative wing, but on the national scene as well, among those who wanted to ensure that America's political landscape would be remade "from the bottom up."[22]

Perhaps Graham was right to suggest, then, that large-scale political forces combined with the ingenuity of a new generation of "hillbilly preachers" would permanently alter the religious and political culture of Southern California. The southern evangelist was surely justified too in harboring a belief that plain-folk evangelicalism's success in the Southland would have much broader regional and national implications. Indeed, already conspicuous in Graham's 1949 Los Angeles tent revival were signs that the "southernization" of Southern California Protestantism was going to help redraw the political map of the West and ultimately thrust this region into the lead of a conservative movement destined to redefine American politics in the postwar years.[23] But what even Graham himself could not fully appreciate in his moment was the degree to which the mainstreaming of plain-folk evangelicalism was first and foremost a social movement. Three demographic forces unique to the Cold War West guaranteed this would indeed be the case: migration, suburbanization, and the rise of the defense industry.

EMBATTLED AND THRIVING

At a fundamental level, plain-folk evangelicalism's improved institutional standing in the Southland was a direct result of postwar migration that began in the late 1940s and continued unabated until the late 1960s.[24] World War II had already sparked this process of social change by facilitating the movement of 4.5 million people into the state, an astounding number that, at that time, represented a 50 percent increase in California's population.[25] Yet wartime migration was merely a precursor of a greater demographic sea change yet to come. Buoyed by government spending in the defense sector, particularly in the aerospace industry, Southern California's economy grew exponentially during the early Cold War years, boasting at times a rate of employment growth that was four times greater than the national average.[26] Opportunities afforded by this economic boom hastened population growth on an unprecedented scale. By the mid-1950s an average of 1,000 people moved into the state every day, 70 percent of whom settled in the expanding residential tracts of the Southland.[27]

What was truly impressive about the Cold War migration, however, was the way it altered the regional alignment of Southern California. Prior to World War II migration patterns to the Southland had been dictated largely by white middle-class Protestants from the country's eastern seaboard and midwestern heartland. A notable shift began in the 1930s as increasingly large numbers of migrants from the "West Central" states of Texas, Oklahoma, and Arkansas filtered in,[28] but it was the massive influx of these migrants during the 1940s that altered this region's demographic profile completely.[29] In contrast to the 1920s and 1930s, when the largest wave of migrants were sun-seeking Iowans and Illinoisans, by 1950 Texas had become the largest contributor to California's population boom, with Oklahoma and Missouri following closely behind.[30] The pace of this demographic change quickened in the Cold War years, so much so that by the late 1960s the entire state of California counted in its populace more white southerners (1.7 million) than Arkansas could claim residents.[31] By 1970 there were more white southerners living in Los Angeles and Orange counties than in Little Rock, Arkansas, and Oklahoma City, Oklahoma, combined.[32]

Considering that the primary source of postwar migration was the most densely Protestant region of the county, it is no surprise that with the increased flow of population from the South to Southern California came a remarkable upsurge in the number of southern religious institutions on the West Coast. What started out in the 1930s as a trickle quickly became a torrent of institutional expansion. At the time of its organization in 1940, the Southern Baptist General Convention of California, for example, could boast no more than a dozen small congregations scattered throughout central and southern California. By 1970 this body numbered over a quarter of a million members, making it the third-largest denomination in the state, and within another ten years it would represent the largest Protestant organization in California.[33] The story of the southern takeover of California religion, however, is more than a Southern Baptist tale. Other predominantly southern religious institutions, including the Assemblies of God and various independent churches that appealed directly to southern evangelical Protestants, experienced similarly dramatic growth rates in the postwar period. No less important in this equation were the thousands of white southern migrants and their leaders who found their way into the countless Pentecostal Holiness and Churches of Christ congregations clustered on quiet street corners throughout the Southlands' blue-collar suburbs, or into other nondenominational "megachurches" that were already flourishing on the West Coast by the early 1950s.

Adding to the momentum of postwar migration from the South to Southern California was the suburbanization of plain-folk evangelicalism. White flight to new middle-class suburbs was a common feature of most American cities in the postwar period, but in Southern California the trend was realized with remarkable suddenness and intensity. Contrary to popular assumptions, suburbanization strengthened rather than weakened institutional bonds within local religious bodies. Foremost on the agenda of defense migrants from the South was an imperative to build strong homes and churches in which the communal needs of believers could be met and from which the light of "true belief" and "true Americanism" could be cast over their neighborhoods. Amid the tumult of postwar Southern California this imperative was greatly aided by a rapidly expanding urban grid that remained remarkably flexible in its legislation of space and relatively powerless in its ability to enforce land-use laws. Enlivened by the air of freedom that came with uncontrolled, postsuburban sprawl in the 1950s, evangelicals eagerly and strategically targeted their neighborhoods for church growth and did so with little heed to the designs of civic or denominational officials. In this way they soon took ownership of their neighborhoods in physical as well as theological terms.

Suburbanization facilitated the rise of strong congregations and communities, and it also allowed evangelicals to bask in their ascent out of Depression-era poverty. The arrival in the late 1940s of a new, highly motivated, and upwardly mobile membership coupled with the brisk climb of earlier southern sojourners into Southern California's middle class provided plain-folk evangelicalism with a degree of institutional wealth and power unseen at any other time during its history. Fresh encounters with success in fact caught many in the pulpits and pews off guard. Having struggled for much of the 1940s to bring order to their surroundings, Southern California Pentecostal leaders, for example, found themselves in strange territory by the early 1950s, marveling at the organizational, financial, and statistical triumphs of their church. They had much to feel good about. By 1955 Southern California Assemblies of God churches were dominating the national body in missions giving, church construction, and several other measurements of financial well-being.[34] And when denominational leaders declared a campaign for "1,000 New Assemblies Churches in 1955," Southern California Pentecostals responded by far outpacing every other district in the country, a pattern that continued for the rest of the decade.[35]

Fully cognizant of the revolution underway out west, meanwhile, the Assemblies of God's national media decided to look for the revolution's source and found it in the Southland's middle-class residential tracts, such as those located in Orange County. "In 1955 more housing units went up in Orange County, California, than in all but eleven of the forty-eight states," the *Pen-*

tecostal Evangel explained to its national audience, adding, "Remarkable gains have been made by the Assemblies in this area, for in its report on this county, *Christian Life* says, 'Fastest spreading group, without doubt, is the Assemblies of God.' In 1940 we had three churches in Orange County. In 1949 we had eighteen. Now we have forty two!"[36] Church scribes made clear too that signs of advancement on the West Coast were far more eye-catching when viewed in person. Once relegated to shacks and garages on unkempt residential streets in Los Angeles, Pentecostal congregations now commandeered meeting space on palm-tree-lined boulevards in buildings constructed out of concrete and steel rather than cinder block and particleboard.

The effect of new wealth was immediate and far-flung in the way it helped plain-folk evangelicalism gain access to the Southland's vibrant marketplace of religion and acquire new lines of communication across the Southwest. On the West Coast, southern evangelicals took the lead in forming larger transdenominational and para-church organizations; venturing more boldly into the world of multimedia by acquiring print, radio, and television outlets; and popularizing old-time religion through the promotion of high-profile evangelists and gospel singers. By the 1950s, meanwhile, southern transplants could share the spoils of California's prosperity with their brethren "back home" by way of shared investments in education and media. No one was more successful in carrying out these strategies than John Brown, the evangelist from Arkansas who, in 1948, purchased Long Beach radio station KGER, principally to help him supply his flagship institution—John Brown University, in Siloam Springs, Arkansas—with a self-sustaining endowment.[37] The move paid off in other ways. It was KGER that in 1949 first broadcast word of the impending arrival of Billy Graham and that continued to provide a home for the region's new slate of local evangelists.[38]

The backdrop of this remarkable surge in institutional expansion was, of course, the emergence of Southern California's military-industrial complex, a third defining social experience for plain-folk evangelicalism.[39] Fully cognizant that the fortunes of their religious establishments were contingent on the continued rise of national defense and its expanding economic web, high-profile evangelical leaders like Graham and Brown encouraged their followers to celebrate the melding of Bible-belt religion with the political interests of the gun belt. In Graham's case this was accomplished more subtly through the strengthening of personal ties with leading industrialists favored by government and convinced by God to extend American military interests abroad. For Brown the agenda was clearer. In addition to building his institutional wealth through an expanded media empire Brown satisfied his economic and patriotic goals by purchasing a number of military academies, each of which trained the Southland's most promising young men to be upstanding Christian gentlemen and effective soldiers. It was at the grassroots level, however, that the fusing of these two interests first took place. Often built within sight of local military depots, airplane factories, and high-tech defense manufacturers, Southern Baptist, Pentecostal, and other southern-based churches came to reflect the patterns of corporate life dictated by the Pentagon. In this setting, where congregational ties to national defense were evident in membership roll calls and weekly bulletins, praying for "God's army" took on added meaning.[40]

Heavy institutional investment in national defense in turn created for these evangelicals a self-fulfilling, self-reinforcing sense of entitlement that assured them of their rightful duty as protectors of Christian America. Products of a culture that asserted the privileges of whiteness, toughness, and the pioneering ethic and heirs to the promise of divine chosenness and burden of Christianization, white southern defense migrants came to Southern California already confident of their unique place in history. Now, political and economic conditions unique to the Cold War West convinced them that their "errand" had to assume weightier proportions as a mission for God and country. Reading popular religious literature, listening to weekly sermons, and attending large crusades, these evangelicals imbibed a message that convinced them that they had been called to be pilgrims *and* patriots. This destiny entreated them not only to cast spiritual light on a morally darkened frontier but also to propagate the message of true Americanism. In the welter of the Cold War West, the tale of expanding horizons within plainfolk evangelicalism was blended early and intently into the unfolding saga of American nationalism.

White southern evangelicals thus found in Southern California's unique landscape reasons to feel both entitled and embattled, sensibilities upon which their religious subculture ultimately thrived.[41] Galvanized by the process of migration, emboldened by the freedom of postwar affluence and suburban sprawl, and determined to carry out its mission of Christianization, plain-folk evangelicalism held within it the impulses to flourish not only as a religious movement but as a champion of anticommunist conservatism in the Southland. Ensuring that this would indeed be the case were the thousands of preachers who moved west during the Cold War years to meet the pulpit needs of the Southland's growing churches. Thanks to the rise in fortunes of their constituents and the impressive breadth of institutional and media support, as well as the growing sense that Southern California would dictate political and cultural patterns in the postwar period, these clerics recognized quickly that the future of their ministries could only be enhanced by increased investment in the Southland. In the immediate wake of Graham's 1949 crusade, an entire generation of like-minded plain-folk evangelical leaders emerged ready to invent themselves on the West Coast.[42] Theologically conservative, culturally innovative, and politically outspoken, these modern-day saddlebag saints, like the itinerant preachers who spread their gospel by horseback in the nineteenth century, remained true to the precepts of "Texas theology" but gained fame by adapting this system of belief to the sensibilities of the Southland's new suburban middle class.

That their quest to remake Southern California in their own image was successful is evidenced in the biographies of J. Vernon McGee and Robert "Bob" Wells, two of Southern California's proudest and most famous "hillbilly preachers" during the 1950s and 1960s. Products of the western South's expansive middle class that was hit hardest by Depression-era poverty but energized most by Southern California's postwar economic boom, these self-made men offered personal testimony to the virtues of rugged individualism, democracy, and free enterprise, values that rang true with the collective experience of their constituency. Inspired personally by Graham's prophetic call for all-out war with communist forces, McGee and Wells not only offer testimony to the proficiency with which plain-folk evangelicalism used this mandate to assume leadership within Southern California's burgeoning conservative movement in the 1950s and 1960s but also provide clues as to how political developments in the West ultimately transcended regional boundaries in their importance.[43]

"THE COUNTRY PREACHER WHO CAME TO TOWN"

Born in Hillsboro, Texas, in 1904, McGee was the product of an austere rural environment and a family life that was equally trying.[44] McGee's childhood was inalterably shaped by his father's ongoing personal struggles with alcohol and financial failures as a sharecropper in West Texas, but it was molded most dramatically by the tragedy that beset his family during his early teens. Settled in southern Oklahoma for the longest duration of his adolescent years, McGee's life eased into a regular pattern of attending school, chopping cotton for a dollar a day, and hunting possum on the banks of the local creek, a routine that was close to ideal for any youngster. Boyhood bliss was cut short, however, when his father died tragically while repairing a local cotton gin. Forced into manhood by his father's death, McGee and his mother moved to Nashville, Tennessee, to live with relatives. There he renewed the innocent pledge to serve God that he had made while huddled over his father's grave. Following his religious encounter,

McGee began to look harder for ways to follow through on his promise. With much encouragement and financial support from dedicated friends, McGee eventually took the step toward full time ministry by finishing undergraduate studies and then completing a doctorate in theology at Dallas Theological Seminary. Following a short stint as a radio preacher on a country-music station and extended pulpit ministries in two modest-sized churches—one "located on a red clay hill in the corner of a cotton patch in Midway, Georgia," the other on Main Street in Cleburne, Texas—McGee eventually found his way to the West Coast, where, in 1941, he became senior pastor of Pasadena's esteemed Lincoln Avenue Presbyterian Church.[45] Eight years later, in the fall of 1949, McGee took yet another leap forward in his career when he assumed the pastorate of the Church of the Open Door (COD) in downtown Los Angeles.

The move to COD elevated McGee to the pinnacle of his profession. Founded in 1915 as a supporting ministry of the Bible Institute of Los Angeles (BIOLA) and modeled after the famed Moody Memorial Church in Chicago, COD quickly assumed a reputation of its own as the citadel of West Coast evangelical Protestantism.[46] Several of its most important features assured it of this status, including its impressive size (COD's membership of 4,500 made it the largest nondenominational church west of Chicago) and its ties to Anglo-American evangelicalism's most powerful men.[47] In its immediate setting in downtown Los Angeles, however, nothing distinguished COD more than its physical dimensions. Built in a distinctive "Italian style" replete with carved archways and lush rooftop gardens, COD's concrete-and-steel structure consisted of a three-tiered auditorium with over 4,000 theater-style seats, an eight-story-high skylight that illuminated the entire ceiling, and the city's grandest pipe organ. COD's exterior, meanwhile, did its best to draw in the hesitant. While the largest set of chimes on the Pacific Coast rang out from above the north tower, COD eventually added modern panache to its classic facade by erecting two giant neon signs that proclaimed "JESUS SAVES."

When McGee entered COD's venerated pulpit for the first time as pastor and, in his soft drawl, introduced himself as but "a plowboy from . . . Texas," he effectively gave notice to his parishioners that their institution's classical heritage was less of a concern to him than its future.[48] Upon taking over, McGee immediately set out to reform the institutional culture of COD according to his own vision of evangelicalism. The path he laid out for his congregation was a reflection of the personal journey that had brought him to Los Angeles. Lessons learned from the poverty of his childhood, fundamentalist teachings of his seminary years, and pastoral training in his early career all informed the religious system he sought to inculcate into his new congregation. At once gritty and disarming in his persona, informal and unbending in his demeanor, McGee truly personified the new "Texas theology" that promised to refashion Southern California religion in the postwar period.

A shrewd promoter in the marketplace of religion, it was McGee's laid-back style as a preacher that ultimately set him apart. When taking in his words, either in person or daily on his popular KGER radio program, the country preacher's audience quickly found themselves drawn in by a voice that seemed strangely but endearingly out of place in a sprawling metropolis like Los Angeles. Remembered fondly by those who listened regularly as distinctively "folksy" and "catchingly different" for its nasally timbre and gentle undulations, McGee's voice transported the willing listener back to a simpler time and place.[49] Many California suburbanites were looking for nostalgia alone when tuning in; others were seeking a familiar gospel.[50] For his part, McGee did all he could to embellish the down-to-earth quality of his homiletic style. An early convert to the use of visual aids while preaching, McGee loved nothing more than to pull out his trusty "electric blackboard" (his designation for the overhead projector) and "photographic slides" to help him illustrate a parable or passage from the New Testament.[51] Pictures of an adolescent boy fishing on the banks of a river or hunting possum in the woods on the edge of town, illuminated either by words or on the white screen behind him, were not infrequent "homely additions" to one of his Sunday evening sermons or Thursday night bible studies.[52] And like a true southern preacher, McGee preferred to draw out from his text the story and its redemptive qualities rather than to overwhelm his listener with doctrinal complexities. "When the plain sense of Scripture makes common sense, seek no other sense" was a maxim McGee preached often to his congregants.[53]

It was this same folksy, black-and-white approach that made McGee a champion of Christian anticommunism and his church a staging ground for countersubversive activity. Beginning in the early 1950s and continuing with increased frequency and intensity as the decade wore on, McGee entered the pulpit with an arsenal of words and images that he was prepared to unleash against "atheistic communists" at a moment's notice.[54] His convictions reflected a growing fixation among most evangelical citizens that the communist Leviathan would be the tool used by Satan to systematically eradicate the Christian democratic values that undergirded their society.[55] The totalizing tendencies of this belief system left plenty of room in McGee's imagination for conspiratorial thinking, including that of the most rabidly right-wing, nativist kind.[56] Although far less "reactionary" than the "vengeful countersubversives" who worked hard to promote this type of thinking,

McGee was, nevertheless, always willing to entertain theories of world conquest by "fifth columnists."[57]

More representative of McGee's mind-set, however, was an eschatological line of reasoning that explicated international communism in the unfolding of providential history. Exegetical renderings of history and prophecy thus became McGee's favorite approach to this subject. When speaking out against communism, McGee often guided his reader back through time in a way that demonstrated both his impressive breadth of study and the single-mindedness of his thought. For example, in one of McGee's favorite sermons, titled simply "Origin of Communism," congregants were offered a history lesson that began with the Confrérie de la Paix in the late twelfth century and continued through Jean-Jacques Rousseau, Adam Weishaupt, Gracchus Babeuf, Louis Blanc, Anacharsis Clootz, French Freemasonry, Thomas Paine, Robert Owen, and anarchy, to end with extended comments on Karl Marx, Friedrich Engels, Vladimir Lenin, and the commendable efforts of the Dies Committee (the House Committee on Un-American Activities). This foray into the historical development of radical philosophy and its champions was "scheduled to provoke serious minded Christians to recognize the menace," not to alarm his audience, McGee assured. In case the evidence overwhelmed them, however, the preacher always concluded such sermons by spelling things out simply: Communism was rooted in lawlessness, anarchy, and Satanism. Consistent too was McGee's policy of closing services of this foreboding nature with words of comfort and invitation: "It is dark in the world just now [but] never too dark for [a] child of God. . . . Where are your sins tonight?"[58]

McGee's fear of communism also grew out of a deep-seated belief that popular democracy was fragile. Therefore, he and others had to maintain constant vigilance on the part of its defenders; after all, the very strength of democracy—freedom—was, he liked to point out, its very weakness.[59] For contemporary liberal critics like Daniel Bell and Richard Hofstadter, whose scholarly assessments of Cold War conservatism were widely accepted in the 1950s and continued to inform studies of the Republican Right into the 1980s, McGee's belief system was hardly legitimate; antimodern, irrational, and dangerously reactionary, McGee's worldview was, according to them, nothing more than a by-product of psychological and sociological imbalance.[60] This appraisal falls short, however, of appreciating the historical breadth and theological depth of McGee's thinking. Neither paranoid nor disenfranchised, McGee looked at the world lucidly as a product of his religious and political heritage, convinced that freedom itself might be threatened at every turn. This was, he readily acknowledged, a reality that America's forefathers grappled with constantly, a worry that beset his ancestors in the nineteenth-century upper South, and therefore a threat citizens in the twentieth-century West needed to take seriously.[61]

His style of homiletics was a product of this worldview. By exhaustively cataloging history's "false philosophies," McGee was able to expose the multiple dangers communism posed to America's most cherished values of private property, patriotism, family, and community.[62] The method behind his sermons, on the other hand, also allowed him to make a subtler point. The people best equipped to fight communism were those who had the least amount of patience for mental games played by smart people, commoners who were not encumbered by the complexities of humanist ideas but who saw things clearly and simply in black-and-white terms, plain folk schooled by life rather than the Ivy League university. It is in their practical application especially, therefore, that McGee's anticommunist lectures assumed a distinctively populist tone. When looking for examples of anticommunist crusaders, McGee intimated, his congregants would be wise to look to the farms of Georgia and Texas first before turning to bustling streets of New York and Chicago. Here stories of farm-boy heroism helped enhance his pedagogy. Fully aware by the late 1950s of the legend of John Birch, the Baptist missionary and American Military Intelligence Officer killed by Chinese communists in 1945 whose life was being made famous in political circles by Robert Welch's ultraconservative grassroots organization, the John Birch Society, McGee weighed in on the subject to describe in his own compelling way how a young, dedicated Baptist boy from the South acquired the courage of his convictions that would turn him into a martyr for the "Christian, democratic cause." Birch was truly heroic for his selfless acts behind enemy lines in China, but his heroism, McGee was quick to emphasize, was the product of core values upheld every day by good, honest southern folk like Birch's parents and grandparents.[63] Much more than an abstract political symbol to embrace, therefore, Birch was, first and foremost for McGee, a model to emulate.

When verbal cues failed to drive this point home, McGee regularly turned to his trusty visual aids for help. In many of his sermons McGee let projected images of his own past reveal the keys to overcoming the communist menace. "Will Russia Destroy the U.S.?" and "A Nation at the Crossroads," two of McGee's more popular anticommunist homilies, for example, were delivered with the help of the pastor's "stereopticon." "I wish I could take you to your home town tonight [but the] best I can do is take you to mine" was how McGee began the second of these sermons before leading his congregation on an elaborate slide-show tour of Oklahoma and Texas. Beginning with images of his childhood home in Ardmore, Oklahoma, McGee moved slowly through a repertoire of thirty slides, talking all the while about the values each image portrayed and their potential power in helping ward off communism. Reserved for the end was a picture of the Dallas skyline. As if to emphasize the relevance of traditional thinking to modern living, McGee spent an extended period of time on this image, talking about the moral centeredness of Dallas that made it "truly one of [the] great cities of America." With the slide dimming, McGee made one final tug at his congregants' hearts by inviting them to sing the "Battle Hymn of the Republic."[64]

Whether through story, picture, or sound, an artless comportment allowed McGee special access to the hearts of his audience, and this is what made him so valuable to the anticommunist Right. The simplicity of his preaching, in truth, belied the extent to which he intended to shape the minds of his congregants by imparting usable facts and analysis of current politics. Prior to each of his sermons McGee spent hours researching his chosen topic by perusing journals, newspapers, and other popular forms of literature, all in addition to his regular study of scripture. Among his favorite periodicals were conservative journals like the *Manion Forum, American Mercury, Christian Economics,* and *Reader's Digest.* When gathering word on current events was of primary concern, however, nothing supplanted the *Dallas Morning News* in McGee's weekly routine; attached clippings and highlighted quotes from this conservative newspaper were common addendums to McGee's sermons, suggesting the trust this Texan continued to place in his hometown newspaper.[65]

Fighting communism made research a priority in McGee's life, and he sought to instill the same intellectual discipline in the lives of his parishioners. Among the many changes made to COD's weekly routines, in this regard, were the afternoon sessions held each Sunday during which anticommunism, current events, and other pressing matters in political life were discussed in an open forum. Often leading these sessions were religious activists or politicians, and frequently the scheduling of these meetings allowed for the viewing of anticommunist films ranging in popularity from the mass-produced *Operation Abolition* to lesser-known documentaries on Iran, Cuba, and the Middle East.[66] Produced by various anticommunist organizations, these films also served as an invitation for COD congregants to participate in the larger crusade that was taking place outside their church doors. Fred Schwarz's School of Anti-Communism, an organization begun in Los Angeles in the early 1950s with the help of local preachers like McGee, was among the more famous of the anticommunist movements to benefit directly from COD's focused concerns with regional and national political trends.

In all of these endeavors McGee rarely shied away from partisanship. Increasingly agitated in the early 1950s by an "intrusive" government that continued to furnish "no incentive at all even to those who wanted to get out of the poverty level,"[67] McGee grew convinced by the last years of the decade that "only an immediate and continuous uprising of conservative thought [could] halt our nation's plunge into socialism."[68] This was a conclusion McGee was first drawn to early in the 1950s as he came to the realization that the American political landscape had shifted dramatically. Like other evangelicals from the South, McGee had initially welcomed the New Deal as a necessary, temporary correction to the excesses and failings of capitalism. But when evidence began mounting in the immediate postwar years that New Deal liberalism had full intentions of becoming the established order, McGee recoiled. He saw the New Deal as a wolf in sheep's clothing that was now exposed for what it had always been: a collectivist enterprise and a halfway house to communism.[69]

Here the personal once again became political. Constantly referencing his own political awakening, which had caused him to turn away from his Democratic roots, McGee offered his followers a formula for grassroots political action.[70] Symptoms of the last days were everywhere, he pointed out, from the lack of a national commitment to Christian economics to rampant moral degeneracy in the home to the disappearance of traditional curricula in the classroom. Animated by the very same impulse that operated at the center of communism—namely, a desire to suppress Christian democracy and replace it with a centralized, secular, and humanist system—each of these developments, McGee ventured to say, could be traced to New Deal Democrats.[71] He believed that at this juncture the current state of affairs in American society demanded that he and his parishioners not "wring our hands... not push [the] panic button... and not sit on our hands either."[72] Besides doing all they could to reverse these trends in their neighborhoods, schools, and city halls, McGee averred, his listeners needed to begin thinking of ways they might make an impact on state and national politics. His testimonies of faith never left much doubt that political action of the sort he imagined would only be effective if carried out on behalf of conservatism and the Republican Party.

THE COWBOY PREACHER AND GOLDWATER CONSERVATISM

His frequent partisan commentary aside, McGee generally preferred comforting the weak and saving the lost to political barnstorming. Sustained demonstrations of aggressive politicking were left to a related group of "cowboy preachers" who, by the late 1950s, were taking plain-folk evangelicalism further to the right in its theology and politics. For these men, the transition from plough to pulpit to political stump was a natural progression. Connected in a loose network that stretched from the Deep South through the Southwest, the mountain West, and Southern California, these fundamentalist pastors secured their audiences through a variety of modern methods, none more important than the radio. They were most successful, however, in securing their empires through the construction of strong, independent churches. Like Harvey Springer, Denver's infamous "cowboy preacher," whose Baptist congregation was the largest in the West in the 1950s, some of these men dabbled in the racist politics of the Far Right, associating at times with Gerald L. K. Smith, the anti-Semitic red-baiter who found his own political career rejuvenated in postwar Southern California. At no point, however, were they marginalized in the way Gerald L. K. Smith and other reactionaries were; nor were they relics of a prewar fundamentalist world.[73] Although these preachers celebrated an idyllic past, they saw in the postwar West vast potential for modern empires built with new money and premised on new fears generated by America's Cold War with communism.

No one was more successful within this network than Bob Wells. Born in Alabama during the interwar years, Wells grew up in an environment where self-initiative and self-inventiveness were core values. These traits served him well as he tried to carve out a career in Depression-era Texas, first as a banker and then as an evangelist. Following a five-year stint as pastor of the Galilean Baptist Church of Dallas, a church founded by fundamentalist legend John R. Rice, Wells embarked on a modest career as a second-tier evangelist.[74] Throughout the late 1940s and early 1950s, Wells crisscrossed the country speaking to large crowds in midsized cities like Grand Rapids, Michigan; Toledo, Ohio; Lynchburg, Virginia; and Anaheim, California.[75] It was his stops in Lynchburg and Anaheim that proved most critical to his own professional fortunes. While in Lynchburg, Wells was instrumental in helping an earnest but conflicted young convert by the name of Jerry Falwell realize his calling as a Baptist preacher. From this encounter emerged a friendship that would continue throughout the 1960s and 1970s, one that would see Wells consult frequently with the young rising star on matters of religion and politics and result in Falwell's frequent visits to Orange County.[76] Wells's introduction to Anaheim during a West Coast swing in the mid-1950s, however, confirmed his vocational aspirations. Impressed with the religious energy and entrepreneurial zeal of the place, two dynamics that spoke to the core of this businessman-turned-evangelist, Wells decided to return to Southern California for good in 1956. Convinced by demographic trends and local culture that he could soon build an independent church in Orange County that would rival any within the southern fundamentalist network he operated, Wells pitched a revival tent amid thirteen acres of orange trees in western Anaheim and christened it Central Baptist Church.[77] His personal drive paid collective dividends. By the time it celebrated its tenth anniversary in 1966, Central Baptist proudly boasted a weekly average Sunday school attendance of almost 4,000, making it the largest church in the county and the second-largest Baptist church west of the Rockies.[78]

It was Wells's agenda more than his ambition, however, that guaranteed Central Baptist's success in the new residential tracts of Orange County and made it a staging ground for Christian anticommunism and, ultimately, Goldwater conservatism. Foundational to the mission of the church was an open desire to meet all the spiritual, political, and educational needs of the community, an agenda neatly summed up by Wells's three-headed maxim of "Evangelism, Patriotism, and Christian Education."[79] In this arrangement, evangelism was Central Baptist's lifeblood, at least initially. Under Wells's watch Central Baptist assumed an aggressive program of outreach in the community that sought to draw in those from the neighborhood who were unsaved, unchurched, or "in-between churches." Several tactics were employed toward this end, but none were most successful than the annual Operation Outreach crusade that brought in students from Bob Jones University (South Carolina) during the summer months to help Central Baptist canvass Orange County's sprawling subdivisions. During one summer alone, Operation Outreach campaigners knocked on 50,000 doors.[80]

If evangelism brought locals into the pews, a political culture of Christian patriotism kept them there, which first became evident in cradle-to-grave ministries in Christian education. Equally important to Wells was Christian education. Like so many Christian conservatives of the day, Wells heralded the words of J. Edgar Hoover when, in 1960, the FBI director proclaimed, "The youth who has experienced old-fashioned religious training and who has received sound efficient Bible teaching in Sunday School will be able to meet and resist temptation" and will not "become involved in juvenile criminal violations."[81] Central Baptist used this decree as motivation to build an entire K–12 school system that would allow area children to be taught the basics of reading and writing in an environment that recognized the "Bible and Christian philosophy of life as the pervasive core of all knowledge and experience."[82] The jewel in the crown of this private educational system was Heritage High School, which opened in the fall of 1963 with the help of Wells's fellow Texan, good friend, and church benefactor Walter Knott. Against the "pagan sin capital of the world" where "the pressures of Hollywood, attractions of the beach, and the casual way of life" had caused the "erosion of character and dependability" among Southern California's youth, Heritage High School stood as a bastion of traditional pedagogy.[83] Here, under the guidance of teachers trained in the South's leading Christian universities, Knott's grandchildren along with 700 other students learned from a curriculum that melded liberal arts education with biblical training, character building, and full emersion in a program of Americanism meant to instill "a real love of country . . . and the Christian principles upon which our country was founded, including a clear understanding of our free enterprise system."[84]

Heritage High School was designed first and foremost for purposes of academic instruction in Christian patriotism, but it also served a broader political role as the epicenter of political activity in the community. Besides solidifying ties with a local parents' textbook-reform association, the Rossmoor Parents for Better Education, and helping make it one of the leading organizations of its kind in the state, Heritage High also promoted its own Parent Teacher Fellowship (PTF) as an alternative to the local PTA. During the early 1960s, regular meetings of the PTF usually featured lectures by Wells and his political friends on the strategies of anticommunism. These talks were often supplemented by "surveillance reports" provided by Central Baptist's own spies, pastors and parents who infiltrated and recorded curricular activities at nearby Fullerton College (now California State University, Fullerton) and later at the University of California, Irvine.[85] According to fundamentalist ideals of gender roles, men always exercised official headship over the PTF, but in reality the educational and surveillance activities undertaken by this organization were usually led by women whose domestic responsibilities compelled them to enter the public and political spheres in defense of family, home, and neighborhood. Other related initiatives carried out by these female congregants in the name of Christian anticommunism, such as prayer groups and textbook-evaluation panels, further connected them to the remarkably expansive orbit of female political activism, which, as historians like Michelle Nickerson and Donald Critchlow have documented, provided much energy and direction for the postwar conservative movement.[86]

As evidenced in the broad vision of its female crusaders, anticommunist subterfuge was not, therefore, the only political tactic employed by Heritage High's PTF; concerns with communism, in fact, encouraged political awareness on several levels. Central Baptist's legion of concerned parents ventured out from their fundamentalist fortress to protest the Anaheim Public School Board's liberal educational standards in subjects as far ranging as history and sex education.[87] Increasingly concerned with a loosening of sexual mores in society, Heritage High parents and Central Baptist members also joined forces in the mid-1960s with their counterparts at Christian Heritage schools in San Diego—institutions guided by Wells's good friend and fellow southern fundamentalist Tim LaHaye—to seek legislative action against obscenity.[88] These efforts resulted in the sponsorship in 1966 of Proposition 16, a measure that sought to bring obscenity laws under the jurisdiction of local governments and citizens. Although the effort failed at the polls, the initiative succeeded at giving notice to all Americans that evangelical voters were now on the march.[89] Much more than simply a place of academic instruction, Heritage High was, in short, a home base for conservative activism on multiple fronts.

As vital as it was to local political efforts, Heritage High also proved to be a linchpin in a much broader network of educational institutions that spanned the country's southern rim from San Diego to Searcy, Arkansas. Using postsecondary institutions to inculcate young people with Christian American values, these academies simultaneously promoted a united anticommunist front in defense of free enterprise, states' rights, and family values, all galvanizing principles of Barry Goldwater's presidential campaign. George Benson's Harding Academy in Searcy (recognized by some as the "West Point of the Radical Right") was one of the more famous of these, but countless others bolstered this network too, including Pepperdine College and John Brown University.[90] Through interpersonal ties between Wells, Knott, Benson, and many of the leading institutions in this network, Central Baptist was soon recognized as an important link in this chain of Sunbelt fundamentalist institutions. Lecture tours of leading spokespersons from within the network were usually designed to include Central Baptist on their West Coast itineraries. It hardly mattered who was in Central Baptist's pulpit—whether radio personality Paul Harvey, anticommunist crusader Billy James Hargis, or another political firebrand—for their messages were substantively the same. To be sure, partisan politics were never left outside when these men entered Central's sanctuary.

"Educational" enterprises of the sort Heritage High's administrators and parents endorsed proved that politicization was not simply a trickle-down affair at Central Baptist, but it was Wells's commanding presence that proved to be the congregation's most vital contribution to local political culture. Determined to reveal "the truth" about American politics and society by tearing asunder the "feather curtain" of leftist propaganda in the mainstream media, Wells created an intricate web of programming and organizations that were consciously designed to counteract the "leftist establishment." When the American Civil Liberties Union (ACLU) and the Anti-Defamation League began challenging racialized patterns in housing, Wells formed his own Christian Anti-defamation League; when news coverage became inundated with pictures of Berkeley radicals and civil rights protestors, Wells started his own magazine, radio, and television programs; when the local media began criticizing Governor Ross Barnett's policies in Mississippi during the 1962 fight over desegregation, Wells appeared in a televised debate—in defense of Barnett—and accepted an invitation to speak at the local chapter of the California Republican Assembly (CRA).[91] As self-designated prophet of the Right, Wells reveled in every opportunity to speak his mind on pressing political matters of the day, and by all accounts there were many in the community eager to listen.

It was in his weekly preaching, however, that Wells was most effective in helping the southern migrants and local defense workers who called the church home come to terms with the historical processes that had led them into the middle-class suburban landscape of Orange County.[92] On Sunday mornings and evenings Wells used several homiletic strategies to turn his congregants into anticommunist combatants and Goldwater conservatives, many of which mirrored techniques embraced by the secular Right. Robert Goldberg has effectively demonstrated how modern marketing of Old West symbols helped galvanize grassroots support for cowboy conservatism and its leaders, Barry Goldwater and Ronald Reagan. In fact, independent-minded preachers like Wells were no less successful than their political heroes in tapping the politics of western symbolism to stir their constituents to action. From the pulpit and with his pen, Wells effectively portrayed himself as a maverick cut from the same cloth as the Southwest's venerated saddlebag saints, who, in frontier times, had always demonstrated a readiness to fire their "gospel guns" against advancing threats of apostasy. Always left for congregants to decide after listening to Wells's biblical bravado was whether they could muster the courage necessary to follow in their fearless leader's tracks.

Meanwhile, armed with a theology and political philosophy that ensured the sanctity of the individual, celebrated the entrepreneurial spirit, and boldly called for a re-Christianization of America, Wells in his sermons offered congregants more than just symbols. They also offered them an intellectual framework that seemed sensible in its ability to translate the concerns of "plain folk" into modern political discourse and enticing in the way it offered theological legitimacy to the modern conservative cause. During Sunday morning services, Wells accomplished this through subtle references to an idyllic past when Americans had been allowed to live free of the constraints of centralizing and secular forces, to flourish as pioneers for the gospel of Christ and Christian democracy.[93] Far less nuanced, however, were Wells's evening sermons. Advertised in bold lettering in local newspapers and attracting audiences that often spilled out of the auditorium into the parking lot, Wells's evening sermons offered interpretations of current political events through the lens of biblical prophecy and supplemented them with explicit, uncompromising calls for political mobilization in the name of the new conservatism. As one can imagine, sermons such as "Be Sure to Vote Right in the Election," "Did Nixon Help or Hinder," and "Why the John Birch Society Is Right" left little to the political imagination, and that is the way this religious maverick with the booming voice wanted it.[94]

That was certainly the way Wells's congregants preferred it—hard-nosed and uncompromising, with little room for abstraction. Central Baptist, after all, was where they came looking for and found a faith community that might cater to their long-held beliefs *and* their new middle-class needs; here, while the gospel choir and fire-and-brimstone preaching of each Sunday morning service reminded them of their roots in Oklahoma and Texas, the sprawling church plant they helped build on prime real estate underscored their status as well-adjusted suburbanites. Under Wells's tutelage they discovered yet another identity as political activists. While their pastor's strident anticommunism confirmed for them long-held suspicions that New Deal liberalism and its collective impulses were evil, his concessions to the dignity of hard work and plain living convinced them that the interests of common folk would be best served by a leader like Goldwater. So it was that in the summer of 1964 Central Baptist parishioners responded to their pastor's urgings by setting up Goldwater tables on the sidewalk outside their church (just off church property so as not to threaten the church's tax-exempt status), canvassing for their candidate and his conservative causes (including Proposition 14, the Republican anti–fair housing initiative), and organizing a bus convoy to the Arizona senator's rally at Knott's Berry Farm in nearby Buena Park.[95]

As impressive as it was at the time, grassroots momentum of the kind witnessed in 1964 only grew in intensity as Central Baptist drove deeper into the political fray during the late 1960s. While at the local level Central Baptist congregants continued to act out their pastor's political creed by leading grassroots campaigns for Reagan initiatives in matters of education and public decency, in higher circles of power Wells joined other southern clerics in providing leadership at the party level. By the late 1960s a number of preachers like Wells were asserting influence in such partisan affiliates as the CRA, and through their involvement in Sunbelt evangelical networks, they acted as liaisons between Southern California and southern Republicans.[96] Other uprooted southern clergy affected California's GOP more directly by running for office. In the case of southern-based religious institutions like Pepperdine College, leadership in the California Republican Party became almost a rite of passage for its highest executives, all of whom were respected lay preachers within the Church of Christ.[97]

Another of Wells's friends and a fellow Christian anticommunist crusader was W. Stuart McBirnie, the itinerant Baptist evangelist who arrived in the Southland during the late 1950s. By 1963 McBirnie was pastor of the United Community Church of Glendale, one of the largest congregations in the area, and the voice of the Glendale Crusade for Americanism and the popular talk show *The Voice of Americanism*. Each of these enterprises helped forge McBirnie into a respected consultant for conservative Republican politicians. Even before assuming a leading administrative role in the local Goldwater campaign, McBirnie had gained the ear of Ronald Reagan and soon became one of the politician's close advisers. Struggling to find an appropriate slogan around which he could mobilize conservatives for the 1966 run at the governorship, Reagan turned to McBirnie, who subsequently coined the term "Creative Society" as a phrase that might capture the imagination of voters. Reagan's gubernatorial victory not only proved McBirnie's hunch correct but also forged a relationship between the candidate and California's plain-folk evangelicals, a relationship that would last for years to come.[98]

"SALVATION IN THE SOUTHLAND"

In 1949 Billy Graham boldly prophesized that the Southland would be changed by "a hillbilly, a country boy," who would "sound forth in a mighty voice" a plan of redemption for those caught in the throes of sin and paralyzed by fears of communism. Surely he could not have imagined the extent to which his predictions would come true. During his first visit to Los Angeles in 1949, the relatively unknown Graham preached old-time religion in his endearing "folk style" to locals gathered in a makeshift tent on an empty city lot. Twenty years later Graham was a powerful "insider" in his own right, armed with a success story that resonated with Southland evangelicals who had already helped transform him into an emissary of the Right and who had translated his message into action for the new conservatism.

Graham, moreover, was not the only southern evangelical preacher to enjoy such success. As witnessed in the life stories of McGee and Wells, thanks to the confluence of unprecedented, large-scale demographic, social, and economic forces, postwar Southern California proved to be a launching pad for aspiring itinerant preachers and for empire-minded clerics, as well as a base from which to spread plain-folk evangelicalism across the land. Indeed, it was from the far reaches of Southern California, the leading wedge of the gun belt and the tip of the Bible belt, these leaders believed, that they would vitalize the West and, in the process, awaken an entire nation to the gospel of Christ and the populist conservatism of the new Republican Party. The pace of their ascent out of the margins and into the cultural and political mainstream was truly impressive. In stark contrast to their humble beginnings in the 1940s, when they were dismissed or simply ignored by most who heard them, these country preachers had, by the late 1960s, become power brokers within the Republican Right, ultimate champions of an anticommunist agenda that had already proven critical to Goldwater's run for the presidency in 1964 and that was proving even more vital for the fortunes of California's own cowboy conservative, Ronald Reagan.

Evidence of this metamorphosis was there for all to see on Graham's return visit to Southern California in September 1969, when a record-breaking crowd gathered in Anaheim's Big A stadium.[99] Religious, political, and popular icons of Sunbelt conservatism were there en masse to greet him. In the days surrounding the crusade, the residents of Orange County were treated to appearances by a bevy of their favorite entertainers, including Pat Boone, John Wayne, Johnny Cash, and audience-favorite Norma Zimmer, star soloist of the *Lawrence Welk Show*. A highlight for others was the special appearance of Ruth Graham at a women's luncheon staged at the Anaheim Marriott's Grand Ballroom. Hosted by Nancy Reagan, the luncheon served 11,000 women (the largest sit-down meal ever served under one roof west of the Mississippi), all of whom seemed to find Graham's soft, conversational voice pleasing to the ear and her practical words of wisdom on God's design for Christian living in the home easy to digest.[100] Yet for others, the highlight came on the crusade's second evening when, at the conclusion of Lieutenant Cleve McCary's stirring testimony of faith and patriotism, all 54,000 people in attendance spontaneously erupted into heartfelt, standing applause. Of the Marine's courage in overcoming multiple wounds from Vietnam, wounds that included the loss of an arm, an eye, and half his teeth, Billy Graham too could not help but respond emotionally: "He can stand up here and talk about the joy of the Lord with a smile on his face. Christ can do that, and he can do it for you."[101]

Emotional too were Graham's parting words after the close of the crusade. By the end of the ten-day extravaganza, the Graham team had not only established new records and captured the attention of the national media[102] but had also thrust Graham onto a stage, literally and figuratively, alongside some of the most powerful cultural and political figures of the day, including Governor Reagan.[103] Having had Reagan open the proceedings with words of welcome was no doubt a matter of pride for Graham, but at a final press conference organized in the immediate wake of the crusade, "an obviously ebullient Graham" could only speak in general terms as being grateful *for all* of the happenings and special guests that had made this crusade the high point of his career. "I feel more at home here than any place I've ever been" were the unsolicited words spoken with absolute sincerity by a country preacher truly enamored with what life in the Southland had to offer.[104]

NOTES

1. Excerpt from Billy Graham's sermon, delivered in Los Angeles, September 1949. See Graham, "Prepare to Meet Thy God," reprinted in *Revival in Our Time* (Wheaton, Ill.: Van Kampen Press, 1950), 124.

2. Excerpt from Billy Graham's sermon, delivered in Los Angeles, September 1949. See Billy Graham, "Amos the Hillbilly Preacher," Tape 235, Audio Tape Collection, Billy Graham Evangelistic Association Papers (hereafter BGEA), Billy Graham Archives, Wheaton College, Wheaton, Illinois.

3. John Pollock, *Billy Graham: The Authorized Biography* (Grand Rapids, Mich.: Zondervan, 1966), 50; Marshall Frady, *Billy Graham: A Parable of American Righteousness* (Boston: Little, Brown, 1979), 197–204. For a vivid description of Graham's preaching antics during the 1949 Los Angeles crusade, see William Martin, *A Prophet with Honor: The Billy Graham Story* (New York: William Morrow, 1991), 112–119.

4. John Pollock, *To All the Nations: The Billy Graham Story* (New York: Harper & Row, 1985), 39–48.

5. Robert Shuler, "The Spiritual Upheaval in Los Angeles," *Pentecostal Evangel*, 4 February 1950, 12; Pollock, *To All the Nations*, 47.

6. For insight into the evolution of the New Evangelicalism in the immediate postwar years, see especially George Marsden, *Reforming Fundamentalism: Fuller Seminary and the New Evangelicalism* (Grand Rapids, Mich.: Eerdmans, 1987), and Richard Quebedeaux, *The Young Evangelicals: The Story of a New Generation of Evangelicals* (New York: Harper & Row, 1974).

7. Assessments of Graham's career that have glorified the southern preacher include Pollock, *To All the Nations*, and Frady, *Billy Graham*. Other evaluations that have come close to vilifying him include James Morris, *The Preachers* (New York: St. Martin's Press, 1973). Critical but more scholarly assessments have been provided by William McLoughlin, *Revivals, Awakenings, and Reform: An Essay on Religion and Social Change in America, 1607–1977* (Chicago: University of Chicago Press, 1978), and Martin, *Prophet with Honor*.

8. A similar question is answered differently in Richard W. Etulain, "Regionalizing Religion: Evangelicals in the American West, 1940–1990," in *Religion and Culture: Historical Essays in Honor of Robert C. Woodward*, ed. Raymond M. Cooke and Richard W. Etulain (Albuquerque, N.M.: Far West Books, 1991), 79–103.

9. Here I am borrowing the phrase "burned-over," popularized by Whitney R. Cross when describing the proliferation of revivalism in early-nineteenth-century upstate New York. See *The Burned Over District: The Social and Intellectual History of En-*

thusiastic Religion in Western New York, 1800–1850 (1950; repr., New York: Octagon Books, 1981).

10. On the cultural dominance of Baptists in Texas and the western South after 1870, see Linda K. Pritchard, "A Comparative Approach to Western Religious History: Texas as a Case Study, 1845–1890," *Western Historical Quarterly* 19, no. 4 (November 1988): 417, 421.

11. On the intellectual underpinnings of commonsense realism, see George Marsden, *Fundamentalism and American Culture: The Shaping of Twentieth-Century Evangelicalism 1870–1925* (New York: Oxford University Press, 1980), esp. pt. 2.

12. "Texas theology" was the term used by Baptist moderates at Southern Baptist Theological Seminary in Louisville to describe their aggressively conservative brethren at Southwestern Baptist Theological Seminary in Fort Worth. See Paul Harvey, *Redeeming the South: Religious Cultures and Racial Identities among Southern Baptists, 1865–1925* (Chapel Hill: University of North Carolina Press, 1997), 151. The term resonates, however, with evangelical sentiments and styles in other prominent denominations of the Southwest.

13. As quoted in John Shelton Reed, *The Enduring South: Subculture Persistence in Mass Society* (Chapel Hill: University of North Carolina Press, 1972), 57.

14. James Gregory, *American Exodus: The Dust Bowl Migration and Okie Culture in California* (New York: Oxford University Press, 1989), 142.

15. On the origins of the democratic spirit in popular evangelicalism, see, for example, Nathan O. Hatch, *The Democratization of American Christianity* (New Haven, Conn.: Yale University Press, 1989).

16. See Samuel Hill, "The Shape and Shapes of Popular Southern Piety," in *Varieties of Southern Evangelicalism*, ed. David E. Harrell Jr. (Macon, Ga.: Mercer University Press, 1981), 99–102.

17. Grant Wacker, "Uneasy in Zion: Evangelicals in Postmodern Society," in *Evangelicalism and Modern America*, ed. George Marsden (Grand Rapids, Mich.: Eerdmans, 1984), 26.

18. John H. Redekop, *The American Far Right: A Case Study of Billy James Hargis and Christian Crusade* (Grand Rapids, Mich.: Eerdmans, 1968), 51.

19. On the breakdown of the New Deal coalition, see, for example, Thomas Sugrue, *The Origins of the Urban Crisis: Race and Inequality in Postwar Detroit* (Princeton, N.J.: Princeton University Press, 1996); Becky Nicolaides, *My Blue Heaven: Life and Politics in the Working-Class Suburbs of Los Angeles, 1920–1965* (Chicago: University of Chicago Press, 2002); Dan T. Carter, *The Politics of Rage: George Wallace, the Origins of the New Conservatism, and the Transformation of American Politics* (New York: Simon & Schuster, 1995).

20. The way the politics of anticommunism helped unite disparate groups of fiscal, social, and religious conservatives for political purposes is well documented. See, for example, George Nash, *The Conservative Intellectual Movement in America since 1945* (Wilmington, Del.: Intercollegiate Studies Institute, 1996), and Richard Gid Powers, *Not without Honor: The History of American Anticommunism* (New York: Free Press, 1995), 252–255.

21. Anticommunism was, of course, a crusade undertaken by a broad spectrum of religious leaders and institutions. For most, anticommunism simply provided added incentive for the preaching of traditional religion. For some—most notably plain folk evangelicals but also Mormons and other religious "outsiders"—the campaign against communism provided entry into the cultural and political mainstream. Determined since the early twentieth century to prove their worth as true Americans, Mormons, for example, appropriated the language and activism of anticommunism as a way to gain legitimacy (and leverage) in Cold War American society. On anticommunism's usefulness as a evangelistic device within Catholicism and mainstream Protestantism see, for example, Mark Stephen Massa, *Catholics and American Culture: Fulton Sheen, Dorothy Day, and the Notre Dame Football Team* (New York: Crossroads, 1999); Carol C. R. George, *God's Salesman: Norman Vincent Peale and the Power of Positive Thinking* (New York: Oxford University Press, 1993). Mormonism's employment of anticommunism for cultural gain is discussed in Bryan T. Smith, "Toward Respectability and Peculiarity: Mormon Anticommunism Rhetoric, 1936–1960" (unpublished paper, in the author's possession).

22. On the capture of the Republican Party by western conservatives, see, for example, Kurt Schuparra, *Triumph of the Right: The Rise of the California Conservative Movement, 1945–1966* (Armonk, N.Y.: M. E. Sharpe, 1998); Mary C. Brennan, *Turning Right in the Sixties: The Conservative Capture of the GOP* (Chapel Hill: University of North Carolina Press, 1995).

23. James Gregory, *The Southern Diaspora: How the Great Migrations of Black and White Southerners Transformed America* (Chapel Hill: University of North Carolina Press, 2005).

24. For brief analysis of these trends, see Southern California Research Council, *Migration and the Southern California Economy*, Southern California Research Council, report 12 (Los Angeles: Occidental College, 1964), 19–24, and Warren S. Thompson, *Growth and Changes in California's Population* (Los Angeles: Haynes Foundation, 1955), 152.

25. Thompson, *Growth and Changes in California's Population*, 4.

26. Southern California Research Council, *Migration and the Southern California Economy*, 21–24.

27. Center for Planning and Development Research, *Characteristics of Metropolitan Growth in California*, vol. 1 (Berkeley, Calif.: Institute of Urban and Regional Development, University of California, 1965), 7. The Southern California Research Council's study *Migration and the Southern California Economy* notes that while 700 of every 1,000 migrants landed first in Los Angeles and Orange Counties, 300, on average, would eventually relocate to other counties in the state (16).

28. Donald J. Bogue, Henry S. Shryock Jr., and Siegfried A. Hoermann, *Subregional Migration in the United States, 1935–40*, vol. 1 (Oxford, Ohio: Scripps Foundation, Miami University, 1957), 11.

29. U.S. Bureau of the Census, *Census of the United States, Population: 1940, State of Birth* (Washington, D.C.: GPO, 1940), 17–18.

30. Thompson, *Growth and Changes in California's Population*, 68.

31. James Gregory, "The Southern Diaspora and the Urban Dispossessed: Demonstrating the Census Public Use Microdata Samples," *Journal of American History* 82 (June 1995): 118.

32. According to census totals for 1970, the population of Arkansas was 1,923,295 and Oklahoma 2,559,463; Little Rock and Oklahoma City reported populations of 381,123 and 718,737 respectively. These two figures combined fall short of matching the estimated 1.2 million white southerners living in Los Angeles and Orange Counties.

33. Douglas W. Johnson, Paul R. Picard, and Bernard Quinn, *Churches and Church Membership in the United States* (Washington, D.C.: Glenmary Research Center, 1974), table 2; Martin B. Bradley et al., *Churches and Church Membership in the United States, 1990* (Atlanta: Glenmary Research Center, 1992), 13–14.

34. Southern California churches regularly led, for example, in the annual rate of giving to the Assemblies of God Foreign Missions Department and the denomination's publishing enterprises. See, for example, "Interesting Statistics," *Informant*, May 1956; "Where the Evangels Go," *Pentecostal Evangel*, 25 March 1950, 9.

35. See "'Go to the Lost . . .': 1,000 New Assemblies of God Churches in 1955," *Pentecostal Evangel*, 30 January 1955.

36. See "Progressing in One of Our Fastest Growing Counties," *Pentecostal Evangel*, 16 September 1956, 16–17.

37. "Radio KGER Presents," KGER-Brown Radio File, John Brown University Archives (hereafter JBU), John Brown University, Siloam Springs, Arkansas. By 1949 Brown was reporting to his constituents that his California investments were providing 90 percent of the university's operating costs. See untitled report, *John Brown University Bulletin*, April 1949, JBU.

38. Bill George, interview by author, 4 April 2003, Siloam Springs, Arkansas.

39. A helpful overview of California's heavy investment in the defense sector is provided by Roger Lotchin, *Fortress California, 1910–1961: From Warfare to Welfare* (New York: Oxford University Press, 1992).

40. For example, purposely located within range of Orange County's El Toro Marine Base so that it could meet the religious needs of enlisted men and their families was Bristol Street Baptist Church, an institution whose internal workings were dictated by the exigencies of defense mobilization: When training sessions at El Toro began, Bristol Street's membership ranks expanded; when a new batch of recruits was shipped off to the front or tours of duty ended, membership ranks fell. See "Enrollment Book," Bristol Street Historical File, First Baptist Church, Tustin, California.

41. See Christian Smith, *American Evangelicalism: Embattled and Thriving* (Chicago: University of Chicago Press, 1998).

42. The variety of ministries started in this quest was as striking as the capitalist verve that drove them. Bill Bright, Tim LaHaye, James Dobson, John Wimber, Ralph Wilkerson, Hal Lindsey, Henry Morris, all household names within American evangelicalism by the 1960s for their innovations in youth, family, charismatic, prophetic, and educational ministries, saw their careers benefit early from the same combination of social forces that set Graham on his way in 1949.

43. For fuller treatment of preceding themes see "Evangelicalism Becomes Southern, Politics Becomes Evangelical: From FDR to Ronald Reagan," in Mark Noll and Luke Harlow, eds., *Religion and Politics in America*, Second Edition (New York: Oxford University Press, 2007), 297–325; Darren Dochuk, "From Bible Belt to Sunbelt: Plain Folk Religion, Grassroots Politics, and the Southernization of Southern California, 1939–1969" (Ph.D. diss., University of Notre Dame, 2005).

44. Details of McGee's life as presented here are drawn from his short biography compiled in Gertrude L. Cutler, ed., *The Whole Word for the Whole World: The Life and Ministry of J. Vernon McGee* (Pasadena, Calif.: Thru the Bible Radio Network, 1991), and from miscellaneous biographical material located in the McGee Historical Collection, Thru the Bible (hereafter TTB), Pasadena, California.

45. Cutler, *Whole Word for the Whole World*, 8.

46. Details of the history of the Church of the Open Door and the Bible Institute of Los Angeles are taken from G. Michael Cocoris, *70 Years on Hope Street: A History of the Church of the Open Door, 1915–1985* (Los Angeles: Church of the Open Door, 1985), and G. Ted Martinez, "The Rise, Decline, and Renewal of a Megachurch: A Case Study of Church of the Open Door" (D.Min. diss., Talbot School of Theology, Biola University, 1997).

47. Behind the founding of COD was Lyman Stewart, a transplanted oil baron from Pennsylvania who, soon after relocating to Los Angeles in the winter of 1882, founded the Union Oil Company. See "Black Oil and Souls to Win," *King's Business*, February 1958, 10–29. For a useful introductory glance at this Anglo-American network of evangelicalism, see Mark Noll, David Bebbington, and George Rawlyk, *Evangelicalism: Comparative Studies of Popular Protestantism in North America, the British Isles, and Beyond, 1700–1990* (New York: Oxford University Press, 1994). For insight into the class dimensions of Anglo-American Protestantism in early twentieth-century Los Angeles, see Gregory H. Singleton, *Religion in the City of Angels: American Protestant Culture and Urbanization, Los Angeles, 1850–1930* (Ann Arbor, Mich.: UMI Research Press, 1979).

48. As quoted in Cocoris, *70 Years on Hope Street*, 81.

49. See unsigned letters from listeners in J. V. McGee History File, TTB.

50. See "Radio Reactions from Burleson, Texas," *Open Door News*, June 1969, *Open Door News* Collection, Church of the Open Door Archival Material (hereafter CODA), Church of the Open Door, Glendora, California.

51. See "News Release" for the *Los Angeles Examiner*, 50th Anniversary folder, "A" Misc. Box, CODA.

52. Cutler, *Whole Word for the Whole World*, 55.

53. As quoted from Dr. David Cooper in McGee's *Guidelines for the Understanding of the Scriptures* (Pasadena, Calif.: Thru the Bible Radio Network, n.d.), n.p., McGee—Printed Sermons File, TTB.

54. "Atheistic communists," an often-quoted assessment of communism provided by J. Edgar Hoover, comes from "Communism's Offensive against God," *Pentecostal Evangel*, 7 January 1951, 11.

55. Powers, *Not without Honor*, 252–255.

56. On the conspiratorial dimensions of evangelical and countersubversive anticommunism in the early Cold War period, see, for example, Robert Alan Goldberg, *Enemies Within: The Culture of Conspiracy in Modern America* (New Haven, Conn.: Yale University Press, 2001).

57. "Vengeful countersubversives" is a label used by Richard Powers to characterize the "reckless," anti-Semitic, radical anticommunist wing of the Republican Party in the late 1940s and early 1950s. Powers, *Not without Honor,* 192. The alternative designations are "extremist" and "respectable" anticommunist conservatives. On the fluidity of these categories, see Donald T. Critchlow, "Conservatism Reconsidered: Phyllis Schlafly and Grassroots Conservatism," in *The Conservative Sixties,* ed. David Farber and Jeff Roche (New York: Peter Lang, 2003), 108–126.

58. See copy of written notes for "Origin of Communism," McGee Sermon Notes File, TTB.

59. See sermon notes for "'Foul Weather' or 'The Time of Tribulation,'" McGee Sermon Notes File, TTB.

60. See, for example, Daniel Bell, ed., *The Radical Right,* 3rd ed. (New Brunswick, N.J.: Transaction Publishers, 2002); Richard Hofstadter, *The Paranoid Style in American Politics and Other Essays* (New York: Alfred A. Knopf, 1965).

61. See sermon notes for "The United Nations and Prophecy," McGee Sermon Notes File, TTB.

62. "Origin of Communism," McGee Sermon Notes File, TTB.

63. See "John the Baptist and the John Birch Society," audio recording of J. Vernon McGee at Church of the Open Door (date unknown), TTB. McGee refrained from endorsing the John Birch Society but spoke sympathetically about the anticommunist organization.

64. See copy of written notes for "A Nation at the Crossroads," McGee Sermon Notes File, TTB. Included in these sermon notes are instructions written out by McGee to indicate when and how the homily would utilize illustrations to emphasize a key point.

65. The numerous clippings attached to each of McGee's filed sermons evidence his resourcefulness in seeking out articles and editorials from his favorite newspapers and magazines. McGee was on the mailing list of the *Manion Forum,* receiving and using newsletters regularly distributed by this conservative organization. See, for example, general letter from *Manion Forum,* 24 April 1961, attached to "Modern Man and the Moral Muddle," McGee Sermon Notes File, TTB.

66. On the showing of *Operation Abolition,* see COD Bulletin, 4 September 1960, Bulletin Collection, CODA. *Iran, Brittle Ally* was shown the week following, and *Castro, Cuba, and Communism* was shown on 26 April 1964. Sunday afternoon sessions at COD attracted a veritable who's who in the world of evangelical anticommunist activism, but also on occasion local and state politicians. A favorite at COD was Kenneth Hahn, supervisor of Los Angeles County during the late 1950s and 1960s. See "What Does the Future Hold for America?" COD Bulletin, 3 June 1962, CODA.

67. Cutler, *Whole Word for the Whole World,* 8.

68. See clip from *Manion Forum*, 12 December 1958, attached to sermon notes for "What Can Happen to the Christian in 1962"; McGee Sermon Notes File, TTB.

69. See sermon notes for "'Foul Weather' or 'The Time of Tribulation,'" "Can America Survive?" and "Will America Go Communist or Roman Catholic or Is There a Third Alternative?" McGee Sermon Notes File, TTB.

70. See sermon notes for "The Crisis of This Present Hour," McGee Sermon Notes File, TTB.

71. See sermon notes for "Can America Survive?" and "'Foul Weather' or 'The Time of Tribulation,'" McGee Sermon Notes File, TTB.

72. See sermon notes for "The Crisis of this Present Hour," McGee Sermon Notes File, TTB.

73. There are a number of useful studies of the "racist," or old Christian, Right. Among the most useful are Leo Ribuffo's *The Old Christian Right: The Protestant Far Right from the Great Depression to the Cold War* (Philadelphia: Temple University Press, 1983) and Michael Barkun's *Religion and the Racist Right: The Origins of the Christian Identity Movement* (Chapel Hill: University of North Carolina Press, 1997). Both of these works place men like Springer and his fundamentalist contemporaries on the religious and political fringe of Cold War America. While some cowboy preachers who operated within this network were indeed on the fringe, I would contend that the networks of these pastors were larger and more significant than previously assumed, and that the ideological orbits in which these men operated often intersected with the broader movement for political conservatism.

74. See "Bob Wells, an Orange County Leader since 1956," *Baptist Bible Tribune*, 24 October 1985, 12.

75. See "Down through the Years, 1956–1985: A Tribute to Our Pastor-Founder," Church Annuals and Special Events File, Central Baptist Church Archival Material (hereafter CBA), Victory Baptist Church, Anaheim, California.

76. Falwell made a number of visits to Orange County on Wells's behalf. Causing the biggest storm of media attention was Falwell's keynote address at Central Baptist Church's twentieth-anniversary celebration, held in the 8,000-seat Anaheim Convention Center in 1976. See *Register*, 2 October 1976.

77 Central Baptist was affiliated with a consortium of independent fundamentalist Baptist churches (the Baptist Bible Fellowship) that stretched from the South northward through Tennessee and Kentucky to the upper Midwest and westward along Route 66 to Southern California. Outside the South and the Southwest these churches—often called temples or tabernacles—catered to white southern migrants who had relocated midcentury to cities like Akron, Ohio; Detroit; and Los Angeles to work in the auto industry. While some of these churches often boasted (with some exaggeration, no doubt) memberships of 25,000 in the 1940s and 1950s, most could, as late as the 1960s and 1970s, still claim to have Sunday schools that were among the largest in the land. One survey taken in 1968, in fact, found nine of the ten largest Sunday schools in the nation operating within this fellowship of independent Baptist churches. For further background information on the Baptist Bible Fellow-

ship, see James O. Combs, ed., *Roots and Origins of Baptist Fundamentalism* (Springfield, Mo.: Baptist Bible Tribune Publications, 1984).

78. See "10 Largest Sunday Schools in the U.S. Today," Newsletters File, CBA.

79. See *Voice of Truth and Freedom*, April 1967, CBA. The *Voice of Truth and Freedom* was produced by Central Baptist Church for public distribution. Its readership was limited but nevertheless extended from Southern California to the Deep South.

80. Central Baptist Newsletter, 26 August 1965, Church Notes File, CBA.

81. Central Baptist Newsletter, 4 May 1960, Church Notes File, CBA.

82. Bulletin of Heritage High School, Promotional File, CBA.

83. This description of Southern California comes from the mouth of Denver Klaassen, the principal of Heritage High School. "Heritage High School Far from 'Ordinary'!" *Voice of Truth and Freedom*, November 1966, 6, CBA.

84. Bulletin of Heritage High School, Promotional File, CBA.

85. Other than Wells, Walter Knott was one of the more frequent guest speakers at the PTF. See, for example, "P.T.F. Notes," 4 November 1965, *Central Baptist News Letter*, News Letter File, CBA. Central Baptist "surveillance" of local colleges increased as Vietnam protests became more common. See, for example, "Do We Want Another Berkeley in Fullerton?" *Central Baptist Church News Letter*, 16 February 1967, and "Should Filth and Perversion Be Permitted under Guise of Academic Freedom?" *Central Baptist Church News Letter*, 26 January 1968, both CBA.

86. On the political power of women in the conservative movement and the Republican Right, see, for example, Donald Critchlow, *Phyllis Schlafly and Grassroots Conservatism: A Woman's Crusade* (Princeton, N.J.: Princeton University Press, 2005); Michelle Nickerson, "Domestic Threats: Women, Gender, and Conservatism in Cold War Los Angeles, 1945–1966" (Ph.D. diss., Yale University, 2003); Sylvie Murray, *The Progressive Housewife: Community Activism in Suburban Queens, 1945–1965* (Philadelphia: University of Pennsylvania Press, 2003); Lisa McGirr, *Suburban Warriors: The Origins of the New American Right* (Princeton, N.J.: Princeton University Press, 2001). On conservative women and the Religious Right, see, for example, C. Manning, *God Gave Us the Right: Conservative Catholic, Evangelical Protestant, and Orthodox Jewish Women Grapple with Feminism* (New Brunswick, N.J.: Rutgers University Press, 1999).

87. See, for example, the call to action in "The Immorality of Our Public School System," *Church Notes*, 30 September 1965, Church Notes File, CBA. Their experience in the trenches, for example, made Heritage High's PTF an important ally of the California Citizens Committee and California Families United. These two organizations were among those determined to ban SIECUS (Sex Information and Education Council of the United States) and its implementation of sex education in Anaheim high schools, an initiative that drew national attention in 1968 but that had, in fact, surfaced earlier in the decade. For more on Orange County's war with sex-education advocates, see William Martin, *With God on Our Side: The Rise of the Religious Right in America* (New York: Broadway Books, 1996), chap. 4. On Central Baptist's involvement in this local battle, see, for example, "School Sex Class Conflict With Bible Doctrine Cited," *Anaheim Bulletin*, 5 December 1968; "The New Morality

Is Immorality" and "Shall We Teach Sex in Public School?" both in *Central Baptist News Letter*, News Letter File, CBA; "Sex Education," *Voice of Truth and Freedom*, April 1967, CBA.

88. For further background on LaHaye's educational efforts, see, for example, Eugene F. Provenzo Jr., *Religious Fundamentalism and American Education* (Albany: State University of New York Press, 1990); Sara Diamond, *Spiritual Warfare: The Politics of the Christian Right* (Boston: South End Press, 1989), chap. 3; Michael Lienesch, *Redeeming America: Piety and Politics in the New Christian Right* (Chapel Hill: University of North Carolina Press, 1993), chap. 7.

89. This ongoing fight helped preachers like Tim LaHaye and politicians like William Dannemeyer assume a more important role in Southern California conservatism. For a brief overview of these developments, see McGirr, *Suburban Warriors*, 226–228. See also Sara Diamond, *Roads to Dominion: Right-Wing Movements and Political Power in the United States* (New York: Guilford Press, 1994).

90. On George Benson's vital contribution to Goldwater conservatism, see L. Edward Hicks, *"Sometimes in the Wrong, but Never in Doubt": George S. Benson and the Education of the New Religious Right* (Knoxville: University of Tennessee Press, 1994).

91. Wells never shied away from a fight; quite the opposite, he thrived on it, and this is what made him, according to a *Newsweek* article, an essential cog in the Orange County conservative machine. "Orange County California: A Little Piece of America," *Newsweek*, 14 November 1966.

92. Membership records for Central Baptist Church are not available. However, Wells's extensive records of funeral services conducted for members provides a useful glimpse of the demographic makeup of the church. While the church did attract people from other regions of the United States, the primary group represented in the congregation was migrants from Oklahoma, Arkansas, Texas, and other areas of the Southwest. In terms of class, this church seemed to appeal to a solidly middle-class constituency as well as to a cross-section of blue-collar workers, many of whom had come to California to work in the local defense industry. See Funeral Directory, CBA.

93. Sermons available in tape form, CBA.

94. "Be Sure to Vote Right in the Election," "Did Nixon Help or Hinder," and "Why the John Birch Society Is Right," sermons available in tape form, CBA.

95. On the centrality of the Proposition 14 campaign to Goldwater's success in Southern California, see Matthew Dallek, *The Right Moment: Ronald Reagan's First Victory and the Decisive Turning Point in American Politics* (New York: Free Press, 2000). On the role of religious conservatives in this campaign, see Darren Dochuk, "'From Bible Belt to Sunbelt': Plain Folk Religion, Grassroots Politics, and the Southernization of Southern California, 1939–1969" (Ph.D. diss., University of Notre Dame, 2005).

96. On Wells and the CRA, see, for example, "Dr. Wells to Speak on 'Isms,'" *Anaheim Bulletin*, 29 November 1965. The records of the CRA, held in Special Collections at the University of California, Los Angeles, offer further evidence of clerical involvement in this organization.

97. In the late 1950s and early 1960s, Pepperdine firmly aligned itself with the Republican Party by securing ties to Republican donors, hosting conservative forums, and offering leadership. Among those who served in leadership both at Pepperdine and in the GOP were Bill Teague, school vice president, who ran unsuccessfully on the Republican ticket in Orange County, and Bill Banowsky, president of Pepperdine in the early 1970s, who assumed several official posts within the California and national Republican Party. Information on Pepperdine's involvement with the California Republican Party stems in part from Bill Banowsky, interview by author 2 May 2006, Malibu, California. For a general inside history of Pepperdine, see Bill Henegar and Jerry Rushford, *Forever Young: The Life and Times [of] M. Norvel Young and Helen M. Young* (Nashville, Tenn.: 21st Century Christian, 1999).

98. For further background on McBirnie and his activities, consult unprocessed material in the Marie Koenig Collection, Huntington Library, San Marino, California, and in Box 34 of the Radical Right Collection, Hoover Institution on War, Revolution, and Peace, Stanford University, Palo Alto, California. On McBirnie's role in the Goldwater campaign as well as his relationship to Reagan, see Dallek, *Right Moment*, 118–119, 226–227, and "Reagan Charges Democrats Stole McBirnie Letter; Candidate Admits Pastor Conceived His Campaign Slogan 'Creative Society,'" *Los Angeles Times*, 14 October 1966.

99. *Southern California Crusade Bulletin*, September 1969, BGEA; Team Office—Executive Assistant for Team Activities, collection 12, box 16, folder 39, BGEA.

100. See "Mrs. Billy Graham: Lunching with 11,000," *Christianity Today*, 24 October 1969; "11,000 Women Hear Mrs. Billy Graham's 'Design for Living,'" *Fullerton News*, 16 September 1969.

101. "Anaheim Crusade: At Home with the Angels," *Christianity Today*, 24 October 1969, 40.

102. The total attendance for the ten-day crusade was 384,000, with 20,336 professing to have had a salvation experience. These numbers paled in comparison to Graham's four-week Los Angeles Crusade of 1963, at which more than 900,000 people went through the turnstiles. But on average, the Anaheim crusade brought in more people per night than previous crusades and was thereby considered a marked success. See Team Office—Executive Assistant for Team Activities, Southern California 1969, box 16, folder 46, BGEA. Team Office—Executive Assistant for Team Activities, collection 12, box 16, folder 39, BGEA.

103. Governor Ronald Reagan gave the welcome on the opening night of the crusade. See Team Office—Executive Assistant for Team Activities, Southern California 1969. A full account of the proceedings was offered in "At Home With the Angels," *Christianity Today*, 24 October 1969, 40, 45.

104. "Anaheim Crusade," 45.

PART TWO

I was having lunch in San Francisco's Chinatown on the day the International Olympic Committee announced that Beijing would host the 2008 Summer Olympics. From my table at a sidewalk café, I watched as suddenly and quite unexpectedly the streets filled with thousands of cheering and flag-waving Chinatown residents. Within minutes, banners celebrating Beijing's status as host city stretched across the narrow streets, and vendors hawking Beijing Olympics T-shirts appeared as if by magic on nearby street corners. Amid the revelry, I could imagine North Beach, San Francisco's traditionally Italian neighborhood in summer 1955, when residents found out that Rome would host the 1960 Summer Olympics, or four years later, when people in Japantown heard that Tokyo would become the first city in Asia to host the games, or in 1963 in the Mission District, when Latinos celebrated Mexico City's choice as the 1968 Olympic site. Here in the West's densest city, the diversity of the region comes into remarkable focus. The West is home to many of the nation's largest populations of Latinos, Asian Americans, and Native Americans, and it has been the destination for much of the postwar emigration of African Americans.

The incredible diversity of the West has created a modern political dynamic that is, in most cases, radically different from that of the rest of the nation. Huge numbers of immigrants from Central and South America moving into the South and the Midwest have only recently forced residents to rethink the biracial model that has defined so many American, especially southern, communities. As Indian casinos pop up across the nation, more Americans are coming to realize what westerners have known for decades: that Native Americans have a special legal relationship with the state and federal governments. As the rest of the nation begins to look more western in its racial and ethnic diversity, the political models that have evolved in western cities, such as San Francisco (and Denver, Seattle, and Albuquerque), will become more and more common nationally. In this section of essays, our contributors examine the graphic transformation of the West's minority communities and discover an emerging political pattern that is no longer provincial but, rather, national and transformative.

While historians of western politics have long looked to the Populist and Progressive movements as the sources of western liberalism, our next set of essays explores a newer form of liberalism that celebrates diversity and articulates claims for racial and social justice. Michael Steiner argues that it was the moral geography of western multiculturalism as expressed by writer, thinker, and regionalist Carey McWilliams that provided the catalyst for a political ideology that celebrated difference as central to western identity. Through McWilliams, Steiner wrests the idea of regionalism from its parochial and reactionary definitions and reworks region into a space where cultures, people, and ideas come together to create a place marked by a new regional consciousness that is greater than the sum of it parts.

Ignacio Garcia helps us understand the complexities of western politics as he looks through the prism of Chicano political culture. In this analytic overview, he not only lays out the progression of Chicano political involvement but also explains how and why a complex and often contradictory constituency has been and is still too often portrayed as a blunt, monolithic force. By delving into the historical and contemporary nuances of what he calls the "rural metropolis," Garcia reveals the generational, economic, and social forces that drive this most significant ethnic constituency.

With the incredible growth of Indian casinos across the nation (in 2007, thirty-one states had Indian gaming), the issues and ideas that dominate the discourse of intertribal politics have entered the national political consciousness. In his essay on the development of a national Native American political culture, Bradley Shreve explains how the cornerstones of intertribal Indian politics—tribal sovereignty, treaty rights, self-determination, and cultural retention—revolutionized Indian Country. Focusing on national intertribal organizations, Shreve also shows how Native American politics have reflected and influenced federal and state policy.

Unpacking the biracial model that has for too long dominated our discussion of the politics of race, Scott Tang demonstrates the practical reasons that racial coalitions in western cities worked or did not work, according to circumstances. Basing his study in postwar San Francisco, Tang explains how the civil rights movement unfolded in a city with many different races and ethnicities and far from the centers of the movement in the American South. With different racial groups, each with its own history of subordination, contests over physical spaces often became battles over each group's place in the city's racial hierarchy.

CHAPTER 5

The Politics of Place: Carey McWilliams and Radical Regionalism

Michael Steiner

There are healthy forms of regionalism, but rigid, ideological regionalism is usually dangerous. Nothing is more anathema to a serious radical than regionalism.
Henry Nash Smith, 1980[1]

In the 1930s I became, and have remained, an unreconstructed, unapologetic radical.... In a sense I have been a socialist for many years, but I have never known a socialist party or movement with which I could identify.... And I have never been a member of the Communist Party.... But had I been accused of being a radical (western style), I would readily have pleaded guilty.
Carey McWilliams, 1979[2]

"America is West," poet Archibald MacLeish famously declared in 1929.[3] These three simple words highlight the persistent belief that everything exceptional about the United States is rooted in the western experience. The West—as an idea, process, and place—is seen as the source of American distinctiveness, and as this book demonstrates, American politics have always had a distinctly western flavor. From the mid-nineteenth-century clash over free-soil and slave frontiers to the subsequent sprouting of Populist, Progressive, New Left, New Right, environmental, and racial-ethnic causes into our own times, the West has been a seedbed of American political development.[4] There are many reasons why the West has been our political wellspring and testing ground, and a useful way to grasp the region's pivotal role is to consider fundamental questions about the relationship between place, people, and politics. Perhaps the most effective way to bring such abstract issues down to earth is to examine moments of history when Westerners became keenly aware of the political dimensions of their regional identity and to explore the work of self-conscious regionalists who forged political positions from their western sense of place.

There have been many periods when questions of place became paramount, and westerners from across the spectrum have pondered the political implications of these questions. The 1920s and '30s were such an era, and social critic Carey McWilliams (1906–1980) was such a regional thinker and activist. As authentic a westerner as Barry Goldwater or Ronald Reagan, his near contemporaries and ideological opposites, McWilliams grew up on a ranch working with cowboys yet never felt the need to wear a cowboy hat to prove his western credentials. Growing up in mountain ranchlands in Colorado and coming of age in multicultural Los Angeles, he embraced a vast cross-section of the West. His career as an agrarian- and proletarian-rooted regionalist breaks stereotypes about the role of place and politics in the American West. Rather than waxing nostalgic about the western land and folk, Carey McWilliams delighted in puncturing regional myths, stirring a sense of injustice, and inspiring younger western writers to uncover challenging features of their region. Among those he directly motivated were Theodore Roszak and Hunter S. Thompson, whom he encouraged to write about the 1960s counterculture and the Hell's Angels, respectively.[5]

Fittingly described as "a sardonic Galahad, constant to the democratic grail,"[6] McWilliams fearlessly defended persecuted minorities, from unjustly condemned Mexican American youths and relocated Japanese Americans during World War II to blacklisted ex-communists and civil rights advocates during the McCarthy and Nixon eras. McWilliams was both a self-proclaimed "chauvinistic westerner" and an "unreconstructed, unapologetic radical."[7] His social justice politics and radical regionalism—are embedded in a profound sense of people and place and in a critical understanding of the complex interaction between groups of people and the geographic settings of their lives. As we will see, McWilliams was a regionalist by virtue of his vision of California as a testing ground for labor and race relations, and he was a "radical" in the deepest sense of the term: His fierce sense of injustice drove him to the root of social problems and demanded thorough social change.

Drawing on a neglected nineteenth-century tradition of utopian and socialist protest that he perceived as "the hidden spring of California progressivism,"[8] McWilliams's radical politics of place underscore the fact that regionalism can be rooted in urban as well as rural landscapes, can be inspired by immigrant and working-class concerns, and can be steeped in a critical as well as an elegiac love of the land. As we will see, his distinctive radical regionalism defies the standard image of regionalism as an inherently conservative impulse and offers a progressive alternative to politics in the West. To weigh the larger significance of such radical western regionalism and McWilliams's role within it, it is important to place regionalism within a larger historical pattern and to trace the emergence of his politics from particular times and places within California and the West.

VARIETIES OF WESTERN REGIONALISM

The 1920s and '30s marked the golden era of American regionalism. Broadly defined as a people's sense of belonging to the portion of the earth they inhabit and an awareness of the interaction between people and place at the subnational level, regionalism and regional awareness can evolve into a conscious cultural impulse and social cause.[9] Beginning in the wake of World War I and fading by the early years of World War II, regionalism captured the imaginations of artists and intellectuals, policy makers and politicians. The title of a 1933 essay by Benjamin Botkin, "We Talk about Regionalism—North, East, South, and West," captures a glimpse of this widespread concern, and assertions of regional consciousness and sense of place were especially strong in the trans-Mississippi West.[10]

Cropping up all over the western map, self-proclaimed regionalists ranged from cliques of English professors in New Mexico, Oklahoma, Montana, and California to groups of New Deal planners in the Columbia, Colorado, and Missouri river basins, from maverick intellectuals as different as J. Frank Dobie, Bernard DeVoto, and Walter Prescott Webb to writers as varied as Mary Austin, Mari Sandoz, and Vardis Fisher. During the 1920s, scores of little magazines began promoting the spirit of western place, and by the 1930s footloose journalists, novelists, and photographers—often stirred by the racial, economic, and environmental tumult in the West—scoured the landscape to discover, in Alfred Kazin's words, "a whole world of marvels on the continent to possess—a world of rivers and scenes, of folklore and regional culture, of a heroic tradition to reclaim and of forgotten heroes to follow."[11]

This was neither the first nor the last time Westerners would study the land and declare their pride of place. Like American regionalism in general, western regionalism has had an episodic history with a sharp political edge. Regional consciousness emerged in the trans-Mississippi West toward the end of the nineteenth century in many forms—including local color writing, architecture, and arts and crafts in parts of the West—but regional consciousness was most powerfully expressed as fierce indignation against the moneyed powers of the East. What Robert Hine has described as "a cultural voice as strong and dominant as a prairie wind" resounded across the West.[12]

The region that would become a bastion of the New Right by the late twentieth century was once a stronghold of the Left. Describing the "periodic bouts of leftism" that convulsed early Kansas—the fiery protests of John Brown and Carry Nation, the wide readership of the socialist journal *Appeal to Reason*, the lionization of Eugene Debs and Robert LaFollette—Thomas Frank has speculated that "it was as though the blank landscape prompted dreams of a blank-slate society, a place where institutions might be remade as the human mind saw fit."[13] Henry George's and Frank Norris's California-based crusades against land and railroad oligarchies, Elizabeth Mary Lease's fiery Kansas Populism, Oklahoma's socialist Green Corn Rebellion, and William "Big Bill" Haywood's Rocky Mountain–rooted labor radicalism—these movements capture the essence of western regional protest as the nineteenth century gave way to the twentieth.

A hundred years later, self-conscious western regionalism is again riding high. A complicated tangle of New Right and New Left politics, environmental protest, racial-ethnic awareness, and intellectuals touting a "New Western" regionalism on public and academic stages, this current incarnation echoes both the political fervor of the turn of the century and the cultural rediscovery of the interwar decades.[14] To chart the political dimensions of self-conscious western regionalism over the past century is an immense task, but the best place to begin is with the interwar decades, when the topic was most widely debated and when a spectrum of westerners grappled with the meanings of this protean impulse.

Scholars who have mapped the contours of interwar regionalism usually interpret these regionalists as cranky reactionaries building foolish barriers against the acids of modernity and the tides of pluralism and progress. Western regionalists—especially when they move from aesthetic to ideological stands—seem susceptible to such antimodern excesses. From Webb, Dobie, Fisher, and Austin in the 1930s to Edward Abbey, Mike Foreman, Barry Goldwater, Ronald Reagan, George W. Bush, and other voices of the sagebrush, Earth First! the counterculture, the New Right, and the neoconservatives in our own times, western regionalists often fit an intransigent, antiurban, even xenophobic mold.

Reactionary regionalists abounded in the 1930s and in our times. Such proclamations as Austin's neoprimitivist praise for the bracing tonic of "the aboriginal poetic orgy," for example, or Dobie's assertion that it is better for a Texan "to go out and listen to coyotes singing at night in the prickly pear" than to read classic New England writers—whom he called "dreary creatures . . . utterly foreign to the genius of the Southwest"—reflect the diehard stance often taken by western regionalists. Webb's paean to the Texas Rangers and condemnation of the "ditch water" blood and "cruel streak in the Mexican nature" echoes the racism often heard among regionalists. "The one thing we could do for a country like Mexico," Abbey fumed in 1982, "is to stop every illegal immigrant at the border, give him a good rifle and a case of ammunition, and send him home. Let the Mexicans solve their customary problems in their customary manner."[15] Certainly not every western regionalist has been a hidebound racist and reactionary, and certainly Austin, Dobie, Webb, Abbey, and others were often purposely provocative, but Botkin's 1937 observation that "regionalism has received a black eye from its association with lost causes" rings true as a warning to any one attempting to forge a progressive regional stance.[16]

Denunciations of western regionalism as treacherous sectionalism or narrow-minded provincialism have been standard fare from the time that prairie Populists were derided as "Calamity Howlers" bent on dismembering the union in the 1890s, or New Mexico regionalists were mocked for "retreating into the kiva" in the 1930s.[17] Though some observers bluntly dismissed regionalism as "a petty patchwork carried on by misfits," others detected in it more ominous problems, charging, for example, "almost every one of the ideas of the regionalist credo could be matched more or less verbatim from the writings of Nazi experts on art."[18]

Such retorts continue in our own times as critics warn that "once in the bloodstream, regionalism is as hard to expunge as dengue fever." Some condemn western regionalism as a misguided rejection of modernity; others argue that it "concocts for us a pacifying, relaxing, New Age image of organic traditions and communities" and is stone deaf to the "multicultural Babel" of contemporary life.[19] If it isn't rejected as a reactionary retreat, regionalism is disdained, in the words of another observer, as a form of "boosterism, a fatuous puffing of merely local talent—a kind of literary chamber of commerce juxtaposed to the three national congresses of race, class, and gender."[20] Musing about the potentially "poisonous" consequences of regional appeals to the land, the folk, and "listening to the purposeful earth," erstwhile western regionalist Henry Nash Smith bluntly told me in 1980 that although "there are healthy forms of regionalism, ideological regionalism is usually dangerous. Nothing is more anathema to a serious radical than regionalism."[21]

Despite the persistence of a truculent, reactionary strain in the West, there are other western regionalists who deserve greater attention. As we have seen, Smith's close friend and fellow cultural critic, Carey McWilliams, was the most prominent spokesperson for what can be seen as an alternative radical leftist regionalism that found its strongest voice in California. Although western regionalism has been saddled with reactionary baggage, there has also been a vital countertradition of a pluralistic, even proletarian regionalism in the West, and McWilliams's early career, from the early 1920s to the late 1930s, offers a case study of the tangled politics of western regionalism and a prime example of how a devoted regionalist could achieve a progressive political stance.

Keenly aware of both the strengths and weaknesses of regionalism, McWilliams would forge a powerful brand of western regionalism by drawing upon, in his own words, a "deeply-rooted indigenous radicalism, which has been consistently 'socialist' and 'utopian', with the emphasis on social and racial equality." As we will see, McWilliams's mature sense of being a "western-style" radical and his critical regional stance and passionate sense of place would pioneer the way for pluralist, cosmopolitan versions of western regionalism that have become increasingly possible in our own time.[22] As a precursor of the progressive regionalism of contemporary cultural critics Richard Rodriguez, Joan Didion, Patricia Limerick, Daniel Kemmis, Barbara Kingsolver, Terry Tempest Williams, Gloria Anzaldua, Luis Valdez, Ronald Takaki, John Sayles, and others, McWilliams's effort to forge regionalism on the left offers a key insight to the tangled politics of place in the West.

A REGIONALIST ON THE LEFT

At first glance, regionalism seems a small part of McWilliams's monumental legacy. Usually remembered as the feisty, long-term editor of the *Nation* and chronicler of California's quirky culture, McWilliams is now being celebrated for even more heroic feats. After years of relative neglect, McWilliams's star is on the rise as scholars rediscover his role as public intellectual, pioneer in race relations, precursor of the "new western" history, prescient environmentalist, and fearless advocate for civil rights. Although Forrest Robinson has complained that few students of the American West, especially those under forty, would recognize McWilliams's name, it is clear that he is now emerging as a patron saint of regional and racial history. Deeply impressed with McWilliams's all-embracing geohistorical vision, Mike Davis has extolled him as "the Walter Prescott Webb of California, if not its Fernand Braudel," while Kevin Starr has declared, "All efforts to interpret California through narrative analysis . . . are a series of footnotes to Carey McWilliams. . . . every writer on California becomes . . . a toiler in the vineyard that McWilliams first surveyed and planted."[23]

McWilliams has recently been reclaimed as a pioneer in understanding the cultural construction of race and praised for seeing beyond the traditional black/white dichotomy to envision the role of Latinos, Asians, Pacific

Islanders, and Native Americans in our racial system. A proponent of multiculturalism and diversity decades before the words became overused clichés, McWilliams stands out, in Matthew Frye Jacobson's words, "for his refusal to lose sight of the overall complexity of the American mosaic and for his refusal to make 'race' identical with 'the Negro' in American political life."[24] According to Michael Willard, McWilliams's prescient work on borderlands migration and on race and labor relations in California prefigured "central concerns of the environmental justice movement" and "anticipated American studies' attention to racialized representation, cultural exchange, and hybrid identity in national and transnational contexts."[25] Asserting that "McWilliams is that rarest of chroniclers of a time and a place who gets more, rather than less, important with each passing decade," William Deverell simply concludes: "We are all his students." He was a versatile thinker and brilliant writer who could be both hilariously funny and fiercely indignant, a champion of the underprivileged and a gadfly of the establishment. It is inspiring to encounter such a mind and learn from such a teacher, and it is easy to understand how talk of McWilliams can, in Catherine Corman's words, quickly soar "into a pure love-fest, ending with blanket endorsement."[26]

Love-fests and blanket endorsements do not cover every portion of McWilliams's career, however. Scholars are not likely to celebrate his early years as a literary regionalist and contributor to the aesthetic regionalism so rampant during the interwar decades. Carey's writing career was sparked in the mid-1920s by a Whitmanesque urge to trumpet the gaudy wonders of Los Angeles, his adopted city, over the rooftops of the world. Inspired by two seemingly antithetical mentors—Mary Austin and H. L. Mencken—young McWilliams began publishing zesty regionalist essays in the late 1920s and early 1930s. With their unlikely mixture of Austin's earthbound mysticism and Mencken's smart-set cynicism, these youthful efforts seem to have little relation to the passionately engaged, politically charged masterpieces that McWilliams produced by the late 1930s.

In a ten-year burst of Herculean productivity between 1939 and 1949, McWilliams wrote eight prophetic books devoted to searing public issues. *Factories in the Field* (1939), *Ill Fares the Land* (1942), *Brothers under the Skin* (1943), *Prejudice; Japanese-Americans: Symbol of Racial Intolerance* (1944), *Southern California: An Island on the Land* (1946), *A Mask for Privilege: Anti-Semitism in America* (1948), *North from Mexico: The Spanish Speaking People of the United States* (1949), and *California: The Great Exception* (1949)—these penetrating, impassioned works changed the American intellectual landscape. Written amid a frenzied public life as a crusading civil rights attorney and a progressive state official that made him a lightning rod for right-wing fury, this spirited outpouring is rightly viewed as McWilliams's intellectual legacy. Deeply

Carey McWilliams as an H. L. Mencken–inspired literary regionalist, early 1930s. As a young lawyer and man-about-town in the late 1920s and early 1930s, McWilliams published sharp-edged, sardonic portraits of cultural and literary landscapes in Los Angeles, California, and the West. Photograph by Will Connell, 1933. UCLA Department of Special Collections, courtesy of Will Connell Jr.

probing yet widely accessible, imbued with a sense of injustice and ironic irreverence, these books stand as prose masterpieces. In many ways a potent blend of George Orwell, Howard Zinn, and Patricia Limerick at their best, they are a model of engaged radical writing, a continual wellspring of ideas, and the direct inspiration for scores of contemporary historians and cultural critics.[27]

In light of this monumental achievement, McWilliams's early regionalist

Carey McWilliams as public figure and politically engaged regionalist, early 1940s. By the early 1940s, McWilliams was deeply immersed in California-based social and political causes. After capturing national attention through *Factories in the Field* (1939), with its radical proposal to redistribute extensive agricultural holdings, McWilliams served, among other commitments, as chief of the state's Division of Immigration and Housing (1939–1943), national chair of the Sleepy Lagoon Defense Committee (1942–1944), and spokesperson against wartime racism and Japanese relocation (1942–1945). Courtesy of Nancy McWilliams, Daniel Geary, and the estate of Wilson Carey McWilliams.

efforts seem trivial and even at cross-purposes with most of his career. As I have already noted, interwar regionalism, which launched him as a writer, is usually dismissed as a narrow-minded, backward-yearning impulse. Whether chided as precious primitivists hiding from the world or indicted as dangerous fascists evoking the land and folk, western regionalists were pummeled from the center and the left of the political spectrum. Against this onslaught, it still seems treacherous for anyone on the left to be a regionalist.

McWilliams, while acknowledging regionalism's penchant for poisoning Progressive ideals, was nonetheless drawn to many of its values. Immersed in literary regionalism yet attracted to left-wing radicalism, Carey experienced and understood the inner workings of what might be called the regional dilemma as profoundly as any public intellectual, then or now. Over a five-year period, from 1927 to 1932, he experienced a tug-of-war between literary and political commitments, between local and national contexts. He was torn between a deeply felt sense of place that demanded focused regional narration and an unswerving sense of injustice that compelled broad political action.

Toward the end of his life, McWilliams looked back over these pivotal years and his solution to the dilemma. "I got interested in this regional thing in part through Mary Austin," he recalled in a 1978 interview. "The Southern Agrarians were around and making noises. . . . And this was not quite like that, but it was the feeling that there should be more attention paid to western history, western writing. . . . It seemed . . . as though this might develop into something important. It had the potential of that, but as the Depression deepened, regionalism was sort of pushed aside." In his autobiography he wrote, "These literary interests swiftly receded as the Depression deepened. After 1932 I was writing almost exclusively about social issues, politics, and labor."[28]

Although McWilliams seemed to renounce self-conscious regionalism in favor of left-wing activism early in his career, a deep-seated critical regionalism—a profound sense of the interaction of people and place—remained the driving force and focal point of McWilliams's best work. His magisterial books on California, the West, labor, and race relations are grounded in the immediate experiences of people in place—individuals and groups interacting in Los Angeles barrios and movie lots, San Joaquin Valley cotton fields and Orange County citrus groves, San Francisco's waterfront, and the Sierra goldfields. This dynamic vision of things taking place and critical affection for the teeming land and life around him imparted rare power and poignancy to McWilliams's writing. By the late 1930s he had forged a distinctive radical regional voice and had become the most prominent spokesman for an alternative pluralistic regionalism that found its strongest voices in California and the West.

Beginning in the mid-1920s as a Mencken-inspired aesthete debunking the vulgarity of mass culture, McWilliams had become a fierce champion of the downtrodden masses by the mid-1930s. By 1939, with the publication of *Factories in the Field*, with its advocacy of statewide collectivization of all large-scale farms, McWilliams would be denounced by agribusiness as "Agricultural Pest No. 1, worse than pear blight or boll weevil."[29] With this sweeping, passionate account of economic, racial, and environmental injustice, McWilliams found his radical regional voice. Championing civil rights and free speech and forging a link between the abuse of nature and the mistreatment of minority groups, McWilliams directly inspired Cesar Chavez and helped lay the groundwork for the California-based student, countercultural, and environmental movements of the 1960s and '70s. Drawing attention to the capitalist exploitation of the land and of the Chinese, Japanese, Mexican, Filipino, and poor white migrants who worked it, he demonstrated the power of regionalism on the left for the 1930s and for the present.[30]

How McWilliams achieved this radical regionalism and his relationship to other self-styled proletarian western regionalists, including Louis Adamic, John Steinbeck, Paul S. Taylor, Benjamin Botkin, Kenneth Rexroth, Tillie Olson, Woody Guthrie, Carlos Bulosan, Jack Conroy, and others, is but one chapter in an astonishingly active, widely involved life. In tracing the emergence of McWilliams's voice of regional dissent between 1923 and 1937 and finally evaluating its relevance for our own times, I will focus on crucial moments—turning points and epiphanies—that marked his evolution from an aesthetic to a politically impassioned regionalism.[31]

THE EDUCATION OF A WESTERN RADICAL

On 18 March 1922, seventeen-year-old Carey McWilliams arrived by train in Los Angeles from his home state of Colorado. He had just been expelled from the University of Denver after a disastrous St. Patrick's Day drinking spree, and his fall from grace paralleled the collapse of his family's fortunes. His father, Jerry McWilliams, a prosperous rancher and state legislator from Steamboat Springs, lost everything in the post–World War I agricultural depression, and when he died penniless and unexpectedly in 1921, Carey's mother and older brother moved to Los Angeles to restart their lives. Memories of his father crushed by indifferent economic forces haunted Carey throughout his life and ignited his sense of social injustice, but when he joined his mother and brother in Los Angeles in 1922, his mind was occupied by more immediate impressions. In the 1920s, Southern California was bursting at the seams as the final gathering point for the westering frontier, and after the initial shock over the contrast between the panoramic beauty of his birthplace and the tawdry squalor of Los Angeles, young McWilliams embraced his new region with wonder-struck gusto.

His diary, begun on New Year's Day 1923 and continued through the 1970s, quickly filled with the high-spirited notes of an eighteen-year-old keenly sensitive to the exotic landscape and surging spectacle of the place. Fittingly enough, the first two entries introduced themes that would preoccupy him throughout his life: the creation of regional identity and the dynamics of racial prejudice. The Rose Parade, he noted, "is a big advertising campaign . . . in such a superb setting, the Arroyo Seco Bridge hanging like a pattern of lace in the night!" And a few days later, after riding a streetcar back from his clerking job at the Los Angeles *Times*, he recalled how "an old, middle-class Jew was being made fun of by a conductor, and he replied, 'Ah, But I respect everything—even every little child'—Beautiful sentiment,—precisely what I would think *were I a Jew*."[32]

Carey's first job, hunting down deadbeats who refused to pay their advertising bills to the *Times*, thrust him into the city's less respectable underside; at the same time, taking courses at the University of Southern California (USC) introduced him to the region's literary cliques and budding intelligentsia. In nearly the same breath as describing streets swarming with "Bums, drunks, fruiters and the scenes of God's creation," Carey also noted the joy of reading H. L. Mencken, Mary Austin, George Sterling, Robinson Jeffers, and Ambrose Bierce and of hearing Upton Sinclair speak to the USC Quill Club on literature and "the social revolution."[33] Within the space of a few weeks in early 1923, he witnessed Sister Aimee Semple McPherson preaching at the Angelus Temple and expressed "the mad desire to laugh, to drink, to jazz around," and got "drunk as an idiot pauper" at the "Turkish Village,—danced with cabaret belle."[34]

A prolific wunderkind, McWilliams began law school in 1926 even as he started running with the Los Angeles bohemian fast set. He also began publishing scores of articles on literary regionalism in magazines across the country and launched his first book, a biography of Ambrose Bierce. The frenzied years between 1926 and 1929 marked the peak of Carey's career as a literary rebel and self-conscious regionalist. A lively intellectual circle—described as a "sizzling sort of fellowship"[35] including poet Hildegarde Flanner, painter Kim Weber, book dealers Jake Zeitlin and Stanley Rose, writers Herbert Klein, John Fante, William Saroyan, and Louis Adamic—broadened his experience and expressive skills. More-distant literary mentors—

Mencken, Austin, and Bierce—sharpened his fascination for capturing the quirks and varied textures of the American land and folk.

But most of all, the surging land and life of the region precipitated his creative genius. One of his earliest essays, simply titled "Los Angeles" (1927), is filled with attraction and repulsion for the place. "Los Angeles is a harlot city—gaudy, flamboyant, richly scented, sensuous, noisy, jazzy," he wrote. "More and more the place takes on the aspect of a gigantic three-ring circus. . . . a mad world—a democratic brothel. . . . The very showiness of the place attracts, like an enormous scarlet beetle or the huge amethyst ring of a bishop."[36] Young McWilliams soaked up the spirit of the place with boundless fervor, and twenty years later he would lovingly recall 1920s Los Angeles as "a great circus without a tent" where "ducks waddled along the streets with advertisements painted on their backs; six-foot-nine pituitary giants with sandwich board signs stalked the downtown streets; while thousands of people carrying Bibles in their hands and singing hymns marched in evangelical parades. With its peep-shows, shooting galleries, curio shops, health lectures, and all-night movies, Main Street became a honky-tonk alley that never closed."[37]

And in one of the most powerful passages in American regional writing—a paragraph now etched in granite in Pershing Square in Los Angeles—McWilliams recounted how his conflicted feeling about "this weirdly inflated village" changed one morning in 1929 after seven years of exile "haunted by memories of a boyhood spent in the beautiful mountain parks, the timberline country, of northwestern Colorado":

> I had spent an extremely active evening in Hollywood and had been deposited toward morning, by some kind soul, in a room at the Biltmore Hotel. Emerging next day from the hotel into the painfully bright sunlight, I started my rocky pilgrimage through Pershing Square to my office in a state of miserable decrepitude. In front of the hotel newsboys were shouting the headlines of the hour: an awful trunk-murder had just been committed; the district attorney had just been indicted for bribery; Aimee Semple McPherson had once again stood the town on its ear by some spectacular caper; a University of Southern California football star had been caught robbing a bank; a love-mart had been discovered in the Los Feliz Hills . . . there was news about another prophet, fresh from the desert, who had predicted the doom of the city, a prediction for which I was morbidly grateful. In the center of the park I stopped to watch, a little self-conscious of my evening clothes, a typical Pershing Square divertissement: an aged and frowzy blonde, skirts held high above her knees, cheered by a crowd of gri-

macing and leering old goats, was singing a gospel hymn as she danced gaily around the fountain. Then it suddenly occurred to me that in all the world, there never was nor would there ever be another place like the City of the Angels. Here the American people were erupting, like lava from a volcano; here, indeed, was the place for me—a ringside seat at the circus.[38]

With equally loving descriptions of the region's dazzling natural landscape and of money-mad migrants mistreating it, McWilliams hoped that Westerners might someday learn to live up to the promise of their land and finally create the "great city on the Pacific, the most fantastic city in the world."[39] Written in 1946, this clear-eyed critical affection for a people and a place—this sardonic portrait of a weirdly wondrous place that deserves more from the people who dwell in it—represents the zenith of McWilliams's regional vision and stands as a hallmark of American regional writing.

McWilliams remembered his rocky pilgrimage across Pershing Square in 1929 as an epiphany and turning point in his sense of place and power as a writer. Yet it would take at least three more years—a period marked by an intensifying political consciousness and a widening geographic perspective—before he found his voice of radical regional dissent. By the late 1920s, he had gained some fame for publishing a host of articles on local Los Angeles color and folklore and on cultural regionalism throughout California and the West. Appearing in magazines ranging from *Overland Monthly, Frontier,* and *Southwest Review* to *American Mercury, Harper's,* and *Saturday Review of Literature,* many of these articles championed the clusters of poets, painters, playwrights, folklorists, and editors who proclaimed themselves "new regionalists" in defiance of East Coast cultural domination. Mary Austin's influence is clear as McWilliams praises artists who learned to "Stay West" and evoke the spirit of their native grounds, while Mencken's voice echoes as he paints the wondrous possibilities and crude excesses of such art, extolling, for example, "the note of determined and powerful revolt" in Montana fiction yet debunking "the local poetess complex" in the Northwest, the "passion for western Americana" in the Southwest, and the infatuation with foolish "myths of the West" that hover "above and around all of us like a disembodied spirit murmuring strange incantations."[40]

Even such cynical regionalism would seem precious in light of the withering events of the 1930s. McWilliams's early cultural rebellion—even at its most biting moments—had little political content and only limited contact with the Left. Yet he sprinkled his writings with seeds of doubt about the power of art to change what seemed to be an increasingly corrupt, unjust society. On 23 August 1927, the day Nicola Sacco and Bartolomeo Vanzetti were executed, McWilliams interviewed Upton Sinclair in a dank cafeteria in Long Beach, and he recalled the sense of despair and deep anger toward the system that filled their conversation. A year later, in the summer of 1928, Carey and his close friend Louis Adamic drove up the Pacific Coast from Los Angeles, each gathering writing material—McWilliams for his Bierce biography, Adamic for *Laughing in the Jungle* (1932), his sprawling tragicomic treatment of the American scene. They stopped at Carmel to visit Robinson and Una Jeffers, and after walking the grounds of Tor House overlooking the rugged shoreline, both young writers were profoundly struck by Jeffers's bleak image of America as a "perishing Republic" and his dark prophecy of a civilization-ending decade to come. Jeffers's premonition marked a realization for both men that the Lost Generation world of the 1920s was ending and would "be followed by a time of turbulence and upheaval."[41]

The year 1929 brought further political awakening and geographic widening. By July McWilliams was reading extensively in the works of Lewis Mumford, Floyd Dell, Max Eastman, Waldo Frank, Mike Gold, and other East Coast radicals and musing at length in his diary "about the nature of radicalism."[42] In October, he traveled to New York City for the first time, beginning a complicated, lifelong relationship with the place where he would live and work for the last thirty years of his life.

Carey's first New York visit coincided with the stock market crash on 29 October 1929. But he was preoccupied with other things, especially going through the galleys for his book on Bierce and meeting as many of the city's radical intelligentsia as possible through Adamic, who had just moved there. He enjoyed seeing Louis and his Greenwich Village dancer friend, Stella Sanders, and he was exuberant about the birth of his first book, but he was disillusioned with New York's intellectual scene, whose radicalism struck him as rootless, superficial, and infected with insufferable condescension toward anyone or anything west of the Hudson River. He described Hart Crane, for example, as "a smart young ass with a cane," and he dismissed New York intellectuals who professed a Whitmanesque faith in "the redeeming efficacy of an indigenous culture" yet remained in "the dingy recesses of New York apartments" where they "prayed for the unregenerate hinterland."[43] McWilliams's New York immersion and train trip back across the continent magnified his western pride and sense of place. Looking through train windows as he swept past Chicago and Kansas City and through New Mexico, McWilliams dashed off rhapsodic, Jack Kerouac–like poems to such places and the sprawling immensity of the land. "The west, the west," he wondered, "what will come of the country here?"[44]

Back in Los Angeles, he began answering such questions about the West by intensifying his focus on the local scene and its vibrant cultural mixture.

He was also haunted by doubts about the social significance of his writing. In a journal entry for 12 December 1929, for example, in nearly the same paragraph as he noted the grotesque architecture along Wilshire Boulevard—"There is a great upwelling of puerile emotion and fancy; noisy, gaudy, blatant"—he also wondered about the larger importance of writing about such things. "Writers and artists should strive to be more in the foreground of events," he argued. "They should write things that *do*,—that act. . . . To merely write is a decoration but of doubtful value. There is a certain pleasure in action and reaction."[45]

This deepening fascination with the regional spectacle combined with concern that he write things "that *do*,—that act" redoubled over the next year. Searching for meaning in the seething, multiethnic city, he would write a two-page "Rhapsody on Entering the Arcade Building," describing its kaleidoscope of "cafeterias, lunch counters and soda fountains, cheap haberdasher shops," or he would simply note, "Los Angeles at lunch time . . . a nation of munching jaws."[46] "A chimerical land," he concluded, "swift-changing, fluid, time-annihilating . . . such a raucous strip—and the great lands to the West." He noted in a later entry that "The frontier historians should make a neat chapter out of Los Angeles, as the end of the trail. . . . Thousands coming here under such amazing conditions, it is not remarkable that confusion, and insanity, and great fear resulted."[47]

McWilliams's urge to write radical, socially significant regionalism filled his thirty-nine-page chapbook, *The New Regionalism in American Literature*, published late in 1930. A sweeping survey and stinging indictment of much of the regionalist movement, it also projected hope for a more critically engaged regionalism. Lambasting what Mumford, DeVoto, and others would decry as the "besetting weakness" of regionalism and its many backward-yearning enthusiasts, McWilliams complained, "The new regionalists reveal a typical modern tendency in their attempt to escape from the tumultuous present into a glamorous past." He continued, "In times so strenuous as ours, it is rather annoying to discover intelligent men devoting their talents to such tasks as listing the animals and plants in Oklahoma folk cures and noting, with infantile delight, the eroticisms in the folk-speech of taxi-drivers." The new regionalists, he argued, "have shown little interest in the proletarian heroes of the modern age." They "shun present problems with even greater dexterity" than had the old local colorists, and they seemed to have only the most superficial connection to the land and life around them. "California, of course, has a poet for every realtor," he mocked. "Just how deep and abiding," he asked rhetorically, "is the infatuation of the regionalists for their land and its folk?"[48]

Despite such withering criticisms, McWilliams's manifesto contained seeds for a more grounded, socially significant regionalism. Properly practiced, regionalism gives the artist "familiarity with his environment," satisfies a thirst for community, and inspires critical affection for the land and life around him—a vigorous contrast to the typical eastern writer trapped "in some cul-de-sac from which he emits faint and waspish denunciations of his native land." "Despite its extravagant ambitions and occasional lapses in sense," McWilliams concluded, "regionalism has made Americans stand on their own legs," and, beginning in 1930, he would forge a radical, politically charged regionalism that helped Americans understand the deeper workings of their strenuous times.[49]

McWilliams's political education after 1930 was swift and dramatic. There is a world of difference, for example, between the flippant sarcasm of his 1930 essay "Swell Letters in California," a send-up of sentimental art, and the fierce indignation of the 1933 work "Getting Rid of the Mexican," an angry account of Mexican repatriation.[50] Of his shift from literary regionalist to labor journalist, McWilliams recalled that "if anyone had said in 1929 when the Bierce book was published that a few years later I would be writing a book about farm labor in California, I would have said they were off their rockers. . . . But it all changed so fast."[51]

Like his contemporary John Steinbeck, McWilliams was swept up in tidal waves of injustice and social ferment that reached their fiercest heights in California and the West. With its fervent strikes, migrations, and political radicalism, California was at the center of things, and, again like Steinbeck, he found it impossible to ignore the upheaval and outrage surging around him. His respectable life as a successful establishment lawyer and literary critic seemed pale and meaningless. "I'm quite discouraged about everything," he noted in his diary in August 1932. "I'm not pleased with my life, prospects, or achievements." Aroused by social injustice and dissatisfied, even bored, with his personal and professional life, McWilliams left his constraining marriage and lucrative law practice in 1934 to devote himself to labor activism and legal advocacy for victims of prejudice and poverty.[52]

A PLURALIST POLITICS OF PLACE

Heightened political and racial awareness imbued McWilliams's growth as a radical regionalist. His expressive power soared with his appreciation of the rich multiplicity of people and places and with his rising social consciousness and decision to join ranks with the underdog—the submerged multitudes that Adamic would describe as "shadow America." Through another friend, writer John Fante, McWilliams explored Bunker Hill's lower-class and ethnic neighborhoods, and he was introduced to the growing Filipino community in Los Angeles through the young writer Carlos Bulosan. His long-standing attraction to the region's seething cultural landscapes extended into prisons, ethnic neighborhoods, fields, and factories. Doing legal work in a prison, he was struck by its mixed multitude—"Negroes laughing, Mexicans, whites"— and visiting Boyle Heights on another legal errand, he noted that "You pass through the Japanese element. . . . Then you come to Mexican town. It is an amazing place. . . . a riotous disorder about everything."[53]

As early as 1932 McWilliams's journal entries were peppered with distress about Mexican repatriation, the rise of racial hate crimes, jobless friends pleading for money, and the brutal treatment of striking farm and factory workers across the state, often contrasting these struggles to California's stirring natural landscape. A scathing portrait of Depression-battered encampments in Riverside, for example, ends with the sight of "Temescal Canyon, the cottonwoods shimmering in the light," and his litany of violent strikes sweeping the state concludes with a description of wildflowers "in riotous bloom."[54] His anger toward the system reached a crescendo in January 1934. "If the times don't change soon," he wrote, "we'll be driven to desperate expedients. . . . You reach a point finally when you feel a responsibility to go out and bang tables, shout, and raise hell." He continued, "Here I am doling out help to a friend, and I have exactly $40.00 in the bank! The temptation at times is strong, to go out and *do something* for these people. . . . They are not to blame for being poor and jobless. . . . What they want is a set of ideas and a fight."[55]

This outburst marked a turning point for McWilliams. Beginning in 1934, he devoted himself to disturbing the established order; he worked as a labor lawyer and investigative writer; he was willing to "bang tables, shout, and raise hell" to help underrepresented people fight for more equitable lives, to give "shadow America" "a set of ideas and a fight." He recalled, "No experience did more to shape my political point of view than this brief engagement with labor. It pushed me beyond the liberalism of the period in the direction of a native American radicalism with which I could readily identify." He represented unions throughout the state—including Mexican American citrus workers in Orange County in 1934 and 1936, potash miners in the Mojave Desert in 1935, rank-and-file studio hands in Hollywood in 1936, and Filipino domestic workers in 1937.[56]

In May 1935, he took a twelve-day back-roads tour of California in a broken-down Dodge Roadster with journalist and schoolteacher Herbert Klein investigating labor relations and the rise of "farm fascism." Their experiences interviewing agricultural workers of every race and ethnicity and witnessing their abject poverty and appalling working and living conditions culminated in a series of fiery articles in 1936 that were incorporated three years later into *Factories in the Field* (1939)—a monument of multicultural proletarian regionalism and the beginning of his decade-long output of equally powerful conscience-driven, place-related masterpieces.[57] The 1935 tour was a deciding moment in his life. "Carey became a radical," his close friend Alice Greenfield McGrath recalled in 2005, "when he actually saw how migrant workers lived. ... The sight of those people—that's what transformed Carey's life."[58]

McWilliams was involved in a gamut of political activities during the 1930s, including participation in Upton Sinclair's ill-fated EPIC (End Poverty in California) campaign for governor in 1934, involvement in the defense committee for labor leader Harry Bridges and in numerous antifascist organizations, and four tumultuous years as director of the California Division of Immigration and Housing.[59] By the mid-1940s, amid the racial ferment of war, McWilliams developed a farsighted vision of multicultural regionalism—of the West Coast as America's "racial frontier" where "groupings of all the racial strains that have gone into the making of the American people," including Anglos, African Americans, Hispanics, and Asians, would interact, developing complex patterns of fusion and separation that would have vital implications for postwar America.[60] But two events in 1936 and 1937 signaled his deep commitment to a radical regionalism and reveal the roots of this pluralistic perspective. Carey's central role in the Western Writers' Congress in November 1936 and a series of impassioned letters written a year later mark the achievement of a forward-looking regionalism in which a fervent sense of justice was grounded in profound sense of place.

In July 1936, McWilliams agreed to be the key Southern California organizer for a gathering of progressive and left-wing writers to be held in San Francisco.[61] A regional offshoot of the first American Writers' Congress held in New York City in April 1935, the Western Writers' Congress was conceived as a forum for artists and intellectuals to discuss their relationship to pressing social, economic, and political problems. Part of the wider antifascist and Popular Front movements, the congress called upon "writers of America, particularly writers of the West, where the liberty-loving tradition of the pioneers is still fresh," to consider how their work could help workers and minorities in their struggle against the rising "forces of reaction."[62]

From his office on the eighth floor of the Arcade Building on Spring Street, McWilliams became a zealous promoter: calling local meetings, soliciting advice from organizers of a similar writers' congress in the Midwest, dashing off earnest invitations to all the progressive writers and intellectuals he knew in Hollywood, academia, and elsewhere.[63] Some 250 writers from across the West attended the three-day congress, which opened at San Francisco's Scottish Rite Auditorium on 13 November 1936. A cross-section of speakers—including Harry Bridges, Upton Sinclair, Humphrey Cobb, Dorothy Parker, Donald Ogden Stewart, Ella Winter, Sara Field, William Saroyan, and Nathanael West—talked on topics ranging from labor and race relations to fascist and progressive trends in the film industry. Although few focused upon the issue of regionalism and left-wing politics—McWilliams, for example, spoke about his experiences as a labor lawyer—the need for a radical western regionalism was a pervasive, unifying theme.[64] Poet Kenneth Rexroth came closest to confronting the issue directly. Declaring that "insofar as we are poets, we are enemies to this society" and noting that the "conditions for a regional renaissance are strong in the West today," he wisely concluded that the most compelling regional art may *seem* the least political. "It is quite conceivable," he argued, "that a sonnet about the moon, written by someone thoroughly aware of what he is talking about, might be much more effective than an agitational lyric by someone not so blessed."[65]

Two prominent communist writers who could not attend gave ringing though far less subtle endorsements of proletarian regionalism in the West. Singing a paean to western literary mavericks Mark Twain and Jack London as rebellious antifascist archetypes, Mike Gold avowed, "I am a Western writer only by adoption ... but I can feel the high beauty and terror and epic power of the region." Decrying the "spurious regionalism of the 'little' magazine" and the "reactionary regionalism" of many southern and western writers, Meridel LeSueur called for a forward-looking "regionalism of class roots, class history." She enjoined progressive writers to nurture such consciousness in their own regions "to create stronger and richer roots for the growth of the creative personality, a wider and richer audience."[66]

McWilliams was in many ways the catalyst for this groundswell of left-wing regionalism in California and the West, and with the publication of *Factories in the Field* in 1939, he emerged with Steinbeck as one of the two most powerful and accomplished spokespersons for this movement. Rather than analyzing the dynamics of this and the seven other regional masterpieces he published between 1939 and 1949—the subject of a book in itself—I will end with two 1937 letters that capture the essence and sweep of his newly found radical regional voice. One, written to McWilliams by a young professor, pays tribute to Carey's accomplishments; the other, written by McWilliams to one of his most intimate friends, relates an experience as momentous as his rocky pilgrimage across Pershing Square.

In early July 1937, Dudley Wynn, an English instructor at the University of New Mexico who had recently published several incisive critiques of the Southern Agrarians, Mary Austin, and the southwestern regionalists, wrote a striking letter to McWilliams. Praising McWilliams's and Louis Adamic's recent work and thanking Carey for his advice in writing about Mary Austin,

Wynn registered his disgust with the nostalgia-drenched, fascist-scented regionalism emanating from Nashville, Santa Fe, and other genteel enclaves. Calling for a full-blooded regionalism that would honor "this brawling, inchoate continent of ours" and evoke the peculiar energy "of our machines and our non-bookish hordes of people," Wynn paid homage to McWilliams's work. "The sympathies of the far-seeing American," he continued, "have to lie with the machine-tenders, the sit-down strikers, the gum-chewing stenographers, the hard-drinking, aimlessly fornicating mass—all of whom, to genteel eyes, look so hopeless, but with whom the future lies." Describing the need for a redeeming regionalism with "a good infusion of Whitman-like, Adamic-like lustiness and economic radicalism," Wynn extolled Carey McWilliams's achievements.[67]

Three months later, in early October 1937, Carey wrote a remarkable letter to his close friend Louis Adamic. It had been nine years since their Carmel meeting with Robinson Jeffers, which had been a harbinger of harsher, yet more electrifying, times. Adamic had dedicated his 1935 novel *Grandsons: A Story of American Lives* to McWilliams, and he in turn had published a laudatory monograph, *Louis Adamic and Shadow America,* later that year. In this letter, however, McWilliams shifted direction and took his friend to task for being duped by the United Fruit Company into writing a book, *The House in Antigua* (1937), that could be read as a romanticized account of economic imperialism in Guatemala. Concerned that Adamic had lost his critical edge and fervor, McWilliams vehemently complained, "There are no revolutionaries in America anymore! Don't you know that, following the new line, the Communists are defending the Constitution; draping themselves in the flag, etc. I confess that I'm somewhat intransigent, and that I like the old line better."[68]

After registering his disappointment with watered-down radicalism, Carey recounted what can only be termed a personal political epiphany—an experience he would reemphasize throughout his life. As a union lawyer, Carey had addressed 1,500 women walnut workers from a kaleidoscope of cultures gathered in a large hall in East Los Angeles. His words were translated into Armenian, Russian, Spanish, and Polish. "You should have been there," he wrote to Adamic, "to *feel* this thing: the excitement, the tension. And you should have watched some of those women as they got to their feet and tried to tell their experiences. . . . What profound meaning they conveyed! I felt, honestly, very weak, meaningless, and ineffectual." Many of the women held up fists that were swollen, bruised, and blackened from cracking walnuts by hand, and they complained that they would often slip on the scattered shells. A young, blond woman jumped up laughing, raced down the center aisle, bent over and lifted her skirt high to show McWilliams "a large black and blue mark right where you would expect it to be." The exuberant workers would applaud every time they heard the word "Organize!" "You felt stirred, profoundly stirred.... Such extraordinary faces!" he told his friend.[69]

This is the voice of radical regionalism at its best. If Carey's 1929 Pershing Square revelation revealed an astonishing love of place, his 1937 epiphany among the East Los Angeles walnut workers illuminated his impassioned urge for social justice. It was through such experiences in union halls, waterfronts, factories, and fields, in ethnic and working-class neighborhoods, among poor whites, Mexicans, Filipinos, Japanese, African Americans, and many other ethnic groups that McWilliams reached such expressive heights. And it was through a maelstrom of political events and a myriad of friends that he evolved from literary to political dissent and developed a profound grasp of the interaction between people and place within the city, state, and region he had grown to love so fiercely.

California in the 1930s was a racial frontier and a focal point of radical regionalism. Issues of race, class, and environment have always stood out more vividly in the West than in the rest of the nation. As Carey McWilliams hoped, the fires of social protest that flared so brilliantly in California in the 1930s are alive in other forms today. His environmental sensitivity, vision of racial diversity, maverick temperament, and passion for social justice—all firmly rooted in California, yet part of a larger though less visible liberal political tradition in the American West—seem increasingly relevant today.

In 1965, fourteen years after leaving Los Angeles to become editor of the *Nation,* McWilliams looked back on his career from his vantage point in New York. Proudly asserting his regional credentials as the first person from west of the Mississippi—indeed, the first person from west of the Bronx—to edit the hundred-year-old magazine, he then listed the most significant concerns in his life. "Somewhat in the order of their emergence," he wrote, "my special interests have been: organized labor and civil liberties, migratory farm labor, race relations, demagogic mass movement and, of course, all things related to California, its history, sociology, folkways, cults, population dynamics and politics—not to mention its coastline, mountain ranges, desert areas and lush valleys."[70]

A profound love for California—for its teeming cultures and matchless landscapes—was clearly the driving force of McWilliams's life as a writer and activist. A deep sense of place inspired his prose, and California (and to a degree, the entire West) provided a necessary framework for observing the grounded experiences of social movements and people's lives. Often the region's harshest critic, he could also be its strongest advocate. For McWilliams, California was not only a "racial frontier" and possible seedbed for America's multiracial future but also a testing ground for pressing issues of migration, labor, civil liberties, and the environment, among others. De-

Striking women cotton pickers, California's Central Valley, late 1933, photographed by Ralph H. Powell, 1933. Courtesy of the Bancroft Library, University of California, Berkeley, BANC PIC 1945.007:4.

claring that California's "population includes every ethnic strain, every racial type, every social class," McWilliams stressed that "sequences that take decades to unfold elsewhere are often enacted here in a few years—you can see the process taking place before your eyes, as though in slow motion."[71] Using California as a multicultural test case with inclusive possibilities for the nation and indeed the world as a whole, McWilliams's radical regionalism serves as an example of progressive politics of place that might emerge from any portion of the earth's surface.

By the late 1930s, Carey McWilliams had created a forward-looking, pluralistic regionalism that stands as a model for writers, artists, scholars, and ordinary people in our own time. In doing so, he was one of the rare Americans who could truly answer "yes" to Walt Whitman's haunting questions:

> Who are you indeed who would talk or sing to America?
> Have you studied out the land, its idioms and men?
> Have you learn'd the politics & geography, pride, freedom, friendship of the land? . . .
> Are you faithful to things? Do you teach what the land and the sea, the bodies of men, womanhood, amativeness, heroic angers teach?[72]

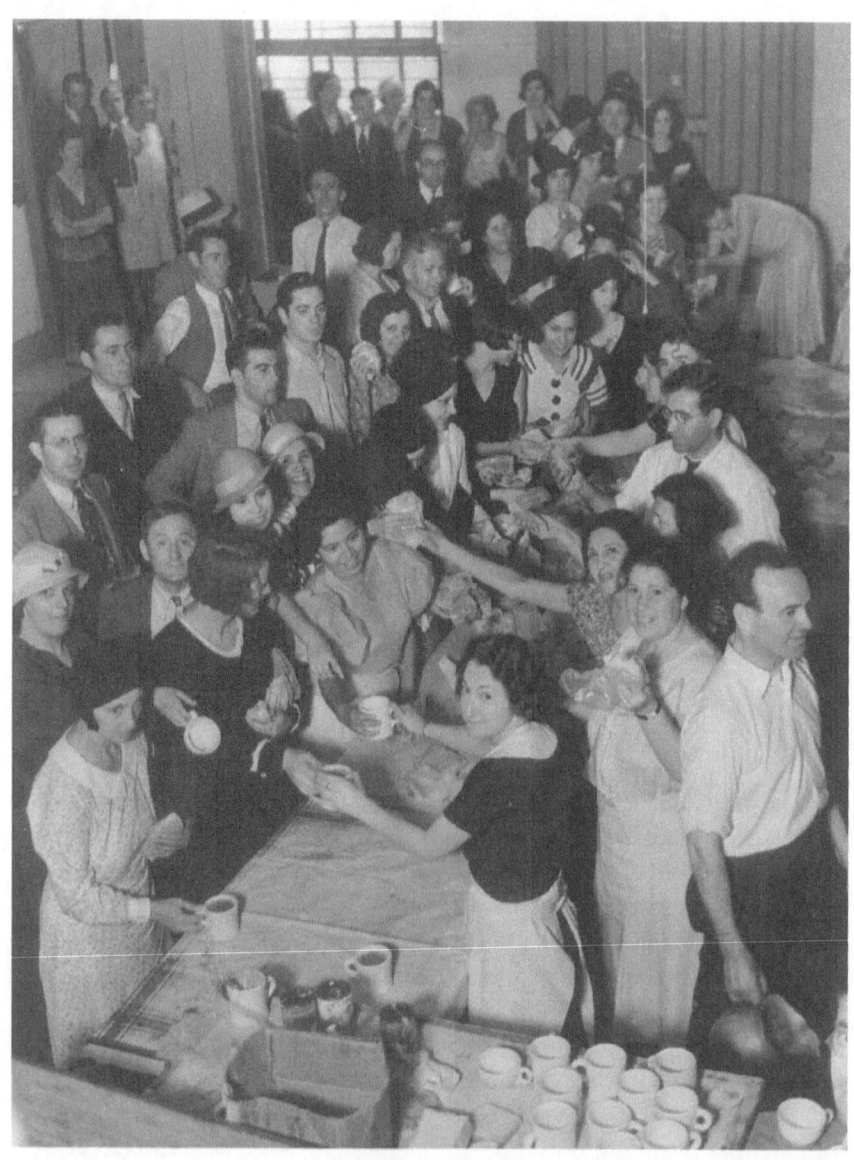

Striking Los Angeles garment workers and pickets being served lunch at strike headquarters, 19 October 1933. Courtesy of the Los Angeles Public Library, *Herald Examiner* Collection, HE-000-729.

As students of America's western political culture, we should find Whitman's provocative questions itching at our ears until we understand and answer them. Responding to the tumult of his times, Carey McWilliams truly "studied out the land"—learning to be faithful to its broad amplitude, its politics, geography, and "heroic angers." His powerful sense of place, his critical affection for the land and the astonishing diversity of people upon it, his grounded, politically engaged prose—all might stand as a prototype for a critical regionalism that could shape American politics and American life in general.

The radical regionalism that grew out of the 1930s might inspire us today. "The fires that burned so brightly—if briefly—in the best days of the 1930s," McWilliams observed in 1970, "will never be wholly extinguished."[73] And his larger desire to forge "a program for a better America, a better civilization organically developed out of the soil and energy of this continent" echoes what progressive critics Michael Denning, James Baldwin, Richard Rorty, and others mean when they urge us to truly "achieve our country, and change the history of the world."[74] Carey McWilliams's ability to merge a deep-seated love of place with a passion for racial equality and social justice holds promise for regional, national, and global politics in the twenty-first century.

NOTES

1. Henry Nash Smith, interview by author, 18 July 1980, Berkeley, California.

2. Carey McWilliams, *The Education of Carey McWilliams* (New York: Simon & Schuster, 1979), 320–321.

3. Archibald McLeish, "American Letter," in *Collected Poems of Archibald MacLeish* (Boston: Houghton Mifflin, 1985), 163.

4. Scanning the American political landscape since the 1940s, Richard White argues, for example, that "the New Right and the New Left, hippies and environmentalists, the new immigration, even aspects of the civil rights movement, all were western in important ways." White, *"It's Your Misfortune and None of My Own": A History of the American West* (Norman: University of Oklahoma Press, 1991), 575. For a succinct summary of the West's political centrality, see William Deverell, "Politics and the Twentieth Century West," in *A Companion to the American West*, ed. William Deverell (Oxford: Blackwell, 2004), 442–459.

5. Looking back at his years as editor of the *Nation* magazine, McWilliams recalled launching Hunter S. Thompson's career by suggesting that he write a book about California's Hell's Angels and encouraging Theodore Roszak to write *The Making of a Counter Culture*. See Carey McWilliams, *The Education of Carey McWilliams* (New York:

Simon & Schuster, 1979), 235–236, 248–249. For a vivid account of coming of age among cowboys and ranch hands, see "Growing Up in Steamboat," in ibid., 27–38.

6. Wilson Carey McWilliams, foreword to *Fool's Paradise: A Carey McWilliams Reader*, ed. Gray Brechin (Berkeley, Calif.: Heyday Books, 2001), xvii.

7. Carey McWilliams, *California: The Great Exception* (1949; repr., Berkeley and Los Angeles: University of California Press, 1998), 342; McWilliams, *Education*, 321.

8. McWilliams, *California*, 189.

9. Michael Steiner, "Regionalism in the Great Depression," *Geographical Review* 73 (October 1983): 432, and "Regionalism," in *American Heritage Encyclopedia of American History*, ed. John Mack Faragher (New York: Henry Holt, 1998), 774.

10. B. A. Botkin, "We Talk about Regionalism—North, East, South, and West," *Frontier* 13 (May 1933): 286–296.

11. Alfred Kazin, *On Native Grounds* (New York: Doubleday, 1942), 394.

12. Robert V. Hine, *The American West: An Interpretive History* (Boston: Little, Brown, 1984), 358.

13. Thomas Frank, *What's the Matter with Kansas? How Conservatives Won the Heart of America* (New York: Henry Holt, 2004), 31–32.

14. Regarding the more recent surge of western regionalism, see Richard Maxwell Brown, "The New Regionalism in America, 1970–1981," in *Regionalism in the Pacific Northwest*, ed. William G. Robbins, Robert J. Frank, and Richard E. Ross (Corvallis: Oregon State University Press, 1983), 37–96, and Michael Steiner and David Wrobel, "Many Wests: Discovering a Dynamic Western Regionalism," in *Many Wests: Place, Culture, and Regional Identity*, ed. Michael Steiner and David Wrobel (Lawrence: University Press of Kansas, 1997), 1–30.

15. Mary Austin, *The American Rhythm: Studies and Reexpressions of Amerindian Songs* (Boston: Houghton Mifflin, 1930), 37; J. Frank Dobie, *Guide to Life and Literature in the Southwest* (Austin: University of Texas Press, 1943), 11; Walter Prescott Webb, *The Great Plains* (New York: Ginn, 1931), 126, and *The Texas Rangers: A Century of Frontier Defense* (New York: Houghton Mifflin, 1935), 14; Edward Abbey, *Down the River* (New York: E. P. Dutton, 1982), 17.

16. B. A. Botkin, "Regionalism and Culture," in *The Writer in a Changing World*, ed. Henry Hart (New York: Equinox Press, 1937), 140.

17. "Calamity Howlers," editorial, *Decatur (Tex.) Times*, 22 March 1893, reprinted in *The Populist Mind*, ed. Norman Pollak (Indianapolis: Bobbs-Merrill, 1967), 56–57; Kyle Crichton, "Cease Not Living," *New Mexico Quarterly* 5 (May 1935): 74.

18. Dudley Wynn to Carey McWilliams, 2 July 1937, box 1, Carey McWilliams Papers (Collection 1319), Department of Special Collections, Charles E. Young Research Library, University of California, Los Angeles (hereafter McWilliams Papers–YRL); H. W. Janson, "Benton and Wood, Champions of Regionalism," *Magazine of Art* 39 (May 1946): 186.

19. Horace Sutton, "Sunbelt vs. Frostbelt: A Second Civil War?" *Saturday Review*, 15 April 1978, 37; Roberto M. Dianotto, *Place in Literature: Regions, Cultures, Communities* (Ithaca, N.Y.: Cornell University Press, 2000), 23

20. Michael Kowalewski, "Writing in Place: The New American Regionalism," *American Literary History* 6 (Spring 1994): 175.

21. Henry Nash Smith, interview by author, 18 July 1980, Berkeley, California.

22. McWilliams, *California*, 189; McWilliams, *Education*, 321.

23. Forrest Robinson, "Remembering Carey McWilliams," *Western American Literature* 34 (Winter 2000): 411; Mike Davis, *City of Quartz: Excavating the Future in Los Angeles* (New York: Verso, 1990), 35; Kevin Starr, "Carey McWilliams's California: The Light and the Dark," in *Reading California: Art, Image, and Identity, 1900–2000*, ed. Stephanie Bloom (Berkeley and Los Angeles: University of California Press, 2000), 15.

24. Matthew Frye Jacobson, *Whiteness of a Different Color: European Immigrants and the Alchemy of Race* (Cambridge, Mass.: Harvard University Press, 1998), 258. Other recent glowing appraisals of McWilliams as a pioneering multiculturalist include Nikhil Pal Singh, "Culture/Wars: Recoding Empire in an Age of Democracy," *American Quarterly* 50 (Fall 1998): 471–522, and Kevin Allen Leonard, "'Brothers under the Skin'? African Americans, Mexicans, and World War II in California," in *The Way We Really Were: The Golden State in the Second World War*, ed. Roger W. Lotchin (Urbana: University of Illinois Press, 2000), 187–214.

25. Michael Neven Willard, "Nuestra Los Angeles," *American Quarterly* 56 (September 2004): 809, 933.

26. William Deverell, "Privileging the Mission over the Mexican: The Rise of Regional Identity in Southern California," in Steiner and Wrobel, *Many Wests*, 235, 238; Catherine A. Corman, "Teaching—and Learning from—Carey McWilliams," *California History* 80 (Winter 2001–2002): 205.

27. In the past two years alone, three pathbreaking studies of California labor and race relations are brilliant evocations of ideas pioneered by McWilliams: See Mark Arax and Rick Wartzman, *The King of California: J. G. Boswell and the Making of a Secret American Empire* (New York: Public Affairs, 2003); Richard Stevens Street, *Beasts of the Fields: A Narrative History of California Farm Workers, 1769–1913* (Stanford, Calif.: Stanford University Press, 2004); and William Deverell, *Whitewashed Adobe: The Rise of Los Angeles and the Remaking of Its Mexican Past* (Berkeley and Los Angeles: University of California Press, 2004). Don Mitchell's *The Lie of the Land: Migrant Workers and the California Landscape* (Minneapolis: University of Minnesota Press, 1996) is also instilled with McWilliams's spirit.

28. Carey McWilliams, "Honorable in All Things," interview by Howard Gardener, 10 July 1978, Los Angeles, McWilliams Papers–YRL; McWilliams, *Education*, 66, 67. "Most of my writing in the first years of the Depression continued to be on literary themes and subjects," he recalled. "I was for a time intensely interested in regionalism and regional culture, much in the manner of the Southern Agrarians, but with a Western emphasis" (ibid., 66).

29. McWilliams proudly cited the Associated Farmer's condemnation in *Ill Fares the Land: Migrants and Migratory Labor in the United States* (Boston: Little, Brown, 1942), 13, and in *Education*, 77. His scathing exposé, published within months of John Steinbeck's *Grapes of Wrath*, was widely vilified by the establishment. Condemn-

ing *Factories* as "so grossly incorrect and misleading that it has no historical value" and declaring that "it should be returned to the garbage can from whence it emanated," Dr. George Clements, the Los Angeles Chamber of Commerce's "Mexican expert," echoed the opinions of many business leaders. Cited by Douglas Monroy, *Rebirth: Mexican Los Angeles from the Great Migration to the Great Depression* (Berkeley and Los Angeles: University of California Press, 1999), 152.

30. For perceptive treatment of McWilliams's pioneering work in environmental justice and of his direct impact upon Cesar Chavez and other activists, see Aaron Sachs, "Civil Rights in the Field: Carey McWilliams as a Public-Interest Historian and Social Ecologist," *Pacific Historical Review* 73 (May 2004): 215–248.

31. For detailed accounts of McWilliams's intellectual development, see two articles by Greg Critser, "The Making of a Cultural Rebel: Carey McWilliams, 1924–1930," *Pacific Historical Review* 45 (May 1986): 226–255, and "The Political Rebellion of Carey McWilliams," *UCLA Historical Journal* 4 (1983): 34–65. The first book-length biography of McWilliams, Peter Richardson's *American Prophet: The Life and Work of Carey McWilliams* (Ann Arbor: University of Michigan Press, 2005), appeared after my article was completed.

32. Carey McWilliams, Date Book for 1923, entries for 1 January and 5 January, box 51, McWilliams Papers–YRL.

33. Ibid., entry for 13 January; Date Book for 1924, entry for 3 April, for the quotations, ibid. Exuberant notes about discoveries of writers and artists are scattered throughout the early journals.

34. Ibid., entries between 28 January and 28 March.

35. McWilliams, foreword to *Fool's Paradise*, xiii.

36. Carey McWilliams, "Los Angeles," *Overland Monthly and Out West Magazine* 85 (May 1927): 135.

37. Carey McWilliams, *Southern California: An Island on the Land* (1946; repr., Salt Lake City: Peregrine Smith, 1973), 133.

38. Ibid., 375–376.

39. Ibid., 377, 135, 136.

40. Carey McWilliams, "Young Man, Stay West," *Southwest Review* 15 (Spring 1930); "A Letter from the Northwest," *Saturday Review of Literature*, 12 July 1930, 1193; "Letters from the Southwest," *Saturday Review of Literature*, 6 December 1930, 434; "Myths of the West," *North American Review* 232 (November 1931): 432.

41. McWilliams, *Education*, 50, 63. Writing to McWilliams seven years later, Jeffers expressed a political despair at odds with his friend's newly found activism. "It seems to me," Jeffers wrote, "that in a degenerate society the individual has got to isolate himself morally ... or else degenerate too. He can keep up his morale; he cannot save society's." Robinson Jeffers to Carey McWilliams, 17 May 1935, box 3, McWilliams Papers–YRL. For Louis Adamic's account of the 1928 meeting with Jeffers, see Adamic, *My America, 1928–1938* (New York: Harper & Brothers, 1938), 463–476.

42. Carey McWilliams, Date Book for 1929, entry for 9 July, box 51, McWilliams Papers–YRL.

43. Carey's disaffection with what he perceived as Louis's newly gained superficial

New York radicalism and his quip about Hart Crane are in his Date Book for 1929, entries for 19 and 30 October, ibid.; his critique of New York condescension is in Carey McWilliams, "Localism in American Criticism: A Century and a Half of Controversy," *Southwest Review* 14 (July 1934): 426. The New York intellectuals mentioned here are Randolph Bourne, Van Wyck Brooks, Sherwood Anderson, Mumford, and Frank.

44. McWilliams, Date Book for 1929, entries for 19 and 30 October and what appears to be 2 November, box 51.

45. Ibid., entry for 12 December.

46. Carey McWilliams, Date Book for 1930, entries for 20 March and 20 April, McWilliams Papers–YRL.

47. Ibid., entries for 20 March and 28 December.

48. Carey McWilliams, *The New Regionalism in American Literature*, Chapbook No. 46 (Seattle: University of Washington Book Store, 1930), 23, 24, 26, 10–11, 38–39.

49. Ibid., 35, 36, 32.

50. Carey McWilliams, "Swell Letters in California," *American Mercury*, September 1930, 42–47; McWilliams, "Getting Rid of the Mexican," *American Mercury*, March 1933, 199–201.

51. McWilliams, "Honorable in All Things."

52. Carey McWilliams, Date Book for 1932, entry for 31 August, box 51, McWilliams Papers–YRL. He touches upon this turning point in his *Education*, 65–67, 85–86.

53. Ibid., entries for 2 March and 4 June, box 51, McWilliams Papers–YRL.

54. Carey McWilliams, Date Book for 1931, entry for 24 October; Date Book for 1933, entry for 13 October, McWilliams Papers–YRL.

55. Carey McWilliams, Date Book for 1934, entry for 16 January, McWilliams Papers–YRL. Carey's personal life also hit rock bottom at this point. After separating from his wife and child in late 1934, he took a second train trip to New York and back, and brooding over his dissolving marriage, he asked, "How am I to be alive? Perhaps I am dead and dreamed this turgid dream. . . . Can I still go on living? And on what terms, and where?" Carey McWilliams, Date Book for 1935, entry for 12 March, McWilliams Papers–YRL.

56. McWilliams outlines many of his labor organizing activities in *Education*, 74–86. The quotation is from page 85.

57. Ibid., 75.

58. Alice Greenfield McGrath, interview by author, 23 January 2005, Ventura, California. McGrath was McWilliams's close friend and associate for nearly thirty years, beginning in 1943 when he invited her, as a twenty-four-year-old social activist, to become the executive director of the Sleepy Lagoon Defense Committee.

59. For a thoughtful analysis of this dimension of McWilliams's career, see Daniel Geary, "Carey McWilliams and Anti-Fascism, 1934–1943," *Journal of American History* 89 (December 2003): 912–934.

60. Carey McWilliams, "Critical Summary," in "Race Relations on the Pacific Coast," special issue, *Journal of Educational Psychology* 19 (November 1945): 194. McWilliams's *Brothers under the Skin* (Boston: Little, Brown, 1943) is filled with this perspective.

61. Barbara Chevalier to Carey McWilliams, 29 July 1936, in "Material Relating to the Western Writers' Congress, 1936–1937," Carey McWilliams Papers, BANC MSS C-H 46, Bancroft Library, University of California, Berkeley (hereafter McWilliams Papers–BL).

62. "Call to a Congress of Western Writers," in "Material Relating to the Western Writers' Congress," McWilliams Papers–BL. Regarding the first of four national gatherings of writers on the left, see Henry Hart, ed., *American Writers' Congress* (New York: International Publishers, 1935). Three valuable discussions of this version of literary radicalism are Daniel Aaron, *Writers on the Left* (New York: Avon Books, 1961); Michael Denning, *The Cultural Front: The Laboring of American Art in the Twentieth Century* (New York: Verso, 1997); and Alan M. Wald, *Exiles from a Future Time: The Forging of the Mid-Twentieth-Century Literary Left* (Chapel Hill: University of North Carolina Press, 2002).

63. Of particular interest is the exchange between McWilliams and Meridel LeSueur in which McWilliams asks her about the June 1936 Conference of Midwestern Writers held in Chicago, and she describes some of the proceedings, especially her opinions as well as Mike Gold's on the need for a proletarian regionalism. Meridel LeSueur to Carey McWilliams, 16 August 1936; McWilliams to LeSueur, 4 September 1936 and again, 12 September 1936; McWilliams to LeSueur, 21 September 1936, in "Materials Relating to the Western Writers' Conference," McWilliams Papers–BL.

64. Ella Winter, "Western Writers' Congress," *Pacific Weekly*, 30 November 1936, 145–146.

65. Kenneth Rexroth, "The Function of Poetry and the Place of the Poet in Society," paper delivered at the 1936 Western Writers' Conference, in *World outside the Window: The Selected Essays of Kenneth Rexroth*, ed. Bradford Morrow (New York: New Directions, 1987), 6, 7.

66. Mike Gold, "Why a Writers' Congress," *Pacific Weekly*, 9 November 1936, 308; Meridel LeSueur, "Midwestern Writers' Conference," *Pacific Weekly* 16 November 1936, 320. Also see LeSueur, "Proletarian Literature in the Middle West," in Hart, *American Writers' Congress*, 135–138.

67. Dudley Wynn to Carey McWilliams, 2 July 1937, McWilliams Papers–YRL.

68. Carey McWilliams to Louis Adamic, 3 October 1937, ibid.

69. Ibid. McWilliams recalled the detail about the "large black and blue mark" in his *Education*, 84.

70. Carey McWilliams, "Personal Note," *Nation* 201 (September 1965): 25.

71. Ibid., 25.

72. Walt Whitman, "By Blue Ontario's Shores," in *Works of Walt Whitman*, vol. 1, *The Collected Poetry* (New York: Minerva Press, 1969), 314–315.

73. Carey McWilliams, "Steinbeck & the 1930s," thirty-two-page typescript, box 5, McWilliams Papers–YRL.

74. Carey McWilliams, *Louis Adamic and Shadow America* (Los Angeles: Arthur Whipple, 1935), 92; Richard Rorty, *Achieving Our Country: Leftist Thought in Twentieth Century America* (Cambridge, Mass.: Harvard University Press, 1998), 13. Rorty's title

comes from James Baldwin's *The Fire Next Time* (1963). While considerably less hopeful than Rorty, Michael Denning, in *Cultural Front*, provides glimpses of hope in the ruins of the grassroots leftist "cultural laboring" of the 1930s. Rorty's project to rebuild our society by drawing on the progressive, cooperative commonwealth legacy of Abraham Lincoln, Whitman, John Dewey, and other progressives echoes McWilliams's pluralistic regional perspective.

CHAPTER 6

Latinos in the Politics of the West
Ignacio M. García

In spring 1977, Raul Villarreal, an underemployed bartender running for city council in Kingsville, Texas, approached a serious-looking older gentleman who was sitting outside on his porch. Using the best of his South Texas Spanish, Raul laid out his plan to change the way the city government responded to the needs of the Mexican American community. Nodding several times and even interjecting some of his own ideas, the older man seemed in total agreement with the young, unkempt candidate of La Raza Unida Party. Sensing a solid vote, Villarreal confidently asked, "Can I have your vote then?" The older fellow responded, "Sorry, but I can't." "Why?" asked a perplexed candidate. "I can't vote, I'm Jehovah's Witness," answered the man.

Slightly frustrated but still anxious to get the "Chicano vote," Villarreal moved on to the next house. After a similar few minutes, another older fellow put up his hand and said, "I can't vote for you." Again Villarreal asked why. "Because I don't vote for someone *mas pendejo* [more of an idiot] than I am," said the man. "Look at yourself, unruly hair, worn-out jeans and a five o'clock shadow on your face." Totally frustrated, but the wiser for the experience, Raul went home, changed his clothes, cut his hair, and never again left the house without shaving. He also avoided Jehovah's Witnesses. One month later, he was elected to the city council by five votes.[1]

Raul's experience reflects the larger Latino political experience. No matter how often politicians believe they "understand the community," they are confronted with its diversity. Religion, ideology, propriety, partisanship, and economics combine to create a complex social and political community that seems accessible to many politicians seeking the "Hispanic vote" but that turns out to be more unyielding than expected. The Latino vote is more than multifaceted; it is one without a firm unanimity in terms of political direction. Consider the last several decades, during which Latinos have divided over candidates, propositions, and immigration issues. With the exception of the 1960 presidential election, Latinos have never been as loyal to one particular party as African Americans have been to the Democratic Party.[2]

Without doubt there are commonalities. It would be impossible for there not to be, given that many Latinos continue to face common problems and often receive common responses when they agitate for answers. The majority of Latinos in the West are lower middle class at best; their children drop out of school before graduation, and those who don't do not go to college in large numbers. Latino barrios are still afflicted with drugs, gangs, poor schools, inadequate housing, and poor political representation. More important, especially for the middle class, they are all but ignored in the intellectual life of the nation. Most Latinos, then, see their experience in American society as either half-empty or half-full, neither of which is considered a fulfillment of the American dream.

Still, over time, Latinos have found different political ways to respond to this unfulfilled dream. This has always been true in Latino politics in the West, though it is much easier to see this diversity in political action in the recent battles over immigration, driver's licenses, benefits for immigrants, bilingual education, affirmative action, and the new, so-called moral issues. I will argue that Latino diversity—and in this essay I will concentrate on Mexican Americans—is based on class differences, the time they have been in the United States, where they live, and military experience. These differences have at times coalesced around the issues of race and legal or constitutional status. Yet it is important to note that even within this diverse political setting, Mexican Americans in the West have much in common in their struggle for rights of full citizenship.

To set the stage for understanding Mexicano politics in the West, it is important to start at the signing of the Treaty of Guadalupe Hidalgo at the end of the U.S.-Mexico War in 1848. While the treaty ended the war, settled war reparations, and provided citizenship to those Mexicans who stayed in the newly acquired territory, it fell woefully short of dealing with the complex situation of a newly conquered people who were to grow in numbers very fast in a very few years. The United States not only acquired territory but also developed a voracious need for Mexicano labor. This need for labor would be the cornerstone of the "foundation of conflict" that would soon arise.[3]

Because of the need for labor, Mexicans and Mexican Americans on both sides of the border became submerged in a sea of second-class citizenship. Initially, this need for labor meant opportunities for Anglos; it led to the transfer of jobs and of ranches, farms, and other small-scale business enterprises from their Mexican owners to Anglo newcomers. Even before the treaty's ink was dry, newly arrived white settlers found ways to dispossess these "new" residents of the American nation from their lands through court challenges, dishonest business dealings, and violence. As they lost their jobs, businesses, and land, Mexicans became disenfranchised, poor, and second-class human beings. Whatever rights they had gained under the treaty that ended the war vanished along with their livelihood. The marginalization of Mexican Americans made the poorest of them unwanted and politically powerless. The more fortunate survived through intermarriage or sheer tenacity, but they lost most of their independence and came to rely on alliances with Anglos or on Anglo benevolence for their survival.[4]

From the early years after the treaty was signed to about the end of the nineteenth century, the process of Mexican dispossession made the former Mexican territories into a white man's land. Anglos owned the land and the businesses, and they gave out the jobs. They also wrote the laws, and while Mexican Americans did not face a legally endorsed Jim Crow system, local rules kept Mexican Americans oppressed. For example, in Uvalde, Texas, city leaders created a law that required Mexican Americans to have a "passport" in order to enter the city.[5] In many communities, farmers and ranchers controlled the mobility of Mexicano workers. In other places the law was blind to the lynching of Mexican Americans caught committing crimes. The first fifty years after the Treaty of Guadalupe Hidalgo, Anglos "solved" the so-called Mexican problem by marginalizing them and keeping them out of sight. But the expansion of agriculture, manufacturing, and mining would soon undermine that strategy and create divisions within the Anglo community itself over what to do with the unwanted but much-needed Mexican labor.

The 1920s and 1930s saw the split of the Mexicano population into those who were citizens or had legal residency and those who were temporary workers or undocumented residents. The creation of the border patrol and the efforts at immigration restriction created a political and eventually an ideological boundary between the two groups. Prior to the border's development into a restrictive legal and political boundary, these diverse communities had occupied the same space and confronted Anglo hostility in much the same manner. But with the solidifying of the border, the two communities began moving away from each other. The hostility of white residents forced both communities to develop strategies to defend their interests. For immigrants and temporary workers, this usually meant the expansion of mutual aid societies and the formation of workers' unions and associations. It meant calling upon the Mexican consulates to do more and creating internal communities to develop a civic life unavailable in the larger society.[6]

For Mexican Americans and long-time resident aliens of Mexican descent, the reaction to a heightened sense of hostility took a different route. Two things affected the direction: One was the large number of immigrants and temporary workers who came during the first twenty years of the twentieth century. The other was World War I. The former had two immediate effects: the competition with Mexican Americans for low-paying jobs, particularly agricultural work, and a severe increase in hostility toward Mexicano workers from those Anglos who believed they were being overrun by the large numbers of new Mexicans. These Anglos drew few distinctions between long-term residents and recent arrivals. It was during this time, according to social historian David Montejano, that a culture of segregation began developing in Texas and much of the rest of the Southwest.[7]

Service in World War I for a small group of Mexican Americans, did, however, create a distinguishing experience for the new leaders in the native-born community. Serving as officers and senior enlisted men, this group of Mexican Americans found that in combat they more than held their own among Anglos. More important, the experience in war, defending American interests, created within them a strong sense of patriotism. They saw themselves as part of the nation in a way they had not before, and they became convinced that their future, and that of their community, was in the United States, and not Mexico.[8] Within a few years of being back in the United States, they began establishing organizations geared toward developing the "best, purest and most perfect type of a true and loyal citizen of the United States of America."[9]

This focus on the obligations and benefits of citizenship began a slow but steady departure from the Mexicano politics of the past. While less noticeable at the grassroots level, this change was clear among upper- and middle-class Mexican Americans. Their organizations began promoting English-language skills, encouraging the elimination of child labor, celebrating American holidays, and writing a complementary history that tied them to American society.[10] By the 1940s, the leaders of these groups had also begun demanding the end to illegal immigration and the hiring of undocumented workers, particularly in the fields.[11] Still, on a local level, Mexican Americans and Mexicans lived in most of the same barrios, shopped at the same places, and often celebrated life in the same space. They mostly spoke Spanish and confronted the same hostilities, making them a mixed community of native-born and recent arrivals.

The diversity of western Mexican Americans was compounded by where and how they lived. While 1960s activist Rodolfo "Corky" Gonzales would argue—in seeking political unity—that in spite of diversity, Mexican Americans "look the same . . . feel the same . . . cry and sing the same," that was and is only partially true.[12] Mexicans and Mexican Americans were more tied to a local space and even to a homeland (if, for some, only a cultural touchstone) in Mexico than they were to each other across the spaces of the Southwest. Before the 1950s, any Mexicano national identity stemmed from ties to Mexico and the occasional concern that Mexican officials expressed over its citizens "in exile." Their common experience in the West— exploitation, poverty, and racial discrimination—does not invalidate the fact that there were many communities of Mexican Americans in the West. While all the Mexicano communities in the West were affected by the major economic enterprises of the region—ranching, farming, mining, and construction—these experiences were tempered by urban-to-rural ratios, state politics, diversity of population, immigration patterns, native-born or immigrant leadership, and a host of other factors that gave each community a uniqueness that should not be overlooked.[13] Acknowledging this diversity still permits us to search for common geography. "Placing them" allows us to define the place of confrontation between Anglos and Mexican Americans and helps us identify what sociologist Tomás Almaguer calls "fault lines," those places where the struggle over constructed space occurs.[14]

For Mexicans and Mexican Americans, this space was neither rural nor necessarily urban. It was a space I will call the rural metropolis. Most Mexicanos lived in towns. While some worked in rural enterprises tightly connected to urban centers, others inhabited cities while eking out a rural life by working in the fields or in canneries, packing plants, or slaughterhouses. Still others left the cities annually to take part in the migrant waves across the West, the Northwest, and the Midwest, working from crop to crop and harvest to harvest. The dusty roads, the migrant fields, the little towns, the foremen, and the pay by cash provided a cultural space that Carey McWilliams once described as "neither town nor country, neither rural nor urban . . . a world of its own."[15]

Historian Gilbert González and economist Raul Fernández ask us to envision a rural world of Mexican Americans that, when engulfed by urban sprawl, transforms itself into a series of barrios.[16] There were mining towns, citrus camps, copper towns, sharecropping communities, and Mexicano villages on the edges of cities and towns with industrial centers. Thousands of Mexicano workers lived in these sometimes stable, often shifting communities. And it is here where the foundational space for Mexicano activism and politics was created.[17] The majority of barrio organizations, political leaders, and ideals came out of this environment. This is so not because most lived in rural communities at the time but, rather, because it was in rural communities that Mexicans and Mexican Americans could best understand their dilemma as a conquered and marginalized people.[18]

Ruralization, then, becomes a social construct based on an attachment to the space that Mexican Americans occupy, a space profoundly affected by poverty, unrewarding work, mistreatment, and constant reminders of its inhabitants' landlessness. But it was in this space, this construct, that a continual renewal of Mexicano rural culture emerged, regardless of the demographic reality of its physical presence within urban boundaries.[19] While this might seem to challenge the urban focus of Chicano studies, it is important to understand that I am talking about the coexistence of a rural culture within an urban reality. No one should question that the middle-class reformist politics and the university activism all speak to a strong and profound urban experience, but for now, the rural metropolis and its connotations for the urban Chicano/Latino experience must be a starting point in understanding Mexican and Mexican American activism of the past century.

The rural metropolis was a segregated space, immensely more important in keeping whites white than in keeping Mexican Americans separate.[20] In early western communities, agricultural, ranching, and mining endeavors made it almost impossible to completely segregate Anglos from Mexican Americans, but by the beginning of the twentieth century, this segregation was becoming more commonplace. Pressure from their white constituencies prompted many white politicians to "encourage," promote, and coerce the development of a separate and separated Mexicano world. This effort began with labor practices that not only kept Mexican Americans separated from other peoples of color in the fields and the factories, but also locked them in low-wage jobs, forcing them to create their own affordable communities on the outskirts of the white world. Eventually, Anglos established Mexicano schools to institutionalize segregation.[21] Alongside this separation came a greater—though de facto—effort to keep the races apart. While few laws existed to segregate Mexican Americans from public accommodations, no laws existed to include them either, and thus public theaters, swimming pools, barbershops, restaurants, parks, and a host of other public entities were kept off limits to them without fear of legal ramifications.[22]

In the 1830s, Texan entrepreneur Stephen F. Austin wrote, "My object, the sole and only desire of my ambitions since I first saw Texas, was to redeem it from the wilderness."[23] Keeping whites out of the "wilderness" meant keeping them away from Mexican Americans, seen by most Anglos as not only a foreign people but also as part of the "color" of the wilderness. By the twentieth century, this wilderness had little to do with nearness to the land or the individualism of Turnerian thought; rather, it referenced illiteracy, poverty, coloredness, and dependence on the economics of low wages and low self-esteem. This segregation served not only a social but also a political function because these segregated, poor, and disdained communities in the West scarcely influenced the electoral process and the body politic. When Mexican American civil rights organizations developed, their leaders first sought to urbanize their constituencies, to bring them out of the wilderness. As one reformer claimed years later, Mexican Americans would progress and become better citizens with "newspapers, radio and television" as well as assimilation campaigns that made them better Americans.[24] Becoming American really meant becoming non-Mexican in the context of citizenship status, as when Hector P. García, founder of the American G.I. Forum, counseled veterans to not mark "Mexican" on their job or census forms.[25]

Keeping Anglos out of the barrio except in administrative or policy capacities allowed a strong asymmetric relationship to develop. Mexican Americans saw Anglos only when they confronted authority, when they voted, and when they went to work or school. The "meeting place" thus reaffirmed each group's place in the social hierarchy. In places like Central Texas, where blacks, poor whites, and Mexican Americans initially worked and lived in close proximity, whites in authority decided that only Mexican Americans would be kept to pick the cotton. Poor whites were replaced because they weakened the social hierarchy, and African Americans were fired because they were seen as too demanding, while Mexicans and Mexican Americans were seen as much more manageable because many could not speak English, few understood the law, and they had no allies among the labor unions, whose members saw them as foreign workers taking American jobs.[26]

Having Mexican Americans and Mexicans do the low-pay work allowed white westerners to maintain a sense of superiority, but without the discomforts of a de jure system of discrimination as existed in the rest of the South. In the land of freedom, democracy, and individualism, all men were equal, except, of course, those who weren't. Even in places like Arizona, Southern California, New Mexico, or parts of South Texas, where not all Mexican Americans were illiterate or poor, the asymmetric relationship was maintained. Every Mexicano elite understood that for every one of them who was well off or had survived Anglo racism, hundreds of their countrymen were poor, uneducated, and "foreign." This put pressure on the elites to conform to the status quo. Given this pressure, it is not surprising that the Mexican American Generation (1930–1960) initially created a political philosophy that sought to reaffirm that they were good citizens and good neighbors, that they were in essence "another white race."[27]

Being good citizens was important to these reformists because it allowed them into white political space. They believed that over time their civic participation would bring them social acceptance and provide them an opportunity to interact and mingle with their Anglo counterparts. Many Mexican Americans believed that if Anglos knew them, they would like them or at least tolerate them. To many whites, however, Mexican Americans' political participation was trespassing on the public space that justified Anglo superiority. Their resistance to any sign of Mexicano political power only served to convince Mexican American political leadership that they were on the right path. It became even more important, consequently, to be seen as white. It is important to point out, however, that even the strongest proponent of this approach rarely argued for a denial of racial origins. The code of the oldest Mexican American organization, the League of United Latin American Citizens (LULAC), "Love the men of your race, be proud of your origins and maintain it immaculate, respect your glorious past, and help to defend the rights of your own people."[28] Mexican American reformers were able to speak to two identities at the same time, and they often emphasized one over the other according to which was more politically advantageous at the time.

It must be pointed out that in American anthropological circles, there was no real category for mestizo, a classification accepted in Latin America, referring to the mixed Indian and Spanish origins of those from that region. Thus, in the United States, anyone not Asian or Native American was either black or white. Mexican Americans had to choose one or the other in that binary, and there were simply no—in their minds—biological, social, or even economic benefits to choosing to be black. Over time, for these middle-class reformers, whiteness would prove more beneficial, especially when struggling for civil rights, simply because only whites had full rights.

The struggle for the benefits of whiteness stretched back into the mid-nineteenth century. The former Mexican citizens' first encounter with the U.S. constitutional interpretation of race happened only a few years after the U.S.-Mexico War, when a former Mexican citizen named Ricardo Rodríguez applied for U.S. citizenship in Texas.[29] His action forced the federal judiciary to take up the question of whether Mexicans were white, because at the time only whites could naturalize. In 1866, few might have believed that a century later the nation's courts would still be struggling with the racial status of Mexican Americans. In fact, the *Rodríguez* naturalization case became part of the fifty-two-plus prerequisite cases that would be heard in the courts from the 1860s to the 1950s. Not surprisingly, most of these cases originated in the West. Central to each case was the question, "Who was white?"[30]

Western politicians were as perplexed by immigration as were their eastern counterparts, but Anglo westerners confronted an influx of newcomers from the west (Asians) and the south (Mexicans). California courts (and eventually the federal courts) had to decide exactly what characteristics made a person white. Was it skin color, facial features, national origin, language, or culture? Or was there some scientific data that could be relied upon to make a judgment? Even popular opinion or "common knowledge" became part of the filter. As legal scholar Ian Haney-López has argued, "In short, the courts were responsible for deciding not only who was white, but why someone was white."[31] While this process took place on both coasts, the determination was much more critical in the West because the authorities did not believe that immigrants from Mexico and further south were "whiteable." And that has proven to be the case. No one speaks today of Poles, Italians, Greeks, or Jews as "people of color," yet that is exactly how Mexican Americans and other Latinos are depicted in scholarly literature.

Rodríguez eventually received permission to naturalize, even though the court judge expressed his misgivings that Rodríguez, "if the strict scientific classification of the anthropologist should be adopted . . . would probably not be classed as white." Unfortunately for the judge and others who opposed the naturalization of Mexican Americans, the nation's treaties with Mexico conferred citizenship on the former residents of that nation. This made Mexican Americans white by treaty, but not by "common knowledge" or "scientific evidence." This then, would create the foundation for the de facto segregation and discrimination that Latinos—still mostly Mexicans and Mexican Americans—suffered in the West. Walter Benn Michaels, a literary theorist, described this as an effort not to defend the "white state" but actually to create "the state through whiteness." In the West that is exactly what happened.[32] In the process, white westerners created in their minds and in their social structures a permanent "colored" mass. Mexicans and Mexican Americans responded by "empowering" this notion of difference in order to develop survival strategies, thus guaranteeing a pulling away on both sides.[33]

Mexican Americans became the great social problem of the West. Their numbers, the Anglo demand for their labor, and their early resistance to being treated poorly by Anglos created a careful balance in the social structure of the West. This structure came under the purview of the judicial system again and again, mostly because both the courts and the political leaders went back and forth in deciding on the "color" of Mexican Americans. Nearly seventy years after *In re Rodríguez*, the U.S. Supreme Court wrote, "whether a person of [Mexican] descent may be naturalized in the United States is still an unsettled question."[34]

Mexican Americans simply did not fit the western taxonomy of whiteness. It took until the 1940s for Mexican Americans to be accepted as white in the nation's courts. In the years between the *Rodríguez* case and World War II, the term "Mexican" had been racialized to mean "foreigner" and "nonwhite." Yet most Mexicano civil rights advocates resisted being classified as something other than white. In the 1930s, when the U.S. Census Bureau created "Mexican" as a racial category, Mexican Americans protested so loudly, and they were assisted by the Mexican government, that by the 1940 census they were again classified as white.[35] The subsequent growth of the Mexican American middle class, their mass participation in World War II, and the numerous legal victories in the field of education forced government agencies and some political leaders to finally recognize that Mexican Americans were not simply another group of nonwhites. But if the legal and sometimes political classification of Mexicans as nonwhites proved difficult to promote, the social classification of Mexicans as foreigners and nonwhites persisted until the mid-1950s.

The racialization of Mexican Americans reflected the belief among Anglos that Mexican Americans were going to remain a constant problem. While segregation and de facto discrimination had become the principal means of defining a white political and social geography, by the late 1920s and into the 1930s, both the courts and social scientists approached race in the West in a different way. A culture of disadvantage and inferiority became the way to exclude Mexican Americans from the functions of the larger society. Discouraged from voting, gerrymandered into segregated school districts, discriminated against in most public spaces, and treated harshly by law enforcement officials, Mexican Americans had been further marginalized. Social scientists took to describing Mexican Americans as clannish, confused, and linguistically illiterate, thus making them not-good-neighbors. For more moderate and liberal Anglos who recoiled from the racism of earlier periods, this was a way to "redeem white attitudes" by blaming Mexican Americans for their problems.[36]

It would be well to state that not all Anglos were intent on institutionalizing racism or on marginalizing Mexican Americans. They rarely, however, questioned the idea that Anglo culture and values were "neutral." This perception of neutrality, constructed from the early beginnings of the Republic and reinforced at every encounter with people of color, established Anglo culture as "western" culture. By this measure, Mexican Americans, as well as other people of color, were always found wanting. In what Asian American scholars have called "the redeeming of whiteness," any effort to make things better for "others" in the West always maintained the asymmetric relationship between the races by never abdicating this neutrality.[37] It is this "neutral" measuring stick that continues to maintain the asymmetric relationship between whites and peoples of color in the modern West. Mexican Americans still do not measure up to "neutral standards" of civic duty, and thus they rarely gain the full benefits of American society.

Mexicano advocates, especially those representing mainstream civil rights organizations, had limited success when fighting accepted notions of whiteness. Understanding that whiteness was the path for widespread acceptance, they consistently pointed out that Mexican Americans were white within, and only within, the white/black binary, and they promoted Mexicano achievements and service to the nation.[38] By the late 1940s, a renewed LULAC and the new American G.I. Forum continually stressed Mexican Americans' war service, their education, and their Americanism. But to do so, they codified Mexican Americanism away from Mexicanism. They did not so much reject their origins or ethnic background as create political and social classifications within them. They found it convenient to reaffirm the U.S.-Mexico border as a political and social boundary. They began a campaign to "save the Mexican American worker from the consequences of illegal immigration."[39]

While justifiably concerned with the lowering of wages created by the Bracero Program—a labor agreement between the United States and Mexico that lasted from the 1940s to the early 1960s—and by illegal immigration, Mexicano civil rights advocates tried to frame the wage problem in a way that might create empathy among Anglos. In doing so, however, they tended to blame the immigrant workers for low wages, poverty, and crime, thereby distinguishing longer-term residents of Hispanic descent from the Mexicans coming north to work. Using the same terminology that Anglos used, they categorized these people as "foreigners," "wetbacks," "illegals," "dirty," and "disease-infected." After a while, many working-class Mexican Americans, whether legal or not, became part of this "culture of disadvantage." Said one G.I. Forum activist while describing his own community: "We have a lot of people in San Marcos (Texas) who don't care [about] school. They want their children as 'assets' to make them work so that they can buy new cars and get drunk on Saturday nights and brag about their not knowing how to read or write."[40]

Describing working-class Mexicans and Mexican Americans this way allowed those in the middle class to distinguish themselves. While Anglos sought to racialize Mexicans away from the larger society, Mexican Americans sought to define themselves toward American society by disassociating themselves from those characteristics that made them "Mexicans." Too many Mexican American reformers used "merit" as a distinguishing factor. Said one young Mexican American, "We have concluded that our Mexican youth are not meeting the social and intellectual requirements of our highly progressive American civilization. . . . We are blaming no one else but ourselves . . . for our backward conditions."[41]

There were many Mexican American civil rights advocates who did not like criticizing their fellow Mexicans, and they usually did not distinguish between legal and illegal, poor or rich when they called for protection of civil rights. Still, most Mexican American civil libertarians found it difficult to find acceptance by the larger society if they continued to stress a connection to the "other" Mexicans. Historian Mario T. García argues that constructing an Americanism based on education, respectability, and whether or not one was a veteran created both a "meritorious" status for Mexican Americans and a way to overcome those characteristics least acceptable to American society.[42] Taken to the extreme, Americanism could work to both discriminate against Mexican-origin people outside the barrio and to distinguish them within.

This struggle with whiteness complicated the politics of the Mexicano middle class in the West. Squeezed between Anglo whiteness and Mexican American brownness, these middle-class advocates and their adherents used doublespeak to navigate the dangerous political waters of American civic duty. Their political role depended on their connection to a brown constituency, but their ability to deliver for that constituency depended on accessibility and nearness to whiteness. Thus, they continually juggled political rhetoric that found them at times "proud of their ancestry" and later as "white Americans" demanding full rights. This juggling act meant that Mexican Americans would never really become fully white as some European immigrants did.

Whiteness did not affect the Latino working class in the same way. Contrary to the experience of many other "potentially white" ethnics as well as of working-class whites, Mexican American workers did not gravitate toward conservative politics or politics of race. This does not mean that Mexican-origin workers did not have prejudices against African Americans, Asian Americans, and other people of color; rather, those prejudices were not a foundation used to "whiten" their status. Mexican workers, while normally socially conservative, were more likely to look toward liberal reformers and even radicals for political direction, and they continued to defend their racial origin throughout the twentieth century. Their resistance to whiteness can be seen in the promotion of their mestizo and indigenous past, their establishment of workers' organizations, their maintenance of the Spanish language and Mexicano culture, and their willingness to use violence to defend themselves and their Mexicano space. In a precursor to the politics of Chicanismo and somewhat to the Latino politics of today, these working-class Mexicans and Mexican Americans wanted their rights as residents and citizens respected, even as they clung to their *mexicanidad*. Thus, for many, whiteness was simply not an attraction. This attitude continued to be held, to a large extent, by many working-class Latinos in the twentieth century.

The refusal of the Mexicano working class to move toward whiteness made it even easier for the middle class to continue to play the politics of whiteness and yet maintain a connection to the brownness of the community. The reality was that to serve as a bridge between groups made them more useful politically and allowed them to be able to distinguish themselves from "other" whites. This ability would become important by the late 1950s, when they began to demand rights of participation as members of a group of loyal Americans who were different and could be useful in dealing with Latin Americans during the Cold War.

For whites, the defense of de facto discrimination became critical by the 1930s and 1940s. Because of the difficulty of establishing or maintaining a politically endorsed segregation, most national and state political leaders (who publicly claimed to favor integration of Mexican Americans) acceded to the demands of their white constituents who were satisfied with the separation of the races. Legally, however, the courts began ruling against school segregation of Mexican Americans as early as the 1930s.[43] But even if Mexican American schoolchildren were being allowed piecemeal into integrated schools, their parents were still denied the basic rights of citizenship. It was clear that few western state governments were anxious for an engaged Mexican American constituency.

For example, while Mexican Americans could litigate, testify, and seek redress from the courts, they could not sit in the jury box in much of the West. The exclusion was not comprehensive, and no law or judicial guideline was enacted to ensure it, but social practice provided a good insurance against wholesale participation by Mexican Americans. Mexican Americans began challenging this practice as early as the 1920s, but it was not until 1954 that the Supreme Court ruled in their favor. Before that, both state and federal courts used two defenses in thwarting any legal precedence on the issues.[44]

From the 1920s until 1946, the courts used the notion of "qualification" to justify exclusion from juries. Mexican Americans, they argued, simply did not meet the requirements for participation: education, voter registration, language proficiency, or intelligence. Mexican Americans were simply not up to the task. Consequently, as long as court officials could make the claim that these "deficiencies" were the reason for disqualification, no discrimination on race, national origin, or ethnicity could be alleged. By the 1940s, however, Mexican Americans were seen as white by the courts, and those keeping them off juries argued that they could not claim racial discrimination if they were excluded. The reasoning went that if an all-white jury tried a Mexican American, it was a jury of peers since both the jury and the defendant were white. This approach basically nullified the ruling in *Norris v.*

Alabama, which had placed the burden on the state to prove that the absence of any African American or other person of color in the jury box was not discrimination.[45]

Mexican Americans were then discriminated against dually. They did not "qualify" to be jurors, and they could not protest their absence from the jury box because they were white. Although Mexican American lawyers tried repeatedly to challenge this notion, they were shot down each time by a court system that accepted only a white/black binary in the equal protection clause of the Fourteenth Amendment. It was not until the Warren Court's ruling in *Hernandez v. Texas* that Mexican Americans were indeed protected by the Fourteenth Amendment as a "class apart."[46] Legally, Mexican Americans were white but different, or white but brown. And brown was neither a race nor a color; it was just different. It was complicated then and remains so today.

This complicated racial position retained the ambivalence of whiteness within the barrios. It is interesting that in retelling his part of the story in a posttrial pamphlet, Pete Hernandez's lawyer Carlos C. Cadena emphasized that "this decision is based strictly on a question of national origin—not race." At the same time, he chided those in his community for not seeking alliances with other people of color.[47] His ability to speak to both sides of the issue reflected barrio politics as a mix of brown and white, stirred into the other measures of identity: class, citizenship status, and recentness of arrival. While brownness provided Mexican Americans with an identity and their uniqueness, whiteness gave them more opportunities and the possibility of eliminating prejudices. For that reason, Cadena and Hernandez's other lawyers argued for whiteness of a "class apart" or what the justices referred to as a "separate class."[48] But because "class apart" did not constitute race, it had neither the permanency of blackness nor the benefits of whiteness. Try as they might, Hernandez's lawyers had little option but to take what they could achieve and continue to struggle for a better solution.

Seemingly, Anglos have neither been comfortable nor familiar with this notion of white and brown. Because Mexicano voters could not be fitted neatly in one camp or another, most politicians and political parties simply made them a "constituency," to be wooed during elections but to be ignored when the spoils were divided. Constituency politics meant never having a voice but always having a presence. This became so exasperating for Mexicano reformers that it caused educator and civil rights notable George I. Sánchez to declare, "I don't give a damn what liberals want" shortly after castigating conservatives for seeking Mexican American support without offering anything significant in return.[49]

The conflict over brown or white became more complicated in the twentieth century with the continued growth of the immigrant population from Mexico. A nearly constant regeneration of Mexican immigrants made it even more imperative that Mexican American elites make a conscious effort to distinguish themselves from the newcomers. Whatever accommodation had been negotiated with Anglos in the latter part of the last century was threatened by the increase in the number of noncitizens from Mexico. For the first thirty or so years of the twentieth century, Mexican American elites, civil rights advocates, and politicians sought to be seen as Americans only. They asked mostly for the chance to be accepted as Americans and to shed the label of "foreigners." This was the period of the politics of inclusion.

During this period, middle-class advocates avoided attention seeking and sought instead acceptance. They fought discrimination not by critiquing the status quo but by critiquing their exclusion from it. This meant they were unwilling to speak for inclusion of all and explains why, at the elite level, they shunned alliances with other people of color. It should be pointed out that as these middle-class reformers sought inclusion, working-class activists were fighting for labor rights and respect as Mexicanos. The two approaches differed and created tensions between the Mexican Americans who identified with their national origin and those who saw themselves as Americans first.[50] The former recognized that they were people of color, and the latter underscored their "separate class" whiteness.

These conflicts rarely reached the point of being all-out war. After all, both groups believed that they were discriminated against, and they shared much of the same perception of their circumstances. Their differences lay in their analysis of the solution. Working-class leaders saw unionism, nationalism, and resistance as a way to confront Anglos' rampant racism. They sought a place-within-a-place for themselves and did not necessarily reject American society. But they saw the doors closed and chose to engage in bread-and-butter issues relevant to their barrios. Middle-class reformers, on the other hand, believed that integration was the only workable solution. To be fully included in American society meant better educational, employment, and social opportunities.

As recipients of American values—and American ambitions—the middle-class reformers saw no benefits in looking south to Mexico or in creating a place-within-a-place. Even more important in this discussion was the fact that identity—or Mexicanness—became absent from much of their rhetoric and philosophy. They became defenders of their people, while maintaining an "American first" persona. They accepted the term "Mexican American" because it spoke to their political and social placing, but they made sure that the emphasis was on "American." As New Mexican senator Dennis Chávez would argue during the 1960 presidential election, "When a boy named González goes off to war, he doesn't wear a Mexican uniform. He wears the uniform of the United States of America. There's nothing for him as a Mexican, but there is everything here for him as an American."[51]

The battle for the leadership of the western Mexican American community changed in favor of the middle-class reformers beginning in the late 1920s and solidified by the early 1940s. This resulted from Anglo repatriation and deportation campaigns during this period.[52] These crusades to rid the nation of unwanted Mexican workers destroyed a number of working-class organizations by deporting a large number of immigrant leaders. For the first extended period, American-born Mexicans had the leadership arena mostly to themselves. That, plus the rise of the first significant American-educated population, provided for the birth of a barrio Americanism that challenged the once-dominant immigrant politics.[53] That the New Deal provided some political openings for Latinos only strengthened the position of the middle-class reformers.

By the early 1950s, Mexican American political organizations began pressuring politicians to deal with the needs of the urban barrios across the country. New leaders arose. They were a new breed of Mexican American politicians and reformers who advocated beyond the local level. Within a decade, these individuals were running for statewide office and creating alliances with Anglo politicians. In 1960, they formed the Viva Kennedy Clubs that launched a national campaign to help elect John F. Kennedy president. They followed that effort by establishing or reinvigorating statewide organizations throughout most of the West. They saw themselves as representative of all Mexican Americans. While far from being national spokespersons, they did extend Mexicano issues beyond the normal political boundaries of their own base.[54]

During this period the politics of inclusion gave way to the politics of similarity. These politics were as much about being "similar" as they were about being constitutionally equal. Mexican Americans now cast themselves and their history in Anglo terms. For example, historian Carlos Castañeda described Mexicano history as a pioneer story and cast it within terms that most Anglos could understand: Christianity, democracy, and individualism. These new political values more easily fit the politics of the emerging Cold War, when all Americans "came together."[55] Latino politicians and reformers took advantage of national conditions to promote a mainstream politics that sought to make them more acceptable to whites and moved them away from the working-class nationalism that emphasized their differences from white Americans.

As we have seen, such a mainstream politics had been part of Mexicano political culture since the turn of the century, but they took even firmer hold in an expanding community whose strong ties to the old country had been badly mauled by repatriation and subsequent deportation campaigns. This shift was accelerated by the labor circumstances of the West, where the agricultural and mining industries' appetite for new workers created opportunities for unionization.[56] Even immigrant organizations began clamoring for their rights as residents or workers of this nation. Equality or similarity became a reward for good citizenship and for service to the nation in World War II.

Much has begun to appear recently on Mexican American participation in World War II and its impact on returning veterans. The points of emphasis should be threefold: The war brought Mexican Americans from all over the country together, allowing a sense of their Mexican Americanness to overcome their regionalism. It brought them into contact with whites in a different context and under different ground rules. And last, it provided them an assertiveness based on their military service. They came out of the war believing that they were brave, they were defenders of the nation, and they were equal. For many, the clock could not be turned back.[57]

After the war, western politics and continuing immigration greatly influenced the proponents of both inclusion and similarity by forcing them into the politics of reaction. The incredible increase in population threatened to overwhelm the older Mexican American communities in southern Colorado, Arizona, California, and New Mexico. Mexican American politicians and civil rights advocates had to choose how to define the two communities within the barrio. Repatriation and subsequent deportation campaigns—including Operation Wetback in the 1950s—continued to deplete the immigrant leadership.[58] The rise of Anglo conservatism in the late 1950s and early 1960s, which sought to redefine the issue of minorities in ideological and class terms rather than in strictly racial ones, served as the catalysts for this new climate.

For example, conservatives saw Mexican American civil rights crusades and politicians as part of an expansion of "liberal socialism." To them, the region's underbelly seemed to be revolting and threatening to exacerbate the West's unresolved dilemma of the "Mexican problem."[59] By ignoring past progress, they blunted any further advancement of the politics of similarity. But even as they turned red-baiting full force on liberal Mexican American reformers, they attracted many moderates with promises of inclusion.

Thus, the 1950s were years of both progress and retrenchment. Mexican Americans made inroads at the political grass roots by winning local elections, by working as political lieutenants for state and national figures, and by becoming national spokespersons for Mexicano and Latino issues. But in giving up their identity as a people of color and by muting any fundamental criticism of the American political system, they became political gadflies, unable to be anything more than a nuisance at the policy-making level. Their efforts did much to attract Mexicano voters to the electoral process, but at the price of limiting their own effectiveness at stimulating fundamental reform.

Yet by the late 1960s, Mexican Americans in Arizona, California, New Mexico, and Texas were again the "loudest" minorities in demanding civil rights and in supporting liberal and radical causes. More important, these new advocates for Mexicano rights were much more nationalistic, were more focused on the working class, and were immensely more scathing in their critique of American society. In what seemed a clear succession of events, Mexican Americans began identifying themselves as "Chicanos," spoke Spanish more frequently, promoted their culture constantly, and launched the United Farm Workers Union in California, the Alianza Federal de Pueblos Libres in New Mexico, the Crusade for Justice in Colorado, and La Raza Unida Party in Texas.[60] In Arizona, a group of militant Latino Democrats became a force in state politics, while the Spanish Speaking Organization for Community, Integrity, and Opportunity (SOCIO) became a fairly successful advocacy group in Utah.[61] Almost out of nowhere—for those whites who had ignored prior efforts—Mexicano protests sprang up loudly and irreverently. These Chicanos seemed to be demanding everything from cultural rights to land, from political power to bilingual education, and from respect to open borders.

This phase became the politics of nationalism and "otherness." Mexicano activists redefined their strategy in regards to their civil rights struggle. While the more radical organizations led this new movement, they were followed at least part of the way by mainstream leaders who saw their own effectiveness blunted by the new conservatism. In almost every instance, these new organizations and leaders came out of the rural metropolis. Even Rodolfo "Corky" Gonzales of the Crusade for Justice, headquartered in Denver, spoke to Mexican American rural issues such as land, dignity, history, and local control. All presented people in struggle, fighting for the landless and dispossessed.[62]

This new style of politics changed historical icons and Mexicano history itself. Chicanos did not need to connect to World War II—as earlier generations had done—to find heroes. Instead, they looked toward Meso-America, the Mexican Revolution, and early Tejano revolutionaries for their inspiration. More important, their starting point was not Americanism but a new-found Chicanismo, or, for moderates, a new Mexican Americanism that was more militant in nature. Having fought their civil rights struggles within gringo parameters for most of the century, these young Turks sought to change the playing field. For them, success was measured not by upward mobility but, instead, by cultural survival. They rejected the "culture of disadvantage" and the ahistorical interpretations of most liberal and conservative social scientists writing on the barrios. These new Chicanos rejected the politics of their predecessors and of liberal Anglo politicians because they had failed to "arrest poverty in the barrios, to educate the children, to end discrimination, to respect the culture, or to create indigenous leadership."[63]

The Chicano movement established alternative political parties, created Chicano studies programs, rewrote the history of Mexican Americans in the United States, and led to a resurgence of the cultural arts in the barrios. Chicano leaders "rhetorically" reclaimed a large part of the West and renamed it Aztlán, the mythical homeland of the Aztecs. Rejecting traditional American politics, they developed a myriad of ideologies that saw them as a people rather than a minority group, and that saw them as something other than white Americans. By reaffirming the primacy of class and race, they reignited the debate over identity and called for a rejection of whiteness as the only alternative to success. They racialized the terms "Mexican" and "Latino," recognizing a racialization that had always been just below the surface even during the height of the Mexican American Generation.[64]

The politics of "otherness" or nationalism sought to take Mexican Americans out of their forgotten niche in western politics and put them in their own political orbit, and it represented an effort to destroy the asymmetric relationship between Mexicano politics and western politics. Only by being seen as a separate political entity, beholden to no one and focused on the barrio, could Mexican Americans (and Latinos) gain the attention of white America.[65] They would—in the later stages of what have come to be known more generally as Latino politics—become a group to be catered to and spoken to in its own language. Latino politics became a new version of the politics of constituency—a voting bloc to be added to the totals of either party or particular candidates, but with its own agenda and its own leaders.

These politics astounded western Anglos. The "Mexicans" they knew were not like this. They might have been prone to violence, and their leaders were always whining about the conditions of the barrio, but they had always seemed controllable, either because they were not citizens, because they did not vote in large numbers, or because they were overly concerned with legitimacy and about being seen as good Americans. These new Chicanos were both citizens and unafraid. Many were also in college, and some were Vietnam veterans. They spoke the language, and they knew American history well enough to turn it against American society. Not integrationists, they used rhetoric outside the boundaries of traditional U.S. civil rights language. Anglo politicos found Chicano efforts to become part of a larger

Third World cross-pollination of activism particularly disturbing. This trend tended to expand the discussion of such issues as segregation, discrimination, police brutality, land, and cultural rights. From Reies López Tijerina's land issues at the United Nations to La Raza Unida's flirtation with communist Cuba, Chicanos were now internationalizing their politics.[66]

Yet this internationalization was hardly new. Mexicans and Mexican Americans had been thinking internationally for most of the century. In 1959, a mixed group calling itself the American Committee for Protection of Foreign Born petitioned the United Nations to focus attention on the problems of the Mexican immigrant. The notion of "immigrant," however, was not limited to recent arrivals but, rather, took in anyone of Mexican origin. Committee members asked the United Nations to investigate "because repeated attempts [by government and private entities had] failed to overcome the serious deprivations of the human rights of the Mexican immigrant in the United States."[67] Before that petition, Mexican Americans and other Latinos had looked toward their individual consulates for help in addressing their treatment in the United States.

Every Latino generation has seen a need to look toward the international community for help in its struggles for civil and human rights. While some in the Mexican American Generation were uncomfortable going outside the United States, others were conscious of the eyes of those outside the nation, who looked to see how the United States treated its Mexicans. Hector P. García, and probably the most successful civil rights advocate of the G.I. Generation, constantly wondered what his Mexican neighbors thought of the way the United States acted toward its Mexican-origin population.[68] Mexican and Mexican American leaders understood something that scholars have only recently come to realize: that the experience of Mexicans and Mexican Americans (and most Latinos) has been a transnational one. Latinos are tied to their mother country not just by relatives or citizenship status but also by the immigrants who constantly pour in from the south.[69]

The Chicano movement's transnationalism did not succeed in building the kind of strong bridge with Mexico that many activists had hoped for, but it did reawaken many Mexican nationals' consciences about their responsibility to those *mexicanos de afuera* [those in foreign lands]. From Luis Echeverría to Felipe Calderon, Mexican presidents have had an interest in what happens to their citizens on the U.S. side of the border. The concern has been political and economic, and has sometimes been about posturing to the world, but it has frequently served the interests of Mexican American and Latino leaders and activists. Since the late 1990s, Central American governments have also become involved in the social politics of their immigrants in the United States.

But both the liberal version of transnationalism as well as its leftist and nationalist alternative created a climate conducive to recruitment from the right. Those Mexican Americans and Latinos who saw openings in society and had become beneficiaries of the activism of the past were no longer so anxious to critique American institutions and their founding principles. Sensing that much of the Chicano movement and the liberal middle-class attack was based on a distancing from the mainstream, they reacted by voting for more mainstream politicians and opened their minds and hearts to conservative politics. The Republican Party, initially slow to react, quickly made up for lost ground to take advantage of the split within the community. Stressing "similar values," they established the Hispanic Republican Committee and hired Latinos for their election committees.

For Mexican Americans, transnationalism has been a double-edged sword. It keeps their status ambivalent because in the transnational arena they are neither completely foreign nor fully American. As transnationals, however, they can claim a sense of peoplehood and thus remove from themselves the stigma of being a small and powerless group of hyphenated Americans. Here, in this arena, they can play the politics of constituency in the West just as Puerto Rican Americans do in New York and Cuban Americans do in Florida. That is why immigrant status and immigration politics have recently been at the core of the Mexican American and Latino political agenda. Where they came from, why they are here, what they will do in relation to the old country, and whether they will or will not assimilate is of concern not only to Americans at large but also to the Latino communities across the nation. Immigration politics are also a testament to westerners that globalization means more than selling their goods and making their investments in global markets. It is also about letting in the world. Anglo politicians have slowly become sensitive to this important issue, as witnessed by both political parties' pandering to Hispanics with proposals for immigration reform and through friendships with Latin American leaders.

This political posturing by both Anglo American politicians and Mexican American advocates is part of the fourth phase of Mexicano politics, which I call the "Hispanic integration phase." During this phase, Mexican Americans—now referred to as "Hispanics"—have moved into the political mainstream; have been elected to Congress, to governorships, and to mayoral offices; and have developed national organizations. They have also become an important constituency for both political parties. Their appointments to the president's cabinet and their consideration for federal judgeships, even the Supreme Court, have become a political fact. More important, there is now an assumption that their participation is crucial to the political process, though admittedly still far from reaching its potential.

One reason for this emerging political importance has been population growth. Yet this growth has been more diversified than in the past. Immigrants now come not only from Mexico but also from Central and Latin America and the Caribbean. Los Angeles, San Francisco, Houston, Dallas, Phoenix, Salt Lake City, Las Vegas, and other communities have entered a Latino-ization phase in which not only the larger community but the barrios too are becoming more diverse. This diversity has sparked debates and contentions about what at one time were Mexican immigrant or Mexican American issues. Immigration to the West is no more just a Mexican issue, and neither are bilingual education, political representation, inadequate housing, or job discrimination. Even in higher education, debates now rage in California, New Mexico, Texas, and Arizona on whether universities should have Chicano studies or Latino studies. Latino politics—when neatly separated by nationality—had been in large part about what happened in the mother country and about immigration issues particular to the country. Now Puerto Ricans—who are citizens—talk about immigration and legal and illegal status. Cubans—for the most part better educated and more affluent—talk about poverty and poor schools. Central Americans worry not only about the Central American Free Trade Agreement but also about what concessions Mexico's president can get from his American counterpart. The issues of language accessibility, education, political representation, judicial fairness, and identity have taken on a more diverse perspective at the same time as they are becoming homogenized "Latino issues."

One important feature of this "Hispanic integration" is that the tenacity of the politics of similarity and the belligerency of the politics of nationalism have merged and become politics of recognition. Not only do Latino politicians today want civil and cultural rights, but they also want recognition and a rewriting of the nation's history that underscores their contributions. This phase combines the years of struggle with the optimism of the more affluent and educated Latin American immigrants who feel more confident about competing with the Anglo.[70] The business community and the national politicians have homogenized a Latino political agenda and force fed it to the diverse Latino community through both the Spanish and English Latino media, and when possible, through the mainstream media.

This integration, of course, resonates mostly at the national level. As the last major poll of Latinos indicated, most Cubans are Cubans first, most Mexicans are either Mexican or Mexican American first, and so on. Politics at the grassroots level are about grassroots issues and always have been. At the end of the twentieth century, most of the issues for Latino communities in the West remained the same. Some might have taken on more urgency than others, but the list has neither grown nor shrunk significantly. Jobs, education, housing, health, political representation, judicial hostility, immigration, and lack of substantive visibility remain issues of importance to Latino organizations throughout the West.[71] Compounding Latino problems has been a push among western conservatives, who have become more willing to use raw power to turn back Latino political ambitions.

For Latinos, this conservatism has become more sophisticated and to some even enticing. While still based on some form of racialism, this western conservatism is more ideologically and economically based and has proven capable of reaffirming class and racial divisions within the Latino community. The more there is diversity within the Latino community, the greater the probability of internal divisions within it. Latinos moving toward the Republican Party are still a significant minority, but they are a crucial one. The difference today is that among some sectors of the nation's conservative leadership, there is a Latino-friendly constituency that uses political appointments and friendly gestures toward Mexico and Central America to argue for a "place" in the Republican Party for Latinos. Accelerating the move among some Latinos toward conservatism has been the rise of immigration as a divisive issue in the discussions over national security. This is a plus for a Republican Party that cannot grow much larger without Latinos.[72]

Not surprisingly, issues such as English-only legislation, bilingual education, affirmative action, immigration reform, benefits for resident aliens, social cost of undocumented families, and culture wars are defining battlegrounds for the two largest groups in the West. These issues are not new. Texas passed English-only injunctions in the 1920s, most of the Southwest has been debating bilingual education for over fifty years, affirmative action—in another rhetorical form—was part of the politics of similarity, immigration has been debated in the West since the beginning of the twentieth century, and the culture wars have been fought from the moment the first white settler moved into the Mexican part of the West. Anglo politicians have tried exclusion, coercion, co-option, and now courtship to control Latino political power. In some form or another, all of those methods are applied today in different parts of the region as the Latino population continues to grow at an astronomical rate. Latino reaction has also been multifaceted, as some groups and leaders use some or all of the earlier-mentioned approaches: inclusion, similarity, nationalism, and integration.

Using Oscar Martínez's notion of a border region moving constantly northward with the spread of people of Mexican origin, we can say that the Latino political West also continues to expand nationally.[73] Latinos outside the West bring their own experiences into the mix, but they understand that what happens in the West will have a great impact on them. In a sense, what happens to Mexican Americans in the West will determine much of what happens to all Latinos in the United States. This is so not only because people of Mexican origin are the largest Latino group by far, but also because the region remains a crucial political space. Becoming an important part of the political agenda of this region makes them a crucial element of national politics.

Latino politics, however, remain *in* the West but not *of* the West. Whites in the West continue to pass legislation and play politics to limit Latino political power, while denying that they are doing so. Recently passed English-only laws and other restrictive propositions are described as attempts to control "illegal immigrants" or to "maintain American culture," but they are in reality attempts to control the growth of Latino political power. Latinos, on the other hand, have yet to mount a successful and sustained response to such western politics because they confront a political dilemma. To play integration politics—and defuse charges of "foreignness"—is to lose their special constituent status, but to continue to play that status makes them targets of these same attacks.

More significantly, as Latinos continue to seek political integration at all cost, the more likely it is that the schisms within the community will deepen. Latinos who are doing well or who see opportunity in the mainstream may not only drop out of the Latino drive for civil rights, but may well become its opponents. This development is pushed along by another element that has come into play in the last two decades: Latinos are now represented in most of the echelons of government in the West, and some have powerful white allies. Thus, the "Latino agenda" is multifaceted and much more difficult to implement. Also, Latinos in the West are not simply a political nuisance or just another group to be appeased. They are a potentially dominant group, and most other political groups are conscious of that. It is quite possible that Latinos in the West and across the country will soon be entering a new phase that will have profound ramifications for the nation's politics.

Before that occurs, however, Latinos will have to increase their voter-participation rates, get more of their compatriots to become citizens, and avoid the potential split of their community into liberal and conservative camps. A Latino leadership will have to evolve that sees itself as national in scope and that speaks to issues that are not only "Latino issues" but peripheral issues created by the Latino presence. These Latino political leaders must also accept that their politics will be influenced by border issues, globalization, and Latin American politics and economics, as well as by a new nativism that has arisen over undocumented workers. Unlike those of earlier Mexican American and immigrant generations, this new generation of Latino political leaders will have to lead from both the top and bottom and respond to these issues with a much more coherent political stand.

Something that is likely to help is the growth of the nativism that has surged into conservative politics and that has become so anti-immigrant that even some former Republican Latino constituencies are gravitating toward more moderate or liberal positions. More important, this anti-immigrant fervor has energized Latinos to become citizens and to participate in the electoral process. This heightened participation will no doubt lead to a greater clout among the political parties, and probably to the election of more Latino officeholders and to more political appointments. At the same time, this heightened nativism is moving Latinos and Mexicanos to re-affirm their identity as well as their "otherness," and to become hypersensitive to the disadvantages they continue to encounter in the United States. Thus, even as they become more integrated into American society, they are becoming less traditional Americans because they are expanding the notion of what it means to be an American. This means that Latino politics in the West will become *of the* West when the West becomes more Latino and not the other way around.

NOTES

1. Raul Villarreal was a student friend during my time in college. For more on him and the activities of La Raza Unida Party in Texas, see Ignacio M. García, *United We Win: The Rise and Fall of La Raza Unida Party* (Tucson: University of Arizona Press, 1989), esp. 161–164.

2. See Ignacio M. García, *Viva Kennedy: Mexican Americans in Search of Camelot* (College Station: Texas A&M University Press, 2000).

3. For a fuller discussion of the Treaty of Guadalupe Hidalgo, see Richard Griswold del Castillo, *The Treaty of Guadalupe Hidalgo: A Legacy of Conflict* (Norman: University of Oklahoma Press, 1992).

4. David Montejano, *Anglos and Mexicans in the Making of Texas, 1846–1986* (Austin: University of Texas Press, 1987).

5. See Rodolfo Acuña, *Occupied America: A History of Chicanos*, 5th ed. (New York: Pearson Longman, 2004), 64.

6. For a more detailed discussion of the internal community built by Mexican Americans, see Antonio Ríos-Bustamante, *Los Angeles, Pueblo y Region, 1781–1850* (Mexico City: Instituto Nacional de Antropología e Historia, 1991), and Emilio Zamora, *The World of the Mexican Worker in Texas* (College Station: Texas A&M University Press, 1993).

7. See Montejano, *Anglos and Mexicans*, 220.

8. For more on Mexican Americans in World War I, see Carole E. Christian, "Joining the Mainstream: Texas's Mexican Americans during World War I," *Southwestern Historical Quarterly* 92 (April 1989): 559–595.

9. See Mario T. García, *Mexican Americans: Leadership, Ideology, and Identity, 1930–1960* (New Haven, Conn.: Yale University Press, 1989), 25–61; quotation on 31.

10. Ibid., 231–251.

11. See Ignacio M. García, *Hector P. García: In Relentless Pursuit of Justice* (Houston: Arte Publico Press, 2003), 74–103, 196, 198–201.

12. Quoted in Ignacio García, *Chicanismo: The Forging of a Militant Ethos among Mexican Americans* (Tucson: University of Arizona Press, 1997), 92.

13. For a short discussion of this characteristic, see García, *Viva Kennedy;* Acuña, *Occupied America;* and Juan Gómez-Quiñones, *Chicano Politics: Reality and Promise, 1940–1990* (Albuquerque: University of New Mexico Press, 1990). These works as well as others deal with the subject of differences in the Mexican American communities of the West and Southwest. No extensive work has been done specifically on this topic, but it is mentioned quite often in the works published on Mexican Americans.

14. Tomás Almaguer, *Racial Fault Lines: The Historical Origins of White Supremacy in California* (Berkeley and Los Angeles: University of California Press, 1994).

15. Carey McWilliams, *Southern California: An Island on the Land* (New York: Duell, Sloan & Pearce, 1946), 207. This was true even in those parts of the mountain West where mining predominated. Most Mexicano workers in mining regions lived in small company towns, segregated, close to rural communities and outside the reach of larger urban institutions. For all purposes, they were out in the sticks. Not much has been written on this subject, but Mario T. García's "Border Proletariat: Mexican Americans and the International Union of Mine, Mill, and Smelter Workers," in *Mexican Americans,* 176–179, provides some discussion of this mining ruralization, though he does not describe it as such.

16. See Gilbert G. González and Raul A. Fernández, *A Century of Chicano History* (New York: Routledge, 2003), 92–94.

17. For one of the best and most extensive statistical works done on Mexican Americans in the city, see Leo Grebler, Joan W. Moore, and Ralph C. Guzmán, *The Mexican American People* (New York: Free Press, 1970).

18. See F. Arturo Rosales, *Testimonio: A Documentary History of the Mexican American Struggle for Civil Rights* (Houston: Arte Publico Press, 2000).

19. See González and Fernández, *A Century of Chicano History,* 92–94.

20. Ian Haney-López, *White by Law: The Legal Construction of Race* (New York: New York University Press,1996), 1–9.

21. For a discussion of the so-called Mexican problem as it pertained to the public schools, see Guadalupe San Miguel Jr., *"Let All of Them Take Heed": Mexican Americans and the Campaign for Education Equality in Texas, 1910–1981* (Austin: University of Texas Press, 1987), 103–108. For an excellent discussion of the "culture of segregation," see Montejano, *Anglos and Mexicans,* 220–234.

22. Montejano, *Anglos and Mexicans,* 235–256.

23. Quoted in Arnoldo De León, *They Called Them Greasers: Anglo Attitudes toward Mexicans in Texas, 1821–1900* (Austin: University of Texas Press, 1983), 3.

24. García, *Viva Kennedy,* 167.

25. García, *Hector P. García*, 96.
26. Neal Foley, *The White Scourge: Mexicans, Blacks, and Poor Whites in Texas Cotton Culture* (Berkeley and Los Angeles: University of California Press, 1997), 183–214.
27. García, *Mexican Americans*, 25–61.
28. Ibid., 25.
29. See Arnoldo De León, *In re Ricardo Rodríguez. An Attempt at Chicano Disenfranchisement in San Antonio, 1896–1897* (San Antonio, Tex.: Caravel Press, 1979), and Fernando Padilla, "Early Chicano Legal Recognition: 1846–1897," *Journal of Popular Culture* 13 (Spring 1980): 564–574.
30. See Haney-López, *White by Law*, 1.
31. Ibid., 3.
32. See Walter Benn Michaels, "Race into Culture: A Critical Genealogy of Cultural Identity," *Critical Inquiry* 18 (1992): 655–663.
33. This notion of empowering difference is the foundation for the building of an internal community, for cultural identity, and for ethnic pride.
34. See *Morrison v. California*, 291 U.S. 82 (1930), 95n5.
35. See "The Social Security Classification" and "A Poignant Defense of Whiteness of Mexicans," both in Rosales, *Testimonio*, 172–173.
36. See Haney-López, *White by Law*, 21–22; Sumi Cho, "Redeeming Whiteness in the Shadow of Internment: Earl Warren, Brown, and a Theory of Racial Redemption," *Boston College Third World Law Journal* 19 (1998): 73–120; and, for a discussion on the "neutrality" of whiteness, Barbara Flagg, "Was Blind, but Now I See: White Race Consciousness and the Requirement of Discriminating Intent," *Michigan Law Review* 91 (1993): 953.
37. Cho, "Redeeming Whiteness."
38. See Dennis Chávez's letter to Texas State Prison, 1 June 1954. In this letter, Senator Chávez takes issue with the prison system for classifying Andres Viera as "Mexican" instead of "white." He wrote, "I am sure it is not the practice of the Prison Department to list a man by his nationality, or his descent, as the case might be, in an official document such as this." Letter found in Dennis Chávez Collection, Box 32, Folder 3, Special Collections, Zimmerman Library, University of New Mexico, Albuquerque.
39. See García, *Hector P. García*, 198–201; see also *What Price Wetbacks?* pamphlet of the American G.I. Forum and the Texas State Federation of Labor (AFL). Austin, Texas, undated, Hector P. García Papers, Special Collections, Bell Library, Texas A&M University, Corpus Christi, Texas.
40. García, *Hector P. García*, 156.
41. This quote is found in Carlos Muñoz Jr., *Youth, Identity, Power* (New York: Verso, 1989), 33. The full text of the statement is found in Paul Coronel, "Where Is the Mexican Youth Conference Aiming?" *Mexican Voice*, February 1940, 1.
42. García, *Mexican Americans*, 33–38.
43. For a good discussion of litigation against segregated schools, see San Miguel, *Let All of Them Take Heed*.
44. Haney-López, *White by Law*, 67.

45. See Clare Sheridan, "Another White Race: Mexican Americans and the Paradox of Whiteness in Jury Selection," *Law and History Review* 21 (Spring 2003): 4–7; *Norris v. Alabama*, 294 U.S. 587 (1935).

46. *Hernandez v. Texas*, 347 U.S. 475 (1954).

47. See Ruben Munguía, comp., *A Cotton Picker Finds Justice! The Saga of the Hernandez Case* (San Antonio: Munguia Press, 1954). The pamphlet is unpaginated but the reader should take note of the section written by Carlos C. Cadena, "Legal Ramifications of the Hernandez Case."

48. See the ruling in *Hernandez v. Texas*.

49. Quoted in García, *Viva Kennedy*, 133.

50. Gómez-Quiñonez, *Chicano Politics;* Richard García, *The Rise of the Mexican American Middle Class: San Antonio, 1929–1941* (College Station: Texas A&M University Press, 1991).

51. Quoted in "Chavez Says Rich Get Richer under GOP," *Fresno Bee*, 5 October 1960.

52. For an excellent discussion of the repatriation campaigns, see Francisco E. Balderrama and Raymond Rodríguez, *Decade of Betrayal: Mexican Repatriation in the 1930s* (Albuquerque: University of New Mexico Press, 1995).

53. For more on barrio Americanism, see García, *Hector P. García*, 74–104.

54. García, *Viva Kennedy*, 60–74, 123–130.

55. Mario T. García, "Carlos E. Castañeda and the Search for History," in *Mexican Americans*, 232–234.

56. García, "Border Proletariat,"175–198.

57. See Lorena Oropeza, *Raza Si! Guerra No!* (Berkeley and Los Angeles: University of California Press, 2005); Maggie Rivas-Rodríguez, *Mexican Americans in World War II* (Austin: University of Texas Press, 2005); and Raul Morín, *Among the Valiant* (Alhambra, Calif.: Borden, 1963).

58. See Juan Ramón García, *Operation Wetback: The Mass Deportation of Mexican Undocumented Workers in 1954* (Westport, Conn.: Greenwood Press, 1980), for more on the effort among Mexicano reformers to deport undocumented workers.

59. For an excellent discussion of this conservatism, see Lisa McGirr, *Suburban Warriors: The Origins of the New American Right* (Princeton, N.J.: Princeton University Press, 2001); see also Mary C. Brennan, *Turning Right in the Sixties: The Conservative Capture of the GOP* (Chapel Hill: University of North Carolina Press, 1995).

60. For a discussion of this period, see Acuña, *Occupied America;* Armando Navarro, *La Raza Unida Party* (Philadelphia: Temple University Press, 2000); Gómez-Quiñonez, *Chicano Politics;* and García, *Chicanismo*.

61. For some discussion on the movement in Arizona and Utah, see Navarro, *La Raza Unida Party*, 202–230. For work on SOCIO in Utah, see Jorge Iber, *Hispanics in Mormon Zion, 1912–1999* (College Station: Texas A&M University Press, 2000), 85–114.

62. Navarro, *La Raza Unida Party*. Also see Reies López Tijerina, *They Called Me "King Tiger"* (Houston: Arte Publico Press, 2000), and Antonio Esquibel, *Message to Aztlán* (Houston: Arte Publico Press, 2001).

63. See García, *Chicanismo*, 19–42.

64. See Mario T. García's discussion of this generation in *Mexican Americans*.

65. Chicano militants clashed among themselves in developing politics of independence. Some sought to completely shun the American political arena, while others simply sought to rearrange the relationship. For a discussion of this debate among the activists of the national La Raza Unida Party in 1972, see García, *United We Win*, 91–116.

66. Ibid.

67. See Griswold del Castillo, *Treaty of Guadalupe Hidalgo*, 146–148.

68. See García, *Hector P. García*, 276.

69. For one of the best general discussions of Latino transnationalism, see Juan González, *Harvest of Empire: A History of Latinos in America* (New York: Penguin Books, 2000). Also see Carlos G. Vélez-Ibañez and Anna Sampaio, *Transnational Latina/o Communities* (New York: Rowman & Littlefield, 2002).

70. One only has to peruse the pages of *Hispanic Monthly* and *Hispanic Business* to see the tremendous growth of this sector and its recruitment of the best and the brightest of the Latino community. Interestingly, unlike traditional business magazines that might seek a homogeneous clientele, these periodicals see the economic benefit of Latino diversity.

71. See Rodolfo O. de la Garza et al., eds., *Latino Voices: Mexican, Puerto Rican, and Cuban Perspectives* (Boulder, Colo.: Westview Press, 1992).

72. See Richard Santillan and Federico A. Subervi-Vélez, "Latino Participation in Republican Party Politics in California," in *Racial and Ethnic Politics in California*, ed. Bryan O. Jackson and Michael B. Preston (Berkeley, CA: University of California Press, 1991), 285–319.

73. Professor Oscar Martínez was a mentor, and one who taught me about borderlands and their "extension" northward. See his *Troublesome Borders* (Tucson: University of Arizona Press, 1988) and *Mexican-Origin People in the United States* (Tucson: University of Arizona Press, 2001).

CHAPTER 7

The Evolution of Modern American Indian Politics
Bradley Glenn Shreve

On 3 March 2007, the Cherokee Nation of Oklahoma held a special election to determine whether the descendants of former slaves owned by Cherokee elites were, in fact, legally tribal members. According to an 1866 treaty, black freedmen within the tribe were full citizens of the Cherokee Nation. Indeed, those freedmen who came of age after the Civil War grew up speaking Cherokee, participating in traditional ceremonies, and attending tribal schools. Many married full-blooded tribal members, and some even went on to hold tribal office. Despite this history, voters rejected the initiative, effectively banning all descendants of freedmen from claiming membership in the tribe.[1]

Critics throughout Indian Country assailed the results of the plebiscite as racist, rightly pointing out that many predominantly white tribal members, who can claim only a small amount of Indian blood, continued to be counted as full citizens of the Cherokee Nation. Still, few have questioned the tribe's legal right to hold such an election or to make such a determination on its membership. The recent decision may be "a reckless application of sovereignty," as Cherokee leader Taylor Keen stated, but ultimately the tribe has the right to determine its membership. Treaties brokered between the U.S. government and the Cherokee Nation have guaranteed the tribe its unique independent status. As *Indian Country Today* columnist Steven Newcomb argued, "The Cherokee Nation is free to do what it wants with its reputation and its legacy. And if that includes throwing out the descendents of slaves that some Cherokees once owned . . . that's its business."[2]

This debate over tribal inclusion—or exclusion, as it may be—reveals the parameters and underlying assumptions that inform contemporary intertribal political culture. It is a political culture that differs dramatically from that of other racial minorities. In order to understand American Indian politics we must, as Scott Tang argues in chapter 8, toss out the binary racial rubric that quite often imprisons our thinking. Differing radically from the goals of their Japanese, Chinese, Mexican, or African American counterparts, Native American political actors today subscribe to an unquestioned ideological foundation of tribal sovereignty, treaty rights, cultural retention, and self-determination. The first principle, tribal sovereignty, stands as perhaps the most integral. The notion that all Indian tribes, bands, and pueblos exist as distinct, independent autonomous entities shapes the political discourse in Native America and defines the dialogue between the First Nations and the federal and state governments.

From this first principle stems an unflinching belief that the treaty is the highest law of the land. Agreements between the federal government and the First Nations have established reservations, guaranteed territorial integrity, and recognized a body of political rights that Native people have, which distinguishes them from other Americans. The cornerstone principle of cultural retention remains equally significant throughout Indian Country. Although in the past both newcomers and Natives have argued for the acculturation and assimilation of the American Indian, today belief in the importance of preserving traditional languages, customs, arts, and spiritual beliefs is simply unquestioned. Finally, all Native political actors in the public sphere stand firm in espousing self-determination—the right of Native people to decide what is best for themselves.

Today, it may seem obvious that such principles would form the basis of the political discourse in Native America, but this foundation only took form over the past seventy years or so. It has been those intertribal organizations that work to define Indian peoples' relations with federal and state governments that have formed contemporary Native political philosophy and ideology. Such organizations, however, do not operate in a vacuum. In fact, just the opposite is true: Native political culture is inextricably linked to the larger political climate. Of particular importance to the contours of American Indian politics are the two greatest changes in twentieth-century American political culture: the rise of the New Deal order in the 1930s and the movement for decolonization, inclusion, and social change that began in the wake of World War II and accelerated in the 1960s.

The emergence of the welfare state fundamentally altered the direction of federal Indian policy and tribal politics. Before the succession of Franklin Roosevelt to the presidency, government officials and self-proclaimed reformers—both white and Native American—sought to assimilate or incorporate the First Peoples into American society by breaking up tribal landholdings and destroying Native traditions, customs, and languages.

Roosevelt's commissioner of Indian affairs, John Collier, launched what was nothing short of a revolution with his Indian Reorganization Act, disposing of the former policies of land allotment, assimilation, and acculturation while embracing self-determination, cultural retention, and tribal sovereignty. From the founding of the National Congress of American Indians in 1944 up to the present, every intertribal political organization of any standing has promulgated these cornerstone principles.

With the onset of the Cold War and the culture of conformity that followed, the federal government renewed its efforts to integrate and assimilate Native people into the mainstream of American society. The civil rights movement and other movements for social change and justice influenced Indian activists to employ new tactics to secure the basic premises of the Indian New Deal. Through civil disobedience, demonstrations, and occupations, the red power warriors of the National Indian Youth Council, the Indians of All Tribes, and the American Indian Movement forcefully brought the concerns of Native people to the political consciousness of the nation at large. In the 1970s, after years of agitation on the part of these activists, allies in Congress drafted and passed a slew of federal legislation that repositioned sovereignty, cultural retention, treaty rights, and self-determination as key features of Indian policy.

That intertribal organization and the political discourse in Native America have been intertwined with greater social and economic transformations occurring on the national stage should be obvious. However, only recently have scholars broken with the insular view of the American Indian experience that has dominated historical writing for generations. Historian Daniel Cobb's work stands as a milestone in this regard, revealing how President Lyndon Johnson's War on Poverty shaped Native politics and the struggle for self-determination in the 1960s. In this essay, I likewise seek to show the evolution of American Indian politics within the larger national context, while also stressing that Native peoples rose above tribal differences and found a common set of principles that united them.[3]

Recognizing Indian history and politics as part and parcel of American politics remains essential, but it is equally important to place the struggle for sovereignty, treaty rights, cultural preservation, and self-determination in a regional context. The fact is that the vast majority of Native people reside in the West, and hence their story is undeniably a western one. In many ways, American Indian politics, like the West itself, are a product of the often heavy hand of the federal government. As historian Richard White has shown, federal influence in the West has been all pervasive. And such influence in tribal communities, whether in the city or on the reservation (which itself is very much a western construct) is no exception.[4]

Before Franklin Roosevelt and his cadre of innovative minds took control of the White House in 1933, federal Indian policy and Native American politics adhered to a mold set during the 1880s, when white reformers called for the incorporation of Native people into the mainstream of American society. They believed that Indian reservations allowed for the continuance of Native culture and were thus impeding rather than facilitating progress. Organizations such as the Women's National Indian Association and the Indian Rights Association lobbied for the dismantling of reservations and the assimilation of Indians into mainstream American society. Their efforts culminated in the Dawes Severalty Act, which divided tribally owned land into individual plots granted to each head of family. All excess land was sold off to white settlers, resulting in the loss of millions of acres of land.

Progressive reformers used the immigrant experience as their model. Like the Germans, Irish, and Italians, they argued, American Indians would become fine upstanding citizens if placed in the right environment and given proper education, which meant boarding schools far from tribal influences. In 1879, the Office of Indian Affairs opened the Carlisle Indian School in Carlisle, Pennsylvania, under the supervision of Richard Henry Pratt. A former army officer, Pratt firmly believed in racial equality, but he maintained that Indian identity and culture needed to be wiped away. He argued that all people were born blank slates; hence, if Native people were placed in a Euro-American environment, they would shed their tribal background and adopt white customs and habits. Pratt distilled this philosophy down to the famous slogan "Kill the Indian, and save the man," which was exactly what he tried to do by placing Native children in white homes and educating them at Carlisle.[5]

It was graduates of Carlisle who later formed the first intertribal organization, the Society of American Indians (SAI). Echoing earlier progressive reformers, SAI leaders such as Carlos Montezuma (Yavapai Apache), Charles Eastman (Sioux), Sherman Coolidge (Arapaho), Gertrude Bonnin (Sioux), and Thomas Sloan (Omaha) believed that Native people should reject tradition and custom and embrace Euro-American culture. The federal government, they argued, could work to the First Peoples' benefit by breaking up reservations, allotting lands, and educating Native children. While Indian politics at the local level varied dramatically by tribe, the SAI dominated the national political scene and defined the discourse on American Indian political culture in the public sphere.[6]

Passage of the Citizenship Act in 1924, which conferred all the rights and privileges of American citizenship on Native people, eventually led to the dissolution of the SAI, as many within the organization believed it no longer served a legitimate purpose. Indians went without a viable, Native-led intertribal association for the next ten years. During this time, Collier founded the American Indian Defense Association to uphold Native landholdings and advocate for political rights. Unlike the reformers before him, Collier rejected assimilation and acculturation, believing there was something of great value in traditional Native cultures. Collier's work established him as one of the greatest critics of federal Indian policy and as the foremost defender of Indian rights. When a nation ready for change elected Roosevelt president in 1932, Collier landed the job as the commissioner of the Bureau of Indian Affairs (BIA).[7]

During Collier's administration, federal Indian policy stressed renewed tribalism, self-determination, cultural preservation, sovereignty, and treaty rights. The Indian Reorganization Act (IRA)—the centerpiece of the Indian New Deal—incorporated these principles and completely transformed Indian affairs. Tribes formed new governments that in theory would eventually assume the duties held by the Department of the Interior. The IRA also sought the preservation of Indian culture through an educational program that rejected the assimilative notions of the past and encouraged children to embrace their Native heritage. Another section called for the restoration of large portions of allotted Indian land.[8]

Many Native people who found employment in the BIA during the Indian New Deal refocused their political thinking, rejecting assimilation and embracing cultural revival, sovereignty, and treaty rights. Others, however, fought the reorganization plan and the Indian New Deal, lobbying for the IRA's immediate revocation. This faction, which fundamentally disagreed with Collier's vision, adhered to the SAI's philosophy of assimilation, allotment, citizenship, and acculturation. They believed the new direction in Indian policy denied Native peoples' ability to succeed in American society. Forcing traditional tribal structures and communal land ownership on American Indians was nothing short of racist, they argued, amounting to a "back to the blanket" policy. These women and men formed the American Indian Federation (AIF), and through this organization they fought the commissioner for the future of Native America.

Headed by O. K. Chandler (Cherokee), Joseph Bruner (Creek), and Alice Jemison (Seneca), the AIF attracted mostly those Native people who had been economically successful. Many of its founding members came from the Society of Oklahoma Indians and the Indian National Confederacy of Oklahoma, assimilation-minded organizations that advocated progress through self-help. Other federation members, such as Thomas Sloan, had been leaders in the Society of American Indians. In a sense, the AIF was the logical extension of the SAI, as its platform called for the integration of Native people into mainstream white America.[9]

Most AIF members believed individual landownership and American citizenship remained the most viable political course for Native people. Like other conservative critics, they attacked Collier's IRA and other reforms as a "communistic scheme." Bruner contended that Collier had been "an associate and admirer of radicals, liberals, free thinkers, and communists for the past twenty years or more." Meanwhile, Chandler declared that "red radical forces" had infiltrated the federal government, were undermining America's Christian heritage, and were imposing a state of communism on Indian tribes. He accused Collier of segregating Native people on reservations and forcing a primitive tribal structure on them. Moreover, he believed that BIA schools under Collier's direction had replaced Christian education with the instruction of Indian languages, music, and art that was harmful and perpetuated antiquated Indian traditions. Alice Jemison elaborated on Chandler's contentions before the House Committee on Indian Affairs. According to the AIF secretary, the IRA was "taking Indians backward to the time before Columbus," while Collier was attempting to preserve the "primitive ways of our ancestors for the entertainment of the American public, just the same as wild animals in a zoo." Indians, the AIF believed, needed liberation from federal control so they could enter the mainstream of American society.[10]

By the mid-1940s, internal discord, along with associations with such far-right organizations as the James True Associates and the Silver Shirts of America, led to the demise of the AIF. The organization's central message of assimilation, antitribalism, and integration, however, had gained widespread appeal among lawmakers in the House and Senate. Directly after World War II these neo-assimilationists began advocating for the establishment of an Indian claims commission, which would pay off tribes for past injustices and get the government "out of the Indian business." This new impetus reflected the emergent civic nationalism and conformity that arrived with the onset of the Cold War. While the recent global conflagration had made clear the dangers of fascism and racial nationalism, the emerging competition between the United States and the Soviet Union for global influence forced policy makers to open the nation's doors to minority groups whom they had previously shut out. For the new generation of Indian leaders who subscribed to the tenets of the IRA, this integrationist milieu posed a direct threat to tribalism and the very existence of Native people and culture.[11]

In May 1944, D'Arcy McNickle (Flathead), Archie Phinney (Nez Percé), Ruth Bronson (Cherokee), Charles Heacock (Sioux), and other Indians who worked in the BIA during the Indian New Deal organized themselves into a steering committee with the intention of creating a new intertribal organization. Months later, they held the inaugural convention of the National Congress of American Indians (NCAI) at the Cosmopolitan Hotel in Denver, where they registered eighty-one delegates from twenty-seven states and fifty tribes, making the meeting the largest intertribal conference to date. Delegates hammered out several resolutions. Most significant, they created a legal aid bureau that would represent tribes in need of counsel in land-claims cases. The NCAI also determined to lobby Congress on key social, economic, and political problems facing Indians, including issues of territorial sovereignty and treaty rights.[12]

Like the Society of American Indians during the Progressive Era or the American Indian Federation of the 1930s, the NCAI fashioned itself as the voice of all Native people, ignoring, in a sense, the overwhelming diversity in Indian Country. The organization's leaders identified the key principles of sovereignty, treaty rights, cultural preservation, and self-determination as crucial for all Native people. Whether or not the NCAI was correct in its assessment proved to be a moot point. The organization successfully established an entirely new set of parameters, which every intertribal association of any significance has worked within since the mid-twentieth century.

In its formative years, the NCAI concentrated on Indian claims and on protecting territorial sovereignty. Soon, a new and even greater threat emerged out of the Cold War conformity and integrationist impulse that gripped the nation. The passage of House Concurrent Resolution 108 in 1953, which called for the termination of the federal government's trust responsibilities, threatened to eliminate all social services and Indian tribes' status as sovereign, federally recognized, political entities. Termination proved to be the greatest menace to tribalism, treaty rights, Indian identity, and the protection of Native people's land base since the passage of the Dawes Severalty Act in 1887. The NCAI leaped into action when the federal government effectively terminated the Menominees of Wisconsin, the Klamaths of Oregon, and the Alabama-Coushattas of Texas as federally recognized tribes in 1954. Under the leadership of executive secretary Helen Peterson, the organization drew up the Declaration of Indian Rights, which rejected forced termination and proclaimed the organization's support of federal guardianship and the reservation system. For the NCAI, reservations or a tribal land base were essential to Indian identity and cultural preservation.[13]

The NCAI fought forced termination through the 1950s and well into the 1960s. It employed attorneys to challenge the policy in the nation's courts and lobbyists to work within the halls of Congress. Many members of the organization, however, prepared for the worst and sought to prepare tribes for a future without federal services. D'Arcy McNickle founded American Indian Development, Inc. (AID, Inc.) to help tribes attain self-sufficiency through economic progress. The AID's first annual report stated that it was of "critical importance" that Indians develop management skills and assume control over tribal resources. The organization later elaborated on the point, noting that health, education, a lack of hospitals, underdeveloped resources, and rampant poverty remained serious problems facing Indian Country. If American Indians were to survive as a people, they must "organize and manage industrial and business enterprises utilizing [their] own resources." Relying on funding from a host of philanthropic foundations, McNickle held exploratory workshops in Brigham City, Utah; Tahlequah, Oklahoma; and Phoenix, Arizona, calling for participants with "leadership potentialities" who would eventually help their respective tribes in development.[14]

The AID eventually turned its attention to preparing Indian youth for leadership roles, and in so doing it laid the ideological foundation for future Native student activists. The organization's primary youth project was the Workshop on American Indian Affairs, a six-week intensive course held in Boulder, Colorado, that critiqued assimilation and acculturation and instilled in its participants the principles of tribalism, cultural renewal, treaty rights, sovereignty, and self-determination. In a report drafted shortly after the first workshop in 1956, instructor Fred Gearing forcefully argued that one of the endeavor's primary goals must be fostering a sense of cultural pride among Native students. "They should develop greater competence and assurance in interpreting themselves as Indians," he argued. McNickle built upon this assumption, asserting, "The design of the project should be to provide the young people with a sound working philosophy," which they would use to "benefit their people" and defend "against erroneous ideas."[15]

In the workshops, held in the late 1950s and 1960s, instructors carefully planned lectures and assigned readings to push their agenda. Indian-centered histories, such as John Collier's classic book *Indians of the Americas* and D'Arcy McNickle's and Harold Fey's account *Indians and Other Americans,* offered a different view of the American experience, one that highlighted Indian achievements and documented European atrocities against indigenous peoples. Felix Cohen's writings on colonialism bolstered these volumes. Cohen, who had also served in the BIA under Collier, painted the United States as a colonial power that sought only power over Native people and exploitation of their resources. He called for full self-determination in Indian communities and an end to the policy of forced termination.[16]

Workshop instructors employed a number of social-scientific studies as a means to give students a theoretical framework through which to view their condition. Students read such sociological staples as Robert Redfield's essay "The Folk Society" and Alfred Schuetz's piece "The Stranger." One work regularly assigned at the workshops over their fifteen-year span was Ruth Benedict's famous treatise from 1934, *Patterns of Culture.* A student of anthropologist Franz Boas, Benedict was an early proponent of cultural relativity. She purported that all cultures must be viewed on an equal plane and that one could not judge one society by another society's standards. While Benedict's thesis may seem obvious to a twenty-first-century observer, it was radical fodder during the 1950s, a time of conformity and consensus.[17]

The students who took part in the workshops came from throughout Indian Country, giving the project a truly intertribal flavor. Although some participants grew up in urban areas such as Los Angeles or Albuquerque, the majority were from reservations or rural tribal communities. Such overall diversity among the attendees meant that some students came from highly traditional backgrounds, while others were fully assimilated. Regardless of their upbringing, most left the workshop with a newfound pride in their Indian ancestry. In their responses to postworkshop questionnaires, students reported positively on the workshop agenda and indicated that they had come to view the condition of Native people in an entirely new light. "[Pride] is the most important thing I have learned in these six weeks," declared one participant. "The Indian is more than a dirty, poor, underprivileged person allowing his life to be wasted away in idleness. The Indian for me has become a person rich in a way of life that is fast being swept away by others."[18]

We can gain further insight into the effectiveness of the workshop by examining the students' newsletter, *Indian Progress*. Probably the first intertribal student publication to circulate on a national level, the newsletter reported on events from around Indian Country, but it also gave workshop participants a chance to voice their opinion on issues facing Native people. Editorials reflected the students' co-optation of the cornerstone principles of treaty rights, sovereignty, self-determination, and cultural preservation. At times, they even revealed an emerging nationalism and identified with movement politics, as when one student reported, "With the coming of the white man up to the present the American Indian has been in constant danger of losing his rights. . . . Indian people are beginning to realize that together they will stand a better chance of protecting their rights."[19]

For many of the young women and men who participated in the Workshop on American Indian Affairs, such sentiments were more than just empty rhetoric. The Indian students who participated in the workshops—like the politicized young people who formed the Student Nonviolent Coordinating Committee (SNCC) and the Students for a Democratic Society (SDS)—came of age in a much different sociopolitical environment than had the founders of the NCAI. They were, in the words of Maurice Isserman and Michael Kazin, part of a "superheated ideological atmosphere" that painted a black-and-white political landscape of good versus evil. Viewing the world through such a lens created a sense of superidealism and spurred these young women and men to challenge actively the injustices they saw in the society around them. As such, they went on to turn ideology into action. They took the principles of self-determination, sovereignty, treaty rights, and cultural preservation as promulgated through the six-week session and formed the first Native student activist organization, the National Indian Youth Council (NIYC). Workshop participants Clyde Warrior, Mel Thom, Herb Blatchford, Joan Noble, Bruce Wilkie, Karen Rickard, Robert Dumont, and many more became active members and officers in the NIYC.[20]

Such united action required a spark. In 1961, McNickle and the officers of the AID decided to invite the enrolled workshop participants to the American Indian Chicago Conference. Workshop organizers declared that the gathering would be "an exceptional opportunity for learning and for participating in a major conference on Indian affairs." The conference proved to be more than just a learning experience; it was the powder keg that launched the NIYC and, hence, the Native activist movement.[21]

The main purpose of the Chicago Conference, however, was not to establish a new youth movement. Rather, organizers hoped to draft a new policy statement on Indian affairs that would reposition the basic ideals of the Indian New Deal as the foundation of federal Indian policy. The recent election of John F. Kennedy afforded organizers a prime opportunity to break with the past. The Indian Claims Commission had proven a failure, as the government had inadequately compensated tribes for lost lands. Even more pressing was the disastrous policy of termination, which left tribes without federal services and led to an erosion of traditional culture and community. Something had to be done, and Kennedy offered Native leaders, who were alarmed by the erosion of tribal sovereignty and treaty rights, a chance for reform.

Organized by anthropologists Sol Tax and Nancy Lurie, along with NCAI leaders D'Arcy McNickle and Helen Peterson, the Chicago Conference would bring Native people together to discuss the major problems facing their communities and to devise new strategies to alleviate them. Tax relied on BIA roles, NCAI membership lists, and word of mouth to recruit as many participants as possible. Held in June 1961, the gathering was a huge success. Over 800 Indians from some ninety tribes, bands, and pueblos met in Chicago for the conference, eclipsing the NCAI's inaugural meeting as the most diverse and largest pan-Indian assembly held in modern times.[22]

In theory, the conference participants would outline their ideas for a new direction in federal Indian policy in a statement they would present to President Kennedy. But Tax recognized that with such a wide array of attendees, such a task would be next to impossible. He therefore asked McNickle to draft a preliminary statement, which conference participants would use as a blueprint and a source of discussion. The NCAI founder jumped at the project, realizing the conference offered him an ideal opportunity to control the debate and define the parameters of Indian politics. McNickle's preliminary statement, which the main assembly adopted essentially verbatim, rejected assimilation and acculturation, embraced traditional Native culture, disavowed the policy of forced termination, and called for federal acknowledgment of treaty rights and tribal sovereignty. In short, the former bureau employee and disciple of John Collier had ingeniously reestablished the principles of the Indian New Deal as the foundation of modern Indian politics. Chicago Conference representatives later presented McNickle's statement, dubbed "The Voice of the American Indian," to the president.[23]

Equally significant, the Chicago Conference, perhaps contrary to the intentions of the organizers, led to the formation of the NIYC. Native students, many of whom had attended the Workshop on American Indian Affairs, came together to discuss alternative strategies for dealing with problems facing Indians. They observed and learned from their elders and even had the opportunity to serve as chairpersons of smaller group discussions. Ultimately, they resolved to form a youth caucus to give the younger generation in attendance a united voice in the conference proceedings.

As the week progressed, many members of the youth caucus concluded that the conference was overly bureaucratic and was "going out on a tangent," deviating from its original intention. Future NIYC president Mel Thom (Paiute) complained of the "uncle tomahawks" who failed to take a strong enough stand and instead were "fumbling around, passing resolutions, and putting headdresses on people." Thom, Herbert Blatchford (Navajo), Shirley Witt (Mohawk), Clyde Warrior (Ponca), Karen Rickard (Tuscarora), and others thought that the youth should come up with a separate statement of purpose to redirect the conference's aims. At the final mass gathering, members of this new generation of Indian leaders—the 1960s generation—forced their way onto the main stage, seized the microphone, and delivered their statement demanding a stronger, even militant stance on sovereignty, treaty rights, self-determination, and cultural preservation.[24]

After the Chicago Conference, several of the student attendees headed to Colorado for the summer workshop. Others who were a part of the youth caucus returned to their tribal communities to begin planning a national youth gathering in Gallup, New Mexico, later that summer. Following the lead of other activist-oriented student organizations, such as SNCC and SDS, the founders of the NIYC believed they could infuse a youthful vivacity into their larger struggle. As charter member Joan Noble (Ute) put it, "One thing about the young people is that they are more apt to go out and do what they think is right than the older group."[25]

Although those who established the NIYC were very much a part of the generation that also founded SNCC and SDS, Native students' goals stood in stark contrast to those of their white and black contemporaries. Rather than seeking inclusion in American society, civil rights, or a more participatory democracy, the red power warriors of the 1960s adhered to the political tradition of their elders. Hence, treaty rights, tribal sovereignty, self-determination, and cultural preservation remained their ideological pillars, even while they pursued these goals in a more forceful, even militant manner that mirrored that of SNCC and SDS.

At their founding meeting, the students set up the framework for their new organization. They penned articles of incorporation, resolved to support the position of their elders in the NCAI, set guidelines for membership, identified possible sources of funding, elected a slate of officers, and launched a quarterly newsletter. Despite such steps, the NIYC struggled during its formative years to find its niche. Both officers and members hoped to make an impact through some form of direct action or civil disobedience, but they were unable to devise a strategy or find a pressing issue on which to make a stand. In the meantime, staffers used the organization's publication, *Americans before Columbus,* as a sounding board for ideas and as a vehicle to express the rising tide of American Indian militancy.[26]

When the dynamic young leader Hank Adams joined the NIYC's ranks, they found the issue they were searching for. In Washington State, Adams reported, game authorities had begun arresting members of the Muckleshoot, Puyallup, Nisqually, and Quinault tribes for fishing off-reservation without a permit. According to a series of nineteenth-century treaties brokered between the tribes and the federal government, however, the Native people had the right to fish at "all usual and accustomed places" in exchange for surrendering a large portion of their traditional land base. An article published in the December 1963 edition of *Americans before Columbus* reported that Washington State's game department had "virtually declared war on Indian fisheries." Through use of an "armed militia," wardens had confiscated boats and nets, essentially denying the Northwest Indians their traditional subsistence. "The facts are plain," the NIYC reported. "The Indians have treaty rights to fish and the moral right of every person in this country to make an honest living."[27]

As the crisis over fishing rights in the Pacific Northwest heated up, NIYC president Mel Thom called a special midyear meeting to determine how and when to take action. Respectful of each tribe's sovereignty, council leaders resolved to wait for a petition from the tribal leadership requesting their assistance. Such an appeal came in February 1964. At an emergency meeting, the young Native activists took a page from their African American counterparts, who had launched the sit-in movement in the Deep South. They planned to hold a series of "fish-ins" to demonstrate against Washington State's violation of the Northwest Indians' fishing rights as guaranteed by federal treaty.[28]

And like civil rights activists, or perhaps even like the Yippies who burst onto the scene just a few years later, the NIYC recognized that the media could be used as a tool to propagate the issue of treaty rights and bring it to the fore of public conscience. The NIYC deftly secured the support of movie star Marlon Brando and contacted a host of media outlets to give the demonstrations and the issue of treaty rights the widest possible publicity. "We knew the game wardens would make arrests," Thom later recalled; all they needed to do was ensure that the riverbanks where the fish-in would occur were lined with news correspondents to capture the authorities on film harassing and handcuffing peaceful Native fishermen and celebrities like Brando.[29]

On 1 March, NIYC activists, local Indian fishers, reporters, and game wardens all gathered on the banks of the Puyallup River, waiting for someone to make the first move. As the tension mounted, some Indians began snapping photographs of the straight-faced game wardens. Soon the seriousness of the situation evaporated, as children began to play along the river and protesters continued taking pictures of the increasingly irritated authorities. When actor Marlon Brando cast the first gill net, the fun ended and the arrests began. As anticipated, news of the fish-ins—and especially the arrest of Brando—made both local and national headlines.[30]

The NIYC followed the fish-ins with a massive protest held at the state capitol building in Olympia, where between 2,000 and 5,000 people attended to show their support or simply to observe what had to be one of the largest protests ever held in Washington's capital city. Traditional war dances performed by the Makah tribe energized the crowd, as did the speeches of Indian activists who demanded respect for treaty rights and the creation of a new state-level Indian advisory committee headed by local Native people. The fiery NIYC leader Clyde Warrior accused the state of Washington of reneging on the government's trust responsibilities and of destroying "the sacred relationship between the Indian and God." A separate statement issued to the governor read:

> The past and present history of treaties between the federal government and their captive Indian nations exemplify a treaty as a "convenient way of license to steal" for the government. If this be so, then perhaps our next appeal must be to the governments and people of the world. For it would seem that Hanoi, or Moscow, or London, or France should be

deeply concerned with the United States treaties and the violation of them. For if Justice is denied to us today because we are weak and defenseless by you who have the power to mete justice, then the day will come when you or our children will also appeal for justice to the deaf ears of your conquerors. "The seeds you sow are the crops you reap."[31]

The governor responded predictably, refusing to meet the demands of the protestors and insisting that Native fishers adhere to state game laws.[32]

Thus, the NIYC fish-ins and protests failed to bring about an immediate change in Washington State's policies. It would take another ten years of fish-ins, demonstrations, and lobbying before a federal judge, Judge George Boldt, upheld the treaty rights of the Northwest Indians and guaranteed their right to 50 percent of the catch. What the fish-ins did do was begin the Indian protest movement of the 1960s and '70s. The events that unfolded on the banks of the Puyallup and Nisqually rivers proved to be the first instance of modern intertribal direct action. The NIYC quickly gained national recognition as one of the foremost intertribal organizations in operation, inspiring a new generation of angry Native youth to employ alternative strategies to bring attention to the cornerstone principles of treaty rights, sovereignty, self-determination, and cultural retention.

Through the remainder of the 1960s, the NIYC continued its fight for these ideals. In 1968, the organization moved its main office to Berkeley, California, and then to Albuquerque, New Mexico, a year later. Reestablishing itself in the city inevitably led to a change in membership and new foci for the NIYC, as the council turned its attention toward confronting issues facing urban Indians. Unemployment, lack of job training, discrimination, and inadequate housing were a few of the more pressing problems, but the lack of tribal structure and community, along with a sense of alienation and marginality, also plagued many Native people who had relocated to such western and midwestern cities as Denver, Albuquerque, San Francisco, and Minneapolis.

The NIYC developed new programs to confront these problems. The organization actively fought discrimination and racism through protest and legal action, while also developing a job-training and job-placement program. Despite these changes, the organization never deviated from the cornerstone principles that had guided intertribal politics since World War II. Tribal sovereignty, treaty rights, self-determination, and cultural preservation remained the ideological foundation of the NIYC. The same was true for other intertribal political organizations that formed in the cities. Perhaps nowhere was this more evident than with the Berkeley-based United Native Americans (UNA).

In early 1968, Lee Brightman, LaNada Means, and Jack Forbes founded the UNA to give Native students at the University of California a political voice and base. Forbes had worked closely with NIYC president Mel Thom and educational specialist Robert Dumont in developing a series of model demonstration schools that would employ a new Native-based curriculum. Like Thom, Forbes and other UNA leaders subscribed to the increasingly militant orientation of youth politics of the late 1960s. Just as black power proponents called for a separate African American nation, the UNA demanded sovereignty and an end to the colonialism and racism that they felt imprisoned Native people.

In the same way as the Black Panthers in neighboring Oakland restricted its membership, the nationalist UNA reserved full membership for Natives only, allowing, however, an associate membership for whites. Calling for "the brotherhood of all Indian peoples without regard to the whiteman's boundary lines," the organization backed the preservation of Native culture and languages, which could be facilitated through the establishment of Indian-controlled educational institutions, Office of Economic Opportunity programs, and the founding of a separate American Indian university. The UNA stood firm on treaty rights as well, declaring unequivocal support of the Pacific Northwest Indians in their fish-in struggle.[33]

Means, Brightman, and Forbes went a step further in their militancy, insisting that a nonprofit, Indian-controlled organization replace the BIA. As it stood, they said, the BIA was a "colonial office" controlled by "white bureaucrats and their Indian collaborators." To illustrate their point, they called for the creation of a "Bureau of White Affairs," which would give non-Indians a taste of the paternalism and oppressive oversight that Native people had to cope with on a daily basis. "It is obvious that whites are being badly discriminated against," the UNA reported with Yippie-like sarcasm. "They are also becoming too soft and need to go through a toughening experience with the help of the ever-ready federal government."[34]

The UNA launched the periodical *Warpath* to serve as its mouthpiece for propagating the message of "Indian Power!" Like the NIYC's publication *Americans before Columbus*, *Warpath* printed articles that reflected its platform of treaty rights, self-determination, sovereignty, and cultural preservation, as well as its anti-BIA position. *Warpath* often vacillated between measured critiques of Indian policy to outright condemnations of American society. Forbes's article "U.S. Indian Equality: A Proposal" affirmed the trust relationship between the United States and America's First Nations and maintained that the government needed to extend services to urban Indians.[35]

Just one issue later, however, the article "Indians' Religion Superior" switched tactics by blasting the "White imperialists and brainwashed Indians, anxious to destroy Indian personality." The anonymous author wondered how "American Indian peoples had succeeded in producing so many Superior Persons, so many noble men, who respected nature and lived a holy life while at the same time Europe was producing so many killers, fanatics, and thieves." Affirming the greatness of Native culture, the author asked, "Why was it that most Indian leaders were compassionate, dignified, honest men while almost all of the kings, popes, and other leaders of Europe were completely selfish, unscrupulous, cruel, and immoral?" The answer was "Indian religion was far superior to European religion."[36]

As the UNA pushed its nationalist agenda in *Warpath*, on the other side of the San Francisco Bay the American Indian Nation, another intertribal organization founded to help Indians adjust to an urban environment, began plans for transforming the abandoned and dilapidated federal prison on Alcatraz Island into an American Indian national center. The center would serve as a "living cultural memorial" to all Indians in the United States, while the actual construction project would act as a sort of domestic Peace Corps–type venture that would give the American Indian in the Bay Area "the opportunity to pull his own bootstraps rather than federal apron strings." The federal government could live up to its democratic ideals and redeem itself from "100 years of shame" by authorizing such a center.[37]

The UNA took notice of the American Indian Nation's efforts and, along with Native students from the University of California, Los Angeles, and San Francisco State College, joined the cause. Their efforts were further invigorated when the San Francisco Indian Center burned to the ground in October 1969, leaving the Native people in the city without a central community center. Realizing that the federal government would never hand over title to Alcatraz, Indian leaders in the Bay Area decided to take matters into their own hands. Like the white radicals who stormed and occupied administration buildings on college campuses around the country, Native students in the Bay Area would simply seize the island. On 20 November 1969, Native students calling themselves Indians of All Tribes landed on Alcatraz and commenced an occupation that lasted until June 1971.

Garnering wide support from the NIYC and other intertribal organizations throughout Indian Country, the Indians of All Tribes issued a proclamation laying claim to the former prison for all Indian peoples "by right of discovery." "We wish to be fair and honorable in our dealings with the Caucasian inhabitants of this land," they asserted. "We will purchase said Alcatraz Island for twenty-four dollars in glass beads and red cloth, a precedent set by the white man's purchase of a similar island about 300 years ago." The occupiers went on to declare they intended to develop a center for Native American studies where young people could learn about Native culture and art; an American Indian spiritual center to rejuvenate ancient religious practices; an Indian center of ecology to train Native youth to restore Indian lands and water resources; an Indian training school that would include a center for arts and crafts, as well as a restaurant that would serve Native foods for the public; and finally, an American Indian museum to "show the noble and tragic events of Indian history."[38]

The Indians of All Tribes ultimately failed in their bid to make Alcatraz "Indian land forever," but they succeeded in inspiring a new wave of Indian activism and pushing the Indian activist movement into the American conscience through massive media exposure. As the dramatic occupation of Alcatraz unfolded, urban Indians in Minneapolis likewise took action to improve living conditions, combat racism, and protest federal Indian policy. Former Ojibwe convicts Clyde Bellecourt, Dennis Banks, and Edward Benton Banai established the American Indian Movement (AIM) in the Twin Cities to bring these issues to light. Despite its urban orientation, AIM adhered to the same overarching philosophy as the NIYC, the UNA, and the Indians of All Tribes.

Sharing the same political foundation allowed these competing intertribal organizations to work together. AIM entered into an alliance with the NIYC in late 1969, when the two organizations resolved to cooperate in their efforts and support one another's programs. Former NIYC associate director Sam English recalled Clyde Bellecourt "running around" at the annual NCAI meeting in Albuquerque hoping to meet Mel Thom. "You could see the excitement on his face," noted English. On 10 November of that year, AIM, the NIYC, the NCAI, and other intertribal organizations joined together to form the American Indian Task Force to present Vice President Spiro Agnew with a statement calling for greater Native involvement in shaping federal Indian policy. Although AIM and the NCAI differed sharply in the tactics they employed, both organizations subscribed to the same principles of treaty rights, tribal sovereignty, self-determination, and cultural preservation, allowing for a general statement that included the signatures of both Dennis Banks and D'Arcy McNickle. Such cooperation stood in sharp contrast to the African American struggle, which experienced acute divisions in the mid-1960s between black power proponents calling for separation and moderate leaders advocating integration.[39]

The alliance between such disparate factions of the Indian movement failed to hold together through the 1970s. The breakdown, however, resulted from disagreement over tactics rather than over ideology. In 1972, AIM and the NIYC led a caravan they termed the "Trail of Broken Treaties" from California to Washington, D.C. When the activists reached the capital in late October, just days before the 1972 presidential election, they issued a twenty-point proposal that called for the restoration of treaty rights and the treaty-making process. The demonstrators also insisted a new organization, to be called the "Office of Federal Indian Relations and Community Relations," replace the outdated and ineffective BIA. Finally, they demanded the protection of Native religions and the preservation of Indian culture. Fish-in organizer Hank Adams penned the proposal in hopes of achieving some sort of agreement with the Nixon administration before the upcoming election.[40]

Matters, however, descended into chaos when the activists marched to the BIA building and attempted to negotiate with bureau officials. Security officials demanded the protestors leave the premises at once. The rebuttal, coupled with the inability of the caravan leaders to find adequate lodging, led to the forced occupation of the building. Holed up for a week, the occupiers erected a teepee on the front lawn and unfurled a banner that read "Native American Embassy." When word spread that the bureau would not meet their demands and that the police planned on expunging the caravan from the building, the protestors took out their anger and frustration on the building itself—violently destroying furniture, artwork, office machinery, and file cabinets full of records. Leaders in both the NIYC and the NCAI condemned the sacking of the BIA building as wanton destruction. A year later, when AIM members went on to occupy the hamlet of Wounded Knee in South Dakota, neither organization gave its support.[41]

While AIM continued to engage in activities that garnered media exposure, the NIYC filed numerous lawsuits at the state and federal level. The NCAI and other intertribal organizations such as the Native American Rights Fund also worked for treaty rights, sovereignty, and self-determination in the courts, as well as through vigorous lobbying efforts in Washington, D.C. Indeed, by the 1970s, the Indian movement was a vast kaleidoscope of organizations—each the product of a different era—employing radically different methods to achieve the same basic goals.

America's turn toward the right with the election of Ronald Reagan in 1980 dampened the spirit of vigorous social protest that had characterized the previous two decades, but not before the movement had forcefully brought the cornerstone principles before lawmakers and into the public conscience. As Native leaders worked from the outside, key insiders in Congress and the White House alike came to realize that the assimilationist policies of the postwar era had failed miserably. Senator Edward Kennedy's 1969 report "Indian Education: A National Tragedy—A National Challenge" called for greater tribal recognition and self-determination. Even President Richard Nixon, who had served as vice president during the peak years of Cold War conformity and assimilation, issued a pointed statement that flatly asserted, "The policy of forced termination is wrong." Under Nixon's watch, federal Indian policy underwent a sea change as lawmakers rejected the integrationist impulse and embraced the cornerstone principles that intertribal activists and leaders had been fighting for since the inception of the NCAI in 1944.[42]

Indeed, the list of legislation passed during the decade is impressive: the Blue Lake Restoration Act of 1970, the Alaska Native Claims Settlement Act of 1971, the Indian Education Act of 1972, the Indian Financing Act of 1974, the Indian Self-Determination and Education Assistance Act of 1975, the Indian Healthcare Improvement Act of 1976, the Indian Child Welfare Act and the American Indian Religious Freedom Act of 1978. These acts and others restored the tribal land base, gave Native peoples a greater degree of self-determination, and recognized Indian sovereignty, drastically changing Native American communities' relationship with the federal government and with white society. Perhaps even more impressive was the movement's success in preserving, even rejuvenating, Native American cultures. Sociologist and Indian scholar Joane Nagel has shown how the Indian activist movement of the 1960s and 1970s led to a swell in Native self-identification and promoted what she calls "a native cultural renaissance." Nagel's research vividly underscores her assertions, revealing that the number of Native people claiming Indian ethnicity tripled between 1960 and 1990.[43]

Today, American Indians live with a political legacy that was set in place during the Indian New Deal and secured with the rise of the Indian activist movement of the 1960s and 1970s. Scholars of Indian studies and history constantly stress the cultural, social, and political diversity within Indian Country, warning against generalizing about Native people in any respect. This may be a good rule of thumb, but it is equally important to recognize that virtually all intertribal organizations of any significance, as well as the overwhelming majority of Native people, are of one mind in their support of tribal sovereignty, treaty rights, self-determination, and cultural retention. These cornerstone values unite Native people today and inform politics in Indian Country.

Probably the greatest single issue in Native America today reflecting this political milieu is the controversy over gaming. The issue first came to the fore in 1979 when the Seminoles of Florida began holding high-stakes bingo games. State law prohibited gambling, leading authorities to shut down the Seminoles' operation. In response, the tribe filed suit and won the case in federal court. The U.S. Supreme Court eventually weighed in on the matter in the 1987 case *California v. Cabazon Band of Mission Indians,* ruling that state laws did not apply on Indian land.[44] The following year, the U.S. Congress passed the Indian Gaming Regulatory Act, which called on tribes seeking to open casinos to work with state governments in devising gaming compacts.

The lucrative gaming industry has led to unprecedented profits, but it has also caused problems within many tribes. In two successive, highly contested referendums, the Navajo Nation rejected gaming in the mid-1990s. Many traditionalists within the tribe believed that gaming would compromise the tribe's sovereignty, as it would require that the tribe negotiate with the states of Arizona and New Mexico. However, more recently, under the leadership of Joe Shirley Jr., the Navajo have reassessed their position and voted for limited gaming on the reservation. Perhaps even more controversial is the case of the Mission Indians of California. Since the 1980s, many of these bands have opened casinos on tribal lands throughout the state, quickly discovering the immense windfall that gaming brings. Some Mission Indians have therefore begun implementing restrictions on tribal membership and, in some cases, disenrolling people to maximize profits for the select few. Lawsuits have resulted, but as with the Cherokee Nation's vote to prohibit those on the freedmen rolls from claiming membership in the tribe, few in Indian Country have questioned the Mission Indians' sovereignty and right to self-determination.

The gaming controversy has highlighted how tribes' sovereign status can benefit Indian nations economically. Outside forces, however, seeing only the advantages of sovereignty and ignoring the widespread poverty that plagues many reservations, have called for reform and a new direction in federal Indian policy that mirrors the assimilative approach of the past. Many have championed the supremacy of a state's law over Indian nations within its borders and have argued, like the proponents of termination, that Native people should be fully incorporated into the dominant culture. But while lawmakers may debate the future of treaty rights, tribal sovereignty, cultural preservation, and Indians' right to self-determination, Native people themselves have remained resolute in their fight to maintain these principles, principles that for seventy years have stood as the foundation of intertribal politics.

NOTES

1. Brian Daffron, "Freedmen Descendants Struggle to Maintain Their Cherokee Identity," *Indian Country Today,* 4 April 2007, A4.

2. Ibid.; Eric Cheyfitz, "The Case of the Cherokee Freedmen: Identity Politics in

Indian Country," *Indian Country Today,* 4 April 2007, A3; Steven Newcomb, "The Cherokee Nation's Contradictory Stance," *Indian Country Today,* 4 April 2007, A3.

3. Moreover, Cobb shows how the greater process of decolonization sweeping the globe influenced politicos and activists alike in their efforts to bring about change in Indian Country. See Daniel M. Cobb, "Community, Poverty, Power: The Politics of Tribal Self-Determination, 1960–1968" (Ph.D. diss., University of Oklahoma, 2003).

4. Richard White, *"It's Your Misfortune and None of My Own": A New History of the American West* (Norman: University of Oklahoma Press, 1991), 633.

5. Margaret Connell Szasz, *Education and the American Indian: The Road to Self-Determination since 1928,* 3rd ed. (Albuquerque: University of New Mexico Press, 1999), 9–10; Hazel W. Hertzberg, *The Search for an American Indian Identity: Modern Pan-Indian Movements* (Syracuse, N.Y.: Syracuse University Press, 1971), 16. For more on Indians and the boarding school experience, see David Wallace Adams, *Education for Extinction: American Indians and the Boarding School Experience, 1875–1928* (Lawrence: University Press of Kansas, 1995), and Basil H. Johnston, *Indian School Days* (Norman: University of Oklahoma Press, 1988).

6. Szasz, *Education and the American Indian,* 9–10; Hertzberg, *Search for an American Indian Identity,* 16, 37, 60, 67, 117, 156.

7. For more on Collier's early career as a reformer and founder of the American Indian Defense Association, see Laurence C. Kelly, *The Assault on Assimilation: John Collier and the Origins of Indian Policy Reform* (Albuquerque: University of New Mexico Press, 1983), and John Collier, *From Every Zenith: A Memoir and Some Essays on Life and Thought* (Denver, Colo.: Sage Books, 1963), 40–132.

8. For a detailed assessment and breakdown of the Indian New Deal and the IRA, see Kenneth R. Philp, *John Collier's Crusade for Indian Reform, 1920–1954* (Tucson: University of Arizona Press, 1977), and Graham D. Taylor, *The New Deal and American Indian Tribalism: The Administration of the Indian Reorganization Act, 1934–1945* (Lincoln: University of Nebraska Press, 1980).

9. Marci Jean Gracey, "Attacking the Indian New Deal: The American Indian Federation and the Quest to Protect Assimilation" (M.A. thesis, Oklahoma State University, 2003), 7. Though a preponderance of the AIF's initial membership was from Oklahoma, other areas of Indian Country were also well represented. Many members claimed affiliation with the Mission Indian Federation of California, New York's Intertribal Committee for the Fundamental Advancement of the American Indian, and the Black Hills Treaty Council of South Dakota. Laurence M. Hauptman, "The American Indian Federation and the Indian New Deal: A Reinterpretation," *Pacific Historical Review* 52 (November 1983): 380.

10. Statement by Joseph Bruner, n.d., in *Native Americans and the New Deal: The Office Files of John Collier* (microfilm), ed. Robert E. Lester (Bethesda, Md.: University Publications of America, 1993), reel 1, frame 465; AIF statement to "the American citizenship," n.d., in ibid., reel 1, frame 468; microfilm reel 1, frame 374; O. K. Chandler, *Now Who's Un-American? An Exposé of Communism in the United States Government* (Washington, D.C.: American Indian Federation, n.d.), 3–4, 17, 20. U.S. Congress,

House, Committee on Indian Affairs, *Wheeler-Howard Act—Exempt Certain Indians: Hearing before the Committee on Indian Affairs,* 76th Cong., 3rd sess., 10–20 June 1940, 23, 30, 179, 418, 505.

11. Collier, *From Every Zenith,* 315–316, 362; Dorothy Parker, *Singing an Indian Song: A Biography of D'Arcy McNickle* (Lincoln: University of Nebraska Press, 1992), 106; Peter Iverson, *"We Are Still Here": American Indians in the Twentieth Century* (Wheeling, Ill.: Harlan Davidson, 1998), 116. For more on post–World War II civic nationalism, see Gary Gerstle, *American Crucible: Race and Nation in the Twentieth Century* (Princeton, N.J.: Princeton University Press, 2001).

12. Thomas W. Cowger, *The National Congress of American Indians: The Founding Years* (Lincoln: University of Nebraska Press, 1999), 40–42; "Proceedings of the National Congress of American Indians," 1944, Records of the National Congress of American Indians (hereafter, RNCAI), National Anthropological Archive, Smithsonian Institution, Washington, D.C., series 1, box 1.

13. Cowger, *National Congress of American Indians,* 114–116. For an in-depth look at the genesis and consequences of the federal government's policy of termination, see Donald L. Fixico, *Termination and Relocation: Federal Indian Policy, 1945–1960* (Albuquerque: University of New Mexico Press, 1986).

14. "American Indian Development: A Project Sponsored by the National Congress of American Indians, First Annual Report," 1952, *The John Collier Papers, 1922–1968* (Sanford, N.C.: Microfilming Corporation of America, 1980), CSWR, microfilm reel 54, frame 758. The Ford, Carnegie, Rockefeller, Whitney, and Marshall Field Foundations were the primary contributors to AID. "American Indian Development, Second Annual Report," 1953, Library of Congress, Washington, D.C., 5, 27–28.

15. "Report on Summer Workshop on American Indian Affairs," 9, 19, Robert Rietz Papers (hereafter Rietz Papers), Native American Educational Service College, Chicago, Illinois, file drawer 5, 1956 folder; letter to Sol Tax from D'Arcy McNickle, 19 February 1957, D'Arcy McNickle Papers, Newberry Library, Chicago, Illinois (hereafter Newberry), box 25, folder 214.

16. "Report on Summer Workshop on American Indian Affairs," Rietz Papers, file drawer 5, 1956 folder. See John Collier, *Indians of the Americas* (New York: W. W. Norton, 1947); Harold Fey and D'Arcy McNickle, *Indians and Other Americans: Two Ways of Life Meet,* rev. ed. (New York: Harper & Row, 1970); Felix Cohen, "Colonialism: A Realistic Approach" (1945), in *The Legal Conscience: Selected Papers of Felix S. Cohen,* ed. Lucy Kramer Cohen (New Haven, Conn.: Yale University Press, 1960), 369, 378, 381–382.

17. See Alfred Schuetz, "The Stranger: An Essay in Social Psychology," in *Identity and Anxiety: Survival of the Person in Mass Society,* ed. Maurice R. Stein, Arthur J. Vidich, and David Manning White (Glencoe, Ill.: Free Press, 1960), 98–109. Robert Redfield, "The Folk Society," *American Journal of Sociology* 52, no. 4 (January 1947): 293–308; Ruth Benedict, *Patterns of Culture* (New York: Mentor Books, 1949).

18. "Report on Summer Workshop on American Indian Affairs," 5–6, n.d., Rietz papers, file drawer 5, 1956 folder. Workshop instructor Rolland Wright analyzed the demographic background of all the participants during the workshops' span. He reported

88 students from the Southwest, 55 from the Dakotas, 52 from Oklahoma, 41 from the Midwest, 27 from the Great Basin, 23 from Alaska, 16 from the East, 14 from the Northwest, 11 from the Southeast, 7 from California, and 6 from Canada. Rolland H. Wright, "The American Indian College Student" (Ph.D. diss., Brandeis University, 1972), 16, 104–105; Rosalie Wax, "Recommendations for Recruitment of Students," 5, 7, n.d., Rietz Papers, file drawer 5, Wax folder; "American Indian Development, Inc. Assessment of the Workshop," 1, n.d., Rietz Papers, file drawer 5, assessments folder.

19. *Indian Progress*, no. 7 (23 July 1962), American Indian Chicago Conference Records, National Anthropological Archives, Smithsonian Institution, Suitland, Maryland, box 9, D'Arcy McNickle folder.

20. Maurice Isserman and Michael Kazin, "The Failure and Success of the New Radicalism," in *The Rise and Fall of the New Deal Order, 1930–1980*, ed. Steve Fraser and Gary Gerstle (Princeton, N.J.: Princeton University Press, 1989), 218; Rosalie Wax, "A Brief History and Analysis of the Workshops on American Indian Affairs," 24 October 1961, Murray Wax Papers, Newberry, box 33, folder 635.

21. AID, Inc. pamphlet, *Education for Leadership*, RNCAI, series 4, box 144, AID folder.

22. Although well over 800 people attended the conference, only 467 officially registered. American Indian Chicago Conference Registration, n.d., National Indian Youth Council Records (hereafter NIYCR), CSWR, box 1, folder 10.

23. "Preliminary Statement," prepared 26–30 April 1961, NIYCR, CSWR, box 1, folder 8.

24. Stan Steiner, *The New Indians* (New York: Dell, 1968), 36, 37; notes on Herbert Blatchford, n.d., Stan Steiner Papers (hereafter Steiner Papers), Department of Special Collections, Green Library, Stanford University, Palo Alto, California, series 1, box 23, folder 10; notes on Herbert Blatchford, n.d., Steiner Papers, series 3, box 15, folder 14; Shirley Witt to Herbert Blatchford, 28 June 1961, Shirley Witt Papers, CSWR, box 2, folder 25; Editor's note, *Aborigine* 1, no. 1 (1961) (El Paso, Tex.: Southwest Microfilming, 1996).

25. Minutes of the National Indian Youth Council meeting, 10–11 August 1961, NIYCR, CSWR, box 1, folder 11.

26. Ibid.

27. "Washington State Shifts War Strategy," *Americans before Columbus* 1, no. 2 (December 1963): 5.

28. Mary B. Olson, "Social Reform and the Use of the Law as an Instrument of Social Change: Native Americans' Struggle for Treaty Fishing Rights" (Ph.D. diss., University of Wisconsin, 1984), 587; "National Indian Youth Council Highlights for 1963–64," *Americans before Columbus* 2, no. 3 (27 July 1964): 2.

29. David Farber, *Chicago '68* (Chicago: University of Chicago Press, 1988), 212; "National Indian Youth Council Highlights for 1963–64," 2; Mel Thom, "For a Greater Indian America," *Americans before Columbus* 2, no. 1 (March 1964): 2; notes on the fish-ins, n.d., Steiner Papers, series 1, box 28, folder 5; Steiner, *New Indians*, 50.

30. Notes on the fish-ins, n.d., Steiner Papers, series 1, box 28, folder 5; Steiner, *New Indians*, 50; "Marlon Brando, S.F. Cleric Arrested for Fishing Illegally," *Seattle Times*, 2 March 1964; Mike Conant, "What Kind of a Guy Is This Actor Brando?"

Daily Olympian, 3 March 1964; "Marlon Brando, Episcopal Minister Arrested, Released during Fish-In," *Bellingham Herald,* 2 March 1964.

31. NIYC statement, 3 March 1964, NIYCR, CSWR, box 19, folder 4.

32. Notes on the fish-ins, n.d., Steiner Papers, series 1, box 28, folder 5; memo from Bruce Wilkie to the NIYC, 12 March 1964, NIYCR, CSWR, box 19, folder 4; Steiner, *New Indians,* 57; "Governor Refuses to Yield to Pressure from Indians," *Daily Olympian,* 3 March 1964; "Tribes Request Attention," *Americans before Columbus* 1, no. 1 (5 May 1964): 4; "Ponca Protests Treaty Breaking by Washington," *Americans before Columbus* 1, no. 1 (5 May 1964): 3.

33. "Proposed General Principles for United Native Americans," *Warpath* 1, no. 2 (1968): 4; "UNA Supports Fish-In Struggle," *Warpath* 1, no. 2 (1968): 1.

34. "Colonialist BIA Exposed," *Warpath* 1, no. 2 (1968): 9; "Bureau of White Affairs," *Warpath* 1, no. 2 (1968): 6.

35. Jack Forbes, "U.S. Indian Equality: A Proposal," *Warpath* 1, no. 2 (1968): 6.

36. "Indians' Religion Superior," *Warpath* 1, no. 3 (1969): 2.

37. Petition for American Indian National Center, n.d., Steiner Papers, series 1, box 26, folder 7; American Indian Nation's petition for tax exemption, n.d., Steiner Papers, series 1, box 26, folder 7; American Indian Nation to the President's Commission on the Disposition of Alcatraz, n.d., Steiner Papers, series 1, box 26, folder 7.

38. "Alcatraz Island Reclaimed by Indians," *Americans before Columbus* 2, no. 1 (December 1969–January 1970: 8; [Indians of All Tribes] Proclamation, in *Red Power: The American Indians' Fight for Freedom,* ed. Alvin M. Josephy Jr., Joane Nagel, and Troy Johnson, 2nd ed. (Lincoln: University of Nebraska Press, 1999), 40–43.

39. Brief History of AIM, n.d., Witt Papers, CSWR, box 3, folder 4; Akard, "Wocante Tinza," 16; letter from Gerald Wilkinson to Clyde Bellecourt, 3 December 1969, NIYCR, CSWR, box 3, folder 33; letter from Clyde Bellecourt to Gerald Wilkinson, 7 January 1970, NIYCR, CSWR, box 3, folder 34; Sam English, interview by author, 27 February 2007, Albuquerque, New Mexico; "American Indian Task Force statement Presented to Vice President Spiro Agnew and White House Staff, November 10, 1969, " in Josephy, Nagel, and Johnson, *Red Power,* 94–97.

40. "The Twenty-Point Proposal of Native Americans on the Trail of Broken Treaties," in Josephy, Nagel, and Johnson, *Red Power,* 45–47.

41. Paul Chaat Smith and Robert Allen Warrior, *Like a Hurricane: The Indian Movement from Alcatraz to Wounded Knee* (New York: New Press, 1996), 153–162.

42. George Pierre Castile, *To Show Heart: Native American Self-Determination and Federal Indian Policy, 1960–1975* (Tucson: University of Arizona Press, 1998), 79, 91.

43. Joane Nagel, *American Indian Ethnic Renewal: Red Power and the Resurgence of Identity and Culture* (New York: Oxford University Press, 1996), 5, 13. More specifically, 523,591 people reported Indian ethnicity in 1960, compared to 1,878,285 in 1990. After statistically analyzing the data, Nagel noted that such a change could not be due to a natural increase in the population. Nagel, "American Indian Ethnic Renewal: Politics and the Resurgence of Identity," *American Sociological Review* 60 (December 1995): 947.

44. *California v. Cabazon Band of Mission Indians,* 480 U.S. 202 (1987).

CHAPTER 8

Becoming the New Objects of Racial Scorn: Racial Politics and Racial Hierarchy in Postwar San Francisco, 1945–1960

Scott H. Tang

Unlike other regions, the pattern of race relations on the Pacific Coast has long assumed a triangular pattern: whites, Negroes, and Orientals; while in Los Angeles the pattern is quadrilateral: whites, Negroes, Orientals, and Mexicans. It is this basic difference in the pattern which serves to make the West Coast our racial frontier. Here, in this one region, are represented important groupings of all racial strains that have gone into the making of the American people. And in this pattern Negroes have now become the key minority group.
Carey McWilliams, 1945[1]

As World War II drew to a close, Carey McWilliams and other racial liberals along the Pacific Coast rhapsodized about the new possibilities that the unsettled state of race relations could offer to people of color. Their guarded optimism drew strength as they witnessed the political awakening of minority groups at a time when civic unity and the welfare of racial minorities were thought to be vital to the war effort. Moreover, as calls for a "double victory" indicate, the war provided a language to critique domestic racism after Americans framed the conflict as a battle against intolerance. Now was the time to bring the fight for equality home. Even as they acknowledged that the forces of intolerance remained strong, racial liberals expressed hope that in the West they had an opportunity to defuse racial tensions and to build relationships among white Americans, Mexican Americans, Asian

Americans, and African Americans. They even imagined that the different minority groups would form powerful interracial political coalitions.

As McWilliams noted, African Americans had become the key minority group in the West Coast's postwar race-relations environment. This position stemmed in part from the black population explosion after African Americans migrated to the region's major metropolitan areas in search of better employment opportunities. Seattle's black population, for instance, rose from 3,789 residents in 1940 to 15,666 residents in 1950. Portland's black population made similar gains, growing from 1,931 to 9,529 residents. Inland urban areas experienced black population growth as well. In the same ten-year span, the number of black residents in Denver went from 7,836 to 15,059. Black migration to the West was even more dramatic in California, where the number of black residents jumped from 4,846 to 43,502 in San Francisco and from 8,462 to 47,562 in Oakland. Los Angeles, the only western city with a large black community prior to the war, saw its black population almost triple from 63,774 to 171,209 residents. While traditional black communities swelled during the war and continued to grow in the years that followed, new black communities popped up where none existed before. The black population in Richmond, California, grew from a negligible 270 residents to 13,289 residents by 1950.[2]

Because of this large influx and because of the increased focus on the discrimination they faced, African Americans came to dominate western discussions of race. More than any other minority group, African Americans made race prejudice and racial discrimination public issues by articulating their social protest in their newspapers and in the streets. Some used direct-action methods to call for minority hiring, fair housing, and civil rights. In 1953, picketing by the Seattle branch of the National Negro Labor Council led Sears, Roebuck and Co. to hire its first black employee. At the same time, moderate organizations participated in antidiscrimination court cases and engaged in lobbying efforts for civil rights legislation. Black leaders always recognized that African Americans would play a crucial role in the advancement of racial relations. Seaton Manning, the executive secretary of the San Francisco Urban League, claimed that African Americans were "the most articulate of all minority groups" and noted the presence of experienced black leaders and established black organizations. He added that these leaders and organizations not only worked to better conditions for African Americans but also actively supported the cause of other minorities.[3]

But these other minorities seldom joined African Americans in the struggle for racial equality in the immediate postwar era. One reason why multiracial coalitions failed to materialize is that African Americans, Asian Americans, and Latinos had different political cultures, each shaped by a unique history of subordination. Barred from naturalization until the middle of the twentieth century, Chinese and Japanese immigrants could not fully participate in politics and could not rely on government authorities to address their needs. This exclusion of the immigrant generation from the electoral system slowed the process of political socialization. In addition, Chinese Americans customarily eschewed personal involvement in the political world outside of Chinatown because many immigrants had entered the country illegally. Rather than draw attention to themselves, they allowed the Chinese Consolidated Benevolent Association, more commonly known as the Chinese Six Companies, to speak for them in all interactions with external political entities. Even after Chinese immigrants gained naturalization and voting rights, the Chinese Six Companies maintained their position as communal mediators and kept the community internally focused as well as outwardly focused on political developments in Asia.

Moreover, African Americans, Asian Americans, and Latinos occupied different positions in the region's racial hierarchies. Despite widespread antiblack sentiment throughout the nation, white westerners did not consider the presence of African Americans, who were both small in number and trapped in undesirable unskilled jobs, to be a serious race problem until the 1940s. As a result, black westerners actually managed to escape the worst expressions of racism while other racial minorities bore the brunt of race hatred and inspired most of the region's racially discriminatory practices and policies from the second half of the nineteenth century through the early twentieth century. Chinese and Japanese immigrants, for example, became the targets of political mobilizations that left them socially, economically, and politically marginalized. By depicting to the rest of the country the evils of Chinese immigration, anti-Chinese groups in the West helped make the Chinese presence an issue of national importance. They not only warned that economic competition from racially inferior Chinese immigrants would downgrade white workers but also portrayed the "heathen" immigrants as physical and moral threats to American families. Congress responded in 1882 with the Chinese Exclusion Act, the nation's first major immigration-restriction law. In the twentieth century, Japanese immigrants faced similar political crusades to prevent their settlement and to undermine their livelihood. Several western states enacted alien land laws to stop Japanese immigrants from controlling land and making inroads in agriculture. At the same time, anti-Japanese pamphlets disparaged the Asian immigrants as unassimilable and even depicted them as an invading army that hoped to colonize America for the Japanese emperor. Many of these negative representations resurfaced after the attack on Pearl Harbor and made their way into arguments for interning approximately 120,000 Japanese Americans living along the West Coast.[4]

By the end of the 1940s, however, the "coolie," the "heathen Chinee," and the Japanese "yellow peril" had long disappeared from respectable political discourse. White Americans appeared to be more friendly toward Chinese Americans, undoubtedly because they associated these Asian ethnics with the nation's wartime ally. Charles Leong, the editor of an English-language community newspaper, the *Chinese Press*, remembered that the war led to feelings of social acceptance among Chinese Americans. "For the first time we felt we could make it in American society," he recalled. Japanese Americans also felt greater social acceptance by the end of the decade. Joe Grant Masaoka, the director of the northern California regional office of the Japanese American Citizens League (JACL), commented on the way race relations had changed since the end of the war. "Within the last three years," he said, "the decline of discriminatory practices directed against Japanese Americans has been truly remarkable. The combination of individuals, organizations, press and radio focusing their pressure has substantially cleared away most anti-Nisei incidents. The difference between wartime hysteria and present sentiment toward Japanese Americans is like night and day." Whether stemming from the publicity given to wartime sacrifices made by Japanese Americans or from the emerging Cold War relationship between the United States and Japan, favorable attitudes repositioned Japanese Americans as a valuable part of America's pluralist culture.[5]

But while white attitudes toward those of Asian descent gradually improved in the 1940s and 1950s, antiblack racism intensified. A 1946 survey of white racial attitudes in Spokane, Washington, revealed that prejudice against African Americans had already eclipsed prejudice against Japanese Americans. On the other side of the state, signs restricting patronage to white customers appeared in Seattle restaurants, theaters, and recreational facilities for the first time. Meanwhile, white property owners, who were often the most vocal critics of the growing black population, organized to prevent African Americans from living in their midst. Whenever they tried to challenge these attitudes, policies, and activities, black political leaders encountered racism that was so virulent that it dispelled any illusions of the West as a potential racial paradise. Evidently, what helped make African Americans the key minority group in the triangular and quadrilateral race-relations patterns of the postwar West was their unfortunate status as the "new objects of racial scorn."[6]

This study examines racial politics and racial hierarchy in postwar San Francisco. It reveals a changing race-relations environment and shares a selection of political activities to show how different nonwhite groups managed their minority status. San Francisco also was home to several Latino and other Asian American groups, but only the experiences of African

Americans, Japanese Americans, and Chinese Americans are included in this investigation. These three groups clearly had some common political interests in the postwar era, but they had different political priorities and different political cultures as well. These differences ultimately made forming a sustained interracial coalition impossible. In the end, black San Franciscans faced numerous obstacles in their struggle to improve their lives, whereas Asian San Franciscans gained greater acceptance in mainstream society and ascended the city's racial hierarchy. Juxtaposing the experiences of black and Asian San Franciscans and examining points of intersection contribute to a better understanding of why marginalized racial minorities who stood on similar ground in 1940 found their common ground eroding by the 1960s.

Although it sheds light on a particular racial dynamic, the San Francisco case study illustrates the complex racial politics that can be found in cities throughout the West, even in areas far away from the Pacific coast. The racial hierarchies may differ from place to place, but similar challenges to coalition building emerge. In postwar San Antonio, Texas, for instance, Mexican American residents had more civil rights and greater access to public accommodations than did their black counterparts. These discrepancies in minority-group status partially explain why Mexican American political organizations did not contribute to black-led desegregation campaigns in the early 1960s. One Mexican American resident commented, "Our roots are different. Our problems have been different, our solutions have been different. Therefore our philosophy is different." The lack of support from the Mexican American community nevertheless frustrated black San Antonians. Harry Burns, a leader in the San Antonio branch of the National Association for the Advancement of Colored People (NAACP) and one of the principle organizers of the local civil rights movement, stated years later, "Sometimes we feel that they [Mexican Americans] are our oppressors. . . . They try stepping on our heads to get ahead." Even though different minority groups were involved, the sentiments expressed in the San Antonio example echo what black San Franciscans and Asian San Franciscans said about one another in the late 1940s and early 1950s.[7]

Most important, the San Francisco case study confirms the necessity of analyzing urban racial politics in ways that address how one minority group can affect another. As our cities become more racially diverse, the traditional focus on the intersecting lives of the white majority and a particular racial minority fails to capture the complete race-relations picture. Through their political actions, racial attitudes, and interracial interactions, black and Asian San Franciscans show that race relations between peoples of color and race relations between whites and nonwhites are intertwined. Understanding the complexities of racial politics in San Francisco, therefore, furthers our knowledge of racial politics in multiracial settings, which most postwar western cities are and which many urban areas across the nation are becoming. This is one reason why Carey McWilliams characterized the West Coast, with its complex rather than binary racial patterns, as our nation's "racial frontier."

San Francisco offers an intriguing site for analyzing western racial politics. Despite being the seedbed for several political movements targeting Asian Americans, San Francisco still maintained a reputation as a place that welcomed ethnic and racial diversity. In 1944, Mayor Roger Lapham made reference to this reputation when he noted the unfortunate development of tension along racial and religious lines and announced the creation of a mayor's committee on civic unity. "To allow such conditions to go unnoticed in America would be deplorable," he said, adding that permitting "such conditions to exist without notice in San Francisco, which has through the years been noted for its cosmopolitan makeup, would be unthinkable." Lapham even refused to believe that existing intolerant attitudes were indigenous to the city and speculated that they were the result of Axis propaganda. The city's reputation as a tolerant place would persist in the postwar era. Herb Caen, a *San Francisco Chronicle* columnist, told readers in 1949:

> I enjoy the knowledge that minorities from all over the world live here, side-by-side, in an atmosphere that is truly "cosmopolitan"—that is, remarkably free from condescension, chauvinism, and petty friction. I like the daily sight of Negroes working at self-respecting jobs for the municipal government, running streetcars, handling the grips of the cable car, driving buses. . . . The Chinese and Japanese have become integral parts of the civic scenery—in almost every kind of job and profession in almost every part of the city.

A few columns may have suggested the existence of intolerance and discrimination, but the overall body of Caen's writings perpetuated this aspect of the city's mystique.[8]

This representation of San Francisco as a city of tolerance required public amnesia concerning the experiences of racial minorities. Black, Chinese, and Japanese San Franciscans faced racial discrimination whenever they looked for housing or employment, and they felt the sting of prejudice on a regular basis before the war. These groups understandably had a different perspective on the city's reputation as a tolerant place. Maya Angelou, who had moved to the city shortly after the attack on Pearl Harbor, later wrote, "San Franciscans would have sworn on the Golden Gate Bridge that racism was missing from the heart of their air-conditioned city. But they would have been sadly mistaken." A Chinese San Franciscan named Wing Ng echoed Angelou's observation when he called prewar San Francisco "the most discriminating city in the whole [of] California."[9]

Although they may have escaped southern bigotry and Jim Crow rules, African Americans still felt the full force of race prejudice and racial discrimination as they migrated to the city during and after the war. For instance, black newcomers encountered housing discrimination and a municipal government that was both ill prepared for the situation and unwilling to alleviate it. The only spaces open to African Americans were those Fillmore district units that had been emptied by the forced uprooting of Japanese Americans or temporary public housing units near the naval shipyard at Hunters Point. In other parts of the city, they found neighborhood groups, merchants' associations, and improvement clubs organized to prevent them from occupying houses and apartments. According to Charles Johnson, the author of a wartime study of black workers in San Francisco, it was these neighborhood mobilizations that would later lead to ghettoization. Johnson's study included several statements to show the antiblack attitudes driving the campaign to prevent black occupancy. "Negroes are lazy and dirty," one respondent said, adding, "It's bad to have them living around white girls." Another respondent stated, "Negroes now coming in are rowdy, thievish, drunken, and quarrelsome. They are dirty and among white women in restaurants and other places of business." One man proclaimed that he would not even want famed opera singer Marian Anderson as a neighbor.[10]

Black San Franciscans also faced considerable resistance from white employers and white workers when they sought work in more prestigious and more lucrative skilled and semiskilled jobs. For example, the Municipal Railway's employee union voted to fine any member $100 for giving Audley Cole, a recently hired black employee, the necessary training for the job. One member who broke ranks to train the new employee received a beating from a fellow worker. Although the union eventually bowed to pressure to admit Cole and to train him, at least one San Franciscan expressed displeasure concerning black streetcar operators and advocated hate strikes to drive African Americans from the workforce. "It's a disgrace to see those black beasts running street cars," he wrote in a letter a few years after the war.

> Of course when a slump comes they will be out and San Francisco people will be back there. It looks terrible to visitors here to see those

niggers on street cars. . . . Where I work, and I have learned in other places, it is catching on. . . . we have told the boss that if he hires niggers we all will quit. Several blacks have been around looking for jobs. But they won't be hired. That is what the solution to the influx of more niggers to this town must be—Don't work with them. Keep them out of unions. . . . They ask for it. now [*sic*] boycott 'em.

From the letter writer's perspective, racial discrimination in the workplace, either by employers or by unions, was the last line of defense.[11]

Black community leaders continually exposed the disjuncture between San Francisco's reputation for tolerance and the status of the city's nonwhite residents. Along with other racial liberals, they participated in private organizations such as the Council for Civic Unity (CCU), which brought together representatives from different community groups into a coalition dedicated to promoting a positive race-relations environment. The CCU used member resources to study racial discrimination in the city, sponsored a radio program focusing on civil rights news, and helped lead several campaigns for a local fair-employment ordinance. Throughout their critiques of the racial status quo, racial liberals argued that city government should play an integral role in combating racial prejudice and creating racial equality.

Unlike their Asian American counterparts, whose inconsistent involvement was issue specific and almost entirely peripheral, black leaders were actively engaged in the CCU and in other organizations focusing on municipal racial issues. Joseph James, president of the San Francisco branch of the NAACP at the end of the war, served as a vice president of the CCU and as a board member for the Urban League. He also worked with local political and community leaders, including individuals from the progressive Left, by serving on the San Francisco Civic Unity Committee created in the mayor's office. James eagerly shared the black community's interests through his participation in these various organizations and tried to work with others to improve the status of all racial minorities. In comparison, Henry Shue Tom, a Chinese American member of the mayor's Civic Unity Committee, barely contributed. If the committee's minutes are an indication of the organization's activities, Tom never revealed issues specific to Chinese San Franciscans. Moreover, apart from a couple of references to discrimination against Japanese Americans, the minutes show that black issues were completely dominating the city government's discussions of race by the middle of the 1940s.[12]

Even if his community's interests received the most attention, James always hoped to move the NAACP away from being an organization that was only concerned with black issues. "Our problem is not an isolated one," he said in his 1944 inaugural address. "We must throw our strength in concerted action with other groups of American citizens whose goals are the same as ours." Besides emphasizing the need to build relationships with others, James showed how African Americans were combining the ideas of racial liberalism with the wartime demand for a "double victory." He said, "The war can be lost for us by our failure to force the extension of freedom and democracy here just as surely as it can be lost by the defeat of our armies abroad. We must make ourselves worthy of the boys who are shedding their blood for us, by carrying on an unceasing struggle to make America a better place for their return." In many ways, the election of James to the presidency of the local NAACP revealed a wartime transition toward a more politically active black leadership that was aggressive in its critiques of racial discrimination and in its calls for racial equality.[13]

James also brought to the branch a perspective that resonated with the black working class. Before taking office, he had worked as a welder at Marinship when he led the San Francisco Committee against Segregation and Discrimination, an organization that initiated lawsuits that successfully challenged the legality of racially segregated auxiliaries in the Boilermakers' Union. During his tenure as president, he acknowledged the value of cooperating with the local trade union movement. He once told readers of the *People's World*, a Communist Party newspaper, that progress for African Americans was linked to advancing the interests of the working classes: "The Negroes as a whole and such organizations as the NAACP are pretty well convinced that the only way the Negro people can make gains is by throwing their weight in with organized labor, and on all issues that effect [*sic*] the people as a whole, instead of making the old-time 'gentlemen's agreement' between high politicians and Negro leaders to get a couple of garbage collectors' jobs with the city."

The San Francisco branch of the NAACP also published an article welcoming the civil rights work of the National Negro Congress (NNC). After commenting that the NNC remained alive largely through the efforts of both black and white communists, the author described the group as an ally in the struggle to better conditions for black Americans, calling it "one more voice raised in the general chorus for freedom and democracy." The author stated, "That voice may be of different quality from those now being heard, but it will be singing the same tune."[14]

Because they embraced ties with the progressive Left, expressed many of the same political beliefs, and even engaged in similar militant protest activities, those black community leaders who associated with "radicals" during the developing Cold War provided critics with an argument to combat the struggle for black rights. This interconnectedness of red-baiting and black-hating was evident in the 1946 protest at the Uptown Theater. Spearheaded by the John Brown and the Fillmore Communist Party clubs, the protest was part of the "Jobs for Negroes" direct-action campaign that placed a dozen black female workers in Woolworth's, the National Dollar Store, and the Owl Drug Store. Doris Dixon, chairperson of a jobs committee composed of members from the two communist clubs, expressed the need to increase employment opportunities in the community. "All you see walking up and down the streets here in Fillmore are Negroes," she said, "but you don't see any Negroes selling in the stores." She noted, "The Negroes live here, spend their money here, and they have a right to get decent jobs here." In fall 1946, Dixon's group formed a joint committee with the local NAACP and the American Veterans Committee to request the hiring of a black usher at the Fillmore district's Uptown Theater. After a series of unproductive conversations, the joint committee, which named itself the Committee for Fair Employment, called for a boycott and established a picket line at the Uptown.[15]

Despite dropping attendance at the Uptown, theater managers refused to negotiate with the Committee for Fair Employment. "If we hired a Negro usherette now, it would be a victory for the Communists," stated one manager, vowing never to allow that to happen. Theater officials instead decided to undermine the picket line by passing out free movie passes. The *People's World* reported that the theater recruited Wesley Peoples, a prominent black Republican and a leader in the local Negro Chamber of Commerce, to facilitate the distribution of the free movie passes and to urge the black community to ignore the picket line. Moreover, Peoples was reportedly the secretary for the George Washington Carver Society, a group that printed leaflets disparaging the direct-action campaign. One Carver Society flyer was highly critical of the NAACP branch's involvement in the Uptown protest. It insinuated that the picketing would never have occurred if the theater had bought advertising space in the city's black newspaper or had paid off local NAACP officials. The Carver Society called the entire campaign a scheme for "the lining of their greasy pockets under the guise of racial unity, solidarity and advancement." It also denigrated the "picketing for jobs" mobilization as another example of "Communist front organizations ... [wanting] to raise 'hell.'" With all capital letters, the Carver Society advised readers, "DON'T BE A SUCKER. ATTEND YOUR NEIGHBORHOOD MOVIE OR SHOW. IGNORE THE PRESENT PICKET LINE."[16]

The Committee for Fair Employment, on the other hand, emphasized the broad support behind its boycott and criticized the red-baiting tactic. "Charges of Communist agitation or interferences [*sic*] are purely a smokescreen to weaken the fight against job discrimination," the committee declared. Although Communist Party clubs, the National Negro Congress, and the American Youth for Democracy were actively engaged in the protest, the campaign to hire a black usher also enjoyed support from the American Veterans Committee and several progressive labor groups. Demonstrating the support of organized labor was especially important since theater officials claimed that picketing for minority hiring violated their closed shop agreement with their employee union. At the same time, the committee branded Wesley Peoples "an 'Uncle Tom' with a consistent record of betrayal to the Republican reactionaries; betrayal to the anti-FEPC [Fair Employment Practices Committee] forces; betrayal to the worst proponents of racial discrimination."[17]

The boycott lasted three months before the Committee for Fair Employment and the theater came to an agreement. A theater manager who had predicted that hiring an African American would lead to disaster reportedly described the first black usher as "very satisfactory, intelligent and efficient." Emboldened by its victory, the Committee for Fair Employment attempted to replicate its success by challenging the hiring policies of two other movie theaters on Fillmore Street. Criticism for its involvement in the Uptown theater protest and its association with alleged radicals did not deter the San Francisco NAACP from continuing to support the use of direct-action methods to expose race prejudice and to expand black employment opportunities. During Carlton Goodlett's presidency, the branch sponsored the formation of the Affiliated Clubs and Organizations of San Francisco, a protest group that used boycotts or the threat of boycotts to pressure businesses such as the Emporium department store and the Borden Dairy to hire black workers.[18]

Picketing for jobs nevertheless remained controversial since it not only angered employers but also had the potential of alienating white workers by upholding racially based hiring in favor of African Americans. Moderate black political leaders believed that the NAACP's traditional methods—legislative lobbying, legal challenges, personal meetings, and publicity campaigns—better served their community interests. They began steering West Coast NAACP branches, some of which were thought to be under Communist Party control, in that direction. Moreover, from the perspective of the national and regional NAACP officials, charges of communism derived from association with alleged radicals were detrimental to the larger campaign. The national NAACP had to contend with the anticommunist attitudes of political leaders not only in the nation's capital but also in the South, where the struggle for black rights appeared most vital. At the end of the decade, the national NAACP would impose political conformity throughout its organization as it sought respectability and became more entrenched in the Cold War Democratic Party.

Besides maintaining relationships with organized labor and the progressive Left, another feature of black politics in postwar San Francisco was a commitment to interracial cooperation with Asian San Franciscans. With the lifting of the West Coast Exclusion Order, for example, Joseph James gave assurances that African Americans would welcome and assist Japanese Americans as they returned from the internment camps. When the former internees encountered violence and discrimination, James told a representative from the JACL that the NAACP offered "an outstretched hand, and invite them to join forces with us and see what we can do about correcting some of these abuses." James, who eventually served as a member of the JACL's local advisory board, characterized the interactions of the JACL and the NAACP as "working together openly and effectively." This cooperation on both the local and regional level was evident in the legislative campaigns that the two minority organizations supported and the amici curiae briefs that they filed. At the NAACP's 1947 West Coast Regional Conference, delegates endorsed the JACL's entire legislative agenda. They voted in favor of granting naturalization rights to Japanese immigrants, repealing California's Alien Land Law, and establishing an evacuation claims commission to study and compensate for losses incurred during the wartime removal. The JACL, meanwhile, filed an amicus curiae brief on behalf of African American petitioners in *Shelley v. Kraemer* (1948), one of several NAACP cases challenging the legality of restrictive covenants.[19]

Their leaders may have worked together, but rank-and-file black and Japanese San Franciscans seldom got beyond superficial interaction and peaceful coexistence. According to a 1949 article in *Pacific Citizen*, the JACL's official organ, the Fillmore district was neither a "unified community" nor "an example of racial harmony." Japanese San Franciscans, who had hoped to rebuild their community, considered black San Franciscans a threatening presence and blamed them for the deterioration of the neighborhood. One African American characterized the Japanese American attitude as "one of contempt mixed with fear." Wilson Record, a sociology professor at Sacramento State College, made the following observation several years later: "Mutual suspicions are hard to dispel, or the feeling that regardless of how hard they try little will come of efforts to realize common goals through common endeavors. Negroes resent the white's more ready 'acceptance' of Japanese as students, workers, and neighbors. They sense that, indirectly at least, Japanese 'acceptability' may have grown out of the Negroes' more frightening challenge to the white community."[20]

Record's observation concerning white acceptance of Japanese Americans suggests the higher position that Asian San Franciscans began to hold in the local racial hierarchy. In contrast to the increased levels of antiblack racism, negative attitudes toward Asian Americans gradually declined in the postwar era. For Japanese Americans, the better race-relations environment emerged in the latter half of the 1940s. When Californians in 1946 voted down Proposition 15, which would have strengthened the state's Alien Land Law, the *Nichi Bei Times* noted that the vote represented "the first time in California's political history, the people of the state have turned down a measure aimed primarily at persons of Oriental ancestry." Saburo Kido, the national president of the JACL, wrote in the *Pacific Citizen* that "the attitude of the voters has progressed from the anti-Orientalism of the 1920's to that of according equal and fair treatment to all."[21]

In this changing race-relations environment, the JACL continually challenged the injustices that Japanese Americans experienced. Through its Anti-Discrimination Committee, it used the courts and other legalistic means to knock down California's ban on alien fishing licenses and land ownership. The organization also successfully lobbied for the 1948 Evacuation Claims Act, a measure that provided partial restitution for losses incurred during the removal process. By highlighting the community's wartime sacrifices, America's partnership with Japan in the Korean War, and the Cold War implications of racial restrictions on naturalization, the JACL and its allies were able to obtain Issei citizenship rights as a clause within the 1952 McCarran-Walter Naturalization and Immigration Act.[22]

Chinese San Franciscans, on the other hand, began to enjoy an improving race-relations environment as soon as the war began. "The crisis of December 7 has emancipated the Chinese in the United States," Rose Hum Lee declared in a *Survey Graphic* article published in October 1942. Lee believed that the war led to greater Chinese American inclusion and assimilation. With Chinese Americans going outside of Chinatown for jobs and with white Americans coming into Chinatown for entertainment, the social isolation that often characterized Chinese American life appeared to be diminishing. "They [Chinese Americans] live on close terms with their American neighbors, enjoy the same recreation and health facilities offered to their fellow citizens," Lee stated optimistically. "No longer do Americans think of the Chinese as mysterious Orientals from a little known land." From the perspective of some white observers, however, Chinese Americans were less mysterious only because they seemed more American. One woman wrote in her master's thesis that Chinatown and its residents had become modernized: "The Chinese people on her streets dress as other Americans; the queue and the lilly [*sic*] foot are never seen; the children playing on the streets converse in modern American slang; modern cars are parked by their Chinese owners along the streets; and, probably most modern American of all sights in modern Chinatown, are the cocktail bars with their 'juke boxes.'"[23]

White acceptance of Chinese San Franciscans in the workforce was also on the rise. Rose Hum Lee noted that Chinese Americans were finding employment outside their ethnic economy, taking advantage of openings in places ranging from shipbuilding factories to downtown offices. The new opportunities represented a departure from the prewar era, when, Lee claimed, one could count all the jobs available to Chinese Americans "on the fingers of the hand—chop suey and chow mein restaurants, Chinese art and gift shops, native grocery stores that sell foodstuffs imported from China to the local Chinese community." In the postwar era, Asian San Franciscans, especially the assimilated American-born generation that came of age in the late 1940s and afterward, finally gained access to jobs that were commensurate with their high educational achievement.[24]

African Americans did not enjoy similar long-term advances in the workforce. Many lost their industrial jobs when wartime production levels were no longer necessary and after returning servicemen received the promise of postwar employment. In addition, a 1946 report from the Committee on Fair Employment Practice noted that the employment situation for Chinese Americans remained good but that discrimination had already curtailed the wartime gains of black workers. African Americans continued to be in a comparatively worse position in the decade that followed. A survey conducted by the Council for Civic Unity in the mid-1950s revealed that private employment agencies believed that referring qualified black applicants was a pointless endeavor. One survey respondent admitted to discriminating against African Americans when she disclosed that her agency would make phone calls on behalf of qualified Asian American applicants but would automatically place black applicants in the "inactive file."[25]

A racial hierarchy that placed African Americans on the bottom rung was also apparent in the different experiences that black and Asian San Franciscans had when they searched for housing. Japanese Americans and Chinese Americans began living in units outside their traditional neighborhoods, with some of them entering what had been all-white neighborhoods. Census figures for one Richmond-district neighborhood indicated that the area had only three minority families in 1950. By the second half of the decade there were many more Asian American families living in the neighborhood. Realtors interviewed for a 1957 study estimated that racial minorities, primarily Asian Americans, represented 15 to 20 percent of the neighborhood's population. White and Asian San Franciscans in the neighborhood did not interact socially, but antagonism between the two groups was minimal. The presence of African Americans, on the other hand, created considerable resentment. One woman said that many residents threatened to move out if any more blacks came into the neighborhood.[26]

Antiblack racism was so strong that even being a famous baseball star failed to ensure better treatment. In 1957, residents in the exclusive Sherwood Heights district pressured a home owner to cancel the sale of his house to Willie Mays. The fact that Mays paid $5,000 over the listing price of $32,500 did not prevent whites from arguing that an African American neighbor would lower property values. Martin Gaewhiler, a builder and a resident in the area, said: "Certainly I objected [to the sale]. I happen to have quite a few pieces of property in that area and I stand to lose a lot if colored people move in. But I didn't force Gnesdiloff [the seller] to do anything. I told him to use his own conscience, but that he'd get a bad name if he went through with this. I certainly wouldn't like to have a colored family near me." When he was reminded that the neighborhood already had a couple of Asian American families, Gaewhiler reportedly drew a sharp distinction between African Americans and other racial minorities. The home sale went through in the end, but the initial objection further tarnished the city's cosmopolitan image in the eyes of black San Franciscans. "It's all a lot of camouflage," Mrs. Mays stated; "they grin in your face and then deceive you."[27]

Realtors confirmed that Asian San Franciscans faced less hostility than black San Franciscans. Citing a broker as his source, Frank Quinn, executive director of the Council for Civic Unity in 1960, related the story of an African American doctor who had his $24,000 offer on a house rejected by the home owner. A Chinese American family reportedly bought the house a week later for $22,000. According to Quinn, "The woman who owned the house had less feeling against Chinese than she did against Negroes, and I was told this by the realtor." Interviews taken in 1955 for a study of racial discrimination in local real estate practices verified that black San Franciscans experienced greater discrimination in their search for housing. The survey elicited the following responses from realtors:

> Generally, the feeling is against non-Caucasians, but most people will qualify this by saying they mind Orientals less than Negroes.
> Mexicans are often not considered a minority and Orientals are generally accepted, but the Negro is a special problem.
> It is easier for Orientals than for Negroes to buy. . . . Japanese and Chinese are often accepted almost like whites.

Asian San Franciscans also had access to more rental units. An estimated 67 percent of the city's rental vacancies in 1961 were open to Asian Americans, whereas only 33 percent were open to African Americans.[28]

With more housing units available to them, Asian San Franciscans could choose to circumvent existing barriers rather than break them down. This accommodation to the racial status quo in housing angered some black San Franciscans. In May 1955, J. Maceo Green, a columnist for the local black newspaper, provided a bitter critique of Asian Americans for their failure to contribute to the fair housing struggle. He told *San Francisco Sun-Reporter* readers that "other groups sat around rubbing their hands in dismay but it was the despised Negroes . . . who broke these covenants." He claimed that those Asian Americans who now live outside their ghettoes had benefited from the black struggle to expand minority rights. Besides chastising Asian Americans for their passivity, Green accused Asian Americans of adopting the dominant culture's prejudice against African Americans. "These groups have a tendency to seek recognition. . . . in many instances Negroes have found them joining in with the others to down Negroes as being pariahs," he wrote.[29]

The charge that most Asian San Franciscans seldom fought for their housing rights had some validity. A survey of 500 Nisei living in San Francisco and Berkeley in the second half of the 1950s found that 61 percent of those questioned would avoid conflict if they learned that others objected to their presence in a particular neighborhood. Responses included "It's not worth the trouble" and "I don't want to be the cause of any unpleasantness." Twenty-three percent claimed they would fight for their housing rights and move in at any cost; 15 percent took positions between these two, including at least one respondent who would poll the neighbors and only move in if accepted. The survey also noted that over half the Nisei had obtained their current residences through friends and Japanese American real estate brokers, and 58 percent of the 300 San Francisco respondents even rented from a Japanese American landlord. These practices guaranteed that their race would not become a problem for either the landlord or the seller.[30]

Although they avoided the direct-action tactics employed by black San Franciscans, Asian San Franciscans were far from passive when interests specific to their communities were involved. For instance, when a proposed immigration bill endangered the entry on a nonquota basis of Chinese wives married to American citizens, Chinatown political organizations mobilized a protest. The Chinese Six Companies sent their representatives to the nation's capital to help modify the bill so that Chinese immigration rights would remain intact. The Cathay Post of the American Legion contributed to the effort by lobbying the California department of the American Legion to support the bill's modification. Meanwhile, the Chinese American Citizens Alliance and the Chinese YMCA's Public Affairs Committee wired protests to California's senators and congressmen. Students from a Chinese-language school even started a petition drive to demonstrate the public's support of Chinese immigration rights. In only two days, they reportedly collected over 2,000 signatures from Chinese Americans and white Americans. All of the aforementioned political activities reveal a preference for private actions and moral suasion over aggressive public protests.[31]

The prominent role of the local JACL in the campaign to modify the 1948 Western Addition redevelopment plan also suggests that Asian San Franciscans willingly worked with other racial groups if common interests existed. Considered the city's worst blighted area, the Western Addition was home to the Japanese American and African American communities. In 1948, twenty-seven blocks of the Western Addition were designated for urban renewal, which for residents meant the loss of homes and small businesses. The JACL characterized the plan as another forced uprooting before stressing its impact on all racial minorities in the Western Addition. "Having experienced the 1942 evacuation," a *Pacific Citizen* writer commented, "they now feel that the redevelopment plan may in actuality be a final evacuation for them, an evacuation from which there will be no return." The writer indicated that the program provided housing for only 75,000 people even though the current population was closer to 86,000. She concluded that the displaced racial minorities would only exacerbate overcrowding in other areas. Other critics noted that the redevelopment program failed to improve housing conditions for lower-income residents. Michi Onuma, the former housing chairman of the San Francisco JACL, pointed out that the plan projected a substantially higher rent for the new units. "We've got to have real slum clearance," she protested, "not slum clearance to provide housing for middle and upper groups alone." The *Pacific Citizen* described public officials as being fully aware of the possibility that higher rents would drive racial minorities from the area. Redevelopment under the current plan, the newspaper said, did not make residential life better for racial minorities. Instead, urban renewal meant nonwhite removal.[32]

The JACL invited Japanese American property owners and businessmen to join its fight against the existing slum-clearance plan. In a letter to San Francisco's Board of Supervisors, it affirmed the necessity of redevelopment but added that the plan needed to be modified to protect the interests of nonwhite and low-income residents. The JACL asked for a provision against segregation and discrimination as well as a guarantee that displaced residents and businesses would get priority in the redeveloped area. It also wanted the construction of low-cost housing for those who could not afford the new rents. Lastly, the JACL thought that the current property owners not only should have more protection in the selling of their property but also should be given the opportunity to participate in the construction of new units. Simply put, the JACL preferred that local residents, business owners, and property owners have greater control in the Western Addition redevelopment process.[33]

In the end, the Board of Supervisors unanimously passed a resolution requesting the redevelopment agency to include "covenants against discrimination or segregation" in its leases and contracts. Unfortunately, the resolution did not include penalties for those who violated these covenants, which meant that the redevelopment agency was not legally obligated to abide by the supervisors' request. Morgan Gunst, the chairman of the agency, nevertheless believed that his agency was "morally" bound to uphold the antibias resolution. Although they wanted compulsory measures, those who opposed the original redevelopment plan considered the resolution a satisfactory outcome. The JACL's *Pacific Citizen* praised it as a step forward in the struggle to protect minority rights. Unfortunately, with all the attention focused on the issue of discrimination, the additional concerns expressed by the JACL—that is, the need for economic safeguards and greater community control—were forgotten. Apart from the nondiscrimination statement, the program emphasizing private sector leadership remained intact.[34]

While the campaign to reform the Western Addition redevelopment plan was an episode of multiracial cooperation, the struggle to end discrimination in public housing reveals that minority groups often had conflicting interests. The San Francisco Housing Authority (SFHA) used the racial makeup of the neighborhood to determine occupancy in its projects and thus excluded blacks from all but one of its permanent housing projects. Only Westside Courts, located in the heart of the Fillmore district, accepted African American tenants. Critics of the segregation policy argued that nonwhite applicants should be able to live in any of the city's housing projects— Chinese San Franciscans should not be confined to Chinatown's Ping Yuen, and black San Franciscans should not be trapped in Westside Courts. They said that preserving the "neighborhood pattern" not only limited the number of units available to nonwhites but also prevented the integration of racial minorities into different neighborhoods.[35]

The housing authority resisted efforts to change this segregation policy. When William McKinley Thomas, a black physician who served as a housing authority commissioner from 1946 to 1950, moved to have the SFHA publicly oppose segregation, no one seconded his motion. Furthermore, the SFHA refused to approve the city's application for a new housing project with an added antidiscrimination stipulation. According to the *Pacific Citizen*, four out of five housing authority members opposed the nondiscrimination measure and employed delay tactics and high-pressure lobbying in an attempt to kill it. The Board of Supervisors and the housing authority eventually reached a compromise in early 1950. Although the board endorsed the dropping of the neighborhood-pattern policy, the supervisors permitted the SFHA to maintain for the time being segregation in existing units and in all "deferred" projects currently ready for construction. These units would gradually adopt the nondiscrimination policy. Future developments, which would not begin construction for another two years, were to be racially integrated from the start. According to the Council for Civic Unity, the voluntary nondiscrimination policy resembled the antibias measure adopted in the Western Addition redevelopment program: It sought to urge rather than legally bind the housing authority to drop its racial steering practices. The supervisors also left open the possibility of restoring the neighborhood-pattern policy should nondiscrimination prove to be a failure.[36]

Shortly after the compromise agreement, fair housing advocates lost their only supporter among the housing authority's commissioners when Mayor Elmer Robinson decided not to reappoint William McKinley Thomas. Charles Jung, the president of the local Chinese American Citizens Alliance, was the chosen successor. The Council for Civic Unity wondered whether the new commissioner would favor the permanent maintenance of the neighborhood pattern in Ping Yuen, a soon-to-be-completed Chinatown project. It commented in its newsletter, "It is to be hoped that the misinformation & confusion as to the effect of nonsegregation on the long-delayed Chinatown housing project will not turn Commissioner Jung against the new [nondiscrimination] policy." The CCU's concern that segregation would persist was not unwarranted. Both the *Chinese Press* and a member of a Chinatown housing committee stated that the retention of the neighborhood pattern in Ping Yuen was a sound policy.[37]

In the summer of 1952, fair-housing advocates again criticized segregation in public housing when the SFHA announced that African Americans would be barred from living in North Beach Place, one of the deferred projects. During a public meeting on housing-related issues, African Americans shared stories of the SFHA's giving them the run-around in an attempt to turn them away from North Beach Place. Mattie Banks told everyone that she had been denied an apartment even though she met all the necessary qualifications. She added that the SFHA offered to place her in a temporary housing unit at Hunters Point after the NAACP filed a discrimination suit on her behalf.[38]

Despite the NAACP's victory in *Banks v. the San Francisco Housing Authority* (1952), the struggle to end segregation in public housing was not complete. Refusing to back down, the housing authority immediately asked for a stay of execution. It argued that existing neighborhoods such as North Beach and Chinatown were integral to the city's charm and its renowned "international flavor" and that they must be preserved. The housing authority not only proceeded to appeal the superior court's decision but also proposed a new Hunters Point project to meet black housing needs without sacrificing the neighborhood pattern. As it stalled for time, the SFHA quickly filled vacancies in North Beach Place and Ping Yuen. All these actions drew criticism from the *Sun-Reporter*, the NAACP, and the Council for Civic Unity. Even a special county grand jury committee chastised the SFHA for contesting the judge's decision, stating that "it marks our city as a center of race bigotry, which it is not in fact."[39]

The *Sun-Reporter* noted that Charles Jung did not initially oppose either the racial steering policy or the attempt to appeal the court ruling. In a veiled criticism of Jung, J. Maceo Green argued that the NAACP's campaign to end the neighborhood-pattern policy "caused other minorities, the Chinese, for instance, to gain both direct and indirect benefits." Referring to Jung directly, another editorial stated, "It is significant that not one member of the whole commission of the Housing Authority raised his voice for democracy, although it has at least one member of a minority group." Two weeks later, the paper made an angrier statement concerning Jung's inaction. "The Negro," it said, "stands in the vanguard of the vigorous struggle against the advocates of this undemocratic practice, whereas members of some other minority groups submit supinely, even request segregation!" Shortly after the publication of this editorial and following an unsuccessful appeal, Jung and another commissioner voted against further legal action to preserve segregation. Though the majority of commissioners still wanted to appeal the decision, this vote represented the first break in the SFHA's united front.[40]

That Chinese San Franciscans neither criticized the housing authority nor made ending the neighborhood-pattern policy an important goal is not surprising. This inactivity reflected the comparatively good relationship that Chinatown organizations had with the housing authority and the municipal government. While the black community thought that the SFHA ignored its needs, Chinatown's leaders viewed the completion of Ping Yuen as evidence of the city's commitment to housing low-income residents of Chinese descent. In addition, low-income Chinese San Franciscans worked, shopped, and relaxed in Chinatown and had little desire to apply for public housing elsewhere. When the SFHA offered replacement housing to families that were displaced for the construction of Ping Yuen, it discovered that almost all the outgoing families refused to be relocated in other areas of the city and found their own housing in the vicinity of Chinatown. Therefore, J. Maceo Green's contention that Chinese San Franciscans should realize that they benefited from the NAACP's legal action against the housing authority was actually off the mark.[41]

The relative inactivity of Chinese San Franciscans was also consistent with the overall political culture within the ethnic community. While politics within the Japanese American community abruptly changed with the arrest and removal of the immigrant leaders and the ascendance of the JACL, the continuity of political elites in Chinatown ensured that the community's political interests and style after the war would not deviate significantly from those in the prewar era. Unlike the JACL and the NAACP, the leaders of Chinatown seldom used the courts to push for civil rights and rarely engaged in public social criticism. They chose instead to lobby white officials in private, a more conservative approach that simultaneously maintained the image of Chinese Americans as law-abiding citizens. Frank Quinn expressed frustration over the relative inactivity of Chinatown's leaders. "They do not look at the idea of asserting themselves in the way that we feel that civil rights must be asserted," he said. Quinn attributed the situation to the phenomenon of illegal immigration, stating at one point, "The people are just plain afraid to get involved because of the fact that there are so many people whose tenure in this country is in great question."[42]

In addition, the leaders of the Chinese Six Companies, the most influential Chinese American organization, eschewed political protest and enforced political conformity to demonstrate both their commitment to anticommunism and their loyalty to America during the Korean War. The absence of social protest in housing issues likewise reflected the class orientation of the Chinese Six Companies, which was dominated by a small set of conservative businessmen. These leaders, as well as the heads of the clans and the district associations, wielded considerable economic power. One study of Chinatown conducted in the early 1970s showed that the community entities they led controlled an estimated 65 percent of the land in the core area of Chinatown. This explains why the displacement of Chinatown businesses was one of the only issues raised by Chinatown leaders during the site preparation for Ping Yuen.[43]

Stanton Jue suggested that class differences and political orientation further explained why Chinese San Franciscans avoided political collaboration. "The conservative middle and lower-middle classes predominantly feel that there is no homogeneous political interests with other minority groups," he told readers of the *Chinese Press*. In reality, shared political interests often did exist, but shared political cultures did not. Voting on propositions showed that Chinese San Franciscans supported liberal policies such as fair-employment legislation and public-housing construction. Voting for political offices, however, confirmed that black and Chinese San Franciscans behaved differently at the polls. In the 1948 presidential election, for example, an estimated 70 percent of black San Franciscans voted to reelect

Harry Truman, while only 13 percent backed Thomas Dewey. The fact that Henry Wallace, the Independent Progressive Party candidate, garnered more black votes than Dewey earned confirms where black San Franciscans were located along the political spectrum. In comparison, Chinese San Franciscans were more conservative. Fifty-seven percent of these voters gave their votes to Dewey, and only 35 percent gave their votes to the Democratic incumbent. If voting behavior is any indication, Chinese San Franciscans were one of the more conservative social groups in the city, whereas black San Franciscans were one of the most liberal if not radical groups.[44]

When they dreamed of multiracial political coalitions, postwar racial liberals assumed that black and Asian Americans had many "homogeneous political interests." Although they saw similar marginalization along racial and class lines, they never considered the different political priorities and political cultures that existed in these minority communities. If these differences were not enough, the educational and occupational gap that continued to widen between black and Asian San Franciscans ensured that these groups did not have much common ground on which to build sustained interracial coalitions. Greater white acceptance and better job opportunities permitted the entry of assimilated and educated Asian Americans into the middle class. Asian American capital accumulation through home ownership was integral as well. These changes in status in turn affected Asian American political interests and political cultures. After decades of exclusion, Chinese American and Japanese American San Franciscans embraced their status as "honorary whites."[45]

As he acknowledged the postwar developments that contributed to the greater inclusion of Asian Americans, Wilson Record speculated that "the appearance of new objects of racial scorn" may have partially paved the way. He later reiterated this claim and cited these words from a Protestant minister of Japanese descent: "A lot of us are congratulating ourselves on working for and securing wide acceptance in the community at large. But I suspect that we have been bailed out by the Negroes. They moved in and frightened the whites, who then found that we Japanese weren't so bad after all. They could stop hating us and start hating the Negroes." By linking antiblack racism with white acceptance of Asian Americans, Record suggested that the improved conditions that enabled Chinese American and Japanese American San Franciscans to climb the local racial hierarchy in the postwar era would not necessarily benefit black San Franciscans. When would another group elevate African Americans by becoming the new object of racial scorn?[46]

Meanwhile, after defining the presence of various Asian American groups as race problems from the late nineteenth through the early twentieth century, local political discussions concerning race and race relations pointed to Chinese Americans and Japanese Americans as the solution to all race problems. Long before Asian Americans as model minorities became a theme in the national media, white San Franciscans were using Asian American San Franciscans to criticize black San Franciscans and black social protest. During a hearing before the Civil Rights Commission in 1960, the city's chief of police expressed his disagreement with those who cited inadequate housing as one of the major factors driving criminal activity. "The basic reason for crime is a moral deterioration," Thomas Cahill said. To support his argument, Cahill commented that Chinese San Franciscans lived in a ghetto and "there are no real crime problems there even though they are together." In other parts of his testimony, Cahill praised Chinese and Japanese San Franciscans, stating that their veneration of the family explained their moral behavior and their obedience to authority. When asked whether he thought black San Franciscans disrespected the law, Cahill responded by stating that they were overly suspicious of the police and the justice system. He elsewhere accused African Americans of wanting the world to accommodate them rather than adjusting themselves to their surroundings.[47]

These racial intersections in San Francisco suggest the value of a multiple-group approach to studying race relations in multiracial settings. Examining several groups in the same moments and spaces can reveal structures, relationships, and experiences that may be less apparent in studies based solely on a particular racial community or on a binary set of white/nonwhite race relations. Scholarly works that continue to use a binary approach to race relations could be missing an interesting story. If the greater presence of African Americans and rising antiblack racism contributed to the improved race-relations environment for Asian Americans, then racial intersections need to be explored for a more thorough understanding of how the racial hierarchy changed in San Francisco and in other western cities. An approach that includes an understanding of shifting racial hierarchies and that analyzes race relations within a larger constellation of intergroup dynamics exposes the gains made by Chinese Americans and Japanese Americans as potential indicators of losses for other social groups. More generally, the positioning of Asian Americans as model minorities validates the American dream and undermines more aggressive demands for public policies to bring about greater social equality, both of which serve to reproduce the racial hierarchy by keeping some groups on the bottom rung while allowing the creation of shared political and economic interests for those on top.

NOTES

1. Carey McWilliams, "Critical Summary," *Journal of Educational Sociology* (November 1945): 193-194.

2. Quintard Taylor, *In Search of the Racial Frontier: African Americans in the American West, 1528-1990* (New York: W. W. Norton, 1998), 254, 267; U.S. Bureau of the Census, *Sixteenth Census of the United States: 1940, Population*, vol. 2, *Characteristics of the Population* (Washington, D.C.: GPO, 1943), pt. 5:1042 and pt. 1:788; *A Report of the Seventeenth Decennial Census of the United States, Census of Population: 1950*, vol. 2, *Characteristics of the Population* (Washington, D.C.: GPO, 1952), pt. 37:51 and pt. 6:47.

3. Quintard Taylor, *The Forging of a Black Community: Seattle's Central District from 1870 through the Civil Rights Era* (Seattle: University of Washington Press, 1994), 184, 170; Seaton Manning, "Housing and Employment: The Minimal Needs for Mental Health," *Beacon* (Winter 1946): 4-6.

4. Tomás Almaguer, *Racial Fault Lines: The Historical Origins of White Supremacy in California* (Berkeley and Los Angeles: University of California Press, 1994), 38-41.

5. Victor G. Nee and Brett de Barry Nee, *Longtime Californ': A Documentary Study of an American Chinatown* (New York: Pantheon Books, 1973), 154; Joe Grant Masaoka, Japanese American Citizens League, Northern California Regional Office report dated 29 November 1948, found in California Federation for Civic Unity, carton 1, no folder name, Bancroft Library (hereafter BL), University of California, Berkeley.

6. Taylor, *Forging of a Black Community*, 174, 282, 168. The phrase "new objects of racial scorn" is from Wilson Record's statement in U.S. Commission on Civil Rights, *Hearings before the United States Commission on Civil Rights. Hearings Held in Los Angeles, California, January 25, 1960, January 26, 1960; San Francisco, California, January 27, 1960, January 28, 1960* (Washington, D.C.: GPO, 1960), 846-850.

7. Robert Goldberg, "Racial Change on the Southern Periphery: The Case Study of San Antonio, Texas, 1960-1965," *Journal of Southern History*, August 1983, 352, 362.

8. Mayor Lapham's statement in the San Francisco Civic Unity Committee Minutes, San Francisco Public Library History Stacks, 27 October 1944; Herb Caen, *Baghdad by the Bay* (Sausalito, Calif.: Comstock Publishing, 1987), 220-221.

9. Maya Angelou, *I Know Why the Caged Bird Sings* (New York: Bantam, 1971), 181; Wing Ng, in *Growing Up in the Cities*, 80/17c, box 1, BL. *Growing Up in the Cities* are the transcripts of tape-recorded interviews conducted in 1977-1979.

10. Charles Johnson, *The Negro War Worker in San Francisco, A Local Self-Survey* (San Francisco: n.p., 1944), 32.

11. *People's World*, 24 January 1942, 14 February 1942, and 9 March 1942; anonymous letter assumed to be dated 1948, in Carlton Goodlett Papers (hereafter Goodlett Papers), reel 2: "NAACP: Correspondence," State Historical Society of Wisconsin.

12. *People's World*, 24 May 1946; minutes of the San Francisco Civic Unity Committee, San Francisco Public Library. The mayor's Civic Unity Committee included not only liberal religious and civic leaders but also community leaders who were left of

center. For example, Matt Crawford, chairman of both the minorities committee of the San Francisco Congress of Industrial Organizations council and the National Negro Congress, and Oleta Yates, the president of the Communist Political Association of San Francisco, served on the Civic Unity Committee.

13. *People's World*, 7 January 1944.

14. Albert Broussard, *Black San Francisco: The Struggle for Racial Equality in the West, 1900–1954* (Lawrence: University Press of Kansas, 1993), 159–165; *People's World*, 21 July 1944; *The N.A.A.C.P. Counsellor*, July 1946, in Goodlett Papers, reel 2: "NAACP: Misc. Materials."

15. *People's World*, 6 June 1946, 28 September 1946, 5 October 1946, and 19 October 1946.

16. *People's World*, 7 December 1946 and 24 December 1946; flyer entitled "Congratulations to Our Loyal Supporters" and Carver Society flyer entitled "Open Letter to the General Public in the Fillmore District," both in Goodlett Papers, reel 2: "NAACP: Misc. Materials"; newspaper stories on the campaign for jobs in *People's World*, 28 September 1946 and 5 October 1946.

17. *People's World*, 25 November 1946, 16 November 1946, 10 December 1946, 24 December 1946, and 18 January 1947.

18. *People's World*, 8 February 1947, 20 February 1947, and 24 February 1947; "Annual Report of the President of the San Francisco Branch of the N.A.A.C.P., December 18, 1949" in Goodlett Papers, reel 2: "NAACP: Misc. Materials"; *People's World*, 20 September 1949, 21 October 1949, 17 November 1949, 9 November 1949, 23 November 1949, 20 December 1949, 22 December 1949, and 28 December 1949.

19. "Report on Conference of California's Councils of Civic Unity and Similar Organizations," 6 July 1945, California Federation for Civic Unity, carton 1, no folder name, BL; Joseph James, "Profiles: San Francisco," *Journal of Educational Sociology*, November 1945, 178; "NAACP West Coast Regional Conference, San Francisco California, March 7–8, 1947," in Goodlett Papers, reel 2: "NAACP: Misc. Materials"; *Pacific Citizen*, 8 May 1948; *Shelley v. Kraemer*, 334 U.S. 1 (1948).

20. *Pacific Citizen*, 1 October 1949; Wilson Record, *Minority Groups and Intergroup Relations in the San Francisco Bay Area* (Berkeley: Institute of Governmental Studies, University of California, 1963), 33.

21. Proposition 15 information and *Nichi Bei Times* quotation in *A Monthly Survey of Events and Trends in Race Relations* (Fiske University Social Science Institute), December 1946, 153; *Pacific Citizen* quotation in ibid., November 1946, 126.

22. Sucheng Chan, *Asian Americans: An Interpretive History* (Boston: Twayne Publishers, 1991), 142; Jere Takahashi, *Nisei/Sansei: Shifting Japanese American Identities and Politics* (Philadelphia: Temple University Press, 1997), 127–129; *Pacific Citizen*, 7 November 1952.

23. Rose Hum Lee, "Chinese in the United States Today," *Survey Graphic* 31 (October 1942), reprinted in Judy Yung, *Unbound Voices: A Documentary History of Chinese Women in California* (Berkeley: University of California Press, 1999), 465–472; Ruth Hall Whitfield, "Public Opinion and the Chinese Question in San Francisco, 1900–1947" (M.A. thesis, University of California, Berkeley, 1947), 71–72, 89.

24. Yung, *Unbound Voices*, 465. Rose Hum Lee, "Chinese in the United States Today," *Survey Graphic* 31 (October 1942) cited in Yung, *Unbound Voices*, 465.

25. Bessie Mae Ferina, "The Politics of San Francisco's Chinatown" (M.A. thesis, University of California, Berkeley, 1949), 89; Irving Babow and Edward Howden, *A Civil Rights Inventory of San Francisco: Part I, Employment* (San Francisco: Council for Civic Unity of San Francisco, 1958), 242, 248.

26. Eddie Barnes et al., "Changing Neighborhoods: A Follow-Up Study of Community Stability in 35 Racially Changing Neighborhoods in San Francisco and East Bay" (unpublished group research project, University of California, Berkeley, 1957), 51, 66–67.

27. *San Francisco Sun-Reporter*, 23 November 1957; Gaewhiler cited in *Pittsburgh Courier*, 23 November 1957; NAACP West Coast Region, carton 39, "Willie Mays," BL.

28. U.S. Commission on Civil Rights, *Hearings*, 551, 556; Constance L. Jensen, John Lindberg, and George L. Smith, "The Minority Group Housing Market in San Francisco, with Special Reference to Real Estate Broker and Mortgage Financing Practices" (unpublished group research project, University of California, Berkeley, 1955), 43–45, 27; Record, *Minority Groups and Intergroup Relations*, 14, 33.

29. *Sun-Reporter*, 21 May 1955.

30. Harry Kitano, "Housing of Japanese-Americans in the San Francisco Bay Area," in *Studies in Housing and Minority Groups*, ed. Nathan Glazer and Davis McEntire (Berkeley, Los Angeles: University of California Press, 1960), 190–195; *Pacific Citizen*, 27 January 1951.

31. *Chinese Press*, 11 March 1949 and 1 April 1949.

32. *Pacific Citizen*, 31 July 1948.

33. *Pacific Citizen*, 3 July 1948 and 24 July 1948.

34. Eric Fure-Slocum, "Emerging Urban Redevelopment Policies: Post–World War II Contests in San Francisco and Los Angeles" (M.A. thesis, San Francisco State University, 1990), 56; *People's World*, 16 May 1949 and 17 May 1949; *Pacific Citizen*, 21 May 1949.

35. Broussard, *Black San Francisco*, 222; Godfrey Lehman, "For Chinese Only," *Frontier* 3, no. 4 (February 1952): 14–15.

36. Broussard, *Black San Francisco*, 223; *Pacific Citizen*, 28 January 1950 and 25 February 1950; *People's World*, 10 November 1949 and 23 November 1949; *Newsletter of the Council for Civic Unity of San Francisco* (May 1950), Institute of Governmental Studies Library, University of California, Berkeley.

37. Council for Civic Unity of San Francisco, *Among These Rights; Chinese Press*, 3 March 1950.

38. *People's World*, 15 September 1952 and 19 September 1952.

39. *Sun-Reporter*, 19 September 1953, 8 November 1952, 15 November 1952, 21 February 1953, 6 June 1953, and 13 June 1953; *People's World*, 9 December 1952 and 26 September 1952; *Banks v. Housing Authority of San Francisco*, 120 Cal. App. 2d 1 (August 26, 1953), Civ. No. 15693.

40. *Sun-Reporter*, 21 February 1953, 5 September 1953, 19 September 1953, and 26 September 1953.

41. *Chinese Press*, 16 September 1949.

42. U.S. Commission on Civil Rights, *Hearings*, 556.

43. Nee and Nee, *Longtime Californ'*, 232; *Chinese Press*, 16 September 1949.

44. *Chinese Press*, 22 September 1950; Ferina, "Politics of San Francisco's Chinatown," 68–73.

45. I use "honorary whites" not only to draw an analogy between Asian American San Franciscans and nonwhites who enjoyed white privileges in South African apartheid, but also to situate my discussion in the scholarly literature on the social construction of whiteness, much of which focuses on how marginalized Americans of European descent claim whiteness by consciously distancing themselves from African Americans.

46. U.S. Commission on Civil Rights, *Hearings*, 846–850; Record, *Minority Groups and Intergroup Relations*, 13.

47. U.S. Commission on Civil Rights, *Hearings*, 756, 761–763.

PART THREE

In 1964, Peter Cohon, fresh out of Grinnell College, left for San Francisco. Despite acceptance to the prestigious Writer's Workshop in Iowa, Cohon, a young man on the make, believed his destiny lay in the West. Intense, curious, and adventurous, he enrolled in graduate school at San Francisco State to become a writer and poet. With his girlfriend in tow, he moved into the only place he thought he could afford, a run-down apartment in Haight-Ashbury, a perch that provided a front-row seat to the massive social upheavals about to mark the period and the region. Over the next decade, Cohon embraced the changes wrought by the 1960s with an enthusiasm that few matched. Inspired by a peyote trip and with his life at a crossroads, he changed his last name to Coyote. He became an integral member of two of San Francisco's most influential and politically active tribes: the San Francisco Mime Troupe and the Diggers, groups committed to challenging every aspect of the status quo. He took drugs, lived in communes, and rode with the Hell's Angels. His wide circle of friends included every major figure in the California counterculture. He was no part-time, thrill-seeking hippie, however; he was committed to bringing about large-scale cultural change by living differently.[1] He and his cohort sought more than anything else authenticity, to live a life without the artifices demanded by civilization. Like generations of Americans before them, they came west to carve out their version of utopia.

Borrowing ideas as old as western thought and articulated by a diverse set of thinkers including Jean-Jacques Rousseau, Walt Whitman, and Frederick Jackson Turner, the West—for Coyote and so many of his fellow counterculturalists—stood for a place where life could be reinvented, where utopias were still possible. As millions poured westward looking to build their own version of paradise, those contests to demarcate western space, to define western culture, and to determine the authentic western character took on serious political import. In our final section of essays, our contributors examine the search for moral authority, especially as manifest in the creation of a new approach to economic and geographic order.

Our final essays reveal the complexity of contemporary western political culture and challenge some long-standing assumptions about the organization of space, the political meaning of our relationship with nature, our definitions of liberal and conservative, and the relationship between politics and memory. The conflict over western space both broadly defined and as specific as a storefront comes to vibrant life in Amy L. Scott's examination of lifestyle politics in Boulder, Colorado. Creating a model that could be applied to "hip" cities across the West, and even to pockets in the rest of the nation, she demonstrates how a counterculture version of politics, society, and economics revitalized and altered the landscape of urban spaces. In crucial ways, Scott's argument about the primacy of place in political discourse is central to understanding the political legacy of the twentieth-century West. Moreover, her vision for urban politics offers exciting new directions for this, the most urban region in the nation.

Andrew G. Kirk shows us the fascinating complexities that await us when we move beyond basic right and left politics. His countercultural libertarians, rock-climbing CEOs, and rock-star conservatives demonstrate a western political diversity that simply cannot be explained by the blunt pronouncements of the punditocracy. Moreover, as he moves beyond the triumphant or declensionist models of much 1960s historiography, he reveals a myriad of paths taken by those political activists whose exploits were less obvious (but perhaps more long lasting) than those of the radicals who found themselves at the center of a media-fueled "sixties." Kirk demonstrates the effectiveness of those who made a quiet commitment to wholesale change and whose politics simply does not fit into tidy categories. And perhaps most important, the politics described by Kirk are uniquely western in their outlook and practice.

In his essay, intellectual and environmental historian John P. Herron unlocks the relationships between environmental history and environmental politics. Using the conversations about the role of technology *in* nature, he demonstrates that it is within competing interpretations about the nature of environmental history that we can find the necessary connections to competing visions of democracy. Our everyday actions reveal our thoughts on nature and how to live in a world of limited resources. Not only does his essay offer a thought-provoking set of directions for both environmentalists and environmental historians, but it also makes clear the underlying philosophic ideals that both promote and limit environmental politics.

Closing out our volume, David M. Wrobel explores the serious connections between memory, myth, history, authenticity, and western political culture. In his examination of "the politics of memory," he shows us that contests over memory and history have very real political ramifications. In creating the Golden West of their memory (and controlling the myth making and history) of their West, pioneer societies and their heirs created a political climate that grew dependent on conflating authenticity with legitimacy. And it is within these contests over authenticity that westerners have continued to define their very unique and growingly powerful political ideas, ideas that are now influencing our national political agenda.

NOTE

1. Coyote has enjoyed a long and illustrious acting career and, of particular interest to those who love western history, served as the narrator for Ken Burns's Public Broadcasting Service series, *The West.* For more on his earlier life see Peter Coyote, *Sleeping Where I Fall: A Chronicle* (New York: Counterpoint, 1999).

CHAPTER 9

Remaking Urban in the American West: Urban Environmentalism, Lifestyle Politics, and Hip Capitalism in Boulder, Colorado

Amy L. Scott

In 1969, Boulder plumber Russell "Bud" Chesebro was driving his brand-new truck down Broadway on his way home from work when he was stopped by 3,000 antiwar protesters. Watching them march down the middle of the street, blocking traffic, yelling, waving signs, and mostly having a good time, Chesebro was not happy. He also opposed the Vietnam War, but he refused to accept that a bunch of hippies and protesters had the right to block the streets of his city. He was not going to watch passively while misbehaving college students and hippie outsiders infringed on his right to conduct business. He slowly drove around the police barricade and into the crowd.[1]

The demonstrators did not respond peacefully. They hurled insults and whatever was handy at the creeping plumbing truck. Pummeled by a bicycle frame, backpacks, and other objects, Chesebro conceded the battle and slammed his truck into reverse. As protestors gave chase, he sped away from danger . . . or so he thought. In forty years as a Boulder resident, Chesebro had never been on the wrong side of the law. But after spending $1,800 to knock the dents out of his truck and repair his busted windshield, he found himself before a municipal judge, answering charges of reckless driving and interrupting a "peaceful protest."[2]

Chesebro could not have been more surprised at the new Boulder. As a forty-year resident, he had enjoyed the postwar boom that had restructured Colorado's economy and doubled its population. As the owner of his own plumbing business, he cheered on residential and commercial development. To Chesebro, growth was the key to his and Boulder's future; growth

251

meant more customers and more money; simply stated, growth was good for business. Most members of Boulder's postwar business community shared Chesebro's enthusiasm. That said, however, Chesebro and his fellow boosters had specific ideas about what type of people were welcome in Boulder. They expected new residents to share their core conservative values and to fit a particular social profile: middle-class status and a civic identity shaped by political moderation, and with traditional ideas about gender roles and sexuality and a trusting deference to elected officials and leaders in the business community.

Moreover, they expected the members of the ever-growing University of Colorado student population to confine their activities, as college students in Boulder traditionally had, to football, fraternities, wilderness recreation, and nearby ski resorts. The heated street encounter between Russell Chesebro and outspoken members of Boulder's youth culture emerged from these presumptions. Ultimately, as the showdown between a determined businessman and the protestors temporarily revealed, Boulder residents would become entrenched in a much larger fight over who had the right to define the city's politics, culture, and future.

Militant protestors marching in the city's streets exploded conservative residents' assumptions about their hold on cultural authority and political legitimacy in Boulder.[3] So did the parade of long-haired hippies who had taken over parks and streets around the university and threatened to occupy retail and living spaces on downtown Pearl Street, the city's auto-friendly shopping district. Protest politics in Boulder mirrored what was happening in much of the rest of the nation. Young people concerned with national and global events acted locally to interrupt the ease of daily routines in university towns like Boulder, bringing local commerce to a standstill and forcing community leaders to accommodate their growing political and cultural power.

Proof of how much life was changing in Boulder was driven home in the 1971 city council elections when an environmentalist, a gay hippie entrepreneur, an African American human rights activist, and a feminist scholar won seats by defeating the old-guard majority of conservatives and moderates who had ruled the city for decades. By the early 1970s, Boulder boasted not only continued growth but also an activist, politicized citizenry. Activists expanded the boundaries of political life as they debated what kind of city they wanted to live in. A coalition of college students, hippies, and urban environmentalists—a group that I refer to as "lifestyle liberals"—began redefining Boulder, transforming the conservative western college town into a progressive micropolitan city.[4]

The remaking of Boulder did not happen quickly or easily. Old-guard conservatives were hardly eager to hand their all-American city over to a new liberal political coalition. Instead, they began to articulate a competing vision for Boulder's future and construct a different narrative about the meaning of equality and the rights and responsibilities of citizenship. They also, not surprisingly perhaps, questioned the political legitimacy of Boulder's liberal newcomers.

Consistent with the traditions of western boosterism, most of Boulder's postwar leaders believed that physical growth produced economic vitality. They hoped to capitalize on the increased federal government spending and military presence in the region. Like leaders in other western cities, they also hoped to attract middle-class home owners and consumers to Boulder by promoting suburban development and annexation. Indeed, in the two decades that followed World War II, promotion was the hottest game in town. Elected officials and businessmen used city resources and the Boulder Chamber of Commerce to sell their city. In promotional literature, they described Boulder as a business-friendly, amenity-rich university town, a promising investment site for federal dollars and for private firms engaged in scientific research and production, and a recreational paradise for middle-class home owners. Conservatives had no intention of giving up on that vision and relinquishing political control of Boulder. Economic growth was celebrated and promoted by conservatives; cultural transformation was not.

By the late 1960s, Boulder's progrowth boosters faced a serious challenge. In the political atmosphere of the 1960s and the decades that followed, an alternative model for building and governing cities seemingly superseded the power of old-fashioned western boosterism.[5] Newly empowered activists selectively applied the politics of the New Left, the counterculture, and the rising environmental movement to the redefinition of their city and began to invent a politics of lifestyle liberalism. The new liberal government laid the plans for a human-scale, environmentally sustainable city by continuing to develop a system for open-space preservation and growth management. Activists in Boulder began to argue that lifestyle difference, or the freedom to "do your own thing," was a basic individual right. Lifestyle politics had broad appeal and could be claimed by student radicals, hippies, rebel rock climbers, environmentalists, Buddhist poets, gays and lesbians, and even by the New Right. In Boulder, both newcomers and old-timers like Bud Chesebro began to understand that leaders who convincingly promised to protect quality of life and to create space for authentic lifestyles in Boulder would claim the authority to define Boulder's future.[6]

The emergence of a liberal coalition dedicated to the creation of human-scale, micropolitan western cities not only complicates our understanding of post-1960s social movement activism but also has implications for the way we think about western urban history. Lifestyle liberals' rise to power in cities like Boulder; Eugene, Oregon; Santa Fe, New Mexico; Carmel, California; and Austin, Texas, counters the declensionist "failure of the sixties narrative," which holds that following the implosion of the New Left, 1960s radicals abandoned social justice movements in favor of self-centered quests for personal liberation.[7] Rather, many channeled their energies into local politics.[8] In Boulder and its western counterparts (and even some midwestern cities, such as Madison, Wisconsin), activists organized politically to remake urban cultures and landscapes. Examining how activists tried to reconfigure patterns of urbanization, connect the environment to politics of lifestyle, and change the meaning of city life in the West by creating dense, human-scale, cosmopolitan urban spaces offers one way to understand these new approaches to liberal politics and Cold War radicalism. Boulder's lifestyle liberals, for instance, embraced the New Left's vision of expansive individual freedom through participatory democracy as well as the counterculture's lifestyle experimentation, and they worked to bring these ideas into everyday practice, or at least acceptance, through political experiments within their bounded urban space. Within this spatial creation of urban participatory democracy, actions from the most minute consumption decisions (such as choosing to recycle) to major life decisions (such as choosing to practice Buddhist-inspired "right livelihood") functioned simultaneously as sources of individual activism, community definition, and an acknowledgment that connections existed between one's local economy and the global environment.

As part of a larger project to create an ideal urban environment, Boulder's lifestyle liberals acted out their political beliefs each day. They rode their bikes to work, invested in recycling, declared the city a nuclear-free zone, battled to close the Rocky Flats plutonium-processing facility, and convinced the city council to disinvest city assets from countries and corporations that turned a blind eye to human rights violations. Activists founded organizations that brought people into the fight for peace, nuclear disarmament, and environmental sustainability. Boulder entrepreneurs marketed holistic and sustainable products that claimed to minimize environmental damage and maximize individual and community health, empowering consumers by offering them the opportunity to promote their chosen cause through product choice.

Lifestyle liberalism and the micropolitan urbanism it fostered became important elements in the creative social and political experiment that many Americans have conducted since the 1960s.[9] Lifestyle liberals' quest for quality of life—their search to maximize individual freedom and human potential within the framework of urban participatory democracy and entrepreneurial capitalism—produced new politics, new markets, and new cityscapes in the American West.

This history of the micropolitan model for western urban living offers an understanding of postwar western cities as more than a cautionary tale of sprawl or an apocalyptic narrative of environmental disaster. Rather, activists redefined western urban spaces according to their political and cultural values, creating a post-1960s political coalition that situated small cities as sites of progressive political and cultural change.[10] The freethinking spaces (often universities), creative entrepreneurs, citizen-diplomats, and tolerant populations that have defined micropolitan cities during the past thirty years fostered locally based yet nationally significant opposition to the growing conservatism of the West and the nation. Citizens of these culturally and politically creative cities generated a useful oppositional political ideology about the culture and economy of America, the future of American democracy, and America's role in the world.[11]

Environmentalists' response to a growth economy based on Cold War militarism, rapid urbanization, population growth, and suburban sprawl represented a set of political conflicts that originated in western cities during the postwar period. In most urban spaces, post-1960s activists did not replicate the electoral victories that allowed lifestyle liberals to control Boulder's city government. Nonetheless, during the 1960s and 1970s, the interconnected issues of economic growth and environmental preservation and the degree to which lifestyle difference should determine urban culture informed political contests in almost every western city with large university populations. Boulder activists' plans for an innovative, creative, and sustainable city became an alternative development model that residents in cities like Burlington, Vermont, and Asheville, North Carolina, began to follow, encouraging cultural diversity and creativity, protecting the environment, and guaranteeing residents access to outdoor recreation.

BUILDING ECOTOPIA'S INFRASTRUCTURE

In many ways, the history of the modern American West is defined by westerners' response to massive urban migration and the reorganization of metropolitan areas during World War II.[12] After 1941, federal defense spending transformed the economic, physical, and human landscapes of the West and "shifted the American center of gravity westward." During the war 8 million Americans migrated to the West, and 22 million arrived over the next twenty-five years. More than 90 percent of these migrants chose to live in towns, cities, and suburbs.[13] While drawing people to Colorado, wartime mobilization also integrated local economies along the Front Range of the Rocky Mountains from Colorado Springs to Boulder into a

160-mile-long linear regional economy centered on the rapidly growing metropolis of Denver. Within this emerging spatial and economic structure, Denver became Colorado's model city for economic expansion and diversification, postwar population growth, and suburban development. Looking to Denver as an example, Boulder's post–World War II leaders schemed to extract their next mother lode not from the gold mines and glacial waters of the Rockies but from Uncle Sam. Boulder promoters planned to bring peacetime prosperity by attracting federal research laboratories and private defense contractors who would collaborate on high-tech projects with research scientists at the University of Colorado.[14]

Micropolitan urbanism in Boulder emerged as grassroots activism in opposition to this business-government partnership dedicated to urban growth, decentralized suburban development, and the stratification of political power that characterized postwar metropolitan development in most of the West. When Boulder's population doubled between 1950 and 1958, many residents, particularly recently arrived University of Colorado professors, complained that Denver's expanding residential developments threatened to trap their community within an indistinct suburban web. In particular, the possibility that developers might build houses or resorts in the foothills that framed Boulder's western skyline prompted professors Al Bartlett and Robert McKelvey to push for a city ordinance protecting the foothills. Both avid hikers who found solace in high-altitude mountain wilderness, they recruited quality-of-life foot soldiers from the Colorado Mountain Club, an organization dedicated to the preservation of wilderness for individual recreation and leisure.

Appealing to a traditional booster strategy—capitalization and commoditization of the western landscape as an amenity and selling point—local environmentalists argued that wilderness access determined residents' quality of life and, therefore, Boulder's economic future.[15] Yet, flipping the script on this traditional free-market strategy, urban environmentalists argued that livability, and therefore economic success, depended on local government's ability to safeguard Boulder's most important commodity: a view of the mountains and access to forests unmolested by suburbia. This could be achieved, activists argued, by limiting the physical size of the city and confining growth to developed areas. Their position—which raised questions about the difficulty of balancing economic growth with environmental preservation—foreshadowed the programmatic contradictions that confronted President Lyndon B. Johnson's Great Society technocrats: Could government simultaneously address Americans' desire for economic abundance and lives of individual meaning and qualitative value?[16]

Boulder's university-affiliated liberal environmentalists believed that local regulations to preserve quality of life in Boulder were imperative. Bartlett, McKelvey, and their supporters organized a grassroots campaign to prohibit officials from granting city water service to mountain properties above a given elevation, designated on their maps with a blue line. Campaigning for a "Blue Line" amendment to the City Charter, environmentalists turned university classrooms and offices into organizing spaces, distributed information on street corners, knocked on doors, and organized day hikes into the foothills to convince residents of the individual and community benefits of environmental preservation. It worked; many in Boulder came to believe that immediate public access to pristine mountain wilderness was essential to quality of life in Boulder.[17] In 1958, voters passed the Blue Line Charter Amendment, seriously harming the booster strategy of promoting suburban development. The foothills-preservation campaign opened a long-term debate about local government priorities, raising questions that Boulderites revisited frequently: Should the government stimulate the economy or protect the natural environment from development? In what ways were these tasks connected in Boulder, and was it possible to do both effectively?

In 1959, Bartlett and other veterans of the Blue Line campaign organized PLAN (People's League for Action Now)–Boulder, creating a permanent organization for Boulder's newly politicized urban environmentalists. Preventing sprawl was PLAN-Boulder's first priority. Environmentalists argued that slow growth, rather than the boosters' traditional program of promotion and growth, was key to Boulder's economic success. PLAN-Boulder's first newsletter explained the group's aesthetically based environmentalism: "We are for green belts, floodplain zoning, natural and developed parklands, underground utilities—in essence, a beautiful, well-planned community with special emphasis on retaining those characteristics which make Boulder unique. We are against haphazard growth, unsightliness, and ugliness in any form."[18] Within ten years, PLAN-Boulder's platform for compact development became local law when residents approved the 1967 Greenbelt and Thoroughfares Program, taxing themselves to purchase rural, agricultural, and industrial land and designating it as permanently protected, natural open space.[19] By creating a plan for a contiguous greenbelt of land around the city, voters rejected growth advocates' master plan for a decentralized city based on "scatteration" development of satellite suburbs. Instead, voters agreed to limit Boulder's physical size by restricting suburban development sites on the city's fringe. By 1967, contained development, urban infill, and greater density had become the operative planning principles of Boulder's micropolitan model of urban development.

Through the Blue Line Amendment and the greenbelt plan, Boulder environmentalists pioneered an alternative spatial design for western city building. Within the micropolitan model of urbanism, the acquisition of open space was central to the physical design of the city and the culture developing within its borders. Environmental activists—concerned mostly with Boulder's scenic landscape—persuaded voters of the necessity of community oversight of land use, development, and design decisions. Under this model for community planning, the public, as well as property owners and developers, would have a say in determining the built environment and the social organization of their city. By limiting suburban development, urban environmentalists in Boulder offered an alternative path to city building, rethinking the relationship between density, social organization, and community definition: "Little boxes made of ticky tacky" where everyone was "just the same" would be minimized in Boulder.[20]

Boulder's open-space policies represented a deliberate mapping out of an institutionalized space in which urban environmentalists, city planners, property owners, and developers resolved conflicts over the proper use of land on the city's borders. The conceptualization and adoption of an open-space program signaled an ecological turn in urban planning discourse through which urban environmentalists attempted to rethink the relationship between city and nature.[21] Planners influenced by the postwar environmental movement were reacting to the growth of standardized, decentralized suburban communities and to a new system of regional-metropolitan politics in which central cities and suburbs competed for resources and power.[22] Urban planners and environmentalists who took the ecological turn began to view decisions about land use, density, and urban design through the framework of community sustainability.[23] They recognized that decentralized development was economically costly and environmentally unsustainable. They concluded that development decisions were too important to be left solely to the discretion of developers. Rather, citizens and planners began to build into the urban landscape an acknowledgment of the connection between city and nature and a recognition of environmental limits.

With a planning vision for a centralized city surrounded by public open space and with a funding mechanism in place, Boulder's newest bureaucracy, the Open Space Department, shaped the city with elements of three iconic American landscapes: the wilderness (mountain parklands); the pastoral, "middle landscape" of small farms and ranches (prairie open space); and the pedestrian village (growth focused around the city center).[24] Since 1967, residents of Boulder have spent $180 million to purchase 39,000 acres of open space and 7,000 acres of mountain parkland. By 2000, Boulder's environmental coalition included aesthetic preservationists, nuclear-freeze activists, dog owners, endurance athletes, animal-rights activists, and deep ecologists. All claimed an interest in determining human use and access to Boulder's public lands.

FREAK CITY: BOULDER'S ARGUMENT OVER THE COUNTERCULTURE

Even as Boulderites used landscape elements to establish the spatial boundaries of their urban ecotopia, they discovered that an aesthetically driven agenda of environmental preservation could not guarantee the quality of life and urban culture they desired. The presence, visibility, and politicization of the counterculture after 1968 altered the nature of the debate over what urbanism meant in Boulder, forcing liberals to expand their quality-of-life politics beyond the preservation of a landscape aesthetic. In the late 1960s, achieving livability began to mean more than preserving the view; it also meant embracing the cultural dynamism and political diversity of national social movements. Specifically, radical politics at the university and Boulder's "hippie problem" forced permanent residents to accommodate counterculture definitions of quality of life. As a result, Boulder's liberals incorporated New Left ideas and counterculture experimentation into the redirection of Boulder's culture and government, expanding the boundaries of politics in Boulder while creating a new western urban ideal.

After the 1967 Summer of Love, many hippies left San Francisco for the interior West. In Colorado, they initially avoided cities and congregated in the mountains. Squatting on abandoned mining claims and holding "live-ins" in national parks, they romanticized the solitude of the Colorado backcountry and enjoyed more than one kind of "Rocky Mountain High."[25] Rifle-toting "rednecks and cowboys"—so named by the hippies—often patrolled the backcountry in jeeps, and they stormed campsites and beat hippie campers with shovels and tire irons. Mountain property owners made it clear that the Rockies would not host the next summer of love. The sheriff's department responded to vigilante attacks with a "hippie hunt" of its own, clearing hippies from private property and restricting their access to state and national parks. In the wake of violent attacks and run-ins with the law, hippies left the mountains for Boulder, swelling an already large population of summer transients and college-aged tourists who had arrived from across the nation.[26] At a meeting led by Boulder city manager Ted Tedesco, hippies asked for police protection and government sanctions against discriminatory business owners. After requesting thirty acres of Boulder open-space property on the edge of town, they announced their intention to stay in Boulder.[27]

The city council's acknowledgment of hippies' concerns and the audacity of the newcomers, particularly their disrespect for private property rights, shocked Boulder residents, many of whom viewed counterculture migrants not as citizens deserving of a voice in local government but as "defiers of law, draft evaders, trespassers, destroyers of property, thieves and violators of dope and narcotics laws." The editor of the *Daily Camera,* Boulder's local newspaper, hinted that "freeloading hippies" were disruptive outsiders who did not meet conventional requirements for citizenship: "The issue is that persons coming into a community are legitimately expected to abide by its laws and not to sponge off those whose labors have created and sustained the community."[28] Pressured from the left by urban environmentalists and from the right by those who opposed government regulations on development, the city council offered policies of moderation. It appeased critics of the counterculture by vowing to prosecute all lawbreakers, and it placated hippies by promising to investigate civil rights violations.[29]

The council's teetering posture signaled the beginning of four years of public debate over hippie's rights to live in Boulder. The hippie presence, along with a newly charged set of radical voices emanating from the University of Colorado, dominated local political discourse from 1967 to 1971. The very presence of hippies in public spaces provided a wedge issue between urban environmentalists, moderates, and conservative businessmen. Those seeking to implement PLAN-Boulder's program of small-scale centralized urbanism formed a natural alliance with university-affiliated urban environmentalists, human rights activists, and cultural liberals. As a result, many liberals tolerated the presence of hippies, or at least "peaceful hippies," whom they characterized as flower children.[30]

Others, primarily businessmen, adopted an exclusionary position toward hippie newcomers. *Daily Camera* editorials, often the voice of conservative Boulderites, stereotyped all hippies as social misfits or deadbeats who drained the community chest. Such assessments misrepresented the diversity of the new population. Many hippies were neither transients nor street people; some were entrepreneurs who intended to stay. Despite opposition from those locals who characterized hippies as temporary nuisances, many counterculture migrants carved out a niche in the community, opening businesses, advocating political reform, and participating in city government.

One hippie collective, Endor Enterprises, founded by twenty-five-year-old Californian Arthur Armstrong, rented a warehouse and several studios near Boulder's busiest commercial district. Endor's presence hinted at the counterculture's potential agency for altering Boulder's economic, cultural, and political landscape. Like many hippie entrepreneurs, Armstrong's business vision was utopian and experimental. He imagined Endor as an alternative community with institutions uncompromised by American capitalism or liberal politics. The very name that Armstrong chose for his experiment, however—Endor *Enterprises*—acknowledged that peace, love, happiness, *and* profits were not mutually exclusive. Endor opened seven shops that sold counterculture products, sponsored a health food store, and cleared a small profit by hosting local bands and traveling light shows. Paul Corey, a member of Endor's board of directors, described Endor as a new society whose mission was capitalism with a human touch. "We want to bring kids up here and turn them on to love. There's nothing else in town people can get involved in on a human level. The people at Endor are totally free and can feel."[31]

Endor contributed to Boulder's economy, renting downtown property that otherwise stood vacant, and it provided social space for the city's youth. Endor's consciousness-raising commerce, however, did not impress the business community; Endor, it seemed, did not represent the right kind of capitalism. City boosters had spent the 1950s and 1960s encouraging high-tech corporations to relocate to Boulder. Hippie capitalists muddied traditional booster visions for growth, progress, and economic viability. Conservatives were concerned not only about the economic competition that hippie capitalists and consumers posed to established businesses but also about what they assumed were dangerous connections between hippies and radical college students. What the Endor founders envisioned as a collective effort to establish a central-city business that provided goods and services to Boulder's growing counterculture community, many locals saw as a nuisance. Following a barrage of complaints, the city planning board suspended Endor's license based on a noise-pollution violation. Confrontations like those over Endor Enterprises and the provision of public services to hippies multiplied. Conservatives pressured authorities to drive hippies from public spaces, prevent them from gaining a foothold in town government, and keep them away from the University of Colorado.

The business community had reason to worry; university students had grown increasingly radical in the latter half of the 1960s. In fact, Paul Danish, editor of the radical student newspaper, put the number of committed student radicals at between 300 and 400. This group led protests against dormitory rules and campus policies, supported the civil rights movement, and, of course, protested against the war in Vietnam. In October 1967, students blockaded the placement center in an effort to prevent the CIA and defense-related corporations from recruiting on campus. In April 1968, students marched on Regent Hall to protest racism, end dormitory regulations, and promote student power in university affairs. In 1969, after two

Students for a Democratic Society (SDS) members disrupted a speech by visiting San Francisco State University president S. I. Hayakawa, the board of regents disaffiliated SDS as a campus organization. Undeterred, twenty SDS members later stormed the Institute of Defense Analysis, vandalized the office, and stole documents. In March 1970, radicals bombed the Air Force ROTC Office, and in April, 400 students occupied Regent Hall to protest the Vietnam War. Soon enough, students took their protests off campus and onto Boulder's streets, where they alienated many Boulder residents. Imagine the horror many "respectable" Boulderites felt when they saw students flying a North Vietnamese flag and displaying on campus banners that read, "LONG LIVE THE VIETNAM REVOLUTION."[32]

Make no mistake, most University of Colorado (CU) students eschewed radical politics. Still, local shop owners' reluctance to accommodate or even recognize the differences between the radicalized students and those college students who just wore their hair long added to the tensions on University Hill. As historian Beth Bailey wrote, "By the late 1960s America's 'youth culture' had come to *look* very much like the counterculture. Longhaired boys and braless girls. Psychedelic music. Pot. Sex. Certainly not everyone fit this mold, but these were the markers of belonging, of being 'hip.' The counterculture and its style purposely violated the tenets of 'respectability.'"[33] In Boulder, retailers near the university failed to realize that many CU students, like the national youth culture, had appropriated hippie aestheticism and fashion, such as flared blue jeans, long hair, headbands, scarves, colorful clothing, and acid-inspired art, without wholly adopting the counterculture's lifestyle or the politics of antiwar radicalism.

Instead of adjusting their inventories to match the desires of youthful consumers, University Hill merchants blamed hippies for decreased sales. "Dirty" hippies whose appearance, smell, and threatening demeanors frightened away respectable paying customers especially offended shop owners. Fred Shelton, owner of Fred's Restaurant, "tried to keep the middle ground" and lost business from straights as a result. He later described the disgust that many locals felt toward "dirty" hippies: "The horrible smell of patchouli, which makes me gag to this day, was part of their thing, because they may have wanted to be clean, but they didn't have the facilities to be clean, so as a result they were unwashed. So they used patchouli oil in quantities to camouflage the fact that they had terrible B.O."[34] Margaret Yeager, a Boulder resident since 1941, believed that Hill merchants had legitimate complaints. She described hippies as "filthy, disreputable, knocked-out, and threatening."[35] They congregated on sidewalks in front of Hill businesses, blocked store entrances, shouted obscenities at customers, fought with each other, and "urinated and defecated on sidewalks and in flower beds."[36]

Yeager's observations confirmed what many of the more politically motivated hippies believed: that their visible presence on Boulder's sidewalks, their alternative lifestyle, their dangerous demeanors functioned as weapons against mainstream American culture. To members of the counterculture, however, such actions imposed new cultural meanings on urban spaces and created zones of public space liberated from the dominant culture.[37] Radical hippies, for instance, might have called such actions "deliberate obnoxiousness," "weapons of cultural aggression," "a total assault on the culture," or a "mind-fuck."[38] Loitering in front of a business, for instance, did not indicate laziness or a lack of effort or interest. Rather, it indicated that a "FREAK OUT" was in progress.[39]

In addition to Endor, other counterculture-friendly businesses came to Boulder. In May 1969, Timothy Fuller, a hippie from California who had spent two summers in Boulder, purchased the Brillig Works—a former Beat bookstore in the University Hill district.[40] The Brillig Works' raison d'être—to offer a pastiche of goods, services, and welcoming social spaces to those engaged in experimental lifestyles—symbolized the emergence of a post-1960s liberal constituency that tied counterculture values and radical politics to personal economic decisions. Unlike its portmanteau namesake—"Brillig," from Lewis Carroll's nonsense poem "Jabberwocky"—Fuller's experiment had a clear purpose: to build an alternative entrepreneurial business model dependent on consumers whose purchasing decisions were determined by their left-leaning political positions, their counterculture lifestyle, and their concern for the environment. Boulder, with its growing contingent of lifestyle liberals and counterculture freaks, contained the combination of political ferment and experimental consumerism necessary to support a new entrepreneurial model of cause capitalism.[41] Like other western cities with growing counterculture populations, Boulder's future would be determined by subcommunities of people determined to "create a lifestyle and defend it."[42]

Fuller's Brillig Works became a cornerstone in the counterculture community. The Works sold leftist political texts, Eastern philosophical tracts, and Beat literature, and Fuller's publishing company released such titles as the *Pot Cookbook*. Patrons also had access to a crowded coffeehouse and a communal crash pad.[43] To meet the growing demand for hip social spaces, Fuller purchased a warehouse two blocks from the Brillig Works and requested a zoning variance for a combination coffeehouse, restaurant, art gallery, and theater company.

Hill businessmen, who had tolerated the Brillig Works and its clientele, simply could not stomach two warehouses of hippies, one at each end of the retail district. They feared long-haired young people would dominate public and private spaces on the Hill. Consequently, the buttoned-down businessmen protested vehemently against Fuller's zoning request. In the spirit of compromise, the zoning board asked the city's Human Relations Commission (HRC) to mediate between Fuller and the Hill merchants and to make a recommendation on the proposal. Established by the city council in 1965 to address racial discrimination, the HRC by the late 1960s increasingly found itself smoothing tensions between Hill merchants and hippies; it had concluded that Boulder's "new minority race of the hippie" faced discrimination similar to that of the city's racial and ethnic minorities.[44]

After studying Fuller's request, the commission decided in his favor, recommending that the city council approve his coffeehouse, art studio, and theater on a six-month trial basis. Director David Haas explained the commission's decision: "Our feeling as a commission was that the board of zoning adjustment is set up to control land uses, not people. . . . The key to our recommendation and the guidelines is we can't consider applications which are to the exclusion of a group of people and the application of a stereotype, i.e., hippies are all bad." The merchants, however, refused to accommodate. "It became very apparent to us," Haas told the *Daily Camera*, "that merchants were not willing to mediate except to get rid of hippies." Following the failed mediation session, the city gave in to Hill merchants' demands and denied Fuller's request for a zoning variance.[45]

As they had done in the case of Endor Enterprises, prominent members of the business community manipulated the city bureaucracy, pressuring local officials to maintain the economic and cultural status quo. In effect, established business owners curtailed Fuller's investments in Boulder property and his attempt to capitalize on the local hip market. By working through city regulatory agencies to contain hippie economic power in Boulder's retail districts, the Hill merchants taught the young entrepreneur an essential lesson in urban politics: Organized citizens with access to city hall induced policies favorable to their interests, thus determining economic and cultural opportunities. After his encounter with the Hill merchants, Fuller decided to channel his influence with Boulder's counterculture community into a city council election campaign. Winning elections, Fuller realized, meant winning the right to reconfigure Boulder as a tolerant urban space with an economic future tied to creative individual enterprise and the open celebration of experimental lifestyles.

Beset by conflict between hippie newcomers and townspeople who wished them gone, city manager Ted Tedesco, a political moderate, began a series of public meetings to prepare for a massive hippie migration to Boulder during the summer of 1969. Frustrated by the toughest problem he had faced as a city manager, Tedesco quipped, "It's not something you send to a municipal consulting service and say 'Please send me an answer for the hippie problem for twenty-five dollars.'"[46] Nonetheless, when the hippies headed for warmer climates and CU students returned to the Hill, Tedesco searched for pragmatic solutions to the culture war that dominated Boulder politics. He wrote 250 letters to mayors across the country asking how they had handled the counterculture migration to their cities. Boston, he discovered, had hired MIT students to mingle with hippies; Ann Arbor, Michigan, had organized activities and free concerts; Carmel and Monterey, California, had jailed hippies with tough vagrancy laws that the U.S. Supreme Court had declared unconstitutional. None of these solutions, Tedesco concluded, suited Boulder's situation. Tedesco and the majority of city council members opposed police harassment and tough sentencing laws and tried to convince Boulderites that the city would not solve the problem with extralegal actions designed to "run hippies out of town" or by passing harsh ordinances that discouraged hippies from spending their summer in Boulder. Instead, Tedesco defined the city's task as encouraging the acceptance of diversity in the community—as "smoothing the conflict of different values, the different lifestyles of the citizen and the hip."[47] With opposition building in the conservative business community, however, Tedesco's rhetoric of tolerance did not translate into social services for hippies.[48]

In fact, the old guard struck back. The University Hill Merchant Association (UHMA) called for police raids on hippie hangouts. And in July 1970, after two months of frustrating confrontations with local hippies and summer visitors, the UHMA, members of Citizens for a Better Boulder, and the Boulder Taxpayers' League initiated a recall campaign against the city council, Mayor Robert Knecht, and Manager Tedesco. The conservative alliance threatened, again, to withhold payment of sales tax until the city removed hippies from Boulder's retail districts.[49]

Despite their philosophical differences, city officials and liberal environmentalists agreed with Boulder businessmen on at least one issue: Violent members of the counterculture and hard-core drug dealers had to be controlled, and if necessary, law enforcement officers should use force. In April 1971, the city council expanded Boulder's drunk-and-disorderly ordinance, making it unlawful "for any person under the influence of any substance to be in any public place."[50] In May 1971, the city responded to a "meaner breed of transient" with a campaign to reclaim public spaces on University Hill. It doubled its law enforcement budget, added twenty-six officers to the force, and located a permanent police substation on the Hill. This increased police presence led to frequent skirmishes and even street brawls between police and radicals, and after a group of street people attacked an officer on the Hill, the city ordered fifteen officers in full riot gear to patrol the Hill commercial district day and night.⁵¹ With so many police on the Hill to enforce city ordinances, arrests of hippies doubled. A reporter for the *Chinook*, Denver's underground newspaper, compared Boulder to a police state.⁵²

The city's adoption of strict vagrancy and loitering ordinances and its willingness to sponsor tough policing tactics demonstrated the limitations of the counterculture's pedestrian democracy. It would not be so easy to liberate, democratize, and occupy Boulder's public spaces through "freak outs." Boulder's antihippie ordinances also signaled the limits of the political alliance between liberals, urban environmentalists, and countercultural newcomers. Boulder's lifestyle liberals had begun to differentiate between good hippies (flower children) and bad hippies (street people and transients) when engaging in public discussions of the town's counterculture population.⁵³

The tensions finally boiled over on 22 May 1971 when the Hill erupted in a three-day riot. It began after a street person and a police officer engaged in a fistfight. Soon a crowd of street people, who claimed they "were willing to die" to hold on to their right to Boulder's public streets, ran wild and, joined by some hippies and university students, ransacked businesses.⁵⁴ Badly outnumbered, Boulder police retreated from the Hill but recaptured it three days later with heavy barrages of tear gas. Estimates of damages to businesses ranged from $25,000 to $50,000. Destruction was targeted. The Jones Drug Store, which had a reputation for high markups and "hostility to hair," incurred thousands of dollars in stolen merchandise, including its entire supply of uppers and downers. Street people claimed, "The stores that got it deserved it." Not surprisingly, Fuller's Brillig Works survived unscathed.⁵⁵

Enraged at hippie lawlessness and dismayed that their all-American city had become a haven for freaks, radicals, and scofflaws, businessmen created an umbrella organization called Citizens United to Restore Boulder (CURB). CURB vowed to take back the town by electing a law-and-order city council in the November 1971 election. As their slogan "Bring back '63" implied, CURB intended to turn back the clock to 1963, when *Look* magazine had named Boulder one of the top ten small American cities, before growth control and the right to develop the urban fringe had become contested political issues, and before hippies had demanded political and cultural inclusion. CURB labeled anyone—Boulder residents, CU students, and street people alike—who wore long hair and adopted the styles of the counterculture as irresponsible, un-American, and undeserving of citizenship in Boulder. Myron LaPointe, a realtor and member of CURB, voiced the frustrations of Boulder conservatives and echoed the polarizing law-and-order rhetoric of President Richard Nixon: "I'm concerned not only for Boulder, but for America. We've got a lot of people running from coast to coast who are not Americans, not good Americans." The organization's primary goal was to drive hippies from Boulder, but its members also opposed city restrictions on development. CURB president James Hunter claimed that PLAN-Boulder, the primary organization of urban environmentalists, was "the number one enemy" of CURB. In a guest editorial in the *Boulder Daily Camera*, Hunter lambasted the agenda of CURB's liberal opposition, pointing to three primary culprits, who, if they united in a political coalition, threatened to transform Boulder city government: liberal professors at the university, the radical youth culture, and advocates of growth management. "We cannot," Hunter asserted, "afford the luxury of permitting Boulder to be a playpen for maladjusted and defiant young people or a laboratory for bleeding heart reformers."[56]

LaPointe and Hunter, like other longtime residents of Boulder with ties to the business community, sensed that they were in danger of falling from the privileged position that granted them the right to control the terms of public debate and determine local standards of cultural permissibility. Conservative businessmen in Boulder held a narrow, traditional view of the proper and acceptable way to practice politics and conduct business; a coalition of liberals, radicals, freaks, and environmentalists—groups with diverse interests and ideologies, but that CURB conflated as "radicals"—threatened their long-standing control of local government. Political decisions and positions of power, they believed, rightly belonged to long-standing community members with propertied interests in the city. Primacy, permanence, and responsibility, rather than the counterculture values of mobility, experimentation, and tolerance of difference, represented their notion of an authentic community and grounded the right to participate in decisions that determined its future. In effect, LaPointe and Hunter argued, freedom and civil rights were rewards for responsible behavior; hippies, who were not "good Americans," deserved neither.

To publicize their campaign and to reach out to Boulder's "great silent majority," CURB ran a series of advertisements in the *Daily Camera*. Demonstrating that Boulder's businessmen no longer believed they could get their message across in meetings at city hall, CURB took off the gloves. They hammered home what they saw as a clear and unambiguous connection between the counterculture, CU radicals, and unpatriotic antiwar protestors who threatened the very fabric of the civic society of Boulder and of the nation. Their first ad, which quickly followed the Hill riot, was simply a large peace sign under which they printed in bold letters, "THE FOOT PRINT OF THE AMERICAN CHICKEN." A second ad, on 28 June 1971, likened cultural and political radicals to a deadly infectious disease, stating, "LAST SUMMER IT WAS BERKELEY,

THIS SUMMER IT IS BOULDER THAT IS INFECTED. . . . Mr. Mayor; What will it take to wake you up and take action to rid Boulder of these lawless elements?" The most creative CURB ad, "Recipe for Instant Slum," lambasted the counterculture for creating ghetto-like conditions in Boulder neighborhoods and called for the swift eradication of communal housing. CURB also ran ads that linked hippies to hitchhiking, shoplifting, bathing in Boulder Creek, and "welfare abuse."[57] An ad on 3 August 1971—"STAMP OUT FREE LUNCHES!"—criticized hippies for accepting welfare payments from the very system they criticized.

By August 1971, CURB claimed 2,000 members. The conservative attack was organized and well publicized, but in reality CURB had little support beyond the business community. Moreover, hippies, liberals, and university students countered CURB's campaign by organizing Boulder United to Register People (BURP). BURP registered thousands of eighteen-to-twenty-one-year-old voters, demonstrating that the majority of Boulder's youthful activists preferred local electoral drama to violent street confrontations with police. The November 1971 election, following the passage of the Twenty-Sixth Amendment in June 1971 making eighteen the voting age, was the first in which the majority of CU students could vote, and as conservatives had feared, 4,500 new voters between the ages of eighteen and twenty-one, representing 13.6 percent of voter turnout, handed Boulder liberals a victory in a watershed election. A letter to the editor of the *Daily Camera* that "the freaks and their leftist CU allies [would] control the city within three years" rang true when all of CURB's candidates and four city council incumbents were defeated in 1971.[58] In their stead, Boulder residents elected hippie entrepreneur Tim Fuller, an outspoken advocate for gay rights; Penfield Tate, a civil rights activist and the first African American member of the Boulder City Council; Karen Paget, a twenty-six-year-old CU graduate student; and Ken Wright, an environmental activist and advocate of growth control.[59] Clearly, Boulder's new leaders did not fit CURB's definition of "good Americans." But in their cultural politics and social activism on behalf of the marginalized, the oppositional, and the alternative, the new leaders embodied the new politics of lifestyle liberalism that would define what some called "the People's Republic of Boulder" in the post-1960s era.

Although political battles over the counterculture were rooted in the immediate details of whether or not hippies and radicals had the right to occupy Boulder's streets, sidewalks, parks, and businesses, the significance of these squabbles was much larger. Events in Boulder were representative of similar competitions for cultural and political power that developed in western urban spaces during the 1960s. Urban historians have offered examples of how immigrant, ethnic, and racial groups engaged in similar struggles for spatially derived political power at the neighborhood level during the twentieth century. In the western cities of postwar America, control of political and cultural power was determined in part by the youth culture's imaginations of a democratic society in which people could freely adopt alternative lifestyles. To residents of micropolitan cities like Boulder, the acceptance of lifestyle difference became measurements of democratic cosmopolitanism. Lifestyle liberals focused initially on making space for differences presented by the counterculture, and Boulder earned a national reputation as a place that encouraged lifestyle diversity—an urban space out west where anyone could let his freak flag fly.

In 1971, this unlikely group of political activists who had emphasized participatory democracy, authentic experience, and liberation politics raised a tie-dyed freak flag over city hall. By aligning their interests with the preservationist agenda of university-affiliated liberal environmentalists, they won an election and wrested power from moderates and conservatives. Perhaps more important, they created a political culture where environmental preservation *and* communitywide tolerance of lifestyle difference became a measure of quality of life and a policy tool through which Boulder residents imagined and shaped the cultural landscape of their city.

THE BUSINESS OF HIP: CONSCIOUSNESS COMMERCE
SUSTAINS THE REPUBLIC

The new city council worked quickly. It accelerated the city's environmental preservation program, proposed a gay rights ordinance, and supported the construction of Pearl Street Mall—a downtown pedestrian market and entertainment space where freaks and straights could shop and mingle.[60] Liberal city council members like Fuller and Tate also worked with community activists to establish a local tradition of citizens' diplomacy, drafting resolutions that stated the community's official position on issues of national and global importance, such as antiwar resolutions and the declaration of a nuclear-free zone within Boulder city limits. Behind the city council's policy initiatives was an attempt to foster a community milieu that encouraged individuals to pursue meaningful, authentic experiences and to maximize their human potential.

The politics of lifestyle liberalism in Boulder depended in large part on activists' belief that they could create an authentic community. In fact, the concept of authenticity and its continuous contestation were central to the creation of a new political constituency, a new political style, and new corporate model in Boulder. To Cold War political and cultural radicals, "authenticity" had several meanings.[61] It described the ways that people should organize and govern themselves to create a genuine, ideal community. Achieving authenticity meant taking collective action toward social justice and demanding the right to live in communities where everyone participated in decision making. For many activists who participated in Boulder's battle over the counterculture, authenticity became central to their expectations of local government.

When activists spoke of authenticity, they were also talking about economy. "Authenticity" became a benchmark term, a means of critiquing the saccharine organization of postwar work, production, and consumption. In this context, authenticity expressed people's search for alternatives to a lifetime of meaningless toil for a bureaucratic corporation and the wasteful acquisition of unnecessary consumer products.

Enter hip capitalists—like Chögyam Trungpa Rinpoche and Mo Siegel, who actualized dreams of authentic community and economy and in the process proved that "*hip* and *business* were not irreconcilable enemies."[62] Hip capitalists thought about relationships between material production, consumption, and environmental sustainability and determined that there was something political about their economic decisions and those of their customers. Boulder activists who were engaged in the work of community redefinition also tried to reframe the material character of the American dream. Many in Boulder maintained that meaningful individual experience and self-actualization were tied closely to specific types of consumption, work, leisure, and activism. Based on the experiential knowledge that the personal is political, activists connected their left-leaning politics to everyday consumer choices, privileging products marketed at achieving individual holism and environmental sustainability. Entrepreneurs and consumers began to insist on socially meaningful work, and they marketed and consumed "holistic" products and developed local standards for livability and sustainable urbanism.

These entrepreneurs did not eschew materialism per se; on the contrary, they promoted products that promised individual and consequently societal improvement, offering lifestyle liberals and progressive consumers a material base from which to enact personal visions of reform. Like the city's many hip capitalist entrepreneurs—there were 100 "hip" businesses in Boulder by 1976—Trungpa and Siegel captured the essence of Boulder's celebration of political authenticity and cultural dissent and sold it for a profit.[63]

Trungpa did more than anyone else to shape the nature of Tibetan Buddhism in the United States, offering an eclectic path to the sacred for those who dared to walk it.[64] Aided by Beat poet Allen Ginsberg, Trungpa masterminded the establishment of the Buddhist-poetics-humanist psychology community in Boulder, channeling this hybrid counterculture spirituality into a lucrative educational enterprise: the Jack Kerouac School of Disembodied Poetics (1974) and the Naropa Institute (1976), now Naropa University.[65]

Following China's military invasion of his homeland, Trungpa fled to Scotland, where he established a Tibetan meditation community in the Highlands. When the University of Colorado Religious Studies Department offered him a position as a guest lecturer, he moved to Boulder in 1970. Trungpa attracted a handful of students from Boulder's communes. Many of them were "heads" who had experimented with acid as a sacrament. They welcomed Trungpa as an experienced spiritual master who might mold their psychedelic visions into a new consciousness. Practitioners congregated at Trungpa's meditation center, dropped acid, listened to Trungpa's lengthy lectures, and meditated on images from the *Tibetan Book of the Dead*.[66]

By 1972, Trungpa and Ginsberg had concluded that by combining the practices of Tibetan Buddhism, the teachings of humanistic psychology, and the spontaneous linguistics of the Beats, they could fundamentally change the way students perceived the world, offering them an alternative path to higher consciousness and self-actualization. Trungpa and Ginsberg brought Boulder's growing freak community to the attention of the nation when they launched the Jack Kerouac School of Disembodied Poetics in 1974. Prominent poets, artists, and scholars volunteered to teach in the first summer, including Allen Ginsberg, William S. Burroughs, Ram Dass, and Gary Snyder. Organizers expected a maximum of 200 locals, but the prospect of enlightenment offered by Beat and counterculture poets, hallucinogenic drugs, and religious gurus drew 2,000 people from across the nation.[67]

Realizing the marketability of their educational and spiritual experiment, Trungpa and Ginsberg founded the Naropa Institute, a contemplative college that offered degrees in Buddhist studies, Western psychology, and secular meditation. Instead of directing students toward a career path and a life of acquisitive materialism, Naropa offered a life of contemplation and service to the community. Courses included history of the Beat poets, transpersonal psychology, organic gardening, and insight meditation.[68]

While Trungpa Rinpoche is Boulder's most colorful ambassador of consciousness commerce, Mo Siegel, the founder of Celestial Seasonings Corporation and a guru of the multibillion-dollar natural-foods industry, is Boulder's most famous hip capitalist.[69] Locals celebrate the Celestial Seasonings creation story by recounting how Siegel spent the summer of 1969 with his friends picking herbs, getting high, and concocting teas. By September, they had conjured their first batch of "Mo's 36 Herb Tea" in a barn outside Boulder, packaged it in hand-sewn bags, and sold it to a local health food store. Perhaps the more meaningful, if less often told, part of the creation story is Siegel's encounter with the CEO of General Mills in 1972. Seeking to procure financing and a national distribution network, Siegel arranged a meeting with former air force general and General Mills CEO Edwin Rawlings, who adhered to the philosophy that "the principles of good management are pretty much the same whether you are dealing with Wheaties or jet bombers."[70] Rawlings explained to Siegel that the future of the food industry rested on the development and production of scientifically engineered food, sharing with Siegel that these perfectly nutritious foods would be grown not on farms but in laboratory test tubes. "Son," he said, "if you really want to change the way Americans eat, why don't you just dismiss this idea of natural herbal teas and come join our team." This moment, in which Rawlings advised him to get a haircut and a real job, convinced Siegel that developing a natural-foods industry would be nothing less than a radical venture in American enterprise, and it crystallized his mission statement: "to create and sell healthful, naturally oriented products that nurture people's bodies and uplift their souls, and to make the world a better place by unselfishly serving the public."[71] Not only was Celestial Seasonings radically creative, but it was wildly profitable. In 1970, Siegel earned $2,000; by 1978, his company employed 200 people and was earning $9 million per year.[72]

As Trungpa and Siegel built their businesses into national success stories, it became clear that hip capitalism meant more than "an occasional hippie selling drug paraphernalia and posters."[73] Not unlike traditional corporate executives, Trungpa and Siegel realized that power resided in centralized corporate structures, but they believed that leaders guided by a progressive consciousness could use their economic power to uplift individuals and strengthen communities. Both men conducted business based on the idea that their enterprises could make money *and* have a social agenda. Trungpa and Siegel established their businesses with the awareness that a connection existed between material production, consumption, and the individual desire to explore human potentialities and individual authenticity. They did not accept at face value the critiques that 1960s radicals had leveled at American materialism; on the contrary, Trungpa and Siegel turned their energies toward producing material goods, services, and working conditions that they believed were essential to authentic everyday experiences. In a city where an activist's political values influenced her purchasing decisions, hip capitalists provided the material base for individual experiments in cultural and political authenticity.

Finally, Trungpa and Siegel's success depended on their ability to appeal to Boulder's community values by situating their companies as socially useful, morally legitimate institutions. Unlike traditional corporations that lacked a social agenda and based managerial decisions about where to locate solely on economic concerns, hip corporations became connected to their communities for what these places represented culturally and politically. Before expanding into national markets, Boulder's hip capitalists created a corporate soul that reflected the dominant values of their local community, meeting consumer demand while contributing simultaneously to Boulder's image as a progressive city.[74]

Boulder's hip capitalists and their values fit well with city government's task of balancing urban growth and design with environmental preservation. By the 1990s, Boulder was being lauded by many as a model of desirable, sustainable, and economically viable city building. Boulderites had articulated a visionary spirit of place: micropolitan urbanism based on environmental preservation and sustainability, the celebration of tolerance and difference, and an economy powered by creative entrepreneurs offering products for health and sustainability.

Activists influenced by counterculture values, leftists critical of Cold War liberalism, and urban environmentalists determined to prevent sprawl had tried to create a human-scale, sustainable city. Absorbing the critiques of 1960s radicals but working within traditional urban political structures, university-affiliated liberals, outdoor enthusiasts, and counterculture migrants wrested government power from culturally conservative, progrowth businessmen and launched a long-term public experiment to establish an innovative, sustainable, and tolerant cityscape in the American West. A collective determination to achieve "quality of life" stood at the center of activists' experiment in micropolitan city building. The city was their vehicle for thinking about how development patterns determined quality of life. Lifestyle liberals advocated a program of micropolitan urbanism based on broadly defined environmental politics, tolerance of lifestyle diversity, and a local economy sustained by creative capitalism through which entrepreneurs worked for individual, community, and societal reform. They worked to create a compact, human-scale, cosmopolitan city that encouraged individual freedom and fulfillment and rewarded creativity and innovation. Within the micropolitan model, activists searched for solutions to the economic and environmental paradigm that had been addressed superficially by national liberals, and local entrepreneurs addressed anxieties about the tenuous position of the ecologically concerned consumer within an expanding system of global capitalism.

Yet like the conservative businessmen who had held power before them, Boulder's lifestyle liberals inherited the task of preserving the city's beautiful scenery while maintaining a viable economy. In Boulder, becoming micropolitan meant constructing the ideal place in which to live. But were there limits to Boulder's brand of human-scale urbanism: Could the pursuit of the ideal, sustainable city lead to exclusionary social policies?

As the median cost of housing in Boulder topped $500,000, bashing newcomers from Texas and California became a local pastime, indicating that many believed primacy of place carried a privileged status in Boulder and represented a different kind of authenticity.[75] Echoing the pioneer society members of whom David Wrobel writes in chapter 12, Boulder residents cried "NATIVE" in an effort to dissuade visitors from permanently relocating. Boulder still had hip shops, a summer transient population, and the carnival atmosphere of Pearl Street Mall. But in their quest to build a desirable community, had lifestyle liberals preserved hippie aestheticism and hip consumerism at the expense of the complex diversity they had defended during the Age of Aquarius?

Critics claimed that the city, with its moat of open space, had become a gated community harboring wealthy liberals and their trendy cults of self-improvement. Others argued that the city's marketplace focus on authenticity represented an idealism gone clueless and narcissistic, decrying the fact that the social consciousness of many Boulderites extended only so far as a daily shot of wheatgrass juice, trendy yoga workshops, and the most fuel-efficient sport-utility vehicle.

Arguments about the success or failure of Boulder's long-term community experiment indicate that the definitions of "quality of life" and "authentic community"—both goals of lifestyle liberalism in Boulder—are changing and contested. Despite its imperfections, Boulder remains a model for a alternative human-scale urbanism in the West. Boulder continues to experiment with growth management for sustainability, instituting new policies such as permanent affordable housing, inclusionary zoning, green building initiatives, and affordable mass transit. Boulder's experience demonstrates that building sustainable, democratic cities—places where the public participates in the political debates and choices that structure their lives—is a deliberate process made up of daily political choices. Citizens can adopt progressive development models to replace unrestrained, haphazard growth; dedicated activists can consciously determine the physical landscape and urban culture of their cities; and corporate executives can think "more like ecologists than generals."[76]

NOTES

1. Chesebro was not alone in using his car as a weapon against antiwar protestors who obstructed city streets. Presidential candidate George Wallace expressed these sentiments in the extreme. "If when I'm President, any anarchists lie down in front of my automobile," Wallace said, "it'll be the very last time they lie down in front of anything." Phillip Crass, *The Wallace Factor* (New York: Mason/Charter, 1976), 95.

2. Russell "Bud" Chesebro, interview by Ann Bramhall, 28 October 1987, OH 371, Maria Rogers Oral History Collection (hereafter MROHC), Carnegie Branch Library for Local History, Boulder, Colorado.

3. According to David Farber, "Cultural authority—the power to set the rules of proper conduct and behavior—was up for grabs" in the 1960s. "By the late sixties," he writes, "local customs and local power elites were being challenged and often radically subverted by national and international forces." Farber, ed., *The Sixties: From Memory to History* (Chapel Hill: University of North Carolina Press, 1994), 2.

4. A number of historians have written about the connections between cultural rebellion, lifestyle choices, and political radicalism during the 1960s, most notably Doug Rossinow, *The Politics of Authenticity: Liberalism, Christianity, and the New Left in America* (New York: Columbia University Press, 1998); W. J. Rorabaugh, *Berkeley at War: The 1960s* (New York: Oxford University Press, 1989), 141; David Steigerwald, *The Sixties and the End of Modern America* (New York: St. Martin's Press, 1995), 184; Rusty L. Monhollon, *This Is America? The Sixties in Lawrence, Kansas* (New York: Palgrave Macmillan, 2002), 7, 8, 289.

5. David Ley, *The New Middle Class and the Remaking of the Central City* (New York: Oxford University Press, 1996).

6. Chesebro, interview.

7. Julie Stephens, *Anti-disciplinary Protest: Sixties Radicalism and Postmodernism* (New York: Cambridge University Press, 1998), 2–3.

8. Van Gosse, "A Movement of Movements: The Definition and Periodization of the New Left," in *A Companion to Post-1945 America*, ed. Jean-Christopher Agnew and Roy Rosenzweig (Malden, Mass.: Blackwell, 2002), 277–302.

9. Samuel P. Hays, "From Conservation to Environment: Environmental Politics in the United States since World War II," in *Out of the Woods: Essays in Environmental History*, ed. Char Miller and Hal Rothman (Pittsburgh, Pa.: University of Pittsburgh Press, 1997), 104, 114.

10. Richard Florida, *The Rise of the Creative Class, and How It's Transforming Work, Leisure, Community, and Everyday Life* (New York: Basic Books, 2002); AnnaLee Saxenian, *Regional Advantage: Culture and Competition in Silicon Valley and Route 128* (Cambridge, Mass.: Harvard University Press, 1994); Peter Wolf, *Hot Towns: The Future of the Fastest Growing Communities in America* (New Brunswick, N.J.: Rutgers University Press, 1999); William H. Hudnut III, *Cities on the Rebound: A Vision for Urban America* (Washington, D.C.: Urban Land Institute, 1998).

11. Thomas Frank, *The Conquest of Cool: Business Culture, Counterculture, and the Rise of Hip Consumerism* (Chicago: University of Chicago Press, 1997) and *One Market*

under God: Extreme Capitalism, Market Populism, and the End of Economic Democracy (New York: Anchor Books, 2000); David Brooks, *Bobos in Paradise: The New Upper Class and How They Got There* (New York: Simon & Schuster, 2000).

12. Robert Self, *American Babylon: Race and the Struggle for Postwar Oakland* (Princeton, N.J.: Princeton University Press, 2003), 27, 334.

13. Carl Abbott, *The Metropolitan Frontier: Cities in the Modern American West* (Tucson: University of Arizona Press, 1993), 26; Gerald D. Nash, *The American West in the Twentieth Century: A Short History of an Urban Oasis* (Englewood Cliffs, N.J.: Prentice Hall, 1973), 198.

14. Carl Abbott, "The Metropolitan Region: Western Cities in the New Urban Era," in *The Twentieth-Century West*, ed. Gerald Nash and Richard Etulain (Albuquerque: University of New Mexico Press, 1989), 82.

15. On boosters and capitalization of the western landscape, see Mike Davis, "Sunshine and the Open Shop: Ford and Darwin in 1920s Los Angeles," in *Metropolis in the Making: Los Angeles in the 1920s*, ed. Tom Sitton and William Deverell (Berkeley and Los Angeles: University of California Press, 2001), 115; Michael Logan, *Resistance to Urban Growth in the Southwest* (Tucson: University of Arizona Press, 1995), 147–148.

16. Robert Collins discusses growth liberals' ambivalence about the relationship between quantity and quality of life in *More: The Politics of Economic Growth in Postwar America* (New York: Oxford University Press, 2002), 61–65.

17. Abbott, *Metropolitan Frontier*, 145–147.

18. *Highlights of PLAN-Boulder County: 1959–1986* (Boulder, Colo.: PLAN-Boulder County, 1986), 45.

19. James Bowers, Tom Pugh, and Trafton Bean, *Boulder's Fringe Area Objectives* (Boulder, Colo.: Boulder Planning Department, 1964); Daniel McLoughlin, "In Pursuit of the Common Green" (1974), Open Space Collections, Municipal Government Reference Center (hereafter MGRC), Boulder Public Library, Boulder, Colorado.

20. The lyrics for "Little Boxes," written by Malvina Reynolds in 1962 and performed by Pete Seeger in 1963, can be accessed at Charles H. Smith and Nancy Schimmel, "Malvina Reynolds: Song Lyrics and Poems" http://www.wku.edu/~smithch/MALVINA/mr094.htm (Accessed 28 April 2008).

21. On the development of an ecological urban planning tradition in the West, see Greg Hise and William Deverell, *Eden by Design: The 1930 Olmsted-Bartholomew Plan for the Los Angeles Region* (Berkeley and Los Angeles: University of California Press, 2000), 11. Also useful is William Cronan's discussion of Americans' tendency to "see city and country as separate places, more isolated from each other than connected." Cronan, *Nature's Metropolis: Chicago and the Great West* (New York: W. W. Norton, 1991), xiv.

22. Carl Abbott, *The New Urban America: Growth and Politics in Sunbelt Cities* (Chapel Hill: University of North Carolina Press, 1981), 14; Self, *American Babylon*, 27, 33.

23. Timothy Beatley, "Green Urbanism in the Lessons of European Cities," in *The City Reader*, ed. Richard LeGates and Frederic Stout, 3rd ed. (New York: Routledge, 2003), 399–408; Stephen Wheeler, "Planning Sustainable and Livable Cities," in LeGates and Stout, *City Reader*, 486–496.

24. Oliver Gillham, *The Limitless City: A Primer on the Urban Sprawl Debate* (Washington, D.C.: Island Press, 2002), 144.

25. "Cabins, Mines, Now 'Pads': Owners Urged to Check," *Boulder Daily Camera*, 24 February 1968; "Hippies," MGRC, vertical files; anonymous interview by Stephen Gassaway, 1986, Carnegie Branch Library for Local History, Boulder, Colorado.

26. Pete Goter, "Mountain Search Nets Few Hippies," *Boulder Daily Camera*, 5 June 1968, and "Sheriff Scatters Mountain Hippies; Reaction Is Mixed," *Boulder Daily Camera*, 6 June 1968; "Sheriff Nelson Warns against Vigilante Action," *Boulder Daily Camera*, 10 June 1968.

27. Peter Goter, "Investigation Set on Hippie Abuse," *Boulder Daily Camera*, 19 June 1968.

28. "Who's Harassing Whom?" editorial, *Boulder Daily Camera*, 12 June 1968.

29. Goter, "Investigation Set on Hippie Abuse."

30. Ibid.; "Who's Harassing Whom?"

31. Ann Topp, "The Hippie Movement in Boulder: Endor—A New 'Society' for Today's Youth," *Boulder Daily Camera*, 23 June 1968.

32. Bill Brand, "Speakers at CU Rally Urge Armed Revolt against U.S." *Boulder Daily Camera*, 11 September 1969. For accounts of campus unrest, see Frederick S. Allen et al., *The University of Colorado, 1876–1976* (New York: Harcourt Brace Jovanovich, 1976), chap. 6, and Ronald A. James, *Our Own Generation: The Tumultuous Years, University of Colorado, 1963–1976* (Boulder: University of Colorado Press, 1979). On the SDS's storming of the Institute of Defense Analysis, see "20 Radicals Disrupt Top Secret Meeting," *Boulder Daily Camera*, 29 July 1969.

33. Beth Bailey, *Sex in the Heartland* (Cambridge, Mass.: Harvard University Press, 1999), 141.

34. Fred Shelton, interview by Stephen Gassaway, 1987, OH 524, MROHC; Fred Shelton, interview by Evalee Gress, 30 September 1988, OH 408, MROHC.

35. Margaret Yeager, interview by Rose Marie Khubchandani, 13 October 1995, OH 773, MROHC.

36. "Police Begin Hill Foot Patrol as Council Considers Hippies," *Boulder Daily Camera*, 18 June 1969; Ruth Correll, interview by Dorothy Hale, 11 March 1986, OH 316; MROHC; Ruth Correll, interview by Stephen Gassaway, 1987 OH 513, MROHC.

37. Sociologist Daniel Foss defined a "freak out" as "an event in which dissidents impose their own cultural meanings on the environment. . . . They are at the same time effacing the cultural meanings imposed forcibly as manifestations of the cultural-political enemy." The desired result, he wrote, was a "free commune or liberated area." Foss, *Freak Culture: Life-Style and Politics* (New York: E. P. Dutton, 1972), 134.

38. According to Foss, a "mind-fuck" was "a deliberate attempt to shock, infuriate, confuse, or terrorize the 'straights' by perpetrating inconceivable weirdness upon them. . . . This normally involves the wholesale violation of rules and canons of polite behavior, dress, and language; it is an eruption of an intensified version of the freak life-style into environments where the 'straights' are supposedly secure." Foss, *Freak Culture*, 134, 155, 156, 160.

39. Bailey, *Sex in the Heartland*, 146, 167. Ed Sanders, a New York musician and the

publisher of *Fuck You: A Magazine of the Arts*, suggested ways in which counterculture radicals could freak out: "Large numbers of freaks will, in good weather, sprawl miscellaneously over the sidewalk, cavort in the middle of the street oblivious to traffic, and in general, infest an environment to the obstruction and hindrance of purposeful effort and gainful commerce." Sanders, quoted in Foss, *Freak Culture*, 155.

40. Fuller purchased the bookstore from Clancy Sheehan. Sheehan's store was rumored to have been a stopover for Neal Cassady and Jack Kerouac on their cross-country journeys, and most locals were familiar with its history as a space frequented by political and cultural radicals from the university and the community at large.

41. Daniel Foss described freaks as "walking counterenvironments" to conventionality and argued for their political significance. He argued that the consciousness developed by freaks—"turning on to where it's at"—entailed understanding that "a provisional political truth" emerges from "efforts to safeguard the continuing development of the self." Foss also alluded to the flexibility of the word "freak," pointing out that it can also refer to an addict, a compulsive, or one who emphasizes order and hierarchy at the expense of spontaneity (speed-freak, bike-freak, "violence-freak," "power-freak," or "structure-freak." Foss, *Freak Culture*, 12, 68, 132–134.

42. Peter Coyote, *Sleeping Where I Fall* (New York: Counterpoint, 2001).

43. Mark Perlgut, "Colorado's Longhairs: Up on the Mountain and Down in the Town," *Village Voice*, 27 November 1969, 39.

44. "New City Human Relations Officer Protects Blacks, Chicanos, and Hippies," *Boulder Daily Camera*, 26 November 1970. Examples of the tendency of the counterculture and observers of the counterculture to compare their hipness, marginalization, and cultural isolation to that of African Americans, often through racist rhetoric, abound. For one example, see Tom Wolfe: "Big Nig, the poor pathetic spade wants his rent. A freaking odd thought, that one. A big funky spade looking pathetic and square. For twenty years in the hip life, Negroes never even looked square. They were the archetypical soul figures. But what is Soul, or Funky, or Cool, or Baby—in the new world of the ecstasy, the All-One . . . the Kairos. . . ." Wolfe, *The Electric Kool-Aid Acid Test* (New York: Bantam, 1968), 239.

45. "Zoning Board to Consider Coffee House on Thursday," *Boulder Daily Camera*, 9 July 1969.

46. Jane Cracraft, "Boulder Manager Denies Encouraging Hippie Influx," *Boulder Daily Camera*, 15 April 1970; *City Council Position Statement, October 1969*, MGRC, City Council Files; Ann Nye, "Beverly Hills Police Chief Describes 'Aquarius Age,'" *Boulder Daily Camera*, 21 November 1969.

47. "City Officials Discuss Problems of Transients," *Boulder Colorado Daily*, 9 April 1970.

48. "Mayor Emphasizes City Is Not Soft on Hippies," *Boulder Daily Camera*, 29 April 1970; "Hippies," MGRC, Vertical Files.

49. Ron Tollefson, "Hill Group Starts Petition to Recall City Councilmen," *Boulder Daily Camera*, 9 July 1970, and "Council Recall Effort Awaits Legal Review," *Boulder Daily Camera*, 10 July 1970; "Recall Postponed for Talks with Groups," *Boulder Daily Camera*, 11 July 1970.

50. Boulder City Council minutes (20 April 1971), City of Boulder Central Records, Boulder, Colorado.

51. Richard C. Mclean, interview by Marvin Wolf, 5 March 1996, OH 816, MROHC.

52. "What Are Our Alternatives?" *Denver Chinook,* 2 September 1971.

53. Paul "Bear" Donahue, interview by Stephen Gassaway, 20 February 1992, MROHC.

54. Elmo Fitz-Randolph, interview by Ruth Major, 22 October 1993, OH 650, MROHC.

55. "A Heavy Stone," *Denver Chinook,* 27 May 1971.

56. James M. Hunter, "Statement to Council, Administration," guest editorial, *Boulder Daily Camera,* 13 June 1971; Robert Knecht, "It's a Time for Reason," guest editorial, *Boulder Daily Camera,* 20 June 1971.

57. Collection of CURB Advertisements, MGRC, Associations: CURB; CURB, "The Mayor Says Boulder Has a Tough Policy," *Boulder Daily Camera,* 28 June 1971, MGRC, Associations: CURB; CURB, "Recipe for Instant Slum," *Boulder Daily Camera,* 1 July 1971, MGRC, Associations: CURB; Collection of CURB advertisements, MGRC, Associations: CURB.

58. E. C. Pickett's letter to the editor of the Daily Camera is quoted in Phyllis Smith, *A Look at Boulder: From Settlement to City* (Boulder, Colo.: Pruett, 1981), 201.

59. Correll, interview by Gassaway.

60. Conservatives defeated Boulder's first sexual-orientation ordinance and recalled Tim Fuller, who had cosponsored the measure with Penfield Tate, demonstrating the real limits of lifestyle liberals' platform of tolerance.

61. Charles A. Reich, *The Greening of America* (New York: Random House, 1970); Theodore Roszak, *The Making of a Counter Culture* (Garden City, N.Y.: Anchor Books, 1969); Wolfe, *Electric Kool-Aid Acid Test;* James Miller, *Democracy Is in the Streets: From Port Huron to the Siege of Chicago* (New York: Simon & Schuster, 1987); Rossinow, *Politics of Authenticity* and "The Revolution Is about Our Lives": The New Left's Counterculture," in *Imagine Nation: The American Counterculture of the 1960s and 70s,* ed. Peter Braunstein and Michael William Doyle (New York: Routledge, 2002), 99–124; Gosse, "Movement of Movements," 277–302.

62. Quotation from Frank, *Conquest of Cool,* 18.

63. For the statistic on the number of hip businesses in Boulder, see Jane Cracraft, "Establishment 'Bread' Fattens 'Hip' Businesses in Boulder," *Denver Post,* 25 March 1976.

64. James Coleman William, *The New Buddhism: The Western Transformation of an Ancient Tradition* (New York: Oxford University Press, 2001); Charles S. Prebish and Kenneth K. Tanaka, eds., *The Faces of Buddhism* (Berkeley and Los Angeles: University of California Press, 1998); Richard Hughes Seager, *Buddhism in America* (New York: Columbia University Press, 1999).

65. Sam Kashner, *When I Was Cool: My Life at the Jack Kerouac School. A Memoir* (New York: HarperCollins, 2004).

66. One participant in Boulder's early Buddhist community remembered, "It was

like, in San Francisco, we took so many drugs that it started to seem that the trips were the same over and over again and that everybody was burning out! So we decided that we'd better get into spirituality. . . . For the first few years, Rinpoche just kept letting us do our drugs or whatever. But then he came down real heavy on us and did not want us doing drugs at all! He didn't even want us smoking a joint! So we all started drinking." Anonymous, Stephen Gassaway, 1987, Oral History Interview 511, Carnegie Branch for Local History, Boulder, Colorado.

67. Steve Krugman, "Naropa Institute, or Notes from a Manure Heap," *Loka*, Summer 1974, 11–17.

68. *Naropa Institute Catalogue*, Manuscript Collections, Naropa, folder 3, Carnegie Branch Library for Local History, Boulder, Colorado.

69. For an introduction to the early history of the natural-foods industry, see William Belasco's discussion on the countercuisine—the counterculture's desire for healthy foods with no synthetic ingredients, minimal processing, and in as close to a whole and natural state as possible. Belasco, *Appetite for Change: How the Counterculture Took on the Food Industry, 1966–1988* (New York: Pantheon Books, 1989).

70. "General Mills: The General and Betty Crocker," *Forbes*, 1 October 1963, 23–24.

71. Mo Siegel, interview by author, 18 November 2004, Boulder, Colorado.

72. Mo Siegel, interview by Betty Anderson, 1989, MROHC.

73. Frank, *Conquest of Cool*, 26.

74. Roland Marchand, *Creating the Corporate Soul: The Rise of Public Relations and Corporate Imagery in American Big Business* (Berkeley and Los Angeles: University of California Press, 1998).

75. Tom Kenworthy, "Housing Costs at a High Altitude," *USA Today*, 9 March 2004.

76. Paul H. Ray and Sherry Ruth Anderson, *The Cultural Creatives: How 50 Million People Are Changing the World* (New York: Three Rivers Press, 2000), 61.

CHAPTER 10

Free Minds and Free Markets: Counterculture Libertarians, Natural Capitalists, and an Alternative Vision of Western Political Authenticity

Andrew G. Kirk

The consumer has more power for good or ill than the voter.
Stewart Brand, *The Last Whole Earth Catalog*, 1971

In the winter 2004 Patagonia company catalog, sandwiched between a colorful layout of women's Capilene high-performance "Tech Panties" and a page dedicated to the new PCR "Get Down Jacket" made from long-filament polyester fabric from recycled plastic bottles, is a thoughtful article by Yvon Chouinard, the founder and owner of Patagonia, "On Corporate Responsibility for Planet Earth." Beginning with a quotation from the late environmentalist and longtime Sierra Club president David Brower that sensibly warns, "There is no business to be done on a dead planet," Chouinard outlines his philosophy as an alpinist, surfer, fly fisherman, environmentalist, and wildly successful "reluctant businessman."[1]

Central to Chouinard's notion of corporate responsibility is a faith in the value of individual and corporate agency over centralized hierarchy. "I don't trust my government," Chouinard argues. "I support the front-line activist, the river keepers and tree sitters who save a single patch of land or stretch of water." As the owner of a successful corporation, Chouinard could put his philosophy into action, most notably with his "1% for the Environment" campaign that encouraged corporations to contribute tens of millions of

281

dollars to environmental causes over the last decade. This independent thinking and desire to focus on the grass roots rather than on institutional or government reform is in keeping with Patagonia's history as a maverick western company that never fit any standard business model. From the beginning, Patagonia used cutting-edge appropriate technologies wedded to liberal social values and a strong environmental ethic to create a fabulously successful market niche and loyal consumer base. According to cofounder Tom Frost, "our business activities mirrored our rock climbing philosophy that emphasized the style and purity of the activity. Keeping the products simple and pure with designs that came from nature and worked with nature drove our business model."[2] While building their company from a tiny garage operation that produced high-quality specialty hardware for rock climbers to an international success and a flagship of green consumption, Chouinard and Frost blazed a path for an eclectic assortment of counterculture entrepreneurs who followed them.

Should we be surprised to find a thoughtful political essay in an outdoor sports catalog? What is the connection between underwear, jackets, and politics? How does consumption fit with protests, voting, political organization, and other forms of traditional political activity? We might not conjure up images of catalogs when we think of politics in the West, but there is a significant universe of alternative western politics that lives on the pages of catalogs and between the lines of corporate reports. Patagonia catalogs have featured op-ed pieces by Robert Kennedy Jr., Jared Diamond, Bill McKibben, and a host of prominent environmental thinkers. In addition, the company dedicates much of its print and Web space to voter registration and political information. As Amy Scott's work on Boulder, Colorado, so nicely illustrates (chapter 9), consumption is political, and so are the business philosophies and practices that drive and facilitate consumption. Most significantly for this study, the connection between politics and consumption is not always driven by what we think of as traditional conservative or liberal politics. Starting in the 1960s a generation of significant western entrepreneurs created a "new economy," and with it a new and influential libertarian-leaning western politics different from the Populism and Progressivism of the first three quarters of the twentieth century. The best-known aspect of the new economy is the world of cyberspace that grew out of California garages and university labs into the culture-changing force that we all live with, like it or not.

Former Wyoming cattle rancher and Grateful Dead lyricist John Perry Barlow famously referred to cyberspace as the "electronic frontier" and was only one of many who framed the new world of Web-based economy and culture in terms of western history and the frontier mythology.[3] Barlow founded the Electronic Frontier Foundation and penned the classic libertarian statement on cyberspace in his "Declaration of the Independence of Cyberspace." The declaration was widely circulated on the Web and became a manifesto for free information and free markets. An outspoken libertarian, Barlow nonetheless passionately avoided traditional politics, arguing that "to engage in the political process was to sully oneself to such a degree that whatever came out wasn't worth the trouble put in."[4]

As cyberspace grew into a significant force, it spawned a particularly western political philosophy characterized by a "left-right fusion of free minds and free markets" melded with a strong environmental ethic that critics have called the "California Ideology" or "cyberlibertarianism."[5] The term "California Ideology" appears most often as a pejorative label used by new and old leftists who were deeply troubled by the libertarian right turn of many in the computer world and who were particularly disturbed that this move to the right was so directly connected to the counterculture.[6] A more neutral and accurate label for the politics represented by Barlow and his cohort of western new frontier technophiles is "counterculture libertarians" or maybe the "Hip Right." It is important to note that this western libertarian sensibility was "different than the libertarian movement, which like the Libertarian Party tends toward orthodoxy, rigidity, and therefore irrelevance."[7] Counterculture libertarians blended the individualism and liberal social values of the counterculture with a conservative distrust of big government and centralized authority. This seldom-recognized aspect of western political thinking borrowed some of the ideals of the counterculture and some of the ideas about hard work of an older generation. They exhibited an embrace of high technology unique to their era while rejecting the centralized authority that characterized the Right and Left of the 1960s. They valued individual agency over collective action, and they championed the free flow of information and "access to tools" as the best means of empowerment and equality. They also incorporated a strong environmental ethic in their philosophy, with a special emphasis on the possibilities of technologically facilitated green living. They tended to lean to the right of many in their generation but were hip in a way that the budding leaders of the New Right could never comprehend or achieve. This countercultural evolution of western politics blurred the traditional lines between Left and Right and created some unusual political coalitions. Try, for example, to envision a direct relationship between the Grateful Dead and Dick Cheney, and you will start to see how weird these connections can be.[8]

The philosophy of Patagonia that evolved during the 1970s provides a good example of a powerfully countercultural model of consumption and business activism that is not often discussed as a part of western history. Although Chouinard and his generation of outdoor entrepreneurs would not be likely to consider themselves countercultural (they came of age mostly in the 1950s and represent a precountercultural bohemian sensibility), his politics mesh nicely with Barlow and his countercultural libertarian cohort. In the history of western politics, the counterculture is often depicted as the free-spirited sibling of the briefly brilliant but sadly failed New Left. The counterculture was the carefree, drug-addled, nonpolitical, lifestyle-oriented half of an otherwise seriously politicized generation.[9] The hippie counterculture appears political in western history usually only when cast as a foil for conservatives like Ronald Reagan, Richard Nixon, or Amy Scott's worried Boulderites, who feared the chaos that drugs, long hair, and infrequent bathing represented. The stoned hippies of Haight-Ashbury seemed to have almost as little in common with serious New Left activists as they did with Nixon and his crew-cut cabinet. A more cutting critique of the counterculture comes from those who assume that their lifestyle was nothing more than a sad sellout to savvy marketers who quickly co-opted their lifestyle and philosophy and turned it into a tool to get their hooks into the expanding youth market. In this telling, the counterculture becomes a frivolous false consciousness on the part of spoiled middle-class white kids and a distraction from real political contribution. That distraction helped cement the failure of the New Left and ultimately led to the rise of a powerful new western conservatism that enabled the careers of Nixon, Barry Goldwater, Reagan, and the Bush dynasty.

Is the political legacy of the western counterculture this simple? Sellouts or dropouts? Not really. There is an alternative version of the story of the counterculture in which various aspects of this diverse movement coalesce as a significant factor in the shaping of western political culture between the 1960s and the early twenty-first century. Dismissing the counterculture as the apolitical sellout half of the 1960s and 1970s misses the rich contributions the movement made to American politics and culture.[10] The argument can be made that, particularly in the West, the counterculture entrepreneurs who skipped the protest movement and the polls were the ones who made the most lasting contribution to the politics of the last decades of the century. Not unlike the evangelists Darren Dochuk explores in chapter 4, these entrepreneurs turned outsider status to their advantage in a changing political landscape. Their libertarian hybrid political philosophy was not a fringe movement. While it represents a political trend very different from the Populist and Progressive traditions of the region, it captured the spirit of western myth and updated it for a new generation searching for individualism and community reinvention through the electronic frontier of cyberspace, the promising world of alternative technology, the freedom of small business, and the conscience-soothing release of green consumption.

To understand the political landscape of the twenty-first-century West, it is necessary to look more closely at the politics that simmered beneath the psychedelic veneer of the counterculture. These politics don't take a traditional form, and many of the individuals who made significant contributions to the evolution of politics in the West did so through alternative means. These westerners are hard to trace in politics because they often did not vote or participate in political activism in any direct way. Some may not even fit within standard definitions of political, but behind the scenes they were building on many deep western political tendencies: the search for new frontiers, a utopian desire for a new beginning, individualism, escape, distrust of federal government. They embraced individual agency and inventiveness above all and worked to open markets to innovative models of production and consumption. Figures like Stewart Brand, the creator of the *Whole Earth Catalog;* Barlow, rancher and rock legend; and Chouinard are all examples of westerners who did not fit the mold of traditional political actors and yet played a role in shaping the political landscape of the modern West. Their efforts created a new and extremely marketable vision of western authenticity that reconfigured the use of western mythology in American politics and challenged some long-standing political alliances. Through their actions, not their advocacy, they brought a counterculture version of environmentalism and social responsibility into the boardroom and the marketplace.

Much of what has been written about counterculture libertarian thought focuses on the role of libertarian politics in the business and culture of the Internet, thus the term "cyberlibertarians."[11] Counterculture libertarian thinking, however, is also evident in the contentious world of environmental politics. There was a grassroots libertarian strain of environmentalism that differed dramatically from the Progressive model of government-legislated reform that so changed the landscape of the American West. Counterculture libertarian environmentalists focused their energies on grassroots and individual action and on technologically sophisticated entrepreneurship to move environmentalism out of the wilderness and into the market and the home. These environmentalists were more likely to take their inspiration from Edward Abbey's *Monkey Wrench Gang* or Robert Heinlein's *The Moon Is a Harsh Mistress* than from John Muir or Aldo Leopold.[12]

This libertarian-leaning environmentalism arose as a response to the Progressive model of environmentalism, which worked very well for protecting land but not as well for modifying consumption or regulating quality of life.

There is only so much that centralized government can do to convince people to recognize their own self-interest in protecting the environment. The fundamental conundrum for American environmentalism has always been the tension between capitalism and consumption. Despite the remarkable successes of mainstream environmentalism, it has never succeeded in resolving the problems with American materialism; environmentalism requires government regulation but also personal responsibility. For technologically minded counterculture innovators like Stewart Brand, much of what traditional environmentalists advocated just did not make sense. "I did not understand the urban romantic wilderness based environmentalism. I thought we needed to take responsibility and use our abilities to make change. Technology and technological research is critical to environmentalism."[13] John Herron's analysis of changing attitudes toward technology in more recent years (chapter 11) highlights the importance of avoiding the trap of declension stories in which technology is the foil for environmental politics.

A thoughtful reevaluation of the beneficial ways that alternative technologies could be used to create a sustainable future is perhaps the most significant contribution of the counterculture to American culture. Best known for music and drugs, they should be remembered as a new generation of innovators and tool builders. This trend manifested itself in many ways: from elder statesman Buckminster Fuller designing affordable and environmentally sympathetic geodesic domes to Steve Jobs and Steve Wozniak developing personal computers to put the power of free information in individual hands.[14] Working toward similar goals, other counterculture environmentalists, sympathetic scientists, and engineers focused on alternative energy, earth-friendly design, recycling, and creative waste management as the best ways to subvert the large industrial structures most damaging to the environment and to attempt to equalize the world power structure. This design- and engineering-driven environmentalism coalesced into the holistic field of ecological design.[15] Together, these efforts contributed to a growing sense of utopian optimism that tapped into a deep vein of western political thought and a long tradition of "fantasies of Western independence and fresh starts."[16]

In 1975 Ernest Callenbach released his popular science fiction novel *Ecotopia*.[17] Set in northern California, Callenbach's novel portrayed an environmental utopia based on counterculture political and social values and, most significantly, new trends in "appropriate technology." Callenbach's novel painted a picture of an eco-libertarian revolution resulting in the secession of Washington, Oregon, and northern California and the formation of an ecological paradise. *Ecotopia* is an old-fashioned western dressed in counterculture clothes; it is full of tough, gun-toting hippie environmentalists finding freedom on a new frontier. Despite an emphasis on collective ownership of the means of production, the book incorporates a lot of the libertarian-leaning desire for free markets. The characters in *Ecotopia* are not drugged-up flower children interested in peace and love. They are savvy feminists and counterculture Ben Franklins tinkering and innovating while they debate politics and culture.

On the surface, Callenbach's novel might seem like a vehicle for understanding the environmentalism of the early 1970s and the potential of new green technologies. While this is true, there is much more at work in this fantastic tale than a fictionalization of environmentalist hopes. Like other American utopians, Callenbach spent a great deal of his book talking about free markets, consumerism, and the politics he felt best facilitated each.[18] He worked hard in his story to explain the connections between politics, environmentalism, consumption, and authenticity. Callenbach's western utopia was not so much a story about a return to wilderness as a vision for a future based on appropriate technologies and earth-friendly economies and governments. The ecotopian vision was aimed at city-dwellers looking for a new type of enlightened consumerism that accommodated their environmental concerns, individual creativity, and social politics. The novel is an excellent example of the meeting ground of left social values and right distrust of big government that has played such a central role in western politics. *Ecotopia* melded the counterculture lifestyle and social values with a strange brew of libertarian politics, collectivism, states rights, and technologically enthusiastic environmentalism in the same counterculture science fiction tradition as Robert Heinlein's *The Moon Is a Harsh Mistress*. Heinlein paints a futuristic western set on a lunar colony populated by innovative misfits ready to break from the tyranny of centralized authority and realize the potential of thoughtful anarchy. Their battle cry of "TANSTAAFL!" ("There Ain't No Such Thing as A Free Lunch!") captured the imagination of a generation of counterculture entrepreneurs who valued hard work and innovation and individuals who empowered themselves through their actions rather than their words.

In 1975, when *Ecotopia* first appeared, Callenbach's vision tapped into a growing counterculture-libertarian ethos that fueled a host of counterculture publications. Along with the fiction of Callenbach, Heinlein, and other popular writers, the *Whole Earth* publishing empire and its host of imitators provided millions of readers with the latest counterculture thinking. This ferment of counterculture publication also shaped the early stages of the cyber revolution. While Callenbach's ideas were classic counterculture, his use of the myth and symbol of the West as a political tool was in keeping with a long tradition of western politics. What made the book interesting then and now is the way Callenbach used the traditional mythology of western history but reconfigured the story to include countercultural insights on politics and environmentalism. At the heart of this new western narrative is what now would be called green consumerism. In Callenbach's vision, green consumption was just a part of a revolutionary change. In the real world of the mid-1970s, green business and green consumption were emerging as a very pragmatic back door to political influence.[19]

Western utopian visions, often depicted as hopelessly romantic and unrealistic, usually reflect deep truths about the role of myth and perception in shaping western politics. Callenbach's Ecotopians joined a long line of real and fictional western visionaries who choose the West as the stage for their utopian plays not because it is a tabula rasa but because it is a region loaded with malleable and powerful myths and imagery that lends itself well to a redefinition of self and reinvention of politics. Western utopians, like Callenbach, have often been dismissed and derided by mainstream political analysts as frivolous escapists, malcontents, or misfits whose seeming obsession with obscure technologies and mundane futuristic consumerism detracts from their political message. While this may have been the case for many who occupied the expansive western utopian fringe from both sides of the political spectrum, western utopians, both conservative and liberal, often put ideas into play that later moved into the mainstream, shaping national culture and politics. For utopian thinkers like Ernest Callenbach, technology and consumer concepts proved to be the most compelling aspects of his political agenda.[20] More important, ideological movements that appeared utopian in the sense that they represented a hope for a distant but unlikely future often masked very pragmatic research and work that was put into practice quickly and efficiently. One of the ways the counterculture fringe moved toward the center by the late 1980s was by entering the marketplace. By moving their message to the market and situating their innovations within the existing framework of western mythology, they changed the way people think about what it means to be authentic.[21]

But how is this political maneuvering a western phenomenon? How does it fit into the broader trends in the political history of the region? The West played a well-recognized role in the transformation of American politics during the second half of the twentieth century. The rise of western conservatism in particular has been closely studied. Most analysts agree that after World War II, the massive demographic and economic transformation of the region instigated by the war economy created a new and powerful block of white-collar, middle-of-the-road conservative western voters who played a large, perhaps even a defining, role in national politics. The Republican Party shifted its focus to these new westerners and used them as the cornerstone of a very successful political strategy. In fact, Republicans were so successful that a complete transformation seemed to have occurred within the West, with powerful progressive and liberal western constituencies like blue-collar miners and populist farmers being replaced by white-collar workers and conservative entrepreneurial capitalists who had little sympathy for unionism or the old liberal causes that had energized the region for so long. Even the environmental movement, which drew much of its strength from western states, was eclipsed for a time by the conservative response of the sagebrush rebellion.[22]

The Republican Party did an excellent job of recognizing changing demographic and cultural trends in the 1950s and 1960s, and it capitalized on the growing power of the West. Just as important, conservatives recognized the power of western myths and symbols in political marketing. As Robert Goldberg demonstrates in chapter 1, Ronald Reagan's presidential career epitomized the conservative use of the western icon of the rugged individual as a political marketing tool. Reagan often staged press events at which he dressed as a cowboy and demonstrated his riding skills. In so doing, he was participating in a long-standing American political tradition dating back to the legacy of the log cabin campaigns of the 1800s. Traditional conservatives, however, were not the only politicians in the post–World War II era to use western iconography for political marketing. Democrat Lyndon Baines Johnson was Reagan's equal at what historian Anne Butler has called "putting on the hat"—the long-standing tradition of donning western wear to send a political message.[23]

Still, the symbols and myth of the West relate to national politics in ways that are better recognized for traditional conservative politics than for liberal politics. This is particularly true for the significant shifts in western contributions to the hybrid left/right politics that came out of the counterculture milieu and spawned a new type of environmental politics energized by ideas from the appropriate technology movement and the western cyberlibertarianism. Notwithstanding the dot.com and tech bust of the early 2000s, cyberlibertarianism remains a force in shaping western and national politics. The appropriate technology and green consumerism that grew out of the counterculture in the West provided a powerful political legacy and a new twist to the traditional conservative use of western mythology in marketing and politics.[24]

Just after LBJ rode his ranching roots into the White House and while Reagan was gearing up his conservative western political imagery, a growing segment of the western population was putting on the Patagonia Synchilla jacket, made from recycled plastic soda bottles, for the first time. By the mid-1980s, for many westerners putting on the "Pat" took the place of "putting on the hat." Chouinard added a new wardrobe to the closet of western politics, and in the process tapped into a new western iconography whose success rivaled that of the cowboy-hat-wearing individualist favored by traditional politicians. Chouinard's high-tech clothing, tested in the harshest environments on earth, became a political statement for millions who never intended to use the clothes for anything more hazardous than a trip to the store. The burgeoning outdoor industry began clothing a legion of new westerners in outfits as laden with political and cultural symbolism as was the western wear that preceded them. The outdoor-sports industry exploded in the late 1970s, and the American West was the focal point for much of the recreation and the business.[25] The western libertarian sensibility, coupled with consumerism, innovation, and business acumen, found its finest expression on the pages of the *Whole Earth Catalog*. Under the inspired leadership of Stanford biologist and political dropout Stewart Brand, *Whole Earth* gathered together a new universe of goods and philosophies that coalesced into a potent new type of individualistic production and consumption that spawned a counterculture publishing empire. Over time, the libertarian sympathies that fueled *Whole Earth*'s early success reached full flower on the DayGlo of *Wired* magazine.[26] In *Wired*, the libertarian new western politics reached its zenith of influence during the dot.com boom of the 1990s when flip-flop-wearing Silicon Valley CEOs crashed the gates of the corporate world, average Americans felt empowered by purchasing business machines, and a powerful new voting block of what conservative critic David Brooks called BoBo's (bourgeois bohemians) ushered in a new era of mass consumption.[27] For critic Brooks, the orgy of technoconsumption of the 1990s was further proof that the counterculture was a fraud and that its adherents were dupes who did not understand that consumption was consumption whether the products were BMWs or bamboo floors for home yoga gyms. But this view misses the entrepreneurial spirit built into the fabric of the counterculture and overlooks the fact that the consumption trends of the 1980s and 1990s were not so much evidence of a liberal sellout as examples of the extent of the influence of this hybrid left/right counterculture politics.[28]

The marketing savvy and business genius of the counterculture has been a fruitful topic for discussion among historians and cultural critics. Much of this literature is critical of the counterculture "sellouts" who traded in their souls for a buck or of the cynical marketers who stole the soul of the counterculture and used it to hawk Nike shoes to poor kids and yuppies.[29] Of these, Thomas Frank's *Conquest of Cool* stands out as the most thoughtful. Frank highlights the ways counterculture mixed perfectly with capitalism from its earliest days. There were many in the "movement" who forcefully asserted their business interests and forged an alternative business network that built a strong foundation for future political activism. Counterculture entrepreneurs were very consistent in their drive to make products and deliver services that they believed in and that they thought could make a difference in the world. As Stewart Brand related later, "As they followed the mantra 'Turn on, tune in and drop out,' college students of the '60s also dropped academia's traditional disdain for business. 'Do your own thing' easily translated into 'Start your own business.'"[30] These new entrepreneurs stuck with their ideals as they moved away from traditional politics and toward business ventures built on values that allowed them to work toward political goals through alternative means. Young entrepreneurs, Brand insisted, "brought an honesty and a dedication to service that was attractive to vendors and customers alike. Success in business made them disinclined to 'grow out of' their countercultural values, and it made a number of them wealthy and powerful at a young age."[31] History seems to suggest that in western politics dropping out was perhaps as effective as tuning in.

The particular brand of western green consumerism and entrepreneurial enthusiasm epitomized by the *Whole Earth Catalog* was very effective in enabling its participants to reinvent powerful western symbols and negotiate or advance a hybrid left/right political agenda via the market economy. The political realism of green consumerism provided an easily digestible version of western left/right politics—individualistic, rugged, cool, hip, antiestablishment, and yet still closely linked with the traditions of the region. The focus on lifestyle and intellectual exploration of Brand and his generation of creative entrepreneurs and thinkers provided an alternative model for political activism. Their model of political activism was far different from the contentious union liberalism and polarizing protest movements that characterized much of liberal politics in the West during the twentieth century and sent many middle-of-the-road westerners scurrying toward Ronald Reagan. One of the central ideals of the hybrid counterculture alternative to traditional politics was the greening of production and consumption.

Convincing American producers and consumers that there was a middle ground between capitalism and environmentalism was no easy task. Some good examples of those working toward this reconciliation include Paul Hawken, Amory Lovins, and Hunter Lovins, who provided a captivatingly simple model for this reconciliation in their influential book *Natural Capi-*

talism (1999). Building on Hawken's earlier work in *The Ecology of Commerce* (1993) and *Growing a Business* (1987), they argued that an environmental ethic based on realistic use of existing appropriate technologies was the key not only to the health of the planet but also to the future of corporate success and profitability.[32] Of course, what these contemporary authors propose is not without precedent. In some ways their model of "natural capitalism" harkens back to the "gospel of efficiency" of Teddy Roosevelt and Progressive conservationists. Unlike Roosevelt's cohorts, however, natural capitalists argue that environmentalism is best left to individuals and corporations who will use the free market to correct environmental waste and abuse. Much of the political debate about how to best reconcile commerce and environmentalism has been played out on the pages of the *Whole Earth Catalog*s. Despite Brand's desire to keep politics in the background of his catalog, by the 1970s *Whole Earth* was very much engaged in politics.

When he started *Whole Earth*, Brand asked for advice from his mentor, designer and intellectual Buckminster Fuller. Fuller advised Brand to avoid politics; "I took Fuller's advice to make *Whole Earth* non-political. That was the idea throughout." A good example of an important counterculture figure, Brand participated in Ken Kesey's infamous Acid Tests and put together the landmark Trips Festival, two of the wildest happenings of the early San Francisco counterculture. He seems to conform to the standard interpretation of apolitical lifestyle-oriented counterculturalists. "I was not really political at all," Brand remembered. "Like Kessey and others [I was] just kind of looking on. I saw marchers in Berkeley and thought, cool, glad they're doing it. But I was not one of the marchers."[33] Brand may not have started political, but his life and work made very significant contributions to politics, and by any measure his long-term success in the realm of politics surpassed that of many who led the marches. Brand was a natural leader and built a counterculture business model that facilitated the exercising of politics through both sides of the marketplace, consumption and production.

The *Whole Earth Catalog* and its successor, *CoEvolution Quarterly*, became a nexus of hybrid left/right politics, environmentalism, appropriate-technology research, alternative lifestyle information, and communitarian anarchism.[34] First published in 1968, *Whole Earth* brought a wide range of divergent counterculture trends under one roof. Commune members, computer designers and hackers, psychedelic drug engineers, and environmentalists were but a few of those who could find something of interest in the pages of *Whole Earth*. Brand's founding goal was to create a survival manual for "citizens of planet Earth" and "hippie environmentalist spacemen."[35] The subtle political strategies of *Whole Earth* drew on a long tradition of indirect politics through publication going back to eighteenth-century philosopher Denis Diderot's *Encyclopédie*, "A tremendous storehouse of fact and propaganda that swept Europe and taught it what 'reason,' 'rights,' . . . and related social principles are or should be. The work was subversive in its tendency, not in its advocacy."[36] According to Brand, *Whole Earth* was a "movable education" for his counterculture friends "who were reconsidering the structure of modern life and building their own communes in the backwoods." Under his direction, *Whole Earth* and its successors extolled the virtues of steam-powered bicycles, windmills, solar collectors, and wood stoves, alongside the new "personal computers," satellite telephones, and the latest telecommunications hardware. Brand and his followers were convinced that access to innovative and potentially subversive information and energy technologies was a vital part of changing the cultural perceptions that contributed to environmental decay.[37] Most significantly, *Whole Earth* provided a guilt-free outlet for a new generation of socially aware consumers. While *Whole Earth*'s readers learned about social, cultural, and technological alternatives to the old world of their parents, they also got an implicit and explicit lesson in green capitalism and green consumerism. Starting in 1968, *Whole Earth* and spin-off publications made significant contributions to the reevaluation of capitalism, consumerism, technology, and the environment. In the pages of the *Whole Earth Catalog*, appropriate technology, advice on business, and counterculture politics happily and effortlessly commingled. Had Daniel Bell studied the ideal of capitalism espoused in the catalogs, or more important, embodied by the project of making and selling the catalogs, he might have found a rough model for resolving what he called "the cultural contradictions of capitalism."[38] In the left/right world of counterculture libertarianism, there were no contradictions of capitalism; the so-called contradictions were all a part of the same sensibility.

What would it really take to change the world? What practical everyday kind of service could one offer to those who wanted to nurture the environmental health of the planet, change the political status quo, and in the process save their collective souls? In March 1968 twenty-nine-year-old Brand asked these big questions of himself while flying over Nebraska returning from the funeral of his father. At that point Brand was best known for distributing buttons that read "Why Haven't We Seen a Photograph of the Whole Earth Yet?" His buttons contributed to the release of photos of the earth from space; historians rank the dissemination of those photos high on the list of events that have shaped environmental awareness since the late 1970s.[39] Brand stood out within the counterculture both for his clean-cut and bookish appearance and for his organizational prowess. Even as a young man adventuring with some of the most colorful and eccentric characters on the scene, Brand valued practical solutions, realistic schedules, and well-thought-out blueprints and business plans, and considering his consciousness-altering circumstances, he made some remarkably clearheaded decisions about how to invest his money. He learned the basics of capitalism and sound business practices from watching drug dealers ply their trade. "We all had experience with drug dealing and saw supply and demand first hand," he later recalled. Trained as a biologist at Stanford University, Brand learned early that access to good data and tools was critical to accomplishing goals and producing productive results.

As Brand sat on the plane returning from his father's funeral, he concocted an idea and scrawled it over the end pages of Barbara Ward's *Spaceship Earth*.[40] He envisioned a blueprint for an information-delivery system modeled on the L. L. Bean catalog (a publication he viewed as a priceless and practical "service to humanity").[41] Brand's counterculture version of the catalog would be a "catalog of goods that owed nothing to the suppliers and everything to the users."[42] He hoped to create a service that would blend the liberal social values of the counterculture with the technological enthusiasm of his Stanford classmates and professors. *Whole Earth* would also, from the start, advocate decentralized organization, heterarchy over hierarchy, free markets, and free information. This goal required a service that "eschewed" traditional New Left politics and instead "pushed grassroots direct power—tools and skills" in the most straightforward way: a list of goods, services, information, and how-to guides.[43]

Brand pictured a collection of information covering all aspects of the ever-expanding universe of alternative and appropriate technologies, products, publications, and events. Unlike participants in the active underground press, who tended to focus on politics and culture, Brand wanted to highlight new technologies and tools.[44] For the most part, the politics of the catalog were captured in the access to tools, but there was always a significant portion of the catalog dedicated specifically to libertarian thinking and politics. The catalog was aimed at counterculturalists and communitarians of all sorts, but from its conception it transcended the counterculture and distanced itself from New Left critiques of capitalism. Brand wanted to focus his efforts on a particular segment of the counterculture, the "doers" like him, "with a functional grimy grasp on the world."[45] Brand's project was a lofty one: to create a system of moral marketing and green capitalism produced by a hippie corporation that used the power of money and marketing for an altruistic end and provided access to markets without marketing and answered the question "Where to lay hands on a computer without forfeiting freedom."[46] Over the years many aspects of the catalog changed, including the title, but never the subtitle: "*Access to Tools.*" This phrase captures Brand's philosophy and sets his efforts apart from many of his contemporaries. By tools, Brand meant not only hammers and saws for building geodesic domes, but IBM Selectrics and Selectric Composers, Polaroid MP3 cameras, and, most important, personal computers. While the New Left resisted many of these technologies and the New Age segment of the counterculture "despised" them, Brand and his cohort embraced appropriate technologies as the key to social change and environmental health.[47]

Brand was one of many who rejected the antimodernism of some environmentalists and counterculturalists. *Whole Earth* represented a large segment of the counterculture that simply did not fit the model of neo-Luddite nature children popularized by the media. There is a great deal of evidence that the preoccupation with technology and its consequences was one of the central features of 1960s social and environmental movements and of the counterculture in particular.[48] In 1968 Theodore Roszak published his influential study of the youth movement, *The Making of a Counter Culture*. According to Roszak, the counterculture was a direct reaction to "technocracy," which Roszak defined as a "society in which those who govern justify themselves by appeal to technical experts, who in turn justify themselves by appeals to scientific forms of knowledge."[49] The counterculture radicals of the 1960s, he argued, were the only group in America capable of divorcing themselves from the stranglehold of 1950s technology and its insidious centralizing tendencies. Roszak's position on technocracy mirrored the philosophy of intellectuals like Jacques Ellul and Herbert Marcuse.[50] For Roszak the most appealing characteristic of the counterculture was its rejection of technology and the systems it spawned. Charles Reich, in his bestseller *The Greening of America* (1970), also highlighted the youth movement's rejection of technology as a fundamental component of the counterculture ideology.[51] For both Reich and Roszak, it was bureaucratic organization and complexity that made the technocracy evil.

Roszak's counterculture, with its antimodernist bent and distaste for technology and science, is the counterculture best known by the American public and the scholarly community. While Brand was equally distrustful of bureaucracies and of big government's co-option of technology, in all other respects *Whole Earth* represents a very different trend. In Brand's view, technology in the right hands was the best hope for a more democratic future. Appropriate technology in particular could help, according to Brand, to create socially conscious businesses, like the *Whole Earth Catalog*, and create information like the photos of the Earth that could change the way people perceive their environments. In retrospect, the embrace of technology by an icon of the counterculture might surprise many. Even more surprising, and the most striking aspect of *Whole Earth*, was the business model it created. In hindsight it is clear that *Whole Earth* was at the forefront of a new trend in

American business, a trend that resonates in our own time. Brand was a pioneer in the greening of American business, and his corporations were a harbinger of a new political calculus at least two decades ahead of its time.

On the pages of *Whole Earth* and in his own books, Brand articulated a world of libertarian counterculture capitalism while many of his contemporaries were still advocating a socialist revolution. Brand was not alone in business or philosophy. The founders of Ben & Jerry's, Apple Computers, Smith & Hawken, Williams-Sonoma, Virgin Group, and Patagonia all shared parts of this political vision. Those who created these successful companies all shared some direct connection or general affinity for the counterculture and used their knowledge of cultural trends to create powerful corporations, find new market niches, and reshape the American economy and American business. They perfected the cause-based and liberation marketing that is now preached at Harvard Business School. A generation of young Americans educated at elite universities have learned from them that life as a corporate capitalist can be OK if one has liberal social values.[52] It requires, however, doing something one loves, practicing inconspicuous consumption, and focusing on marketing a natural product or contributing to the liberation of information and expanding access. Which brings us back to Patagonia.

Rock climbers like Royal Robbins and Chouinard are examples of bohemian extreme-sports enthusiasts who turned their passion into successful businesses. These legendary pioneers of rock climbing, the first to scale the seemingly impossibly vertical granite of Yosemite's El Capitan, are significant for their contributions to the worldwide evolution of rock climbing as a sport as well as for their technical innovations and contributions to a major economic revolution in outdoor equipment and apparel.[53] Chouinard in particular, along with several business-savvy partners, including climbing pioneer Tom Frost, linked extreme sports, environmental advocacy, and consumerism in a manner similar to Brand in the *Whole Earth Catalog*, but he aimed at a very different constituency. Together he and his partners founded the wildly successful outdoor-apparel company Patagonia and changed the dress code for the new West.[54] Slightly older than Brand, Chouinard spent a good part of the 1950s and 1960s living a bohemian dropout life in Yosemite's legendary climbers' hangout, Camp 4. During this period, Camp 4 was full of young men who had given up on materialism and headed to the mountains in search of "authentic experiences." What distinguished this generation of wilderness truth seekers was their decidedly entrepreneurial genius. The dusty and dirty picnic tables of Camp 4 produced no fewer than three founders of internationally successful corporations during the five-year period between 1958 and 1973 alone. Chouinard,

Chouinard Equipment Co. "Skunk Works," Ventura, California, 1969. Photo Courtesy Tom Frost.

Frost, and Robbins all founded companies that went on to great success and helped create the multibillion-dollar outdoor-sports industry.

Patagonia, started as the Great Pacific Iron Works with $600 Chouinard borrowed from his mother, was the quintessential garage business. Dissatisfied with the quality of European pitons (the metal spikes climbers use), Chouinard started making his own high-quality "chromoly" units in his garage for his own use. Word spread, and soon the demand grew and a business was born. Chouinard expanded his operation to include clothing and formed two companies, Chouinard Equipment and Patagonia. Both were successful almost from the start, in part because Chouinard found a real need and filled it, but also, and more important, because he built his businesses around a powerful set of political and social concerns. Early on, that concern was "clean climbing," the idea that rock climbing and other outdoor activities had to take care of the resources they used and do as little damage to the environment—in the case of clean climbing, the rock itself—as possible. Clean climbing was a revolution that reshaped the sport worldwide and opened the door for the mass marketing of what had been up to that time a fringe sport for serious eccentrics and dropouts.

The clean-climbing revolution had implications beyond the climbing community. Chouinard became a leading proponent of the clean-climbing ethic, developing a host of thoughtful and environmentally sensitive products for climbers. More significant, Chouinard was among a pioneering group of American businessmen who, in the 1970s, built a business philosophy that united environmentalism, outdoor sports, social responsibility, libertarian-leaning views on government, and huge profits. Like Brand and the counterculture entrepreneurs who followed them, these climbers were socially liberal, "hated the Feds," and had very little desire to work for any traditional political movement.[55] The politics of the climber-entrepreneurs were embedded in their engineering and marketing. Chouinard, for example, worried that the successful technological developments of the postwar period had made access to the rarified cliffs of Yosemite a little too easy and environmentally harmful. He argued, "No longer can we assume the Earth's resources are limitless; that there are ranges of unclimbed peaks extending endlessly beyond the horizon. Mountains are finite, and despite their massive appearance, they are fragile."[56] He helped reinvent his sport and in the following decades infused politics into the apparel industry and got his message out to a large audience. Chouinard's is just one example of a green business model that shaped American consumerism in the late twentieth century.[57] By the 1990s, Camp 4 alumni Frost, Chouinard, and Robbins wielded considerable political power and used their influence to help preserve the park they had grown to love as disheveled climbing bums. Like many of their generation, they had used their disengagement from politics very productively and found themselves moving to positions of political power from the most unlikely of trajectories. Like Brand, it was their lack of participation in traditional politics and their disengagement from the traditional political process that, ironically, gave them political power and influence later in their careers.

In the 1970s, scholars like Daniel Bell were arguing that capitalism was on the verge of collapse, doomed to destroy itself as the tenuous balance between consumption and production was becoming unsteady as the Protestant ethic faded in the hedonistic climate of the day.[58] In hindsight it is easy to see how one might fail to perceive a future where capitalism would be reconciled with liberal social values, environmental concerns, and hedonistic self-expression. Similarly, it was pretty clear by the late 1970s that the age of the organization man was on the wane, but it was not clear to most what would rise up to take its place. While many liberals wrung their hands over the hedonism and seeming lack of political engagement of the counterculture, Brand, Chouinard, and a host of innovative entrepreneurs had already created a model for integrating their social politics within the existing framework of the capitalist market.

Reading the first few *Whole Earth Catalog*s reveals nothing less than an attempted reconciliation of nature and capitalism, freedom and safety, technology and environment, the rural and the urban, adventure and domestication, the holy and the profane. And central to this encompassing reconciliation was a casual acceptance of capitalism. "You many not think capitalism is nice," Brand wrote in anticipation of criticism, "and I don't know if it's nice. But we should both know that the *Whole Earth Catalog* is made of it." Long before many in his cohort, Brand was willing to utter, in a positive way, the most profane word of his generation: "money": "So along with shit, fuck . . . and the rest, I wanted to say among my friends money, not to swear but to honor its function."[59] This willingness to be open about the business and capital side of his endeavor provided a powerful, and often emulated, counterculture business model. Brand and *Whole Earth* helped invent the "weird hybrid zone where creativity and commerce intersect" that epitomized the dot.com boom of the 1990s and the parallel "greening" of American business.[60] While they worked without shirts and played volleyball every noon, the crew at *Whole Earth*, like their Silicon Valley colleagues who followed, were deadly serious about achieving their goals and thought nothing of putting in eighty-hour workweeks.

By the late 1970s, Brand's notoriety as an innovative thinker made him a sought-after adviser to politicians and business leaders and ultimately led to his appointment as an adviser to California governor Jerry Brown between 1977 and 1979. In that role, Brand was able to provide political access for many of the influential counterculture and environmental thinkers published in *Whole Earth*. Brand arranged meetings between Brown and such creative intellectuals as futurist Herman Kahn and such technologically enthusiastic environmentalists as Amory Lovins.[61] Brand sent a steady stream of iconoclastic intellectuals to Brown's office, and Brown shaped California energy policy partly according to their recommendations. By the late 1970s, Brand's political cachet enabled him to move from the fringes of western politics to the center. Valuable as a political adviser because he was not a traditional politician or supporter of the traditional political process, he remembered, "I was able to work directly with Jerry Brown because I was out getting experience and not marching." He added that there were "lots of examples of counterculture business people who became very successful and have influence in many different ways."[62]

The combination of technological enthusiasm, market savvy, conservative views on government regulation of economy, and environmental and social consciousness helped *Whole Earth* become one of the most successful publications of its time. *Whole Earth* and its business model and work ethic have provided inspiration for a new generation of business leaders. In fact, it is in the realm of business where *Whole Earth* has left its most lasting mark. By the end of the 1970s, the *Whole Earth Catalog* brought together some of the most innovative members of the counterculture to attempt to reconcile nature and the machine. The research promoted by Brand and other appropriate-technology enthusiasts, in both alternative energy and alternative information systems, appeared to succeed in substantially altering the way Americans thought about the power of technology as a benevolent force for environmental protection, ecological living, and personal liberation. In many ways, the reconciliation of ecology and technology, individualistic lifestyle, and libertarian politics popularized by *Whole Earth* provided a more integrated and realistic model for environmental politics in the West. By demonstrating that there were possibilities for a middle ground between modern technology, socially conscious consumerism, and at least one strain of conservative politics, the *Whole Earth Catalog* and other like-minded businesses contributed to the acceptance of environmentalism in mainstream American culture.

Environmental consumerism and the desire for environmentally friendly alternatives drove very successful national efforts to change American business practices without altering the fundamental economic system. One of the most successful of these was the 1989 grassroots "McToxics" campaign aimed at McDonald's restaurants' use of Styrofoam packaging. American consumers found it unacceptable that a corporation like McDonald's would dump 1.3 billion cubic feet of chlorofluorocarbon-laden styrene foam into landfills each year. This effort soon went national, with consumers engaging in boycotts and "send-it-back" efforts against McDonald's franchises that refused to switch to cardboard and paper packaging. Ultimately McDonald's capitulated, and the foam was replaced with paper wrappers. The McToxics effort illustrated the degree to which environmentalism had successfully infiltrated consumer culture and provided a model of an alternative type of consumer-based political action. It also demonstrated that while Americans were willing to use their economic power to advocate environmental issues, they were unwilling to challenge the basic economic system: They still wanted the hamburger, and they were willing to buy it from an enormous corporation; but they preferred that it not be wrapped in Styrofoam.

The power of the counterculture libertarians peaked with the dot.com boom of the 1990s. Their techno-utopian rhetoric and enthusiasm for the "new economy" and the electronic frontier lost some of its luster in the stock crash and scandals of the early 2000s. The rise of the neoconservatives and the strong connection between the administration of George W. Bush and social conservatives severed many of the ties between the Hip Right and the Republican Party. John Perry Barlow, an outspoken critic of traditional participatory politics, changed his mind about his politics in 2004 as it became clear that America was experiencing another in a long sequence of culture wars that pitted liberal against conservative social values. At the same time, political policy and other gauges of success and failure became subservient to entrenched and seemingly irreconcilable social beliefs. The songwriter for the countercultural house band the Grateful Dead, Barlow worked on Dick Cheney's Wyoming campaign when he ran for Congress as a small-government and free-market fiscal conservative. He especially appreciated Cheney's environmental views and policies and considered him an ally in his Wyoming environmental activism.[63] Their alliance was troubled at times, most famously leading to the lyrics for the Grateful Dead song "Throwing Stones." By the early years of the twenty-first century, Barlow could not stomach the Bush administration's "very authoritarian, assertive form of government . . . in the guise of Libertarianism."[64] Nonetheless, Barlow continued to appreciate Cheney's "pragmatic ecology" and his credentials as a westerner who was willing to work for a type of environmental protection Barlow valued. Barlow fished with Cheney on his ranch and felt they shared a "realistic environmentalism" characterized by a deep love of the land and respect for those who knew it through work.[65]

By the late 1990s, Stewart Brand had also carefully distanced himself from the Libertarian Party and conservative trends of recent years. When asked about being branded as a Libertarian, he made it clear that "I think that's fair, historically, not now."[66] For counterculture libertarians like Barlow, the Bush administration was a dangerous failure on two counts. First and foremost, the administration demonstrated "an unwillingness to engage in any kind of mitigation of the free market," and second, they were intensely adversarial to the liberal social values that characterized the "hippie-mystic strain" of libertarianism that had contributed to the left/right fusion of the cyberlibertarians. It is an interesting moment in American history when hippies are saddened by the lack of core conservative values evidenced by fundamentalist Republicans.

The criticism runs both ways. While Barlow and others on the Hip Right became disenchanted with the New Right, they were themselves much condemned, especially from the Left. For liberal critics the blurring of political lines risked a dilution of liberal claims to social responsibility in return for a hybrid libertarianism that seemed unlikely to appeal to social conservatives or traditional liberals. Further, the wave of social conservatism and antienvironmentalism that swept the nation in the aftermath of 9/11 demonstrated some of the limitations of thoughtful consumption and renegade business models as a political strategy. In many respects, the utopian rhetoric of *Ecotopia*, the early editions of the *Whole Earth Catalog*, and even fairly recent editions of *Wired* magazine seems as hopelessly optimistic as the long-past visions of western utopias of the late 1800s. Still, the recent rumblings of blue-state federalism lends the fantasy of *Ecotopia* new appeal. In the wake of the 2004 election, blue-state liberals on both coasts started talking like Ecotopians—advocating giving up on the red states and going one's own way. This wistful thinking taps into a long western tradition of fearing unjust outside influence and unfair use of western resources—now money, not trees or minerals—for the benefit of other regions.

Events since the turn of the new millennium seem to indicate a return to the polarized politics that have so characterized the West and the nation for much of the second half of the twentieth century. George Bush also appears to have wrestled the iconography of the West back as well. He and key members of his administration "[put] on the hat" very effectively. In the 2004 election, the images that resonated with the media and the public seemed to be George W. clothed in traditional western wear chopping down trees on his Texas ranch. John Kerry was seen in the latest high-tech outdoor wear snowboarding down the slopes with remarkable style. Clearly in 2004, the traditional "putting on the hat" worked better than the new West version of "putting on the Patagonia." But even the polarization of 2004 is not as simple as it seems. While the fight between left and right appeared more entrenched than ever, the hybridization of the 1990s remains a force in western politics and will probably complicate things further in the future. Green Party success in local and state elections in New Mexico during the 1990s demonstrated the ability of western politics to move beyond left and right and provide an alternative model of political activism that scrapped the "packaged deal" of the party system.[67]

Thoughtful counterculture libertarians may pose the most direct threat to the neoconservatives who solidified their power in 2004. Western liberals might wonder if the hybridization of left and right politics of the counterculture libertarians contributed to rise of the "neocons" while diluting liberal constituencies by moving probusiness moderates to the right. The fight between liberals and Green Party candidate Ralph Nader demonstrated the level of concern over so-called third-way views. A more neutral view could argue that the hybrid movement represents the best bet for a popular consensus. By holding neocons to the conservative traditions of fiscal responsibility and protection of the free market while standing firm on their liberal social agenda, counterculture libertarians offer an avenue for a different type of conservative politics that could appeal to politically moderate westerners from the Left or the Right. Moreover, the natural capitalism of companies like Patagonia still represents a means of integrating social responsibility into daily life that even during periods of intense political polarization appeals to a wide spectrum of Americans from both sides of the political fence.

In fact, the model of politically realistic environmentalism of the counterculture might provide the best hope for a meeting of political minds in the West of the future. Conservation and preservation evolved into environmentalism because of a collective realization that protecting the environment was a personal choice that influenced quality of life. Millions of Americans love the outdoors and go there as often as they can. A decent percentage of these outdoor enthusiasts support environmental protection and give money to groups that lobby on behalf of the environment and work toward progressive legislation. Many average outdoor fans may even vote for candidates who have some sense of an environmental ethic. But are those actions more or less important than walking out of their way to recycle a can, or reading the label of a new jacket to find out what it was made of, or giving a few seconds of thought to how their consumption fits into the chain of ecology that we are a part of, despite how divorced we are from the production side of the capitalist equation? It is no revelation that the personal can be political. Conservatives have done a good job lately of recognizing that personal choices and preferences for quality of life and values can, and often do, supersede American interests in policy plans and decisions. The counterculture libertarians recognized this also and helped shape a political response based on individual agency. Reconciliation and meeting on middle grounds is always a goal—could this hybrid philosophy of politics be a model? Or is it just another utopian dream that played out on the well-used western stage? William Carlos Williams famously said, "The pure products of America go crazy."[68] Western political history generally proves this true, which makes it likely that the future of western politics will be some hybrid of the Left and the Right.

NOTES

1. Yvon Chouinard, "On Corporate Responsibility," *Patagonia: The Edge Book Winter 2004 Catalog*, Winter 2004, 36–37, and *Let My People Go Surfing: The Education of a Reluctant Businessman* (New York: Penguin Books, 2005), 129–133, for specifics on catalog politics.

2. Tom Frost, phone interview by author, 4 February 2005.

3. John Perry Barlow, "Crime and Puzzlement: In Advance of the Law on the Electronic Frontier," *Whole Earth Review* 68 (Fall 1990): 44–57.

4. John Perry Barlow, interview by Brian Doherty, "John Perry Barlow 2.0: The Thomas Jefferson of Cyberspace Reinvents His Body—and His Politics," *Reasononline*, August–September 2004, http://www.reason.com/news/show/29236.html.

5. Quotation is from Louis Rosseto, "Rebuttal of the Californian Ideology," *Alamut Bastion of Peace and Information,* http://www.alamut.com/subj/ideologies/pes simism/califIdeo_II.html. Lots of online debate centers on the California Ideology and cyberlibertarians. For the most thorough critique, see Richard Barbrook and Andy Cameron, "The Californian Ideology," http://www.hrc.wmin.ac.uk/theory-cal ifornianideology.html. Much of the discussion of the politics of cyberspace happens, no surprise, on Web discussions. For cyberlibertarians, see Langdon Winner, "Cyber-Libertarian Myths and the Prospects for Community," in *Cyberethics: Social and Moral Issues in the Computer Age,* ed. Robert Baird, Reagan Ramsower, and Stuart E. Rosenbaum (Amherst, N.Y.: Prometheus Books, 2000), 319–331, and Thomas Streeter, "That Deep Romantic Chasm: Libertarianism, Neolibertarianism, and the Computer Culture," in *Communication, Citizenship, and Social Policy,* ed. Andrew Calabrese and Jean-Claude Burgelman (New York: Rowman & Littlefield, 1999), 49–64.

6. Barbrook and Cameron, "Californian Ideology," in particular.

7. Jennifer L. Burns, "O Libertarian, Where is Thy Sting?" *The Journal of Policy History* 19, 4 (Fall 2007): 453–71.

8. John Perry Barlow, phone interview by author, 1 November 2005. Barlow was one of Dick Cheney's campaign managers during his first run for Congress. Both Barlow and Stewart Brand, creator of the *Whole Earth Catalog,* have received awards from the leading Libertarian journal, *Reason,* over the years for their contributions.

9. Counterculture as defined in Peter Braunstein and Michael Doyle, "Introduction: Historicizing the American Counterculture of the 1960s and '70s," in *Imagine Nation: The American Counterculture of the 1960s and '70s,* ed. Peter Braunstein and Michael Doyle (New York: Routledge, 2002), 5–14.

10. On the complex relationship between the counterculture and the marketplace, see David Farber, "The Intoxicated State/Illegal Nation," in Braunstein and Doyle, *Imagine Nation,* 17–40. Farber offers the most nuanced and sophisticated reading of the counterculture/culture relationship—an excellent essay.

11. There is an ocean of writing from the mid-1990s forward on the computer revolution and the politics it grew out of and spawned. Much of this writing looks at the politics that lurked beneath the technology. Particularly useful for this essay were Stewart Brand, *The Media Lab: Inventing the Future at MIT* (New York: Viking, 1987); Bruce Sterling, *The Hacker Crackdown: Law and Disorder on the Electronic Frontier* (New York: Bantam, 1993); Steven Levy, *Insanely Great: The Life and Times of Macintosh, the Computer That Changed Everything* (New York: Viking, 1994); Stewart Brand, "We Owe It All to the Hippies," *Time,* March 1, 1995, 96.

12. Edward Abbey, *The Monkey Wrench Gang* (New York: Perennial Classics, 2000); Robert A. Heinlein, *The Moon Is a Harsh Mistress* (New York: Orb, 1997). First published in 1965 as novella in the magazine *The Worlds of If,* Heinlein's vision of a libertarian revolution on the new frontier of the moon became an instant classic that influenced a generation.

13. Stewart Brand, phone interview by author, 9 September 2004.

14. Steven Levy, *Hackers: Heroes of the Computer Revolution* (New York: Penguin Books, 1994).

15. Sim Van Der Ryn and Stewart Cohen, *Ecological Design* (Washington, D.C.: Island Press, 1996); Chris Zelof, ed., *Design Outlaws on the Ecological Frontier* (Easton, Pa.: Knossus, 2000); and David Orr, *The Nature of Design: Ecology, Culture, and Human Intention* (New York: Oxford University Press, 2002).

16. Patricia Nelson Limerick, *The Legacy of Conquest: The Unbroken Past of the American West* (New York: W. W. Norton, 1988), 94.

17. Ernest Callenbach, *Ecotopia* (New York: Bantam, 1977).

18. Compare Callenbach's *Ecotopia* to Edward Bellamy's *Looking Backward: 2000–1887* (1888; repr., New York: Signet Classics, 2000). Both books spend more time on the reconciliation of consumerism and politics than on any other single issue.

19. I do not want to imply that Callenbach was a consumer sellout, just that an important part of his philosophy included an attempt to move his readers toward a new type of socially and environmentally sensitive consumerism. In his *Living Cheaply with Style: Live Better and Spend Less*, 2nd ed. (San Francisco: Ronin Publishing, 2000), he goes to great lengths to discourage consumerism and present alternative ways to "live better" without being a slave to consumerism.

20. Here too there are many similarities with other utopian writers, Bellamy and Upton Sinclair in particular. Both of these utopian authors presented a case for socialism that was embraced by very few, whereas the consumer issues they discussed as a vehicle to present the socialism provided compelling food for thought and a cause for action for millions.

21. Stewart Brand, "We Are as Gods," in "Thirtieth Anniversary Celebration: *Whole Earth Catalog*," special issue, *Whole Earth Review* (San Rafael, Calif.: Point Foundation) 95 (Winter 1998): 3. This folio issue, edited by Peter Warshall, contains a complete reprint of the first edition of the 1968 catalog and a large section of essays written in 1998 reflecting on issues and themes explored in the various *Whole Earth* catalogs over the years.

22. Paul Kleppner, "Politics without Parties: The Western States, 1900–1984," in *The Twentieth-Century West: Historical Interpretations*, ed. Gerald D. Nash and Richard W. Etulain (Albuquerque: University of New Mexico Press, 1989), 295–338; Michael P. Malone and F. Ross Peterson, "Politics and Protest," in *The Oxford History of the American West*, ed. Clyde A. Milner, Carol A. O'Connor, and Martha A. Sandweiss (New York: Oxford University Press, 1994), 501–533. See also Richard D. Lamm and Michael McCarthy, *The Angry West: A Vulnerable Land and Its Future* (Boston: Houghton Mifflin, 1982).

23. Anne M. Butler, "Selling the Popular Myth," in Milner, O'Connor, and Sandweiss, *Oxford History of the American West*, 784.

24. Trends in appropriate technology are explored in Carroll Pursell, *The Machine in America: A Social History of Technology* (Baltimore: The Johns Hopkins University Press, 1995) and "The Rise and Fall of the Appropriate Technology Movement in the United States, 1965–1985," *Technology and Culture* 34 (1993): 629–637. For another view, see Thomas P. Hughes, *American Genesis: A Century of Invention and Technological Enthusiasm, 1870–1970* (New York: Penguin Books, 1989). "Key alternative technology" concepts were popularized by Ernest Callenbach's novel *Ecotopia*. The relation-

ship between environmentalism and technology is specifically explored in Jeffrey K. Stine and Joel A. Tarr, "At the Intersection of Histories: Technology and the Environment," *Technology and Culture* 39, no. 4 (1998): 601–640. For two classic and influential perspectives on the subject, see Barry Commoner, *The Closing Circle: Nature, Man, and Technology* (New York: Alfred A. Knopf, 1971), and E. F. Schumacher, *Small Is Beautiful: Economics as if People Mattered* (New York: Harper & Row, 1973). The best of the more recent work in this area is William McDonough and Michael Braungart, *Cradle to Cradle: Remaking the Way We Make Things* (New York: North Point Press, 2002). The *Whole Earth Catalog* had many incarnations. The most useful single issue is the "Thirtieth Anniversary Celebration: *Whole Earth Catalog*." A very good and more recent overview of appropriate technology and politics is Jordan Benson Kleiman, "The Appropriate Technology Movement in American Political Culture" (Ph.D. diss., University of Rochester, 2000).

25. Outdoor Industry Foundation and Pew Charitable Trusts, "Outdoor Recreation Participation and Spending Study: A State-by-State Perspective" (Outdoor Industry Foundation and Pew Charitable Trusts study, 2002). For more information, see the Outdoor Industry Foundation's Web site at: http://www.outdoorindustry.org/media.oia.php?news_id=71&sort_year=2003.

26. Theodore Roszak, *From Satori to Silicon Valley: San Francisco and the American Counterculture* (San Francisco: Don't Call It Frisco Press, 1986). Frederick Turner, *From Counterculture to Cyberculture: Stewart Brand, the Whole Earth Network, and the Rise of Digital Utopianism* (Chicago: University of Chicago Press, 2006). John Markoff, *What the Dormouse Said: How the 60s Counterculture Shaped the Personal Computer Industry* (New York: Viking, 2005).

27. David Brooks, *BoBos in Paradise: The New Upper Class and How They Got There* (New York: Touchstone, 2000).

28. For a compelling look at the complexities of 1960s political identity and particularly the intersections of liberalism and conservatism among the counterculture generation, see Rebecca E. Klatch, *A Generation Divided: The New Left, the New Right, and the 1960s* (Berkeley and Los Angeles: University of California Press, 1999). Klatch argues against the "sell out" view of 60s political activists who moved away from political activism and toward traditional careers in business and industry. Mirroring the writings of those, like Brand, who lived through it, she argues that the politically active youth of the sixties took their ideologies with them to the market place.

29. For a subtle and detailed analysis of the relationship between the business world and counterculture, see Thomas Frank, *The Conquest of Cool: Business Culture, Counterculture, and the Rise of Hip Consumerism* (Chicago: University of Chicago Press, 1997). Also of interest is Joseph Heath and Andrew Potter, *Nation of Rebels: Why Counterculture Became Consumer Culture* (New York: Harper Business, 2005). Ken Goffman and Dan Joy, in *Counterculture through the Ages: From Abraham to Acid House* (New York: Villard, 2004), provide a very broad overview with thoughts on consumption along the way. Also indispensable is Sam Binkley, "Consuming Aquarius: Markets and the Moral Boundaries of the New Class, 1968–1980" (Ph.D. diss., New School University, November 2001).

30. Brand, "WE OWE IT ALL TO THE HIPPIES," 12.

31. Ibid., 12.

32. Paul Hawken, Amory Lovins, and L. Hunter Lovins, *Natural Capitalism: Creating the Next Industrial Revolution* (Boston: Little, Brown, 1999); Paul Hawken, *The Ecology of Commerce: A Declaration of Sustainability* (New York: HarperCollins, 1993) and *Growing a Business* (New York: Simon & Schuster, 1987); *Growing a Business* is the companion volume to Hawken's seventeen-part PBS series. See also, McDonough and Braungart, *Cradle to Cradle*.

33. Brand interview; ibid.

34. The first edition was published in 1968 as *The Whole Earth Catalog: Access to Tools*, edited by Stewart Brand and published by the Portola Institute with distribution provided by Random House. Several revised versions, all with Brand as the lead editor, followed between 1969 and 1971, when *The Last Whole Earth Catalog* (Menlo Park, Calif.: Portola; New York: Random House, 1971) appeared. *The Last Whole Earth Catalog* won the prestigious National Book Award in 1972. All of the *Whole Earth* catalogs were reprinted many times, and often there were seasonal editions. Between 1972 and 1999 there were several notable editions. See, especially, Stewart Brand, ed., *The Next Whole Earth Catalog: Access to Tools* (San Rafael, Calif.: Pont Foundation, 1980; distributed by Rand McNally in the United States and Random House in Canada). This particular edition is notable for its shear size, 608 oversized pages, and breadth of coverage. There were also several *Whole Earth*–type companion volumes, such as J. Baldwin and Stewart Brand, eds., *Soft-Tech* (New York: Penguin Books, 1978), that focused on particular issues. Brand relinquished the editorship in the 1980s, and several editors have since shepherded the perennially popular publication through several more editions. Most notable among these are Howard Rheingold, ed., *The Millennium Whole Earth Catalog* (San Francisco: Harper San Francisco, 1994); Warshall, "Thirtieth Anniversary Celebration: *Whole Earth Catalog*"; Kevin Kelly, ed., *Signal: Communication Tools for the Information Age. A Whole Earth Catalog* (New York: Harmony Books, 1988).

35. Langdon Winner, "Building a Better Mousetrap: Appropriate Technology as a Social Movement," in *Appropriate Technology and Social Values: A Critical Appraisal*, ed. Franklin A. Long and Alexandra Oleson (Cambridge, Mass.: Ballinger, 1980), 33.

36. John A. Garraty, *The Columbia History of the World* (New York: Columbia University Press, 1990).

37. For more on Brand's larger philosophy, see his published works. Although on very different subjects, together they show some clear links between his early and his recent work on these issues. Brand, *Media Lab; How Buildings Learn: What Happens after They're Built* (New York: Penguin Books, 1994); and *The Clock of the Long Now: Time and Responsibility* (New York: Basic Books, 1999).

38. Daniel Bell, *The Cultural Contradictions of Capitalism* (New York: Basic Books, 1996). In this landmark book on the twisted relationship between capitalism and modernism, Bell dismisses the counterculture as a "children's crusade" that sought to "eliminate the line between fantasy and reality" (xxvi–xxvii). Oddly, in an otherwise provocative and well-thought-out book that seeks to reveal the complex contra-

dictions inherent in American culture, Bell reduces the counterculture to a monolithic and meaningless rehash of old bohemian ideas.

39. Neil Maher, "Shooting the Moon," *Environmental History* 9, no. 3 (July 2004): 526–531.

40. Brand interview. The Whole Earth philosophy of money is spelled out clearly in the records of the nonprofit Point Foundation created to distribute the profits from the catalogs. Point Foundation Records, M1441, Department of Special Collections, Stanford University Libraries, Stanford, California.

41. Barbara Ward, *Spaceship Earth: The Impact of Science on Society* (New York: Columbia University Press, 1966).

42. Brand, *Last Whole Earth Catalog*, 439. This version of the catalog contains Brand's version of *Whole Earth*'s genesis and evolution, along with a wonderful discussion of money and capitalism. The history continues in the *Whole Earth Epilog*, ed. Stewart Brand (Point Foundation, September 1974), 752–753. See also Stewart Brand biographical materials, Whole Earth Catalog Records, M1045, Department of Special Collections, Stanford University Libraries, Stanford, California.

43. Brand, "We Are as Gods," 3.

44. To satisfy readers looking for cultural, spiritual, and political fare, Brand launched the *Whole Earth Supplements*. The first, and most notable, of these was edited by Brand's friend Ken Kesey and focused on such subjects as politics, religion, art, and poetry.

45. Brand, *Last Whole Earth Catalog*, 112.

46. Ibid., 429.

47. Brand, "We Are as Gods," 3.

48. For more detail on counterculture views on technology, see Andrew Kirk, "Machines of Loving Grace: Alternative Technology, Environment, and the Counterculture," in Braunstein and Doyle, *Imagine Nation*, 353–378.

49. Theodore Roszak, *The Making of the Counter Culture: Reflections on the Technocratic Society and Its Youthful Opposition* (New York: Doubleday, 1968); ibid., 8.

50. Jacques Ellul, *The Technological Society*, trans. Joachim Neugroschel (New York: Continuum, 1980); Herbert Marcuse, *One Dimensional Man: Studies in the Ideology of Advanced Industrial Society* (Boston: Beacon Press, 1964).

51. Charles A. Reich, *The Greening of America: How the Youth Revolution Is Trying to Make America Livable* (New York: Random House, 1970).

52. The literature on business and the environment is vast. See Hawken, Lovins, and Lovins, *Natural Capitalism*; Hawken, *Ecology of Commerce* and *Growing a Business*; *Harvard Business Review on Business and the Environment* (Cambridge, Mass.: Harvard Business School Press, 2000); Hamish Pringle and Marjorie Thompson, *Brand Spirit: How Cause Related Marketing Builds Brands* (Chichester, U.K.: John Wiley & Sons, 1999); Sue Adkins, *Cause Related Marketing: Who Cares Wins* (Oxford: Butterworth Heinemann, 1999); John Elkington, *Cannibals with Forks: The Triple Bottom Line of 21st Century Business* (Gabriola Island, B.C.: New Society Publishers, 1998); Andrew Crane, *Marketing, Morality, and the Natural Environment* (New York: Routledge, 2000); Alasdair Blair and David Hitchcock, *Environment and Business* (New York: Routledge,

2001); Jacquelyn A. Ottman, *Green Marketing: Opportunity for Innovation* (Chicago: NTC Business Books, 1998); Carl Frankel, *In Earth's Company: Business, Environment, and the Challenge of Sustainability* (Gabriola Island, B.C.: New Society Publishers, 1998).

53. There is lots of wonderful writing about this history of rock climbing and outdoor sports from the 1940s to the 1990s. Especially important for those interested in the critical period of innovation in Camp 4 (the legendary climbers' hangout in Yosemite) is Steve Roper, *Camp 4: Recollections of a Yosemite Rockclimber* (Seattle: Mountaineers Books, 1994). See also Gary Arce, *Defying Gravity: High Adventure on Yosemite's Walls* (Berkeley, Calif.: Wilderness Press, 1996); Chris Jones, *Climbing in North America* (Berkeley and Los Angeles: University of California Press, 1976); Paul Piana, *Big Walls: Breakthroughs on the Free-Climbing Frontier* (San Francisco: Sierra Club Books, 1997); Doug Scott, *Big Wall Climbing: Development, Techniques, and Aids* (New York: Oxford University Press, 1981); Ed Bennett, "The Bay Chapter and the Birth of Modern Rock Climbing," Sierra Club Rock Climbing section of the *San Francisco Bay Yodeler*, June 1999; Jim Bridwell, "Brave New World," *Mountain* 31 (1973); Layton Kor, *Beyond the Vertical* (Boulder, Colo.: Alpine House, 1983); Chouinard, *Let My People Go Surfing*.

54. Hawken, *Growing a Business*, 61–63.

55. Steve Roper to author, personal communication, 13 January 2004.

56. Yvon Chouinard and Tom Frost, "A Word," *Chouinard Equipment Catalog*, October 1974: 2.

57. Kirk, "Machines of Loving Grace," 353–378; Hawken, Lovins, and Lovins, *Natural Capitalism*.

58. Bell, *Cultural Contradictions of Capitalism*.

59. Brand, *Last Whole Earth Catalog*, 438; ibid.

60. Brooks, *BoBos in Paradise*, 41.

61. Brand's work as Brown's adviser and the intellectuals and ideas he brought into the governor's office are discussed in Stewart Brand, "The New Class: Herman Kahn, Governor Jerry Brown, Amory Lovins," in *News That Stayed News: Ten Years of CoEvolution Quarterly*, ed. Art Kleiner and Stewart Brand (San Francisco: North Point Press, 1986), 89–112, and Art Kleiner, *The Age of the Heretics: Heroes, Outlaws, and the Forerunners of Corporate Change* (New York: Doubleday, 1996).

62. Brand interview.

63. John Perry Barlow, interview by Aaron Davis, "John Perry Barlow: Wyoming's Estimated Prophet," *Planet Jackson Hole Online*, 28 July 2005, http://www.planetjh.com/news/A_100072.aspx.

64. Doherty interview with Barlow, *Reasononline*.

65. Barlow, phone interview by author.

66. Brand interview.

67. Jay Kinney, "Beyond Left and Right," *Whole Earth* 101 (Summer 2000): 22–29.

68. A. Walton Litz and Christopher MacGowan, eds., *The Collected Poems of William Carlos Williams*, Vol. 1: 1909–1939 (New York: New Directions Books, 1986), 217.

CHAPTER 11

The Call in the Wild: Nature, Technology, and Environmental Politics

John P. Herron

The increasingly common headlines are almost always the same: "Lost hiker discovered after cell-phone call."[1] From Mount Rainer in Washington to Mount Wilson in California to Mount Harvard in Colorado, rescue teams are searching for wayward natural travelers by way of cellular phone and global-positioning satellite. The accompanying stories have also assumed newsprint uniformity: "Local sheriff finds dehydrated climber (or lost Boy Scout troop or misguided European vacationer or suburban mother of three) wandering in nearby wilderness area." The individual facts of the stories are insignificant. In this lost-and-found drama, locales and participants are neatly interchangeable. More interesting is that cell phones are now as common on nature expeditions as backpacks and sleeping bags. The presence of cell phones in nature may appear trivial. At best, it is further evidence of modernity's continuing saturation of experience. But examined seriously, their arrival suggests a change in American attitudes toward nature, the role of technology, and, most significant, the direction of regional environmental politics.

That Americans would bring their phones into the wild is hardly surprising. According to the Computer Industry Almanac, a Chicago-based market research firm, more than 180 million Americans used cellular phones in 2002. Data from the U.S. Census confirms that between 1995 and 2003, cell phone usage surged more than 300 percent. Given current rates of market expansion, we can expect 95 percent of Americans to own cell phones by 2010.[2] The endless sound of ringing cell phones has become the musical score to everyday life in our homes, businesses, restaurants, and even our forests, parks, and wilderness areas. The embrace of this technology reveals that Americans are reconciling nature and society in new ways. Yesterday, an uneasy alliance between technology and society created a bifurcated approach to the environment marked by both reverence and fear. Today, technology is so ubiquitous as to appear almost natural.

Historically, Americans rarely doubted that technology could manage nature's vagaries, and they embraced industrial technology with religious fervor. From the first swing of the English ax to the genetic alteration of foodstuffs, technology transformed nature from what many saw as a static environment into a world of continuous change where technical progress assured economic growth.[3] Such a belief sits at the foundation of American culture; the master narrative of this nation's history is continual development through the technological improvement of the natural world.[4] In an age of technological enthusiasm, citizens derived a common feeling of awe from the large-scale application of technology within nature, even when these applications came with environmental costs. Historian David Nye labeled the preoccupation with the machine the "technological sublime." In an often-cited example, Nye describes the way Americans celebrated the dirt and noise of the nineteenth-century industrial landscape, "with its cavernous factories draped in smoke," not only as a sign of economic health but also as confirmation of their new powers of environmental transformation.[5]

Life in modern America, however, added new dimensions to the technological sublime. In contemporary society, it is difficult to find an aware citizen who does not regard the smoke from the factory with distaste. Complex counternarratives abound from those Americans for whom disruption, not progress, was the result of their contact with technology. But for as much as the by-products of technological growth cause alarm, few question the underlying principle of remodeling the environment to suit human tastes.[6] Cell phones do not belch dark clouds of smoke, but like other forms of technology, they do have an impact on our environment. They can alter our sense of space and question our modernist definition of what counts as natural. Cell phones can also serve contrasting ends. By connecting distant outposts, they can strengthen community bonds, just as they can accentuate individuality by breaking the technological limits that anchor us to the local. And for our purposes, a cell phone in nature can also short-circuit traditional environmental stories. Rooted in particular places, most narratives of environmental action attempt to understand how people are linked to their landscape. Introduce technology into these stories, and the narrative culminates in a high-modern moment—the construction of a dam, the arrival of big science—and the impact of new technologies on environmental health. Cell phones, however, defy easy categorization, and by illuminating the once remote, and often masked, connections between technology and nature, the cell phone, and all that it represents—personalized technology, consumption, dependence, mobility, and connectedness—brings a new sensibility to the discussion of environmental politics.

The debate over the role of the technological sublime within American life has serious implications for modern environmental politics. For more than a century, the contours of regional environmental politics were influenced by two modes of perception: one emotional, yet illusive; the other practical, yet immoral. As the pendulum of public opinion swayed back and forth, Americans repeatedly debated the proper relationship between economics, aesthetics, use, and preservation. How Americans understood and employed technology shaped this political conversation as well as the understanding of nature's role within society. The result was a market-driven political course that drifted between stewardship and exploitation.

In the effort to understand the formation of this political dynamic, historians and environmental scholars usually choose one of two explanatory theories. The first views environmental politics as a response to an explosion in production during and after World War II. When nuclear power, agricultural chemicals, and industrial synthetics burst upon the national scene, with them came new environmental dangers. Concerned Americans responded with a political movement to protect themselves from these hazards. The second argument shifts causation to new modes of consumption. In the affluent days of the 1950s and beyond, millions of Americans had the time, resources, and inclination to focus on what are now labeled quality-of-life issues. Instead of preserving resources for efficient use or creating defenses against the excesses of industrial society, many Americans put a premium on the reinvigorating and redemptive benefits of an experience in pristine nature. As more Americans tried to find refuge in nature from modernization, the movement to protect the environment grew in political strength.[7] These twinned positions, and their multiple variations, provide much of the foundation needed to understand the motivations behind modern environmental politics. But for all their appeal and utility, these arguments are also increasingly narrow and less effective as analytical tools to understand current environmental dynamics.

In this essay, I argue that contemporary environmental politics, especially in the American West, have less to do with concerns over production or preservation than with competing theories of democracy. For all the emotive responses to nature that celebrate the sublime or even the material, ideas about nature always reflect a political consciousness. Americans have long debated the proper role of nature within human affairs, but it is the content of these debates—more than their resolution—that remains significant. Advocates for natural development correctly understood that resource use provided the wealth necessary to support American democracy, just as those pushing for natural preservation found in the physical world the source for national values and morals.

Linking nature to politics is not original. Thomas Jefferson did so 200 years ago (as did Plato a few years before that), but a political perspective must be reintegrated into environmental dialogues. The skeptical might rightly assert that environmental affairs are already fully politicized. Indeed, it is difficult to envision how environmental concerns could become more overtly political. But such claims misrepresent the role of nature in American political life. Look at just one example: our understanding of such luminary environmental figures as the nineteenth-century writer Henry David Thoreau and the twentieth-century ecologist Aldo Leopold. As charter members of the canon of environmental heroes, these men, their lives, and their legacies have been investigated in detail. And there is little debate that such work, including the inquiry into the ideological foundations of environmental thought in America, represents some of the best scholarship in the field. But less scholarly attention has been directed at examining these individuals and their positions from a political perspective.[8] For instance, most observers interpret Thoreau's retreat to Walden as a flight from overcivilization. Yet *Walden* is not only an escapist tract; it is also political criticism. Thoreau certainly looked to nature for moral instruction, but the lessons learned were intended for greater human society. Thoreau's political positions on commerce, economic utilitarianism, and the role of the state all took shape from his experiences in nature. Similarly, Leopold's conservation ideal, an ethical position that stressed the need for balance between humans and nature, also had a significant political dimension. Leopold's conservation plan emphasized proper natural-resource management not only as a means to achieve natural harmony but also as a way to create a political alternative to the American market system. As a political educator, Leopold combined his understanding of natural systems with his views on citizenship and community to create a workable form of democratic liberalism.

Thoreau and Leopold, however, are easy marks. Perhaps a more apt comparison would examine the well-known divide between naturalist John Muir and forester Gifford Pinchot. Muir's message to America was to avoid materialism and embrace the wild as a means to personal and social improvement. The Progressive Pinchot, by contrast, argued that the technical administration of natural resources would limit government corruption and ensure material prosperity for all citizens. Oversimplified as morality versus commodities, these opposing traditions took shape more than a century ago and continue to influence the direction of environmental disputes in America. We readily understand their differences, but we overlook their similarities, especially their common political foundation. Both Muir and Pinchot pushed for a political program that would protect nature's abundance and guide the interaction between humans and nature. And both shared in the goal of advancing American prosperity, protecting personal liberty, and cultivating national virtue.

In modern America, both these positions have become more sophisticated. Muir's moralism is better informed by ecology, biology, and other natural sciences, and Pinchot's utilitarianism includes respect for nature's aesthetic rewards; the result is a new narrative that pulls these once divergent positions closer together. But such accommodation has come at the cost of losing the original political dimension of their ideas.[9] When Muir's political criticism and Pinchot's commitment to public service are divorced from their natural context, we are left with an incomplete understanding of how nature contributed to American political history. Whether Americans were innocents in search of a noble agrarian dream or smallholding capitalists carving a competitive marketplace out of the physical world matters little. What does matter is the recognition that perceptions of humanity's relation to the natural world contributed to the creation of both mainstream and alternative American political traditions.

Political undercurrents inform many discussions of environmental action, yet still needed, I believe, are environmental studies that reconnect perceptions of the environment to America's political heritage. Democratic theory resists external constraint; the goal of the system is to maximize individual opportunity. Such a structure is predicated on the assumption of expanding natural abundance. Nature, however, has limits, and it is within these limits that "the context [of] human life takes place."[10] It is necessary, then, to chart a course that finds balance, not just in terms of the nation's conservation ethic but also within the scope of America's political economy. By using cell phones in nature as an entry into the complex web of relationships inherent in this modified landscape, this essay argues that to better understand environmentalism as a social force, we need to shift our attention away from deconstructing conceptualizations of nature to uncovering the linkages between our daily actions and the role of nature within American political thought.

In the West, such efforts will find especially fertile ground. As a project, environmental practices were once indelibly linked to the American West. In the region's many battles over preservation, its abundance of resources, and its strong federal presence, the West embodied the central questions of nature's impact on American life. Modern environmental concerns now transcend the bounds of region, but in the context of politics, the West still remains primary. For more than two centuries, statesmen and scholars from Jefferson to Frederick Jackson Turner and beyond put great faith in the West to anchor the nation's future within a participatory democracy. In the American mind, authenticity and individualism were coded as western, and the West was envisioned as the location to fulfill the democratic ideal. The West of myth and hope was always Edenic, the foundation of the American recovery narrative. In reality, of course, the region was never that pure. But placing the debate over technology, nature, and politics within a western space not only illuminates how Americans have apprehended nature but also engages fundamental questions about liberty, restraint, and political value.

As we might expect, the arrival of cell phones in the natural world has not come without controversy or complaint. For every voice touting the safety advantages of hiking with cell phones, there is another shouting that cellular technology poses a danger to the health and sanctity of nature. Some of this criticism is rooted in urban annoyance transferred to a natural setting. Larry Nickey, search and rescue director for Olympic National Park, remarked that he is tired of hearing the sounds of stock trades, dinner reservations, and "Guess where I am now?" conversations atop remote western peaks.[11] Others complain of a lack of outdoor social etiquette. Gary Paull, trails coordinator at Mount Baker–Snoqualmie National Forest in Washington State, spoke of his growing impatience with cell-phone use in nature. "It's just common courtesy," an exasperated Paull complained, "if you're going to [make] a phone call, go behind a tree."[12]

But other critics level more serious charges that illuminate a conflicted relationship between nature and technology. These comments help us understand how many Americans, schooled in an Enlightenment view of the sublime, apprehend the natural world that surrounds them. Writing in the *New York Times*, for example, outdoor adventurer John Markoff recounted a backcountry ski trip in the Sierra Nevada where a companion fell several hundred feet down an icy chute, breaking his back in the process. A cell-phone call brought a California Highway Patrol helicopter for an immediate evacuation. Rather than feeling relief that his friend was safe, however, Markoff reported that he hesitated before placing the emergency call and that using his cell phone "felt like cheating." What makes nature "real," he continued, "is that you have to have the skills to get yourself out of whatever predicament you've gotten yourself into." Had it been Markoff lying in the snow with a broken back, a rescue made possible by cell phone might not have seemed so troubling, yet his views, however uncompassionate, stand as representative for those Americans who define nature's authenticity in contrast to society's artifice. His reliance on a cell phone, what he termed a "wireless umbilical cord," corrupted his natural experience. More significantly, the unchecked spread of cellular technology, Markoff concluded, was evidence that nature in America "is a rapidly vanishing ideal."[13]

It is one thing to worry about the disposal of 130 million lead- and arsenic-laden cell phones that add 65,000 tons of waste to American landfills annually, or to protest the construction of another cell-phone tower, or to fear its effects on the landscape or on the millions, perhaps tens of millions, of migratory birds that, according to the Fish and Wildlife Service, die each year flying into cell towers.[14] But it is quite another to conclude that cell phones are destroying nature's idyll, especially since in most parks, wilderness areas, and remote nature sites, traditional cellular phones do not work. For instance, in North Cascades National Park outside of Seattle, one of America's most wired cities, less than 10 percent of the park's 750,000 acres are cell-phone accessible. Still, such a dramatic position is becoming increasingly popular within environmental thought.

Further exploring the theme of nature's contamination by technology, *Sierra* magazine, the print outlet of the Sierra Club, one of the largest environmental advocacy organizations in the country, asked for reader opinions on cell phones in nature. The range of responses included the expected. Cell-phone users, one Idaho reader volunteered, "have forgotten that a fundamental reason we seek out wilderness is to reconnect with nature and the wondrous parts of ourselves that these devices have so brusquely cut us off from." Another reader from California compared the serenity of nature to the calm of a house of worship and asked "would we [ever] consider . . . accepting cell calls while in church, mosque, or synagogue?" A final reader was even bolder: "If I saw someone carrying a cell phone . . . I'd say, Go Home! Take a vacation in some flashy resort. You are not suited for the wilderness."[15] The idea that cellular phone use makes the appreciation of nature difficult also finds considerable traction within the literature of environmental politics. Christina Nealson, reporter for the *High Country News*, the leading environmental newspaper in the American West, put that sentiment in print. "I go into wilderness to leave linear time behind," she wrote. "I also leave behind the world of instant access, where phones, e-mail, cars and airplanes provide fast contact with anyone in the world. It is a step from the planned, organized, domesticated world into the realm of the unexpected. . . . a cell phone changes all of this." Cell phones "fill solitude with instant access to the technological world" and, Nealson concluded, change nature "as much as forbidden roads and chainsaws."[16]

Put aside the likelihood that these comments come from adventurers wearing Gore-Tex jackets, biomechanically designed hiking boots, and Global Positioning System receivers on their wrists. Such opinions are evidence that despite the best efforts of environmental scholars to illustrate the connections between humans and the natural environment, many Americans continue to view nature as a pristine place apart from the stain of humanity. The basic outline of this position is well-known. Whereas civilization is corrupt, nature is unspoiled. Whereas the values of civilization are based on development, nature is the depository of virtue. According to this antimodernist understanding of the global environment—itself a product of participation in modern life—human action, intentional or otherwise, is often destructive, technology is a tool for exploitation, and nature, if only left undisturbed, would exist in balance and harmony.[17]

Such ideas draw on a long history of western thought and action. When Europeans arrived in America, they found in nature both paradise and wildness. The theological maxims of the founders dictated that nature be purged of evil influences. At the same moment, economic necessities drove these same early Americans to use all technical means to squeeze the natural environment for its bounty. In the eighteenth century, as scholars such as Perry Miller, Richard Slotkin, and Henry Nash Smith have suggested, Americans shifted their religious gaze and placed God inside, rather than outside, nature. During this American Enlightenment, as nature remained a source of wealth, it also became a site of spiritual renewal.[18] The tension between these two positions—nature as product and nature as pristine—explains much of the nation's political development. By defining the accepted uses of property, relations between the individual and the state, and the role of commodities and exchange, the American understanding of nature as material shaped the politics and culture of capitalism.[19] Americans acknowledge nature as a cultural force in literature, romance, and mythology but often underestimate the equally significant role of nature in American political formation. Despite the founders' belief in the virtue of small republics, most Americans saw a future based on economic growth. With the resources available to make growth possible, western nature was privileged as the location of that increase. As the nation prepared to unfold itself onto the lands of the distant West, it would also attempt to institutionalize and formalize the relationship between nature and culture. Given the special place reserved for nature, such antagonism between the natural world and intrusive technology—from the mill to the locomotive to the cell phone—is not unusual. In the American mind, the enduring perception is that nature and technology have been frequent foes.

The best examination of this duality in American life is still Leo Marx's *Machine in the Garden* (1964). Marx argued that for much of their history,

Americans embraced pastoral nature as their ideal. As inheritors of a long tradition that snaked through Virgil's Italy and Elizabeth's England, Americans took Old World images of New World nature and created a national identity based on their place as tenders of the utopian garden. From politics to literature, these Americans constructed their vision of society from nature's cues. As long as the nation remained preindustrial, such an Edenic vision of natural harmony survived in the American mind. By the middle of the nineteenth century, however, industrialization, immigration, and urbanization—to cite the holy trinity of change—had fundamentally altered the landscape. In their reaction to this transformation, some Americans insisted, even in the face of escalating technological growth, that the nation could remain preindustrial; others jettisoned their earlier faith in pastoralism. But it is a third approach that Marx finds most compelling. The majority of the nation, he argued, redefined their understanding of nature to meet changing industrial circumstances. In the process they created a "middle landscape," an industrial version of the pastoral ideal that made room for the machine within the garden. In this transformed environment, nature was modified, but not obliterated.[20] The machine brought order to the physical world. Americans defined the landscape as a fusion of different impulses to create a Jeffersonian-style republic free from the ills of European industrial blight.

By the conclusion of the Civil War, however, rapid industrialization had made this accommodation a fading dream. Even as many in American life celebrated the arrival of new technologies as evidence of manifest destiny and progress, other prominent Americans bemoaned the loss of the garden fable so critical to political mythology. Marx investigated the lingering contradictions embedded in this understanding of the environment to illustrate the continuing pervasiveness of nature in American society. Debates about technology and society maintain a special resonance within environmental politics because, as Marx explained, "the machine's sudden entrance into the garden presents a problem that ultimately belongs not to art but to politics." It is, Marx concluded, "the great issue of our culture."[21]

Marx's thesis is not without its critics, but his argument that in its symbols and vocabulary the American political tradition is anchored in pastoral nostalgia, agrarian dreams, and wilderness regeneration has special appeal within environmental thinking. From founding figures like Benjamin Franklin and Alexander Hamilton to literary icons such as Herman Melville's Ishmael and James Fenimore Cooper's Leatherstocking to social commentators like Daniel Boorstin and Richard Hofstadter, we find evidence that Americans locate a unifying significance in the natural world. Whether to distinguish American democracy from European feudalism or natural rights from law, nature has become the nation's political covenant.[22]

Return then to the cell-phone invasion. When we broaden our examination of the impact of this technology on nature, we find a range of political perspectives from the right as well as the left. Despite the best efforts of some park officials to restrict cell-phone use and the desire of many environmentalists to minimize technological intrusion, the fight to keep cell phones out of nature is a losing battle. And not just because cell phones, like kudzu, have invaded every corner of American society, but because a new generation of nature travelers *want* their cell phones in the wild. In a recent survey of equipment needs for nature trips, for example, readers of *Backpacker* magazine put cellular phones near the top of the list.[23]

The debate over cell phones in nature is, of course, one part of a much larger discussion. Placed within the context of modern environmental politics, however, it illuminates the significant tensions inherent within the environmental movement. For several decades, environmental scholars investigated the multifaceted nature of environmental political activity in American history. The majority of these studies conclude that environmental politics—although often lacking a unified platform—remain a provocative element of the American social dynamic.[24] In a short time, environmental politics moved from fringe to mainstream and achieved remarkable results in the process. Need proof? Look around. Vigilant Americans of all ages are constantly on the lookout for human-made threats to the environment. Air quality in cities is improving, protection of limited resources is commonplace, and you couldn't start a fire on the Cuyahoga River if you tried. Environmental advocates promoted this activity as a counter to the ills and abuses of technology. Considered part of the effort to return nature to its natural and balanced state, environmental politics found common cause in a shared desire to ensure that nature's benefits were protected for the enjoyment of future generations of American society. Such a position illustrates one of the paradoxes about environmental politics: They promote a forward-looking reform effort that attempts to preserve a vision of the natural world that exists largely in backward-looking nostalgia. But as political theorist Wilson Carey McWilliams noted, in language and practice, environmental politics are "intensely contemporary." The main thrust of environmental politics, he continued, is driven not by romance but "by the dynamics of technology and global economics."[25] McWilliams's brief definition of environmental politics is well structured, yet as the comments of those wishing to keep their natural experience cell phone–free suggest, modern environmental politics are affected less by macroeconomics than by a wistful desire to save unspoiled nature.

That such a position would become so dominant is not unexpected. Within the history of environmentalism, antimodernists abound. Many important environmental figures of the last two centuries were critical of America's faith in machine technology. And rightfully so, for industrial technology contributed much to the declining stability of the environment. Yet despite steady and consistent warnings to the contrary, many more Americans believe that technology will solve the unforeseen problems of the future. If oil reserves run low or if essential materials become scarce, inventive American scientists, these optimists believe, will find a solution to the crisis. Finding a fantasy technical fix has become an all-too-common element of the environmental dialogue.[26] By contrast—and further complicating this dynamic—being antitechnology was never a prerequisite for membership in green political circles. A cast of leading players from Thoreau to Rachel Carson tried to rein in the excesses of modernism but were hardly antitechnology. But in modern America even these muddy divisions no longer seem appropriate, as it is increasingly possible to bridge the once large gap that separated technology from nature, even when such a marriage leads to unexpected offspring. In recent years, the ever-strengthening bond between technology and nature created hybrid positions that have altered the shape of the political debate.

One such transitional position is illustrated in the concept of a "cell-phone naturalist," a term coined by Julia Redpath Buckley, a correspondent and producer for National Public Radio. Symbolic of the merge between all things natural and technical, Buckley's cell-phone naturalist is at once protechnology, procapitalism, and proenvironment. Such a combination was once thought to be as anachronistic as a present-day William Jennings Bryan—a political leftist and an evangelical Christian. Or to put it in current political speak, someone with red-state values and a blue-state voting record.[27] In the first years of the twenty-first century, the arrival of the cell-phone naturalist has supercharged the debates of environmental politics.

Conservative politicians, for example, have focused on the contradictory influences inherent in the idea of a cell-phone naturalist to advance an agenda of resource use. In a speech delivered before the Alaska Resources Development Council in 2002, for instance, Deputy Secretary of the Interior J. Steven Giles provided a sketch of this new kind of modern environmentalist:

> He [wears] a parka with double-rip-stop nylon supplemented with ceramic particles and polyurethane coat-welded seams. The rest of his clothing includes various pieces made from micro filaments [and] micro fleece. . . . He is carrying a cell phone . . . and using a laptop to stay connected to the internet. [His] canoe . . . is made from DuPont's

patented Kevlar. All of this goes into or on top of the largest sturdiest sports utility vehicle he can find. [He] sees no contradiction in terms of the products he uses that are made from petroleum products and mined ores and his cause against the source of those products.... the more energy he uses with his high-tech gadgets, the more we need.

"I have this reoccurring nightmare," Giles continued, that cell-phone naturalists will have "complete success in stopping all energy and resource development," we will lose all access to technology, and, he concluded, Americans everywhere will be "reduced to items of clothing made from cotton or wool."[28]

God forbid Giles's nightmare comes true and we abandon spandex. Giles, not surprisingly, proves an ideal foil for environmentalists. In addition to his Chicken Little approach to environmentalism, he often makes wacky James G. Watt–style pronouncements about public lands while privately maintaining a close relationship with the oil and gas lobby. But the concept of the cell-phone naturalist he outlined is not so easily dismissed. The phrase, now a popular tag line in political dialogue, has appeared in everything from debates on the floor of the U.S. Senate to publications as diverse as the *Weekly Standard* and the *Utne Reader*.[29]

Within this environment, the political Right has grabbed the cell-phone naturalist with both hands. To the unsympathetic, the cell-phone naturalist is proof that environmental politics in America are driven by elitists unable to recognize the irony of their hypertechnological lives. In an effort to promote development, conservative politicians trot out the image of the cell-phone naturalist as a way to shrink the distance between the cartoon portrayals of the greedy developer and the romantic environmentalist.[30] The Left too has used the cell-phone naturalist not to demonstrate the Left's own duplicity but to illustrate the inability of big business and federal regulatory agencies to grasp the stakes and structures at play in American environmental politics.

Beyond this rhetoric, however, the cell-phone naturalist stands as an effective metaphor with which to view the changing dynamic of environmental politics. I hesitate to embrace the cell-phone naturalist as an investigative tool because the term has increasingly been used pejoratively by conservatives against their opponents, yet it does enable us to reposition our understanding of contemporary environmentalism. In most standard histories, environmental politics are portrayed as a long debate on the merits of various natural management policies. The narrative begins in the 1890s and its lead characters—from Theodore Roosevelt and Gifford Pinchot to Lewis Mumford and Robert Marshall to David Brower and Terry Tempest

Williams—engage in debates over the proper relationship between consumption and preservation of the natural world. Science and religion, ethics and economics, and natural rights and democratic theory all take turns influencing the tone and direction of America's environmental dialogue. Much of this deliberation was interpreted as a referendum on purity. Political actions that conserve nature slid to one side of the scale of virtue, while positions that advance development or include a technological imperative moved to the other. In the public mind, perhaps even in the view of the self-identified environmentalist, environmental activity in the postwar West was a struggle to preserve nature from development and urban growth, especially the ever-dwindling locations of wild nature. In this high-stakes battle, right-thinking nature advocates were pitted against wrongheaded corporate interests in a fight for control of the environment and the nation's moral compass.

Such a dichotomous approach to understanding environmental debates is not without standing, but environmental politics in the West were never so bipolar or clean-cut.[31] The perception that nature and technology are locked in political battle will never disappear, but the arrival of the cell-phone naturalist suggests that this dichotomy is losing relevance. After all, the cellular phone is more than the latest machine to enter the garden. The cell-phone naturalist, and its associated implications, situates environmental politics directly within the bounds of the middle landscape. And by so doing, the cell-phone naturalist transforms our examination of environmental politics from an obsession with the reverential to a workable reconciliation with the accelerating forces of modern industrial life.

Few question the transformative power of technology on nature. And the reaction to cell phones in the wild repeats a plotline found often in postwar environmental debates. New innovations, once celebrated as technical marvels, become environmental liabilities. The classic example is DDT. With the ability to eliminate lice and mosquitoes, and therefore typhus and malaria, DDT was credited with saving the lives of thousands of soldiers as well as tens of thousands of civilians during World War II. The importance of DDT was confirmed in 1948 when Swiss scientist Paul Müller was awarded a Nobel Prize for Physiology or Medicine for his research with the powerful insecticide. Working from the "If a little is good, then more is better" mantra, American chemical manufacturers heavily promoted DDT for civilian and agricultural use until its extensive application led to an ecological catastrophe. Cell phones, as I have already suggested, are not DDT. Nor are they as disruptive as bulldozers, roaring locomotives, or even, despite the *High Country News* report, chainsaws. But new technologies always create new forms of politics, and the cell phone in nature deserves more attention if only to expand the traditional parameters of the debates that mark and define modern environmental politics within the region.

Critics of the cell-phone naturalist charge that environmentalists are oblivious of the consequences—unintended or otherwise—that the introduction of technology has on the environment and that their politics adhere to an ethical standard not supported by their actions. But such an attack is off center, because by taking a cell phone into nature, these travelers are also building connections between technology, nature, and the lived experiences of natural interaction. A cell phone in the wild simultaneously marks one's personal independence and one's communal dependence. Despite the openness of the American West, few of its landscapes are free from anthropocentric markers; rather than artificially separating these spaces, environmental politics need to make the accommodation of nature and culture a priority. Situating human meanings within the natural world will challenge assumptions about the boundaries that traditionally divided the human and nonhuman worlds and will give value to peopled places. If the politics of nature in America are to recognize that the natural environment is as much a cultural place as it is a natural space, then we must shift our attention away from the established debates around conservation and preservation and toward a recognition that environmental politics reflect how Americans imagine social relationships and cultural institutions.[32] An approach that blends technology and the environment rejects the traditional view that claims recovery and redemption come through nature and finds a replacement in the belief that humans belong to nature.[33] Not all the criticism of the cell-phone naturalist is shortsighted, as the arrival of technology has costs. And it would be a mistake for the modern machine to become a replacement for the garden, but if regional environmentalism is to find a place at the grown-up table of American politics, its practitioners must find a way to reconcile the competing claims of the party of nature and the party of technology in a postindustrial age.

This desire to blend environmental politics with a lived history is not new. More than a decade ago, environmental historian William Cronon published "The Trouble with Wilderness," an essay that sparked both applause and condemnation from its readers.[34] At the head of the debate was Cronon's declaration that the concept of nature is not as natural as people think. Nature is often assumed to be a certainty, clear, uncontested, and pure. Yet the way Americans act, think, and write about nature is deeply entangled with human values and ideals. More important, Cronon criticized the romanticism and primitivism within American thought that privileged select wilderness areas over the broader nature where most Americans lived and worked. The problem with wilderness, then, was that as sacred space it demanded special protection. At the end of the twentieth century, the American environmental movement committed itself to the defense of a limited nature largely free of human presence, excepting those few with the means to find refuge in distant wilderness. The danger of a wilderness-first approach to conservation, Cronon argued, was that it detracted environmentalism away from its true mission: developing a sustainable economy and improving the health of America's everyday nature. Critics charged that Cronon's essay—which forced environmentalists to defend their philosophy against charges of hypocrisy and elitism—exposed the environmental movement to political attacks. That claim is at least partially true, for his essay appeared at a time of resurging political conservatism in America. But more significant is that the reaction to Cronon's essay revealed how reluctant many environmentalists and environmental politicians were to bring cultural landscapes into play for environmental politics. Despite mounting academic work that suggests otherwise, popular conceptions of nature continue to reflect the belief that the nature that matters most is, to invoke an overworked phrase, "out there." The devotion to a favored landscape that exists apart from American society is naive, but it is perhaps more understandable given the continuing pervasiveness of the antitechnology position that exists within much of environment politics.

Yet the links between nature, technology, and environmental politics have always been complex in American history. At the beginning of the twentieth century, as Samuel Hays demonstrated, technological enthusiasm was an integral part of environmental politics. Seen as a counter to the destructiveness and waste of previous management techniques, well-applied technology became a solution to America's declining natural resources.[35] In the 1930s, a decade-long effort to reverse economic and natural misfortune thrust millions of Americans into nature. Programs such as the Civilian Conservation Corps (CCC) and the Tennessee Valley Authority (TVA) and agencies like the Soil Conservation Service and the Bureau of Land Management (BLM) addressed national needs through environmental means. The low-tech work projects of the CCC became a focal point of recovery efforts, but it was the high-tech intervention of the TVA, the BLM, and the U.S. Army Corps of Engineers that most dramatically demonstrated the impact that managed nature could have on American life.

In the 1940s, as the demands of war accelerated resource use, Americans exhibited an unflagging faith in the power of technology to revolutionize social affairs, including their relationship to nature. When the war ended and the atomic age began, an awareness of the costs of technological development became more prominent within American society. Checking the impact of technology to protect threatened nature became politically viable, and environmental politics were enmeshed in a larger campaign for social health. Over the next four decades, and punctuated by efforts to restrict technological excess such as the clean air and water mandates, American environmental politics matured into a moral crusade.

This brief overview treads familiar ground. Born of the same conditions that animated other social movements of the 1960s and 1970s, environmentalism evolved and matured into a political force in modern America. But still, the impact of this movement on American affairs is not universally accepted as significant. Much of the historiography of change and protest in postwar society has, for instance, overlooked the escalating concern for environmental issues. Vocal environmental scholars have demanded a corrective. Robert Gottlieb, Kirkpatrick Sale, Philip Shabecoff, and others argue that environmental activity must be understood against the backdrop of the multiple social and political movements of the twentieth century.[36] More recently, historian Adam Rome pushed for a reconceptualization of the 1960s that better incorporates environmentalism into the "driving forces of change in the period."[37] Further, Rome uses the diverse constituencies and varied motivations within environmental politics as evidence of the wide appeal of the environment in American life. Through their call for a more nuanced understanding of cultural dynamics through environmentalism, environmental scholars have attempted to better situate environmental politics within the social milieu of postwar America.

But it is equally, perhaps even more, important to frame this analysis in the opposite direction. A critical approach to social change that considers the linkages between nature, cultural mores, and social structures can be the means to increase the footprint of environmental politics within modern American life. And part of this effort to better understand the environmental movement necessarily includes integration of environmental politics into social and cultural affairs. To that end, investigating the points of contact between environmentalism and other movements in postwar America can be illuminating. But to fully incorporate environmental politics into the larger movements of the era is to ignore important areas of divergence. After all, in the nature of protest, in the motivation of its advocates, and in the goals of its participants, the politics of the environment share less common ground with the civil rights crusade or the campaign for women's rights than was once believed. To approach environmental politics on its own terms is to better understand how the politics of nature is part of the desire to redefine the public interest. More appropriately, this effort can also establish the importance of nature to human affairs. And where the assimilation of the social and the technical can again be instructive is in pushing environmental politics to break free from the declensionist stronghold that dominates environmental narratives. A serious examination of the intersection of nature and technology will not conclude that technophiles are in harmony with nature's economy or that technology has been a benign force on the landscape. It could, however, push environmental actors to avoid economic determinism and create narratives that recognize the complex interaction between the human and nonhuman worlds to address natural issues that have contemporary standing.

Humans tell stories to make sense of their world. These stories necessarily contain social assumptions about the structured relationships between citizens and the natural environment. But to change the understanding of those relationships, we need to change the narratives.[38] Writing a new story of environmental politics is not easy; declension remains "the grand narrative" of environmental affairs in America.[39] Historian Richard Judd labeled declensionist environmental stories part of the "western synthesis," since so many of the classic works in the field explore the preservation battles for control of the landscape of the American West.[40] Declension is, however, more than just a western tale. Rather, as one scholar argued, the declension narrative sits at the center of the "most important mythology humans have developed to make sense of the relationship to the earth."[41] In the attempt to chronicle the history of natural use by human cultures, declension stories have a universal appeal. Whether we begin with Adam's fall from grace and the technological efforts to recover the garden, or with a pristine Eden slowly corrupted by technological abuse, or with a more modern benchmark, we find that Americans have created different (and often competing) environmental origin stories that conceptualize the human manipulation of nature.

Declension stories are not dead yet.[42] Nor should they be, as the effort to trace the impact of the market economy on the landscape is far from over. But environmental politicians still need to prove that nature matters. By introducing narratives that expand participation and challenge assumptions, it may still be possible to alter the accepted telos of American politics. A more complete understanding of contemporary environmental politics must recognize that among the changes introduced to the American political landscape in the late twentieth century was a very different understanding of what counts as "political." From New Left and feminist politics to the reinvigoration of more traditional ideological positions, participation in the American political process has broadened. The expansion of the franchise is especially apparent within environmental debates, for issues ranging from social justice to the meaning of private property have become fundamental to the maturation of environmental politics.

This idea is by no means new within environmental circles, but it does require deft political gymnastics. Environmentalists, for example, have long feared the impact of materialism and consumerism on nature. In response, they crafted a defense of environmental rights based on nature's moral values. The standard refrain for environmentalists included the belief that costs and sacrifices required to find environmental balance were outweighed by the benefits returned to nature. Such an approach is conventional wisdom within environmental methodology, but it may also miss the mark. Appeals to morality and the intrinsic value of the environment are fodder for antienvironmentalists who claim that environmental practices are dedicated to the protection of nature at the expense of the human. But an awareness of environmental politics needs to inform both sides of this dialogue. Environmentalists, for example, have all but abandoned discussions of property rights and economic development, just as issues of tax reform and campaign financing are almost never embraced by environmental reformers. On the other side, critics of environmental advocacy miss the importance of resource conservation in guaranteeing equality of opportunity. Importantly, the reestablishment of the borders of environmental politics could frame the discussion back to the linkages between nature and culture. Because most critically, what an understanding of the larger dynamics of environmental politics provides is an understanding that regardless of language, environmentalism in America is rooted in public health.[43] It is less flashy, to be sure, but to talk of human health within a worked landscape is to engage the full spectrum of American political values.

Not all environmental scholars welcome a revised script for natural affairs. Environmental journalist Mark Dowie spoke for many when he argued that if environmental politics are "to remain a vital force in the next century," they would not do so because they adopted a radical perspective on the political landscape but "because [the] leaders returned to the fundamentals of the original movement."[44] Dowie's commentary reflects a popular position among environmental advocates working to build stable political coalitions. And in truth, it would be hard to argue against injecting modern environmental politics with the passion of Thoreau or Muir, or even Theodore Roosevelt. But "original" ideas of conservation and preservation have been recycled into modern debates. Environmental politics, however, are so much more encompassing that to search for the moral space of Thoreau's nature in twenty-first-century America is to court political irrelevance. Americans believe that nature is a bounded place where they can discover an innocent past. Most Americans tend to believe that, in contrast to the messiness of politics that operate on a level far removed from their daily experience, independence and individualism spring forth from nature like an artesian well. It is against the dense picture of politics as complex market dynamics that environmental politics, its supporters claim, offer an alternative tradition. I disagree. I argue not with the position that environmental politics are part of an alternative tradition but, rather, with the position that politics are exclusively market driven; it is critical to recognize that nature remains at the heart of the American political experience. Placing a narrative of environmental concern next to the narrative of American politics does little to bridge the gap that separates social structures from nature. What is needed, and hopefully what a serious examination of technology in nature provides, are narratives that use the insights of environmental history to tell us things we do not yet understand about American political development.

NOTES

1. I would like to thank the members of the Nature and Culture seminar at the Hall Center for the Humanities, University of Kansas, especially Greg Cushman, Karl Brooks, and Don Worster, for their comments on an earlier draft of this essay. Jeffrey Sanders, James Sheppard, and Patrick Dobson also suggested important revisions. Most noteworthy was the assistance that came from the other contributors to this volume, especially Jeff Roche.

2. On cell phone usage, see *Statistical Abstract of the United States: 2004–2005* (Washington, D.C.: Government Printing Office, 2005). See also the annual reports from the *Computer Industry Almanac;* their reports can be found at: www.c-i-a.com/pr0206.htm.

3. Carl Mitchum, *Thinking through Technology* (Chicago: University of Chicago Press, 1994), 59–60.

4. David E. Nye, "Technology, Nature, and American Origin Stories," *Environmental History* 8 (January 2003): 8.

5. David E. Nye, *American Technological Sublime* (Cambridge, Mass.: MIT Press, 1994), 125.

6. Arnold Pacey, *Meaning in Technology* (Cambridge, Mass.: MIT Press, 2001), 133.

7. Hal K. Rothman, *Saving the Planet: The American Response to the Environment in the Twentieth Century* (Chicago: Ivan Dee, 2000), 5–10, and Adam Rome, *The Bulldozer in the Countryside: Suburban Sprawl and the Rise of American Environmentalism* (Cambridge: Cambridge University Press, 2001), 3–7. I am especially indebted to Rome for this broad overview of the development of environmental politics.

8. Bob Pepperman Taylor, *Our Limits Transgressed: Environmental Thought in America* (Lawrence: University Press of Kansas, 1992), 1–4, 23–26. See also Taylor, "Aldo Leopold's Civic Education," in *Democracy and the Claims of Nature: Critical Perspectives for a New Century,* ed. Ben A. Minteer and Bob Pepperman Taylor (Lanham, Md.: Rowman & Littlefield, 2002), 173–187, and Curt Meine, *Aldo Leopold: His Life and*

Work (Madison: University of Wisconsin Press, 1988), 165–170. Consider also Grant McConnell, "The Conservation Movement—Past and Present," *Western Political Quarterly* 7 (September 1954): 463–473, and Roderick Nash, *Rights of Nature* (Madison: University of Wisconsin Press, 1989).

9. Taylor, *Our Limits Transgressed*, 24–26.

10. Samuel P. Hays, *A History of Environmental Politics since 1945* (Pittsburgh, Pa.: University of Pittsburgh Press, 2000), 234.

11. James Gorman, "The Call in the Wild: Cell Phones Hit the Trail," *New York Times*, 30 August 2001.

12. Claudia Rowe, "Ah, Wilderness! Ah, the Sound of Cell-Phone Gossip! Ah, Nuts!" *Seattle Post-Intelligencer*, 20 April 2004.

13. John Markoff, "Wilderness Is Becoming Less Wild," *New York Times*, 21 December 2003.

14. Estimates vary widely, but it is generally agreed that between 4 million and 40 million birds perish annually in collisions with towers, wires, and other support structures. See the U.S. Fish and Wildlife Service (USFWS) guidelines regarding cell-tower placement and bird health at http://migratorybirds.fws.gov/issues/towers/comtow.html. The regulations originated, at least in part, with the creation of an Avian Powerline Interaction Committee, a joint venture of the Edison Electric Institute, the Audubon Society, and the USFWS. Among the many government publications on this committee, see "Electric Utility Industry Service Team to Protect Birds" (Washington, D.C.: USFWS Office of Public Affairs, 2003). These guidelines have also been controversial. The Forest Conservation Council, the Friends of the Earth, and the American Bird Conservancy sued the Federal Communications Commission (FCC) in federal court in 2003 claiming that the government-approved tower guidelines fail to protect migratory birds. Information on cell-phone waste comes from Inform Inc., an environmental research organization. See section "Cell Phone Waste Is Toxic," in *Cell Phones: A Poster Child for Extended Producer Responsibility* (January 2004), 1 (http://www.informinc.org/fact_cellEPR.pdf). See also Lisa Guernsey, "Phones in the Drawer or in the Trash, or to a Good Cause," *New York Times*, 28 February 2002, and Jonathan Sidener, "Recycling, Legislation Are among Efforts to Reduce Phones Dumped in Landfills," *San Diego Union-Tribune*, 17 May 2004.

15. "Last Words," *Sierra*, May–June 1997.

16. Christina Nealson, "In Wilderness, Don't Phone Home," *High Country News*, 17 August 1998.

17. For more information on antimodernism, see T. J. Jackson Lears, *No Place of Grace: Antimodernism and the Transformation of American Culture, 1880–1920* (New York: Pantheon Books, 1981).

18. The literature on this transition is vast, but as a start, consult these classic works: Perry Miller, *Nature's Nation* (Cambridge, Mass.: Belknap Press/Harvard University Press, 1967); Richard Slotkin, *Regeneration through Violence: The Myth of the American Frontier, 1600–1800* (Middletown, Conn.: Wesleyan University Press, 1973); and Henry Nash Smith, *Virgin Land: The American West as Symbol and Myth* (Cambridge, Mass.: Harvard University Press, 1950).

19. Michael Paul Rogin, *Ronald Reagan, the Movie, and Other Episodes in Political Demonology* (Berkeley and Los Angeles: University of California Press, 1987), 175–177.

20. Pacey, *Meaning in Technology*, 138.

21. Leo Marx, *The Machine in the Garden: Technology and the Pastoral Ideal in America* (New York: Oxford University Press, 1964), 353.

22. Rogin, *Ronald Reagan*, 178–180. I rely heavily on Rogin's interpretation of political thought in this section, more so than this single footnote suggests.

23. Baxter State Park in Maine, for example, was one of the first to ban the use of cell phones on park grounds. See Michael Hill, "Cell Phones Invade Wilderness," *USA Today*, 19 October 1999.

24. Among the vast literature on this movement, see Stephen Fox, *The American Conservation Movement: John Muir and His Legacy* (Madison: University of Wisconsin Press, 1981); Samuel P. Hays, *Beauty, Health, and Permanence: Environmental Politics in the United States, 1955–1985* (Cambridge: Cambridge University Press, 1987); Kirkpatrick Sale, *The Green Revolution: The American Environmental Movement, 1962–1992* (New York: Hill & Wang, 1993); and Hal K. Rothman, *The Greening of a Nation? Environmentalism in the United States since 1945* (New York: Harcourt Brace, 1998).

25. Wilson Carey McWilliams, preface to Minteer and Taylor, *Democracy and the Claims of Nature*, vii.

26. One of the classic examinations of the American belief in technological progress is Lynn White Jr., "The Historical Roots to Our Ecologic Crisis," *Science* 155 (March 1967): 1203–1207. This essay is usually referenced by religious scholars, but it also speaks to issues of technology and development.

27. See Thomas Frank, "Lie Down for America: How the Republican Party Sows Ruin on the Great Plains," *Harper's*, April 2004, 36.

28. The full text of Giles's speech is available from several sources. For a favorable review, see Steve Sutherlin, "Giles Blasts the Cell Phone Naturalist," *Petroleum News*, 1 December 2002, 2. Giles's commentary also sparked concern. Citizens for Responsibility and Ethics in Washington, Defenders of Wildlife, and Friends of the Earth are among the organizations that petitioned the White House for Giles's removal. A transcript of Giles's speech is available through the Alaska Resource Development Council page, www.akrdc.org/membership/events/conference/2002/presentations/griles.html.

29. See David Brooks, "Cell Phone Naturalists," *Weekly Standard*, 26 October 1998, 20–25. An abridged version of Brooks's article was reprinted as "Cell Phone Naturalists: Affluent Adventurers Are Changing the Face of Environmentalism," *Utne Reader*, March–April 1999, 75–80. I acknowledge a large debt to Brooks's work. His article was very helpful in the organization of this essay. For Senate references to the cell-phone naturalist, see U.S. Congress, Senate, *Gale Norton Nomination: Hearings before the Committee on Energy and Natural Resources*, 107th Congress, 1st sess., 18 January 2001 (Washington, D.C.: GPO, 2001), 3.

30. Brooks, "Cell Phone Naturalists," *Utne Reader*, 77.

31. Andrew Kirk, "Appropriating Technology: The *Whole Earth Catalogue* and

Counterculture Environmental Politics," *Environmental History* 6 (July 2001): 375–376.

32. Luis A. Vivanco, "Conservation and Culture, Genuine and Spurious," in *Reconstructing Conservation: Finding Common Ground*, ed. Ben A. Minteer and Robert E. Manning (Washington, D.C.: Island Press, 2003), 59.

33. Max Oelschlaeger, *The Idea of Wilderness: From Prehistory to the Age of Ecology* (New Haven, Conn.: Yale University Press, 1991), 133–134.

34. For one version of this essay, see William Cronon, "The Trouble with Wilderness, or Getting Back to the Wrong Nature," in *Uncommon Ground: Toward Reinventing Nature*, ed. William Cronon (New York: W. W. Norton, 1995), 69–90.

35. Samuel P. Hays, *Conservation and the Gospel of Efficiency: The Progressive Conservation Movement, 1890–1920* (Cambridge, Mass.: Harvard University Press, 1959).

36. Robert Gottlieb, *Forcing the Spring: The Transformation of the American Environmental Movement* (Washington, D.C.: Island Press, 1993); Sale, *Green Revolution;* and Philip Shabecoff, *A Fierce Green Fire: The American Environmental Movement* (Washington, D.C.: Island Press, 2003).

37. Adam Rome, "'Give Earth a Chance': The Environmental Movement and the Sixties," *Journal of American History* 90, no. 2 (2003): 527.

38. William Cronon, "A Place for Stories: Nature, History, and Narrative," *Journal of American History* 78 (1992): 1372–1376, and Nye, "Technology, Nature, and American Origin Stories," 8.

39. Brian Donahue, "Environmental Stewardship and Decline in Old New England," *Journal of the Early Republic* 24 (July 2004): 234.

40. Richard Judd, "Writing Environmental History from East to West," in Minteer and Manning, *Reconstructing Conservation*, 19–21.

41. Carolyn Merchant, *Reinventing Eden: The Fate of Nature in Western Culture* (New York: Routledge, 2003), 2.

42. Donahue, "Environmental Stewardship," 234, and Ted Steinberg, "Down, Down, Down, No More: Environmental History Moves beyond Declension," *Journal of the Early Republic* 24 (July 2004): 262.

43. For a commentary on the link between mainstream environmentalism and the elitism associated with the preservation of the pristine at the expense of the human, see Matthew Klingle and Joseph E. Taylor III, "Caste from the Past," *Grist*, 8 March 2006, http://www.grist.org/comments/soapbox/2006/03/08/klingle/index.html.

44. Mark Dowie, *Losing Ground: American Environmentalism at the Close of the Twentieth Century* (Cambridge, Mass.: MIT Press, 1995), 225.

CHAPTER 12

The Politics of Western Memory
David M. Wrobel

In April 1849, a group of thirty-six young men left Illinois and joined the California Gold Rush. The Jayhawkers, as they called themselves, crossed the Great Plains and the Rockies and joined up in Salt Lake City with a much larger party of about 200 men, women, and children.[1] The entire group left Salt Lake City at the end of September, planning to travel via the Spanish Trail to Los Angeles. But by early November, the Jayhawkers had become concerned that traveling with the larger party would slow them down and prevent them from reaping their fair share of California's precious metals harvest. Seeking a shorter route to the promised land, the Jayhawkers and a few other groups split from the main party and tried a shortcut through the Sierra Nevadas by way of the Walker Pass cutoff.

The shortcut was not fortuitous. The Jayhawkers and various other smaller groups who had joined them, altogether totaling eighty or so men, women, and children, ended up in what is now known as Death Valley (in southwestern Nevada and eastern California). Nearly 280 feet below sea level at its lowest point, Death Valley is the hottest and driest place on the continent; temperatures of 134° have been recorded there. In that desolate place, albeit in winter, not summer, the Jayhawkers suffered the ravages of hunger, thirst, and physical exhaustion. With their food supply running out, they made it to the western edge of the valley and camped near the 11,000-foot Telescope Peak, but they could not find a pass to lead them through the Panamint Mountains. On 13 January 1850, two Jayhawkers died from exhaustion and dehydration. A third Jayhawker died two weeks later, after the group had made it out of the valley, probably from drinking too much cold water at the first spring they found.[2]

On 4 February 1850, three months after separating themselves from the larger group, the Jayhawkers emerged from their nightmarish journey, quite literally stumbling onto the San Francisquito Ranch in California's Santa Clara Valley. The survivors, by all accounts, looked like walking skeletons, the contours of their teeth clearly visible through the stretched skin and flesh of their gaunt, hollow cheeks. Some had reportedly lost a full 100 pounds in weight. The youngest member of the original Jayhawker party, John Burt Colton, a man more than six feet tall who normally weighed between 150 and 160 pounds, was said to have weighed only 64 pounds at the end of the ordeal. Ironically, the Jayhawkers may have headed south toward Death Valley because of what had happened to the Donner Party further to the north a few years previously.[3]

The Jayhawkers' journey is a memorable one with all the ingredients of grand drama: hope, faith, charity, greed, pain, suffering, endurance, heroism, death, and salvation. Unlike the Donner Party's terrible ordeal, the Jayhawkers' journey was not marked by cannibalism, though one member of the group seems to have suggested it before being run out of the camp by the others.[4] But for all the drama it is hard to find a moral to accompany this tale. The young pioneers were driven by a desire to get rich quick, and they chose their ill-fated route in an effort to get rich even more quickly.

But the real story, for our purposes, is not the journey itself but the surviving Jayhawkers' shared memories of it. The group formed a pioneer society and held annual reunions every 4 February (the date of their deliverance from Death Valley) from 1872 until 1909, when there remained fourteen of the original party, with an average age of eighty-three and a half. Mini-reunions occurred until 1918, when only two, John Burt Colton and Lorenzo Dow Stephens, were still alive. It was at these reunions and in their correspondence that the Jayhawkers defined themselves as "true westerners" by emphasizing how they had endured hardships in the old frontier West that younger people, enjoying the modern comforts and conveniences of the safe, tamed new West, simply could not understand. They reminded each other that their suffering was the very foundation of the authentic frontier. The aging Jayhawkers equated "westernness" with the trials and tribulations of pioneering. Their organized memories of their frontier ordeal tied them into a wider world of frontier reminiscences, one that included correspondence with Theodore Roosevelt (both prior to and during his presidency), living frontier legend and mythologizer William F. "Buffalo Bill" Cody, frontier illustrator Frederic Remington, and a host of other pioneer dignitaries and chroniclers.[5]

Colton, chief organizer of the Jayhawker reunions, also corresponded with the organizers of many other California pioneer societies, including the New England Associated Pioneers of '49 (formed in 1888), Boston's Associated California Pioneers of 1849 (1889), New York's Associated Pioneers of the

Territorial Days of California (1875), and the Maryland Society of California Pioneers (1887). The members of these groups who did not end up settling in the West certainly felt a strong attachment to their western frontier past. These California gold rushers who had long since returned to Boston, New York, and other eastern cities wrote to Colton about their efforts to "[show] future generations what it has cost to add what was once wild and uninhabited country, to [the] present grand possibilities [of the United States]."[6] These past pioneers, sensitive about public perceptions of their motivations, recalled not a shared desire to strike it rich but, rather, their role in the more noble and heroic endeavor of taming a wilderness. Gold is not the primary focus of gold rush reminiscences; rather, they tend to revolve around the theme of frontier heroism, the suggestion that participants were part of a great historic moment and movement.[7] Emphasizing the materialistic ambitions that drove them to the goldfields might have undermined the historical significance of the endeavor and the moral character of the participants.[8]

The Jayhawkers' collective efforts to sustain the memory of their journey, along with renewed press coverage of their story, elevated the group's survivors to the status of pioneer heroes. In the 1880s, as expressions of concern over the perceived closing of the American frontier became a part of the national cultural milieu, newspapers and magazines became eager for stories of past pioneer struggles, such as those of the Death Valley emigrants. During the 1890s, such expressions of "frontier anxiety" became more prevalent and acute as the nation experienced a terrible economic depression, heightened agrarian protest, industrial strife, urban squalor, and continued political corruption.[9] A mountain of accounts of the exploits of old pioneers appeared in books and magazines throughout the decade. In 1893, the *San Francisco Chronicle* published a feature story on the Jayhawkers' ordeal, based on Colton's memories. In 1894, William Lewis Manly published his personal account of the events, *Death Valley in '49*. It was Manly who, with another man, had set off for the California settlements and returned to rescue some of the families still lost in Death Valley.[10]

While Manly is clearly the star of his own account, another hero emerges from the pages of his book and from the recollections of other Jayhawkers. Juliet Wells Brier has been largely forgotten to history, but thoroughly deserves a resurrection. Mrs. Brier, along with her husband, the Reverend James Welch Brier, and their three young boys, tagged along through Death Valley behind the Jayhawkers. Manly wrote that the Jayhawkers all agreed that Mrs. Brier was "by far the *best man* of the [Brier] party."[11] Mrs. Brier, Manly wrote, "did all sorts of work when the father of the family was too tired, which was almost all of the time."[12] The Jayhawkers found the "holier than thou" attitude of Reverend Brier rather irritating, but they found Juliet

Brier inspirational. They thought, Manly added, that the reverend ought to "assert his manliness, take the burden on himself, and not lean upon his delicate and trusting wife."[13]

But Juliet proved not to be so delicate. Each day she loaded and unloaded her family's oxen and sometimes those of the Jayhawkers when they were too tired or weak to do it themselves. Participant accounts note that Juliet "carried" her family (that is, took primary responsibility for their welfare), and for parts of the journey, it seems, she did literally carry the children, aged four, seven, and nine. At times she cradled one of them in her arms, led a second by the hand, and carried the eldest, and weakest, on her back.[14] She was the hardiest of all the Death Valley pioneers, not just the "best man" of the Brier family. Most of the Jayhawkers spoke far less highly of her husband. James Brier does not seem to have recognized the full magnitude of his wife's bravery and her vital contribution to the family's survival. Furthermore, according to most accounts other than his own, he does not seem to have shown much bravery or been of much assistance himself.

But Juliet was a quiet heroine, disinclined to harp on her own incredible valor. She did not give her first newspaper interview on the Death Valley crossing until December 1898, almost a half century after the event. The Christmas Day edition of the *San Francisco Call* featured Juliet's reminiscences of the journey.[15] Notably, the piece appeared less than two months after her husband's death. Shortly before he died, Reverend Brier had disassociated himself and his family from the Jayhawkers. He was upset over Manly's criticisms of him in *Death Valley in '49*. Perhaps the unfavorable contrasting of his weakness with the great fortitude and heroic sacrifices of his wife particularly embarrassed Reverend Brier. Whatever the case, the reverend had the Brier family officially removed from the list of Jayhawkers.[16]

Interestingly, a few months later, the 1899 Jayhawker reunion was held in Lodi, near San Francisco, at the home of the Briers' son, John Wells Brier, and his wife. Juliet Brier was present, and she also attended the reunions of 1903, 1908, 1911, and 1913, all held at her son's home. She died on 26 May 1913, just a few weeks before her hundredth birthday. Whether her half-century-long silence concerning the events of 1849 resulted from her own deference to patriarchy and respect for her husband or from her own preference for privacy is difficult to ascertain.[17] What is clear is that the Jayhawkers considered Juliet Brier to be one of them. In their memory, she had suffered, and endured, and contributed selflessly and bravely to the Jayhawkers' cause. For them, she was indeed the "best man" of the Brier family, a true pioneer whose actions and attitude, like the Jayhawkers' (but not her husband's), ought to inspire younger generations who had not experienced the rigors of frontier life.[18]

In 1918, the forty-seventh and final Jayhawker reunion and the sixty-ninth anniversary of the party's deliverance took place when the two surviving Jayhawkers, Colton and Stephens, met at Stephens's house in San Jose, California. Colton passed away the following year at the age of eighty-eight.[19] Stephens, the last of the original Jayhawker group, died in 1921, at the age of ninety-five. A decade later, in 1928, the Jayhawkers' offspring (the Sons and Daughters and Grandsons and Granddaughters of the Jayhawkers of '49) began to hold annual reunions in their honor.[20] A few surviving descendants continue to meet annually as part of a group called the Death Valley '49ers. They can be found at the annual meetings of the Los Angeles Corral of Westerners, which in turn is part of a larger network of corrals throughout the nation and the world known as Westerners International, which continues to memorialize the nation's frontier heritage.

While the terrible ordeal of the Donner Party has certainly overshadowed that of the Jayhawkers in public memory, the Jayhawkers have not been completely forgotten by history, as they feared they might be.[21] An elaborate hoax that occurred around the 150th anniversary of their ill-fated journey put the Jayhawkers back on the historical map. On New Year's Day 1999, the first of many newspaper accounts appeared about the discovery of a trunk full of Jayhawker belongings in a cave near the Panamint Mountains in Death Valley. The trunk, as it turned out, was "bunk," which was quite embarrassing for Jerry Freeman, an amateur archeologist and substitute high school teacher who claimed to have made the great discovery. The superintendent of Death Valley National Park brought in professional archeologists from the Smithsonian Institution in Washington, D.C., and the Western Archeological and Conservation Center in Tucson, Arizona, to study the contents of the trunk, and they found various indisputable pieces of evidence proving its inauthenticity—including glue in clothing items that was clearly manufactured in the twentieth century, a porcelain bowl made in 1914, and tintype photographs that could not have been processed before 1856. Freeman appeared on the *Good Morning America* television show and national news programs featured the story prior to the determination that the trunk was a fake.[22]

The discovery—or better, constructed discovery—of the trunk is doubly ironic. The Jayhawkers had labored relentlessly, for nearly half a century, from 1872 to 1918, to memorialize their frontier heroism, their pioneering virtue, and their true westernness, and they had urged their descendants to do the same. Their shared memory of their own past, however, was a recreation, just like the trunk; neither were quite what they appeared to be. But unlike the contents of the trunk, the Jayhawkers' vivid memories of their pioneering past were not pure fabrication, but something far more subtle and intriguing. Their remembered story was not fake, though it was surely marked in places by exaggeration of some details and by the conscious effort to forget certain others. Most important for our purposes, the Jayhawkers' collective recollection of their past was what they needed it to be. They remembered with a purpose, for their place in the present depended on the public's perception of their past.[23]

The Jayhawkers craved public recognition of their heroism. Jerry Freeman almost certainly craved public recognition too, as he tried to position himself within the contours of a great historical legacy. But there was a crucial difference between the old pioneers who experienced the terrible journey to the western promised land and the amateur archeologist who sought to make a name for himself. The Jayhawkers, to use a contemporary phrase, had been there and done that, but later generations could not do the same, the old pioneers insisted, because the time for such blood-stirring adventures had long since disappeared with the old western frontier. They wanted the public to remember them as the last of the great pioneers, the final frontiersmen, the only living links to a terribly dangerous but indisputably glorious past. They wanted to live out their twilight years in the warm glow of public admiration. But admiration alone was not enough; they wanted to be deemed relevant to the present age while also being recognized as heroes of a past age.

There was little conflict among the Jayhawkers about the meaning of their shared past experience; aside from the Reverend Brier, all seemed in general agreement.[24] But there were times when the shared memory of the pioneers clashed with the accounts of their chroniclers. A second story illustrates the clash of collective memory and professional history. In 1893, the same year that Frederick Jackson Turner delivered his paper "The Significance of the Frontier in American History," which would become the single most influential piece of writing by any American historian, the Society of California Pioneers formally struck another historian, the renowned Hubert Howe Bancroft, from its list of honorary members. The California Pioneers took this action because Bancroft's massive seven-volume *History of California* (1886–1890) had, in their estimation, darkened the proud heritage of the state's early Anglo settlers. Bancroft, with the help of his extensive staff, was a veritable publishing machine. Prior to 1893, he had completed more than fifty large volumes on the Americas, covering more than seven feet of shelf space.[25] He was one of the best-known historians of the late nineteenth century, but certain elements of his version of the California past were at odds with the purposes of the Society of California Pioneers.[26] The society was particularly incensed by Bancroft's very critical treatment of John C. Frémont and other key participants in the Bear Flag revolt, and of General John A. Sutter.[27]

The Society of California Pioneers published a special booklet about Bancroft's dismissal. Society member and prosecutor Willard B. Farwell wrote in this report that Bancroft had "wantonly and maliciously wrong[ed] the old Argonauts" in his "quasi-history." As "living witnesses" to the events that Bancroft described in his work, California's old pioneers had a duty to "correct misstatements and misrepresentations of so-called historians." Bancroft had produced a "monstrous series of libels upon the memories of departed illustrious Pioneers and [a] monstrous perversion of the facts of history." His misreading of the past could not be allowed, Farwell continued, to stand as the official version of the events, the one that would shape the public consciousness of later generations. The society sent Farwell's report to Bancroft and invited the historian to defend himself at Pioneer Hall in San Francisco on 12 December 1893. Bancroft did not appear to face the charges. He also refused to appear at rescheduled meetings on 26 December 1893 and on 9 January 1894. Not surprisingly, the reviled historian was not in attendance at the next rescheduling of the hearing on 16 January. The Farwell report was finally submitted to the organization's members for action on 5 February, with Bancroft absent for the fifth time. The resolution to strike Bancroft from the list of honorary members unanimously carried. Members also recommended that the society's report be distributed to "the Public Libraries of the United States and elsewhere" to serve as a "vindication of the memories of the many early pioneers."[28]

What is the significance of the society's action? One might argue that no great harm was done when a group of grizzly old Anglo settlers sought to make an example of a historian who had constructed a western past that conflicted with their own shared memory of the same events. Bancroft, who did not bother showing up for any of his "trial" dates, was clearly not particularly pained by the events. But it is interesting that Bancroft's loss of pioneer status and Turner's first public articulation of his thoughts on the frontier's significance took place at around the same time. Turner argued that the frontier experience had shaped American democracy, nationalism, and individualism and had created a distinctive national character. But he also emphasized that the frontier had closed and that its closing marked the end of the first great period of American history. Turner would spend much of the rest of his career (nearly four decades) concerned about the future of a frontierless America. Would the nation become less democratic now that the frontier wellspring had run dry? Would America become a sorry mirror of its European progenitors, beset with class divisions, industrial violence, and urban blight?

While Turner was concerned by what would happen to America without its most significant attribute—the frontier—the members of the pioneer societies that sprang up across the West in the second half of the nineteenth century, such as the Society of California Pioneers, were concerned that they themselves would become less significant as the frontier period passed into the dim recesses of the national memory. Those old Anglo settlers were seeking to maintain their relevance in a changing nation and a changing West. Their efforts to keep their frontier stories at the forefront of the national consciousness constitute one of the most significant elements in the construction of westernness. The tens of thousands of speeches delivered at pioneer-society meetings in the late nineteenth and early twentieth centuries combined with many thousands of published and unpublished book- and article-length reminiscences of the old western settlers amounts to one of the most significant examples of the power of collective memory in the nation's history.[29]

Indeed, in underscoring their own ruggedness, individualism, self reliance, bravery, and moral fortitude; their role in taming the frontier wilderness and making the "desert blossom like a rose" (a ubiquitous phrase in western pioneer reminiscences); and their place at the forefront of the nation-building process, and in contrasting the hardships of their frontier past with the comforts of the postfrontier present, the nation's pioneer memorialists emphasized just about every single element of Turner's frontier thesis long before he had formulated it. Indeed, Turner's essay gave scholarly legitimacy to a set of deeply held sentiments that were very much a part of the cultural milieu of the late nineteenth century.[30] But the true significance of these pioneer reminiscers lies not in their foreshadowing of Turner but in their laying the foundations of the politics of westernness that persist into the present. The Society of California Pioneers asserted the validity of their collective memory, the significance of their frontier experience, against a historian whose account threatened to undermine the authenticity of their memories.

Western pioneer societies were the formal organs through which older generations of westerners (and nonwesterners who had spent time in the West) sought to establish and maintain their status in a changing world.[31] These organizations conferred legitimacy on their members, confirming their vital place in the building of the nation. The societies sprang up all over the West, as well as outside of the West (the Chicago, Maryland, New York, and New England societies of California Pioneers are examples), in the late nineteenth century and generally remained active into the early decades of the next. They usually developed within a couple of decades after the first permanent white settlers arrived in a particular western region, about the same time that individual settlers began to record and publish their reminiscences.[32]

The organizations varied in size, from larger ones, such as the Los Angeles County Pioneer Society (LACPS), with its 1,143 members (682 living and 461 deceased) in 1923, to the Jayhawkers of '49, with just a few dozen members at its founding in 1872. Some of them were formed on the county level (the LACPS, founded in 1897, is an example); others on the state level (including the Society of Colorado Pioneers, in 1872; the Historical Society of Idaho Pioneers, in 1881; and the Society of Arizona Pioneers and the Society of Montana Pioneers, both in 1884); and some, such as the Jayhawkers, bore no relation to units of political organization. Certain state historical societies, including Arizona's, evolved from pioneer societies, a point worth considering in accounting for the endurance of the frontier legacy.[33] These state historical societies continued to promote the virtues of their states' respective pioneers well into the twentieth century, playing a kind of politics of western memory that operated outside formal political channels.

The politics of western memory were marked by competitiveness among the pioneer societies and state historical societies of different states as they all concurrently laid claim to the frontier heritage. These organizations debated the severity of the frontier process in their respective western places, all of them claiming to have played host to the most dangerous, demanding, and inhospitable conditions that the frontier West had to offer. As well as being characterized by an elevated generational pride, pioneer reminiscences are marked by a heightened subregional or state-level pride—a sort of "I'm more authentically western and frontiersman-like than you" syndrome. Oregon settlers contrasted themselves with those in California, emphasizing that the latter had arrived later and entered a landscape and climate too mild for them to be considered true frontiersmen and women. California's pioneer reminiscers contended that they had experienced greater dangers and privations in the course of their journeys to the Golden State—"separated as it was by such vast wastes of desert lands and pathless mountain heights peopled by hordes of savage Indians"—and that they should thus be considered the greatest pioneers of all.[34] The Jayhawkers, who contrasted the horrors of their journey through the valley of death with their deliverance in the promised land of Southern California, are a part of this tradition.

Midwestern pioneers claimed that they had arrived in their states ahead of the railroads and thus were the true frontiersmen, the real westerners. "A man can't be a pioneer and travel in a railroad car," the governor of Illinois proclaimed before the Old Settlers Association of Illinois, Missouri, and Iowa in 1885, and he went on to exclude Kansas, Nebraska, and Colorado from the category of "pioneer states."[35] The following year, 1886, the members of the Old Settlers' Association of Johnson County, Iowa, were reminded that they had completely transformed their environment, breaking the prairies and felling the forests, whereas other pioneers had the good fortune to arrive in ready-made agricultural paradises, such as California. Furthermore, the Johnson County pioneers were reminded that the motivations behind their settlement of Iowa—to live on the land, work hard, and harvest their crops— were more honest and noble than those of settlers driven to California by lust for gold, or driven to Kansas and Texas by politics.[36]

There was a remarkable continuity across time and space in these respective claims to elevated westernness; the issue of the acuteness of the frontier setting was always at their center. An 1897 *Old Timer's Hand Book* for Butte, Montana, claimed that the town's pioneers were the most rugged and frontiersman-like of all pioneers since they had overcome the most "forbidding surroundings . . . a rigorous climate, an unprolific houseless waste, an obstinate nature."[37] As late as 1944, old Wyoming settlers were trumpeting that same theme, emphasizing that they, unlike the pioneers of other neighboring states, "did not move in social, political, or religious groups," but, rather, "were individualists, the products of an environment never to return."[38] The reminiscers' insistence on the authenticity of their experience, on their heightened westernness, has had an enduring legacy that is still evident in contemporary debates in the West.

Since frontier authenticity was vital to a sense of westernness, pioneer societies were often quite restrictive in their admission requirements, and membership in these organizations was eagerly sought. Membership itself was the mark of authenticity. Membership in the Oregon Pioneer Society was limited to those who had arrived prior to statehood (1 January 1853). The Society of California Pioneers reserved admission privileges for those who had arrived before or during the Gold Rush, and the society actually created two separate categories of members (first class: those who had arrived prior to 1 January 1849; and second class: those who had arrived prior to 1 January 1850). The Society of Colorado Pioneers set 31 December 1860 (that is, within a year or so of the 1859 Colorado Gold Rush) as the cutoff date. For the Arizona Pioneers, the legitimacy line was drawn at 1 January 1870; for the first Wyoming pioneer association, the date was 1 July 1884. The admission dates were supposed to mark watershed moments, the defining lines between the unsettled frontier past and the safer, more comfortable modern age. The dates were the boundaries of authenticity; on one side lay those who had endured the hardships of the frontier process and on the other the newcomers who had lived in the lap of luxury, enjoying the fruits of the pioneers' labor. Thus, the frontier period was deemed a thing of the past in much of the far West long before the Census Bureau (which Turner cited in his essay) declared in 1890 that the frontier line was so broken up by isolated bodies of settlement that it would not be referred to in future censuses.

Interestingly, during the 1890s, members of the Society of Montana Pioneers debated the date set for admission into the association, getting it pushed forward from 26 May 1864 to 31 December 1868, thereby allowing more people to lay claim to the title of "pioneer."[39] Most of the pioneer societies renegotiated the original cutoff dates, moving them forward to accommodate the membership wishes of would-be pioneers and, presumably, to sustain the organizations' numbers as members began to die off. One would-be pioneer, Hiram Knowles, had experienced no small degree of frustration over these cutoff dates. Knowles wrote to the Tri-State Old Settlers Association of Illinois, Missouri, and Iowa in 1885, thanking them for inviting him to join their organization and gladly accepting. He lamented that he had not been eligible for the Lee County, Iowa, organization because he arrived there in 1844 and the date for eligibility was 1840. Similarly he missed the California cutoff (1849) by a year, and each of the cutoffs in Nevada (1860), Idaho (1863), and Montana (1864) by two years. As a very old and well-traveled settler, he was honored to finally belong to a pioneer society.[40] That membership conferred legitimacy, authenticity, and, ultimately, meaning to what might otherwise have been dismissed as the aimless wanderings of his younger years.

One of the benefits of membership in a pioneer society was the opportunity to share formally in the collective (and selective) memory of the frontier process. These orchestrated memories of the western past played a significant role in forging a sense of place and a sense of belonging among members of these older generations.[41] Sharing their remembered experiences of journeying and adjusting to western places surely provided a degree of self-validation for individuals and for the groups as a whole. The new, settled West seemed a far cry from the old, pioneer West of their youth. But celebrating their role in building the foundations of contemporary comfort and prosperity probably helped alleviate old reminiscers' sense of disconnection from the modern West, even as they drew striking contrasts between past and present. Indeed, through emphasizing their role as the true architects of the postfrontier West, these old settlers were arguing their centrality to the present. Furthermore, by presenting their own past experiences as pioneers as object lessons for later generations, these old settlers were seeking to establish themselves as the arbiters of authenticity and moral goodness.

Indeed, the true significance of the frontier in American history may in fact lie less in any role the frontier actually played in shaping a national character and institutions than in the powerful selective memories of the frontier's influence.[42] Dime novels and more significant literary works such as Owen Wister's 1902 novel *The Virginian;* works of western art by Albert Bierstadt, Frederic Remington, and others; the historical reenactments of Buffalo Bill, movies, and advertisements—all played a vital role in forging a mythic West in the American national consciousness. The West of our contemporary imagination is filled with these evocative images of wild landscapes and rugged frontier types. But would these powerful representations of the winning of the West have sunk so deep into the public memory if they had not rested on a broad foundation of collective recollections of those white Americans who actually participated in the nation's westward expansion and who vigorously organized their recollections? There was power and purpose in the organization of memory.

While the content of these reminiscences focused on the frontier past, their message was directed toward the postfrontier present. As old pioneers recounted their struggles in bygone ages, they hoped that readers would better comprehend their significance to the contemporary West. In a statement typical of those collective efforts, James Sanders, secretary of the Society of Montana Pioneers, reminded the organization's members in 1917 that they had "carried the last frontier to the crest of the Rocky Mountains ... [and driven] the savage red man and bandit from this land ... and dedicated these hills and vales to civilization so that we could come here and build homes for our children."[43] Such actions, this speech and thousands of others like it implied, demanded respect and underscored the relevance of the generation of old settlers to the new era.

However, in forging the politics of western memory, these old settlers performed a delicate balancing act. While insisting on their own centrality to the present and seeking the reverence of younger generations, they also laid claim to their superiority over their descendants. They insisted that their actions demonstrated that they were braver, more rugged, and more manly than the generations that followed. One writer proclaimed in 1890 that the beneficiaries of the safe and civilized West they had created were "in danger of reclining upon the couch of luxury and cultivating [a] spirit of effeminacy."[44] The days of the frontier were commonly described as "times to test men's souls"; and, as Mrs. Brier's example reminds us, it was not just men's souls that were put to the test. Perhaps the Reverend Brier was most incensed by William Manly's questioning of his manliness when he decided to remove his family from the Jayhawker roll and break off communication with the group half a century after their shared journey.

While speeches at pioneer gatherings and published pioneer reminiscences tended to present pioneer achievements within a markedly male frame of reference, there was a good deal of acknowledgment of the achievements of women pioneers, such as the indomitable Juliet Brier.

Women's involvement with pioneer societies came largely in the form of auxiliary organizations, including the Native Daughters of the Golden West (formed in California in 1887), the Territorial Daughters of Colorado (1876), the Pioneer Ladies Aid Society of Colorado (1889), and the Ladies Auxiliary of the Society of Arizona Pioneers (1902). These auxiliaries often ended up merging with the main, male organizations on a full or partial basis. For example, women who met the temporal requirements for admission into the Society of Colorado Pioneers were, after 31 January 1881, declared "honorary members" of that organization.[45] Women were full members of the Oregon Pioneer Association from the very beginning.[46]

Women were generally present at pioneer society meetings, albeit primarily attending with their husbands. These gatherings generally featured at least one speech on the "pioneer women" or "pioneer mothers," in which male speakers lauded the contributions of their female counterparts. Just as old pioneers reminisced about the object lessons for contemporary American manhood in the more rugged and demanding frontier past, so the speeches detailing the contributions of women pioneers painted them as hardier, more resilient, more self-reliant, and more moral than contemporary women, who had not experienced the trials and tribulations of the frontier. Pioneer women had fought "savage Indians," endured long journeys across "trackless wastes," and then established homes in largely unsettled places at the journey's end; they had proven resourceful enough to meet their families' needs under the most trying conditions.[47] Modern women, the speeches exclaimed, had experienced no such baptisms by fire. Like their male counterparts, pioneer women were also eulogized in published reminiscences—many of which they authored and edited—as a superior breed, an example for later generations of white women to emulate.[48] In fact, this emphasis on the hardiness of the nation's pioneer mothers—which became an increasingly common feature of the genre in the early twentieth century—was partly a response to the emergence of the "new woman" of the Progressive and post–World War I eras.[49] Yet surely, it was that same emphasis on the centrality of women's efforts to the success of pioneering that helped lay the groundwork for earlier Progressive reforms, including women's suffrage, which came first to the western states—Wyoming (1869), Utah (1870), Colorado (1893), Idaho (1896), Washington (1910), California (1911), Arizona, Kansas, and Oregon (1912), and Montana and Nevada (1914).

These old pioneer men and women must have been pleased by the organizational efforts of their offspring. "Young settlers' societies" were formed, in part for the purpose of sustaining community recognition of their parents' achievements. The Native Sons of the Golden West, formed in 1875, stated that its purpose was "keep[ing] alive the memories of the historic valor of the pioneers, their trials, sufferings and grand achievements and by teaching to the young men the glory of our past excit[ing] them to an enthusiastic effort to advance the prosperity of California."[50] Unfortunately, the Native Sons' professed purpose of advancing present prosperity through the adulation of their pioneer predecessors was actually manifested in their nativistic rhetoric that fueled anti-Chinese passions in the state.[51] The Sons of Colorado (organized in 1905) published a journal featuring the reminiscences of their forbears, which would serve as lessons "for the benefit of those who would emulate the heroism and bravery of the little horde that invaded Colorado when the territory was a vast area in possession of the red man." The journal would serve that purpose for more than a generation, proudly pointing to the pioneers' legacy of conquest.[52] Terms such as "invasion" and "conquest" were used unabashedly as the Sons of Colorado wrote history in the service of memory validation, even if, unlike the Native Sons of the Golden West, they were not primary instigators of actual violence against peoples of color. Both organizations of pioneer descendants were playing the politics of western memory, and their efforts have had lasting significance. The 316 active "parlors" of the Native Sons of the Golden West that exist today all across California and engage in various charitable and historic preservation endeavors are a testament to the endurance of the pioneers' legacy.[53] But that legacy is far broader and deeper than these continuing efforts of pioneer descendants to memorialize the frontier past. The politics of western memory have developed around notions of exclusion, authenticity, and longevity, notions that are inextricably linked, in their western American context, to the remembered past of pioneers.

The same politics of western memory that inspired the Native Sons of the Golden West to engage in anti-Chinese rhetoric and action in the late nineteenth century (and resulted in the Chinese Exclusion Act of 1882, renewed in subsequent decades) were fully evident in California in 1913, when the state legislature passed the Alien Land Law with minimal opposition. The state's self-described "Progressives" feared competition from Japanese agriculturalists, who were able to produce considerably more per acre than the average white farmer. In addition, the Native Sons of the Golden West (which had merged with the Native Daughters of the Golden West) once again raised the specter of the "Asiatic peril" to fuel public fear over Japanese competition. Legislation was crafted that prohibited the Japanese from buying agricultural land or leasing it for more than three years. When the Nisei (American-born Japanese who held U.S. citizenship) began acting as guardians for their noncitizen Issei parents, the state of California overwhelmingly passed a referendum prohibiting such acts of guardianship. Similar legislation was passed in Washington State.[54]

In the 1920s the second Ku Klux Klan, which had reemerged on the American landscape in the previous decade, spread nationwide and expanded its circle of hate to include Asians, Hispanics, Catholics, Jews, and southern and eastern European immigrants in addition to African Americans. This revived Klan was especially strong in the South and the Midwest, but it was also significant in the Southwest and the far West, where Asians and Hispanics were the primary targets.[55] The politics of westernness obviously cannot account for the lamentable growth of the Klan to perhaps as many as 5 million dues-paying members at its height in 1925 (the entire U.S. population was only 100 million at the time of the 1920 census); cultural intolerance effortlessly transcended regional boundaries in 1920s America. But the fires of bigotry fed by the Klan in the 1920s were still smoldering when the Depression hit, and the southwestern states enthusiastically supported the deportation (which took as its official label the kinder, gentler term "repatriation") of Mexican Americans. Historian Walter Nugent notes that 450,000 to 1 million Mexican Americans (between one-third and two-thirds of the entire Mexican and Mexican American population residing in the United States), many of them U.S. citizens who had never been to Mexico, were transported there between 1929 and 1935, making it "the largest involuntary mass migration under American auspices up to that time."[56]

In the same decade, voluntary migrants from the poverty-stricken agricultural wasteland of the southern Great Plains, "Okies," "Arkies," and other unfortunates, were subjected to the kind of cultural intolerance in California that was normally reserved for peoples of color.[57] Just a few years later, in 1942, with the Depression winding down and the American war machine winding up, the most infamous act of involuntary mass migration in twentieth-century American history occurred: the relocation of more than 110,000 Japanese and Japanese Americans (400,000 Issei and 700,000 Nisei) from their homes on the Pacific coast to internment camps, which some scholars have labeled concentration camps, in the interior West. Easily identifiable as a race, the Japanese and Japanese Americans lost homes and businesses as well as their democratically guaranteed freedoms during World War II. The fate of other, less easily racially classified, enemy aliens, most notably Italians and Germans, was not nearly so harsh during the war.[58]

The West has developed quite a legacy of exclusion and expulsion in the nineteenth and twentieth centuries, and that legacy has provided the foundation for the anti-immigrant measures of more recent years, such as Proposition 187, passed by Californians in a 1994 referendum and designed to prohibit large numbers of noncitizens from gaining access to state services, including education and health care. A little more than a decade later, in 2005, various private-citizen border-patrol groups, such as California Border

Watch and the Arizona-based American Border Patrol, were making the headlines again, asserting their democratic right to defend the nation's borders, or, to be more precise, the U.S.-Mexico border, since such paranoia is rarely directed toward the U.S.-Canada border. These modern-day border vigilantes vehemently deny that their actions might be motivated by racial prejudice, even as they seek to highlight supposed cultural differences between today's Hispanic immigrants and earlier generations of European immigrants, thus dismissing the potential Americanness and westernness of Hispanics.[59] The links between the frontier memorialists of our story and this long chain of western exclusion and expulsion are far from invisible or insignificant.

Scholars have tended to dismiss the genre of pioneer reminiscence. After all, what can we learn from the triumphal and often tall tales of nearly dead white males and females? As with the fisherman whose catch grows ever larger in his story as time passes, the veracity of old settlers' memories is questionable. These pioneer voices have been regarded—or discarded—by historians as part of the fabric of the mythic veil that needs only to be lifted for the true face of the western past to be revealed. But heritage is a difficult thing to eradicate, and history and memory are inextricably linked. For better or worse, the legacies of western memory shape politics in the contemporary West.

Take, for example, the opponents of growth and development in the contemporary West who reminisce about the way their cherished western communities used to be in the "good old days," before the arrival of super-affluent multiple home owners, mini-homestead compounds, and metropolitan sprawl. Residents of Boulder, Colorado; Jackson Hole, Wyoming; Sun Valley, Idaho; Corvallis, Oregon; Santa Fe, New Mexico; and hundreds of other western "hot spots" tell their own stories that follow the same contours. These contemporary reminiscers, the self-designated official representatives of the true spirit of the West, recall (in their own selective memories, it should be added) simpler, more civil, more moral, more scenic, and more authentically western places and seek to block any further change to their wests. The sentiment is an essentially conservative one, even in cities such as Boulder, where a more liberal constituency opposes growth.

Drawing on their power of primacy—the notion that length of residence in place (that is, chronological proximity to an earlier age of authenticity) confers the right to speak for the "spirit" of that place—these modern day "pioneers" have, in recent decades, expressed their disdain for new arrivals, particularly those coming from California.[60] Their "Caliphobia" (or fear of "Californication") constitutes a good example of the process by which regional identity is nurtured through reaction against other, ostensibly less western, people.⁶¹ Such turn-of-the-millennium concerns are not such a great departure from those at the turn of the last century. Perhaps, like the pioneer reminiscers of earlier generations, today's selective western rememberers are worried mostly about maintaining social status in the new West, even as they present themselves as the protectors of the true spirit of the Old West. Their rhetoric brings to mind the restrictive, time-based requirements for membership in pioneer societies, qualifications that placed a cultural premium on primacy.

The old pioneer reminiscers of a century ago—expressing the fundamental interrelatedness of the ideas of frontier and region—did not just remember the hardships of their westward journeys and play up the object lessons that younger generations could learn from their trials on the trails; they also emphasized the fact that they had been "in place" for longer than other white residents. Since, in their estimation, their racial and cultural affiliation outweighed any claims to primacy that nonwhite groups might have, the fact that Indians and Hispanics had often been in place prior to white pioneers rarely factored into the white pioneers' ruminations about quintessential westernness. A key contour of the white pioneer reminiscence genre was the conferral of primacy on those white Americans who had experienced difficult journeys, transformed formerly inhospitable wastelands, arrived in those places during the frontier period, and, in many cases, displaced the Indians and Hispanics who had arrived before them. This contour has its parallel in contemporary western claims to heightened sense of place based upon primacy.

Different people, of course, have widely varying understandings of the places they live in, and it is difficult to determine whether one person's sense of, or attachment to, a place has more validity than another's, whether one person's identification with a place is deeper, richer, or purer than someone else's. Sometimes people exhibit their attachment to a place and its cultural legacies in the most antagonistic, atavistic, nativistic, and violent ways. Neo-Nazi groups in the northern West seeking to "preserve" a "white homeland" serve as instructive cases in point.⁶² Drawing direct connections between such ugly strains of regional expression and the white pioneer heritage would be too simplistic—the reminiscence genre is hardly monolithic with respect to discussions of race. Nonetheless, it is worth considering the dark underside (as well as the positive side) of these elevated attachments to place.

Claims to heightened "westernness" need to be questioned. Simply to accept the notion that one group's identification with a place is purer than another's, or more rooted in the landscape, more at one with nature, more "real," more western, ignores the purposes behind such claims to attachment. Remember that in the late nineteenth and early twentieth centuries, Anglo pioneers commonly compared the harshness of the particular western environments and frontier journeys that they had experienced with those faced by the settlers of other parts of other western states and regions. Each group of old settlers insisted it had conquered the most barren, inhospitable environment imaginable. Such needs for regional one-upmanship—fostering an "I'm more western than you" mentality—lead us to ask whether sense of place is really so positive a phenomenon in light of the fact that a group's intense attachment to a place, its heightened regional consciousness, may help explain its unwillingness to share that place with others.

The impulse of some intermountain and Pacific northwesterners in the 1980s, 1990s, and 2000s to express their Caliphobia and lament the Californication of "their" promised lands serves as an instructive example of the bolstering of regional identity through expressions of intolerance—an example of regionalism through reaction.[63] Some westerners express these anti-Californian impulses by sporting bumper stickers and T-shirts with such slogans as "Don't Californicate Oregon," "Washington Is Full. Get Out," and "Native Coloradoan."[64] However, any black humor in such printed statements is overshadowed by the fact that they are expressions of regional identity formed through reaction to others. Such expressions of anger or anxiety over the development and destruction of pristine landscapes and the eradication of simple, affordable lifestyles were presumed, in the 1990s, to be a direct consequence of the presence of Californians, whom *Seattle Times* columnist Emmett Watson described as "nitwits," "neurotics," and "sun-bleached barbarians."[65]

The Californication issue helps illustrate the problem of "westernness," or why the politics of westernness or western memory are so problematic and convoluted.[66] California out-migrants have been motivated in part by their perceptions of intermountain and Pacific northwestern places as refuges from pollution, congestion, high property values, high costs of living, crime, and racial tension in Southern California; some of the same factors help account for out-migration of white Californians from the Bay Area, too. Their destinations have been a set of quintessentially "western" safe houses, "last best hiding places," exits on the "white flight highway" from the metropolitan monster lying west of "the West."[67] It has been a back-to-the-land or frontier movement of sorts, displaying a Daniel Boone–esque quality as white Californians flee congested places and head into the relatively wide-open spaces of the intermountain West and coastal Oregon and Washington. But locals draw on the power of primacy (length of residence) to deny the westernness of the newcomers, questioning whether they can ever assimilate and "become western." They view the Golden State expatriates as the great (wealthy) unwashed, people tainted beyond redemption by their former place of residence. Ironically, they are deemed to be a danger to the very same western identity and western surroundings they have come in search of.[68]

Residents' assessments of former Californians as unwestern are based in part on the perception that these comparatively rich migrants bring all the accoutrements—the technological baggage and luxury automobiles—of their old life with them as they begin their presumably simpler, less harried lives in the wide-open (or, to be more accurate, less densely peopled) parts of the West. Even in the twenty-first century, notions of the West as wilderness and "pristine," of untrammeled landscapes as somehow more authentically western than the sprawling metropolises that actually characterize the region and house the vast bulk of its residents are common. We forget that wilderness is less a concrete reality than our own cultural creation and that even the earliest western pioneers dreamed of landscapes dotted with great cities and industrial operations before they looked back wistfully to the days of wide-open frontier landscapes.[69] And in those acts of forgetting, we replay the processes of selective memory construction that characterized those earlier generations. The mere act of having arrived in a western place at an earlier date, when that place was less developed, less "settled," still confers a sense of authentic westernness on residents.

In addition to serving as an illuminating case study in the power of primacy as a determinant of westernness, the rhetoric surrounding the migration of Californians (and Texans, New Yorkers, New Jerseyans, Illinoisans, and others) to the West also highlights the power of rural western imagery as a barometer of identity, and the perceived importance of whiteness to the same. California perhaps seems less western than the intermountain West and the Pacific Northwest to many white Californians because the Golden State has become so racially diverse: Caucasians are now a "minority majority" there.[70] It is less the landscape per se than the mixture of peoples standing against the backdrop of the landscape that nurtures perceptions and misperceptions of westernness. If western mythology does not develop beyond its defining characteristics of white-centeredness and rural-centeredness—if the mythology does not diversify to reflect the region's demographic makeup and its metropolitan character—then how can westernness serve as a thematic construct for a truly inclusive and representative understanding of a contemporary sense of place in the region?

Unfortunately, sizable fractions of the population within certain parts of the West still crave only the "right kinds of people," if they seek population growth at all. The antimigration sentiment leveled at ex-Californians, while far less severe and marked merely by bumper stickers and barbed comments rather than by violence and oppression, nonetheless brings to mind the perceptions that white westerners and easterners alike held of immigrants from other countries starting in the mid-nineteenth century. Similarly dubious notions concerning the unassimilability of newcomers have also driven anti-immigration sentiment. What is more, successive waves of immigrants have, as part of the process of assimilating, themselves laid claim to the constructs of primacy and authenticity.[71] At least the casual expression of anti-immigrant sentiments is no longer as socially acceptable as it was in the late nineteenth and early twentieth centuries. Perhaps the anti-immigrant, antimigrant, anti-Californication sentiments of residents of the intermountain and Pacific Northwest will become less fashionable, too, as time goes on and people adjust more comfortably to the changes going on around them.

Perhaps the rural-centric (or open space–centric) aspect of the politics of westernness will in time also dissipate. Over 80 percent of "westerners" resided in metropolitan areas by 1990. By 2000, the figure was closer to 90 percent.[72] Yet the prevailing influence of frontier mythology—which emphasizes comparatively empty places (for example, "wilderness" areas), thereby rendering them quintessentially western—ensures that the metropolitan spaces, where most westerners live, seem somehow inauthentic, unwestern. It is natural to think about rural spaces as deeply authentic places and more difficult (but essential) to consider seriously the experience of all westerners, from ranchers to reservation residents to suburbanites to high-rise-condo dwellers as "western."[73]

The politics of westernness or western memory are so malleable a construct that they can incorporate green entrepreneurs, cell-phone-phobic adventurers, cowboy conservatives, moralistic liberal agriculturalists and individualistic conservative agriculturalists (including Sagebrush Rebels), oil-industry wildcatters, antigrowth Boulderites, and many others besides. The nation's frontier heritage has created a powerful legacy of westernness, a deep, rich rhetorical well from which groups of all political persuasions have been able to draw in support of their myriad agendas.[74] And while this essay has generally emphasized the less venerable side of this frontier heritage, the ways in which it has nurtured politics of westernness centered on notions of primacy, authenticity, and reaction to change, it is important to emphasize again the concept's flexibility, which may hold the key to more constructive uses of the frontier heritage. In her essay "The Adventures of the Frontier in the Twentieth Century" (1994), Patricia Nelson Limerick outlined the ways in which African Americans, Indians, and other nonwhite Americans have adopted the terms "frontier" and "pioneer" to describe the achievements of individuals of color (describing Jackie Robinson as a pioneer in the arena of race relations, for example). She expresses a characteristic hopefulness that "the popular usage of the word ["frontier" will] begin to reckon with the complexity of the westward movement and its consequences," and she suggests that "the [frontier] concept works as a cultural glue—a mental and emotional fastener that, in some very curious and unexpected ways, works to hold us together."[75]

Regionalism, too, can be a wonderfully positive force that has more to do with community integration and cooperation than with opposition to "others." Western regionalism has often manifested itself in ways that would make the late nineteenth-century regionalist, philosopher, and Californian Josiah Royce proud. He advocated a "wise provincialism," an affinity for place devoid of narrow parochialism.[76] The recent efforts of some northern Great Plains residents to move beyond sectional and sectarian differences to establish interdenominational churches, consolidated school systems, and economic enterprises are a good case in point.[77] Still, it is worth emphasizing that such efforts, while they have bridged sectional and sectarian divides, have rarely sought to bridge the broader cultural divides between races.[78] The kinds of healthy attachments to place that naturally lend themselves to interaction and cooperation among and between different cultural groups can form only when residents move beyond the construct of primacy. When residents of western regions stop equating the authenticity of their sense of place with their longevity in place, the kind of wise provincialism that Royce hoped for is more likely to develop.

Perhaps scholars will have to abandon "westernness" entirely as a thematic construct, since it so thoroughly mirrors popular notions about the region that apply only to a portion of its residents. If these popular perceptions of the West and its special promise are largely Eurocentric creations, the mythology of a particular group seeking to explain its past actions and justify its present position of dominance, then can other people buy into the myth and "become western"? Or, to put a more hopeful spin on the matter, as Limerick does, has the reality of the West's tremendous racial and ethnic diversity started to alter popular notions of what it is to "be" western? One can only hope that popular perceptions of westernness are broadened to reflect current (and historical) metropolitan and demographic realities. If this does not occur, the concept of westernness will have little value for scholars, though the concept will, unfortunately, retain its usefulness for those westerners seeking to assert their presumed primacy and authenticity in opposition to change. The politics of western memory will not go away, but more honest, more sophisticated, more inclusive politics of westernness might yet develop in tandem with a fuller, richer, more honest understanding of the frontier and western past. The hopefulness of such western regionalists and public intellectuals as Royce in the nineteenth century, Carey McWilliams in the twentieth, and Limerick in the twenty-first is heartening. All three point to the need for a full reckoning with the region's failings, including its legacy of cultural exclusion, if a healthier politics of westernness is to emerge.

NOTES

1. The term "Jayhawker" would not be applied to Kansans until the late 1850s. The terms "politics of westernness" and "politics of western memory" are used interchangeably in this essay.

2. Information on the Jayhawker deaths is drawn from Richard E. Lingenfelter, *Death Valley and the Amargosa: A Land of Illusion* (Berkeley and Los Angeles: University of California Press, 1986), 46.

3. The exact number of the Jayhawker party is difficult to determine, since people periodically joined and abandoned the group during the course of the journey. L. Burr Beldon provides a "census" of all the Jayhawkers in his book *Goodbye Death Valley! The 1849 Jayhawker Escape* (Palm Desert, Calif.: Desert Magazine Press, 1956). A listing of the Jayhawkers is also available in Jayhawker Photo Album 1, in the Jayhawker Collection, Henry E. Huntington Library (hereafter referred to as JC, HEH), San Marino, California, made up of nine boxes of manuscripts, eight volumes of scrapbooks, and the photo album.

The brief summary of the Jayhawkers' journey provided here is drawn from various sources, including the entry for the Jayhawkers' Collection in the *Guide to Historical Manuscripts in the Huntington Library* (San Marino, Calif.: Huntington Library Press, 1979); J. G., "The Jayhawkers of Death Valley" (Marysville, Kans.: Privately printed, 1938); Federal Writers' Project of the Works Progress Administration of Northern California, *Death Valley: A Guide* (Boston: Houghton Mifflin, 1939), 14–19; Margaret Long, *The Shadow of the Arrow* (Caldwell, Idaho: Caxton Printers, 1941); Beldon, *Goodbye Death Valley*; L. Burr Beldon, ed., *Death Valley Heroine: And Source Accounts of the 1849 Travelers* (San Bernardino, Calif.: Inland Printing & Engraving, 1954); John Walton Caughey, "Southwest from Salt Lake in 1849," *Pacific Historical Review* 6, no. 2 (1937): 142–164; Frank F. Latta, *Death Valley '49ers* (Santa Cruz, Calif.: Bear State Books, 1979); George Koenig, *Beyond This Place There Be Dragons: The Routes of the Death Valley 1849ers through Nevada, Death Valley, and on to Southern California* (Glendale, Calif.: Arthur H. Clark, 1984); Lingenfelter, *Death Valley and the Amargosa*, 39–51; and Benjamin Levy, *Death Valley National Monument: Historical Background and Study* (Washington, D.C.: National Park Service, 1969). Leroy Johnson and Jean Johnson, eds., *Escape from Death Valley: As Told by William Manly Lewis and other '49ers* (Reno and Las Vegas: University of Nevada Press, 1987) provides a good overview of research on the Jayhawkers. Genne Nelson has prepared an excellent bibliography of sources related to the Jayhawkers (copy in author's possession).

4. It is possible that one of the other groups traveling across Death Valley around

the same time as the Jayhawkers did engage in cannibalism.; see Latta, *Death Valley '49ers*, 8.

5. Box 3, folders JA 135–138, 1894–1915, JC, HEH, "Reunion regrets, etc.," William F. ["Buffalo Bill"] Cody to John Burt Colton, three letters and one telegram; box 5, folders JA 273–278, 1898–1902, John Burt Colton to Theodore Roosevelt, in ibid.; and box 4, folders JA 804–807, 1897–1899, Frederic Remington to John Burt Colton, four letters, in ibid. Colton appears in a photograph with Cody, R. H. "Pony Bob" Haslam, Prentiss Ingraham, and Alexander Majors in Prentiss Ingraham, ed., *Seventy Years on the Frontier: Alexander Majors' Memoirs of a Lifetime on the Border, with a Preface by (General W. F. Cody) Buffalo Bill* (Chicago and New York: Rand McNally, 1893), unnumbered page, between pages 152 and 153.

6. George G. Spurr, Secretary, New England Associated California Pioneers of '49, to John Burt Colton, March 5, 1893, box 3, folders JA 891–892, JC, HEH.

7. See, for example, Sharlot M. Hall, "In the Land of the 'Forty-Niners," *Out West* 29 (December 1908): 397–417.

8. Interestingly, the Steven Spielberg–directed television miniseries *Into the West* (TNT, first broadcast June–July 2005) emphasizes the base materialism and the tragic consequences of California gold fever.

9. Fuller coverage of the "crisis of the nineties" and the accompanying "frontier anxiety" is provided in David M. Wrobel, *The End of American Exceptionalism: Frontier Anxiety from the Old West to the New Deal* (Lawrence: University Press of Kansas, 1993).

10. William Lewis Manly, *Death Valley in '49* (San Jose, Calif.: Pacific Tree & Vine, 1894; repr., Chicago: Lakeside Press, 1927). The material in the book was originally published as a series of letters in the *Santa Clara Daily* between June 1887 and July 1890. Manly was not an original member of the Jayhawker group, but he and another teamster, John Rogers, traveled with the Jayhawkers, and various other smaller groups including the Bennett and Arcane families, known respectively as the Bugsmashers and the Mississippians, through Death Valley. It was Manly and Rogers who would travel out of Death Valley to the California settlements and return with food for the Bennett and Arcane families. Manly is included among the Jayhawkers in the Jayhawker Photo Album, HEH, Special Collections, a collection of images taken in 1893. For more on Manly, see Patricia Nelson Limerick, *Desert Passages: Encounters with the American Deserts* (Albuquerque: University of New Mexico Press, 1985), 45–59.

11. Manly, *Death Valley in '49*, 464.

12. Ibid. For an interesting account of the Briers' journey, see Reverend John Wells Brier, "The Death Valley Party of 1849," pts. 1 and 2, *Out West* 18 (March 1903): 326–335, and 18 (April 1903): 456–465. The author of the articles is the son of Reverend James W. Brier and Juliet Brier. See also Grace Leadingham, "Juliet Wells Brier: Heroine of Death Valley," pts. 1 and 2, *Pacific Historian* 8, no. 2 (1964): 61–74, and no. 3 (1964): 121–127.

13. Manly, *Death Valley in '49*, 464. A rare exception to the common criticisms of the Reverend Brier in historical accounts is that of L. Burr Beldon, who, in *Death Valley Heroine*, writes of Manly: "His belittling references to the Rev. Mr. Brier, a sick man who survived despite the loss of one hundred pounds, is shameful. The

Methodist clergyman rendered a semi-invalid due to an intestinal disorder wasted from 175 to 75 pounds in the ordeal, a deliverance for which he ever gave his Creator credit" (13).

14. Charles Lummis, editorial note on the 1903 Jayhawker reunion at the home of Juliet Brier in Lodi, California, *Out West* 18 (March 1903): 326. For further praise of Juliet Brier and a positive view of Reverend Brier, see Charles F. Lummis, *Some Strange Corners of Our Country: The Wonderland of the Southwest* (New York: Century, 1891; repr., Tucson: University of Arizona Press, 1989), 37–42 (page numbers in the 1989 edition); the chapter "Death Valley" in *Mesa, Cañyon, and Pueblo: Our Wonderland of the Southwest—Its Marvels of Nature—Its Pageant of the Earth Building—Its Strange Peoples—Its Centuried Romance* (New York: Century, 1925), 63–78; and Thomas Shannon, "With the Jayhawkers in Death Valley Fifty-three Years Ago—A Little Band of Hardy Pioneers," *San Jose Daily Mercury*, 16 November 1903, reprinted in Beldon, *Death Valley Heroine*, 57–60, 59. George Wharton James's chapters "The Generous Heroes of Death Valley, Manly and Rogers" and "The Unknown Heroes of Death Valley," in *Heroes of California: The Story of the Founders of the Golden State as Narrated by Themselves or Gleaned from Other Sources* (Boston: Little, Brown, 1910), 73–85 and 86–93, make no mention of the Brier family. One suspects that Lummis's extended coverage of the Briers in *Mesa, Cañyon, and Pueblo* was partly a response to James's emphasis on Manly and Rogers.

15. Juliet Brier, "Our Christmas amid the Terrors of Death Valley," *San Francisco Call*, 25 December 1898, reprinted in Belden, *Death Valley Heroine*, 21–28. The *Call* article, along with Brier's second account, which appeared in the *San Francisco Examiner*, 24 February 1901, are reproduced in Long, *Shadow of the Arrow*, 195–215. See also "Mrs. Brier's Last Account," *San Francisco Examiner*, 27 May 1913, and *Stockton Independent* and reprinted in the *Carson City (Nev.) News*, 8 June 1913; this latter reprint is included in Beldon, *Death Valley Heroine*, 31–35. The Reverend John W. Brier died on 2 November 1898.

16. Latta provides some coverage of Reverend Brier's disassociation from the Jayhawkers in *Death Valley '49ers*, 169–186.

17. There certainly seems to have been no lack of media interest in her story.

18. Colton must have felt gratified when an Oregon woman wrote to him in 1914 about this generational contrast: "These days people do not have any of the hardships that our forefathers had to undergo, and still very often you hear of what a hard time some folks have coming across the continent in Palace Cars." Minnie Moeller to John Burt Colton, 16 January 1914, box 6, folders JA 747–51, JC, HEH.

19. The year Colton died, the *Saturday Evening Post* featured an essay that provided extensive coverage of the Jayhawkers: Frederick R. Bechdolt, "How Death Valley Was Named," Stories of the Old West, *Saturday Evening Post*, 19 July 1919, 30–34 and 66.

20. See Long, "Appendix C: The Jayhawker Reunions," in *Shadow of the Arrow*, 277–280, 279. The Huntington Library in San Marino, California, acquired the Jayhawker Papers (including diaries of the journey, correspondence, maps, scrapbooks, and photographs) from the Colton family in 1930.

21. Latta, in *Death Valley '49ers*, refers to the efforts of the Jayhawkers and the seven other small parties to cross Death Valley as "the most astounding of all migratory epics to be recorded in the history of the settlement of America" (6–7). If the extent of scholarly coverage and public interest in an event are yardsticks of its importance, then the story of the Death Valley migrants does not live up to Latta's claim. The Jayhawkers and the approximately fifty other migrants have not been forgotten by history, but neither has their epic journey entered the public consciousness to nearly the same extent as has that of the Donner Party. It is interesting to note that even in late nineteenth-century works of California history—such as Josiah Royce's *California: From the Conquest in 1846 to the Second Vigilance Committee in San Francisco* (Boston and New York: Houghton Mifflin; Cambridge, Mass.: Riverside Press, 1886)—the Donner Party commonly receives coverage, while the Death Valley migrants do not.

22. See Leroy C. Johnson, "The Trunk Is Bunk," in *Proceedings of the Fifth Death Valley Conference on History and Prehistory, March 4–7, 1999*, ed. Jean Johnson (Bishop, Calif.: Community Printing & Publishing, 1999), 252–277, 252. For more on the contents of the trunk, see LeRoy C. Johnson, http://deathvalley.com/gold/goldarticle13.shtml.

23. A mountain of scholarship on the relationship between history and memory has emerged in recent decades. The seminal works on the topic by sociologist Maurice Halbwachs from the 1940s and 1950s have been translated and published in the volume *On Collective Memory*, ed. and trans. Lewis A. Coser (Chicago: University of Chicago Press, 1992). Halbwachs emphasized the essential role that social groups play in the construction of individuals' memories and the variety of memories produced by different groups within any given society.

24. There were disagreements among the early chroniclers of the Death Valley journey. Indeed, a few writers painted the Reverend Brier in a more heroic light; see note 14.

25. For an excellent overview of Bancroft's career, see Charles S. Peterson, "Hubert Howe Bancroft: First Western Regionalist," in *Writing Western History: Essays on Major Western Historians*, ed. Richard W. Etulain (Albuquerque: University of New Mexico Press, 1991), 43–70; the estimation of the shelf space required to house Bancroft's books is in ibid., 51. Peter Novick, in *That Noble Dream: The Objectivity Question and the American Historical Profession* (New York: Cambridge University Press, 1988), 44–46, notes that Bancroft was a transitional figure in the professionalization of American history. While Bancroft was probably the first American to receive a Ph.D. from a German university and clearly took the gathering of evidence very seriously, professional historians of the time generally considered him (as they did Francis Parkman) to be part of the preprofessional class of historians, often referred to as the romantic historians, on account of their proclivity for bringing their ideological convictions to bear on their histories.

26. In retrospect, the society's condemnation of Bancroft seems rather ironic, since historians have identified him as one of the most significant architects of a positive Gold Rush heritage for California. For more on Bancroft's role in the construction of a Gold Rush mythology, see Glen Gendzel, "Pioneers and Padres: Com-

peting Mythologies in Northern and Southern California, 1850–1930," *Western Historical Quarterly* 32 (Spring 2001): 56–79, 60–62.

27. Willard B. Farwell's report, "In the Matter of the Society of California Pioneers vs. Hubert Howe Bancroft, an Honorary Member of Said Society," is in *Proceedings of the Society of California Pioneers in Reference to the Histories of Hubert Howe Bancroft* (San Francisco: Sterett, February 1894), 4–6. In his report Farwell also highlighted what he saw as numerous errors in Bancroft's two-volume *History of Oregon* (1886–1888).

It is worth noting that Josiah Royce's earlier work *California* drew on the documentary sources in Bancroft's Library and produced a damning account of Frémont's central role in the Bear Flag Revolt of 1846. Royce wrote: "He brought war into a peaceful department; his operations began an estrangement, insured a memory of bloodshed, excited a furious bitterness of feeling between two peoples that were henceforth to dwell in California, such as all his own subsequent personal generosity and kindness could never again make good." Royce added, "From the Bear Flag affair we can date the beginning of the degradation, the ruin, and the oppression of the Californian people by our own" (111–112). A good portion of Royce's *California*, 48–150, is devoted to undermining Frémont's own version of his role in the revolt. Compared with Royce's damning treatment of Frémont, and Royce's powerful indictment—in a chapter titled "The Conquerors and Their Consciences" (152–156)—of the glaring hypocrisy of the nation's efforts to explain away its imperialistic acts in California, Bancroft's treatment seems quite tame. Still, for whatever reasons—perhaps it was just that the society members' sensitivities were more acute in 1893 and that Bancroft's history had simply garnered more public attention than Royce's—it was Bancroft who became the subject of the society's ire, not Royce. For excellent coverage of Royce, see Robert V. Hine, *Josiah Royce: From Grass Valley to Harvard* (Norman: University of Oklahoma Press, 1992); "The Western Intellectual: Josiah Royce," *Montana: The Magazine of Western History*, Summer 1991, 70–72; and "The American West as Metaphysics: A Perspective on Josiah Royce," *Pacific Historical Review* 58 (1989): 267–291.

28. *Proceedings of the California Pioneers in Reference to the Histories of Hubert Howe Bancroft*, 31–32. The response of the society to Bancroft's "revisionist" histories serves as an interesting early example of the debate over who owns the past when collective memories collide with historical reconstructions. The most notable recent example of this clash is the controversy that surrounded the Smithsonian Institution's 1995 exhibit marking the fiftieth anniversary of the dropping of atomic bombs on Hiroshima and Nagasaki. In both cases, the memories of actual participants in events that had occurred a half century earlier clashed with the views of historians. For more on the debate over the *Enola Gay* exhibit, see Edward T. Linenthal and Tom Engelhardt, eds., *History Wars: The Enola Gay and Other Battles for the American Past* (New York: Henry Holt, 1996).

29. I am using the term "collective memory" far more loosely than do the cultural-hegemony theorists who draw on the ideas of Antonio Gramsci and Raymond Williams. The western pioneer societies of the late nineteenth and early twentieth centuries were losing political power, and their organized memories were an effort

to maintain their relevance. Old western settlers clearly declined in significance over time, yet their collective memories contributed to the process by which a frontier-centered western heritage developed and sustained itself in the national consciousness. For an excellent brief discussion of collective memory, see John Walton, *Storied Land: Community and Memory in Monterey* (Berkeley and Los Angeles: University of California Press, 2001), 289–295.

30. John Mack Faragher writes that Turner provided "intellectual legitimization for [William F.] Cody's images"; see Faragher's afterword, "The Significance of the Frontier in American Historiography: A Guide to Further Reading," in Frederick Jackson Turner, *Rereading Frederick Jackson Turner: "The Significance of the Frontier in American History" and Other Essays*, ed. John Mack Faragher (New York: Henry Holt, 1994), 225–241, 230. However, it is important to note that Cody's images popularized sentiments that were deeply engrained in the western pioneer reminiscence genre.

31. To the cynical observer, these old pioneer reminiscers might be deemed a good example of "the paranoid style in American politics," which historian Richard Hofstadter wrote about in the 1960s. But the old western reminiscers discussed in the present essay did not really resemble the "clinical paranoids" of Hofstadter's essay, who saw themselves as the last line in the defense of moral righteousness in a "hostile and conspiratorial world." See Hofstadter, *The Paranoid Style in American Politics and Other Essays* (New York: Alfred A. Knopf, 1966), 4. The old pioneers did not hate the postfrontier present or view it as evil; they just preferred the frontier past and wanted society to better recognize the foundation-building role they had played. Indeed, these reminiscers may be better representatives of Hoftstadter's earlier "status anxiety" thesis than the late nineteenth- and early twentieth-century Progressive reformers for whom he coined the phrase in another of his influential works, *The Age of Reform: From Bryan to FDR* (New York: Vintage Books/Random House, 1955). Hofstadter argued that these reformers' efforts to reconstruct society were motivated more by self-interest than by any altruistic dedication to reform. In short, they wanted, through reform, to re-create the kind of society in which their forefathers and foremothers had been the great social, economic, and political movers and shakers. Old western pioneers, through their writings and their involvement in pioneer societies, were trying to maintain their status as frontier heroes in a changing, postfrontier world; they were trying to be players on a new stage.

32. Michael Kammen, in *Mystic Chords of Memory: The Transformation of Tradition in American Culture* (New York: Alfred A. Knopf, 1991), 254–282, provides an excellent discussion of the broader national context surrounding the foundation of pioneer societies.

33. Interestingly, the Oregon Pioneer and Historical Society was separate from the larger Oregon Pioneer Association. The two groups did attempt to merge in 1874–1875, but the effort failed. See Oregon Pioneer Association, "Constitution of the Oregon Pioneer Association," in *Oregon Pioneer Association, Constitution and Transactions, 1st–14th, 1874–1886* (Salem, Ore.: E. M. Waite, Steam Printer and Bookbinder; Portland, Ore.: Press of Geo H. Himes, 1875-1887).

34. The quotation is from John Hyde Braly, *Memory Pictures: An Autobiography* (Los

Angeles: Nuener, 1912), 5, in Graff Collection of Western Americana, Newberry Library, Chicago, 390. For additional examples of California reminiscers' claims to pioneer preeminence, see Frank Mattison's address "The Sturdy Pioneers," delivered to the Native Sons of the Golden West during the Admission Day celebrations of 1897, in *Proceedings of the Twentieth Annual Session of the Grand Parlor of the Native Sons of the Golden West, April 26–29, 1897* (San Francisco: Julius Gabriel, 1897), 63–70.

35. Governor R. J. Oglesby (Illinois), in *Report of the Second Reunion of the Tri-State Old Settlers Association of Illinois, Missouri, and Iowa, September 30, 1885* (Keokuk, Iowa: R. B. Ogden & Son, 1885), 16–21, 18.

36. C. W. Irish, untitled speech at the Twentieth Annual Reunion of the Johnson County, Iowa, Old Settlers Association, 18 August 1886, and a second speech to the same group, 24 August 1887, both in *Proceedings of the Johnson County [Iowa] Old Settlers' Association, from 1886 to 1899* (N.p., d.d. NEW GC 2132—this is the abbreviation for Graff Collection, Newberry Library), 40 and 48.

37. On Wyoming, see Dr. C. G. Countant, *History of Wyoming and the Far West* (Laramie, Wyo.: Chaplin, Spafford, & Mathison, 1899), 17–19. For Montana, see Guy Piatt, ed., *The Story of Butte: Old Timer's Hand-Book*, special number of the *Butte Bystander*, 15 April 1897 (Butte, Mont.: Press of the Standard Manufacturing & Printing Co., 1897), 19. For Washington, see Charles Prosch, *Reminiscences of Washington Territory: Scenes, Incidents, and Reflections of the Pioneer Period on Puget Sound* (Seattle, Wash., 1904), 121–122. For South Dakota, see Jesse Brown and A. M. Willard, *The Black Hills Trails: A History of the Struggles of the Pioneers in the Winning of the Black Hills*, ed. John T. Milek (Rapid City, S. Dak.: Rapid City Journal, 1924), unnumbered prefatory page; Brown and Willard described the Black Hills as "the last real frontier border on the continent," a place marked by "the elemental struggle of man with nature." And for the Mormons as the quintessential western pioneers, see Charles W. Carter, *The Exodus of 1847* (Salt Lake City: Utah Lithographing, 1897).

38. C. P. Arnold, *The Vanished Frontier*, pamphlet reprinted in *Annals of Wyoming* 16 (January 1944): 57–60, 59. Arnold was a past president (1929) of the Wyoming Pioneer Association, an organization that developed in 1925 out of Wyoming's first organization of pioneers, founded in 1884.

39. For more on pioneer society cutoff dates, see Clyde A. Milner II, "The View from Wisdom: Four Layers of Regional Identity," in *Under an Open Sky: Rethinking America's Western Past*, ed. William Cronon, George Miles, and Jay Gitlin (New York: W. W. Norton, 1992), 213.

40. Hiram Knowles to J. H. Cole, Secretary, Tri-State Old Settlers Association, September 15, 1885, in *Report of the Second Reunion of the Tri-State Old Settlers Association*, 73. Knowles regretted that he was unable to make the trip from Butte City, Montana, back to the Midwest to be formally inducted.

41. Milner, "View from Wisdom," 213.

42. The sheer weight of these collective remembrances is astounding. Library shelves are filled with dusty old volumes of reconstructed memories of the West. While antiquarians have examined these sources with great care, professional historians have largely ignored them.

43. James U. Sanders, in *34th Annual Meeting of the Society of Montana Pioneers: Officers, Reports, Address* (Helena, Mont.: Society of Montana Pioneers, 1917).

44. E. G. Cattermole, *Famous Frontiersmen, Pioneers, and Scouts* (Chicago: Donohue, Henneberry, 1890), iii. While not strictly a part of the pioneer reminiscence genre, Cattermole's book does reflect the genre's key themes.

45. See the *Colorado Pioneer Register*, Maria Davies McGrath Collection, Denver Public Library, 27.

46. See "Constitution of the Oregon Pioneer Association," in *Oregon Pioneer Association, Constitution and Transactions, 1st–14th, 1874–1886* (Salem, Ore.: E. M. Waite; Portland, Ore.: Geo. H. Himes, 1875–1887), 1874:4.

47. See, for example, Colonel Wilbur F. Sanders, "The Pioneers," speech delivered in Helena, Montana, 6 July 1902, quoted in Mary Ronan, *Frontier Woman: The Story of Mary Ronan, as Told to Margaret Ronan*, ed. H. G. Merriam ([Missoula]: University of Montana, 1973), viii.

48. Among the many notable instances of recognition of pioneer women are Jacob Ricord, "Reminiscences of Pioneer Women," speech at the twenty-seventh annual meeting of the Johnson County (Iowa) Old Settlers Association, 24 August 1893, in *Proceedings of the Johnson County [Iowa] Old Settlers' Association, from 1886 to 1899*, n.p., and Prosch, *Reminiscences of Washington Territory*, 122. See also Sarah Fell's autobiography, *Threads of Alaskan Gold* (1904; manuscript, Graff 1303). For more on the role of women pioneers, see Annette Kolodny, *The Lay of the Land: Metaphor as Experience and History in American Life and Letters* (Chapel Hill: University of North Carolina Press, 1975) and *The Land before Her: Fantasy and Experience of the American Frontiers, 1630–1860* (Chapel Hill: University of North Carolina Press, 1984); Joan Jensen, *With These Hands: Women Working on the Land* (Old Westbury, N.Y.: Feminist Press and McGraw-Hill, 1981) and *Promise to the Land: Essays on Rural Women* (Albuquerque: University of New Mexico Press, 1991); and Glenda Riley, *The Female Frontier: A Comparative View of Women on the Prairie and the Plains* (Lawrence: University Press of Kansas, 1988).

49. See, for example, Harry Noyes Pratt's poem "The Pioneer Mother," in Elisha Brooks, *A Pioneer Mother of California* (San Francisco: Harr Wagner, 1922), preface (unnumbered).

50. *Proceedings of the Twentieth Annual Session of the Grand Parlor of the Native Sons of the Golden West*, 45.

51. For more on the Native Sons and nativism, see Peter Thomas Conmy, *The Origins and Purposes of the Native Sons of the Golden West* (San Francisco: Dolores Press, 1956), 18–19.

52. Will C. Bishop, "Salutory," *Sons of Colorado* 1 (June 1906): 3. The journal lasted for more than twenty years, the last issue appearing in April 1928.

53. The Native Sons of the Golden West Web site, www.nsgw.org, provides information on the organization's various charitable and preservation-related efforts. While these place the organization in a favorable light in the early years of the twenty-first century, a parallel southern organization of sorts, the Sons of Confederate Veterans, has been the subject of much negative press on account of that society's ties to white-supremacist groups.

54. For a good overview of these restrictive measures, see Walter Nugent, *Into the West: The Story of Its People* (New York: Alfred A. Knopf, 1999), 165–170, and Patricia Nelson Limerick, "Racialism on the Run," chap. 8 in *The Legacy of Conquest: The Unbroken Past of the American West* (New York: W. W. Norton, 1987), 258–292. For fuller coverage, see Roger Daniels, *The Politics of Prejudice: The Anti-Japanese Movement in California and the Struggle for Japanese Exclusion* (1962; repr., Berkeley and Los Angeles: University of California Press, 1977).

55. Numerous state and regional studies of the second Klan are available. Among the most useful are two of the earliest works: Charles C. Alexander, *The Ku Klux Klan in the Southwest* (1965; repr., Norman: University of Oklahoma Press, 1995), and David Chalmers, *Hooded Americanism: The First Century of the Ku Klux Klan, 1865–1965* (Garden City, N.Y.: Doubleday, 1965).

56. Nugent, *Into the West*, 235.

57. The most poignant account of anti-"Okie" prejudice is John Steinbeck's classic novel *The Grapes of Wrath* (1939; repr., with an introduction by Robert DeMott, New York: Penguin Books, 1992). The best historical account of the Okie migration to California is James Gregory's *American Exodus: The Dust Bowl Migration and Okie Culture in California* (New York: Oxford University Press, 1989).

58. For an excellent brief overview of Japanese and Japanese American relocation, see Nugent, *Into the West*, 258–265.

59. Limerick, in *Legacy of Conquest*, wrote about an earlier generation of southwestern border patrollers; see 339–349.

60. Hal Rothman discusses the theme of primacy, or longevity, at length in *Devil's Bargains: Tourism in the Twentieth-Century American West* (Lawrence: University Press of Kansas, 1998); see esp. 376–377.

61. It is important to consider that the recent demographic growth and accompanying development in some western states (Colorado is a prime example) owes as much to intrastate as to interstate migration. See, for example, David Olinger, "Sprawling Colorado—Who's to Blame?" *Denver Post*, 7 February 1999. For more on Colorado's "sprawl," see Michael E. Long, "Colorado's Front Range," *National Geographic*, November 1996, 80–103, and Larry Fish, "Sprawl Spreads across Colorado, Bringing Concerns with It," *Philadelphia Inquirer*, 3 March 2000. It is worth noting, too, that such antimigrant sentiments are as likely to be voiced by urban dwellers as by rural dwellers in states such as Washington, Oregon, Idaho, and Colorado.

62. Richard White provides some discussion of militia groups in his Western History Association presidential address, published as "The Current Weirdness in the West," *Western Historical Quarterly* 28 (Spring 1997): 5–16. For a fuller treatment of the topic, see Evelyn A. Schlatter, *Aryan Cowboys: White Supremacists and the Search for a New Frontier, 1970–2000* (Austin: University of Texas Press, 2006).

63. Clyde A. Milner II explores how regional identity can form through opposition to outside forces in "View from Wisdom," 203–222, and in "The Shared Memory of Montana Pioneers," *Montana: The Magazine of Western History*, Winter 1987, 2–13.

64. For more on the Washington State bumper sticker, see William Celis III, "California Dreamers Who Move to Seattle Get the Big Chill: Locals Blame the Emigres

for Pollution, Congestion, Discos, and Tanning Salons," *Wall Street Journal*, 10 October 1989. In Colorado the "Native Coloradoan" bumper sticker is quite popular. Some of the students at the University of Colorado, Boulder, sport a bumper sticker that reads "Semi-Native Coloradoan," an amusing rejoinder to the original.

65. Quoted in Celis, "California Dreamers," A1.

66. Incidentally, the pervasiveness of the concept of Californication is evidenced by its entry into popular culture. A notable example is the Red Hot Chili Peppers' 1999 CD release *Californication* (WEA/Warner Brothers, 1999), whose title track explores the theme of the malign influence of California culture on the nation.

67. Mary Murphy utilizes the phrases "last best hiding place" and "white flight highway" in her essay "Searching for an Angle of Repose: Women, Work, and Creativity in Early Montana," in *Many Wests: Place, Culture, and Regional Identity*, ed. David M. Wrobel and Michael C. Steiner (Lawrence: University Press of Kansas, 1997), 156–176, quotations on 172. The original term, "last best place," is drawn from William Kittredge and Annick Smith, eds., *The Last Best Place: A Montana Anthology* (Helena: Montana Historical Society Press, 1988).

68. For more on the economic reasons for California out-migration in the late twentieth century, see Nugent, *Into the West*, 351–379.

69. For more on the theme of wilderness as a cultural construct, see the essays in William Cronon, ed., *Uncommon Ground: Rethinking the Human Place in Nature* (New York: W. W. Norton, 1995), especially Cronon's own "The Trouble with Wilderness, or Getting Back to the Wrong Nature," 69–90; and Ethan Carr, *Wilderness by Design: Landscape Architecture and the National Parks Service* (Lincoln: University of Nebraska Press, 1999).

70. By September 2000, Caucasians had become a minority in California. See Mark Balsassare, "California's Majority-Minority Milestone: What Lies Ahead?" *San Diego Union Tribune*, September 7, 2000: http://www.ppic.org/main/commentary.asp?i=227.

71. The scholarly literature on American nativism is enormous and fast growing. Included among these works is John Higham's seminal study *Strangers in the Land: Patterns of American Nativism, 1865–1925* (New Brunswick, N.J.: Rutgers University Press, 1955) and his *Send These to Me: Jews and Other Immigrants in Urban America* (New York: Atheneum, 1975); Ronald Takaki's important edited collection *From Different Shores: Perspectives on Race and Ethnicity in America* (New York: Oxford University Press, 1994); and Dale T. Knobel's *"America for the Americans": The Nativist Movement in the United States* (New York: Twayne, 1996).

72. The statistic on western metropolitanism is from Carl Abbott, *The Metropolitan Frontier: Cities in the Modern American West* (Tucson: University of Arizona Press, 1993), xii. See also Nugent, *Into the West*, 375. Roger Lotchin provides an excellent discussion of the centrality of urban history to understanding the West in "The Impending Western Urban Past: An Essay on the Twentieth-Century West," in *Researching Western History: Topics in the Twentieth Century*, ed. Gerald Nash and Richard Etulain (Albuquerque: University of New Mexico Press, 1997), 53–81; see also Carl Abbott, "The American West and the Three Urban Revolutions," in *Old West/New West: Quo Vadis?*

ed. Gene M. Gressley (Worland, Wyo.: High Plains, 1994), 75–99. For further commentary on the need to move beyond rural imagery and deal with western urban arenas, see Patricia Nelson Limerick, "The Realization of the American West," in *The New Regionalism*, ed. Charles Reagan Wilson (Jackson: University Press of Mississippi, 1998), 71–98.

73. A tiny sampling of sources that address the issue of regional identity in metropolitan places includes Edward W. Soja's *Postmodern Geographies: The Reassertion of Space in Critical Social Theory* (New York: Verso, 1989); Allen J. Scott and Edward W. Soja, eds., *The City: Los Angeles and Urban Theory at the End of the Twentieth Century* (Berkeley and Los Angeles: University of California Press, 1996); Michael Sorkin, ed., *Variations on a Theme Park: The New American City and the End of Public Space* (New York: Hill & Wang, 1992); Edward S. Casey, *Getting Back into Place: Toward a Renewed Understanding of the Place World* (Bloomington: Indiana University Press, 1993). David Goldfield provides an interesting model that western historians might consider in his *Region, Race, and Cities: Interpreting the Urban South* (Baton Rouge: Louisiana State University Press, 1997). Also worth mentioning is Linda Groat, ed., *Giving Places Meaning* (New York: Harcourt, Brace, 1995), a collection of essays on place by environmental psychologists.

74. For a generally more positive assessment of the frontier heritage than this essay provides, see Ray Allen Billington, *America's Frontier Heritage* (New York: Holt, Rinehart & Winston, 1966).

75. Patricia Nelson Limerick, "The Adventures of the Frontier in the Twentieth Century," in *The Frontier in American Culture*, ed. James R. Grossman (Berkeley and Los Angeles: University of California Press, 1994), 66–102, 92, and 94.

76. See Josiah Royce, "Provincialism." This 1902 Phi Beta Kappa Address at the University of Iowa was first printed in the *Boston Evening Transcript*, was then reprinted in *Race Questions, Provincialism, and Other American Problems* (New York: Macmillan, 1908; repr., New York: Arno Press, 1977), 57–108, and was more recently published in *The Basic Writings of Josiah Royce*, ed. John J. McDermott, 2 vols. (Chicago: University of Chicago Press, 1969), 2:1067–1088.

77. See James A. Shortridge, "The Expectations of Others: Struggles toward a Sense of Place on the Northern Plains," in Wrobel and Steiner, *Many Wests*, 114–135.

78. For a good discussion of the range of possibilities—from the most positive to the most negative—associated with regionalism, see Patricia Nelson Limerick, "Region and Reason," in *All Over the Map: Rethinking American Regions*, ed. Edward Ayers et al. (Baltimore and London: Johns Hopkins University Press, 1996), 83–104, especially 103.

Contributors

DARREN DOCHUK is an assistant professor of history at Purdue University. His essay draws upon his award-winning 2005 dissertation at Notre Dame University, "From Bible Belt to Sunbelt: Plain Folk Religion, Grassroots Politics, and the Southernization of Southern California, 1939–1969." His book based on the dissertation is forthcoming.

DAVID FARBER is a professor of history at Temple University. His books include *The Age of Great Dreams: America in the 1960s*, *Sloan Rules: Alfred P. Sloan and the Triumph of General Motors*, *Taken Hostage: The Iran Hostage Crisis and America's First Encounter with Radical Islam*, and *What They Think of Us: International Perceptions of the United States since 9/11*.

IGNACIO M. GARCÍA, the Lemuel Hardison Redd, Jr. Professor of Western and Latino History at Brigham Young University, is the author of several books, including *Chicanismo: The Forging of a Militant Ethos among Mexican Americans*, *Hector P. García: In Relentless Pursuit of Justice*, and *Viva Kennedy: Mexican Americans in Search of Camelot*. He has served as the regional editor of *Nuestro* magazine and is the founding member of the Community Studies Committee at Brigham Young University.

ROBERT A. GOLDBERG is a professor of history at the University of Utah, where he teaches social and political history. He is the author of six books, which include the award-winning *Barry Goldwater* and *Enemies Within: The Culture of Conspiracy in Modern America*. He is the recipient of seven teaching awards and has held a Fulbright lectureship as the Distinguished Chair in American Studies at Uppsala University in Sweden.

JOHN P. HERRON is an assistant professor of history at the University of Missouri, Kansas City. He is coeditor (with Andrew G. Kirk) of *Human/Nature: Biology, Culture, and Environmental History* and the author of the forthcoming *Science and the Social Good: Nature, Culture, and Community*. He is currently writing an environmental history of Kansas City, Missouri.

R. DOUGLAS HURT, a specialist in American agricultural history, chairs Purdue University's History Department. He is the author of more than ten books, including *African American Life in the Rural South, 1900–1950*, *Problems of Plenty: The American Farmer in the Twentieth Century*, and *The Rural West since World War II*.

ANDREW G. KIRK, an associate professor of history at the University of Nevada, Las Vegas, is the author of *Collecting Nature: The American Environmental Movement and the Conservation Library* and *Counterculture Green: The Whole Earth Catalog and American Environmentalism* and coeditor (with John Herron) of *Human/Nature: Biology, Culture, and Environmental History*.

KAREN R. MERRILL is an associate professor of history at Williams College. She is the author of *Public Lands and Political Meaning: Ranchers, the Government, and the Property between Them*, *The Oil Crisis of 1973–1974: A Brief History with Documents*, and the forthcoming *The Oil Crisis* and *The Modern Worlds of Business and Industry: Cultures, Technology, Labor*, as well as many articles on the American West.

JEFF ROCHE, an associate professor of history at the College of Wooster, is the author and editor of several books and essays on American politics, including *Restructured Resistance: The Sibley Commission and the Politics of Desegregation in Georgia*, *The Conservative Sixties* (coedited with David Farber), and the forthcoming *Cowboy Conservatism*.

AMY L. SCOTT is an assistant professor of history at Bradley University. She is the coeditor of the forthcoming *City Dreams, City Scenes* and the author of several essays on western urban and political history.

BRADLEY GLENN SHREVE is an instructor of history at Diné College (formerly Navajo Community College). He is currently preparing his 2007 University of New Mexico dissertation, "Red Power Rising: The National Indian Youth Council and the Origins of Intertribal Activism," for publication.

MICHAEL STEINER is the coauthor of two books—*Region and Regionalism in the United States* and *Mapping American Culture*—and coeditor of *Many Wests: Place, Culture, and Regional Identity* (with David Wrobel). He is professor of American studies at California State University, Fullerton. His essay "The

Significance of Turner's Sectional Thesis" received the Oscar Winther Award from the Western History Association in 1979. He has twice been selected as Distinguished Fulbright Chair of American Studies.

SCOTT H. TANG is an assistant professor of American Studies at Trinity College. His essay draws on his 2002 University of California, Berkeley, dissertation on the intersections of race and politics in midcentury San Francisco.

DAVID M. WROBEL, a professor of history at the University of Nevada, Las Vegas, is the author of *Promised Lands: Promotion, Memory, and the Creation of the American West* and *The End of American Exceptionalism: Frontier Anxiety from the Old West to the New Deal*. He has also coedited two books: *Many Wests: Place, Culture, and Regional Identity* (with Michael Steiner) and *Seeing and Being Seen: Tourism in the American West* (with Patrick T. Long).

Index

Abbey, Edward, 138, 139, 285
Abramoff, Jack, 8
Adamic, Louis, 149, 151, 154
   and Carey McWilliams, 155–156
   as regionalist, 145, 146
Adams, Hank, 206, 212
"Adventures of the Frontier in the Twentieth Century, The" (Limerick), 351–352
Affiliated Clubs and Organizations of San Francisco, 229
African Americans, 177, 351
   discrimination against, 222, 240–241
   and Latinos, 133
   and loyalty to Democratic Party, 167
   migration to the American West, 220
   and multiethnic diversity in the West, 4, 153, 156, 219–221
   in Texas, 172
   See also African Americans in San Francisco; multiethnic diversity
African Americans in San Francisco, 225, 226, 227, 241, 249
   discrimination against, 232–234, 235–237
   and fights against discrimination, 227–229
   race relations with Japanese Americans, 230
   relationships with Asian Americans, 234
Agnew, Spiro, 211
agrarian values, 53–54
agribusiness, 12, 67–68, 145
Agricultural Adjustment Act, 60
Agricultural Adjustment Administration, 60–62
agricultural commodity organizations, 54, 62, 69
   emergence of, 52

   as lobbying groups, 57
   success of, 66
agriculture, 168, 221, 221
   and politics, 12, 51–73
Aguila Oil Company, 78, 79, 88
Alabama-Coushatta Tribe, termination of, 201
The Alamo (film), 41
Alaska Native Claims Settlement Act (1971), 213
Alaska Resources Development Council, 320
Alcatraz Island, occupation of, 210–211
Alianza Federal de Pueblos Libres, in New Mexico, 183
Alien Land Law (California, 1913), 221, 230, 231, 345
Almaguer, Tomás, 170
Ambrose Bierce: A Biography (McWilliams), 146, 149, 151
Amerada Corporation, 79, 88, 90
American Agricultural Movement, 51, 65–66
American Border Patrol, 347
American Civil Liberties Union (ACLU), 117
American Committee for Protection of Foreign Born, 185
American Farm Bureau Federation (AFBF), 61, 64, 65, 70
   and New Deal, 60
   philosophy of, 64
   and politics, 52, 59, 63
American G.I. Forum, 172, 176
American Indian Chicago Conference (1961), 204–205
American Indian Defense Association, 199
American Indian Development, Incorporated, 201–203

American Indian Federation, 199–200, 201
  and anticommunism, 200
American Indian Movement, 197, 211, 212
American Indian Nation, 210
American Indian Religious Freedom Act
  (1978), 213
American Indian Task Force, 211
Americanism, 19, 116
  and conservatism, 14, 106
  and Mexican Americans, 176, 177, 181, 183
  and urban development, 104
American Mercury (magazine), 16, 112, 148
Americans before Columbus (newspaper), 206, 209
American Veterans Committee, 228, 229
American Writers' Congress, 153
American Youth for Democracy, 229
Anaheim Public School Board, 116
Anderson, Marion, 225
Angelou, Maya, 224–225
Angelus Temple, 146
Anglo-Iranian Oil Company, 81, 88, 92
Anglo-Persian Oil Company. *See* Anglo-Iranian Oil Company
anticommunism, 5, 12, 117, 229
  and Chinese Americans, 239
  and Barry Goldwater, 28
  and plain folk evangelicalism, 101, 109, 115, 119
Anti-Defamation League, 117
Anzaldua, Gloria, 140
Appeal to Reason (journal), 138
Apple Computers, 296
appropriate technology, 286, 289, 292–293, 295, 300
Aramco, 80, 84, 88
  in Saudi Arabia, 89–92
Archer Daniels Midland Company, 67
Arizona Highways (magazine), 22
Arizona Portraits (Goldwater), 22
Arkansas, 82
  as source of plain folk evangelicalism, 99, 103, 105
Armstrong, Arthur, 260–261
Arness, James, 18
Asian Americans, 177, 221, 240
  discrimination against, 221–222
  as model minorities, 241
  and multiethnic diversity in the West, 4, 133, 140, 153, 219–221
  See also Asian Americans in San Francisco; Chinese Americans; Japanese Americans; multiethnic diversity
Asian Americans in San Francisco, 223–240
  political activism of, 234
Assemblies of God
  in California, 103
  growth of, 104–105

Associated California Pioneers of 1849
  (Boston), 333
Associated Pioneers of the Territorial Days
  of California (New York), 333–334
Austin, Mary, 146, 147
  influences Carey McWilliams, 141, 148
  as regionalist, 137, 138, 139, 144
Austin, Stephen F., 171
authenticity in the American West, 5, 333
  competing visions of, 4, 14–15, 148, 247–249, 274, 351–352
  and conservatism, 11, 20, 46
  and counterculture, 269–270, 287
  and impact on western politics, ix, 2, 339, 345
  and moral authority, 3, 339, 341, 342, 347, 351
  and western farmers, 12, 70–71
  and western mythology, 285, 287, 315
Autry, Gene, 19
Aztlán, 184

Babeuf, Gracchus, 110
Backpacker (magazine), 319
The Bad Man (film), 32
Bahrain, 80, 81
Bailey, Beth, 262
Baker v. Carr (one man, one vote), 70
Baldwin, James, 159
Banai, Edward Benton, 211
Bancroft, Hubert Howe, 337–339
Banks, Dennis, 211
Banks, Mattie, 237
Banks v. the San Francisco Housing Authority, 237–238
Barlow, John Perry, 282, 283, 284, 285, 300–301
Barnett, Ross, 118
Barrymore, Lionel, 32
Bartlett, Al, 256, 257
Bear Flag Revolt, 337, 357
Beery, Wallace, 32
Behaviorial Science Corporation, 40
Bell, Daniel, 110, 293, 298
Bellecourt, Clyde, 211
Ben & Jerry's Ice Cream, 296
Benedict, Ruth, 202–203
Benson, George, 117
Bible Institute of Los Angeles, 108
Bierce, Ambrose, 146, 147, 149
Bierstadt, Albert, 343
bilingual education, 167, 183, 187, 188
Birch, John, 111
Black Panthers, 209
Blanc, Louis, 110
Blatchford, Herb, 204, 205
Blue Lake Restoration Act (1970), 213
Blue Line Charter Amendment (Boulder, Colo.), 257

Boas, Franz, 202
Bob Jones University, 115
Boilermakers' Union, San Francisco, 227
Boldt, George Judge, 208
Bonanza (television program), 16, 38
Bonnin, Gertrude, 198
Boone, Pat, 121
Boone, Richard, 18
Boorstin, Daniel, 318
boosters and boosterism, 252–253, 256, 257
 and Barry Goldwater, 24
Borah, William, 57
Boston, Massachusetts, 265, 334
Botkin, Benjamin, 137, 139, 145
Boulder, Colo., 3, 248, 251–280
Boulder Chamber of Commerce (Colo.), 253
Boulder Daily Camera (newspaper), 260, 264, 267, 268
Boulder Taxpayers' League, 265
Boulder United to Register People (BURP), 268
Bracero Program, 176
Brand, Stewart, 281, 286
 and appropriate technology, 295, 300
 and counterculture, 293–294
 creates *Whole Earth Catalogue*, 285, 290
 as entrepreneur, 291–296
 and politics, 292, 298, 299, 301
Brando, Marlon, 207
Brannan, Charles F., 63
Brannan Plan, 63
Braudel, Fernand, 140
Bricker, John, 15, 25
Bridges, Harry, 153, 154
Brier, James Welch, 334–335, 337, 343
Brier, John Wells, 335
Brier, Juliet Wells, 334–335, 343
Brightman, Lee, 209
Brillig Works, 263, 266
Bronson, Ruth, 200
Brooks, David, 290
Brothers under the Skin (McWilliams), 141
Brower, David, 281, 321
Brown, Edmund G. "Pat," 40, 41
Brown, Jerry, 299
Brown, John, 105–106
Brown, John (abolitionist), 138
Bruner, Joseph, 199–200
Bryan, William Jennings, 8, 53, 320
Buckley, Julia Redpath, 320
Buckley, William F., 15
Bulosan, Carlos, 145, 152
Burger King Corporation, 67
Burns, Conrad, 2
Burns, Harry, 223
Burroughs, William S., 271
Bush, George W., 138, 300, 301, 302
 on Ronald Reagan, 44, 45

 as Texas oilman, 77
 and western imagery and iconography, 3, 5, 11, 138, 301
Butler, Anne M., 3, 289

Cadena, Carlos C., 179
Caen, Herb, 224
Cahill, Thomas, 241
Calderon, Felipe, 185
California, ix, 3, 6, 12, 57, 139, 148, 350
 Great Depression in, 151
 as multicultural center, 156–157
 nativism in, 345
 postwar economic boom, 102–104
 radicalism of, 154
California Border Watch, 346–347
California Division of Immigration and Housing, 143, 153
California Gold Rush, 332
California Highway Patrol, 315
"California Ideology." *See* cyberlibertarians and cyberlibertarianism
California Proposition 14 (1964), 119
California Republican Assembly, 118, 119
California: The Great Exception (McWilliams), 141
California v. Cabazon Band of Mission Indians, 213–214
Caliphobia, 347, 349–351
Callenbach, Ernest, 286–289
Camp 4 (Yosemite National Park), 296, 298
Canada, as oil-producing nation, 74
Capper, Arthur, 59
Carlisle Indian School (Penn.), 198
Carmel, California, 149, 155, 254, 265
Carnation, 68
Carroll, Lewis, 263
Carson, Rachel, 320
Cash, Johnny, 121
Castañeda, Carlos, 181
Cattle Queen of Montana (film), 34
Celestial Seasonings Corporation, 271–273
cell-phone naturalists, 320–321, 322, 323
Central American Free Trade Agreement, 187
Central Baptist Church (Anaheim, Calif.), 115, 116, 117, 119
Chandler, O. K., 199, 200
Chavez, Cesar, 145
Chávez, Dennis, 180–181
Cheney, Dick, 283, 301
Cherokee Nation of Oklahoma, 195
Chesebro, Russell "Bud," 251–252, 253
Chicanismo, 177, 183
Chicano movement, 183–186
Chicano studies programs, 171, 184, 187
Childs, J. Rives, 92
Childs, William R., 83
China, 28, 98

Chinatown (San Francisco), 133, 221, 231, 234, 237, 238, 239
Chinese American Citizens Alliance, 234, 237
Chinese Americans, 241
  and politics, 221
  postwar acceptance of, 222
  See also Asian Americans in San Francisco; Chinese Americans in San Francisco; multiethnic diversity
Chinese Americans in San Francisco, 223–224
  acceptance of, 231–232
  conservatism of, 239–240
  and housing, 232
  political activism of, 239
Chinese Consolidated Benevolent Association. *See* Chinese Six Companies
Chinese Exclusion Act (1882), 221, 345
Chinese immigrants, discrimination against, 221
Chinese Press (newspaper), 222, 237, 239
Chinese Six Companies, 221, 234, 239
Chinese YMCA's Public Affairs Committee, 234
Chinook (newspaper), 266
Chouinard, Yvon, 97
  as entrepreneur, 284, 285, 296–298
  and politics, 281–282
  and western imagery and iconography, 290
Chouinard Equipment, 297
Christian Anti-Defamation League, 117
Christian Economics (magazine), 112
Christian Life (magazine), 105
Christopherson, Charles A., 59
Church of Christ, 119
  in California, 103
Church of the Open Door, 112
  and J. Vernon McGhee, 108–109
CIA (Central Intelligence Agency), 261
Citizens for a Better Boulder, 265
Citizens United to Restore Boulder (CURB), 266, 267, 268
Civilian Conservation Corps (CCC), 324
Civil Rights Act of 1964, 29, 40
Civil Rights Commission, 241
civil rights movement, 134, 135, 136, 197, 206, 220, 225
class
  in Boulder, 252, 253
  and Carey McWilliams, 154–157
  divisions in the West, 6
  and farmers, 56, 69, 52
  and Latinos, 167, 169, 175, 176–177, 178–181, 183, 184, 186, 188
  and plain folk evangelicalism, 101, 104, 107, 118, 119
  and race in San Francisco, 227, 239, 240
  and regionalism, 136
Clootz, Anacharsis, 110
CNN, 11
Cobb, Daniel, 197
Cobb, Humphrey, 154
Cody, William F. "Buffalo Bill," 333, 343
CoEvolution Quarterly (magazine), 292
Cohen, Felix, 202
Cohen, Meyer "Mickey," 98
Cold War, ix, 5, 12, 98, 178, 181, 200, 227, 255
Cole, Audley, 226
Collier, John, 5, 197, 199, 200, 202, 205
Colorado Gold Rush (1859), 341
Colorado Mountain Club, 256
Colton, John Burt, 333, 334, 336
Committee for Fair Employment (San Francisco), 227–229, 232
Confrerie de la Paix, 110
Connors, Chuck, 39, 40
Conquest of Cool (Frank), 291
Conroy, Jack, 145
Conscience of a Conservative, The (Goldwater), as expression of conservative message, 27–28
conservatives and conservatism, ix, 7, 69, 289, 300, 301, 302, 324
  in Boulder, 252, 253, 255, 260
  and cell-phone naturalist, 320–321
  and counterculture, 266–269
  and environmental politics, 321
  and farmers, 62, 63, 101
  and the Hip Right, 283, 284, 287
  and Latinos, 182
  and plain folk evangelicalism, 97–131
  and power with the Republican Party, 29
  study of, 13–14
  and western mythology, 3, 11, 13–50
consumer-interest groups, 67
Coolidge, Sherman, 198
Cooper, Gary, 18
Cooper, James Fenimore, 318
Corey, Paul, 261
Corliss, Richard, 36
Corman, Catherine, 141
cost-of-production prices (agriculture), 51, 56, 60, 64, 65
  as political issue, 66
Council for Civic Unity (San Francisco), 226, 232, 233, 237, 238
counterculture, 138, 247, 248, 254, 282, 284
  and appropriate technology, 286, 289
  and authenticity, 270
  in Boulder, Colorado, 259–269, 273
  and hip capitalism, 290–296
  as political issue, 260–269
  in San Francisco, 292
  and technology, 295
  and western mythology, 289

counterculture libertarians, 283, 300, 301–303
  and environmentalism, 285–286
cowboy conservatism, 2, 118
The Cowboys (film), 18
Cowdray, Lord, 79, 88, 78
Coyote, Peter (Cohon), 247
Crane, Hart, 149
Critchlow, Donald, 116
Cronon, William, 323–324
Crusade for Justice (Colorado), 183
Cuban Americans, 186
Curzon, Lord, 80
cyberlibertarians and cyberlibertarianism, 283, 285, 289, 301

Daisy Bradford no. 3 (oil well), 82
Dallas (television program), 77
Dallas, Texas, 112
Dallas Morning News (newspaper), 112
Dallas Theological Seminary, 108
Danish, Paul, 261
Dass, Ram, 271
Davis, Mike, 140
Dawes Severalty Act (1887), 198, 201
DDT, 322
Death Valley, California, 332, 334, 335
Death Valley Days (television program), 16, 38–39, 43
Death Valley '49ers, 336
Death Valley in '49 (Manly), 334
Death Valley National Park, 336
Debs, Eugene, 138
Declaration of Indian Rights, 201
DeGoyler, Everette, 76, 78–81, 90, 92
  early career of, 78
  and oil production in the Middle East, 86–89
DeGoyler, Nell, 79
DeGoyler and McNaughton Corporation, 79
Dell, Floyd, 149
Del Monte, 68
Democratic Party, 6, 167, 229
  and farmers, 52, 55–56, 58, 64, 68
  and NPL, 57
  in the West, 1–3
Denning, Michael, 159
Denver, Colo., 208, 256
  African American population of, 220
Deverell, William, 141
DeVoto, Bernard, 137, 150
Dewey, Thomas, 240
Diamond, Jared, 282
Diderot, Denis, 293
Didion, Joan, 140
Dies Committee. *See* House Committee on Un-American Activities
Diggers, the, 247

Dixon, Doris, 228
Dobie, J. Frank, as regionalist, 137, 138, 139
Donner Party, 333, 336
Doster, Frank, 54
Douglas, Kirk, 18
Dowie, Mark, 327
Dumont, Robert, 204, 209

Earth First!, 138
"Eastern Establishment," 5
Eastman, Charles, 198
Eastman, Max, 149
East Texas, as oil-producing region, 78, 82, 90
Eastwood, Clint, 18
Echeverría, Luis, 185
The Ecology of Commerce (Hawken), 292
Ecotopia (Callenbach), 286–288, 301, 302
Egypt, 80
Eisenhower, Dwight David, 15, 25, 27
Election of 1948, 239–240
Election of 1960, 167, 180
Election of 1964, 29, 30
Election of 1972, 211
Election of 1980, 41, 212
Election of 2000, 1, 11
Election of 2004, 5
Electronic Frontier Foundation, 283
Ellul, Jacques, 295
Encyclopédie (Diderot), 293
Endor Enterprises, 260–261, 263, 264
End Poverty in California (EPIC), 153
Engels, Friedrich, 110
English, Sam, 211
English-only laws, 187–188
environmental history, 248, 312
environmentalists and environmentalism, ix, 3, 7, 11, 255, 283, 292, 300, 303
  in Boulder, 256–260, 265–267
  and counterculture libertarians, 285–287
  and farmers, 67
  as political issue, 2, 248
  and politics, 314
  and technology, 311–312, 316–317, 320
environmental movement, 135, 145, 253, 254, 289
  divisions within, 324
  history of, 325
environmental politics, 312, 327–328
  and Americans' views of nature, 310–331
  and other movements of the 1960s, 325–326
  and technology, 322–323
  tensions within, 319
  in the West, 310
Evacuation Claims Act of 1948, 231

Factories in the Field (McWilliams), 141, 143, 145, 152–153, 154

Falwell, Jerry, 114
Fante, John, 146, 151
farm bloc, 59–60
Farmers Union, 52, 53, 56, 57, 58, 60, 61, 63–64, 70
  in Idaho, 57
  in Oklahoma, 58
  philosophy of, 64
"farm holiday," 60
Farm Holiday Association, 65
Farm Security and Rural Investment Act of 2002, 68
Farwell, Willard B., 338
Federal Agriculture Improvement and Reform Act of 1996, 68
Federal Reserve Act, 58
Fernández, Raul, 170
Fey, Harold, 202
Field, Sara, 154
Fillmore Communist Party, 228
Fillmore district (San Francisco neighborhood), 225, 228, 229, 230, 236
Fisher, Vardis, 137, 138
Fish-ins (protest), 206–207, 209
  and NIYC, 206–207
Flanner, Hildegarde, 146
Flynn, Errol, 32
"Folk Society, The" (Redfield), 202
Fonda, Henry, 18
Forbes, Jack, 209
Ford, John, 4
Foreman, Mike, 138
Fourteenth Amendment, 179
Fox News, 11
Frank, Thomas, 138, 291
Frank, Waldo, 149
Franklin, Benjamin, 318
Freeman, Jerry, 336–337
Free Speech Movement, 39
Frémont, John C., 337
Frito-Lay, 67
Frontier (magazine), 148
frontier mythology *See* western mythology
Frost, Tom, 282, 296–297, 298
Fuller, Buckminster, 286, 292
Fuller, Timothy, 263, 264, 268, 269
Fullerton College (California State University, Fullerton), 116

G.I. Generation, 185
Gaewhiler, Martin, 233
Galilean Baptist Church of Dallas, 114
Gallup, N.Mex., and Indian youth gathering (1961), 205
García, Hector P., 172, 185
García, Mario T., 177
Gearing, Fred, 202

gender
  and conservative politics, 116
  and counterculture, 252
  and labor, 155
  and regionalism, 139
  and western authenticity, 335, 343, 344
  westerns and 1950s, 17–18, 46
General Electric Theater (television program), 36, 38
General Mills, 272
genetically modified crops, 67, 311
George, Henry, 138
George Washington Carver Society (San Francisco), 228
Gerber Products Company, 67
Giles, J. Steven, 320–321
Ginsberg, Allen, 270, 271
global warming, ix
Gold, Mike, 149, 154
Gold Rush, the, 20, 332, 341
Goldwater, Baron, 20–21
Goldwater, Barry
  and antagonism towards the "Eastern Establishment," 27
  early life of, 22–24
  as leader of conservative movement, 25–30
  and love of flying, 22–23
  media representations of, 25
  1964 presidential campaign, 29, 30, 117, 121
  and photography of, 22
  political career of, 23–30
  political philosophy of, 27, 28, 29
  and reputation as western adventurer, 22–24
  as western conservative, 3, 5, 12, 20–21, 37, 39, 102, 118, 119, 120, 136, 138, 284
  and western mythology, 14, 15, 20, 21, 26–27, 45–46
Goldwater, JoJo, 20–21, 22
Goldwater, Michel, 20, 21
Gonzales, Rodolfo "Corky," 169, 183
González, Gilbert, 170
Goodlett, Carlton, 229
Good Morning America (television program), 336
Goodwyn, Lawrence, 83
Gorbachev, Mikhail, 41
Gore, Albert, Jr., 1, 11
Gore-Tex, 317
Gottlieb, Robert, 325
Graham, Billy, 101–102, 105, 120, 121–122
  career of, 99
  as catalyst for political movement, 100
  Los Angeles crusade of 1949, 97–100, 107
Graham, Ruth, 121

Grandsons: A Story of American Lives (Adamic), 155
Grateful Dead, 282, 283, 301
Great Britain, 81, 87, 88
Great Depression, the, 24, 31, 60, 78
and deportation of Mexican Americans and Mexican nationals, 152, 181, 182, 346, 151
Great Pacific Iron Works, 297
Great Plains, 55, 57, 59, 64, 65, 332, 346, 352
farmers in, 58
reformers in, 59
Great Society, 256
Green, J. Maceo, 234, 238
Greenbelt and Thoroughfares Program (Boulder, Colo.) of 1967, 257
green consumerism, 282, 285, 288–289, 291
Green Corn Rebellion (Oklahoma), 138
The Greening of America (Reich), 295
Green Party, 302
Grinnell College, 247
Growing a Business (Hawken), 292
Gulf Corporation, 91
Gunfight at the O. K. Corral (film), 16
Gunsmoke (television program), 16
Gunst, Morgan, 236
Guthrie, Woody, 145

Haas, David, 264
Haight-Ashbury, 247, 284
Hamilton, Alexander, 318
Haney-López, Ian, 173
Harding Academy (Searcy, Ark.), 117
Hargis, Billy James, 117
Harper's (magazine), 148
Harvard Business School, 296
Harvey, Paul, 117
Have Gun—Will Travel (television program), 16
Hawken, Paul, 291, 292
Hayakawa, S. I., 262
Hayes, C. Willard, 78
Hays, Samuel, 324
Haywood, William "Big Bill," 138
Heacock, Charles, 200
Heinlein, Robert, 285, 287
Hell's Angels, 136, 247
Hepburn Act, 58
Heritage High School, 115–117
as political institution, 117
Hernandez, Pete, 179
Hernandez v. Texas, 179
Hickenlooper, Bourke, 15
Higgins, Patillo, 90, 91
High Country News (newspaper), 316, 322
High Noon (film), 16
Highway Act of 1921, 59

Hine, Robert, 137
hip capitalism, 263, 269–274, 281–282, 283–284
Hip Right, the, 283, 300, 301. *See also* counterculture libertarians; cyberlibertarians and cyberlibertarianism
"Hispanic integration," 186–187
Hispanic Republican Committee, 186
Historical Society of Idaho Pioneers, 340
History of California (Bancroft), 337
Hofstadter, Richard, 110, 318
Hoover, Herbert, 60
Hoover, J. Edgar, 115
Hopi Reservation, 22
House Committee on Indian Affairs, 200
House Committee on Un-American Activities (HUAC), 110
The House in Antigua (Adamic), 155
Human Relations Commission (Boulder, Colo.), 264
Hunt, H. L., 82
Hunter, James, 267
Hunter, Stephen, 36
Hunters Point (San Francisco neighborhood), 225, 237–238
Hunt Oil Company, 82
Hustwit, William, 42, 44

IBM typewriters, 295
Ickes, Harold L., 79, 80, 86, 87, 83
Idaho, 6, 56–57
Idaho Federation of Agriculture, 56
Ill Fares the Land (McWilliams), 141
immigration, 133, 170, 180, 235, 239, 318, 351
as political issue, 2, 3, 4, 7, 167, 168, 169, 173, 176, 182, 186, 187, 189–190, 221, 231, 234
Independent Progressive Party, 240
Independents (oil producers), 12, 75, 78, 82–86, 89
characteristics of, 82
distrust of government, 83–85
and oil production in the Middle East, 86
in Texas, 90
India, 88
Indian Child Welfare Act (1978), 213
Indian Citizenship Act (1924), 198
Indian Country, 195, 196, 203
diversity within, 201
issues within, 202
politics of, 213
Indian Country Today, 195
Indian Education Act (1972), 213
"Indian Education: A National Tragedy—A National Challenge" (Kennedy), 212
Indian Financing Act (1974), 213

Indian gaming, 133, 213–214
Indian Gaming Regulatory Act (1988), 214
Indian Healthcare Improvement Act (1976), 213
Indian New Deal, 198–199, 200, 204, 205, 213
Indian Progress, 203
Indian Reorganization Act, 197, 199–200
Indian Rights Association, 198
Indians and Other Americans (McNickle and Fey), 202
Indian Self-Determination and Education Assistance Act (1975), 213
Indians of All Tribes, 197, 210–211
Indians of the Americas (Collier), 202
individualism, 284, 315
  as characteristic of the West, 3
  and conservatism, 24, 107
  and counterculture, 283, 285
  and nature, 311
  and New Left, 254
  as western characteristic, 14, 17, 38, 100, 171, 315, 338
  and western farmers, 54, 62
  and western mythology, ix, 172, 181, 327, 339
  and western politics, 5
  and westerns, 19, 39
In re Ricardo Rodríguez, 173–175
interracial cooperation, in San Francisco, 230
interracial political coalitions, in American West, 220, 223
Interstate Commerce Commission, 58
Interstate Oil Compact Commission, 78
Iran, 80, 81, 88, 91
Iraq, 80
Iraq War (2003), 75
Israel, 98
Issei, 231, 345, 346. *See also* Japanese Americans; Japanese immigrants
Isserman, Maurice, 203

Jack Kerouac School of Disembodied Poetics, 271
Jacobson, Matthew Frye, 141
James, Joseph, 226–227, 230
James True Associates, 200
Japanese American Citizens League, 235–236, 239
  Anti-Discrimination Committee of, 231
  and cooperation with NAACP, 222, 230
Japanese Americans, 222, 241
  and internment camps, 221
  internment of, 136, 346
  postwar acceptance of, 222
  See also Asian Americans; Japanese Americans in San Francisco; multiethnic diversity

Japanese Americans in San Francisco, 223–224, 225, 226
  and housing, 232
  and race relations with African Americans, 230
Japanese immigrants, discrimination against, 221
Jayhawkers, 332–337, 340, 343
Jeffers, Robinson, 146, 149, 155
Jeffers, Una, 149
Jefferson, Thomas, 52, 53, 69, 313, 315
Jeffersonian tradition, 59, 65, 69, 70, 71, 314
  definition of, 52
  as political symbol, 53
  and western farmers, 51
Jemison, Alice, 199, 200
Jenner, William, 15, 25
Jim Crow. *See* segregation
Jobs, Steve, 286
John Birch Society, 13, 111
John Brown club, 228
John Brown University, 105, 117
Johnson, Charles, 226
Johnson, Lyndon Baines, 29, 197, 256, 289
Joiner, Columbus Marion "Dad," 82
Jones, Marvin, 5
Judd, Richard, 326
Jue, Stanton, 239
Jung, Charles, 237, 238

Kahn, Herman, 299
Kansas, 3, 61, 138, 340
Kazin, Alfred, 137
Kazin, Michael, 203
Keen, Taylor, 195
Kemmis, Daniel, 140
Kendrick, John, 59
Kennedy, Edward, 212
Kennedy, John F., 181, 204
Kennedy, Robert, Jr., 282
Kerry, John, 5, 302
Kesey, Ken, 292
KGER (radio station), 105, 109
Kido, Saburo, 231
Kingsolver, Barbara, 140
Kings Row (film), 32
Kissinger, Henry, 13
Klamath Tribe, termination of, 201
Klein, Herbert, 146, 152
Knecht, Robert, 265
Knott, Walter, 115, 116, 117
Knott's Berry Farm, 119
Knowland, William, 15, 25
Knowles, Hiram, 342
Knute Rockne, All American (film), 32
Korean War, 15, 231, 239
Ku Klux Klan, in American West, 346
Kuwait, 80, 81

L. L. Bean catalogue, 294
Ladd, Edwin, 59
Ladies Auxiliary of the Society of Arizona Pioneers, 344
LaFollette, Robert, 138
LaHaye, Tim, 117
Lapham, Roger, 224
LaPointe, Myron, 266, 267
La Raza Unida Party, 166, 185
  in Texas, 183
The Last Outpost (film), 32–33
Latino politics, 184
  class divides within, 181
  diversity of, 167
  in 1950s, 182–183
  in Texas, 166
  since 2000, 187–189
Latinos, 4, 133, 221, 348
  civil rights movement of, 176
  civil rights organizations, 222
  class divides of, 177
  class politics of, 178
  and conservatism, 188
  and Democratic Party, 183
  marginalization of, 168
  political activism of, 169
  political identity of, 187
  racialization of, 173–175, 176
  See also Mexican Americans; multiethnic diversity
Laughing in the Jungle (Adamic), 149
"law and order," as political issue, 28, 266–267
Law and Order (film), 33–34
Lawrence Welk Show (television program), 121
League of United Latin American Citizens (LULAC), 173, 176
Lease, Elizabeth Mary, 138
Lee, Rose Hum, 231–232
Left, the. *See* liberals and liberalism
Lenin, Vladimir, 110
Leong, Charles, 222
Leopold, Aldo, 285, 313
LeSueur, Meridel, 154
liberals and liberalism, 3, 113, 119, 135, 273, 287, 301–302, 303, 313
  in Boulder, 255–269
  and Carey McWilliams, 135–159
  and counterculture, 291, 293
  and environmental politics, 321
  and farmers, 63
  and labor, 152
  and Latinos, 183–186
  and race, 227–230
  and regionalism, 139, 140
  and Ronald Reagan, 36
  western tradition of, 5, 134, 138, 144
  See also "lifestyle liberalism"

Libertarian Party, 283, 301
Life and Legend of Wyatt Earp (television program), 16
"lifestyle liberalism," 252–254, 269–274
Limerick, Patricia Nelson, 140, 142, 351, 353
Lincoln Avenue Presbyterian Church, 108
London, Jack, 154
Look (magazine), 266
Los Angeles, 109, 112, 136
  African American population of, 220
  and Billy Graham, 97–98
  and Carey McWilliams, 145–149
  Filipino community in, 152
Los Angeles Corral of Westerners, 336
Los Angeles County Pioneer Society (LACPS), 340
Los Angeles Times (newspaper), 41, 146
Lost Generation, 149
Louis Adamic and Shadow America (McWilliams), 155
Louisiana, 79
Lovins, Amory, 291, 299
Lovins, Hunter, 291
Lubbock, Texas, 65
Lucas, Anthony, 90, 91
Lurie, Nancy, 204

MacArthur, Douglas, 15
Machine in the Garden (Marx), 317–318
MacLeish, Archibald, 135
Majors (oil producers), 75, 82, 84
Makah Tribe, 207
The Making of the Counterculture (Roszak), 295
Malone, George, 25
Manion Forum (magazine), 112
Manly, William Lewis, 334, 335, 343
Mann-Elkins Act, 58
Manning, Seaton, 220
Marcuse, Herbert, 295
Markoff, John, 315–316
Marlboro Man, 16, 27, 41
Marshall, Robert, 321
Martínez, Oscar, 188
Marx, Karl, 110
Marx, Leo, 317–318
Maryland Society of California Pioneers, 334
Masaoka, Joe Grant, 222
A Mask for Privilege: Anti-Semitism in America (McWilliams), 141
Mays, Willie, 233
McBirnie, W. Stuart, 120
McCarran-Walter Naturalization and Immigration Act (1952), 231
McCarthy, Joseph, 15
McCary, Cleve, 121

McDonald's Restaurant, 300
McFarland, Ernest, 24, 25
McGee, J. Vernon, 120
  and anticommunism, 109–113
  early life of, 107–108
  sermons of, 111–112
McGrath, Alice Greenfield, 153
McKelvey, Robert, 256, 257
McKibben, Bill, 282
McKinley, William, 8
McNary, Charles, 59
McNaughton, Lewis, 79
McNickle, D'Arcy, 200, 201, 202, 204, 205, 211
McPherson, Aimee Semple, 146, 147
McWilliams, Carey, 170, 219, 224, 353
  as advocate for working class and poor, 145
  and California, 136–137
  as California writer, 144–145
  celebration of multiculturalism, 156–157
  early life of, 145–146
  as editor of *Nation* (magazine), 156
  education of, 146
  as labor lawyer, 151–156, 152
  and Los Angeles, California, 146–148
  love of California, 156–157
  multicultural regionalism of, 153
  racial views of, 140–141
  as regional writer, 141–145
  and regionalism, 139–140
  regional writings of, 147–151
  social and political activism of, 152–159
  social awareness of, 150
  study of, 140–141
  as voice of progressive western political culture, 135–165
McWilliams, Jerry, 145
McWilliams, Wilson Carey, 319
Means, LaNada, 209
megachurches, 103
Melville, Herman, 318
memory, 249
  and authenticity in the American West, 249
  and early pioneers, 333–334, 337–339, 342–343
  and western mythology, 21, 26
  and western politics, 332–363
Mencken, H. L., 141, 146, 147, 148
Menominee Tribe, termination of, 201
Mexican American Generation, 172, 184, 185
Mexican American identity, 180, 182
Mexican Americans
  civil rights organizations of, 171
  identity of, 170
  and immigration, 169
  legal status of, 167, 168
  political activism of, 171–172
  racial classification of, 173
Mexicanism, 176
mexicanos de afuera, 185
Mexican Revolution, 183
Mexicans in United States, legal status of after U.S.-Mexico War, 167–168
Mexico, 78, 79, 86, 176, 185
  nationalizes its oil industry, 87, 89
  as oil producing nation, 74
Michaels, Walter Benn, 174
micropolitan urbanism, 253–256, 258, 273
Middle East, 75, 76, 82, 84, 87, 92
  as oil producing region, 74, 86–89
  Oil reserves, 80–81
Miller, Perry, 317
Mission Indian Tribes (California), 214
"model minorities," 241
Monkey Wrench Gang (Abbey), 285
Montana, 3
Montejano, David, 169
Monterey, California, 265
Montezuma, Carlos, 198
Moody Memorial Church (Chicago), 108
Moon Is a Harsh Mistress (Heinlein), 285, 287
Moore, E. H., 85
Moral Majority, 13
Mount Baker-Snoqualmie National Forest, 315
Muckleshoot Tribe, 206
Muir, John, 4, 285, 313–314, 327
Müller, Paul, 322
multiethnic diversity, ix, 4, 6, 7, 53, 133–134, 213
multiracial political coalitions, 240
Mumford, Lewis, 149, 150, 321

NAACP (National Association for the Advancement of Colored People)
  and cooperation with JACL, 230
  in San Antonio, 223
  in San Francisco, 226–228, 229, 230, 237, 238, 239
  in West, 229
  West Coast Regional Conference of 1947, 230
Nader, Ralph, 302
Nagel, Joane, 213
Naropa Institute (University), 271
Nash, Gerald, 7
Nation (magazine), 140, 156
Nation, Carrie, 138
national agricultural organizations, 53
  early twentieth century, 56
  failure of, 66
  and lobbying, 53
  political power of, 52, 56
National Congress of American Indians, 197, 200–202, 204, 206, 211, 212, 213

National Farmers Organization, 64–65, 66
National Indian Youth Council, 197, 203, 205–208, 209, 210, 211, 212
　focus of, 208
　founding of, 205–206
National Negro Congress, 228, 227
National Negro Labor Council, in Seattle, 220
National Public Radio, 320
National Review, 15, 16, 19
Native American cultural retention
　as central issue in Native American politics, 196–197, 211, 214
　and NIYC, 206–208
Native American governments, and relationship with federal government, 196
Native American intertribal organizations, 197–199
Native American politics, 134, 195–218
Native American Rights Fund, 212
Native Americans, 348, 351
　Barry Goldwater and, 22–23
　Carey McWilliams and, 141, 152
　and federal government, 4
　and multiethnic diversity, 133
　and westerns, 19
　See also multiethnic diversity
Native American self-determination
　as central issue in Native American politics, 196–197, 211, 214
　and NIYC, 206–208
Native American treaty rights. *See* Native American self-determination
Native American tribal sovereignty. *See* Native American self-determination
Native Daughters of the Golden West, 344, 345
Native Sons of the Golden West, 344
　racism of, 345
Natural Capitalism (Hawken, Lovins, and Lovins), 291–292
nature and technology, 315–323
Navajo Nation, 22, 23, 214
Nealson, Christina, 316
Nebraska, 55–56
Nebraska Council of Defense, 56
Negro Chamber Commerce, 228
neoconservatives, 138, 300, 302
Nevada, 6
Nevills, Norman, 23, 24
Newcomb, Steven, 195
New Deal, the, 5, 15, 24, 54, 83, 85, 101, 113, 119, 137, 196–198
　agricultural support programs, 64
　and cattle-reduction program, 62
　and crop reduction plan, 60–61
　and western farmers, 60–61
New England Associated Pioneers of '49, 333

New Evangelical Movement, 98
New Left, the, 135, 138, 159, 253–254, 259, 284, 294, 295, 326. *See also* liberals and liberalism
New Mexico, 6
New Regionalism in American Literature, The (McWilliams), 150–151
"new regionalists," 148
New Right, the, 101, 135, 138, 159, 253, 283, 301. *See also* conservatives and conservatism
Newsweek (magazine), 43, 98
"New Western Democrats," 2–3
New York Times (newspaper), 88, 315
Ng, Wing, 225
Nichi Bei Times (newspaper), 231
Nickerson, Michelle, 116
Nickey, Larry, 315
Nisei. *See* Japanese Americans
Nisqually Tribe, 206
Nixon, Richard M., 20, 41, 266, 284
　Native American policies of, 212–213
Noble, Joan, 204, 205
Nonpartisan League, 52, 55–56, 57, 58
　in Idaho, 57
　power of, 55
Norris v. Alabama, 178–179
Norris, Frank, 92, 138
North Beach Place (San Francisco neighborhood), 237, 238
North Cascades National Park, 316
North Dakota, 55, 57
North from Mexico: The Spanish Speaking People of the United States (McWilliams), 141
Nugent, Walter, 346
Nye, David, 311
Nyhan, David, 43

Oakland, African American population of, 220
Office of Economic Opportunity, 209
Office of Indian Affairs. *See* United States Bureau of Indian Affairs
Oil and Gas Journal, 84, 85
oil internationalism, 77
oil isolationism, 76, 77, 85
Oklahoma, 6, 57, 77, 79, 84, 85
　agricultural organizations in, 58
　oil production in, 75
Old Settlers' Association of Johnson County, Iowa, 340–341
Old Timer's Hand Book, 341
Olson, Tillie, 145
Olympic National Park, 315
"On Corporate Responsibility" (Chouinard), 281–282
Onuma, Michi, 235
Open Space Department (Boulder), 258
Operation Abolition (documentary), 112

Operation Wetback, 182
Orange County, California, ix, 104–105, 114, 115, 118, 144, 152
Oregon, 6, 287
Oregon Country, 3
Oregon Pioneer Association, 344
Oregon Pioneer Society, 341
Oregon System, 5
Orwell, George, 142
Overland Monthly (magazine), 148
Owen, Robert, 110

Pacific Citizen (newspaper), 230, 231, 235, 236
Paget, Karen, 268
Paine, Thomas, 110
Palestine, 80
Parent Teacher Fellowship, 116
Parker, Dorothy, 154
Patagonia Inc., 15, 281–282, 297, 302
  philosophy of, 283
  and western authenticity, 296–298
Patrons of Husbandry (the Grange), 57
Patterns of Culture (Benedict), 202–203
Paull, Gary, 315
Payne, John, 34
Pearl Harbor, 221, 225
Pearl Street Mall (Boulder), 252, 269, 274
Pearson, Weetman. *See* Cowdray, Lord
Peck, Gregory, 18, 32
Pentecostal Evangel (magazine), 104–105
Pentecostal Holiness Church, in California, 103
People's (Populist) Party, 52
People's World (newspaper), 227, 228
Peoples, Wesley, 228, 229
Pepperdine College, 117, 119
Pershing Square (Los Angeles), 147, 148, 154
Persian Gulf, 76, 77, 84, 91
  as oil-producing region, 75, 81, 90
  oil reserves, 83
Persian Gulf War (1991), 75
Peterson, Helen, 201, 204
Petroleum Administration for War, 79, 80
petroleum industry, politics of, 74–96
Petroleum Reserves Corporation, 80, 81, 85, 87
Phinney, Archie, 200
Phoenix, Ariz., ix
Pinchot, Gifford, 313–314, 321
Ping Yuen (San Francisco neighborhood), 236, 237, 238, 239
Pioneer Ladies Aid Society of Colorado, 344
pioneer societies, 339–345
  and gender, 343–344
  membership qualifications, 341
  and memory, 342
  and moral authority, 342, 343

plain folk evangelicalism
  and anticommunism, 100–101
  characteristics of, 99–100
  and defense industry, 105–106
  political philosophy of, 100
  roots of, 99
  suburbanization and, 103–104
  success in Southern California, 101–102
  and western politics, 97–131
PLAN-Boulder (People's League for Action Now), 257, 260, 267, 268
Plato, 313
Polaroid cameras, 295
politics of western memory, 332–353
  characteristics of, 345
  and pioneer societies, 339–340
Populist Movement, 5, 134, 135, 282, 284
  in Kansas, 138
  political legacy of, 54
  See also People's (Populist) Party
Portland (Ore.), African American population of, 220
Portrero del Llano no. 4 (oil well), 78
postwar emigration to California, 102–105
Pot Cookbook, 263
Pratt, Richard Henry, 198
Pratt, Wallace, 79, 88
Prejudice; Japanese-Americans: Symbol of Racial Intolerance (McWilliams), 141
production-control legislation (agriculture), 66
Progressive Movement, 5, 58, 69, 135, 282, 284, 345
  and conservation, 292
  and western farmers, 58–59
Progressive Party, 57
Proposition 15 (California 1946), 231
Puerto Rican American communities, in New York, 186
Puyallup Tribe, 206

Quinault Tribe, 206
Quinn, Frank, 233, 239

race
  Carey McWilliams views on, 144, 152
  and racism, 346, 348
  and regionalism, 139, 140, 154
  as social and political construct, 172–175
  and western political culture, 7, 134, 156, 166–190, 219–245, 352
  See also African Americans; Asian Americans; Chinese Americans; Latinos; Mexican Americans; multiethnic diversity; Native Americans
railroads, 5, 55, 58, 138
ranchers and ranching, 4, 62, 66, 83, 170, 289, 351
Rawhide (television program), 16

Rawlings, Edwin, 272
Reader's Digest (magazine), 112
Reagan, Jack, 31
Reagan, Nancy, 121
Reagan, Ronald, 13, 119, 120, 138, 212, 284, 291
   and California gubernatorial election of 1966, 39–41
   death of, 43–45
   early life of, 30–31
   early political career of, 39–41
   and election of 1980, 41
   and film career, 31–36
   as political speaker, 37–38
   presidential career of, 41–43
   and television career, 36, 38–39
   as western conservative, 5, 12, 102, 118, 121, 136, 289
   western image of, 39–46
   and western mythology, 14, 15, 30, 36
   western roles of, 32–36
Record, Wilson, 230, 240
"red-blue" political divide, ix, 1, 5, 302, 320
Red Scare, 15. *See also* anticommunism
Redfield, Robert, 202
Reich, Charles, 295
Remington, Frederic, 333, 343
repatriation of Mexican Americans and Mexicans, during Great Depression, 151, 152, 181, 182, 346
Republican Party, 1, 2, 5, 25, 113
   Barry Goldwater and, 25, 26
   in California, 118–119
   conservative capture of, 29, 102, 121
   conservatives within, 27
   Convention of 1964, 29
   Convention of 1980, 41
   and counterculture libertarians, 300
   farmers and, 55, 64, 68, 52
   and Latinos, 186, 188
   the NPL and, 57–58
   Ronald Reagan and, 41
   in West, 289
   western image of, 3
Rexroth, Kenneth, 145, 154
Rice, John R., 114
Richmond, Calif., African American population of, 220
Rickard, Karen, 204, 205
Rickenbacker, William, 16, 19
Right to Life, 13
right wing. *See* conservatives and conservatism
Rio Bravo (film), 16
Robbins, Royal, 296–297, 298
Roberts, James, 26
Robinson, Elmer, 237
Robinson, Forrest, 140
Robinson, Jackie, 351

rock climbing, 282, 296, 297
Rockefeller, John D., 89
Rocky Flats Plant, 254
Rodríguez, Ricardo, 173, 174
Rodríguez, Richard, 140
Rome, Adam, 325
Roosevelt, Franklin Delano, 24, 85
   election of, 60
   Native American policies of, 196, 198
   and New Deal, 15
   and oil production, 79, 80, 81, 89
Roosevelt, Theodore, 17, 333
   and conservation, 292, 321, 327
Rorty, Richard, 159
Rose, Stanley, 146
Rossmoor Parents for Better Education, 116
Roszak, Theodore, 136, 295
Rousseau, Jean-Jacques, 110, 247
Royce, Josiah, 352–353
rural metropolis, 135, 170, 183
   as cultural force, 171

Sacco and Vanzetti, execution of, 148–149
Sagebrush Rebellion, 138, 289, 351. *See also* conservatives and conservatism
Salazar, Kenneth, 2
Sale, Kirkpatrick, 325
Salt Lake City, 187, 332
San Antonio, Tex., 223
San Diego, Calif., 3, 117
San Francisco, 135, 247, 259
   African American population of, 220–241
   race relations in, 222–241
   racial discrimination in, 224–226, 232–238
San Francisco Board of Supervisors, 235–236
San Francisco Call (newspaper), 335
San Francisco Chronicle (newspaper), 40, 41, 224, 334
San Francisco Civic Unity Committee, 226
San Francisco Committee against Segregation, 227
San Francisco Housing Authority (SFHA), 236–238
San Francisco Indian Center, 210
San Francisco Mime Troupe, 247
San Francisco State College, 210
San Francisco State University, 247, 262
San Francisco Sun-Reporter (newspaper), 234, 238
San Francisquito Ranch, 333
Sánchez, George I., 179
Sanders, James, 343
Sanders, Stella, 149
Sandoz, Mari, 137
Saroyan, William, 146, 154
Saturday Evening Post (magazine), 25
Saturday Review of Literature (magazine),148

382   Index

Saudi Arabia, 80, 81, 84, 85, 88
   and Aramco, 89–92
   as oil-producing nation, 74
Sayles, John, 140
Schuetz, Alfred, 202
Schwarz, Fred, 112
Searchers, The (film), 16
Sears, Roebuck and Company, 220
Seattle, 222, 316
   African American population of, 220
Seattle Times (newspaper), 349
segregation, 4, 118, 169, 222, 223, 227, 235–238
   in West, 171–172, 175, 178
Shabecoff, Philip, 325
Shane (film), 16
Shelley v. Kraemer, 230
Shelton, Fred, 262
Sheppard, Morris, 59
Shirley, Joe, Jr., 214
Siegel, Mo, 270, 271–272
Sierra (magazine), 316
Sierra Club, 281, 316
Sierra Nevada Mountain Range, 315
Silicon Valley, 299
Silver Legion of America. *See* Silver Shirts
Silver Shirts, 200
Sinclair, James H., 59
Sinclair, Upton, 146, 149, 153, 154
Sleepy Lagoon Defense Committee, 143
Sloan, Thomas, 198, 199
Slotkin, Richard, 317
Smith, Gerald, L. K., 114
Smith, Henry Nash, 135, 139, 317
Smith & Hawken, 296
Smithsonian Institution, 336
Snyder, Gary, 271
Snyder Act. *See* Indian Citizenship Act (1924)
Society of American Indians, 198, 199, 201
Society of Arizona Pioneers, 340, 341
Society of California Pioneers, 337–339, 341
Society of Colorado Pioneers, 340, 341, 344
Society of Montana Pioneers, 340, 342, 343
Socony-Vacuum (Aramco), 80
Soil Conservation and Domestic Allotment Act, 61–62
Sons and Daughters and Grandsons and Granddaughters of the Jayhawkers of '49, 336
Sons of Colorado, 345
Southern Agrarians, 144, 154
Southern Baptist General Convention of California, 103
Southern California
   defense industry in, 101
   emergence of plain folk evangelism in, 97–107
Southern California: An Island on the Land (McWilliams), 141

Southwest Review (magazine), 148
Soviet Union, 90, 98, 200
Spaceship Earth (Ward), 294
Spanish Speaking Organization for Community, Integrity, and Opportunity (SOCIO), 183
Spencer Roberts, 40
Spindletop (oil well), 90, 91
Springer, Harvey, 114
Standard Oil Company, 82, 89, 90
   of California, 80
   of New Jersey, 79, 80
Stanford University, 290, 294
Stanwyck, Barbara, 34
Starr, Kevin, 140
Steinbeck, John, 145, 151, 154
Stephens, Lorenzo Dow, 333, 336
Sterling, George, 146
Stewart, Donald Ogden, 154
"Stranger, The" (Schuetz), 202
Student Nonviolent Coordinating Committee, 203, 205, 206
Students for a Democratic Society, 203, 205, 206, 262
Summer of Love (1967), 259
Sun-Maid, 68
Sun Oil Company, 84
Survey Graphic (magazine), 231
Sutter, John A., 337
Szasz, Thomas, 36

Taft, Robert A., 15
Takaki, Ronald, 140
Tarbell, Ida, 92
Tate, Penfield, 268, 269
Tax, Sol, 204
Taylor, Paul S., 145
technological sublime, 311, 312
Tedesco, Ted, 259, 264–265
Teeple, Donald, 16, 19
Tennessee Valley Authority (TVA), 324
Tennessee's Partner (film), 34–35
Termination of federally recognized tribes, 201–202
Territorial Daughters of Colorado, 344
Tester, Jon, 2, 3, 6
Texas, ix, 3, 6, 77, 78, 79, 84, 85, 114, 173, 188
   oil production in, 75
   racial segregation in, 172
Texas Company, 80, 91
Texas oilmen, 87, 89
   and Middle East, 76
   mythology of, 75–77, 83–84, 91
   political philosophy of, 84–85
   political power of, 77
Texas Railroad Commission, 78, 85
"Texas theology," 99, 107, 109
Thom, Mel, 204, 205, 206, 207, 209, 211

Thomas, William McKinley, 236–237
Thompson, Hunter S., 136
Thoreau, Henry David, 4, 313, 320, 327
Tibetan Book of the Dead, 271
Tibetan Buddhism, 270
Tijerina, Reies López, 185
Time (magazine), 25, 43, 98
Tinkle, Lon, 79, 80
Tom, Henry Shue, 226
Tompkins, Jane, 17
Townley, Arthur C., 55, 57
Trail of Broken Treaties, 211–212
Transamerica, 68
transnationalism, 185–186
Treaty of Guadalupe Hidalgo, 167, 168
Trinidad, 88
Trips Festival, 292
Tri-State Old Settlers Association of Illinois, Missouri, and Iowa, 340, 342
"The Trouble with Wilderness" (Cronon), 323
Truman, Harry S., 81, 98, 240
Trungpa, Chögyam, 270–272
Turner, Frederick Jackson, x, 4, 17, 171, 247, 315, 337. *See also* Turner Thesis
Turner Thesis, 17, 338–339, 341. *See also* Turner, Frederick Jackson
Twain, Mark, 154
Twenty-Sixth Amendment, 268

Udall, Mark, 2
United Community Church of Glendale, 120
United Farm Workers Union, in California, 183
United Fruit Company, 155
United Nations, 98, 185
United Native Americans, 208–210, 211
United States Army Corps of Engineers, 324
United States Bureau of Indian Affairs, 5, 199, 209
United States Bureau of Indian Affairs Building, occupation of (1972), 212
United States Bureau of Land Management, 62, 66, 324
United States Bureau of Reclamation, 56
United States Census Bureau, 175, 341
United States Department of Agriculture, 59, 63, 67
United States Department of State, 81
United States Department of the Interior, 199
United States Fish and Wildlife Service, 316
United States Forest Service, 62, 66
United States Geological Survey, 78
United States Mexican War (1846–1848), 167, 173
United States Senate Committee on Foreign Relations, 83, 84
United States Soil Conservation Service, 324

United States Supreme Court, 213–214
University Hill (Boulder, Colo.), 262–266
University Hill Merchant Association (UHMA), 265
University of California, Native American students and, 209
University of Colorado, 252, 256, 260, 262, 267
  Religious Studies Department, 271
  and student activism, 261–262
University of Denver, 145
University of Oklahoma, 78
urban development, 251–252, 322
  in Boulder, Colo., 253, 255–257
  in Denver, 255–256
  impact on western farmers, 67
  political impact of, 70
  and sprawl, 2, 4, 170, 255–259, 347
Urban League, 226
  in San Francisco, 220
USA Today (newspaper), 44
Utne Reader (magazine), 321

Valdez, Luis, 140
Vaus, Jim, 98
Venezuela, 86
Vera Cruz (film), 16
Vietnam War, 251
  protests against, 261–262
Villarreal, Raul, 166
Virgin Group, 296
The Virginian (Wister), 343
Vitalis, Robert, 92
Viva Kennedy Clubs, 181
Voice of Americanism, The (television program), 120
"Voice of the American Indian, The" (Statement), 205

Walden (Thoreau), 313
Wallace, Henry A., 60, 240
Ward, Barbara, 294
Warner Brothers, 31
War on Poverty, 197
Warpath (newspaper), 209–210
Warrior, Clyde, 202, 205, 207–208
Washington State, 6, 57
Watson, Emmett, 349
Watt, James G., 321
Watts Riot, 40, 41
Wayne, John, 18, 32, 39, 40, 121
Webb, Walter Prescott, 137, 138, 139, 140
Weber, Kim, 146
Weekly Standard (magazine), 321
Weishaupt, Adam, 110
Welch, Robert, 111
Wells, "Bob" (Robert), 107, 117, 120
  and anticommunism, 115–116
  early life of, 114

Wells, "Bob" (Robert) (*continued*)
  founds Central Baptist Church, 115
  founds Heritage High School, 115–116
  media empire of, 117–118
  political message of, 118–120
  as western hero, 118
West, Nathanael, 154
West Coast Exclusion Order, 230
Western Addition (San Francisco) of 1948, protests against, 235–236
Western Archeological and Conservation Center, 336
Westerners International, 336
western farmers
  conservatism of, 62–63
  and Great Depression, 60
  politics of, 51–73
  and relationship with federal government, 51
western imagery and iconography, 5, 118
  conservatives' use of, 14, 45
western mythology, 11, 283, 284, 287–288, 343
  and the cowboy, 17
  See also western imagery and iconography
westernness, 333, 336, 341, 346, 348–349
  in contemporary political debates, 347–353
  See also authenticity in the American West
western regionalism, 3, 134, 138–140, 141, 144–145, 352
  characteristics of, 137
  criticisms of, 139
  and liberal politics, 154–156
  and Mexican Americans, 182
  and multiethnic diversity, 13, 157
  in 1920s, 137–138
  as political force, 135–136
westerns
  as expressions of conservative ideal, 19
  heroes of, 19–20
  1950s, 16–19
  films, as expressions of conservative ideals, 16
  television programs, 16
Western Writers' Congress, 1936 meeting of, 153–154
West Texas, 75
wheat growers association, 64
wheat reduction program, 60–61
White, Richard, 197
whiteness
  as social and political construct, 179–180
  in West, 173–177

Whitman, Walt, 157, 159, 247
Whole Earth Catalogue, 285, 287, 290
  business model of, 295–296
  and environmental politics, 300
  and green capitalism/green consumerism, 291–293, 298–299
Why Not Victory? (Goldwater), 28
wildcatter (oilmen), 82–83, 84, 92
Wilkie, Bruce, 204
Willard, Michael, 141
Williams, Terry Tempest, 140, 321
Williams, William Carlos, 303
Williams-Sonoma, 296
Wills, Garry, 35
Winter, Ella, 154
Wired (magazine), 290, 302
Wister, Owen, 343
Witt, Shirley, 205
Women's National Indian Association, 198
women's suffrage, 55, 344
Workshop on American Indian Affairs, 205
  and American Indian Development, Inc., 202–204
World War I
  and agriculture, 58, 59
  and oil production, 80, 344
World War II, 4, 6, 75, 219, 312, 322
  and agriculture, 56
  and internment of Japanese Americans, 136, 346
  Mexican American participation in, 175, 182, 183
  and oil production, 78–81, 85
  and urban development, 102–103, 255
Wounded Knee, S.Dak., and American Indian Movement, 212
Wozniak, Steve, 286
Wrage, Ernest, 26
Wright, Ken, 268
Wynn, Dudley, 154–155

Yeager, Margaret, 262–263
Yergin, Daniel, 85
Yippies, 207
Yosemite National Park, 296, 298
Young Americans for Freedom, 13

Zamperini, Louis, 98
Zeitlin, Jake, 146
Zimmer, Norma, 121
Zinn, Howard, 142

www.ingramcontent.com/pod-product-compliance
Lightning Source LLC
Chambersburg PA
CBHW020258240426
43673CB00039B/635